Common Places

Readings in American Vernacular Architecture

Common Places

Readings in American Vernacular Architecture

Edited by

DELL UPTON

JOHN MICHAEL VLACH

The University of Georgia Press
Athens and London

Designed by Sandra Strother Hudson
Set in Mergenthaler digital Ehrhardt
The paper in this book meets the guidelines for permanence and durability of the Committee on Production Guidelines for Book Longevity of the Council on Library Resources.

Printed in the United States of America
89 88 87 86 4 3 2 1

Library of Congress Cataloging in Publication Data

Main entry under title:

Common places.

Bibliography: p.
Includes index.
1. Vernacular architecture—United States. I. Upton, Dell. II. Vlach, John Michael, 1948– .
NA705.C58 1985 720′.973 84-16167
ISBN 0-8203-0749-1
ISBN 0-8203-0750-5 (pbk.)

For Henry Glassie

Contents

Part Three. Function

Part Four. History

Part Five. Design and Intention

Acknowledgments

The editors are grateful for advice, assistance, and encouragement from friends and colleagues, including Jay Anderson, John Burrison, Simon Bronner, Cary Carson, Tom Carter, Paul Groth, Rusty Marshall, John Moe, Gerald Parsons, Orlando Ridout V, Tom Schlereth, and Camille Wells. Leo Bellamy and Mary Ison of the Division of Prints and Photographs in the Library of Congress helped track down illustrations from the collections of the Farm Security Administration and the Historic American Buildings Survey. Pamela S. Hawkes spent many hours chasing elusive footnote references. Many essential editorial tasks were funded by two annual grants from the Committee on Research at the University of California, Berkeley.

We owe a special debt of gratitude to Malcolm Call and John McGuigan for their early encouragement, and to Malcolm for making a welcome home for the project at the University of Georgia Press. Our editor at Georgia, Debbie Winter, helped us to shape an enormous pile of typescript, xeroxes, drawings, and photographs into a real book.

Authors always acknowledge their spouses, and now we know why. To ours, Karen Kevorkian and Beverly Brannan, thanks.

Most of all, we owe a debt to our teachers James Deetz and Henry Glassie, who introduced us to the vernacular environment and who showed us how to study it.

The editors and the publisher gratefully acknowledge the publications in which articles in this volume first appeared.

Kenneth L. Ames, "Meaning in Artifacts: Hall Furnishings in Victorian America," *Journal of Interdisciplinary History* 9 (Summer 1978): 19–46. Reprinted with permission of the *Journal of Interdisciplinary History* and The MIT Press, Cambridge, Massachusetts. Copyright © 1978 by The Massachusetts Institute of Technology and the editors of the *Journal of Interdisciplinary History.*

Catherine W. Bishir, "Jacob W. Holt: An American Builder," *Winterthur Portfolio* 16, no. 1 (Spring

1981): 1–31. Reprinted by permission of The University of Chicago Press.

James Borchert, "Alley Landscapes of Washington," *Landscape* 23, no. 3 (Spring 1979): 3–10.

Edward A. Chappell, "Acculturation in the Shenandoah Valley: Rhenish Houses of the Massanutten Settlement," *Proceedings of the American Philosophical Society* 124, no. 1 (February 1980): 55–89. Reprinted by permission of the American Philosophical Society.

Lizabeth A. Cohen, "Embellishing a Life of Labor: An Interpretation of the Material Culture of American Working-Class Homes, 1885–1915," *Journal of American Culture* 3, no. 4 (Winter 1980): 752–75. Reprinted by permission of the publisher.

Abbott Lowell Cummings, "Introduction," to *Rural Household Inventories, Establishing the Names, Uses and Furnishings of Rooms in the Colonial New England Home, 1675–1775* (Boston: Society for the Preservation of New England Antiquities, 1964), pp. xiii–xl. Reprinted by permission of the Society for the Preservation of New England Antiquities.

Henry Glassie, "Eighteenth-Century Cultural Process in Delaware Valley Folk Building," *Winterthur Portfolio* 7 (1972): 29–57. Reprinted by permission of The University of Chicago Press.

Alan Gowans, "The Mansions of Alloways Creek," *RACAR: Revue de l'Art Canadien/Canadian Art Review* 3, no. 2 (1976): 55–71.

Thomas Hubka, "Just Folks Designing: Vernacular Designers and the Generation of Form," *Journal of Architectural Education* 32, no. 3 (1979): 27–29. Reprinted by permission of the Association of Collegiate Schools of Architecture.

Excerpts from Norman Morrison Isham and Albert F. Brown, *Early Rhode Island Houses: An Historical and Architectural Study* (Providence: Preston and Rounds, 1895), pp. 5–6, 14–18, 21–24, 141–44.

Fred B. Kniffen, "Folk Housing: Key to Diffusion," *Annals of the Association of American Geographers* 55, no. 4 (December 1965): 549–77. Reproduced by permission of the Association of American Geographers.

Fred B. Kniffen and Henry Glassie, "Building in Wood in the Eastern United States: A Time-Place Perspective," *Geographical Review* 56, no. 1 (January 1966): 40–66.

Clay Lancaster, "The American Bungalow," *Art Bulletin* 40 (September 1958): 239–53. Reprinted by permission of The College Art Association of America.

Stewart G. McHenry, "Eighteenth-Century Field Patterns as Vernacular Art," *Old-Time New England* 69, nos. 1–2 (Summer–Fall 1978): 1–21. Reprinted by permission of the Society for the Preservation of New England Antiquities.

Fraser D. Neiman, "Domestic Architecture at the Clifts Plantation: The Social Context of Early Virginia Building," *Northern Neck of Virginia Historical Magazine* 28 (December 1978): 3096–3128.

Fred W. Peterson, "Vernacular Building and Victorian Architecture: Midwestern American Farm Homes," *Journal of Interdisciplinary History* 12 (Winter 1982): 409–27. Reprinted with permission of the editors of the *Journal of Interdisciplinary History* and The MIT Press, Cambridge, Massachusetts. Copyright © 1982 by The Massachusetts Institute of Technology and the editors of the *Journal of Interdisciplinary History.*

Edward T. Price, "The Central Courthouse Square in the American County Seat," *Geographical Review* 58 (January 1968): 29–60.

Theodore H. M. Prudon, "The Dutch Barn in America: Survival of a Medieval Structural Frame," *New York Folklore* 2, nos. 3–4 (1976): 122–42. Reprinted by permission of the New York Folklore Society and the Editor of *New York Folklore.*

Warren E. Roberts, "The Tools Used in Building Log Houses in Indiana," *Pioneer America: Journal of Historic American Material Culture* 9 (July 1977): 32–61.

Barbara Rubin, "Aesthetic Ideology and Urban Design," *Annals of the Association of American Geographers* 69 (September 1979): 339–61. Reproduced by permission of the Association of American Geographers.

Robert Blair St. George, " 'Set Thine House in Order': The Domestication of the Yeomanry in Seventeenth-Century New England," from *New England Begins: The Seventeenth Century,* 3 vols. (Boston: Museum of Fine Arts, 1982). Courtesy of the Museum of Fine Arts, Boston.

Dell Upton, "Vernacular Domestic Architecture in Eighteenth-Century Virginia," *Winterthur Portfolio* 17, nos. 2–3 (Summer–Autumn 1982): 95–119. Reprinted by permission of The University of Chicago Press.

John Michael Vlach, "The Shotgun House: An African Architectural Legacy," *Pioneer America: Journal of Historic American Material Culture* 8 (January–July 1976): 47–70.

For the most part, articles reprinted in this volume are in their original form. A few have been slightly modified by the authors or editors, and several have substitutions for some of the original illustrations.

Introduction

Common Places is a collection of twenty-three previously published essays on vernacular architecture and landscapes. It was our hope in gathering and arranging them to create a work that would be helpful to teachers and students of the subject, and to interested lay people as well. It contains what we consider to be essential and useful readings on the American vernacular environment. As teachers ourselves, we frequently assign or recommend these readings to our students; many other teachers, we have found, do so as well. Often, however, libraries do not subscribe to all the relevant journals, or they do not have the particular issues needed. Our anthology is intended at the simplest level to save you unnecessary legwork, but it has more weighty purposes as well.

Common Places makes an important statement about the interdisciplinary nature of the study of vernacular architecture and landscapes. The field is extraordinarily broad not only in terms of its subject matter but in the way that its subject matter is presented and interpreted. We have taken great care here not to certify a single preferred approach to the structures and environments of ordinary people—what we have identified as "common places"—but we have tried instead to point to the specific strengths to be found in the array of distinct disciplines that care about ordinary, everyday architecture. Included here are the writings of architectural historians, geographers, folklorists, architects, cultural historians, archaeologists, social historians, decorative arts scholars, art historians, preservationists, and American studies specialists. The student of American vernacular architecture (and we use this word to indicate the range of artifactual surroundings from the chair to the settlement pattern) ought to be aware of the efforts made in all these fields. Only with such a diversity of analytical perspectives can one withstand the physical attractiveness of common architecture that so frequently distracts scholars from interpretation, leaving them to squander their talents on mere description.[1] Knowing that there may be over a dozen legitimate ways to understand a house, a barn, or a town plan prevents the student from making the facile assumption that simple forms represent simple realities. It is our view that to study common places in a multidisciplinary manner is to be rewarded with uncommon insights.

There are other books on the vernacular environment that could be used as texts. These might include Amos Rapoport's *House Form and Culture,* Abbott Lowell Cummings's *The Framed Houses of Massachusetts Bay, 1625–1725,* Henry Glassie's *Pattern in the Material Folk Culture of the Eastern United States* or his *Folk Housing in Middle Virginia,* John Stilgoe's *Common Landscape of America* or D. W. Meinig's *The Interpretation of Ordinary Landscapes.*[2] All of these are major works in the field, but for all their insights they are necessarily limited geographically, temporally, or methodologically and hence cannot encompass all that vernacular architecture and landscape studies include. They require supplemental readings of the sort that we present here.

We are not trying to establish a canon of "best and brightest" here, although we do feel that much excellence is included in our selection. Major scholars are unrepresented, and there are many other works worthy of serious attention. Our intention was rather to compile a group of individually strong articles that also worked together. Within the scope of a manageable volume, these essays seem to us to provide the best mix of frequently cited works and less well-known but high quality articles from as many different disciplines as possible. A longer anthology might have been more inclusive, but it might also have been redundant in content and approaches.

Every student of vernacular architecture has his or her favorite articles. No doubt Fred B. Kniffen's "Folk Housing: Key to Diffusion," published in the widely distributed *Annals of the Association of American Geographers,* ranks high on most lists and we have therefore included it here. However, many excellent articles are never read because they appear in obscure or unlikely publications. Since many libraries do not have full runs of regional or local history journals, few of our readers will have seen Fraser D. Neiman's thorough analysis of seventeenth-century Virginia housing in the *Northern Neck Historical Magazine.* Equally unknown because it was not printed in an American journal is Alan Gowans's "Mansions of Alloways Creek," a study of southern New Jersey's patterned-brick houses that was published in *RACAR: Revue de l'Art Canadien/Canadian Art Review.* By contrast, many people may be familiar with the American Philosophical Society's 125-year run of *Proceedings,* but who would ever think of looking there for an article on vernacular architecture? Hence Edward A. Chappell's fine study of German vernacular architecture in the Shenandoah Valley has gone largely unnoticed. We have joined here the obvious with the obscure in hopes of urging students of vernacular architecture and landscapes onward with examples of good work.

This selection of articles presents not only information about the vernacular environment but models for the presentation of research that students might follow in their own work. The study of artifacts requires pictorial and graphic documentation: photographs, maps, and measured drawings. It is evident from the articles included in *Common Places* just how useful the skills of photography and drafting are, and how incomplete, even inaccurate, any description and analysis of artifacts is when it lacks competent visual documentation. While there are several styles of graphic rendering offered in our collection, one cannot miss the rigorous pursuit of accuracy found in all of them.[3] Once vague plans, simple sketches of squares and rectangles, and crude maps commonly served as illustrations of vernacular structures, but today only a precise, scaled drawing will suffice. Similarly, photographs should be abundant and clear so that a landscape or building can be easily understood. High quality graphic presentation is a significant measure of the seriousness and commitment now required in the study of the vernacular landscape. It is unlikely that a clear interpretation can ever be made from evidence that is unclear. Thus we find that while students of vernacular architecture generally define themselves as humanists, they do not shun the meticulous recording techniques of the "hard" scientist. However time consuming a stick-by-stick, down-to-the-inch record might be, contemporary standards will permit nothing less. The discipline signaled by measured plans and maps and clear, in-focus photographs is a statement of intellectual commitment that the examples provided here invite the reader to emulate.

The contents of this collection are arranged to address five questions that are inescapable in the study of the vernacular environment. They are: What is vernacular architecture? How is it made? How does it work? How does it change? and How is it thought? Phrased more tersely, these inquiries involve the issues of content, construction, function, history, and design.

None of the concerns encapsulated in our five questions is peculiar to architectural investigation. Indeed, in his proposal for artifactual study E. McClung Fleming identified five similar avenues of research under the headings material, construction, design, function, and history.[4] Consequently we recommend that you recognize the equivalence of all material things and take note of all levels of the vernacular landscape from the smallest to the largest. In doing so, the linkages among the different disciplines that study and analyze the tangible results of human creativity will become apparent. The anthropologist, the historian, the geographer, the folklorist, and their colleagues, to the degree that they are concerned with artifacts, must also be prepared to communicate with one another. As the questions proposed in *Common Places* are probed more intensively, interdisciplinary exchanges will become increasingly urgent.[5] The remainder of our Introduction will highlight ways in which the articles reprinted here address our five organizing questions.

Definitions and Demonstrations

This issue of definition, apparently so simple, has proven to be one of the most serious problems for advocates of vernacular architecture and landscapes research. A straightforward, convincing, authoritative definition has not yet been offered. Vernacular architecture is a phenomenon that many understand intuitively but that few are able to define. The literature on the subject is thus filled with what might be called non-definitions. Vernacular architecture is *non*–high style building; it is those structures *not* designed by professionals; it is *not* monumental; it is *un*-sophisticated; it is *mere* building; it is, according to the distinguished architectural historian Nikolaus Pevsner, *not* architecture.[6] Those who take a more positive approach rely on adjectives like ordinary, everyday, and commonplace. While these terms are not as pejorative as other descriptive phrases that are sometimes applied to the vernacular, neither are they very precise. For example, the skyscrapers of Manhattan are works of high style architecture, but they are also commonplace in Manhattan. Are they not logically New York City vernacular buildings?

In practice a great many scholars, when they speak of the vernacular, mean the old, the rural, and the domestic. But this definition, while it identifies an important segment of the ordinary built world, also leaves much out. Is there not vernacular architecture in the present? Is it all from historical periods? Is there no vernacular architecture in urban areas? And what about stores, warehouses, churches, depots, stables, workshops, commercial strips, suburban tracts, and other commonplace environments? Are they not elements of the vernacular? Historians of vernacular architecture usually relax their definitions in the face of these questions. They will concede that contemporary housing, even in cities and suburbs, and other sorts of nondomestic structures along with the spaces surrounding them are vernacular even if they cannot say how. So what do they exclude? Rapoport has written that only about 5 percent of the world's built environment—the portion designed by architects and built by engineers—is not vernacular.[7] The fact that vernacular architecture encompasses so much is both a strength and a weakness of the field. Many can rally to the advocacy of the value of the experience of common people, but few can agree on what aspects of the common experience merit their attention.

Like many others, we have attempted to define the vernacular in this volume by enumerating its forms. The first six articles in *Common Places* provide a partial list of the content of vernacular architecture and landscapes studies. Fred B. Kniffen and Edward A. Chappell concentrate on eighteenth- and nineteenth-century rural houses, John Michael Vlach presents the history of a dwelling type that is found in both rural and urban contexts, and Clay Lancaster reviews the history of the bungalow, which has both its high style and plain style and its exotic and local influences. All manner of buildings are thus suggested as potential subjects for vernacular architecture studies. Spaces are also included in our list. Stewart G. McHenry's article on field patterns and Edward T. Price's study of town plans provide examples of large-scale spatial organizations that convey important architectural messages. Many more forms and spaces could be listed, but these six articles make the point that the concept of the vernacular includes much and excludes little.

The articles that we have grouped under other headings will also provide examples of what the vernacular is. You will undoubtedly notice that when taken as a group these twenty-three essays imply that the American vernacular is mostly old, mostly eastern, mostly rural, mostly domestic, and mostly architectural. This should be taken, however, only as a reflection of past practice and not as a directive for future study. In fact, by showing where scholarship has previously been focused, we also suggest where we might turn next. Clearly more investigation of contemporary buildings, including commercial as well as residential structures, is needed. Since the eastern part of the nation has already received much attention, it is now time to look to other regions. As we do, our definition of vernacular architecture is sure to expand.

Closely connected to the question of the definition of the vernacular environment is that of the identity of its builders. If 95 percent of the built world is to be counted as vernacular architecture, then the vernacular builder must be almost anyone that one might name. While it is a rare and exceptional American who can design and construct a building today, many people have ideas about the kinds of spaces they would like to inhabit. In studies of vernacular architecture these wishes and desires, the conventional tastes of common people, are considered to be as significant as the act of building itself. The vernacular builder, usually a local tradesman, creates not so much what he personally thinks is best but what he knows or senses his customers will want. Thus the consumers of vernacular architecture are also important form givers, a circumstance that provides vernacular architecture with a strong popular or social identity. As the creation of local people, vernacular architecture presents less the wants of any single person than what is communally sanctioned. The British scholar Eric Mercer has pointed to this social dimension, observing that vernacular architecture "is common in a given place at a given time."[8] It is the architecture that groups of people make or have made for their daily use. Just as linguists identify a vernacular dialect as the local usage of a standard language, architectural historians often describe vernacular architecture as the local version of a widespread academic style.

The more self-sufficient and socially secure a community is, the more definite is its sense of identity and the more fixed are its architectural conventions. It follows then that while the concept of the vernacular includes many structures, some can be more vernacular than others because the degree to which an artifactual set represents its residents can vary tremendously. Scholars are usually most confident about their definitions of the vernacular when they study structures with a pronounced ethnic character. Several of the articles in our section on definition present the buildings and spaces of ethnic groups. Chappell analyzes the houses of Germanic groups, Vlach investigates an Afro-American house type, and McHenry illustrates how Vermont field forms reveal whether a settlement was Dutch, French, English, or American. While Kniffen and Price examine the ways that regional rather than ethnic identity is manifested by architecture, their focus on the dynamics of group formation and maintenance is clear. All of these authors use historical data as examples of vernacular architecture, not because of an antiquarian or nostalgic interest but because during the eighteenth and nineteenth centuries particular group identities were more overt and more evident in buildings. Old houses are a good choice for study because their vernacular quotient is high—because their social bases are usually more obvious and easier to read. Scholars of vernacular architecture usually find that their evaluations ring true when the local identity of their data is not diluted by extensive outside contact. It is then frequently the case that they will concentrate on the architecture of what the anthropologist Robert Redfield called the "little tradition."[9]

Answering the question, What is vernacular architecture? involves a judgment about the intensity of social representation as well as about appropriate content. The more conservative people are, the more they are attached to older, precedented, local architecture. The structures they control are usually connected to their domestic environments and typically include their houses, barns, and smaller outbuildings. The examples we use here to define the vernacular are domestic structures with a marked local and popular affiliation. Historic Germanic farm houses built with techniques that are centuries old, for example, are unquestionably vernacular statements. Yet the practice of vernacular architecture research is not restricted only to structures that are traditional. Lancaster's study of the American bungalow presents a complex set of twentieth-century developments in which professional architects, real estate entrepreneurs, building tradesmen, and optimistic middle-class residents all had a role to play. Some portion of the bungalow's history is clearly vernacular; other elements are vernacular only in origin. Hence the bungalow, when compared with a nineteenth-century farm house, seems to be "impure." But regardless of the contrast between historical and contemporary buildings, current forms of popular architecture also need to be studied. Because the housing fashions represented by bungalows or "ready-mades" are, in part, more recent attempts to establish new identities, those houses embody collective ideals equivalent to those lodged in any old-fashioned house type. The modern structures may be less successful in winning a long-lived public allegiance, but they still indicate something of their residents' wishes.[10]

Construction

The encounter with objects requires description. One cannot proceed to interpretation without specifying how the artifact at hand came to exist. Vernacular structures can be explained first at the level of their construction, as the scholar identifies the chronological, geographical, and formal qualities of artifactual technologies.

Vernacular builders use whatever materials are available and whatever skills they possess. As a result, techniques of construction vary widely not only with the task at hand but with the locale. In the Southwest, for example, adobe buildings are indicative of the vernacular tradition, while in New England a wooden frame covered with clapboards is most typical. In the Blue Ridge Mountains horizontal log construction is commonplace, but in other places brick or stone masonry may be preferred. The variety of technologies could fill an anthology itself.[11]

The four articles that we present in *Common Places* to illustrate construction all deal with wooden buildings. This is appropriate since American material culture has historically been dominated by wood and because wooden structures are most numerous in the current stock of American buildings.[12] Moreover, wooden structures can be extremely complex, requiring many separate acts such as shaping the timbers, fitting the joints, squaring the corners, raising the posts, securing the beams, nailing on the lath and siding, and applying the paint and plaster, to complete them. Mass-wall construction with stone or brick, while it requires its own particular expertise, is not nearly as complex or as sensitive to chronological and geographical variation. If you can understand framed structures, then surely you can comprehend simpler technologies.

The articles by Norman Morrison Isham and Albert F. Brown and by Theodore H. M. Prudon present examples of timber framing systems. Isham and Brown move through a house from "garret to cellar" reconstructing its original form, and in the process they reveal the many complex tasks that the early builders of Rhode Island had to perform in order to raise even a small dwelling. Similarly, Prudon's analysis of Dutch barns describes the intricacies of their construction while also attesting to the deep ethnic roots of their framing techniques.

The next two articles examine log construction, a technology that was used for only a small portion of American vernacular buildings but that has nonetheless attracted the largest share of scholars' attention. Unfortunately much of the attention given to log structures has been motivated by nostalgic and romantic myths about the American frontier so that the vast literature on log cabins contains more misinformation than usable data.[13] While they treat all the American building techniques that employ wood, Kniffen and Glassie analyze notched, horizontal log construction most extensively. Much of their commentary is aimed at correcting the many erroneous interpretations of log building's origins, forms, and uses. Warren E. Roberts also attempts to revise mistaken notions regarding log houses. He argues that log houses were not simple, primitive structures, but complex buildings skillfully carpentered with a large assortment of tools.

A complete description of the construction of any item would begin with the preparation of the raw materials—in the instance of a house, preparing the framing members. Next, all the steps in assembly or fabrication would be detailed as foundations are laid, walls are raised, the roof is shingled, the doors and windows are hung, and so forth. But the description would not be complete until the building was furnished, landscaped, and lived in and probably modified by subsequent occupants. Biographical details complete the description of a house by plunging it into the active routines of daily life.

Function

Historically, the attention that students of the vernacular have devoted to typological enterprises—to naming and cataloging I-houses, double-crib barns, bungalows, field patterns, town plans—or to tracing the evolution of historical, and preferably exotic, building technologies like braced-frame or log construction, has obscured the issue of use. Where function has entered into discussions of vernacular building, its character has been assumed rather than investigated. That is, rather than attempting to explore how built forms were used, some scholars have adopted a one-dimensional view of function as a way of explaining physical features. For example, the temperature difference between Virginia and New England has traditionally been presumed to explain the tendency to use end chimneys in the South to dissipate heat and central chimneys in the North to retain it. As Neiman notes in the essay included in *Common Places,* the preference for end-chimney houses in Virginia *postdates* the transference of cooking to detached kitchens; a fire would not have been used in an end-chimney Virginia house in the summer.

It is not only that particular explanations are wrong that makes functionalism an inadequate way to approach vernacular architecture. Functionalism presumes a single simple cause for a complex architectural feature, and it fails to suggest why one solution to the functional requirement was chosen over other possible ones. Functionalism usually involves the anachronistic projection of one's own point of view onto the past. The notion that there is only one best way of doing things underlies most functionalist theories, and it is a notion that grows out of the exaggerated reverence for "science" in all aspects of life that was injected into our culture late in the last century and that continues to hold us captive.

If we set aside functionalism, we must not abandon with it the idea of function. People do not, after all, construct buildings or create landscapes primarily as sculptural forms, or as signposts of cultural diffusion, or to impress their descendants with their ancestors' cleverness, but to *use* in their day-to-day activities. Students of the vernacular environment have only recently turned with new interest to the examination of function in all its particularity, but there has always been some interest in use. The first inquiries were attempts to understand room and furniture naming and function through the use of probate inventories. Both the pioneer furniture scholar Irving W. Lyon and the pioneer vernacular architecture students Isham and Brown recognized in probate inventories—lists of a decedent's possessions made immediately after death—a key to understanding the material universe of colonial and early national Americans. Lyon's *The Colonial Furniture of New England* (1890) attempted to match the objects accumulated by early antique collectors with the obscure names found in the inventories and then to draw some conclusions about the origins and uses of various classes of artifacts. Isham and Brown, too, found probate inventories to be valuable sources. They were less interested in individual objects of furniture than in matching architectural spaces with their furnishings, as a way of discovering the original names and uses of those spaces. In their second book, *Early Connecticut Houses,* the two architects went on to use inventories to attempt to reconstruct the forms of long-demolished buildings.

The use of probate inventories in this manner became a staple of museum practice. When a house or a room of paneling is acquired by a museum, one of the first steps in exhibit planning is to search for the probate inventories of former owners. Cummings, in his *Rural Household Inventories,* was one of the first Americans to look at inventories in the aggregate and to draw out of them not only specific data about single buildings, or unsystematic observations, but coherent patterns of spatial naming and use. Cummings was also careful to take into account the social differences among New England decedents and to attempt to recognize class differences in furnishings and house use.

Research of this sort into object and room uses is an important part of vernacular architecture scholarship, but at the same time it takes into account only a part of the "function" of the vernacular landscape. It is founded on a conception of function as the provision of space for social and economic activities like cooking, dining, sleeping, storage, threshing, planting, or just "sitting," that can be thought of as confined in time and space and defined by a recognizable group of physical actions.

Another approach, one that has been particularly favored in the study of more recent vernacular landscapes, is to ask about the less tangible, more pervasive functions of spaces and furnishings in shaping perceptions and social relationships. We are familiar with this notion at the popular level of the status symbol: a large and grandly furnished parlor might be intended to impress on visitors the owners' social standing and economic prosperity. On a more concrete level, many householders tend to place their best—newest, largest, most valuable—possessions in the most public room and often to rely on less prestigious and even less adequate furnishings elsewhere in the house for the sake of display in the formal room.

Observations of this sort are truisms now, of course, but they point to what some of the most subtle vernacular scholars have tried in recent years. In *Common Places,* Kenneth L. Ames's essay painstakingly reconstructs the social landscape of the Victorian hallway, using it to illuminate three outmoded and otherwise mysterious pieces of furniture, the hallstand, the card receiver, and the hall chair. One could sum up his argument simply by saying that it helped to impress the visitor and to keep him, or more often, her, at the appropriate social distance, but that would lose the particularity of the intricate rituals of calling and being called on: the abstract social function of the hall had a specific content that must be understood to grasp the significance of the architectural spaces and their furnishings.

The use of space to structure social relationships is not confined to the level of the room or that of the individual building. Edward T. Hall, in *The Si-*

lent Language and *The Hidden Dimension*, has shown how spatial relationships between individuals work to the same ends.[14] Other scholars have extended the analysis of the social patterning of space to the level of the city.[15]

Nor is the use of objects to make a "statement" confined to the wealthy or to the socially aspiring middle class. The furnishing of spaces, as Lizabeth A. Cohen shows in this collection, is a matter of concern at all social levels, and it serves not only to impress outsiders, but to create comfortable surroundings for its occupants. We assemble around us objects that evoke familiar images of the past, attractive images of the present, and hopeful images of the future.

Cohen's article reminds us that to use a space, it must be transformed into a place, an appropriate setting in which human beings can act. Unlike single-purpose structures such as religious halls, most vernacular spaces must serve many functions—that is, their makers design them to be the settings for a changing variety of human activities. The investigation of function, whether of a city, a rural landscape, a building, or a piece of furniture, must keep in mind this intended variety. It is for this reason that functionalism is inadequate, but that close attention to the particulars of use is necessary for understanding the vernacular environment.

History

It is tempting to people steeped in the rapidly shifting fashions of modern popular culture to think of vernacular architecture, particularly in its traditional forms, as changeless. An emphasis on the enduring as indicative of deeply held values leads us at times to ignore change, or to treat it as unimportant. A nineteenth-century architectural pattern-book writer amused his readers with the tale of a bumpkin who put up a building, then went to the lumberyard to buy the "architecture" to nail onto it. We have a similar tendency to construct a vernacular tradition in which change and historical context are seen as so much superfluous gimcrackery. Alternatively, we imagine a pristine ideal of vernacular building, to which change comes as lamentable deterioration.

Change is in the nature of the vernacular; vernacular buildings and vernacular landscapes are always changing. For one thing, spatial needs change. The essays in this section of *Common Places* by Fraser D. Neiman, Dell Upton, and Robert Blair St. George describe changes in the demands made on buildings by their users in seventeenth- and eighteenth-century Virginia and New England. The social level at which architectural needs are collectively defined shifts as well. In the colonial period, it might have been a village of individuals who emigrated together from a single foreign locality, or a group of slaves on a single plantation sharing common restrictions and liberties in social relations, or the residents of a colony that constituted the significant social group with shared patterns of interrelationships that shaped expectations of buildings and landscapes. In the nineteenth and twentieth centuries, it was more likely to be an economic or an occupational group or a social class, nationally or regionally distributed, that shared common demands on spaces. The groups, rather than the demands of a single group, might change. James Borchert illustrates how the meanings and uses of urban spaces changed in Washington, D.C., when new groups took them over. In any case, as social demands change, spatial responses to them are altered as well. It is not only that new spatial forms are constantly being devised, but the *resources* for doing so are in constant flux. New architectural ideas are conceived, and others are introduced from outside the local setting. Growing economic prosperity or shifting patterns of trade might make new goods—exotic woods, manufactured iron stoves, printed wallpapers, architectural style books, agricultural journals, cheap tools—available to the vernacular builder. While early Americans were *largely* confined to local resources, the vernacular environment since the time of the Industrial Revolution has been characterized by the increased availability of cheap mass-produced tools and materials with which to landscape, build, and furnish. The two trajectories of change—in socially defined spatial needs and in patterns of the consumption of goods and ideas—are of course interrelated, but it is useful to think of the vernacular landscape as a shifting thing located at the confluence of these two historical streams.

It is necessary to go further and to ask what strategies vernacular builders use to draft new goods and ideas into the service of social requirements. Several possibilities exist. Vernacular builders could simply abandon their former practices and adopt new ones. An expensive or time-consuming building technology might be abandoned when a mass-produced equivalent becomes available, for example. A simple illustration of this is the change in nail-making technology. Until the end of the eighteenth century, nails were made entirely by hand. After a period of about thirty years of experimentation, a method of making durable machine-cut and -headed nails was devised around 1830, and hand-made nails were driven out of the market except for a few specialized uses for which machine-made nails were unsuitable.

More common are methods for *adding* the new to the customary repertoire. Some new ideas are adopted when they fulfill a function not performed by any existing vernacular practice, others when they do not interfere with any established habit. Fashionable Gothic cross gables on houses, for example, were adopted because they were visually striking but located where they did not affect the use of the house: they were appendages to the little-used roof space. They thus served the otherwise unmet function of conveying stylish awareness while avoiding disruption of vital household activities. This nineteenth-century aesthetic practice parallels the present-day commercial practice of attaching a large and striking sign to a nondescript utilitarian building to create what the architect Robert Venturi calls the "decorated shed."[16] Other novel ideas were adopted when they were *analogous* to established vernacular practices. Vernacular builders in New England, for example, were accustomed to butting weatherboard siding against plain vertical corner boards. In the mid nineteenth century, a fashionable "Grecian" appearance could be achieved with little trouble simply by substituting a pilaster for the plain corner board.

More complex and more interesting are the numerous ways that vernacular builders rethought new ideas and blended them into traditional practices. Glassie's *Folk Housing in Middle Virginia* is an extended exploration of the confrontation between traditional building and architectural innovation in a small area of Piedmont Virginia. Another view is provided by Vlach in his article on shotgun houses that shows how a constant spatial concept derived from African building was cloaked in whatever structural and decorative materials were available in a given locality. Paradoxically, the intangible spatial qualities were constant, while the physical components of the shotgun house were evanescent.

Design and Intention

Glassie's and Vlach's perspectives on change lead us to ask about the design process in vernacular building. The word *process* is the appropriate one. Just as the past focus on typology and technology has obscured the dimensions of function and change in vernacular environments, so it has often led to the objectification of vernacular building types and the conception of vernacular design as the reproduction by rote of stereotyped forms. Alternatively, vernacular building has been depicted as the spontaneous and instinctive production of idiosyncratic forms.[17]

Both of these points of view are inadequate. While the vernacular buildings of a given area might be roughly similar in appearance, it is rare to find two that are identical in every respect. Rote memorization is incapable of accounting for the variation. At the same time, the variation is usually confined within a relatively restricted range. Spontaneity cannot account for the disciplining of artifactual production. In the last twenty years, some students of the vernacular, inspired by the work of structural linguists, have searched for ways to understand the vernacular environment—particularly at and below the level of houses—that takes into account both variation and constraint. James Deetz, an archaeologist, suggested in his *Invitation to Archaeology* that the makers of artifacts learn mental templates, basic patterns with a range of interchangeable variations that can be fitted into the larger patterns as the individual occasion demands. Other authors have similarly postulated, in a less technical manner, some underlying mental concept governing architectural design. In *Common Places,* Glassie's essay argues for a preference for bilateral, tripartite symmetry introduced into American vernacular architecture in the eighteenth century. This "Georgian" design sense provided a framework that could be used to structure objects of all sorts, from gravestones to houses, without the necessity of supposing the existence of specific learned templates for individual artifacts. Thomas Hubka describes an analytical method of vernacular design that allows for the mental disassembly of new architectural ideas and their reassembly to make novel designs. Vernacular builders voluntarily restrict the range of possible solutions by confining themselves to familiar ideas and by attempting to solve only those architectural problems that are new to each project, rather than striving for a completely original creation.

A major effort at systematizing our understanding of the vernacular design process was made by Glassie in his *Folk Housing in Middle Virginia* (1975), which is one of the key documents of vernacular architecture studies. Like Deetz, Glassie sought inspiration from linguistics, drawing on transformational or generative grammar, an intellectual offshoot of the structural linguistics that Deetz used. Glassie suggested that the residents of his central Virginia locality absorbed from their neighbors a way of thinking geometrically. He codified this way of thinking into a set of "rules" for "generating" or creating a complete house from a basic geometrical kernel. Glassie was not suggesting that Middle Virginians actually knew of these rules or followed them as he set them out. Instead, he put them forward as a convenient means for systematically describing what native builders were able to do in a more direct but less explicit manner. Glassie was arguing that the members of a culture learn the *principles* of their culture rather than merely memorizing its specific contents. This allows them to invent new cultural "performances"—whether those be houses or settlement patterns or speeches or personal encounters—that do not necessarily duplicate any other example but that obviously share the same underlying principles.[18] Thus Glassie introduces and accounts for the phenomenon that Noam Chomsky called "creativity": the ability to create a unique artifact while remaining within culturally determined limits that was posited at the beginning of this section as the fundamental problem for understanding vernacular design.[19]

These arguments bear on *how* the vernacular designer is able to operate. They shift the study of the vernacular from a problem of classifying inert objects as discrete examples to one of understanding a mental process through the examination of groups of artifacts that provide clues to the operation of that recurring, invisible process. The issue of mental process—of thinking the vernacular—has other implications as well. Thinking involves not only the mechanics or "grammar" of design, as Glassie and others have called it, but the question of intention. Vernacular builders presumably have some reason for wanting to build, and any examination of the vernacular environment must address the idea of intention. A person intends to provide shelter or intends to divide fields in a way that permits a just distribution of land in the community. A town plan is intended to facilitate its functioning as an economic and governmental center for the surrounding countryside or, more abstractly, to provide an image of collective magnificence through the dramatic siting of public buildings. A builder intends a bungalow to foster an informal and comfortable domestic life as a way of reinforcing salutary social values, and so on. All of the authors of *Common Places* share this assumption of the importance of intention. They recognize that a vernacular builder, as much as an aesthetically trained designer, knows what he or she wants and knows how to achieve it.

This interest in intention is particularly evident in the remaining essays in this final section of *Common Places*. Gowans introduces the question by showing that for his New Jersey builders, intention has less to do with ethnicity, artistic influence, or economics than with local social relations. In the last three essays, Fred W. Peterson, Catherine W. Bishir, and Barbara Rubin all explore occasions where vernacular builders confront ideas that are new, and in some cases deny the validity of their own ideas. We can get a sense of the builders' intentions by observing what they do where a choice must be made. Peterson's midwesterners adapt popular architectural forms according to their own aesthetic, in the face of prescriptive literature condemning their local design methods and encouraging a wholesale surrender to architectural authority. Bishir's Jacob Holt understands both traditional and popular modes, and he utilizes whichever one the individual occasion demands. Rubin's commercial entrepreneurs reject elite aesthetic ideology and concomitant claims for the control of urban space, choosing self-assertion over submission to the "public good" as defined by upper-class authorities. These articles all make points that are important complements to the discussion of design method. It is even more important to know why vernacular builders do what they do than to know how they do it.

The study of vernacular architecture is fundamentally a humanistic study. We appreciate buildings and landscapes and furniture as handsome objects, but if we really understand them we know that what is most important is to appreciate the people who made them. The study of intention becomes the ultimate one in vernacular architecture studies, because it is the study of people acting. It shows us people in charge of their own lives, people engaged with their surroundings in a critical way, people making their own histories in the face of authorities trying to make it for them. Is it any wonder that in the context of an increasingly authoritarian political and social climate we should turn to the study of the vernacular?

Using This Book

As editors of *Common Places* we have wrestled many hours with its contents and its arrangement. In the introduction we have tried to identify some important themes that we think run through vernacular studies, and we have tried to locate each essay under the heading that we think it addresses most directly. Most of the articles could have been placed in more than one of the sections. At the same time, each stands on its own as a strong investigation of its subject; none requires having read any of the others to understand it. There are many ways to slice through this book, and you will soon discover any number of other themes and linkages and orderings that can be devised, according to your own interests and experience. As you do so, you will begin to understand the richness of vernacular architecture and landscape studies and the possibilities for your own work.

Notes

1. Dell Upton, "The Power of Things: Recent Studies in American Vernacular Architecture," *American Quarterly* 35, no. 3 (Bibliography 1983): 279.
2. See the Bibliography to *Common Places* for these and other works discussed in the Introduction but not cited in full in the notes.
3. For more detailed descriptions of procedures for recording vernacular environments, see the Bibliography, section on Do It Yourself: Research.
4. E. McClung Fleming, "Artifact Study: A Proposed Model," in *Winterthur Portfolio 9*, ed. Ian M. G. Quimby (Charlottesville: University Press of Virginia, 1974), pp. 153–73.
5. Henry Glassie, "Folkloristic Study of the American Artifact: Objects and Objectives," in *The Handbook of American Folklore*, ed. Richard M. Dorson (Bloomington: Indiana University Press, 1983), pp. 381–82.

6. "A bicycle shed is a building; Lincoln Cathedral is a piece of architecture." Nikolaus Pevsner, *An Outline of European Architecture,* 7th ed. (Harmondsworth: Penguin Books, 1963), p. 15.
7. Amos Rapoport, *House Form and Culture* (Englewood Cliffs, N.J.: Prentice-Hall, 1969), p. 2.
8. Eric Mercer, *English Vernacular Houses: A Study of Traditional Farmhouses and Cottages* (London: Her Majesty's Stationery Office, 1975), p. 1.
9. Robert Redfield, *Peasant Society and Culture* (1956; reprint, Chicago: University of Chicago Press, 1960), p. 42.
10. Gwendolyn Wright, *Building the Dream: A Social History of Housing in America* (New York: Pantheon, 1981), pp. 160–61.
11. See Bainbridge Bunting, *Early Architecture in New Mexico,* and Henry Glassie, "The Types of the Southern Mountain Cabin," in the Bibliography, section on Definitions and Demonstrations, and the works by Abbott Lowell Cummings and Harley J. McKee in the section on Construction.
12. Brooke Hindle, ed., *Material Culture of the Wooden Age* (Tarrytown, N.Y.: Sleepy Hollow Press, 1981).
13. Harold R. Shurtleff, *The Log Cabin Myth: A Study of the Early Dwellings of the English Colonists in North America,* ed. Samuel Eliot Morison (Cambridge: Harvard University Press, 1939).
14. Edward T. Hall, *The Silent Language* (Greenwich, Conn.: Fawcett, 1959), and *The Hidden Dimension* (Garden City, N.Y.: Anchor Books, 1966).
15. See the works by Betsy Blackmar, Perry Duis, Paul Groth, and Sam Bass Warner, Jr., among others, in the Bibliography, section on Function.
16. See Robert Venturi, Denise Scott Brown, and Steven Izenour, *Learning from Las Vegas: The Forgotten Symbolism of Architectural Form,* rev. ed. (Cambridge, MIT Press, 1977).
17. For two classic statements of traditional views of vernacular architecture, see Sibyl Moholy-Nagy, *Native Genius in Anonymous Architecture* (New York: Horizon Press, 1957), and Bernard Rudofsky, *Architecture without Architects: An Introduction to Non-Pedigreed Architecture* (New York: Museum of Modern Architecture, 1964).
18. For an elegantly integrated portrait of material and non-material cultural performance, see Henry Glassie, *Passing the Time in Ballymenone: Culture and History of an Ulster Community* (Philadelphia: University of Pennsylvania Press, 1982).
19. Noam Chomsky, *Aspects of the Theory of Syntax* (Cambridge: MIT Press, 1965), p. 6.

Part One

Definitions and Demonstrations

Folk Housing: Key to Diffusion

FRED B. KNIFFEN

In this article Fred B. Kniffen summarizes almost thirty years worth of explorations of folk building. The vast sweep of his architectural concerns, encompassing structures found all over the eastern half of the United States that were built from the earliest colonial times up to the last quarter of the nineteenth century, makes "Folk Housing" valuable reading for every student of vernacular architecture.

As a geographer Kniffen's main concern is what the spatial and temporal distributions of buildings might indicate about human history. In this article he sorts various houses and barns into types and plots them on maps, providing us not only with the taxonomy that is commonly used for folk buildings but also with an outline of the regional locations for these structures. Kniffen attempts to validate his housing regions by comparing his maps with maps previously drawn up for features of dialect and other cultural patterns. Treating buildings as the outcome of human endeavor, Kniffen notes that housing regions were created incrementally as people moved across the land. The cultural patterns they created were determined in large measure by the bundle of traits they had acquired at their original places of residence, zones or areas that Kniffen labels "cultural hearths." In the three major hearths of the United States—eastern New England, southeastern Pennsylvania, and the Chesapeake Tidewater and Carolina Low Country—distinct patterns of living developed. As people moved westward from these hearth zones, houses with special plans and traits began to appear in the newly settled territories signaling the different origins of their builders and creating a measurable regional diversity in American vernacular building. Since many of the older buildings still survive today, Kniffen encourages us to read them as precise texts explaining the specific manner in which the United States grew as a nation. Folk houses, he argues, tell a richly textured tale of how Americans literally built their country.

In Europe, settlement geography occupies an active and respected place among the fields of geographic endeavor. It is treated as basic cultural geography and ecology. In America, settlement geography has somehow failed to find equally widespread acceptance. A major reason, I believe, lies in the brevity of our historical time span. The methods of historical reconstruction employed in Europe are less applicable here. More than once the opinion has been expressed that our settlement elements and patterns are so youthful as to be marked by ferment, mixture, and makeshift to the extent that they are amorphous, that their study can lead to no significant results. I believe I can demonstrate that these doubts and reservations are groundless; more, that the problems, fruits, and pleasures of research in this field are such as to reward the most demanding among us.

Of the several elements of the settlement pattern, I have chosen to concentrate first on folk housing of the different categories into which it falls: human habitations, barns, and the whole variety of other outbuildings, even more specifically in this present discourse on houses and barns. Admittedly I have not gone beyond housing in digesting recently accumulated data on settlement. Notwithstanding, I can affirm honestly with Brunhes[1] and Jackson[2] that housing even considered alone is a basic fact of human geography. It reflects cultural heritage, current fashion, functional needs, and the positive and negative aspects of noncultural environment. These relationships are more easily appreciated for a simpler era when plant and animal husbandry were dominant pursuits, but are no less true today. There is a strong element of urgency in dealing with the older fold housing, for it is largely unchronicled and its overwhelmingly wood composition makes it bighly vulnerable to destructive forces, leaving behind little record of its character.

My interest in folk housing has been constant, at least latently, for several decades, and very much alive during the past four years, when the indulgence of the National Science Foundation and Louisiana State University enabled me to range through the whole eastern United States from the Gulf to the Lakes and from the Atlantic to the Mississippi. To make the most of the opportunity it was deemed necessary to set up concurrently a typology quantified as to numerical importance and qualified as to areal and temporal position, and to seek out origins, routes of diffusion, adaptations, and other processes affecting change or stability. There was purposely no conscious matching of emerging concepts against the record of historic movements of particular peoples. Rather, this study was designed to be a reconstruction of the nature and movement of settlement elements. The areal groupings and other results so derived then might be compared with those based on different cultural criteria, in the present instance, dialectic differences and regional social organization. Agreement with these latter two might suggest that folk housing is diagnostic of whole cultural complexes. Disagreement might prove the contrary, or it might indicate that housing diffusion was at variance with historic migrations of peoples, or even that certain cherished notions held by those in other disciplines are wrong. In short, it is proposed here to record some of the project's field experiences, observations, and conclusions, even into the realm of speculation.

The Subject

Earliest awareness of areal differences in settlement forms and patterns came with the first of a series of almost annual trips between Michigan and Louisiana beginning in 1930. What was true of the settlement forms of southern Michigan was observed to extend into the northern tier of Indiana counties. Here there was a sharp change, the first item of which to catch my attention was the I-house (fig. 1), much to be referred to hereafter. What were recognized as Pennsylvania German barns (fig. 2) appeared as well in central–northern Indiana. Southward the I-house persisted, but out of the otherwise-confused assemblage there gradually emerged a complex that I came to recognize as characteristic of the Upland South. It was only after the nature of the north–south section was better established that there was opportunity to examine an east–west section from southern Michigan through Upstate New York to New England. Here there was the impression of a basic continuum, with

Figure 1. For the basic I-house the structure in the foreground exhibits one-room depth, two full stories, and entrance in the long side. (Illinois HABS *photograph by Albert J. Delong, 1934.)*

gradual changes eastward from familiar to unfamiliar forms.

If this relation of experiences is vague, it is no more so than were the poorly supported impressions of settlement differences and relationships of the early years. Nevertheless, poor as were the results, these early observations engendered a sustained interest in the settlement of the trans-Appalachian area by migrants from east of the mountains. The accelerated experiences of the past four years have served to clarify the original inferences regarding areal segregation of settlement elements and patterns, leading therefrom to the concept of what is called *initial occupance.* The term is borrowed from my colleague, Professor W. G. McIntire, who employed it with somewhat different emphasis in his study of prehistoric Indian sites of the Louisiana marsh.[3] By initial occupance in the present connection is meant the first postpioneer, permanent settlement imprint established in the several sections of the wooded eastern United States by migrants from seaboard source areas, an epoch ending about 1850. The concept is important because it recognizes the initial imprint as long lasting, surviving even where a new ethnic stock has succeeded the original settlers; Germans in New England–settled southeastern Wisconsin provide a good example. Further, initial occupance is the base of reference for all subsequent change. Initial occupance patterns can be identified faithfully only where the time involved is relatively short, as in the United States. It is presumably a concept of little or

Figure 2. Pennsylvania German barn. Note overhang or "forebay" and access for vehicles on second floor.

no value where the time span is so great as to preclude its reconstruction, as in Europe.

It should not have been necessary to go through this whole research experience to appreciate anew the fundamental geographical importance of man's occupance patterns, but somehow it was by seeking out again and again the repeating, integral, functioning parts: housing, field forms, fences, economic activities, routes of transport, that the basic significance of the occupance structure was reaffirmed. With each new locale came the same queries: In what type of structure is meat smoked? How is hay stored? What type of field fence is used? How is water drawn? Universal in time and space as a functioning structure, the occupance pattern sums up better than anything else the nature of man's rapport with the earth. It is a yardstick to employ in comparisons of whatever era or place. So distinctly geographical in character, this would seem to be an area of inquiry that we must keep our own, even against the onslaught of anthropology. Not only does anthropology venture more and more into the study of settlement patterns,[4] but recently an anthropologist expressed regret that in America only nonanthropologists had studied folk housing.[5]

Procedures

Thus the larger task is to determine the character and areal distribution of the initial occupance patterns established by migrants from seaboard source areas. Consideration is limited to the wooded eastern United States to avoid the complications introduced by the grasslands milieu. Although the period of interest for the trans–Appalachian West begins about 1790, it is of course earlier for southward settlement diffusion east of the mountains. This southern cismontane section, despite original intent to exclude it, was found to be inseparable, hence became incorporated into the study. Concern for the rural rather than the urban scene is only incidentally a matter of personal preference, readily rationalized as reflecting the overwhelming dominance of agricultural activity in the newly settled areas and the much greater degree of cultural uniformity of rural complexes. Furthermore, there are, architecturally speaking, two cultures, rural and urban. Along the major routes of travel,[6] housing types characteristic of eastern cities appear in urban settlements as far west as the Mississippi.

Of the great mass of observable data, there was, then, a highly eclectic selection. There was, for example, an interest in the older forms that might belong to the pre-1850 period, and a tendency to neglect anything younger. Concentration on older forms focused proportionally greater attention on human habitations, for they last longest by a considerable margin. Barns and other outbuildings, with the exception of rare brick or stone structures, are less long-lived. Most greatly changed in the last hundred years are fences. The once ubiquitous rail fence has almost completely disappeared in many sections. Even stone-wall fences have in instances been bulldozed to complete obliteration.

In systematic studies, at least, there is no virtue in seeking out in the field what is already adequately described and mapped. Such matters as land division, gross settlement patterns, and relationship to terrain are portrayed quite adequately for wide areas. Precious field time should be devoted to the largely unchronicled forms, not only folk housing and fences, but also to such matters as agricultural practices, all subject to great and rapid change and even extinction. No other field of study is seriously interested in folk housing, or in any other settlement element for that matter. Aside from a few architectural historians, the architect's interest is not in origins, diffusions, and alterations of folk types. It rather focuses on the architectural "period" represented by the more-pretentious structure as reflected in a surficial treatment that may disguise a single old and fundamental form as severally Georgian, Federal, even Greek Revival and Gothic.[7] The architect's angle of interest is that of the New England farmer who, upon completing his unadorned frame house, hurried off to Boston to retain an architect to add the architecture, in this case gingerbread trim. Even housing experts such as those with the Department of Agriculture are much more concerned with the functional efficiency of farm buildings than they are with historical origins and continuities. The study of folk housing in America thus remains a wide-open field that geographers, backed by ample European precedent, may well make their own. The humbler buildings by reason of their adherence to type and numerical superiority are far more important as markers of basic cultural processes than are uniquely designed individual structures. For the systematist and the user of systematic data, here is important raw material that can be divided into well-defined types and counted.

Research in systematic fields is by no means simply a matter of mechanically recording the numbers and locations of the several types, say of dwellings, but, as already hinted at, necessitates prolonged study to determine first what the types actually are. Whereas there is a broad parallelism in all taxonomic procedure, there are frequently differences even within the same category of cultural phenomena. For example, Estyn Evans has pointed out that in dealing with Irish folk housing floor plan is the all-important criterion of type.[8] This is necessarily true when seeking continuity from archaeologic remains where stone foundations or postmold patterns are the only evidence. On the other hand, where in America still-complete structures are ancestral forms, height, pitch of roof, and other destructible features are significant as permitting subtler distinction of type than floor plan alone allows. And, we shall presently cite an example where several floor plans are exhibited in what to folk thinking is a single type. Penetration of this concept of what constitutes a type in the folk mind is far surer with inhabited structures than with evidence consisting of ancient stone foundations. The example in mind is the I-house (fig. 3), so dubbed in the absence of any common term, either folk or architectural.[9]

The I-house was first recognized in Indiana in 1930 as constituting a link with the Middle Atlantic source area. It was recognized again in the middle thirties in Louisiana (fig. 4) in the form of a house introduced into the southwestern part of the state in the late nineteenth century by settlers from Kentucky, Illinois, and Missouri. A generally like struc-

Figure 3. Frame I-house in central southern Kentucky.

Figure 4. Louisiana frame I-house, a type imported from the lower Middle West in the late nineteenth century.

Figure 5. Carolina-type frame I-house with front and rear additions. (Alabama HABS photograph by W. N. Manning, 1935.)

ture showed up in North Carolina, but with a different front porch and a shed-roof rear appendage (fig. 5). Again, suggestively similar houses appeared throughout the Upland South and its extension north of the Ohio River (fig. 6), and abundantly and old in the Middle Atlantic states and the northern Tidewater South.

From section to section the I-house varied in construction material from brick and stone to frame and logs. Chimneys might be central, inside end, outside end, or paired on the ridge, with regional dominance of specific practices. The floor plan was found to be highly variable (fig. 7). Lateral and rear appendages, front and rear porches, galleries, even classical columns appeared in great variety. But these qualities all I-houses unfailingly had in common: gables to the side, at least two rooms in length, one room deep, and two full stories in height. These constant qualities, a continuous distribution, still-extant logical evolutionary stages, and almost exclusive association with economic success in an agricultural society indicate a common fundamental concept and thus describe a type. The few essentials constitute the basic type, beyond which there are several varieties.

But, to hurry to the denouement: The I-house is one of several compounded from the old English unit consisting of one room and end chimney. It is recorded full-blown for the Delaware–Chesapeake section by at least the late seventeenth century. It joined the movement southward along the Appalachian axis, swung westward as far as Texas and northward across the Ohio, there joining a trickle that had come westward through Pennsylvania. Ear-

Figure 6. Stone I-house in central Kentucky. (HABS photograph by Lester Jones, 1940.)

ly in its movement southward the I-house became symbolic of economic attainment by agriculturists and remained so associated throughout the Upland South and its peripheral extensions. The basal structure was often a simple, one-story dogtrot house; with economic affluence a second story was added and the whole structure weatherboarded (fig. 8). Of all old folk types, the I-house is by far the most widely distributed, notably as a rural dwelling.

These broad conclusions are the product of wide field observation. Perhaps in a discourse with pretensions to intellectual respectability it would be unseemly to admit the delights of fieldwork, of the pleasure of speaking leisurely of the old days with those who lived them or know them in oral tradition, of losing oneself in the less-demanding but more-direct concerns of a simpler day. And how easy it would be to lapse into the antiquarian's point of view, as many are doing with cultural items such as covered bridges and Maine logging dams. What an unmixed joy to be the first in one's community to collect a pure type A-7 double log crib or a series C dog-leg fence!

But there are times in the field when a deluge of variant or new types and combinations leads to a state of utter confusion on the part of the observer. There is then no alternative to stopping for as long as is necessary to identify the pieces and fit them into place. There are other occasions when vestiges of the past are rare. In these instances I can agree heartily with Andrew Clark's statement of last year that we who deal with the past "face . . . difficulties in trying to develop for earlier centuries, by whatever ingenuity we can summon, substitutes for the rich base of quantitative data available for the twen-

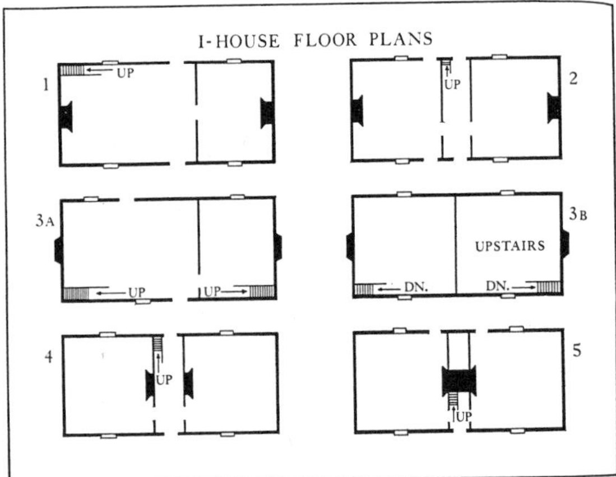

Figure 7. A range of I-house floor plans. Note in 3a two sets of stairs, the one to the right rising from the parents' room. In 3b the room to the right, occupied by the daughters, is inaccessible from the boys' room to the left.

tieth century."[10] If, as I am led to believe, the quantifiers have methods of maximizing the usefulness of scanty data, I am most happy to invite them to apply their procedures. I realize that I on my part must provide them clearly defined things to be treated.

Some Unusual Documentary Sources

I hope it has not been implied that what I have learned of American rural settlement geography has all come through my own fieldwork, for this would slight the important contributions, to mention only geographers, of Trewartha, Zelinsky, Kohn, Brush, Prunty, Mather and Hart, and others. But we are few among many, and we have not carried the systematic treatment of the various settlement ingredients very far. With the work done by geographers you are familiar. I should like here to point out some of the more unusual documentary sources, notably those aiding the study of folk housing.

For the pre-photography age with which we are dealing, collections of contemporary folk paintings are often the only evidence for much-changed areas. The old county histories, with their engravings of individual farmstead scenes, precise dating, and biographical data are invaluable sources. For example, the unexpected appearance of a Pennsylvania German barn in a New England–settled section of Michigan was explained when the text indicated that it was built by one Jacob Gentzler, who had somehow strayed into the area from Pennsylvania.[11] Early travelers' accounts are often less fruitful than might be expected, with vague descriptions, references to "houses of customary sort," and confused reporting of local terminology.

A most valuable collection that includes photographs and plans of older and folk houses is found in the Historic American Buildings Survey files of the Library of Congress. Several folk museums, such as Old Sturbridge Village, Massachusetts, and the New York State Historical Association's Farmers' Museum in Cooperstown, render most valuable aid in "collecting" and displaying authentic and well-documented old structures. In contrast, historical-marker groups are interested primarily in the houses associated with historically important individuals and incidents rather than in the typicality of the structure. We still have nothing to compare with the great outdoor folk museums of Scandinavia and Finland. Finally, I must render homage to the excellent work done by students of Pennsylvania German folk life. So much, now, for the kinds of evidence we have. What has their study yielded?

The Results

By 1790 there were, culturally speaking, three well-defined source areas on the Atlantic seaboard: New England; the Middle Atlantic, centering on southeastern Pennsylvania; and the lower Chesapeake, centering on Tidewater Virginia. The contributions of the Hudson River Dutch and the Delaware Swedes were lost in a sea of alien culture, so that they do not constitute source areas. The Germans of Pennsylvania were saved from cultural extinction especially by their two major contributions: log construction methods and basic barn types, for the principal dissemination of which they enlisted the widely spreading and aggressive Scotch-Irish.

Figure 8. Sided log I-house, Arkansas. The change in the mode of corner-timbering about halfway up suggests that the house was built in two stages. The earlier structure was likely a plain log dogtrot house. (Courtesy of the National Archives.)

Although the present basis of selection of source areas and the extensions of their influences in the eastern United States is folk housing, there is no intent to catalog here the house and barn types for the three great areal divisions into which they fall, nor are the massive accumulations of field data offered in evidence. Rather, there will be a selection for specific purposes. It should be kept in mind that the period of interest begins about 1790 and continues to around 1850.

Farthest north was the New England extension westward, with a very distinct boundary to the south. This was essentially an area of frame buildings, log construction being regarded as a pioneer expedient hardly worthy of any considerable care.[12] An English barn (fig. 9) was introduced in New England;[13] it moved westward to the grasslands with remarkably little change. The permanent frame house, on the other hand, was one of the evolutionary series appearing in New England. Which member of the series was dominant at any specific point on the westward trek follows the principle of *dominance of contemporary fashion.*[14] This principle recognizes simply that for a given period there is a popular fashion, whether dress, house, or whatnot. How does this principle apply to the westward movement out of New England?

In New England there evolved a series of house forms (fig. 10), beginning with a simple one-room

Figure 9. New England English barn. Though New England barns possibly constitute several types, the one illustrated diffused westward almost exclusively.

house in the seventeenth century, a series paralleled at least in its early stages in England. For our period we can pick up the series around 1700, with the two-room deep, two-story, massive-central-chimney house. About 1750 the idea of Georgian symmetry led to the development of a central hall, replacing the central chimney with two set toward the gable ends. Late in the eighteenth century there was great popularity, perhaps better, "revival," of the old story-and-attic, here referred to as one-and-a-half, with central chimney, sometimes yielding to a central hallway and split chimneys. Also in the late eighteenth century began the first rumblings of the classical revival; in the early decades of the nineteenth century it crystallized into a quite different form than its predecessors, with frontward-facing gable and side wings. At first glance this new form seems unrelated to other members of the series, but with further examination its relationship is clearly recognizable in the placement of chimneys, the position of the stairway, pitch of roof, and the exterior proportions and trim.

Now for the diffusion of the series: The oldest type, the two-story central-chimney house, reached slightly into frontier Maine, New Hampshire, and Vermont; the Georgian house more so; the one-and-a-half strongly; the classical form faintly. In Upstate New York the Georgian is still present, the one-and-a-half is dominant, the classical, present. In Ohio's Western Reserve the one-and-a-half is present; the classical is dominant. In Michigan and westward the one-and-a-half was an early introduction, although the classical was overwhelmingly dominant. The barn, keep in mind, came through virtually unchanged.

Thus there was established westward from New England a continuum of initial occupance patterns. With respect to housing, there was a single barn type throughout; dwellings, on the contrary, were selected from the New England evolutionary series in accordance with time of migration, so that the youngest house type was dominant farthest west. Had the area culturally tributary to New England been inhabited during the evolution of the house series, normal diffusion would have carried the oldest house type farthest west.

The Middle Atlantic source area had easily the most widespread influence of all three (fig. 11). The major directions of propagation were southward along the Appalachian axis, with offshoots in every direction, and westward across Pennsylvania, eventually to dominate everything south of the New England stream except for a generally thin Tidewater strip along the outer coastal plain. The Ohio

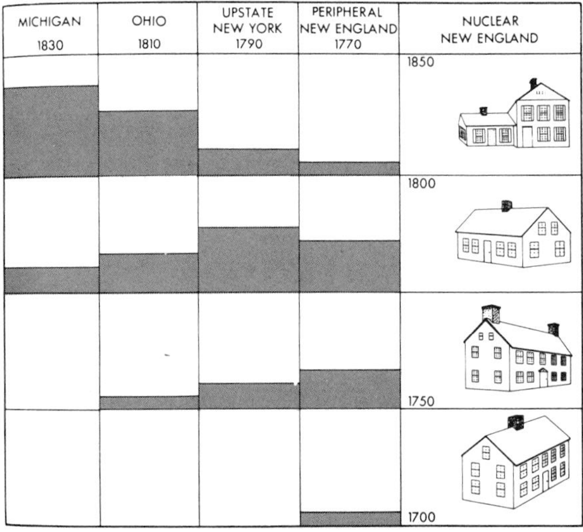

Figure 10. Diffusion of house types from New England. The dates in the vertical column at the right are suggestive of the periods of popularity of the several types in southern New England. The dates in the top horizontal column are approximations of the progress of western settlement. The proportions in the vertical columns are based on field counts.

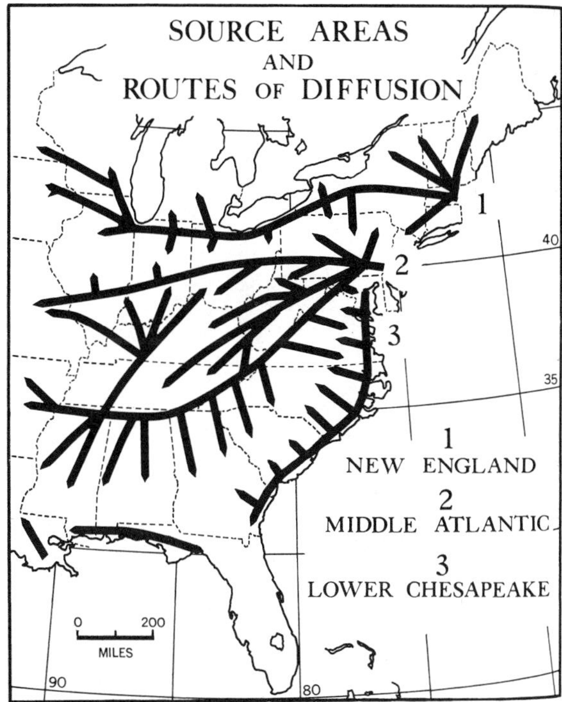

Figure 11. Source areas and diffusion routes. The routes are generally suggestive rather than precise.

Valley Midwest evidenced a strange confusion of influences, those direct from Pennsylvania mixed with many of the same influences that had gone southward from the Middle Atlantic source area and then returned to the Midwest, the two sometimes distinguishable, sometimes not.

The great contributions of the Middle Atlantic source area were the English I-house and German log construction and basic barn types. Note the distinction: Building with logs is a mode of construction, not an architectural type, while a particular type may be produced in any of several media, log, frame, stone, or brick. The central-chimney continental German house (fig. 12) died rather quickly, even among the Pennsylvania Germans themselves, but the primitive German log barn evolved into several types that dominate the Upland South to this day. Here is a case quite different from that of New England, with its evolving house and fixed barn type. South from Pennsylvania the house forms, once crystallized, were reasonably fixed, but the barn evolved quite rapidly and thoroughly.

By the time the log house reached the Valley of Virginia it had pretty well lost its original form. Subject to Tidewater influences, the chimney had moved to the end and outside and the basic plan had become a single ground-floor room (fig. 13). Now there emerged to prominence the first of the two common solutions to the problem of enlarging the unit log house, in this case into what is commonly called a *saddlebag* (fig. 14). This is a widely used method of extending the size of a house by adding another room, its gable set up to the chimney end of the original structure, producing a central-chimney house. The saddlebag house may be built originally as such or it may represent an addition. It may be one story or two; it may have one, two, or three front doors. The one constant feature is its central chimney, and it is generally only one room deep.

We might diverge here for a moment to point out why adding to a log structure poses special problems. Taper and sheer weight normally preclude the use of logs longer than twenty-four to thirty feet. Since logs are rarely if ever truly spliced, the only easy mode of addition is by adding a second story. Even this may not bring sufficient space or it may not be feasible if the original room is small. Adding a second room simply by abutting it against the older is practiced, but not widely. The saddlebag is far more widely distributed, abundantly in West Virginia and Kentucky, less abundantly but throughout the Upland South.

The most familiar solution to adding to a log house is the *dogtrot* (fig. 15), a term, by the way, quite unknown to many of its builders, who may prefer *two-pens-and-a-passage, hallway house,* or other names. Facing gable toward gable, then roofing over the intervening space is so obvious a solution to the problem that it was surely hit upon many times individually, as historic references abundantly

Figure 12. Pennsylvania German, three-room, central-chimney log house. (Courtesy of the Library of Congress.)

Figure 13. Single-room, exterior-chimney log pen. (Virginia HABS photograph by John O. Bostrup, 1936.)

Figure 14. Two-pen, central-chimney log saddlebag house.

Figure 15. Two-pen, end-chimneys log dogtrot house.

affirm. As a well-defined and dominant form it came into being in southeastern Tennessee, in an area where log work developed so highly as to constitute a great secondary source area.

The dogtrot form scarcely worked against the major stream of diffusion, being unknown even as short a distance northward as the old Watauga settlement of Tennessee and North Carolina. It did move south into Florida and the very edge of the Tidewater South, westward into Texas, along the Tennessee River into western Kentucky, Missouri, Arkansas, and occasionally even north of the Ohio River into Ohio, Indiana, and Illinois.

These remarks regarding the modes of overcoming the limitations imposed by log construction apply only to those methods employing corner-timbering or notching. They do not apply to the *pièce-sur-pièce* technique (fig. 16), used from the beginning and throughout early French America and still alive in Canada, where the employment of intermediate and corner posts, into which the tapered log ends are slotted or tenoned, permits the utilization of short logs and imposes no limitation on the size of buildings.

Figure 16. Pièce-sur-pièce *construction, Brown's Valley, Minnesota. (HABS photograph by Charles E. Peterson, 1940.)*

Figure 17. Sided log saddlebag I-house in central Kentucky.

Even with these several variants in the form of log houses, the I-house remained the symbol of economic attainment and, since its only requisites, one-room depth and two full stories, could be in any medium, it was frequently a sided-log, two-story dogtrot or saddlebag house (fig. 17).

The log barns derived from German Pennsylvania we may think of as single or multiple rectangular log units that are called here, contrary to most common practice, *cribs*, to distinguish them from the unit *pens* of log houses. The double log crib (fig. 18) entered early into the streams of diffusion from German Pennsylvania. It much resembled the dogtrot house; the space between the cribs was the heavily planked threshing floor. This simple barn, ancestral to the great Pennsylvania forebay barn, was carried everywhere that Pennsylvania influence reached, throughout the Upland South, westward through Ohio, Indiana, into Illinois and Missouri.

Following generally the same route of diffusion was the large log single crib (fig. 19), simply one unit of the double crib. It frequently was capped with a great sweeping roof that added a shed on either side of the crib, thus producing an end-opening barn, strikingly contrasted to the normal English and German side openers.

The log barns moving southward underwent changes so regular and so directed as to provide an ideal example of progressive evolution. Climatic moderation southward may have contributed to changing attitudes as to form and function of barns. The cribs grew smaller and smaller. From serving as stables they became more and more cribs for the storage of corn (fig. 20). The threshing floor disappeared with a reduction in the growing of small grain and the use of outdoor facilities. Cattle and hogs went largely without shelter (fig. 21). Only horses and mules were sometimes stabled in the sheds that flanked the small single cribs (fig. 22). This diminution in size and change in function did not take place in the westward-moving current out of Pennsylvania.

Figure 18. Double-crib log barn. This is the elemental structure, lacking the sheds that are usually present and adding a door that is more often absent.

Figure 19. Large log single-crib barn. The sweeping roof gives this structure a gable-front orientation, in contrast to the double crib.

Figure 20. Double cribs, for storage at left, for animals at right, eastern Kentucky.

Figure 21. Double-crib barn, both cribs for storage, Alabama.

Figure 22. Small log single-crib structure. The central structure is used for storage; the sheds may be animal shelters.

By manipulating the position and number of cribs, new types emerged (fig. 23). Probably in the same area that produced the dogtrot house, southeastern Tennessee, there arose the four-crib barn (fig. 24), which might be thought of as two double cribs facing each other under a common roof. Unlike its predecessors—the single or double cribs—the younger four-crib barn has not been observed in frame construction. Further, it is abundant only along the Tennessee River.

It was an easy transition from the four-crib barn to what is called here the tranverse-crib barn, simply by adding cribs to occupy the side openings, leaving a long, gable-opening structure with passage through the center, stables and storage provided by the cribs on either side. A further development added sheds on the sides. Log examples of the transverse crib are by no means rare, but frame equivalents are far more widespread (fig. 25). They occur throughout the Upland South and periphery as easily the dominant barn, though increasingly less so northward against the old stream of diffusion out of Pennsylvania.

The Lower Chesapeake source area contributed largely to the Upland South, particularly westward to affect the southward-moving stream out of Pennsylvania. As previously related, houses quickly exchanged interior for exterior end chimneys, both

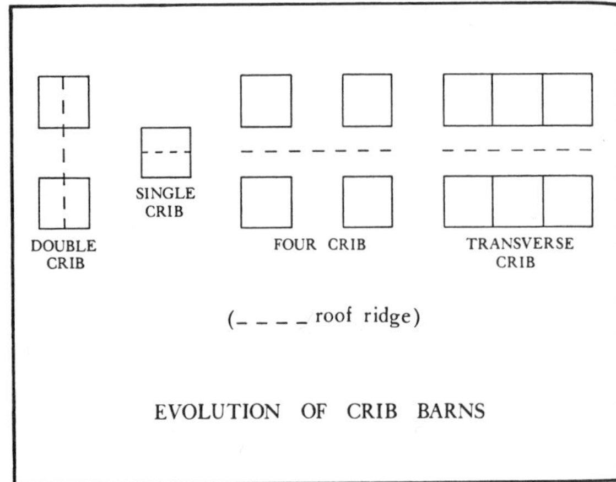

Figure 23. Evolution of crib barns.

Figure 24. Four-crib log barn.

Figure 25. Frame transverse-crib barn.

the I-house and the simpler log structures. The coastal, frame English cottage, in simplest form one room sixteen-feet square with steep roof (fig. 26), was reproduced in log. The evolved coastal cottage consisting of two end-to-end rooms with outside end chimneys may well have inspired the log dogtrot house.

For the Tidewater South as a whole there was a tradition of frame construction, with much early half-timbering. The simpler folk construction was typically clapboarding over frame rather than log. The common and basic house form is the evolved English cottage referred to above: one-room deep; one story and often attic; steep roof; two rooms in length; exterior end chimneys (fig. 27). In its further evolution a shed-roof addition is added to the rear, with an additional pair of chimneys at the ends, and commonly a front gallery (fig. 28). Especially to the south, sometime prior to the Revolution, the cottage was raised as much as a full story on brick foundation or piers (fig. 29).

The Tidewater South, considering its great extent, is remarkably uniform, even in the area of French-Spanish influence from Florida westward (fig. 30). To the north barns are primarily the side-opening English type. Increasingly they are borrowed from the Upland South in the form of single and transverse cribs along the lower Atlantic and Gulf coasts. Aside from the lower Chesapeake–Virginia section, the division between Tidewater and Upland South is incredibly sharp. Here to the south the Upland periphery fronting both Atlantic and Gulf is a dilute form of log culture, almost completely foreign to the coastal strip. Two distinct cultures adjoin for fifteen hundred miles without any considerable mixing.

Getting back to the broader perspective, it must be kept in mind that the three distinctive source areas together with their extensions, New England, Middle Atlantic–Upland South, and Lower Chesapeake–Tidewater South, as here delimited, are based chiefly on field-observed differences in selected settlement elements, specifically house and barn types. It might be interesting to compare them with regions arrived at on some other basis, but still with a cultural-historical orientation. Let us consider first the dialect map (fig. 31) of the eastern United States appearing in M. Pei's *Language for Everybody.*[15] Eastern or northern speech agrees closely with the New England stream as we have delimited it. The line between midwestern and southern dialects is not nearly far enough south as compared with our map of housing types. Hearing what to my untutored ear is good Smoky Mountain speech in the piney-woods areas close to Baton Rouge, lends me some confidence in the greater validity of my division.

Let us compare our division with another, this one dealing with types of communities based on sociological, political, and ethnographic considerations (fig. 32) as found in anthropologist Conrad Arensberg's "American Communities."[16] Though not accompanied by a map, Arensberg apparently accepts the regional divisions of Zimmerman and Du Wors for 1952,[17] based on social organization, though he prefers different nomenclature. Arensberg recognizes the three original source areas, New England, the South, and Middle Colo-

Figure 26. Unit frame Tidewater house, Virginia.

Figure 27. Two-room, frame Tidewater house.

Figure 28. Tidewater house with a two-chimney appendage and a front gallery.

Figure 29. Raised Tidewater house characteristic of the south Atlantic coast.

nies, with the last giving rise to the divergent streams of the Appalachian–Ozark region or Hill South and the Corn Belt or Midwest. Again it seems that the Tidewater South is exaggerated at the expense of the Hill or Upland South, which Arensberg conceded in discussion on the matter.

In view of the fact that our divisions are based primarily on limited material traits, such as house and barn types, and are for no later date than 1850, the agreement is surprisingly good. The differences may reflect, at least in part, changes that have taken place in the last hundred years, since both compared studies are for the present. It seems to me that the agreement attests to the validity of the implications of initial occupance and to the fundamental significance of folk housing as a diagnostic marker of cultural wholes.

Having, I trust, made our major point by confirming the three great culture areas on the basis of folk house and barn types, the division can be substantiated by many other material items. To make a random selection of some of the lesser known: In the New England area trees were initially felled in new clearings; in the Upland South there were initially deadenings of girdled trees. In the New England Northeast river bottoms were usually reserved for meadows; in the South they were planted to corn.[18] One observer noted in pioneer Indiana that northerners built water-powered grist mills, whereas southerners used horse mills. For the same general

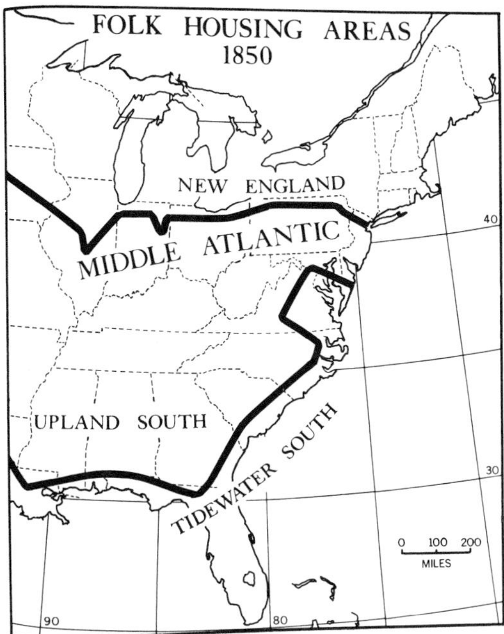

Figure 30. Folk housing areas circa 1850.

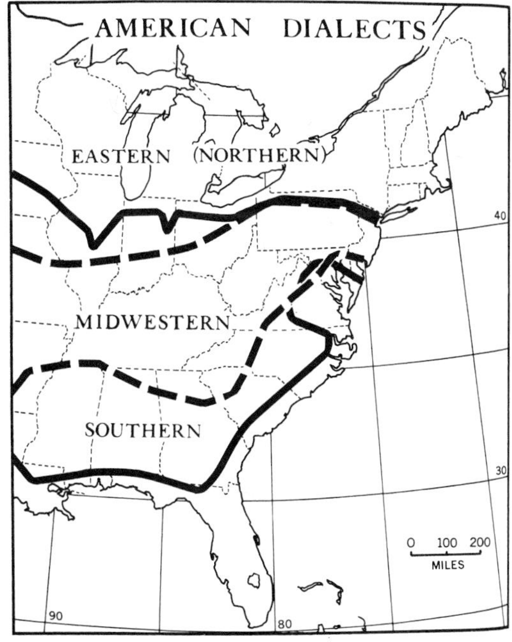

Figure 31. Present-day American dialects and 1850 housing areas. (Dialect areas after M. Pei, Language for Everybody *[New York: Pocket Books, 1958].)*

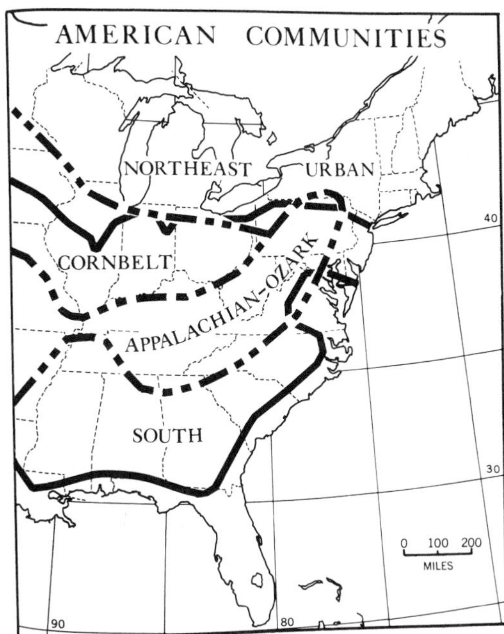

Figure 32. American communities and housing areas. (Community areas after C. M. Zimmerman and R. E. Du Wors, Graphic Regional Sociology *[Cambridge, Mass.: Philipps Book Store, 1952].)*

area, southerners' log houses could be identified by their massive outside end chimneys, the northerners' by smaller inside chimneys. Siding on southern frame barns is commonly, like logs, horizontal; in the northern English frame barns it is almost always vertical. Space precludes consideration of food preferences, which supply interesting and confirmatory evidence. The supply of contrasts is unlimited, although, as with most generalizations, they are not universally true.

One is struck by the strong influence of European precedent over early building in both mode of construction and form. Framing, the use of vertical and horizontal logs and timbers, even the first sod-covered *wigwams* of Plymouth assuredly stem from European sources, as did all the early house and barn types. Even the rail fence is European in all its several forms, probably including the snake or worm fence, which latter has been reported from Tirol.[19] I have every confidence that this typologically primitive form will eventually be fully established as Old World in origin. In reflecting on European antecedents, it may be pointed out that materials and manners of construction, notably those employing a great deal of wood, that were actually vestigial in western Europe, enjoyed a rebirth and a long life in timber-rich America. With respect to housing, this means chiefly construction utilizing closely set horizontal or vertical logs or timbers.

Environmental Differences

So far I have emphasized the importance of cultural origins and continuities, which may serve to stress a fundamental premise that groups will adhere to their cultural traditions unless forced to deviate from them. Still, it is not meant willfully to neglect the unquestioned significance of the environmental milieu. Whether or not one regards environmental adaptation as a creative process is academic; its importance is plain to see. At the same time, an unvarying natural environment demonstrably helps to preserve and extend well-adapted cultural practices. Illustrations of both stability and change can be extracted from the experiences of westward-moving New Englanders, some of the examples drawn from cultural items other than housing.

Westward from New England the range of cultural activities was little affected by natural conditions. If most-useful white pine became scarce westward, it was succeeded by an adequate substitute, the tree called variously tulip, yellow poplar, or whitewood (*Liriodendron tulipifera*). The same crops could be grown, the same orchards planted. The established seafood dishes of New England did suffer decline, but at least salt codfish found its way westward to continue some of the traditional cookery.

Only when the timber began to give way to prairie did natural conditions become assertive.[20] Subtle adaptation to such change is beautifully illustrated from the area of oak openings in southern Michigan. By the time of initial agricultural settlement during the first third of the nineteenth century, perhaps most of the settlers were aware of the advantages of the prairies for cultivation. However, only the affluent could afford to take advantage of them. The first breaking of the sod was expensive, for it might require as many as eight yoke of oxen to accomplish it. Further, the standard cash crop, wheat, could not be grown the first year. There was no immediate income of any sort. If a wet prairie, there was expensive drainage to consider.

Those who settled in the forest faced immediately the demanding task of felling and burning the trees. Yet from the ash they extracted readily salable potash. More important, with a drag they could scratch in seed among the stumps and realize a cash crop of wheat the first year. Resulting from the difference in initial cost and potential as between woodland and grassland, the woodland settlers were the poorer financially, those who had neither means nor time to build pretentious homes initially. The early prairie settlers were normally people of financial means who built substantial homes initially along roads winding through wooded strips adjoining their prairie holdings. The initially established contrast is still plain to see.[21]

More directly concerned with changes in housing is the previously described diffusion southward out of Pennsylvania accompanying a steady modification of climate. Original crops like wheat and flax disappeared in the face of adverse conditions, as did apples and other orchard crops. To match the natural changes and loss of traditional crops was an alteration of barn form and function, from large to small, and from animal shelter for confined stock to storage of corn and other crops not needing a threshing floor, accompanying a new system entailing free-ranging stock the year-round. As storage for corn, the unit cribs of the South were both larger and more poorly ventilated than the corresponding structures in the North. This is possible because corn in the South reaches a greater degree of maturity, hence becomes harder, and so is less subject to spoilage.

Vertical range of natural conditions is reflected in

settlement forms. Hatcher[22] has pointed out that in the mountains there is a declining social status with elevation, from well-to-do valley farms to meager subsistence from steep mountain corn patches. In housing, the range extends from a substantial dogtrot, saddlebag, or I-house and big double-crib barn to the single-pen house and single-crib barn. It has been suggested by some observers of the vertical contrasts that they represent something of selectivity as between those wishing to be farmers and those favoring the older frontier life with hunting a major pursuit. The latter, it is opined, followed the retreating game upward, to the detriment of agricultural potential.

In the Upland South, the type of individual is, or was in 1850, a small farmer, with log buildings, free-ranging stock, and hunting as a serious part of his economy. Contained within this large region were areas where a plantation economy and settlement pattern prevailed. Some of these plantation areas, especially those in more accessible regions, were settled by migrants from a plantation background farther east. They brought with them the "big-house" frame architecture, quarter cabins, and other settlement features of the old Tidewater plantation. Other choice areas were settled by those with an Upland cultural background. If the area possessed favorable natural attributes, notably extensive acreages of good soils, a plantation system arose. However, it began with log houses and barns; with affluence the dogtrot was converted to an I-house (fig. 33), big frame transverse-crib barns

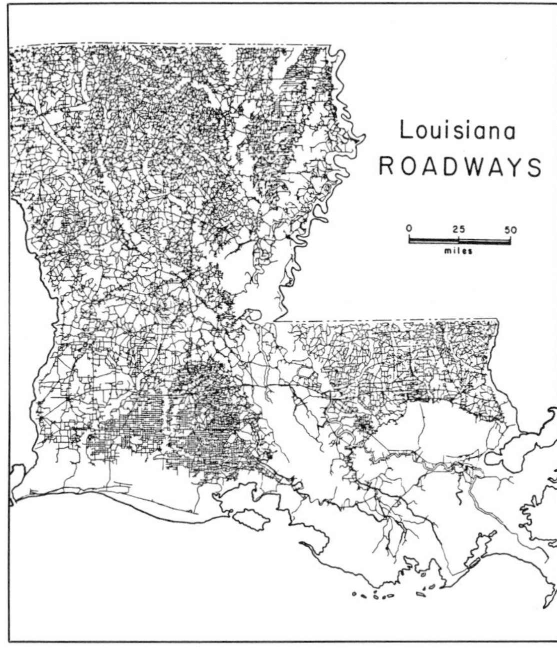

Figure 34. Louisiana roadways. Note the irregular road pattern in hilly northern Louisiana despite a rectangular survey and the regular road pattern in prairie southwestern Louisiana. (Courtesy of the Louisiana Highway Department.)

built, crystallizing into a pattern different enough from the Tidewater assemblage to warrant the title Upland plantation.

For a last example of the importance of environment on the occupance pattern, reference is made to the Ordinance of 1785 and the introduction of the rectangular survey system. The effects of the system in the settlement pattern are beautifully manifested in flat terrain. Yet in hilly areas the effect may be virtually nil, where terrain is so rough as to make roads irregular and to restrict fields to isolated, irregular patches (fig. 34). A very nice compromise between nature and the legal code was noted along the Kankakee River in Illinois, where the houses are set normal to the curving river road whereas the barns in the rear are oriented with the cardinal directions.[23]

Figure 33. Sided log dogtrot, Black Belt, Alabama. Lacks the second story of the true I-house. (Courtesy of Eugene Wilson.)

Cultural Notes

Individual adherence to the practices of one's culture group is so marked as hardly to require further illumination. There is, so the group quite unconsciously assumes, a rationale in their ways, lacking perhaps in all others. For example, consider the matter of how and where a log shall be notched in order to produce the common saddle corner-timbering (fig. 35). In some areas it is invariably on top, if not on both sides. In other areas it is on the bottom only, since any fool knows that to notch the top would provide a pocket for collecting water to rot the log. The notchers could respond that top notching is much easier, and that properly done it collects no water.

Prestige items, then as now, found expression in housing detail. Traquair shows that status of the house in French Quebec was directly proportional to the number of chimneys. It was consequently common practice to add nonfunctioning wooden chimneys to the single central chimney of stone.[24]

Not an unimportant part of my undertaking has been the recognition of vestigial traits and the interpretation of their meaning. There are, for example, the steep roofs and closely spaced purlins of early Virginia house forms pointing to older thatched roofs. There are the white-painted fronts of small frame houses in French Mississippi River areas, relicts of half-timbering and a white, plastered front, with unpainted weatherboarding on the sides (fig. 36). There is fall killing of meat animals in the year-round pasture areas of the South, a practice originating in a time and place where it was necessary to reduce the amount of winter feeding for lack of sufficient fodder.

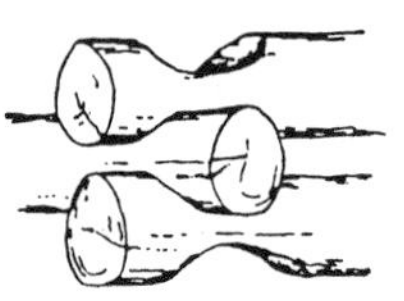

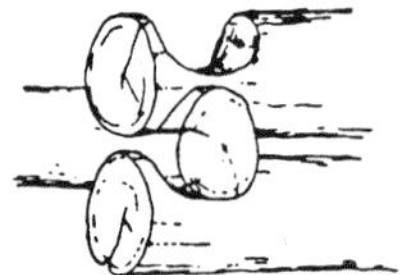

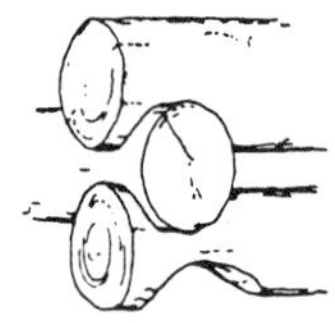

Figure 35. The three common modes of saddle notching logs in building construction: from the top, *on both sides; on top only; on bottom only.*

There is the overhang of second story over first found in many early New England houses. Once explained as devised in Indian-fighting days to give an advantage to the besieged, it was asked how the attack could be confined to the one side of the house where the overhang appeared. It was pointed out that the practice was common in medieval European towns, obviously an accommodation to narrow streets on the ground floor, a means to additional space on the second. Then came a further explanation from Innocent,[25] authoritative student of early English building methods. He noted that the upper stories project on country houses where there is no shortage of space, that the upper story might protect the lower from the weather, but what about the upper itself? He then found that on the earliest timber buildings of western Europe with two stories other than lofts, the upper stories seem to have been towers for defense, having projecting *hourdes* all round. These, he thinks, served as models when dwellings were built with upper stories. Thus the circle is complete; it appears that after all the overhang began as a defensive feature.

Finally, is there any light on what happens in an area of mixed heritage as to the survival value of the older elements? In Illinois, for example, the contrast between older bottomland settlements of southerners and the prairie settlements of easterners is still striking. There is evidence, however, of an eventual greater cultural uniformity. There was a beginning in the form of the locally created square, two-story frame house (fig. 37) of the late nineteenth century, and in the great cupolaed corncrib (fig. 38) of the present. Such examples are many. They suggest survival of old contrasting ways until something completely new submerges them.

Conclusions

This is enough to provide a sampling of what I've been seeing and what I made of the visual evidence. I've painted with a broad brush and generalized beyond certain ground. I hope errors may irritate some readers to vigorous response. I hope readers will consider the merits of the concepts of initial occupance and of the dominance of contemporary fashion and test the diagnostic power of folk housing.

I hope that this kind of evidence will materially aid the evaluation of the ideas of historians such as Turner and Webb. I hope that it may instill, even into popular thinking, a greater respect for the verities of folk practices and brand the popular toy logs and Hollywood misrepresentations as foreign to American traditions.

What I should like to see is a dedicated group of young workers who will with all deliberate haste survey the surviving evidence of the oldest occupance forms and patterns, who will supply us with concepts, terms, and usable quantities, who will be inspired, to paraphrase slightly some now-forgotten source, to think and write about these important things, to be less concerned with sharpening methodological tools, with less playing of closed games with themselves, thereby to raise this very fundamental and satisfying segment of geography to the respected place among American fields of scholarly inquiry that it inherently deserves.

Figure 36. Louisiana Creole house with painted front. (Courtesy of H. J. Walker.)

Figure 37. Square, two-story, pyramidal-roof house that became prominent in the central Corn Belt in the late nineteenth century.

Figure 38. Large cupola corncrib of recent origin in the Corn Belt.

Notes

This article was originally published in the *Annals of the Association of American Geographers* (December 1965).

1. J. Brunhes, *Human Geography* (Chicago: Rand McNally, 1920), p. 74. Brunhes listed the house among his essential facts of human geography, a product of cultural tradition and natural conditions.

2. "The primary study of the human geographer must be the dwelling and the establishment of dwelling types." J. B. Jackson, "The Almost Perfect Town," *Landscape* 2, no. 1 (Autumn 1952): 2–7.
3. W. G. McIntire, *Prehistoric Indian Settlements of the Changing Mississippi River Delta,* Coastal Studies Series, no. 1 (Baton Rouge: Louisiana State University, 1958). McIntire actually uses the term "initial *occupation.*"
4. For example, G. R. Wiley, ed., *Prehistoric Settlement Patterns in the New World,* Viking Fund Publications in Anthropology, no. 23 (New York, 1956). That the cited studies deal with prehistoric settlement patterns in no way removes them from the provenience of geography, as witness the works of contemporary European geographers.
5. N. F. Riedl, in a paper delivered before the Sixty-Third Annual Meeting of the American Anthropological Association, Detroit, November 21, 1964.
6. Noted particularly along the Mohawk, Juniata, and Ohio River routes, but most certainly present elsewhere.
7. See, for example, W. D. Peat, *Indiana Houses of the Nineteenth Century* (Indianapolis: Indiana Historical Society, 1962). Peat recognizes that the basic forms may be different, nevertheless groups the very old I-form with nineteenth-century New England classical revival houses as Greek Revival in figures 46–48 and 58–59. Figures 11–12 illustrating Federal style are respectively an I-house and a New England story-and-a-half.
8. Emphasis on floor plan is evident in all of the work of Estyn Evans. See his *Irish Heritage* (Dundalk: Dundalgan Press, 1943), pp. 58–66.
9. The I-house was first so named in 1936 in recognition of the Indiana, Illinois, or Iowa origin of many of its builders in prairie Louisiana. The *I* seems a not inappropriate symbol in view of the tall, shallow house form it designates.
10. A. H. Clark, in an unpublished paper, "The Coordinates of Historical Geography," delivered at the 1964 meeting of the Association of American Geographers.
11. *History of St. Joseph County, Michigan* (Philadelphia: L. H. Everts Co., 1877), p. 113.
12. In all the eastern United States, only the mixed population of the Upland South and its extension north of the Ohio River thoroughly adopted log construction. Even here the idealized I-house, if log, was disguised by a clapboard covering.
13. M. S. Briggs noted that early New England barn framing is precisely like that of southeastern England in *The Homes of the Pilgrim Fathers in England and America (1620–1685)* (London: Oxford University Press, 1932), p. 62.
14. Dominance of the contemporary fashion is illustrated vividly in modern coastal southwestern Louisiana, where the choice of currently popular slab construction to replace hurricane-destroyed dwellings is an invitation to further destruction. See F. Kniffen and M. Wright, "Disaster and Reconstruction in Cameron Parish," *Louisiana Studies* 2, no. 2 (Summer 1963): 74–83.
15. M. Pei, *Language for Everybody* (New York: Pocket Books, 1958), map, p. 53.
16. C. M. Arensberg, "American Communities," *American Anthropologist* 57, no. 6 (December 1955): 1143–62.
17. C. M. Zimmerman and R. E. Du Wors, *Graphic Regional Sociology* (Cambridge, Mass.: Philipps Book Store, 1952), Basic Regions Map, p. 1.
18. Natural meadows in the North were especially important as sources of hay before hayfields were extensive. Making hay was far less important in the South, where year-round pasturage was possible; one most important source of winter feed, now largely gone, was common cane (*Arundinaria* spp.).
19. H. C. Mercer, *Ancient Carpenters' Tools* (1929, reprint, Doylestown, Pa.: Bucks County Historical Society, 1951), p. 20.
20. An excellent summary of observations and writings dealing with the settlement of the forest-prairie transition belt appears in T. G. Jordan, "Between the Forest and the Prairie," *Agricultural History* 38, no. 4 (October 1964): 205–16.
21. A good example of an old, selective settlement along a prairie-woodland contact occurs some three miles southeast from Mendon, Michigan.
22. J. W. Hatcher, "Appalachian America," in W. T. Couch, ed., *Culture in the South* (Chapel Hill: University of North Carolina Press, 1935), pp. 382–88. Hatcher thought that the more vigorous and alert settlers gained possession of the vantage points, whereas the less highly endowed were shunted off to the less desirable locations.
23. Observed along the left bank of the Kankakee River immediately west of Kankakee, Illinois.
24. R. Traquair, "Old Architecture of French Canada," *Queen's Quarterly* 38, no. 4 (Autumn 1931): 589–608, see esp. p. 595.
25. C. F. Innocent, *The Development of English Building Construction* (Cambridge: Cambridge University Press, 1916), p. 165.

Acculturation in the Shenandoah Valley: Rhenish Houses of the Massanutten Settlement

EDWARD A. CHAPPELL

Because vernacular architecture is mainly the architecture of ordinary people, it commonly manifests their sense of collective identity. In a nation of immigrants like the United States, identity is often shown by a strong allegiance to a particular ethnic group. Edward A. Chappell's study demonstrates how ethnicity was expressed in a set of eighteenth-century vernacular structures built by a German-speaking community in Page County, Virginia.

From the evidence of surviving buildings, Chappell determined that the first Swiss Mennonite settlers built a type of dwelling they called a Flurküchenhaus *or a hall-kitchen house. This building had an asymmetrical floor plan consisting of two, three, or four rooms arranged around an off-center internal fireplace and chimney. Over the course of about seventy-five years these Massanutten farmers modified their Old World building pattern by replacing the internal fireplaces, by shifting room functions, and by balancing the placement of doors and windows. While their new buildings were not exact copies of fashionable English houses, they did have visual features that allowed Rhenish builders to demonstrate their awareness of the trendy double-pile, central-passage Georgian plan.*

Despite these significant changes, there were also significant retentions of German elements. Consequently Chappell suggests that cultural change does not have to be cataclysmic. As long as the will to remain different survives, ethnic distinctions will be manifested in some manner. Only after 1800, at the point when the Massanutten Germans were willing to plunge wholeheartedly into the Anglo culture of Virginia and universally adopted the I-house as their favored dwelling, did German architecture pass from the landscape.

Form in folk architecture is primarily determined by the traditions and the symbolic needs of the people who construct and live in the buildings. For this reason, the identification and interpretation of building patterns in a region can provide a fertile resource for understanding the condition of people's culture. It is evident that much variation within artifact assemblages is the result of individual practical and psychological requirements. Yet patterns of continuity and change in essential forms, such as recurring or changing combinations of spatial arrangements in architecture, reflect corresponding stability or unrest within the culture.[1] This essay presents a group of architecturally similar eighteenth-century Germanic-American houses built in a narrowly limited geographic area within a period of approximately fifty years. The unity of their forms is the result of the cohesive and separatist context in which the houses were constructed. Significant deviation in the form of some structures and later alterations to others are proposed as indications of the impact of acculturation.

The northern Shenandoah Valley, locally called the lower Valley, was settled in the last three quarters of the eighteenth century by Scots-Irish, English, and Germanic people migrating mostly from eastern and central Pennsylvania. The largest group consisted of Germans and Swiss, primarily first and second-generation immigrants from the Rhine Valley. In settling the lower Valley, this group of culturally related Rhenish people brought with them dialects, crafts, and according to contemporary accounts, a personal character that distinguished them from their Scots-Irish and English neighbors.[2] Although people of Germanic background retained numerical superiority in the lower Valley into the nineteenth century, they had, by the beginning of the century, begun to be absorbed into an Anglo-American regional culture. This is not intended to imply that some ethnic characteristics did not survive acculturation, or that some Germanic forms did not for a time affect the artifactual conceptions of the Scots-Irish and English.[3] Yet it was in the period around 1800 that the Germanic people rejected the most visible symbols of their background.

Two instructive examples are language and architecture. Klaus Wust has explained that there existed a bidialectal situation among the Valley Germans before they adopted the English language. The standard German language was used in writing and in public situations while a variety of related dialects, collectively called "Valley Dutch" but actually based on the dialects of the homeland, provided the medium for informal conversation. As a highly visible symbol of separation and as an obstacle to involvement in local business and government matters, the former was largely abandoned in favor of English by about 1830. The more personal use of the dialects survived, in some cases into the twentieth century.[4]

Parallel to the abandonment of the standard German language was the rejection of a general house type that reflected both the aesthetic traditions and the domestic systems of the Rhenish settlers. Even the most casual examination of housing in the Shenandoah Valley reveals a rural landscape dominated by medium-sized farms with a single predominant house form, one that is distinctly nineteenth-century and Anglo-American. Throughout the century, the symmetrical two-story I-house was built in brick and frame in such numbers that its preeminence has not yet been seriously threatened by the tentacles of suburban ranch houses reaching out from the towns.[5] The overwhelming dominance of the I-house in the Valley is striking when compared to the diversity of vernacular house forms that were built in nineteenth-century Piedmont and Tidewater Virginia, where pre-1800 types continued to constitute a significant percentage of the houses built. It can be argued that the tenacious adherence to the I-house form in the Valley housing revolution represents a conscious replacement of the symbols of the old ethnic cultures.[6] For the Germanic people in the Valley, the I-house provided highly visible evidence of at least partial entrance into an acceptable regional culture. As a distinguishing cultural symbol, the form was less important to the relatively homogeneous population of eastern Virginia.

That the ninteenth-century housing revolution in the Shenandoah Valley swept away most of the buildings of the previous century also implies a relative lack of substantiality in the earlier buildings. Except for the most affluent, few nineteenth-century farmers could afford the luxury of replacing a sizable and sturdy old house when it could be altered to accommodate new needs. There is, for example, a relationship with early postmedieval English housing developments, when second floors and chimneys were commonly inserted in earlier open-hall houses.[7] The dearth of eighteenth-century houses surviving in the Shenandoah Valley indicates that, as in the seventeenth-century Chesapeake region, most families lived in buildings that were less substantial than those built by people of average means in the following century.

There was, however, deviation from this pattern of insubstantial Shenandoah Valley housing. In several areas where settlements were established at an early date, farmers and small industrialists within one or two generations reached a level of economic success that led them to build dwellings of sufficient permanence to be occupied through the nineteenth century. An example of such a prosperous enclave is the Massanutten settlement in present Page County. In the 1720s a group consisting predominantly of Swiss Mennonites and led by Adam Müller (usually anglicized to Miller) settled a five-thousand-acre tract along the South Fork of the Shenandoah River east of Massanutten Mountain. Located roughly between Hawksbill Creek and the town of Alma, the land was purchased from Swiss immigrant Jacob Stover, a promoter who at the time of the sale had apparently not gained title to the land.[8] In 1733 eight Massanutten settlers petitioned Virginia Governor William Gooch for confirmation of their ownership. Adam Müller (Miller), Abram Strickler, Mathias Selzer, Philip Lang (Long), Paul Lung (Long), Michael Rhinehart, Hans Rood, and Michael Kaufman stated that after purchasing the land from Stover about four years before, they had sold their properties in Lancaster, Pennsylvania, settled the Virginia land, and "cleared sevl. Plantations and made great Improvements theron."[9]

During the following seventy-five years, the Massanutten settlers or their descendants constructed a group of substantial houses that differ in form from the nineteenth-century houses of the region. Despite variations among the houses, unifying patterns exist that relate them to each other and to Pennsylvania Rhenish buildings. These patterns indicate a cultural distinction among eighteenth-century Germanic people that would diminish in the following century.

Acculturation was not, however, an instant phenomenon that involved the rapid assimilation of the separate ethnic groups of the Shenandoah Valley into a relatively homogeneous population. Some evidence of the gradual process of change is supplied by several of the buildings in the Massanutten group. Before the I-house or one of its formal derivations became virtually the only house type a successful middle-class farmer in the region would build, certain of the ideas it embodied were utilized in combination with familiar Germanic forms. The original form of several of the buildings indicates a movement away from some of the old transported ideas of what a house should be. In addition, later alterations to most of the Massanutten houses are related to the new ideas. Definition of the essential characteristics of the group will help to establish the significant deviations.

The primary house form brought to America by eighteenth-century German and Swiss immigrants was a story-and-a-half or two-story building with a first-floor plan consisting of two, three, or four rooms disposed around an internal chimney.[10] Exposed timber-frame construction called *Fachwerk*, stone, and hewn logs were the materials usually employed for exterior walling. Stone and log construction came to be favored in America, and no examples of *Fachwerk* are known in Virginia. Limestone laid as coursed rubble was generally used for foundations and chimneys.

In this *Flurküchenhaus* or hall-kitchen house a front and often rear door give entry into a narrow kitchen room, or *Küche*, which was served by a large cooking fireplace (fig. 1). Related to the function of the English hall, the room was utilized both for cooking and as the primary informal living space. The *Küche* is located to the right of the chimney in 80 percent of the Massanutten examples. A wider room called a *Stube*, located on the opposite side of the chimney, was apparently used for more formal gatherings, a function similar to that of the Anglo-American parlor. That Valley Germans may have

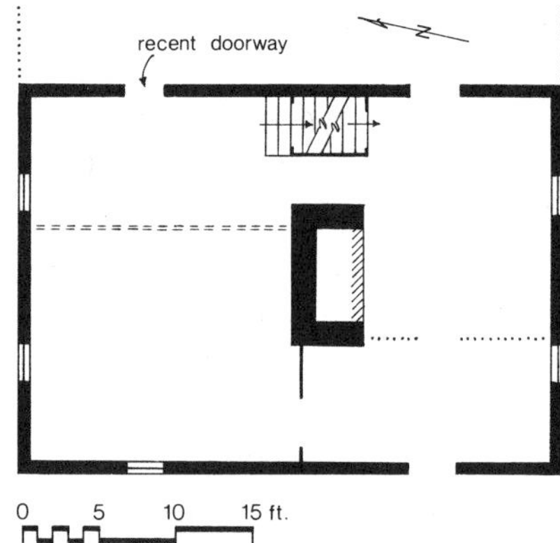

Figure 1. First-floor plan of the Abram Strickler House. For all plans the original fabric is shown as black, later fabric is hatched, and second stage alterations are stippled. The location of destroyed early features is indicated with broken lines, and recent additions are represented with dotted lines. Recent porches are omitted. Wall niches are noted with the letter n.

generally eaten in the *Stube* is indicated by Samuel Kercheval's statement that a long pine table was always located in a corner of the room, with benches permanently fixed on one side.[11] Similar fixed *Stube* furniture has been observed in houses in Switzerland.[12] In most large *Flürkuchenhauser,* the rear of the *Stube* is partitioned to form a narrow unheated sleeping chamber, called a *Kammer* by the Germans and a *Stibli* by the Swiss.[13] Traditionally, the *Stube* was heated by an iron or tile stove that was fed with coals through an opening in the rear of the *Küche* fireplace.[14] All such heating devices were removed when the Massanutten houses were altered, but plates from five-plate iron stoves have survived in the region. An example marked "MARL [BORO] FURN[ACE] 1768" from Isaac Zane's iron works in Frederick County was until recently used as a fireback at Fort Paul Long (fig. 2). At Fort Egypt, the room above the *Stube* was also heated by a stove, which was furnished with coals from a small elevated fireplace on the opposite side of the chimney. In some large-scale variations of the *Flürkuchenhaus* form, the rear of the *Küche* is partitioned to form a fourth room, a space that was utilized as a workroom in Switzerland.[15] Although the fourth room has been identified as a pantry in Pennsylvania, an example at Fort Egypt is provided with a small fireplace (fig. 3b). Evidence of another such fireplace was previously visible at the rear of the *Küche* in Wildflower Farm, a similar house in adjoining Shenandoah County.

The second floor is reached by enclosed stairs most often located in the *Küche,* and in a number of houses an additional stair rises from the *Kammer.* There is considerable variation in second-floor room disposition among the houses in which the original upper-level plan can be determined. Generally, the space is divided axially at the chimney, with one or both of the spaces sometimes divided into two rooms (fig. 3c). Only in one-and-a-half-

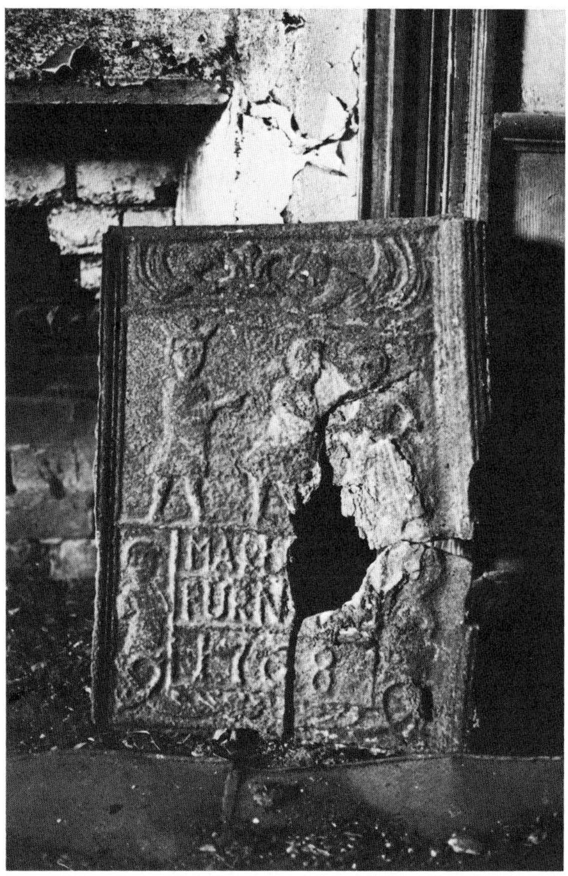

Figure 2. Plate from an iron stove at Fort Paul Long cast at Isaac Zane's Marlboro Furnace.

story Page County houses is the loft space finished. The attics of all single- and two-story houses were originally undivided and the roof framing was left exposed.

The most conservative fenestration of Virginia as well as Pennsylvania *Flurküchenhauser* consists of two openings in each story on the front and rear walls (fig. 4). Three-bay fenestration is also found, and at Fort Rhodes one of the two facade openings into the *Stube* was originally a door. Like eighteenth-century Anglo-American Virginia builders, Germanic builders in the Valley tended to balance exterior openings in relation to internal spaces rather than in relation to the elevation.[16] For example, the facade openings at Fort Rhodes are placed nearly equidistant from the ends of the *Stube* and *Küche,* with less attention given to exterior balance. This grammar of piercing was only loosely followed, however, and concern for external balance is per-

a

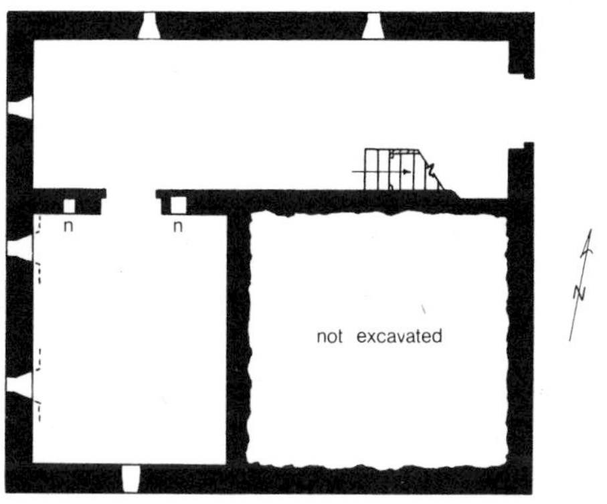

b

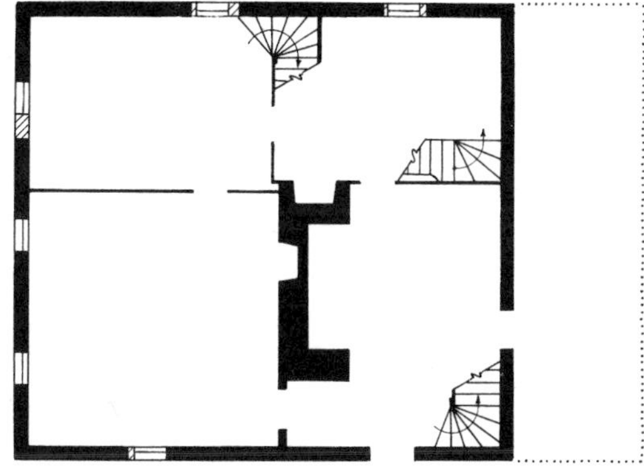

c

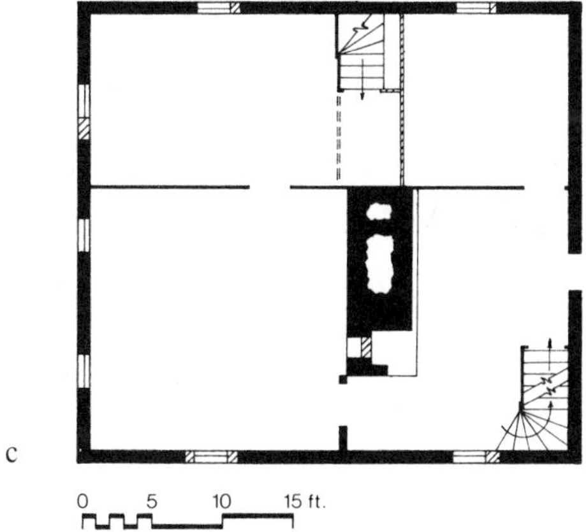

Figure 3. Cellar, first-, and second-floor plans of Fort Egypt. (1940 HABS plans revised by the author.)

Figure 4. Fort Egypt.

ceptible in a number of the houses. Surprisingly, external symmetry is most often found on the gable ends.

Interior finish is characterized by an open expression of the construction methods, a quality that was distinctly avoided by later Valley builders. While the builders of nineteenth-century I-houses created spaces bounded by plastered surfaces and punctuated by nonstructural architectural elements, the ceiling framing and a variety of wall surfaces were left exposed in *Flurküchenhauser* and a minimum of cosmetic details were used. In most examples, interior trim is confined to chair rails, baseboards, and cornice strips over the fireplaces. With the exception of several short sections of masonry and exposed frame walls abutting the chimney, interior walls are of vertical-board construction. An early partition at Fort Egypt is constructed of plain boards and molded battens (figs. 5a, 6). Partitions on the first floor of Fort Rhodes and the second floor of Fort Stover consist of raised panels set into vertical boards with molded edges (fig. 5b). More common among the Massanutten houses, however, are partitions constructed of tongue-and-groove vertical boards with beaded edges (fig. 5c). Only at Fort Stover, a house exhibiting a number of features that deviate from traditional German-American forms, are plastered stud walls found, and there they are confined to the first floor. Consistently, the first- and second-floor interior surfaces of stone walls are plastered, while log walls are usually left exposed and whitewashed. With the possible exception of the first floor at Fort Stover, ceiling framing was originally exposed in all the houses. In buildings of sufficient depth to require bridging beams, summers are used both singly and in pairs (fig. 7, 10). Running between the gable ends, most are set into the chimney masonry, although at the Abraham Heiston House and Fort Stover they are unsupported at the center. Unlike Anglo-American framing, the joists either rest entirely on top of the summers (as at Fort Egypt and Fort Stover) or are only partially set into them (as at Fort Rhodes).

Some of the Massanutten houses preserve roof structures of distinctly ethnic form, while others have simple common rafter roofs that to a certain degree can be recognized as an early acceptance of Anglo-American framing techniques. Two traditional Germanic systems of framing a complex gable roof were used in the Shenandoah Valley, both consisting of common rafters supported by a heavy substructure.[17] In the one method used at Fort Egypt, Fort Rhodes, and the Abraham Spitler House, but surviving unaltered only at Spitler, the supporting structure is comprised of horizontal purlins resting on three pairs of large vertical posts (figs. 8, 9). At the Spitler House and also at Wildflower Farm in Shenandoah County, the posts are connected to the joists by angle braces and to the purlins by arch braces. Collars tie together the posts and common

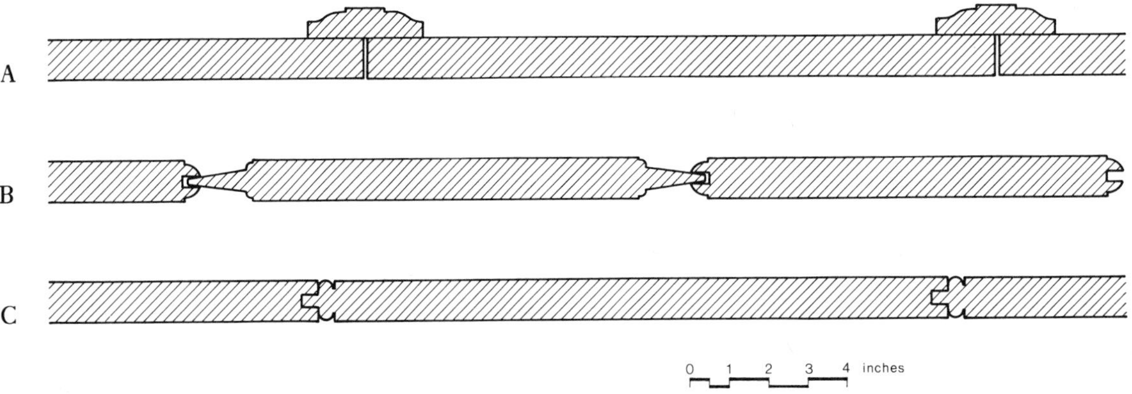

Figure 5. Interior partition details: a, between first-floor rear rooms at Fort Egypt; b, second-floor partition at Fort Stover; c, between the Stube *and* Kammer *at Fort Egypt.*

Figure 6. First-floor partition between the rear rooms at Fort Egypt.

Figure 7. Second-floor north room at Fort Stover.

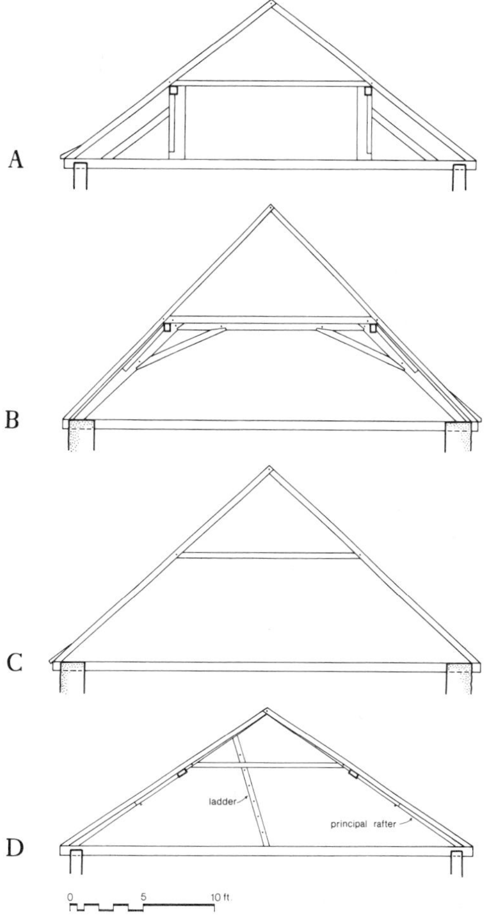

Figure 8. Roofs on Rhenish houses in the Massanutten settlement and nearby: a, the Abraham Spitler House; b, Fort Bowman, Shenandoah County; c, Fort Stover; d, an early nineteenth-century log house at Fort Paul Long. (Roofs a and b were drawn from measurements supplied by Dell Upton; roof c is based on a HABS drawing by Tarquin M. Rachelle.)

rafters above them, but the other rafters are without collars. Not found in the Massanutten houses but used at Fort Bowman in Shenandoah County as well as in Pennsylvania and Maryland buildings is a second system of rafter support which consists of pairs of truncated principal rafters linked by double collars (fig. 8b). The rafters broaden toward the top, where they are slotted to receive the purlins. A lower collar is morticed to the inner sides of the principals, and a larger collar rests on top, tying together the principals, purlins, and common rafters. Principal rafter collars on similar roofs at the Schiefferstadt House in Frederick, Maryland, and the Golden Plough Tavern in York, Pennsylvania, have a slight camber, although those at Bowman are straight.[18] Arch braces add additional stability by connecting the principals to the purlins and lower collars. At Fort Bowman, the common rafters have large 4″ × 6″ collars that are pegged to the purlins, and it is the common collars rather than the rafters that are directly seated on the support system.

In both the post and principal rafter systems, the rafter feet usually rest directly on the joists, without

Figure 9. Roof post and purlin at the Abraham Spitler House.

the false plate intermediary that was popular in Anglo-Virginian framing.[19] Story-and-a-half houses represent an exception, for when the walls are carried above the level of the joists, the rafters must be seated on plates.[20] A feature common to Germanic roofs is a *kick,* or lowering of pitch near the eaves. In the Old World, this broken silhouette was often achieved by placing the rafter feet on the joists directly over the wall and extending the joists beyond. A short partial rafter, or *Aufschifter,* was then framed between the top of the extended joists and the common rafter.[21] Where the kicks are found on American Germanic houses, the rafter feet are often set above the outer face of the wall, and a wedge is merely nailed or pegged to the top of the rafter (figs. 8a and b).

Simple common rafter roofs are known in the Rhineland, and to some extent their use here might be attributed to their cheapness and sufficiency for spanning shorter distances.[22] Yet the size of the building does not constitute the essential factor in the choice of roof type, as illustrated by Moravians' use of the Spitler roof system on relatively small buildings in Salem, North Carolina. While it is true that unsupported common rafter roofs are used on all the smaller Massanutten buildings, they are also found at the Abraham Heiston House and at Fort Stover (fig. 8c), both of which are deeper than Spitler and Bowman. What seems to have happened at the Massanutten settlement and at other Germanic communities in America is a gradual abandonment of the complex roofing systems that were indigenous to Germanic culture. Although the old systems were remembered and aspects of their forms were used on barns and a few other large nondomestic buildings as late as the second half of the nineteenth century, they were apparently abandoned for houses, where simple common rafter roofs usually would suffice.[23] The general demise of the traditional roofs was exemplified by the construction of a log house built by the Long family at Fort Paul Long early in the nineteenth century. The new house was as deep as the Spitler House, and because the roof was to have a low (33°) pitch, it was felt that a common rafter system was not sufficient. The builders eschewed the old systems, however, and instead built an Anglo-American principal rafter roof with butt purlins (fig. 8d).

An essential feature of the Rhenish farm on both sides of the Atlantic is the provision for storage within the body of the house. In some Shenandoah Valley houses an old concept of multi-level attic storage has survived in the utilization of space above the roof collars, reached by a permanent ladder. Kercheval states that garners for grain were a common feature in the upper floor of Valley German houses, and Robert Bucher has described a similar practice in Pennsylvania.[24]

The most dramatic accommodation, however, is a variable cellar form drawn from Rhineland and Pennsylvania precedents.[25] As an integral part of their houses, the Massanutten builders constructed single- and two-room cellars employing techniques that protected large quantities of perishable food from changes in temperature. The cellars housed functions that were relegated to detached spring houses in the nineteenth century, and two Massanutten cellars, as well as a number of Pennsylvania examples, contain springs.[26] The primary insulation method involved construction of a rubble stone barrel vault rising from low walls (figs. 10, 11). These vaulted rooms, or *die Gewölbkeller,*[27] were provided with small vaulted and trabeated window openings that were tapered toward the exterior. Iron and wooden hooks embedded in the

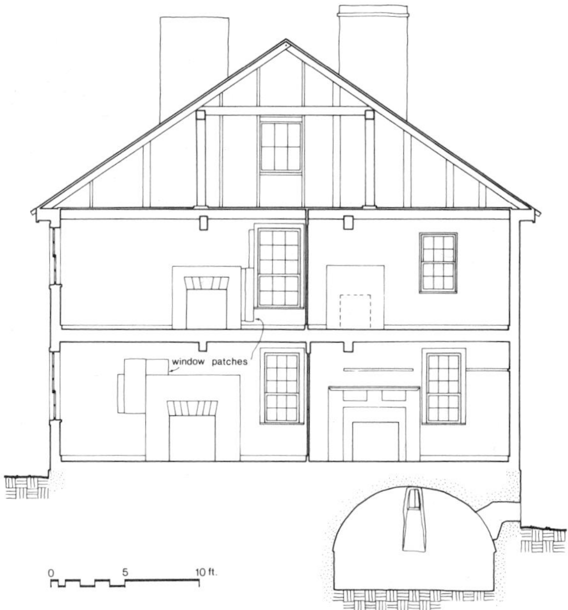

Figure 10. Section of Fort Rhodes.

Figure 11. Cellar of Fort Paul Long.

vaults carried wooden poles for suspension of foods such as meat and cheese.[28] Surviving in two of the Massanutten houses is a second insulation method, which consists of straw and clay infilling between the cellar ceiling joists (fig. 12). The latter method is found in Germanic buildings north of the Shenandoah Valley, both confined to the cellar (for example, at the Alexander Schaeffer House at Schaefferstown and the Golden Plough Tavern at York in Pennsylvania) and extended to insulate the upper floors (Ephrata Cloister in Lancaster County, Pennsylvania and the Schiefferstadt House in Frederick, Maryland). The walls of both cellar forms are pierced with small rectangular niches, which are locally called *pine holes.* The oral evidence that at least some of the niches were used to burn pine knots or other lighting material is supported by one example that has a flue (fig. 29), although it has been suggested that similar recesses in New England Anglo-American cellars were used for cooling.[29] Further, the cooling function is unlikely for two niches that are located in the chimney breasts of the upper floors (fig. 20a). In both Pennsylvania and the Shenandoah Valley, early houses have sometimes acquired the term *fort,* and present use of the prefix may have been encouraged by conjecture about the defensive functions of the vaulted cellars. Despite the improbability of this function, it is of interest that White House was referred to as a "Fort House" as early as 1827.[30]

Several patterns of cellar room disposition and entrance are evident in the Massanutten houses. With the exception of the Andrew Keyser House, all of the cellars have an exterior entrance. The larger houses originally had an additional internal entrance from the first floor. In two-room cellar plans, the external doorway provides entrance to the outer room and the inner room is given the strongest method of insulation, usually by means of a vault. Although it is assumed that both rooms were used for storage, a fireplace in the outer room at the Abraham Spitler House and underground access to a well from the lower of two vertically stacked cellars at Fort Philip Long suggest that those rooms were also the scenes of productive activities. Full-size windows in the cellars at Fort Philip Long and in the outer rooms at the Spitler House and Fort Stover further evidence their use as work rooms. The presence of a cooking fireplace in the outer cellar room at Fort Stover is an indication of changing functions within the *Flurküchenhaus* form, although Robert C. Bucher has interpreted cellar

Figure 12. Outer cellar room of Fort Egypt.

Figure 13. Fort Philip Long.

kitchens in early Pennsylvania houses as survivals of a Swiss *Weinbauern* housing tradition.[31]

Most of the existing houses are sited so that the ground slopes downward at the rear and at one gable end, allowing external entrance to the cellar either at ground level or by way of a short flight of steps. This method of hillside siting, with relatively direct entrance into two floors, is a distinguishing feature of the Rhenish house in America. Multilevel dwellings and farm buildings that take advantage of sloping ground exist in Britain, but the form is seldom found in English-settled areas of Tidewater and Piedmont Virginia.[32] The occasional appearance of the siting choice in nineteenth-century Shenandoah Valley houses can be attributed to the persistence of a Germanic minority trait.[33]

The formal, structural, and functional characteristics of the Rhenish houses in the Massanutten group constitute a set of related traits, most of which were rejected by the builders of similarly scaled houses in the nineteenth century. Structural characteristics include stone and log exterior walling and an honest expression of a diverse assortment of internal construction devices. Formally, the houses often utilize sloping topography to allow direct entrance to cellar and first-floor levels. The first-floors plans consist of two to four rooms grouped around an internal chimney, with an exterior entrance directly into the principal living room, without the mediation of a passage or lobby. The fenestration, like the off-center placement of the chimney, is asymmetrical. Productive and storage functions were contained within the body of the house. Cooking took place in the same room in which the family gathered, and the cellar is equipped with features intended to preserve the food stored there for the family's use. Despite variations, the surviving buildings form a coherent group that is recognizably distinct from the contemporary house forms of other ethnic groups in the region, and that is indicative of the separate nature of Germanic culture in eighteenth-century Virginia. The shared characteristics of the buildings represent an architectural vocabulary that was one aspect of a transported cultural heritage.

Members of the Germanic community, however, became increasingly susceptible to the acculturative pressures of the dominant ethnic group. Because of social and perhaps political aspirations, some wealthy Valley Germans were especially receptive to Anglo-American affectations. Klaus Wust has cited examples of families who in the eighteenth century sought to associate themselves with Anglo gentility by giving properly bucolic, English-sounding names to their estates and by sending their sons to English schools.[34] Jacob Stover even attempted to follow an English-speaking route to heaven by receiving Presbyterian baptism on his deathbed in 1741.[35]

Some of the buildings of the Massanutten group display significant deviations from the *Flurküchenhaus* model, changes that can be attributed to selective cultural assimilation, both aesthetic and functional. The amalgam of Rhenish and English forms does not follow a clear pattern of development towards a formal Georgian model, and a number of disparate English forms can be discovered in different houses. The two surviving Long houses, for example, present a complex mixture of Rhenish and English building types of an equally informal nature.

The original first-floor plan at Fort Philip Long (fig. 14) consisted of two rooms of essentially *Flurküchenhaus* proportions, that is, a narrow *Küche* with wider *Stube* adjoining. Yet the chimneys are located on the gable walls, with the kitchen entrance beside the large cooking fireplace, following the form of some submedieval Western English and Welsh houses.[36] The large irregularly shaped kitchen chimney is placed off center on the gable end and the flue of a corner fireplace in the *Stube* rises through the wall to a small internal stack. Into this informal massing was introduced an unfamiliar form of symmetrical fenestration, with a single door near the center of the front wall giving entrance to the larger room, and three windows evenly spaced in the rear wall. At Fort Paul Long we find an English hall-parlor plan, with the cooking fireplace in the larger room (fig. 15b). There both chimneys are located on the interior of the gable walls, but no attempt has been made toward symmetrical fenestration. Both Long houses utilize sloping ground to provide access to cellars of distinctly Rhenish form.

Gable-end chimneys and multiple fireplaces were also employed in conjunction with the *Flurküchenhaus* plan at three larger, and probably

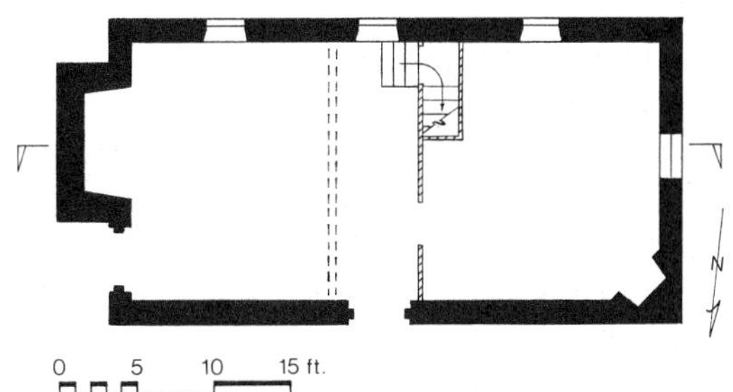

Figure 14. First-floor plan of Fort Philip Long.

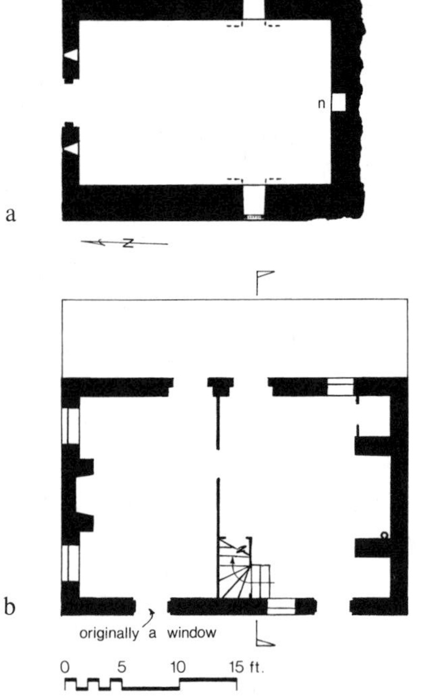

Figure 15. Cellar and first-floor plans of Fort Paul Long.

later, Massanutten houses: the Abraham Heiston House, Locust Grove, and Fort Stover. At the Heiston House the chimneys were simply an affectation of Anglo-American form grafted to a house that retained a two-bay fenestration and traditional interior spacial distribution and functions (fig. 16). But at Locust Grove and Fort Stover, the formal changes were more extensive, and in them we see a desire to present an external facade that more completely resembled the two-story Anglo-American hall-parlor or center-passage house. In both cases, the fenestration of the front wall is ordered in an approximation of symmetrical tripartite form, with windows flanking a doorway. The builders were still designing their houses in accordance with the spatial arrangements of the *Flurküchenhaus* model, however, and rather than placing the front door at the center of the facade, they located it far to one side, so that it still provided entrance to the old *Küche* space (fig. 17). The tripartite fenestration was barely attempted on the rear wall of either house; there the builders were content to utilize more or less traditional patterns of openings.

Locust Grove no longer stands, and insufficient information survives to clearly determine its room uses. Fort Stover, however, exhibits a functional change that indicates that the effects of acculturation within the ethnic community were not confined to a new concern for visual order. That the living patterns within at least one of the familiar spaces had significantly changed is shown by the location of the cooking fireplace in the cellar rather than in the usual first-floor *Küche* location (fig. 18). The separation of food preparation from the primary living space of the house represents abandonment of an essential characteristic of the Rhenish house.

A parallel division of cooking and living spaces that occurred in the English-settled Chesapeake region around the middle of the seventeenth century is considered by scholars to represent an attempt by house owners to separate themselves from the activities of indentured servants and slaves.[37] Although a desire for social division may in fact have been the primary impetus for the detached kitchen in the American South, the expulsion of cooking, with its attendant sounds and smells, conforms with the rationalizing concepts that reached the eighteenth-century American masses as what James Deetz and Henry Glassie call the Georgian world view and Norbert Elias calls an advance in the threshold of delicacy.[38] Whatever its initial stimulus, the suppressed kitchen became a feature common to the households of eastern Virginia slaveowners and non-slaveowners alike, and in the nineteenth century it was part of the regional cultural complex accepted by Germanic people in the Shenandoah Valley. The kitchen occupied a number of positions in relation to the ubiquitous nineteenth-century I-house, primarily at the end of the rear ell, in the basement, or in a detached building, but never within the main body of the house.

All of the Massanutten houses that continued to serve as dwellings in the nineteenth century were altered to accommodate Anglo-American room functions. The general pattern of alteration involved

Figure 16. The Abraham Heiston House.

Figure 17. Fort Stover.

removal of the kitchen and provision of heating fireplaces for two rooms of comparable size, although plan changes were more drastic in some buildings than others (fig. 19). Late nineteenth- and early twentieth-century functions described by informants indicate that the two rooms were used as living room and parlor. At the Charles Keyser House, the larger room was reserved for the entertainment of guests, and it contained the best furniture in the house. The smaller room was used as both a bedroom and family gathering place. The functions of master bedroom and living room were commonly combined in the same first-floor space in nineteenth-century and later Piedmont Virginia houses, a combination that was also found at Fort Rhodes. At Fort Rhodes, the left rear room was utilized as a living room-chamber and the larger left front room was a parlor. In winter, the family living at Fort Rhodes ate in the former *Küche,* and in the summer in the detached kitchen. Alterations to first-floor partitions at the Abraham Heiston House resulted in two rooms of nearly equal size, both

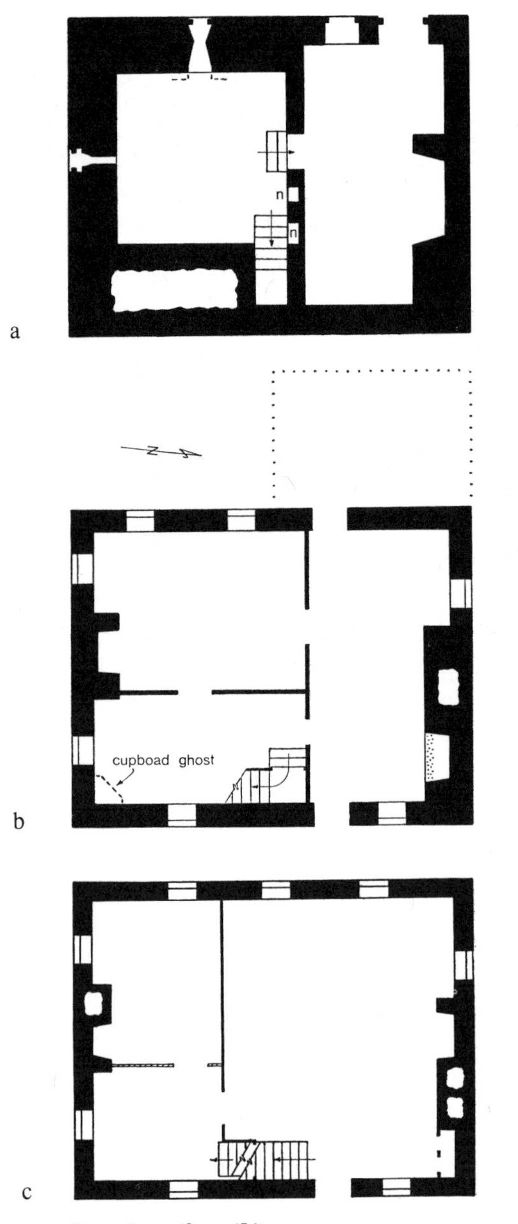

Figure 18. Cellar, first-, and second-floor plans of Fort Stover. (From 1940 HABS plans.)

entered by way of a narrow lateral passage (fig. 20). The right-hand room, occupying part of the original *Küche,* was and still is used as a parlor, and the *Stube* space to the left was used as a living room. A warping frame socket in the ceiling indicates that at one time weaving was done in the living room of the Heiston House.

Henry Glassie has drawn a parallel between transformational linguistic models and artifact analysis that is helpful in understanding the process of change in ethnic cultures. According to Glassie, traditional builders call on conceptual models that provide direction for design.[39] The models consist of both a basic idea of what a house or other artifact should be, and a limited number of ways in which the artifact can be transformed. The builder performs mental operations using the obligatory and optional rules of the model to generate a specific form that fulfills individual need, resource, and fancy. As a result, buildings produced by the members of a culture share characteristics, but are not exactly alike. The transformational model is derived from experience, that is, abstracted from observation of examples. It follows that essential change or replacement of the model is an indication of some disruption in the culture. By studying the nature of model changes, both the forces at work and the systems of response can be approached.

Eighteenth-century German and Swiss immigrants to America established groups of individual farms located in socially related rural enclaves, a pattern that allowed the survival of a strong cultural identity. Germanic settlements presented a sufficiently cohesive ethnic front to be viewed by some English-speaking politicians as threats to the stability of the Anglo-American culture.[40] The continued relationship between families sharing, among other things, a common minority language, resulted in the retention of traditional conceptual models that might not have long survived in a more intensely heterogeneous environment, like those encountered by German immigrants in nineteenth-century American cities. The most prominent artifact model in the mental assemblage brought from

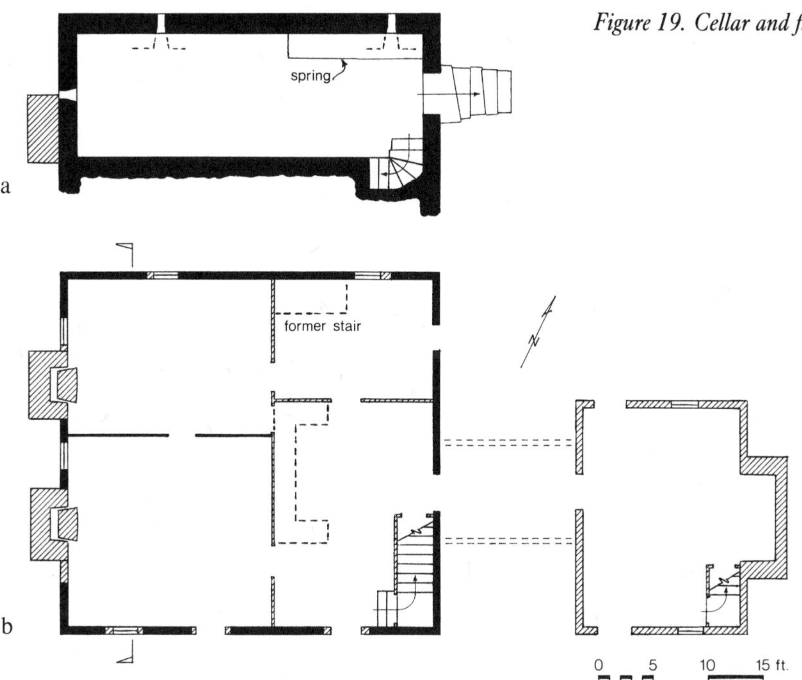

Figure 19. Cellar and first-floor plans of Fort Rhodes.

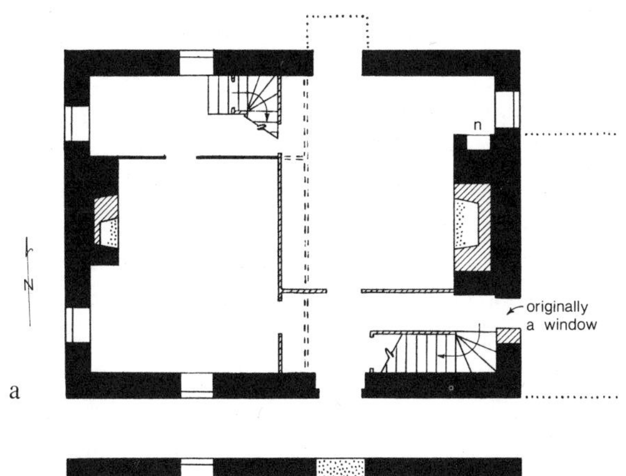

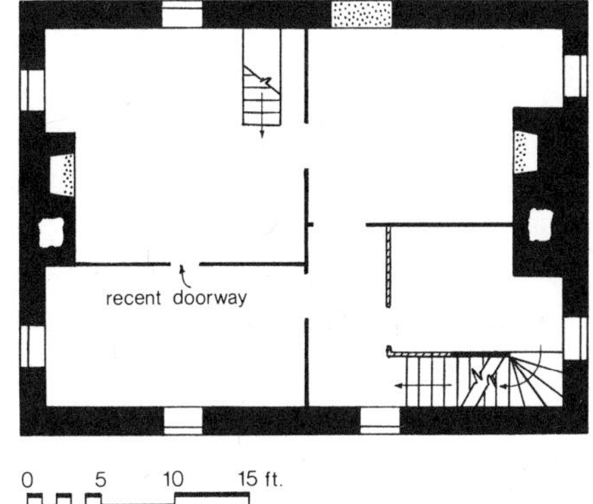

Figure 20. First- and second-floor plans of the Abraham Heiston House.

the Rhine Valley was the *Flurküchenhaus,* a house form with an unbalanced plan, asymmetrical fenestration, an off-center internal chimney, and a kitchen located on the first floor. Available evidence indicates that the *Flurküchenhaus* remained the primary model for German and Swiss houses built in America through most of the eighteenth century.

Contact between cultures and the observation of foreign artifacts allows the assimilation of new models, but as Dell Upton has pointed out, familiarity with new ideas does not necessitate their adoption.[41] The grafting to the *Flurküchenhaus* of some Anglo-American building features, such as simple common-rafter roofs, gable chimneys, and rooms heated with fireplaces rather than with stoves, can be viewed as similar to the use of various stylistic details on vernacular buildings. Although these features represent the acceptance of some parts of a foreign building model, they do not signal a shift in functions within the old house form. The same might be said regarding the quasi-symmetrical ordering of window openings, but where this stylish affectation is found in the Massanutten group, at Fort Stover, a significant functional change has also occurred: the cooking fireplace has been moved from the main floor of the house. This shift in functions suggests that the traditional conceptual model of family activities within the familiar plan has changed, and the occupants have accepted aspects of the domestic patterns of their Anglo-American neighbors.

Soon after 1800, the *Flurküchenhaus* was entirely abandoned for new construction in the Shenandoah Valley, and thereafter moderately successful German and Swiss farmers there would normally build their houses according to the Anglo-American I-house model. Characterized by symmetrical elevations and a balanced plan with rooms of near-equal size flanking an entrance passage, the I-house represented a radical formal change.

More importantly, use of the new form enforced and was engendered by essential functional changes. Similarities exist in the functions of the most prominent rooms in both forms: the *Küche* and *Stube* in the *Flurküchenhaus* and the hall and parlor in the I-house. Unlike the *Küche,* however, the hall is entered only by way of a passage, an intermediate space with psychological and especially proxemic implications that have been discussed by Glassie.[42] Appendages to the I-house further provided for a division of functions that was unknown in the Rhenish house. People most often ate in a room in an ell, and the kitchen was located either in the rear of the ell or in another position distant from the family's living space. In addition, storage and farm-related activities that had once been housed in the attic and cellar were dispersed to detached buildings.

The abandonment of the traditional Rhenish house model and a roughly concurrent replacement of the standard German language are conspicuous indicators of a breakdown in the separate identity of Germanic culture in the Shenandoah Valley. It is because of the highly symbolic nature of the two complex models, however, that they should not be interpreted as signaling the demise of all ethnic distinctions. Rather, the most visible minority distinctions are often the first to fall to the pressure of a dominant group. Although German inscriptions are seldom found on gravestones south of Pennsylvania after about 1800, Germanic motifs continued to be utilized to embellish the stones through the first half of the nineteenth century, and a related decorative aesthetic remains visible in the distinctive interior woodwork of Valley houses from around 1800 to 1840.[43] English inscriptions were combined with old design formulas in *Fraktur* in the early nineteenth century, and the painted decoration of barns remains a prominent feature of the Valley landscape. Dialects survived as a means of communication between close friends into the twentieth century, and distinctions between cultural backgrounds is still a part of the social consciousness of the region.[44]

Beginning in the eighteenth century, Germanic people in America experienced pressure to conform to the culture of the dominant Anglo-American group. That Germanic culture survived as a distinct entity through the century is indicated by the regional sample provided by the Massanutten houses. When acculturation took place, it was not a rapid process that erased all levels of ethnic distinction. Families that first accepted features of eastern Virginia living patterns did so within a familiar building form, although the exterior of the house might resemble an Anglo-American house. The traditional house model, like the German language, was finally replaced because it represented a conspicuous symbol of ethnic division. Other less visible, culturally derived, and ethnically distinct models remained in use.

Partial Catalog

FORT EGYPT

The least altered as well as most complex internal-chimney Rhenish house in Page County is Fort Egypt (fig. 4), located at the middle of a large tract of arable land in a bend of the South Fork of the Shenandoah River, opposite the mouth of Mill Creek. Harry Strickler relates the tradition that Fort Egypt was built by Jacob Strickler, son of Abram, a first generation Swiss immigrant.[45] The nearly square 36′ × 32′2″ house is constructed of logs averaging 9″ × 1′4″ in section, with narrow interstices and dovetail corner notching. Except for the principal facade, the house is now covered with asbestos siding. A nineteenth-century deck-on-hip roof replaces the original gable roof, and the line of the higher old roof ridge is visible on the stone chimney shaft. In the 1940s, a shed-roofed room was added to the east side of the house, in the location of a destroyed nineteenth-century gable-roofed addition.

The first-floor plan (fig. 3b) consists of four rooms disposed around a central chimney, with the front door giving access to the *Küche* to the right. The chimney is brought forward of center, allowing the rear of the *Küche* to be partitioned as another room. The space to the left of the chimney is divided into an 18′3″-square *Stube* and an 11′10″-deep rear *Kammer*, with the partition wall attached to the rear summer beam. An 8′10″-wide cooking fireplace in the *Küche* is now open, although it had been enclosed to form a smaller heating fireplace when the house was recorded by the Historic American Buildings Survey in 1940.[46] The room to the rear of the kitchen is served by a small fireplace that is apparently original, but a roughly finished interior and flue indicate that the *Stube* fireplace is a later insertion. Enclosed stairs rise from both the right front corner of the *Küche* and the right rear corner of the *Kammer*.

A similar four-room plan is found on the second floor, although the partition between the rear rooms has been moved to the right of the stair (fig. 3c). Conspicuous evidence for an original heating stove is found at the front of the chimney stack, where a small recessed fireplace with a raised hearth faces the room over the *Küche*. In the rear of the fireplace is a 1′5″ × 1′4″ opening through which coals could be pushed into a five-plate stove. The opening has been partly blocked, and there are no further indications of the stove's form. The diminutive size of the fireplace suggests that it, like a fireplace in the second-floor passage of the Schiefferstadt House in Frederick, Maryland, was principally intended to provide fuel for the stove rather than to directly heat the room in which it is located.

Recently, whitewash coating has been stripped from the interior surface of the log walls, providing clearer evidence of early fenestration. Log patches indicate that although the original fenestration of the front and rear walls was similar to that of the present nineteenth-century arrangement, the previous windows were horizontal openings measuring approximately 3′ × 2′. The same change in window form is visible at Fort Rhodes, and comparable horizontal openings survive in the log Adam Miller House at Elkton in Rockingham County. Despite the large proportions of the Fort Egypt plan, the house retained a conservative two-bay fenestration, with a single door and window piercing the first-floor facade.

Following the precedent of framing in Pennsylvania Rhenish houses,[47] exposed second-floor and attic joists rest on top of pairs of summer beams extending from the gable walls to the chimney. The edges of both the summer and joists have beveled chamfers. The forward summer on the first floor has been removed, perhaps to facilitate addition of a board ceiling that remains in the *Stube* and *Kammer,* but chamfer stops on the exposed *Küche* joists indicate its original location. The form of interior partitions varies at Fort Egypt. On both first and second floors, the short partition abutting the chimney and separating the front rooms is a frame wall with exposed posts. The partition between the first-floor rear rooms (figs. 5a, and 6) is constructed of vertical boards with 3″ battens enriched with fillets and flattened cymas. All other partitions are of vertical tongue-and-groove beaded boards (fig. 5c). Early doors in the cellar and upper floors are constructed of vertical boards and horizontal battens, and are hung on HL and curvilinear strap hinges. As in other Shenandoah Valley Rhenish houses, latches at Fort Egypt are of a decorative quality that relates them to Germanic latches elsewhere, but they are considerably less rich than the most flamboyant Pennsylvania examples.

Although the original roof was removed in the nineteenth century, a pair of mortices in the top of a joist and corresponding holes in the early attic flooring to the west of the chimney indicate that the house previously had a triple-truss roof frame like that surviving at the Spitler House.

The cellar consists of two rooms (fig. 3a), each incorporating Pennsylvania-German methods for insulating storage space. A 32′4″ × 9′11″ room (fig. 12) at the rear runs the length of the building and is entered through double doors in the east gable wall, and by a recent flight of steps descending from the room behind the *Küche* through an original opening in the ceiling framing. In constructing this room its builders utilized a ceiling form, paralleled at a large number of Rhenish houses in Pennsylvania and at the Abram Strickler House in Page County, that helped provide a constant cellar temperature by insulating the space between the joists. The sides of the 6″ × 8″ joists are slotted to receive wooden slats wrapped with straw and clay, and the surface is plastered and whitewashed, with the lower faces of the joists left exposed. The room is lighted by unglazed windows cut directly through the exterior walls. Toward the end ot this long room is a door to an inner cellar room, which is ceiled with a stone barrel vault and is without exterior entrance (fig. 21). Light shafts taper upward from wide openings in the vault to narrow slots in the exterior wall, and several niches pierce the stone partition wall. Embedded in the vault are iron and wooden hooks for suspension of poles. Until the floor was recently covered with a concrete slab, this room is reported to have had an open spring in the southwest corner. Like the other room, the vaulted room is plastered and whitewashed. The land drops away to the rear of the house, so that the outer room is at ground level and the vaulted room is more than half below grade.

Figure 21. Inner cellar room of Fort Egypt.

FORT RHODES

Closely related to the form of Fort Egypt is Fort Rhodes (fig. 22), located four miles downstream on the west side of the South Fork of the Shenandoah River. Believed to have been built after the house of Mennonite Minister John Rhodes or (Rodes) at this site was burned by Indians in 1764,[48] the large two-story *Flurküchenhaus* was more radically altered in the mid nineteenth century, but it retains details and evidence of a plan similar to Fort Egypt. The 34′9″

Figure 22. Fort Rhodes.

× 32′3″ house has been stripped of its exterior weatherboarding to reveal log walls with dovetail corner notching and chinked interstices. Nineteenth-century alterations intended to remove cooking activities to a detached kitchen building involved the demolition of a large interior chimney, the construction of stone exterior chimneys on the northwest gable wall, and the alteration of the second-floor plan. Interruption of the first-floor ceiling framing indicates the location of the original chimney and cooking fireplace, which served a right-hand *Küche* (fig. 19b). As at Fort Egypt, the rear of the *Küche* is now partitioned to form a fourth room. The partition between the left-hand rooms is constructed of vertical bevel-edged sheathing set between boards with quarter-round molded edges. An original door in this wall is constructed of vertical boards held together with dovetailed tapering horizontal battens, and is hung on HL hinges. Although other first-floor partitions, of flat vertical boards with beaded edges, may be nineteenth-century replacements of eighteenth-century fabric, it is uncertain whether or not the partition between the *Stube* and *Kammer* was moved forward in order to equalize the size of the left-hand rooms.

A patch in the second-story floorboards indicates that a stair rising from one of the two rear rooms was the predecessor of the nineteenth-century stair that now is located on the front wall of the *Küche.* Patches in the log walls demonstrate that the rooms at Fort Rhodes were lighted by horizontal openings like those at Fort Egypt. Evidence appears for two early first-floor windows in both the southwest gable and rear walls, and a single first-floor window in the facade. Front doors entering the *Küche* and *Stube* appear to replace shorter and wider early doors in the same locations.

Representing a slight variation from the framing method used at Forts Egypt and Stover, joists are joined to pairs of summer beams with 3″ slots rather than resting entirely on top of the summers (fig. 10). Both summers and joists are cut with a rough chamfer. The ceiling framing remains exposed on the second floor, but first-floor *Stube* and *Kammer* joists were covered with sheathing in the nineteenth century. Roof framing, which has been reworked using early members, consists of common rafters supported by a pair of purlins and collars seated on vertical posts. The rafters are lapped and pegged at the ridge, and at the eaves they rest on a thin board plate set into the joists. The light framing of the gable visible in figure 10 dates from the twentieth century.

The single-room cellar plan at Fort Rhodes (fig. 19a) is similar to the outer room at Fort Egypt. The 31′6″ × 10′10″ room is located at the rear of the house, where the land slopes downward, and is ceiled with a vault pierced by two window openings. A third window, in the southeast end wall, is partly covered by a nineteenth-century chimney. Entry to the cellar is through an exterior door in the northeast wall, and a blocked series of stone steps beside the door show that originally there was also interior access from the *Küche.* A spring flows from the north corner of the room out through a hole in the rear wall, and an opening in the vault above once allowed water to be drawn up to the first floor.

The ruinous nineteenth-century kitchen is a one-and-a-half story building with gable walls longer than the facade. The walls are constructed of V-notched logs that are smaller and less carefully finished than those of the log Rhenish houses in Page County. Seams in the exterior walls of both buildings indicate that the kitchen was previously attached to the house by an enclosed frame passageway.

ABRAM STRICKLER HOUSE

Located on a knoll that commands a view of the South Fork of the Shenandoah River and White House to the north is the Abram Strickler House, a two-story log building of *Flurküchenhaus* form (fig. 23). Although the exterior is now covered with asbestos siding and the sash and chimney stack are replacements, the house retains its original two-bay facade fenestration and clear evidence of a three-room first-floor plan (fig. 1). The Strickler House measures 25′ × 35′11″, with a 16′7″-wide *Küche* located to the right. Presently partitioned into two rooms, the *Küche* is entered by opposed front and rear doors, and was served by a cooking fireplace that is now sealed. To the left is a single large room that plaster seams indicate was once divided into a roughly square *Stube* and narrow *Kammer.* A stair rises to the second floor from the rear of this room, with steps below it descending from the *Küche* to the cellar. The second-floor room arrangement is modern, and the alterations obscure evidence of the original plan.

Notable surviving details are the two exterior doors, with six raised panels on the exterior surface and horizontal sheathing on the interior, hung on tapering iron strap hinges with decorative ends. The combination of interior board sheathing and exterior panels is a method of door construction found in early buildings in New England and the Chesapeake region, but while it does not commonly appear in later eighteenth-century Anglo-American buildings on the East Coast, it was retained as a standard feature of both Pennsylvania and Virginia Rhenish houses throughout the century.

Floor joists are covered by later plaster ceilings, but those visible from the attic are cut with beveled chamfers and whitewashed. In the roof, common rafters are joined by pinned open-face mortices at the ridge and are stabilized with lap-jointed collars and 1½″ × 6″ diagonal braces set into their upper surfaces at both gable ends.

The ground floor below the north end of the Strickler House provides another variation on the two-room cellar concept found at the Abraham Spitler House and Forts Egypt and Stover. As in those houses, the desire for a storage space buffered from temperature change led the builder to construct two cellar rooms, the smaller inner room provided with a more heavily insulated ceiling and entered only by an interior door from the outer

Figure 23. The Abram Strickler House.

room. The outer room, measuring 20′7″ × 12′6″, is entered by enclosed stairs from the *Küche* and an exterior doorway in the rear wall, and is lighted by windows in the rear and north gable walls. It is ceiled with exposed floorboards and log joists hewn only on the upper and lower surfaces. Rather than being vaulted, the 15′10″ × 7′10″ inner room is provided with an insulated joist ceiling similar to that in the outer cellar room at Fort Egypt. In this case, however, the joists are not structural, but rather are seated below the log joists, on a summer beam just within the larger room and on board sills set into the front exterior wall and atop the interior stone partition. Wooden slats wrapped with straw and clay are inserted in triangular grooves in the sides of the 5″ × 7½″ lower joists, and the interstices are plastered and whitewashed. The house is sited at the edge of a knoll, with the land sloping away to the rear, so the placement of the inner room at the front of the house further buffered its contents from external elements.

ANDREW KEYSER HOUSE

The Andrew Keyser House (fig. 24), survived as a largely intact small three-room plan *Flurküchenhaus* until it was regrettably demolished about 1967. Believed built around 1765 by a first-generation German immigrant, the house was sited on level ground at the edge of a terrace above arable land on the South Fork of the Shenandoah River opposite the mouth of Hawksbill Creek. As with Forts Paul Long and Philip Long, the small size of the Keyser House may have been a major factor in the decision to replace it with a larger house in the nineteenth century. The result of the construction of a new frame I-house at midcentury and the loss of the old building's status as the primary dwelling on the property

Figure 24. The Andrew Keyser House. (From the W.P.A. Collection, Virginia State Library.)

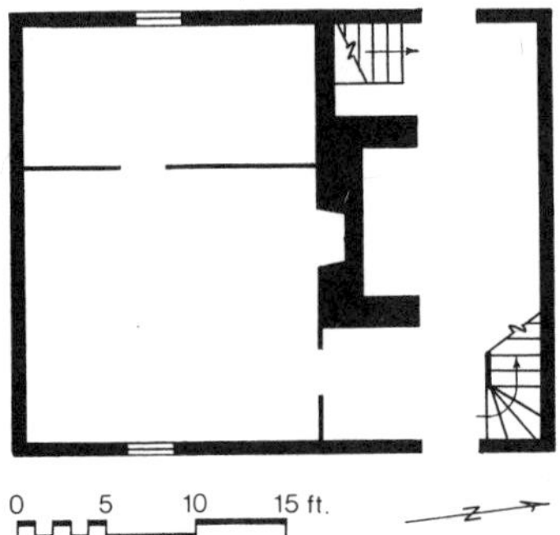

Figure 25. Restored first-floor plan of the Andrew Keyser House.

was the preservation of its original internal spatial arrangement and the retention of the first-floor *Küche* as a room used for cooking.

Photographs show that the house was a story-and-a-half two-bay log structure with dovetail corner notching and narrow interstices. Parts of the foundations remain exposed, and with the owner's description, allow a reconstruction of the first floor plan (fig. 25). Front and rear doors gave access to a narrow *Küche* provided with an eight-foot wide cooking fireplace. An enclosed stair rose to the upper half story from the right corner of the windowless *Küche,* and in the opposite corner a stair descended to the cellar, which survives. The house was divided axially by a board partition in front of the chimney and a masonry wall to the rear. Another board partition separated the roughly square *Stube* from a narrow *Kammer,* each lighted by a single window. The *Stube* was heated by a fireplace in the center chimney, but whether or not the fireplace was a later insertion is unknown. Second-floor joists and the interior surface of the log walls were exposed and whitewashed.

The upper half story was partitioned into three rooms, a room over the *Küche* with no windows and two southern rooms of near-equal size, each lighted by a single window in the gable wall. Second-floor ceilings and end walls were finished with board sheathing.

A 17′2″ × 12′2″ cellar below the northwest corner of the house was entered only by a flight of interior steps passing under the exposed end of the vault. Window openings pierce the south end wall and the west side of the vault, and a small niche is located in the south wall.

CHARLES KEYSER HOUSE

On the same terrace a quarter of a mile west of the Andrew Keyser House is located the Charles Keyser House, a narrowly-proportioned story-and-a-half Rhenish house with an internal stone chimney. Its walls are constructed of log with dovetail corner notching and, except for the weatherboarded rear, are whitewashed on the exterior and interior. Although the building has been extended to accommodate a change in room use, the original two-room *Flurküchenhaus* plan (fig. 26) has remained unchanged. A partition wall located at the rear of the *Küche* fireplace divides the house into almost equal halves. There is no visible evidence that the *Stube* was partitioned, and space used solely for sleeping was probably confined to the upper half story. An uncommon feature of the *Stube* is its gable exterior entrance.

As at the Andrew Keyser House, only single windows pierce the front and rear walls of the *Stube,*

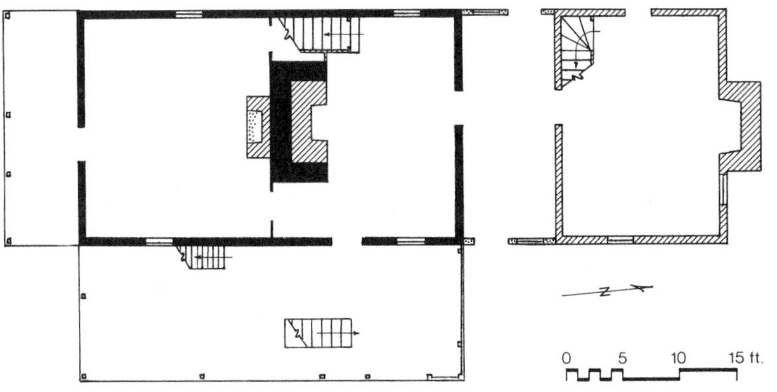

Figure 26. First-floor plan of the Charles Keyser House.

but here the wide *Küche* is also lighted by windows in both long walls. Breaking with the precedent of small window openings at the Andrew Keyser House and Forts Egypt and Rhodes, and perhaps supplying an indication of a later date, first floor windows have six-over-six sash and frames with cyma-molded architrave trim. The *Stube* ceiling received a platerboard covering in the twentieth century, but previously its whitewashed joists were exposed like those of the *Küche* and northern addition.

The second floor is partitioned by board walls into two rooms flanking the chimney and a small lobby containing the stair from the *Küche.* Neither second-floor room has a fireplace. The roof framing, covered by horizontal boards on the interior, consists of common rafters resting on log plates that project from the gable ends. Splayed eaves indicate that wedges were inserted above the ends of the rafters, as at the Abraham Spitler House and Fort Stover.

A 14′7″ × 10′ vaulted cellar is located below the south end of the porch, and is reached by stone steps descending from a trap door in the porch floor. The cellar room is lighted by a window in the south end wall. Reached by an open ladder stair with beaded stringers, space in the pent above the porch was probably used originally, as it is today, for storage.

Early in the nineteenth century, the Keyser House was altered and enlarged in order to remove cooking activities from the main block, and to provide heating fireplaces for the original first-floor rooms. A weatherboarded log kitchen with 15′2″ × 20′4″ dimensions similar to those of the nineteenth-century Rhodes kitchen was built eight feet north of the *Küche,* and the old kitchen fireplace was reduced in size. The two buildings were later connected by a frame hyphen. Stonework was also added to the rear of the chimney to provide a fireplace for the *Stube.* It was probably during this renovation that dormers were added to the old roof, supplying light for the north attic room, which may have previously been lighted by a gable window.

FORT PAUL LONG

Several Massanutten houses combine the *Flurküchenhaus* model with features of the Anglo-American hall-parlor house. Two single-story stone houses that are built into hillsides and have Rhenish cellar forms and first-floor kitchens are provided with chimneys on the gable ends and have rooms heated with fireplaces rather than stoves.

The smaller of the two houses (fig. 27) is locally believed to have been built by Paul Long, or Lung, in the second quarter of the eighteenth century, although a third or fourth quarter date is perhaps more likely.[49] It is located at the edge of the first ridge rising from a wide expanse of bottom land on the northwest side of the South Fork of the Shen-

Figure 27. Rear view of Fort Paul Long.

andoah River two miles above the mouth of Massanutten Run, also called Big Run. The 30′3″ × 20′ house is sited with gable ends facing the slope, allowing direct entrances to the *Küche* through the front wall and to the vaulted cellar in the downhill gable end. Two rear first-floor doors are reached by means of a porch supported by floor joists that cantilever beyond the wall. Wall construction is of coursed limestone rubble. Except at the cellar door, which is spanned by a flat arch of cut voussoirs, the weight above openings is carried by window and door frames and internal lintels. Chimneys project on the interior of both gable walls, each serving a single first-floor fireplace.

The plan (fig. 15b) consists of two rooms divided by a vertical-board partition. The larger room, entered by the original front doorway, contains a 7′-wide cooking fireplace and an enclosed stair to the attic, and the smaller room is served by a small heating fireplace. Joists are now covered with plaster, and aside from rear batten doors with strap hinges hung on pintles, no early interior trim survives. Because the house was replaced as the primary dwelling on the farm by a larger house early in the nineteenth century, however, the *Küche* fireplace was never altered, and iron sockets for a cooking crane remain exposed in its right rear corner. Conforming to a practice found elsewhere in the Shenandoah Valley, the attic joists are seated on thin boards set flush with the exterior surface of the walls, and spaces between the joists are filled with stone. The original roof structure was removed and the walls were raised with wood in the late nineteenth century.

A single cellar room occupies most of the space below the first floor (fig. 15a). The surface of its asymmetrical elliptical vault is unplastered, and seams formed by the centering boards used in its construction remain visible. The cellar is lighted by tapered slots flanking the doorway and by shafts that rise to square openings in the long walls (fig. 28). The western opening retains its original frame with diagonally set, square vertical bars and a solid wooden shutter hung with strap hinges. A breach in the west wall allows examination of the relationship between the first-floor joists and the rough top surface of the vault. Adzed only on their upper and lower surfaces, the joists were undercut at the center in order to clear the top of the vault.

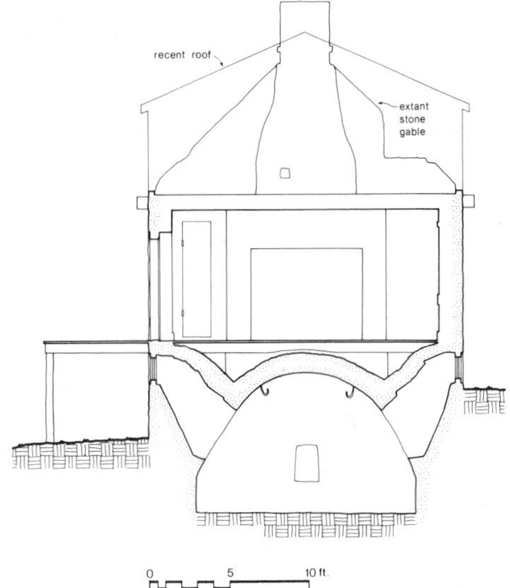

Figure 28. Section of Fort Paul Long.

FORT PHILIP LONG

Related in form to Fort Paul Long is Fort Philip Long (fig. 13), located two miles upstream on the east side of the river. It is a 37′7″ × 19′4″ stone structure that, like Paul Long, has a two-room plan with end chimneys and is built with gable walls facing up a hillside. Details of the form vary considerably from the other Long house, however. The fenestration of Fort Philip Long is more regular, with a single doorway near the center of the facade and three evenly spaced windows in the first floor of the rear wall. A large asymmetrical chimney is located off-center of the exterior of the uphill gable, and a small interior chimney stack protrudes from the roof at the opposite end. Wall openings are spanned with thin wooden lintels, a rare feature in Virginia Germanic houses.

The plan was altered early in the present century, but ghosts of an old interior wall and a stair patch in the attic floor illustrate that it previously consisted of two rooms, the smaller of which was a *Küche,* with a cooking fireplace and exterior door on the east gable wall and a single window in the south wall (fig. 14). The attic stair appears to have risen from this room. Breaking with *Flurküchenhaus* tradition, the front door enters the larger room, which was heated by a corner fireplace and lighted by three windows. Pintles in the orginal frames indicate that the doorway to the *Küche* was hung with a pair of Dutch doors and the front door was a single piece. Nailed to the cooking fireplace lintel is an early shelf supported by a heavy classical cornice consisting of cyma and ovolo moldings separated by a fillet. A plaster ceiling now covers the joists, which have chamfered edges. As at the Andrew Keyser House and Fort Paul Long, this house was replaced by a larger dwelling in the nineteenth century, and as a result its fireplace arrangement has not been altered.

Recently stripped of its modern interior sheathing, the roof structure consists of common rafters morticed and pinned together at the ridge and to the ends of the joists below. Following a common Pennsylvania and Shenandoah Valley practice, the end rafters are seated on pairs of short timbers exposed on the exterior of the gable walls. There were originally no collars, and the attic was unfinished until the twentieth century, when two dormers were added. Previously the space was lighted only by a window in the east gable and a tiny opening in the west gable.

A distinctive feature of this extraordinary house is its cellar arrangement, which consists of two rooms, one beneath the other, the lower of which has underground access to a well through a 44′ tunnel (fig. 29). The upper room is entered by a door in the south long wall, and is lighted by horizontal rectangular windows that are reminiscent of the early openings at Forts Egypt and Rhodes. Unique within the Page County group, a niche or pine hole in the west wall has a small flue that winds upward through the wall to the chimney above. The lower room is entered by a gable-end doorway flanked by horizontal windows with diagonally placed, vertical wooden bars. The present ceiling framing in this room is said to have replaced a system of close-set joists with mud and straw in-fill. A low door in the rear wall opens into a 3′6″ to 5′-tall tunnel cut through the hillside to an opening in the river-cobble lining of a well dug from the surface. There is no evidence of stairs for interior circulation between the cellar rooms and the main floor, so an activity requiring relatively easy access to water is indicated for the lower room.

ABRAHAM HEISTON HOUSE

Three two-story Page County houses of the scale of Forts Egypt and Rhodes combined distinct remnants of the *Flurküchenhaus* plan with internal gable end chimneys. Of the two that survive, the Abraham Heiston House (fig. 16) west of Bixler Bridge on the South Fork of the Shenandoah River retains the closest association with the traditional Germanic form. The substantial stone house is believed to have been built for Abraham Heiston in 1790, and a modern concrete replacement of one of two lost gable datestones is inscribed AH 1790. Soon after construction, the house was obtained by wealthy slaveowner Colonel Daniel Strickler, and it has since remained in the Strickler family. Morris Strickler, the present owner, states the tradition that both Heiston's and Strickler's families were Swiss immigrants who moved to the Shenandoah Valley after first settling in Pennsylvania.

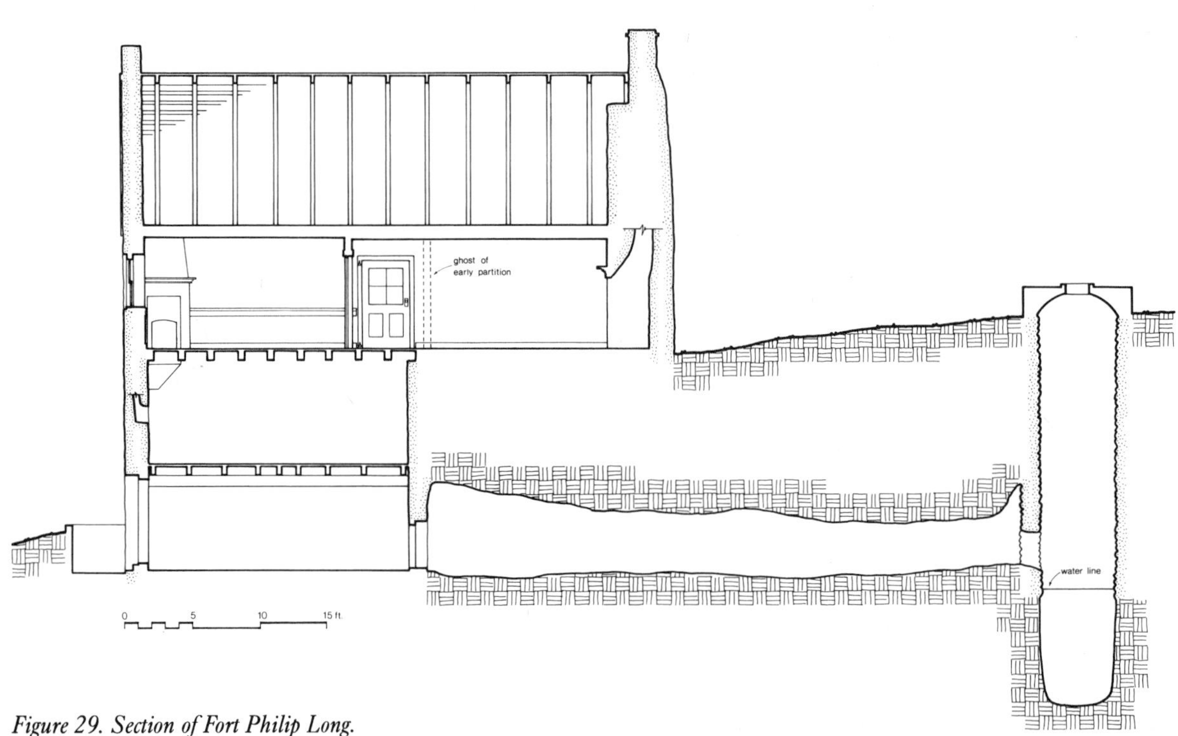

Figure 29. Section of Fort Philip Long.

The house is constructed of coursed rubble limestone with a facade of randomly alternative long and short squared blocks. Both front and rear elevations have a two-bay fenestration, with doorways located to the right. An apparently original doorway, now blocked, once served a second-story rear porch whose marks are visible across the rear wall.

The first floor was altered early in the nineteenth century, but there is evidence that the original plan consisted of three rooms following the *Küche, Stube, Kammer* pattern (fig. 20a). The present vertical-board axial partition appears to be original fabric and seams in the masonry walls indicate it was moved two feet to the left. Originally entered by opposed front and rear doors and not partitioned, the right-hand room served as a *Küche,* with an approximately seven-foot-wide cooking fireplace. The present stair in the front right corner of this room is a successor to an earlier stair that occupied the same location. A reused early post-and-panel door with molded frame serves a closet below the stair, and a lateral vertical-board partition dividing the space to the left of the *Küche* appears to be original. Before being shortened in the alteration, the partition separated a wider heated *Stube* and unheated *Kammer.* Masonry walls in the *Stube* retain the lower part of a plate shelf that extended around two sides of the fireplace breast. During the present owner's childhood, the small room was used as a bedroom for the oldest member of the family.

Dating from the alteration, a stair in the rear room rises between floor joists that, like the summer beam on which they rest, are molded with a bead below a thin cyma. Joists in the two larger first-floor rooms are covered with board sheathing, and the joists in the *Kammer* and second-floor rooms were covered at a later time. The interior first-floor batten doors date from the nineteenth century, but the front door, constructed of vertical boards with tapered battens and hung with three strap hinges on pintles, is original.

The four-room second-floor plan (fig. 20b) remains intact, with vertical board partitions hung with six-panel doors. The larger rear rooms are provided with fireplaces, and an original stair winds up to the attic from the corner of the front right room. Family tradition identifies the smaller left-hand room as "the strangers' room," and previously its only access was from the room in which the stair rises.

The roof is constructed of common rafters with lapped half-dovetailed collars. The rafters are open face morticed and pinned together at the ridge, and morticed and pinned to the joists below.

A 10′11″ × 24′ vaulted cellar beneath the *Küche* space is now entered at the south end through stairs descending from the addition. A five-foot-wide opening in the vault at the southern end of the cellar and patterns in the whitewash of the end wall indicate that interior entrance was previously by way of steps below those at the front right corner of the *Küche.* In addition, there was a 4′10″-wide bulkhead entrance in the rear wall, now blocked and provided with a window. The angle of the vault is unusually low, a factor that combined with an adventurously wide window arch in the eastern wall to cause a fault that has been remedied by timber shoring. The single south window opening has a square aperture similar to that at Fort Paul Long.

FORT STOVER

Fort Stover provides a pivotal example illustrating the change from the traditional concepts that directed Rhenish house building in eighteenth-century America to the popular ideas that affected both later building in the Shenandoah Valley and the alterations that were made to earlier houses. Believed to have been built about 1760 by mill-owner Samuel Stover, the two-story stone house is located at the base of a steep ridge paralleling the South Fork of the Shenandoah River three-quarters of a mile downstream from the mouth of Hawksbill Creek. Except for its front and rear asymmetrical fenestration, the exterior of Fort Stover (fig. 17), with a 36′5″ × 28′ rectangular plan and interior end chimneys, could be mistaken for an Anglo-American hall-parlor house. Yet the fenestration gives evidence that this little-altered house was in fact constructed around a plan that is directly derived from traditional *Flurküchenhaus* spatial distribution. The uphill east elevation, apparently considered the facade, has a three-bay fenestration with first- and second-floor openings ordered one above the other. Eastern exterior doors to both floors are located to the right of center. The piercing of the three-story west elevation is more irregular, with no opening placed directly above another, and first-floor and cellar doors located to the left of the windows. As at the Abraham Heiston House, upper-level doors on both walls must have served elevated porches, and broad stone piers now supporting a modern rear lean-to may be the remains of an early first-story west porch. Despite its asymmetrical composition of wall openings, the exterior of Fort Stover recalls Anglo-American or Renaissance ideas of visual order. Chimneys are built at both ends, and although the plan made a symmetrical tripartite facade impossible, doors placed toward the center of the east wall are flanked by balancing windows, and the second-floor windows of the west wall have nearly equal spacing.

The first-floor plan of Fort Stover (fig. 18b) follows a three-room *Flurküchenhaus* model, with opposed exterior doors giving entrance to a narrow room flanked on one side by two wider rooms of unequal depth. Room use within this familiar spatial distribution had changed, however, for the cooking fireplace is located in an outer cellar room below the first-floor entrance room (fig. 30), and the old *Küche* and *Stube* spaces are heated by small fireplaces. Coexistent with the owner's somewhat schizophrenic concern for external visual order was his desire to separate such productive activities as cooking from the living space of the house, an attitude shared by owners who later altered most of the houses previously examined. At Fort Stover, the unheated first-floor room with narrow proportions is located on the uphill side of the house. Whether or not the room retained its traditional use as a chamber is uncertain, but a plate shelf with hanging pegs and the marks of a built-in corner cupboard indicate that its functions may have included the storage and display of eating accoutrements. An enclosed stair to the second floor rises from this room. The first-floor interior walls are constructed of studs and covered with plaster.

The second-floor plan (fig. 18c) originally consisted of two rooms separated by a paneled wall of the type found at Fort Rhodes. Fireplaces heated both the large 24′7″ × 21′2″ room and the smaller 11′8″ × 21′2″ room, later partitioned into two rooms. The former was provided with a closet with hanging pegs. Although the first-floor ceilings are plastered, the framing is exposed on the second floor, revealing a system of joists resting on a single summer beam extending between the two chimneys (fig. 7). Both the summer and joists have beveled chamfers and are whitewashed.

The first- and second-story trim consists of chair rails, baseboards, and cornice-strip mantels. Standard six-panel doors are hung with strap hinges on pintles. Historic American Buildings Survey drawings and ghosts on surviving doors illustrate that the house retained until recently a group of iron latches of traditional decorative form.

The roof framing consists of common rafters pinned together at the ridge with open-face mortices and resting on the attic joists (fig. 8c). The collars are half-lapped to the rafters.

The two-room cellar pattern seen elsewhere is utilized at Fort Stover, with exterior access to the inner vaulted room through a larger outer room (fig. 18a). Here the outer room served as a kitchen; it has a dirt floor and a ceiling constructed of 10″ to 1′2″ × 7″ hewn timbers laid side by side. It is lighted by a window hung with a batten shutter. The vaulted room is lighted by window slots that taper to 1′4″-wide exterior openings that, like the larger openings, are spanned with flat arches. A partial set of stone steps rising through the northeast corner of the vault indicates that the inner room was also originally entered through an opening below the first-floor stairs. Wooden and iron suspension hooks are embedded in the plastered and whitewashed vault.

Figure 30. Cellar fireplace at Fort Stover.

Notes

This article is a slightly revised version of the one which was originally published in the *Proceedings of the American Philosophical Society* (February 1980). All illustrations are by the author unless otherwise noted.

1. James Deetz, "Ceramics from Plymouth, 1620–1835: The Archaeological Evidence," in Ian M. G. Quimby, ed., *Ceramics in America,* Winterthur Conference Report, 1972 (Charlottesville: University Press of Virginia, 1973), p. 15.
2. Klaus Wust, *The Virginia Germans* (Charlottesville: University Press of Virginia, 1969), p. 174.
3. Dell Upton, "British and German Interaction in the Blue Ridge," paper read at the seminar on Blue Ridge Life and Culture, Blue Ridge Institute, Ferrum College, Ferrum, Virginia, September 1977.
4. Wust, *The Virginia Germans,* pp. 188–89; Elmer Lewis Smith, John G. Steward, and Kyger M. Ellsworth, "The Pennsylvania Germans in the Shenandoah Valley," *Pennsylvania Folklore Society* 26 (1962), pp. 3–5, 243–78.
5. Fred B. Kniffen, "Folk Housing: Key to Diffusion," *Annals of the Association of American Geographers* 55, no. 4 (December 1965): 553–55 (reprinted in this volume).
6. Edward A. Chappell, "Cultural Change in the Shenandoah Valley: Northern Augusta County Houses before 1861," Master's thesis, University of Virginia, 1977, pp. 76–80.
7. W. G. Hoskins, "The Rebuilding of Rural England, 1570–1640," *Past and Present* 4 (November 1953): 44–89; M. W. Barley, *The English Farmhouse and Cottage* (London: Routledge and Kegan Paul, 1961), pp. 57–179.
8. Wust, *The Virginia Germans,* pp. 29–32.
9. William P. Palmer, ed., *Calendar of Virginia State Papers,* vol. 1 (Richmond: R. F. Walker, 1875), pp. 219–20; *Virginia Magazine of History and Biography* 13, no. 2 (October 1906): 121–22.
10. J. Hunziker, *Das Schweizerhaus,* vol. 6, pt. 5, *Das Dreisassige Haus* (Aarau, Switzerland: H. R. Sauer-

lander, 1908–10), p. 137; Robert C. Bucher, "The Continental Log House," *Pennsylvania Folklife* 12, no. 4 (Summer 1962): 14–19; Henry Glassie, "A Central Chimney Continental Log House," *Pennsylvania Folklife* 18, no. 2 (Winter 1968): 32–39.

11. Samuel Kercheval, *A History of the Valley of Virginia,* 2d ed. (Woodstock, Va.: John Gatewood, 1850), p. 136.
12. Richard Weiss, *Häuser und Landschaften der Schweiz,* 2d ed. (Erlenbach-Zurich: Eugen Rentsch, 1973), pp. 135, 152; Thomas Tileston Waterman, *The Dwellings of Colonial America* (Chapel Hill: University of North Carolina Press, 1950), p. 152.
13. William Woys Weaver, "Weizenthal and the Early Architecture of New Strasburge: Swiss Plantations in the Province of Pennsylvania," Master's thesis, University of Virginia, 1973, pp. 9, 54; Weiss, *Häuser un Landschaften,* p. 135.
14. Henry C. Mercer, *The Bible in Iron: or the Pictured Stoves and Stove Plates of the Pennsylvania Germans* (Doylestown, Pa.: Bucks County Historical Society, 1941).
15. Weiss, *Häuser und Landschaften,* p. 135.
16. Henry Glassie, *Folk Housing in Middle Virginia: A Structural Analysis of Historic Artifacts* (Knoxville: University of Tennessee Press, 1975), p. 28.
17. See Weiss, *Häuser und Landschaften,* p. 79; Herman Schilli, *Das Schwarzwaldhaus,* 3d ed. (Stuttgart: W. Kohlhammer, 1977), pp. 170, 222; Adelhart Zippelius, *Das Bauernhaus am Unteren Deutschen Niederrhein* (Wuppertal: A. Martini and Gruttefien, 1957), pp. 115, 145.
18. Historic American Buildings Survey, Schiefferstadt House, Frederick, Maryland, 1974, sheet 11.
19. Marcus Whiffen, *The Eighteenth-Century Houses of Williamsburg* (Williamsburg, Va.: Colonial Williamsburg, 1960), pp. 65–66.
20. Henry Glassie, "The Variation of Concepts within Tradition: Barn Building in Otsego County, New York," in H. J. Walker and W. G. Haag, eds., *Man and Cultural Heritage,* Geoscience and Man, no. 5 (Baton Rouge: Louisiana State University, 1974), fig. 65c; A. Lawrence Kocher, "The Early Architecture of Pennsylvania, part 2," *Architectural Record* 49, no. 1 (January 1921): 36.
21. Weaver, "Swiss Plantations," pp. 68–70; Weiss, *Häuser und Landschaften,* p. 87; Lorenz Johann Daniel Suckow, *Erste Grunde der Bürgerlichen Baukunst* (Jena, Germany: Christian Henrich Cuno, 1763), plate 4.
22. Zippelius, *Das Bauernhaus am Unteren Deutschen Niederrhein,* pp. 147–53.
23. See, for example, Dell Upton, "St. John's Lutheran Church, Wytheville, Virginia," National Register of Historic Places Nomination, Virginia Historic Landmarks Commission, Richmond, 1974.
24. *A History of the Valley of Virginia,* p. 136; Robert C. Bucher, "Grain in the Attic," *Pennsylvania Folklife* 13, no. 2 (Winter 1962): 7–15; see also Eleanor Raymond, *Early Domestic Architecture of Pennsylvania* (1931; reprint, Exton, Pa.: Schiffer, 1977), plates 51, 157.
25. Weaver, "Swiss Plantations," pp. 56–63; Amos Long, "Pennsylvania Cave and Ground Cellars," *Pennsylvania Folklife* 11, no. 2 (Winter 1960): 36–41; Joe K. Kindig III, *Architecture in York County* (York, Pa.: Historical Society of York County, n.d.), p. 7; Henry Chandlee Forman, *Old Buildings, Gardens, and Furniture in Tidewater Maryland* (Cambridge, Md.: Tidewater Publishers, 1967), p. 288.
26. G. Edwin Brumbaugh, *Colonial Architecture of the Pennsylvania Germans,* vol. 41, pt. 2 of the *Pennsylvania German Society Proceedings* (1933), p. 30.
27. Amos Long, *The Pennsylvania Farm* (Breinigsville: Pennsylvania German Society, 1972), pp. 100–101.
28. William Woys Weaver, "A Blacksmith's 'Summerkich,' " *Pennsylvania Folklife* 22, no. 4 (Summer 1973): 26.
29. J. Frederick Kelly, *The Early Domestic Architecture of Connecticut* (1924; reprint, New York: Dover, 1963), pp. 69–70.
30. Shenandoah County Land Tax Book, 1827, located in the courthouse in Woodstock, Virginia.
31. Robert C. Bucher, "The Swiss Bank House in Pennsylvania," *Pennsylvania Folklife* 18, no. 2 (Winter 1968): 5–7.
32. Ronald W. Brunskill, *Illustrated Handbook of Vernacular Architecture* (New York: Universe Books, 1970), pp. 109, 138–39.
33. Upton, "British and German Interaction."
34. Wust, *The Virginia Germans,* p. 52.
35. Ibid., p. 32.
36. Peter Smith, *Houses of the Welsh Countryside* (London: Her Majesty's Stationery Office, 1975), pp. 160, 314; Brunskill, *Handbook of Vernacular Architecture,* p. 53.
37. Cary Carson, "Segregation in Vernacular Buildings," *Vernacular Architecture* 7 (1976): 20.
38. James Deetz, *In Small Things Forgotten: The Archaeology of Early American Life* (Garden City, N.J.: Anchor Books, 1977); Norbert Elias, *The Civilizing Process,* vol. 1, *History of Manners,* trans. by Edmund Jephcott (New York: Urizen Books, 1978).
39. "The Variation of Concepts within Tradition," pp. 228–31; Glassie, *Folk Housing in Middle Virginia,* pp. 19–40.

40. Wust, *The Virginia Germans,* pp. 52, 107.
41. "Toward a Performance Theory of Architecture in Tidewater Virginia," *Folklore Forum* 12, nos. 2–3 (1979): 173–96.
42. Glassie, *Folk Housing in Middle Virginia,* pp. 121–22.
43. Klaus Wust, *Virginia Fraktur* (Edinburg, Va.: Shenandoah Publishers, 1972); Bradford L. Rauschenburg, "A Study of Baroque- and Gothic-Style Gravestones in Davidson County, North Carolina," *Journal of Early Southern Decorative Arts* 3, no. 2 (November 1971): 24–50; Dell Upton, "Kimberlin Lutheran Cemetery, Wythe County, Virginia," National Register of Historic Places Nomination, Virginia Historic Landmarks Commission, Richmond, 1977; Chappell, "Cultural Change in the Shenandoah Valley," pp. 159–70.
44. John Stewart, "The Dumb Dutch in the Shenandoah Valley," *Augusta Historical Bulletin* 3, no. 1 (Spring 1967): 5–6, 17–19.
45. Harry M. Strickler, *Massanutten* (Strasburg, Va.: Shenandoah Publishing Company, 1924), pp. 66–68.
46. Fort Egypt, Luray Vicinity, Page County, Virginia, sheet 2.
47. Waterman, *The Dwellings of Colonial America,* p. 153.
48. Kercheval, *A History of the Valley of Virginia,* p. 91; Frederick County Will Book, no. 3 (1765) (located in the courthouse, Winchester, Virginia), p. 351.
49. Jennie Ann Kerkhoff, *Old Homes of Page County, Virginia* (Luray, Va.: Lauck and Company, 1962), pp. 17–20.

The Shotgun House: An African Architectural Legacy

JOHN MICHAEL VLACH

Like Edward Chappell's essay this article also attempts to tie the identity of vernacular architecture to the identity of its makers. The shotgun house is an example of Afro-American folk architecture. While blacks were acknowledged as the labor source behind some southern mansions and are known to have worked as carpenters and masons in cities and towns all across the South, never were black people credited with building common houses of their own design. John Michael Vlach demonstrates here that the ubiquitous southern shotgun house possesses a long history that is complexly connected to the black experience of the New World.

Moving back through time Vlach retraces the evolution of the shotgun form. He is able to show that proxemic continuities rather than technological factors provide the strongest link between West Africa and the West Indies and that such core cultural values concerning the appropriate use of space survive as a hidden heritage in spite of the hardships of slavery. In Haiti slaves built their own houses and by the early eighteenth century had developed a small rectangular dwelling with a gable entrance that they called a caille. *This house type, the prototype of the shotgun, was then successively built in urban Haiti, New Orleans, and the American South throughout the eighteenth, nineteenth and into the twentieth centuries. The shotgun houses found today all over the South are distinctive then not only because of their thin narrow shape and gable entrance but because of their African roots. The shotgun house type represents a material example of the distinctive cultural heritage of Afro-Americans that is paralleled by a black tradition for music, oral literature, and dance.*

One of the little understood dimensions of American culture has been the material contribution of Afro-Americans. The material achievements of blacks are generally assumed to have been negligible, if not nonexistent. Yet, now and again, diligent scholarship brings to light an Afro-American tradition in basketry, ironwork, pottery, and other crafts.[1] The continued study of Afro-American artifacts will presumably heighten awareness both of black creativity and the existence of Afro-American material culture. Some African artifacts survived the period of slavery because of their similarity to items employed by whites. The mortar and pestle, two African tools, were used for winnowing rice among blacks from the Sea Islands largely because the same implements were also found in the dominant white culture.[2] While the black artifactual repertoire has never dominated the material culture of the United States, it has in some cases provided a central influence in the creation of significant items. Notably, the dugout canoes of the Chesapeake region and the banjo are thought to have benefited from Afro-American influence.[3] There has been a constant interaction of black and white material repertoires leading not only to the sharing of items, but to the borrowing of them as well. It is here argued that in the development of the shotgun house we find an Afro-American artifact that has been adopted by whites and effectively incorporated into popular building practices. The significance of this postulated cultural borrowing cannot be overlooked for it represents an important contribution of Afro-Americans to the cultural landscape. The shotgun house is, moreover, a central building type in the development of an Afro-American architecture.

The assertion that the humble shotgun, the narrow frame shack of cotton fields and mill towns, is an African-derived house will no doubt raise some eyebrows. It is my intention to trace the history of the shotgun house and indicate how it is associated ultimately with an African architectural heritage. The links to Africa are not simple and direct. The story behind the shotgun involves long migrations, the conduct of the Atlantic slave trade, the rise of free black communities, the development of vernacular and popular traditions in architecture, and the growth of American industrial needs. The history of the shotgun extends back at least to the sixteenth century and is too intricate to be treated exhaustively here.[4]

Students of folk architecture have been aware of shotgun houses at least since 1936 when Fred B. Kniffen published his landmark paper "Louisiana House Types."[5] The shotgun house type was one of several building forms that Kniffen found useful as an index for cultural regions. He defined the type as "one room in width and from one to three or more rooms deep, with frontward-facing gable."[6] Since the number of rooms was highly variable and the plan of a minimal shotgun closely resembled trapper and oysterman house types, he might have suggested a historical sequence. But Kniffen was concerned primarily with the interpretation of spatial diffusion so that chronology did not enter directly into his study. He did note that the shotgun was "strikingly" associated with Louisiana's waterways, but again he chose not to comment on the historical significance of this geographical distribution. Twenty years later his student, William B. Knipmeyer, felt confident enough to assert that the shotgun had evolved from Indian dwellings and was itself the evolutionary precursor to the bungalow house.[7] It is probably because Kniffen so stressed the regional affiliation of the shotgun that Knipmeyer constructed a thesis of native origins. Accompanying this theory was the suggestion of recent development; he claimed that shotguns were built only after 1880 when inexpensive lumber was readily available.[8] Yvonne Phillips supported the idea that the shotgun was a late nineteenth-century or early twentieth-century creation by emphasizing the dominance of timber-framed examples.[9] The modernity of the house type was also accepted by John Burkhardt Rehder who, in his analysis of Louisiana's sugar plantations, relied heavily on Knipmeyer's view of the shotgun house.[10] These studies, when taken together, portray this house form as a regional peculiarity, created solely from the idiosyncratic factors of southern Louisiana's cultural and ecological resources, and commonplace only in the twentieth century. It is true that many of the current Louisiana shotguns can be found along the bayous and that most are examples of 1920s and 1930s frame construction (fig. 1). But this viewpoint ignores a major aspect of the building's development. No consideration is given to the matter of origins.

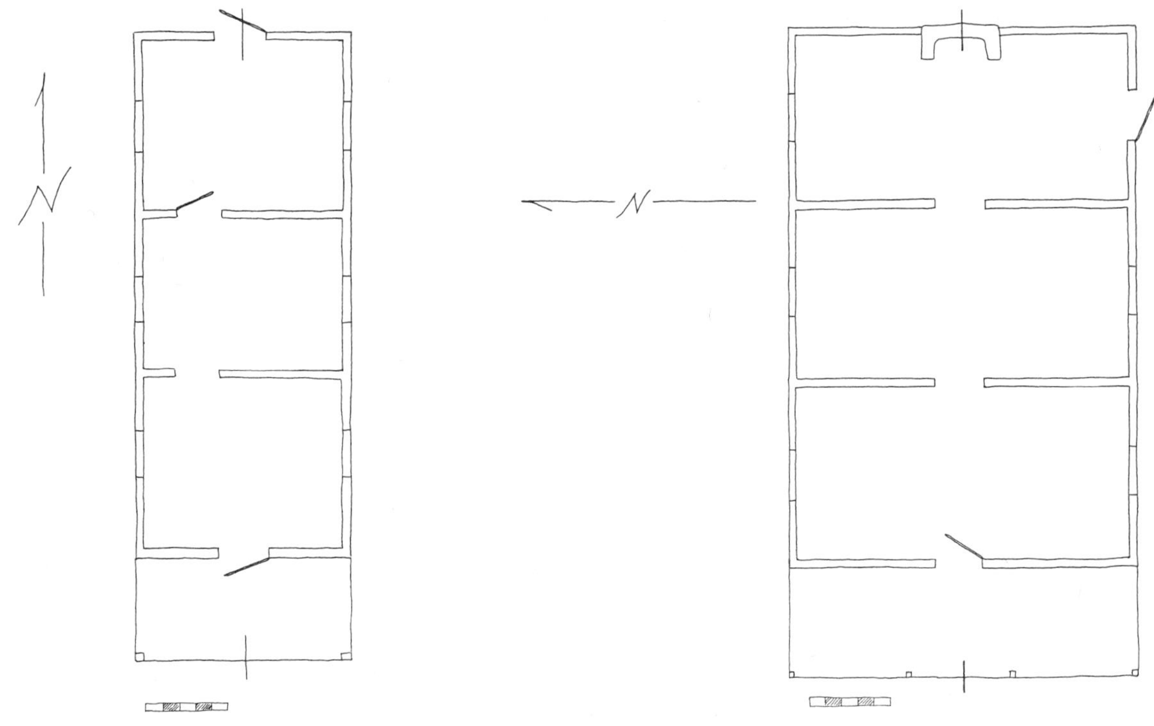
N
N

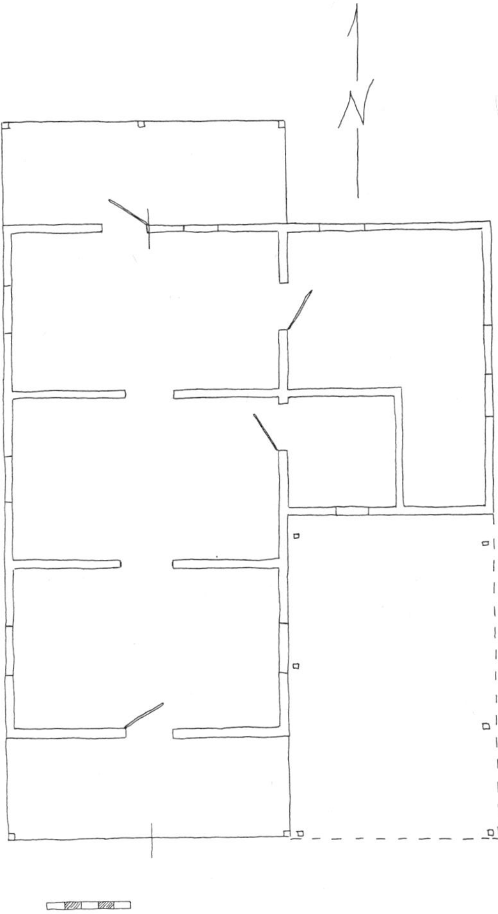

Figure 1. Rural shotgun houses: a (facing page, top), frame shotgun near Fairview, Chicot County, Arkansas; b (facing page, bottom left), plan of a shotgun south of Schriever, Terrebonne Parish, Louisiana; c (facing page, bottom right), plan of a shotgun south of Theriot, Terrebonne Parish, Louisiana; d (top), plan of a shotgun north of Theriot, Terrebonne Parish, Louisiana. (All of these illustrations are from fieldwork by the author in August 1973.)

The origins of the house type remain murky and difficult to comprehend. Yet, it is a history with more antiquity than most have allowed. Geographer Milton B. Newton, Jr., has suggested that the shotgun is an old house form; but he does not state just how old.[11] Architectural historians, while ignoring the rural versions of the type, have shown that the shotgun became common in New Orleans well before the onset of the 1890s lumbering boom.[12]

Three elaborately decorated shotgun houses were illustrated in the 1880 catalog of Roberts and Company, a New Orleans firm that specialized in decorative house trimmings. The sophistication of these examples suggests that the urban shotgun had undergone a much longer period of development than its country cousin (fig. 2). At the very least, the house type must have been around long enough to require updating of its architectural details. With a new set of cornices or balasters an old-fashioned house could appear appropriately stylish. The Roberts company apparently provided the means to keep shotgun houses in step with the flamboyance of changing styles.[13] It would then seem that the shotgun is an older house form and that the search for its origins must involve urban as well as rural versions.

New Orleans should be considered the specific center of shotgun development. This city is the cultural focus of southeastern Louisiana, the region definable by the presence of the shotgun house. The house probably radiated out across the countryside from New Orleans rather than climbing the folk-urban continuum that is assumed to exist in folk architecture. The presence of several subtypes bespeaks the long acquaintance of New Orleans with the shotgun. In addition to the basic single shotgun, there are double shotguns, "camelback" houses, and North Shore houses (fig. 3). The double shotgun, as the name suggests, consists of two single houses built side by side under one roof. Such houses were double-occupancy units that helped to maximize the use of expensive city land. Camelback houses, also referred to as "hump-

Figure 2. An extremely ornate shotgun house illustrated in the catalog of Roberts and Company in 1880. (From Illustrated Catalogue of Moulding, Architectural and Ornamental Woodwork, *compiled by William Bell, Louisiana Steam Sash, Blind, and Door Factory [New Orleans, M. F. Dunn Bro., 1880], p. 81.)*

backs," are single and double shotguns that have two-story rear sections. Since most of the house remains only one story high, these last rooms do resemble "humps." The vertical expansion of these houses is clearly a response to urban crowding. The Louisiana North Shore type, consisting of a single shotgun surrounded on three sides by wide verandas, illustrates how additive secondary features, like porches, can be manipulated to create a regional personality for the standard house type. This subtype occurs frequently across from New Orleans along the north shore of Lake Pontchartrain. What is most significant about the formation of subtypes is that time is required for such variations to develop and become standardized. Folk houses are affected slowly by cultural processes; their basic plans remain relatively fixed and are changed only with cautious innovation. Subtypes arise from experimental attempts to solve problems not initially anticipated when a house form is first used. The proliferation of shotgun subtypes in and around New Orleans would then, in theory, indicate that the house type has long been known in that city.

But the antiquity of the shotgun need not rest on informed speculation alone. There are a few documents that can be used to verify early urban origins. The Notarial Archives of New Orleans maintains a large collection of old posters advertising the sale of property. The posters usually contain a map of the general location of the property, a detailed map of the exact lots which sometimes include measured floor plans, elevations of the fronts of any buildings, and occasionally a perspective view of the property. All of this information is extremely valuable for deciphering the history of old buildings. These records, however, were only kept intermittently for the earlier years of New Orleans history and thus require interpretive analysis. For example, if a house was sold in 1840, it would not be unreasonable to suspect that it existed as much as ten or fifteen years earlier. If a building is a particular subtype of the basic form, it may be further safely assumed that buildings closer to the essential type would have been older.

The oldest shotgun house appearing in these records was located on Bourbon Street near St. Philip in the French Quarter and was sold in November 1833.[14] It is a prototypical shotgun, one-room wide and several deep, with its gable facing the street. The roof was, however, only hipped in the front. Thus, even this early example was already modified by the local roof style, which suggests that this house was patterned on yet older examples. Dimensions for buildings in early contract records suggest that shotguns were being built. A house of three rooms in 1835 was twenty-two feet by fifty-eight feet, including the gallery on the side and rear. Another building constructed in 1837 was sixteen feet across the front and forty feet deep.[15]

A more elaborate variation of the shotgun was

built in the lower Garden District. Four identical houses were built in 1837 at Constance and Euterpe Streets, which were three-room shotguns with two-room additions along the side.[16] A porch surrounded each building on three sides in the manner of a North Shore subtype. These city houses are probably antecedents for the shotguns built in Mandeville and Abita Springs forty years later. This set of shotguns is significant because they are a subtype. Given the time that is required for the development of house variations, early origins for the basic New Orleans shotgun can be posited. The sale of a double shotgun in 1854 in like manner suggests antiquity for the single shotgun house.[17]

These records though sketchy for the early years of the nineteenth century show that the shotgun had taken root as a local type. It has been in New Orleans certainly since the first quarter of the nineteenth century. It is this early origin that allows the shotgun to be associated with Afro-American architectural traditions.

New Orleans had a community of free blacks from its earliest days. They are mentioned in legal records in 1722.[18] Their members grew steadily: 98 in 1764, 353 in 1778, 1,355 in 1803.[19] By the nineteenth century free Negroes, including many mulattoes, constituted one-ninth of the population of New Orleans. The most significant increase in the black community occurred in 1809 with a massive influx of free Negroes from Santo Domingo. After the revolt led by Toussaint l'Overture in 1791, a few black immigrants came to New Orleans and were easily assimilated.[20] But by the time the Louisiana territory was acquired by the United States, Haitian Negroes were considered undesirable. It was thought that they would incite local slaves to rebellion and consequently in 1806 legislation was passed prohibiting the immigration of free blacks from Haiti.[21] But between May 10 and August 19, 1809, some fifty ships brought to New Orleans 1,887 whites, 2,112 slaves, and 2,060 free people of color fleeing conditions in Haiti—6,060 in all.[22] The dimensions of this migration were overwhelming for the local authorities. What was most disrupting about this immigration of Haitian refugees was the change it caused in the racial balance of the city. In 1810 New Orleans had 12,223 people: 4,507 whites, 4,386 slaves, and 3,332 free people of color. The 7,718 Negroes were almost twice the number of whites.[23] The influx of Haitian immigrants made New Orleans a truly black city.

The newly enlarged black community apparently attained both economic success and social recognition.[24] Free blacks were also active in the building trades. By 1850 there were 355 free Negro carpenters and 325 masons.[25] While these figures only represent conditions in the later history of the black community, the large number of Negro craftsmen clearly implies that there were free black house builders from the start of the nineteenth century. The massive increase in the population of New Orleans in 1809 created a severe shortage of housing. Free blacks were in a position to both buy and build houses of their own choosing. They controlled enough financial resources and physical skills to develop their own architectural environment.

Documents in support of this claim are rare but they do exist. In 1787, a free mulatto named Charles was contracted to build a plantation house.[26] Bazile Dede, a free Negro mason, is mentioned in building contracts in 1810 and 1811.[27] James Jolles, a *homme de couleur libre,* in 1835 built a house for Uranie Marsenat Chapieaux that was fifteen feet across the front and forty-five feet long. This house may have been a shotgun and the dwelling that he built next year for Ursin Drouet, described as a one-story frame house, may also have been a shotgun.[28] In 1837, J. B. Joublanc, a free Negro builder, constructed a "typical cottage" for J. B. Massicot.[29]

Of special interest to my thesis are references to the building practices of Haiti, the previous home of many free blacks. In 1839, Francois Ducoing requested that Laurent Cordier build a *maison basse.*[30] This term is used in Haiti for buildings of the shotgun type. This house was built on Elysian Fields, a major street in the Third Municipality which was at that time a black Creole neighborhood.[31] The connection between Haiti and New

518

1023

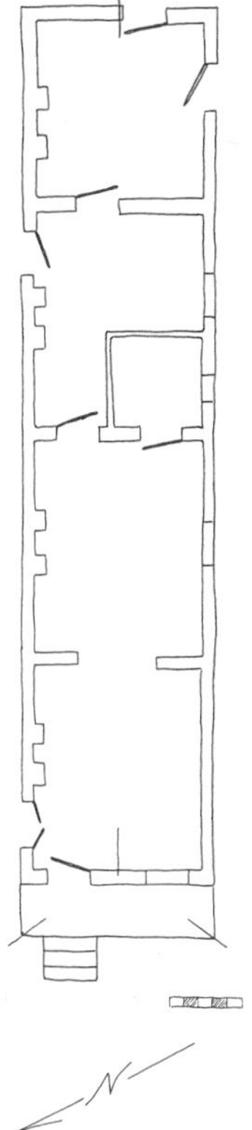

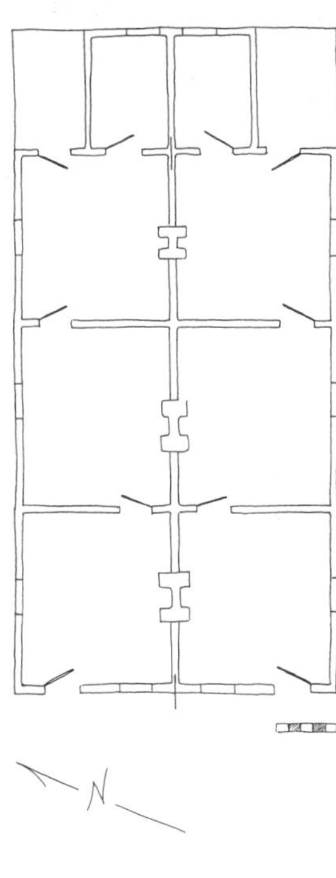

Figure 3. New Orleans shotgun types: a (facing page, top left), single shotgun, Burgundy Street; b (facing page, top right), double shotgun, Bourbon Street; c (facing page, bottom), camelback shotgun, Dumaine Street; d (top), North Shore shotgun, Abita Springs, St. Tammany Parish, Louisiana; e (bottom left), plan of a single shotgun, Chartres Street, New Orleans; f (bottom right), plan of a double shotgun, Eighth Street, New Orleans. (Photographs, August 1973; plans, June 1974.)

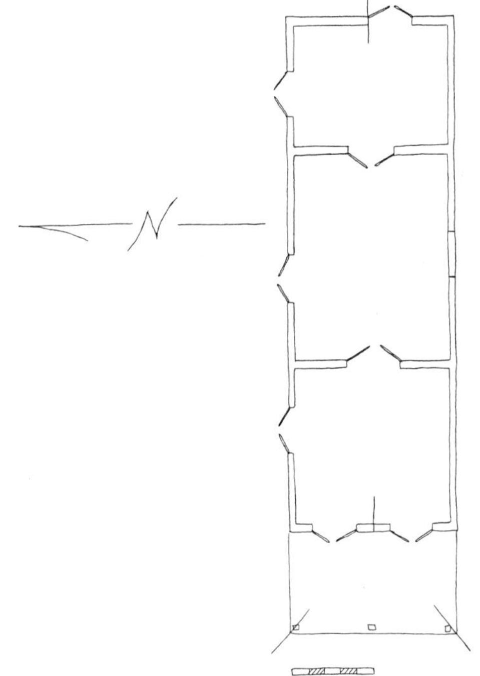

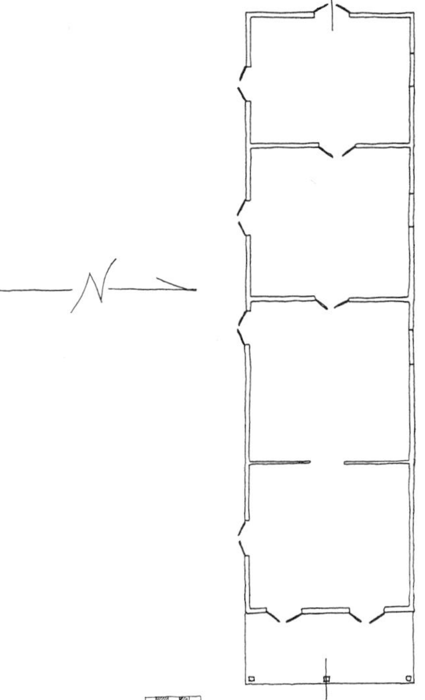

Orleans is more pronounced in the case of Martial Le Boeuf who, in 1840, stated in a contract that his house was to be built after the example of buildings in Santo Domingo.[32] Even viewing these records critically, it must be granted that free blacks were building houses that were sometimes not conventional Creole house types, and that those houses were partially affected by Haitian building traditions.

Kniffen, in wondering where the shotgun could have originated, suggested that either Indians or Haitian slaves were responsible.[33] It would appear, however, that free Haitians built the first shotgun houses. Slave cabins in 1805 were square houses about twelve feet on a side. Although they were constructed with wattle-and-daub like rural Haitian buildings, there is no clear connection between these dwellings and the shotguns that may have been built in New Orleans at the same time.[34] The shotgun house developed in New Orleans about the same time that there was a massive infusion of free blacks from Haiti. This circumstance suggests that the origins of the shotgun are not to be found in the swamps and bayous of Louisiana but in Haiti.

In the towns of southern Haiti there are some houses that are very similar to the shotgun houses of Louisiana. These dwellings (fig. 4), like the shotgun, are one-room wide, one-story high, and have their gable and front entrance facing the road. There is almost always a front porch formed by the forward projection of the gable. Even the same set of shotgun subtypes may be identified in Port-au-Prince. The single camelback occurs with some frequency as well as the double shotgun. Secondary features are also manipulated in the construction of Haitian houses so that some have elaborate verandas resembling those of the North Shore house. On formal grounds these Haitian dwellings must be placed in the shotgun category. The occurrence of the same house types in both Haiti and Louisiana can be explained by the historical links between them via a similar exposure to French culture, trade and commerce, and finally the migration of Haitian Creoles to Louisiana. The shotgun house is perhaps the best document of those ties since the shotguns of Port-au-Prince and New Orleans are similar not only in type but also in specific detail.

Figure 4. Urban Haitian shotguns: a (facing page, top left), frame shotgun, Avenue Magloire Amboise, Port-au-Prince, Haiti; b (top right), half-timbered shotgun, Rue St. Honore, Port-au-Prince, Haiti; c (bottom left), plan of a; d (bottom right), plan of a half-timbered shotgun, Avenue Magloire Amboise, Port-au-Prince, Haiti. This house has a screen of open lattice work between the first and second rooms and thus has a spatial organization similar to the house shown in figure 3e. (All of these illustrations are from fieldwork by the author in October and November 1973.)

The precise size of the floor plans of some Louisiana and Haitian shotgun houses is in some cases almost identical. I found one Port-au-Prince house that measured 13′ × 65′, while two New Orleans shotguns were 13′ × 64′ and 14′ × 64′. The room shapes of New Orleans shotguns are generally squarish, averaging 12′ × 14′. The same rule or proportion holds for Haitian houses. Even though room units are usually smaller in Port-au-Prince, commonly about 12′ × 12′, there is often an exact agreement with the measurements of rooms in New Orleans houses.

The ceiling heights of shotguns are also comparable. Haitian houses are distinctively tall with steeply pitched roofs. They sometimes have the look of small two-story houses. Floor-to-ceiling dimensions are consistently near twelve feet. This height when accompanied by full-length, louvered shutters facilitates the ventilation necessary for comfort in the tropics. Older New Orleans shotguns may have twelve foot ceilings either because of local architectural fashion or because southern Louisiana also has a tropical climate. But since tall ceilings were established in Port-au-Prince as a constant feature, the high ceilings of some New Orleans houses may have been copied as much as an aspect of form rather than function alone.

It certainly seems that formal considerations govern the arrangement of the facades of New Orleans shotguns. A pattern of two frontal openings occurs in most urban Haitian shotguns. The double front "door" pattern occurs repeatedly in New Orleans shotguns. As in Port-au-Prince, the two openings are full-length and shielded by louvered shutters. Even when glass panes are installed, the pattern of two tall, evenly spaced apertures cannot be missed. This type of facade seems to have been copied from the Haitian shotgun. The double-opening pattern was so basic to the early shotgun that it was maintained even when the house plan was significantly altered in the late nineteenth century. At that time it became common for shotguns to have a hallway running the length of one side of the house. However, the door that opened onto the hall was often placed out of rhythm with the other openings. Squeezed against the side of the house, the door could easily be visualized as a part of the addition to the house rather than its entrance.[35] Since the facade pattern endured despite the important modification of the house plan, it must have been a feature firmly established by a traditional precedent. Undoubtedly the houses of Haiti provided a model to be copied and thus served as a basis for the form.

Similarities in internal partitioning of Haitian and Louisiana shotguns is also evident. In the more elaborate shotguns of Port-au-Prince, the first and second rooms are barely divided at all. Instead there is a large opening without doors; sometimes almost ten feet wide. Several houses had screens of lattice work that separated the *salle* from the *salon.* Since these "walls" are not solid partitions, they are essentially decorative rather than functional. Although New Orleans shotguns do not have this type of screen, they do occasionally have wide openings between the first and second rooms. These openings can usually be closed by sliding doors that recede into the side partitions when not in use. Thus, the rooms may be sealed off although normal use habits

Figure 5. Haitian half-timbering patterns (side views): a, symmetrical framing for a shotgun house, Rue Mgr. Guilloux, Port-au-Prince; b, asymmetrical framing for a shotgun house, Avenue Magloire Amboise, Port-au-Prince. (From fieldwork by the author in October and November 1973.)

require that they be left apart. If the doors are left open, a spatial pattern similar to the Haitian shotgun is created. This aspect is not essential to the shotgun form and only occurs in elaborate versions of the house, but it may be related to the social behaviors of the class of elites who required a *salon* for conversation. Since it was the upper class black who migrated to Louisiana, this feature may underline the social as well as the historical circumstances in which the shotgun was introduced into New Orleans.

Haitian shotguns are built with an open-bay framing technique. A strong timber frame is built with a minimum of structural pieces, either 4″ × 4″ or 3″ × 4″ timbers. Sills are laid on the foundation and vertical posts installed only at the corners or along openings in the walls (fig. 5). The walls are braced with diagonals in either a regular or random pattern and capped with plates. All pieces are fitted together with a mortice-and-tenon system of joints. The walls are completed by either covering the frame with siding or filling the spaces with brick and mortar. This building technique, sometimes called half-timbering or *briquette entre poteaux*, is well known throughout Europe and in early America. The technique was introduced into both Haiti and Louisiana by French colonists.[36] Since half-timbering is known in these two areas, a continuity in shotgun construction methods may be suggested, although no half-timber shotguns are known to still exist in New Orleans.

The half-timbering technique may be used to achieve an artistic effect by painting the structural and fill units in contrasting colors. However, this potential is only utilized on the fronts of Haitian shotguns. The X braces that occur on the gable ends are highlighted for decorative reasons. Structural and aesthetic intentions were thus complementary. Yet, it was more common to cover the front with clapboards, which were seven to ten inches wide with a decorative bead at the edge or center (fig. 6). This siding was then painted and thus distinguished the front of the house from its

Figure 6. Decorative framing on Haitian house facades: a, front of house shown in figure 5a; b, front of house, Rue St. Honore, Port-au-Prince. (From fieldwork by the author in October and November 1973.)

sides by both color and medium. The custom of giving special attention to the front of shotguns is also practiced in New Orleans. The side of a house may be unpainted but the front might be given a veneer of brick, painted, or the clapboards on the front will be wider than those on the sides. In rural shotguns one finds instances where only the front of the house will be whitewashed. Creole house types are also treated in the same way but not so much for decorative reasons. Kniffen explains that the "practice harkens back to the days when Creole half-timber houses were weather boarded with unpainted cypress, except for the front which, protected by the porch overhang, was merely plastered and whitewashed."[37] But in the case of the Haitian shotgun, where only the front of the half-timbered house is clapboarded and that part is always protected by a porch, the custom has specific aesthetic intent. The embellishment of the front of shotguns would seem to be a Haitian custom that continued to be associated with specifically Haitian houses even when they were built in Louisiana.[38]

The architectural links between Port-au-Prince and New Orleans cannot be denied. All the nonessential details that are associated with the shotgun in Haiti are also associated with the shotgun in Louisiana, although not always to the same degree. It is evident that the concept of the shotgun house was imported from Haiti, and with the idea of that form came a host of practices that Haitians considered appropriate and fitting for the type. The continuation of these secondary features in Louisiana clearly shows that Haiti provided the basic model for New Orleans' own shotgun culture.

Having linked the New Orleans shotgun to Haiti clearly establishes the involvement of Afro-Americans with the house. The origins of the shotgun, however, lay further back than the late eighteenth century. The urban Haitian shotgun is the end product of a series of transformations and changes. These city dwellings were simply more elaborate versions of a type of plantation house. The largest of these rural houses is almost the same size as the smallest urban examples. The development of the Port-au-Prince shotgun occurs simultaneously on spatial, material, and social levels. The house was expanded from a small two-room dwelling to a sizeable building with as many as four rooms. Sophisticated French half-timbering techniques were used in place of the ordinary wattle-and-daub and thatch. Finally the house became the residence for a freedman as well as a slave. The shotgun had been an element of the slave experience and became an architectural expression with a distinct mulatto identity. The house was a signal of difference and perhaps independence. It has been referred to as an "architecture of defiance."[39]

The prototype for the half-timbered urban shotgun can be found among the small rectangular wattle and thatch huts of rural Haiti.[40] One type is clearly a shotgun house. It is composed of two small rooms which are oriented perpendicularly to the road (fig. 7). Its front entrance is in the gable wall and is shaded by a porch. Occasionally extra rooms are incorporated into the house at the rear or to the side. The dimensions of these houses are remarkably consistent; measurements rarely stray more than two feet from a 10′ × 21′ average.[41] Room volumes are usually ten feet wide and eight feet deep. A space of about four feet is then left for a front porch. Melville J. Herskovits noted that "no house lacks its veranda, however small."[42] The volumetric stability of the rural shotgun indicates that it is a standardized house type constituting a basic pattern for country dwellings. This pattern was established during the plantation era. Pierre de Vaissiere described Haitian slave cabins as "20 to 24 feet long by 12 feet wide and 15 feet high and each of them is divided by partitions into two or three rooms."[43] These dimensions are very close to the measurements of current dwellings and point up the long affiliation of the shotgun house with the history of the New World Negro.

But the shotgun is not simply an Afro-American house even though it has been used repeatedly by New World blacks. The relationship between the Haitian shotgun and black architectural traditions is complicated by the occurrence of a similar house among the Arawak Indians. These indigenous peoples had a house type called a *bohio* by the Spanish that is very similar to a shotgun type (fig. 8). It consisted of one rectangular room with a frontward-facing gable and even had a small front porch. While the mode of construction for the Arawak house is only slightly similar to the Haitian country shotgun, in form it is almost identical.

Early French settlers lived in what amounted to an imitation of this Indian dwelling. Pere Labat, an early traveler to Haiti, built such a house in 1698:

> J'avois envoye nettoyer un place dans le bois, au bord de notre rivière, environ à quinze cens pas de la Maison, ou j'avois fait faire un grand ajoupa, c'est-a-dire, une grande case à la legere & covert de feuilles de balifier & de cachibou, pour s'y retirer en case de pluye.[44]

> (I have tried to clear a place in the woods, at the edge of our river, about 1500 feet from the big house, where I have had built a big ajupa, that is to say, a big thatch house covered with the branches of balifer and cachibou, so one can find shelter in case of rain.)

Even though his description concentrates on the materials used for the construction of the dwelling, the use of an Indian term suggests that the house form might also have been derived from the Indians. A vague engraving showing early French houses presents a structure that is, at least, not contradictory to the design of an Arawak house (fig. 9). Labat notes that it was only in 1705 that half-timbered Creole houses became the preferred type.[45] The French by then had been in Haiti for almost eighty years and during that time they established the *ajupa* or *bohio* as a legitimate, familiar house form. When a profitable plantation economy began to develop in the eighteenth century, they shunned their thatched huts for a building type common to Normandy.

The shotgun was not simply borrowed by African slaves from the Arawak via the sugar plantations. Even if Europeans copied Indian houses to use as slave cabins, those dwellings were satisfactory because of similarities to houses that the African slave preferred. A tight syncretic process links the buildings constructed by the Arawaks, the French, and Africans. Rectangular house forms as well as wattling and thatching techniques are certainly to be found in Europe and West Africa. The Haitian shotgun house was affected by an aboriginal population, European settlers, and unwilling African migrants. In the commingling of peoples each saw in the *bohio* their own type of dwelling. It then is important to look to African house forms in order to understand how and why Haitian blacks adopted the shotgun house type as one of their common houses. The long and intimate association of blacks with the building form suggests that the New World house may significantly reflect the influences of African architectural traditions. It was after all the memory of Africa that guided blacks' first perception of the slave experience.

Philip D. Curtin has noted that the slave trade in the Bight of Benin area of West Africa reaches a peak in the 1780s and suggests that military raids by the Yoruba were responsible for the increase.[46] It was in the decade 1780–90 that French slaving reached its greatest extent when 26,100 slaves were imported annually.[47] Most of the recorded 117 Guinea Coast cargoes for that period were loaded in the Bight of Benin. There is then a significant correspondence in trade patterns. At a time when the Yoruba controlled a large part of the Bight of Benin slave trade, the French were also carrying their greatest number of slaves to Haiti. It seems probable that a large portion of those slaves were Yoruba. They had been brought to Haiti in the beginning of the active slaving period and counted as *Nagos* until 1791. Many were disguised under other names. But what is most important is the pattern of cultural emphasis encouraged by the historical turns of the slave trade. Yoruba and Yoruba-related peoples were brought to Haiti in the first days of slavery in sufficient numbers to preserve many traits of their African culture. The trade then shifted gradually to include more peoples from Central Africa, but toward the end most West African slaves were still Yoruba. The common memory of Africa in 1791, when Haiti became an independent nation, was very likely a reminiscence of the region known

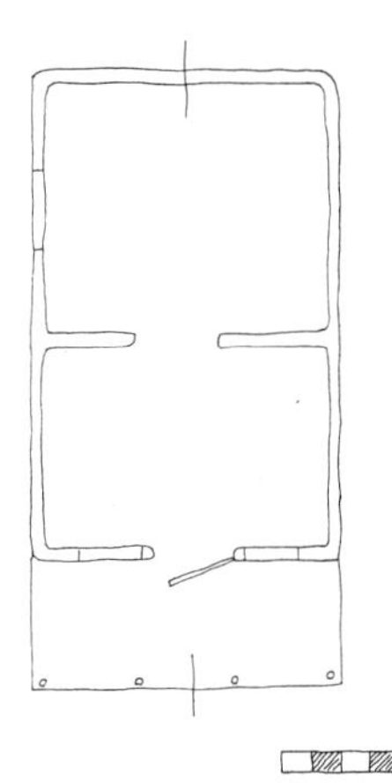

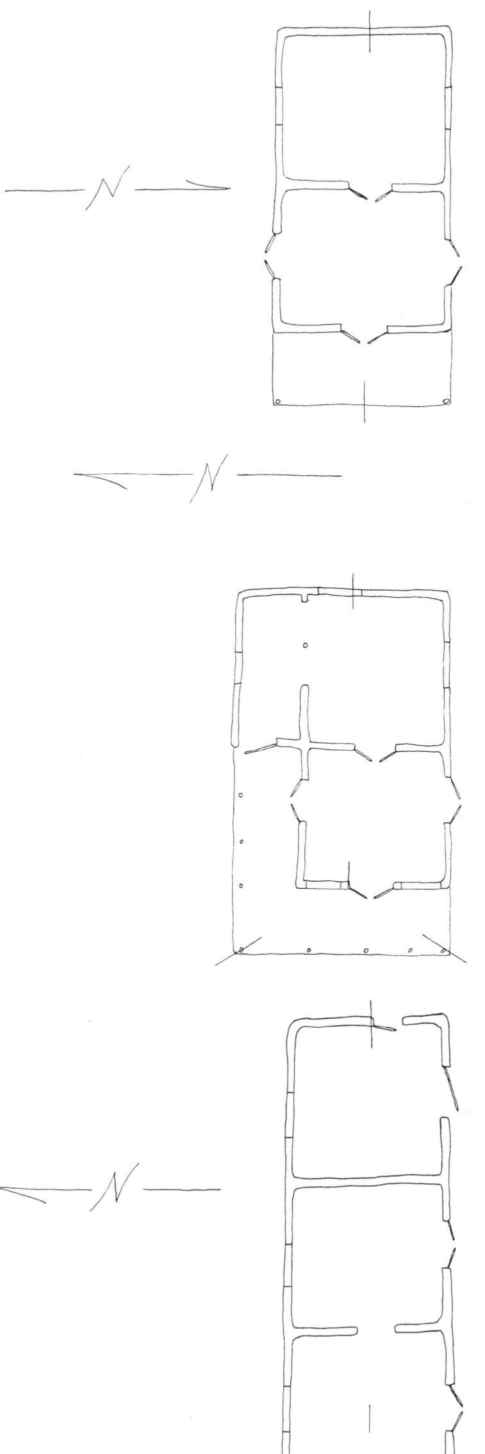

Figure 7. Rural Haitian shotguns: a (facing page, top), wattle-and-daub shotgun, Chancerelles, one-half mile north of Port-au-Prince; b (facing page, bottom left), wattle-and-daub shotgun, Cazeau; c (facing page, bottom right), plan of wattle-and-daub shotgun, Cazeau; d (top), plan of a wattle-and-daub shotgun, Cazeau; e (middle), plan of a wattle-and-daub shotgun, Chancerelles. The small addition to the side of the second room is a bed outshot; f (bottom), plan of a wattle-and-daub shotgun, Chancerelles. This three-room house is a developmental link leading to larger urban shotgun houses. (All of these illustrations are from fieldwork by the author in October 1973.)

Figure 8. A sixteenth-century engraving of an Arawak bohio. *(From Gonzalo Fernandez de Oviedo y Valdes,* Historia General y Natural de las Indias, Islas y Tierra Firma del Mar Oceane *[1535; reprint, Madrid: Imprenta de la Real Academia de la Historia, 1851], plate 2.)*

Figure 9. A seventeenth-century engraving showing the houses of the French Boucaniers. *(From Maurice Besson,* The Scourge of the Indies *[London: George Routledge and Sons, 1929], p. 2.)*

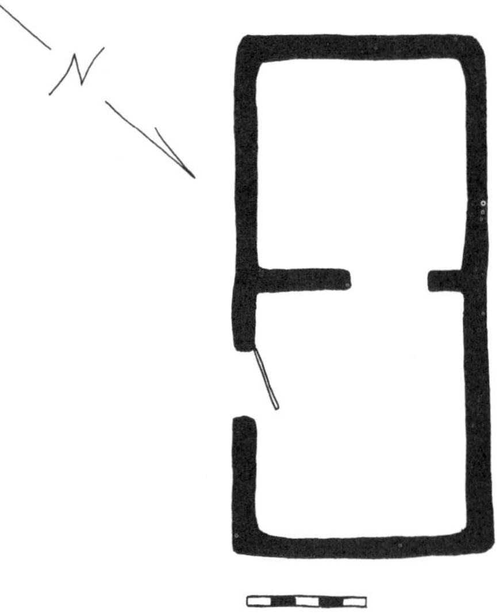

Figure 10. The Yoruba two-room house and related building types: a (top right), a two-room house, Ilefunfun, Nigeria; b (bottom), plan of a two-room house, Aroko, Nigeria; c (facing page, left), plan of a house composed of three two-room units, Atiba, Nigeria; d (facing page, top right), plan of two adjacent compounds in Aroko, Nigeria. The three buildings to the left belong to an Edo family, the remaining two form the household of a Yoruba family. Note the use of two-room modules and the alternative orientations of gable ends with the road; e (facing page, bottom right), plan of an impluvial compound house, Ile Ife, Nigeria. Room volumes here are similar to those used in rural linear houses. Two-room modules are also employed in the urban compound. All of these houses have solid mud walls laid in courses of between 1½ and 2 feet in height and 1 foot thick. (All of these illustrations are from fieldwork by the author in February and March 1974.)

now as Nigeria. The dominant Yoruba elements in Haitian life were reinforced by the newer arrivals. Since they were among the last Africans brought to Haiti, they served as a major link to Mother Africa.

My fieldwork shows that the basic Yoruba house form is a 10′ × 20′ two-room building and is used by both the Yoruba and their Edo neighbors to the southeast. The first room encountered upon entering the house is always a kitchen/parlor, while the second room (without an exterior doorway) serves as bedroom. This double unit constitutes a basic module for the development of other building types (fig. 10). It may be reduced to one room to provide a storehouse for cocoa or if more space is required for a special purpose, a single volume can be added

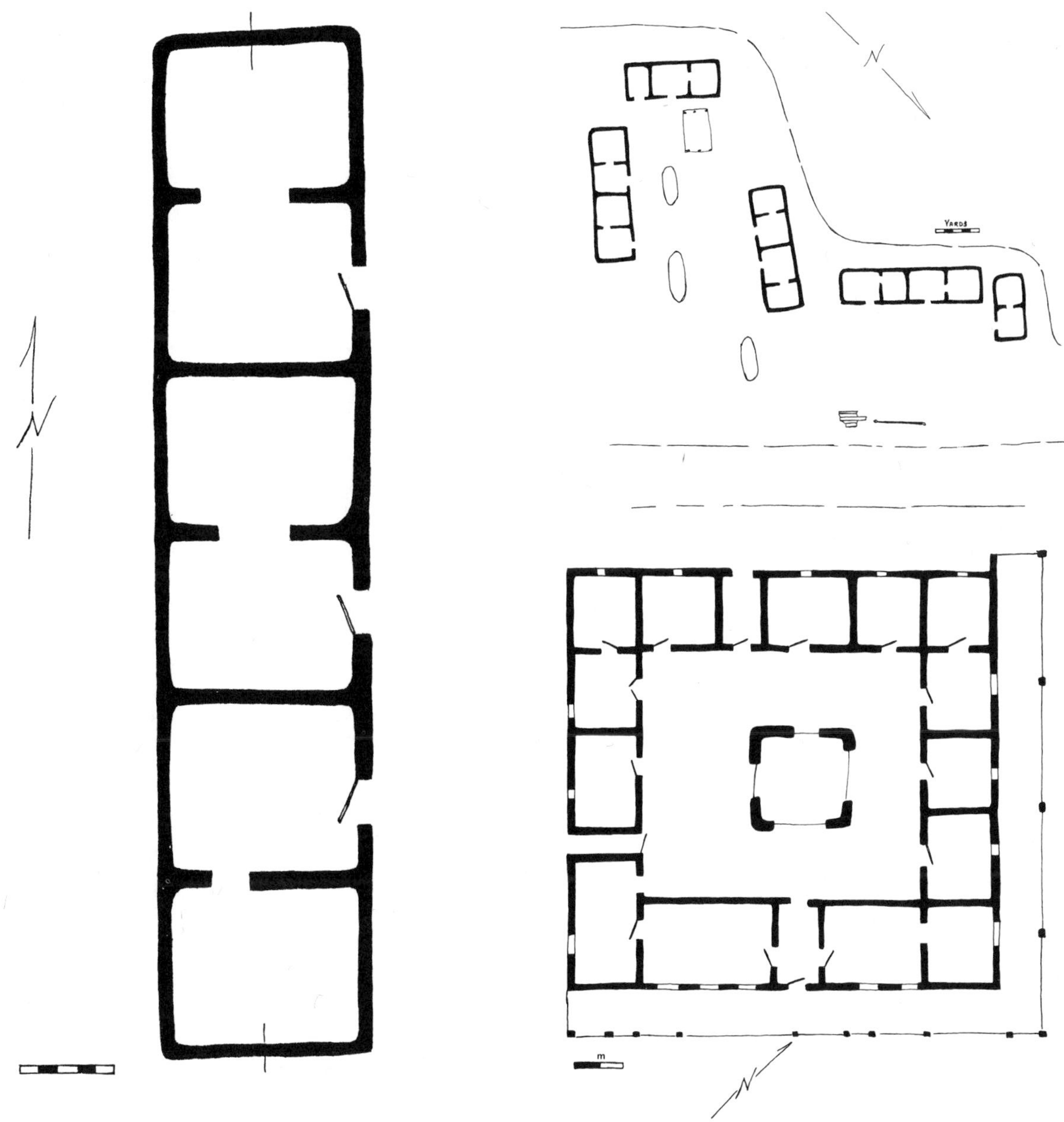
N
YARDS
N
m
N

to the basic house. The two-room module may also be modified by the omission of the partition wall to create a large room that still has the same overall 10′ × 20′ dimensions. The basic unit can also be multiplied; very often a house will consist of two or more two-room units strung out end to end. Even the impluvial compound house contains two-room units.

There are several correspondences between the houses of rural Haiti and western Africa that became clear in my field research. The most striking shared feature is the reliance on the rectangular two-room module. The Yoruba 10′ × 20′ unit coincides closely with the 10′ × 21′ rural shotgun of Haiti. Vertical dimensions are also similar so that wall heights commonly range between six and eight feet in both Haitian and African houses. The Yoruba house thus contains the spatial features of the shotgun. While the aspect of orientation is variable in Yoruba architecture, it does happen that the two-room house will have its gable facing the front like Haitian shotgun houses. In such cases all that is required to convert the Yoruba hut into a morphologically completed shotgun is a shift of the doorway. In the Yoruba house, as in the shotgun, one passes first through a parlor before entering the bedroom; room functions did not need to be shifted. Since the two-room house is a working unit in Yoruba architecture that is intended to be elongated, compressed, and reordered into different building types, the movement of a doorway or the shift from a parallel to a perpendicular alignment is an expected kind of change. Such modifications occasionally occur in the African context and thus the Haitian shotgun may be considered a product of a continuing process of African architectural modification. Haitian houses certainly include in their design the same spatial preferences that are found in West Africa. The rural shotgun thus retained a core of African expectation while satisfying the plantation owners' needs for slave quarters and so there was a meeting of priority and preference.

The form of the shotgun develops essentially from the retention of a version of a Yoruba two-room house, a building form about which several African architectural traditions could cluster. The basic 10′ × 20′ module was first oriented with its gable to the front, and then modified by the shift of the front door to the gable and subsequent incorporation of the gable porch. These latter features were probably copied from the Arawak *bohio.* The new form was often close to 10′ × 21′ with rooms averaging 10′ × 8′. The depth of the rooms was apparently shortened so that the house could include the porch without severely altering the overall dimensions of the Yoruba module. Since the mud wall construction technique used in Nigeria necessitates very thick walls the interior volumes of Yoruba houses are only 9′ × 9′. When compared in terms of square feet, Haitian and Yoruba rooms differ by only one square foot. This similarity suggests a cultural connection between the two house forms. The construction of the shotgun, however, was derived from the French. The roof framing has a system of principal and common rafters that is typical of Norman roof trusses.[48] While the wattle-and-daub method is used in Africa, the technique of making individual panels between posts used in Haiti is more reminiscent of European half-timbering than African modes of construction.[49] Shotgun houses then represent an innovative solution to the problem of shelter. African slaves maintained their own house form by making one morphological change (shifting a doorway), adapting one secondary feature (a front porch), and learning a new technology.

The architectural response to slavery presented here suggests that a people's reaction to adversity can be tenaciously conservative. Africans in Haiti did not drift aimlessly in a sea of alien experiences. Their response was to make sense of their new environment by transforming it so that it resembled a familiar pattern. Cultural contact did not necessitate an overwhelming change in architecture; what was needed was rather an intelligent modification of culture. The shotgun house form is the result of this kind of mental transposition.

The history of the shotgun that has been traced

here has accounted both for the physical development of the type and for some of the cultural motivation behind that development. The Yoruba solution to the problem of plantation shelter was enough like other African house forms that non-Yorubas could also be satisfied with the house in their own terms. The African contribution to the Haitian shotgun thus involves both a form and philosophy of architecture. Because both aspects were part of design process, the shotgun form achieved stability and became deeply imbedded within Haitian culture so that mulattoes used this form while trying to establish their identity as free men. They later carried the idea of the shotgun house to Louisiana. The shotgun of Port-au-Prince then became, quite directly, the shotgun of New Orleans. The shotgun house form has thus been associated with a black population since its first appearance in the United States and it remains largely so today. It can be found in the black sections of almost every southern town. The frequent association of the house with blacks led Glassie to suspect that the origins of the house might be connected to African or West Indian building traditions.[50] Reaching back into the history of the house we have found that the American shotgun is connected directly to Haiti and consequently represents the final product of a set of developments that are ultimately derived from African architecture. Thus by association with black populations and by virtue of African and Caribbean antecedents, the shotgun house is an example of Afro-American architecture.

Notes

This article was originally published in *Pioneer America* (January–July 1976).

1. See Robert Farris Thompson, "African Influence on the Art of the United States," in *Black Studies in the University,* ed. Armstead L. Robinson, et al. (New Haven, Conn.: Yale University Press, 1969), pp. 128–77.
2. Henry Glassie, *Pattern in the Material Folk Culture of the Eastern United States* (Philadelphia: University of Pennsylvania Press, 1968), pp. 116–17.
3. Henry Glassie, "The Nature of the New World Artifact: The Instance of the Dugout Canoe," in *Festschrift für Robert Wildhaber,* ed. Walter Escher, et al. (Basel: G. Krebs, 1972), pp. 153–70; Gene Bluestein, "America's Folk Instrument: Notes on the Five String Banjo," *Western Folklore* 23, no. 4 (October 1964): 241–48.
4. See John Michael Vlach, "Sources of the Shotgun House: African and Caribbean Antecedents for Afro-American Architecture," Ph.D. diss., Indiana University, March 1975.
5. *Annals of the Association of American Geographers* 26 (1936): 179–93, reprinted in Philip L. Wagner and Marvin W. Mikesell, eds., *Readings in Cultural Geography* (Chicago: University of Chicago Press, 1962), pp. 157–69.
6. Ibid., p. 165.
7. "Settlement Succession in Eastern French Louisiana," Ph.D. diss., Louisiana State University, 1956, pp. 68–71, 87.
8. Ibid., p. 177.
9. "The Shotgun House," *Louisiana Studies* 2, no. 3 (Summer 1963): 178–79.
10. "Sugar Plantation Settlements of Southern Louisiana: A Cultural Geography," Ph.D. diss., Louisiana State University, 1971, pp. 174–76.
11. *Louisiana House Types: A Field Guide,* Melanges, no. 2 (Baton Rouge: Museum of Geoscience, Louisiana State University, 1971), p. 6.
12. Bureau of Governmental Research, *Plan and Program for the Preservation of the Vieux Carré: Historic District Demonstration Project,* 1968, p. 33.
13. For a more detailed statement of the activities of the Roberts company see Samuel Wilson, Jr., "New Orleans Prefab, 1867," *Journal of the Society of Architectural Historians* 22, no. 1 (March 1963): 38–39.
14. Plan Book 15, folio 33, New Orleans Notarial Archives.
15. "Collection of Building Contracts and Excerpts, 1800–1900," compiled by Samuel Wilson, Jr. (New Orleans: Tulane University Library, Special Collections Division). All contracts are abstracted on cards and filed chronologically without any reference numbers or other designation.
16. Samuel Wilson, Jr., and Bernard Lemann, *New Orleans Architecture,* vol. 1, *The Lower Garden District* (Gretna, La.: Friends of the Cabildo and Pelican Publishing, 1971), p. 94.
17. Plan Book 87, folio 87, New Orleans Notarial Archives, reprinted in Wilson and Lemann, *The Lower Garden District,* p. 85.

18. Donald R. Everett, "Free Persons of Color in Colonial Louisiana," *Louisiana History,* no. 7 (Winter 1966): 26–27.
19. Edwin Adams Davis, *Louisiana: A Narrative History* (Baton Rouge: Louisiana State University Press, 1971), pp. 131–32.
20. H. F. Sterkx, *The Free Negro in Ante-Bellum Louisiana* (Rutherford, N.J: Fairleigh Dickinson University Press, 1964), p. 84.
21. Robert C. McConnell, *Negro Troops of Antebellum Louisiana: A History of the Free Men of Color,* Louisiana State University Studies: Social Sciences, no. 13 (Baton Rouge: Louisiana State University Press, 1968), p. 46.
22. Ibid., p. 47.
23. Ibid., p. 48.
24. Charles Barthelemy Rousseve, *The Negro in Louisiana: Aspects of His History and His Literature* (New Orleans: Xavier University Press, 1937), p. 24.
25. Robert C. Reinders, "The Free Negro in the New Orleans Economy, 1850–1860," *Louisiana History,* no. 36 (Summer 1965): 275–79, 281.
26. "Collection of Building Contracts and Excerpts, 1800–1900," comp. Wilson.
27. Ibid.
28. Ibid.
29. Ibid.
30. Ibid.
31. Leonard V. Huber, *New Orleans: A Pictorial History* (New York: Crown Publishers, 1971), p. 52.
32. "Collection of Building Contracts and Excerpts, 1800–1900," comp. Wilson.
33. Fred B. Kniffen, "The Physiognomy of Rural Louisiana," *Louisiana History 4,* no. 4 (Fall 1963): 293.
34. C. C. Robin, *Voyage to Louisiana, 1803–1805,* abridged, trans. Stuart O. Landry, Jr. (1807; reprint, New Orleans: Pelican Publishing, 1966), pp. 122–23, 237.
35. For illustrations of this aspect of shotgun facades see Wilson and Lemann, *The Lower Garden District,* p. 98; and Joseph Judge, "New Orleans and Her River," *National Geographic* 139, no. 2 (February 1971): 173.
36. See Fred B. Kniffen and Henry Glassie, "Building in Wood in the Eastern United States: A Time-Place Perspective," *Geographical Review* 56, no. 1 (January 1966): 40–66, reprinted in this volume, for examples of half-timbering.
37. Kniffen, "The Physiognomy of Rural Louisiana," p. 297.
38. Roger D. Abrahams, "Worlds of Action and Order: The Crossroad and the Yard," unpublished manuscript, notes that on St. Vincents there are a whole series of behaviors associated with the facade of a house.
39. Sibyl Moholy-Nagy, *Native Genius in Anonymous Architecture* (New York: Horizon Press, 1957), p. 120.
40. See Alfred Metraux, "L'habitation paysanne en Haiti," *Bulletin de la societé neuchateloise de géographie* 5 (1949): 3–14, for a survey of Haitian house types.
41. These figures are derived from personal fieldwork but also compare closely with the findings of John M. Street who notes that the average Haitian house was 3.6 m × 7.2 m or 10½′ × 21½′. See his "A Historical and Economic Geography of the Southwest Peninsula of Haiti," Ph.D. diss., University of California, 1960, p. 419.
42. Melville J. Herskovits, *Life in a Haitian Valley* (1937; reprint, Garden City, N.J.: Doubleday, 1971), p. 8.
43. Pierre de Vaissiere, *Sainte-Dominique (1692–1789), La societé et la vie creoles sous l'ancien regime,* quoted in Street, "Historical and Economic Geography of . . . Haiti," p. 134.
44. R. P. Labat, *Nouveau voyage au Isles de L'Amérique,* vol. 6. (Paris: Jean de Nully, 1742), p. 9.
45. Ibid., vol. 9, p. 210; see Glassie, *Pattern in the Material Folk Culture,* pp. 120–21, for plans of Creole houses.
46. Philip D. Curtin, *The Atlantic Slave Trade: A Census* (Madison: University of Wisconsin Press, 1969), pp. 178, 225.
47. Ibid., p. 79.
48. See G. Jeanton, *L'habitation paysanne en Bresse* (Paris: Librarie E. Droz, 1935), p. 74, figs. 1–2, for the French mode of roof framing. Compare with Metraux, "L'habitation paysanne en Haiti," p. 9.
49. See Jeanton, *L'habitation paysanne en Bresse,* plates 6, 48, for illustrations of wattle-and-daub filling in half-timbered buildings in rural France.
50. Glassie, *Pattern in the Material Folk Culture,* p. 221.

The American Bungalow

CLAY LANCASTER

The bungalow took middle-class American house builders by storm in the early twentieth century. A drive through any American town will reveal that bungalows and their derivatives make up a high proportion of the existing American housing stock, yet between the initial flurry of interest at the turn of the century and the time Clay Lancaster's article appeared in 1958, this ubiquitous house type received almost no study.

As with many other kinds of popular housing, the term bungalow, *when examined closely, turns out to have been less a descriptive label than an impressionistic qualitative concept that could be applied to a diverse, apparently dissimilar group of dwellings. To call a building a bungalow was not to indicate that it contained specific architectural elements but to conjure up associations with exotic locales—early America, California, and above all the Far East—and of informal, cozy living.*

Whether type or image, the bungalow was not created by a single individual, or even by trained architects in general. It resulted from the blending of a variety of influences—the late nineteenth-century American fascination with the Orient, the romantic and exotic associations conveyed in the very sound of the word bungalow *and the knowledge of its origins in India, a desire for a simpler and less formal style of domestic life, and the attraction to the values and visual forms of early American architecture. All these were grafted onto a long-standing search, dating back to the second quarter of the nineteenth century, for a distinctive form of modest American "cottage" architecture. Great architects like Frank Lloyd Wright and Charles and Henry Greene enter into the bungalow story, but only as a part of it. They were as much followers of a popular movement as were the publishers of bungalow plan books, bungalow magazines, ladies' magazine articles, and other manifestations of the "bungalow craze." In Lancaster's article, the artificial line between vernacular and academic design blurs and we approach a comprehensive understanding of architecture that is faithful to what we encounter "out there."*

The term *bungalow* was frequently used to designate the small American home from about 1880 to the 1930s. The popularity of the word was due to its euphony and vagueness of meaning,

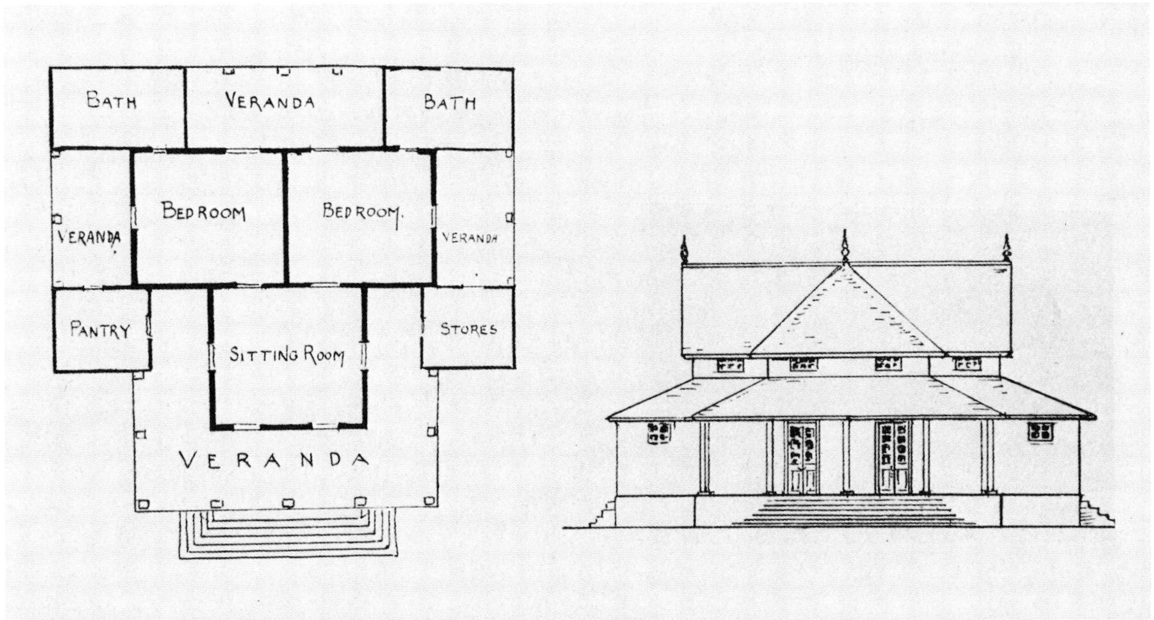

Figure 1. Indian government dāk *or posting bungalow. (From J. Lockwood Kipling, "The Origin of the Bungalow,"* Country Life in America *19, no. 8 [February 1911]: 309.)*

Figure 2. Bungalow, Monument Beach, Mass., designed by W. G. Preston. (From American Architect and Building News *7, no. 222 [March 27, 1880].)*

which made application elastic. In general it may be said to have gradually supplanted the word *cottage*, eventually taking over many of its duties in our common vocabulary for a period upward of half a century. During this time the American house underwent certain changes, changes inherent in the bungalow idea, that brought about the transition to what we know today as the modern house.

The word *bungalow* is of Eastern derivation, coming from the Bengali, *bānglā*, signifying a low house with galleries or porches all around, and identical with the Hindi or Hindustani adjective *banglā*, "belonging to Bengal." Its association with a building type apparently originated among the English in India, native-type shelters being referred to as "Bungales or Hovells" in an India Office diary as early as 1676.[1] About 1825 Mary Martha Sherwood, in *The Lady of the Manor*, describes Indian bungalows (using current spelling) as modest structures "built of unbaked bricks and covered with thatch, having in the centre a hall . . . the whole being encompassed by an open *verandah*."[2] For half a century longer the bungalow continued to be considered a primitive dwelling, at best fit for civilized people only as temporary shelters, or caravanserais, when they were journeying in backward foreign lands.

Writers in American magazines early in this century were aware of the Indian origin of the bungalow. Thus, an article in *American Architect and Building News* in 1908 characterizes the "dāk-bungalow" as "a house for travelers, such as are constructed by the Indian Government at intervals of twelve to fifteen miles on the highroads in many parts of India."[3] The description given coincides with Mrs. Sherwood's. Other authors speak of the bungalow as a "transplantation from the banks of the Ganges to the shores of Saranac Lake," or as migrating from "India to California."[4]

To the British in South Asia the bungalow was no dream house, being "about as handsome as a stack of hay," and giving "the 'irreducible minimum' of accommodation." These remarks came from the pen of J. Lockwood Kipling—father of the poet and raconteur of jungle tales—who illustrated his piece with several sketches and diagrams of authentic examples. Even where the planning was compact all the rooms opened onto galleries and were provided with windows and outside doors for cross-ventilation; in addition there was often a clerestory under the main eaves (fig. 1). The bungalow was, as Kipling remarked, "a purely utilitarian contrivance developed under hard and limiting conditions."[5]

The earliest American house called a bungalow that I have discovered is one at Monument Beach designed by the Boston architect William Gibbons Preston and published in *American Architect and Building News* in 1880 (fig. 2).[6] This house, clapboarded and having a generous verandah, belongs to what has so aptly been termed by Vincent Scully the "stick style," by this time a mode well past its prime.[7] The plan, insofar as it contains a projecting central living room opening onto a gallery and a rear recessed porch, bears some affinity to that of Kipling's Eastern bungalow. Although the arrangement is essentially axial, the massing is quite irregular. The house is two-and-a-half stories in height, but horizontality is emphasized. The design is well adjusted to its setting, which seems to have been taken into positive consideration when the house was designed.

The second bungalow pictured in *American Architect*, in June of 1895, is a more literal interpretation (fig. 3). This is a house for J. D. Grant at Burlingame, California, by A. Page Brown of San Francisco. Brown's bungalow is situated on a hillside, so that there is considerable basement height on the downhill side. With its deep gallery supported on great brackets, and the combination hip and gable roof, the structure suggests an authentic Himalayan chalet. Located on the San Francisco peninsula, the Grant bungalow probably was habitable the year around, unlike the earlier one on Cape Cod.

The *American Architect*'s third bungalow, in the issue of August 22, 1896, brings us considerably closer to the accepted concept of the true American bungalow. It was designed by Julius Adolph Schweinfurth, at this time associated with Peabody and Stearns, for the William H. Lincoln estate at

Figure 3. J. D. Grant Bungalow, Burlingame, Calif., designed by A. Page Brown. (From George G. Bain, "The Congressional Library Building at Washington," American Architect and Building News *48, no. 1015 [June 8, 1895]: 95.)*

Newton Center, near Boston (fig. 4).[8] A sloping site is compensated for by a curving, walled terrace, on which are set potted bay trees, decorative accessories that had become popular because of their adaptation to stylization during the Art Nouveau period. The house itself was low and nestled into the ground at the back, with long, banded windows around the semicircular end of the living room, and tall chimneys having flared caps, an original and attractive composition. The building fit the definition for the "true bungalow" given in a contemporary magazine as a dwelling containing "no more than an absolutely necessary number of rooms," having "no attic, or second story, and no cellar.[9] Its characteristics are: simple horizontal lines, wide projecting roofs, numerous windows, one or two large porches, and the woodwork of the plainest kind."[10] The Schweinfurth scheme shows the dissolution of the older idea that a bungalow is merely a "Summer residence of extreme simplicity, . . . intended for more or less primitive living."[11] The bungalow, rather, was beginning to be recognized as a genuine architectural form, not limited to the bare essentials of the Eastern ethnic shelter, but a creative interpretation based on that type, adjusted to meet modern democratic Western living standards. The article quoted above defining the "true bungalow" goes on to say: "The keynote of the bungalow of the best type is homelikeness and general attractiveness without being pretentious." The assertion also is made that: "The designing of an artistic bungalow which will stand the test of time requires fully as much skill and education along this line as any other style of archi-

Figure 4. Bungalow on the estate of William H. Lincoln, Newton Center, Mass., designed by J. A. Schweinfurth (drawing dated 1895). (From "A Group of Country Houses," American Architect and Building News *53, no. 1078 [August 22, 1896].)*

tecture." In the Schweinfurth design conceived in 1895 the bungalow attained its stride.

That the bungalow vogue was a continuation and an outgrowth of the cottage development in America becomes apparent through a comparison of certain select examples. In 1848 Charles Wyllys Elliott published a book in Cincinnati entitled *Cottages and Cottage Life, Containing Plans for Country Houses, Adapted to the Means and Wants of the People of the United States.* Among the plates was a lithographic view and plan of Frederic Tudor's house at Nahant, Massachusetts, a spreading building with low-pitched roofs and perimeter galleries supported on slender posts (fig. 5). The walls are of stone, the roof covered with bark. We note similarities between this house and the two Massachusetts bungalows (compare figs. 2 and 4). The room arrangement shown, however, is admitted to be Elliott's own invention, recalled some time after visiting the house. Although the house as it stands today has been altered considerably, it is clear that the living room always spanned the entire front of the block, the plan being constituted not unlike that of Kipling's bungalow (fig. 1).[12] Special note should be made of the fact that this house has a real "living room," in the modern sense of the term, rather than the more stilted parlor (imagined by Elliott), then commonly employed. The living room was to become a conspicuous feature of the bungalow. The Nahant House hardly seems adaptable to year-round living on the cool and windswept New England cape. We are informed by A. J. Downing that Tudor was "well known in the four quarters of the world, as the originator of the present successful mode of shipping ice to the most distant tropical countries," and we are left to wonder whether his enterprise extended to Hindustan.[13] More likely it focused on our neighboring islands in the Caribbean.

Our attention is directed to domestic building in that tropic portion of the New World first mistaken by European explorers for parts of India, a false identity perpetuated in the designation "Indies." Perspective and measured drawings of a typical old farm house near Marianao, Cuba, were published in the international edition of *American Architect and Building News* (December 28, 1907), the vacation sketches of Julius Adolph Schweinfurth (fig. 6). The low-hipped roof of the house is double pitched, and the principal rooms form a railroad suite down the long axis of the house; a verandah half as wide extends along one side, and lesser rooms and a

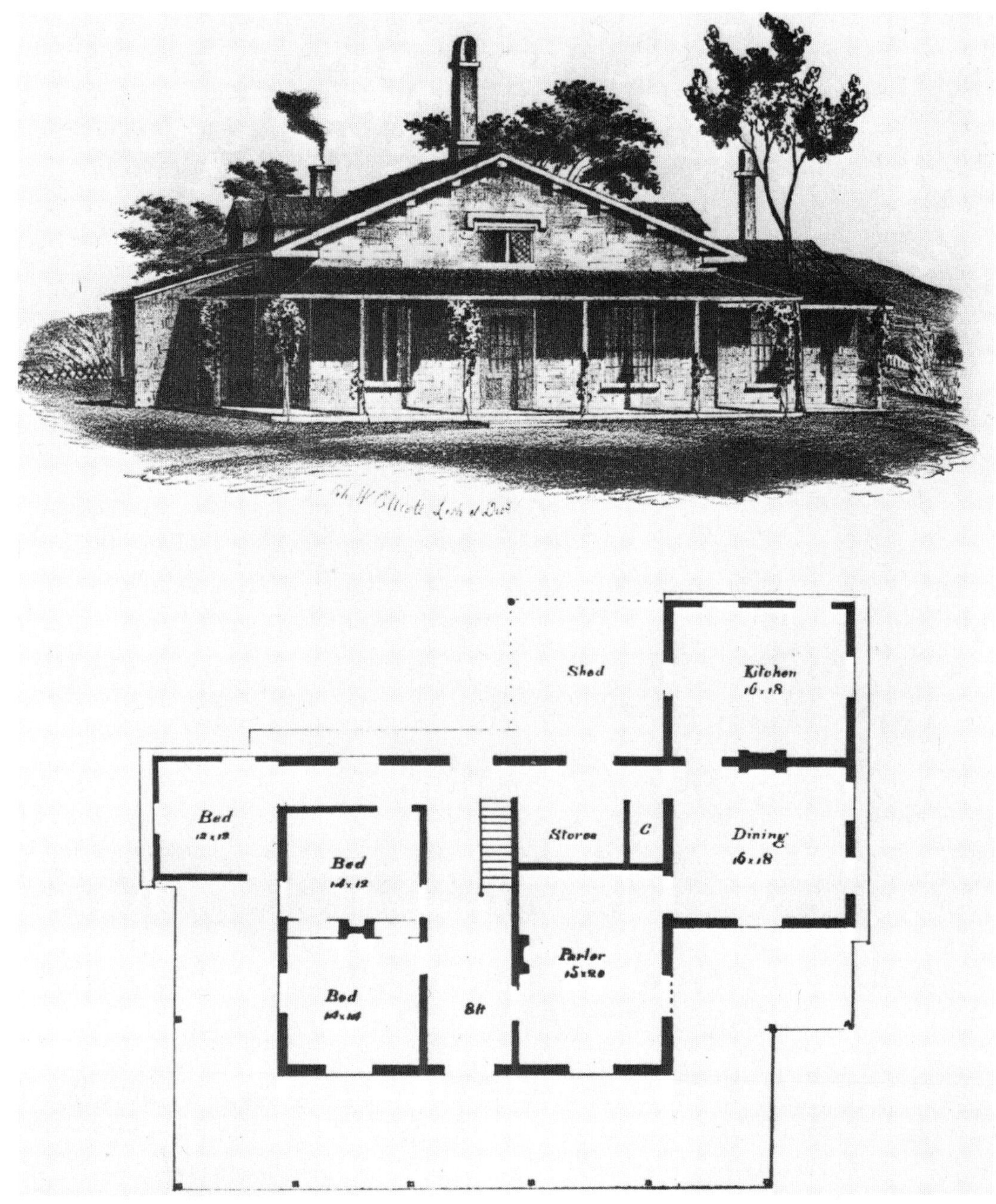

Figure 5. Mr. Tudor's house, Nahant, Mass. (From C. W. Elliott, Cottages and Cottage Life *[Cincinnati: H. W. Derby, 1848], facing p. 133.)*

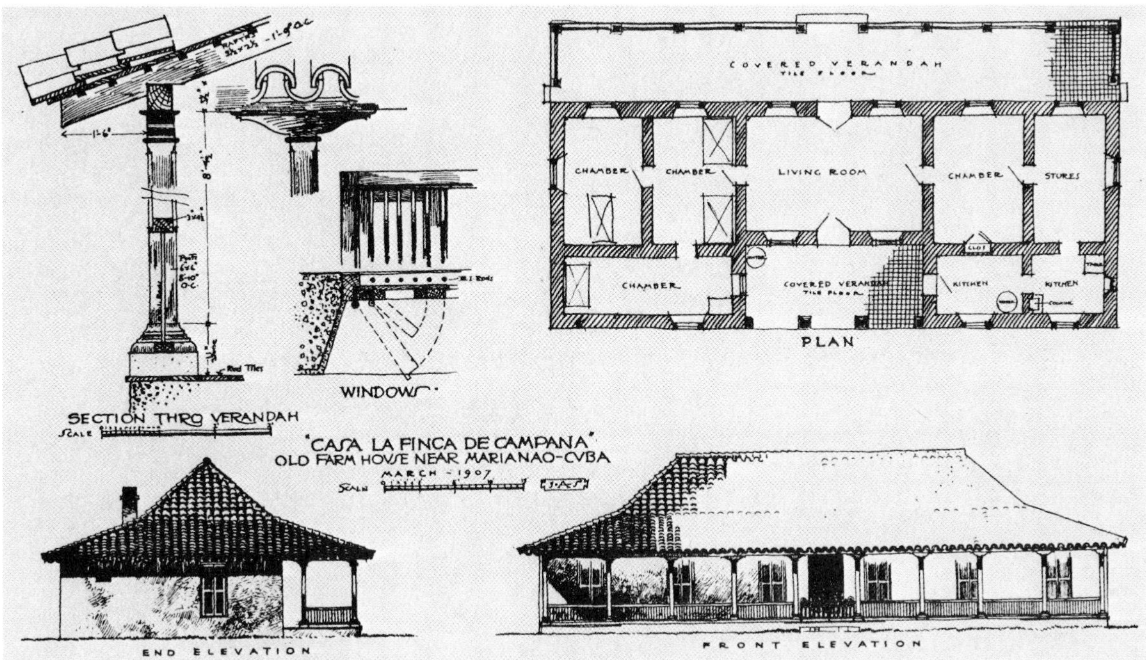

Figure 6. Casa la Finca de Campana, old farm house near Marianao, Cuba. (From "Views of Casa la Finca de Campana," American Architect and Building News *92, no. 1670 [December 18, 1907].)*

recessed porch along the other. This arrangement corresponds in its essentials with a second bungalow plan illustrated in the Kipling article, where the verandah, however, continues partially across the end of the Eastern house, which has two recessed porches at the back (fig. 7). The Indian house, of course, has a clerestory, but the points in common, including similarities in shape, extremely thick walls, and openings placed on axis, make the two houses remarkably alike. Both schemes have resulted more from an aim to satisfy specific requirements than from adopting established forms traditional to the builders, and their similarities is explained by approximately the same climatic conditions. It is not unreasonable that a West Indies house resembling the Cuban building contributed to the design of the Nahant home of the ice exporter.

Of far greater importance than a possible Caribbean influence upon a single mid nineteenth-century house in New England is the impact of early Spanish colonial insular architecture upon a host of dwellings built along the Mississippi River by the French prior to 1762, and afterward by the French and Spanish.[14] "Madame John's Legacy" (ca. 1727), on Dumaine Street in New Orleans, reputedly the oldest existing house in the valley, bears resemblances to the Cuban farmhouse in its gallery, double-pitched roof, plan, and so forth, though the Louisiana house is elevated high above ground level due to the saturation of the soil there.[15] The "raised-cottage" type prevailing throughout the region left many characteristic examples that excited some interest among Americans in the renewed enthusiasm for colonial architecture during the last quarter of the 1800s.[16] Pictures of old houses of the Deep South appeared in magazines (fig. 8). At the World's Columbian Exposition of 1892–93 in Chicago, the Louisiana exhibition was housed in a

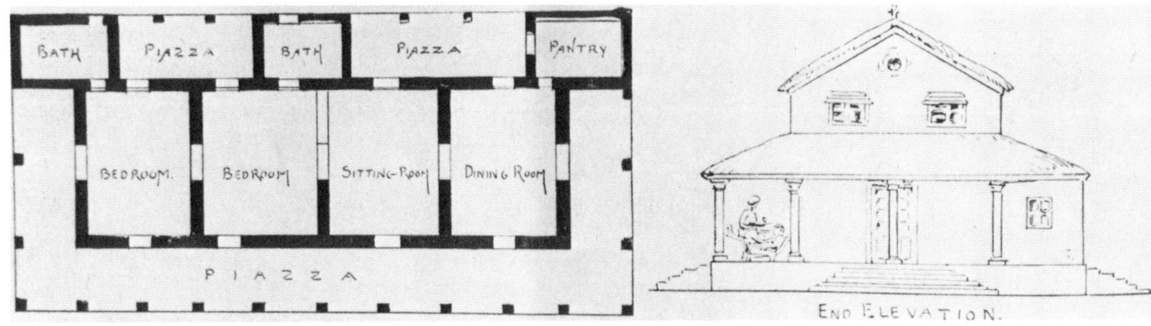

Figure 7. Indian bungalow. (From Kipling, "Origin of the Bungalow," p. 310.)

Figure 8. Residence, Biloxi, Miss. (From Inland Architect *30, no. 1 [August 1897].)*

raised-cottage building styled after Creole plantation residences on the Bayou St. Jean north of the Old Quarter of the Crescent City.[17]

Visitors to the fair from all sections of the country examined the Louisiana pavilion. It was one structure that avoided the classic grandiosity of most of the buildings of the "White City" at Chicago, which, according to Louis Sullivan, would lead American architecture astray for the next half-century.[18] Sullivan already had built himself a single-storied shingled bungalow at Ocean Springs, Mississippi, about midway between New Orleans and Mobile, a hipped-roof, T-plan house with a long piazza facing Biloxi Bay, shaded, and partially concealed, by luxuriant tropic vegetation, and harmonizing in many of its characteristics with indigenous building (fig. 9).[19] During the decade or two following the World's Columbian Exposition, Chicago's north shore became dotted with bungalows of this type.[20]

The other area within the boundaries of the United States offering preexisting models from which elements were borrowed freely by the bungalow movement was the Southwest. The Spanish colonizers here evolved a type similar to that of the Caribbean, through having as a special feature a partially enclosed court or patio, encircled by an inner gallery. The walls of these houses were of adobe bricks, composed of a mixture of loam, sand, clay, straw, and tile chips or other binder, hardened in the sun, and covered with a mud coating that was whitewashed yearly, becoming, in the course of time, a protective lime plaster. Floors and roof were of tile or wood. Buildings in the dry inland region often had flat roofs, like that of the Palace of the Governors at Santa Fe, New Mexico, dating from the early seventeenth century. The plan (fig. 10), of which the major rooms occupied the full width and the others half, had corner fireplaces; it was taken over in abridged form for an adobe residence in the same city built by the architect V. O. Wallingford during the early years of this century (fig. 11).[21]

Early *casas de campo* or *casas de pueblo* (there was little difference between rural and town houses) on

Figure 9. Louis Sullivan's bungalow, Ocean Springs, Miss. (Photograph by Richard Nickel.)

the West Coast were similar to, and equally as plain as colonial adobe houses in the region eastward just noted, though generally belonging to a later period. Few existing houses are known to have been built in what is now California before 1800. Typical of those dating from the second and third decades of the nineteenth century are the single-storied Francisco Avila House (ca. 1818) on Olivero Street, Los Angeles, a narrow rectangular form preceded by a deep wooden gallery, and the Casa Estudilla ("Ramona's Marriage Place," 1824), in Old Town, San Diego, embracing three sides of a patio.[22] The early stage of the Spanish colonial revival along the Pacific often overlooked the simplicity of the original domestic shelters, making use of elaborate details borrowed from Franciscan churches, as in the D. R. Cameron and D. M. Smyth houses in southern California, built in the 1890s.[23] This was the so-called "mission style," the name of which was carried over into furniture that made little pretense of disguising the fact that it was assembled from rectangular pieces of lumber.[24] "Mission" design in furniture was a special branch of the craftsmanship movement, though most of its products did little credit to the high level of skill and sensitivity which the movement purported to advocate. In building, the domestic prototype is remembered today

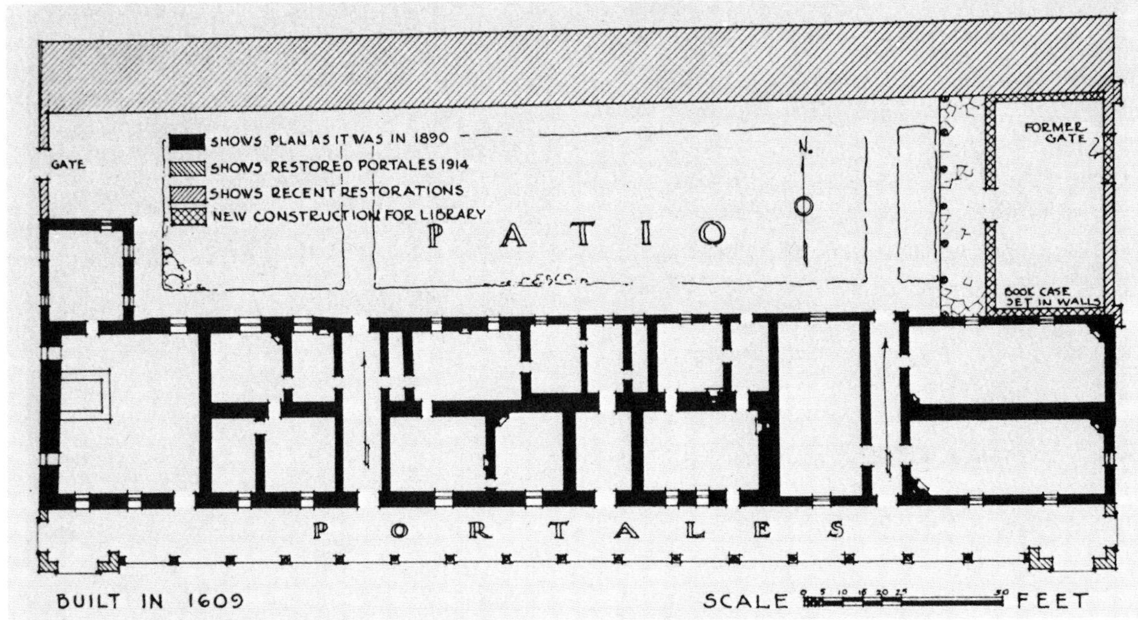

Figure 10. Governor's Palace, Santa Fe, N.M. (From Rexford Newcomb, Spanish-Colonial Architecture in the United States *[New York: J. J. Augustin, 1937], plate 40.)*

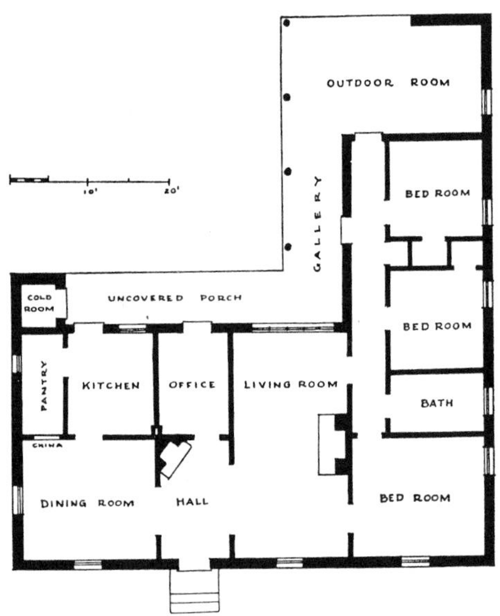

Figure 11. Adobe house, Santa Fe, N.M., designed by V. O. Wallingford. (Drawing by the author, after V. O. Wallingford, "An Adobe House in Santa Fe," House Beautiful *22, no. 1 [June 1907]: 25.)*

through the much overworked—and usually misapplied—designation "ranch house," the predecessor of which was the "ranch bungalow" antedating the First World War, such as the J. C. McConnell House (ca. 1911), built on a small ranch near Burbank, California, by A. S. Barnes and E. B. Rust (fig. 12).[25] The patio, or court, is incidental in this scheme called "modern in every respect." The design is typical of California, where inspiration was drawn freely from many sources, but where the role of the Spanish *rancho* or *hacienda* (farm) house can hardly be overlooked, inasmuch as California furnished the soil on which the bungalow primarily took root and flourished; and the balance of the United States often spoke not of "bungalow" alone, but of "California bungalow" as the more meaningful appellation.

There were several reasons why California became the bungalow hotbed. In the first place the bungalow there was found to be a comfortable perennial home, not limited to summer vacation peri-

Figure 12. J. S. McConnell Ranch Bungalow, near Burbank, Calif., designed by A. S. Barnes and E. B. Rust. (From Charles Alma Byers, "A Ranch Bungalow Embodying Many Modern Ideas," Craftsman *22, no. 2 [May 1912]: 209.)*

ods. A writer framed this idea in the following words: "California, on account of its favorable climatic conditions, affords unending opportunity for variety in the construction as well as in the architecture of the house, large or small."[26] Secondly, Californians were more willing to apply new ideas to house building than were the Atlantic folk: "It is only natural that our first original modern expression of domestic architecture should show itself on the Pacific coast, for the people of the West are above all things pioneers and have a way of dashing aside all tradition and prejudice and getting directly at the thing that meets their requirements in the most practical way. The people of the East are inevitably more conservative, and the fact that Europe is easier of access to them accounts for their more general dependence upon architectural forms . . . they have seen and admired abroad."[27] A third reason for the success of the bungalow in California was sought in the designers themselves. A bungalow proponent of the second decade of the twentieth century stated it this way: "In design there is no special reason why there should be any difference between California and the rest of the country. *But there is*; and it is due to the fact that California architects, and even carpenters and builders are *more generally artists* than those in other parts of our country."[28] Architects predisposed toward designing bungalows naturally gravitated to the state providing appreciation for and patronage of their work.

"The bungalow of the Land of Sunshine is distinctly a California creation," declared an enthusiast in 1906.[29] Some years later another attempted to sketch "The Evolution of the Bungalow" in California:

> In the beginning was the barn. Persons of small means when they first came to California often found it desirable to put all their money into land and the young orchards which were to make their fortunes. They decided to live themselves in a small structure which should be the barn of the future house. These barns were at first constructed with Eastern solidity, with heavy posts and beams, and completely finished on the inside as barns, with stalls, mangers and other like fittings. The human tenant generally decorated the carriage house with burlap,[30] or "Old Government Java" coffee bags, held in place by split bamboo strips; and this with a rough fireplace, a few good pieces of furniture, and the shadows of the rafters overhead,

> made a really delightful living-room. The great barn doors were generally left open, giving an outdoor effect very grateful to the lovers of the sun and space.
>
> The next step was to build only the outside shell of a barn, dividing it into rooms with temporary partitions. . . .
>
> Later, travelers from distant lands noticed the resemblances between these wide-spreading, one-story houses and the East Indian "bungalow," and thenceforward these dwellings ceased to be temporary; but putting on wide verandas and a dignified name, sprang up in every direction, as intentional homes.[31]

Awareness of the affinity to the Indian caravanserai, then, constituted a definite step in the formation of the California bungalow. The Grant House at Burlingame (fig. 3), and another example bearing "a close resemblance to its prototype in India," built at Palm Springs not later than 1910, serve to illustrate the phase.[32] With regard to the latter it was pointed out that inasmuch as hot weather comes to Palm Springs as early as May: "The roof is double, ventilators extend all around, and the inside doors are supplied with large transoms," as in the authentic Hindustan design.[33] However, the California bungalow progressed beyond the literal stage which bequeathed title to the small house that grew out of the barn.

> Eventually some great man discovered that as there was no snow and really no violent storms in California, a house could be made to stand up without a frame, that it could be built of nothing but upright boards reaching from sill to plate, with scantling as cross-ties. . . .
>
> Most of the best bungalows are made of broad redwood boards with weather stripping, and are mill finished inside.

It was stressed that wood was left in its natural finish, or perhaps given a stain, one of the cheapest consisting of asphalt dissolved in hot turpentine, a lump six inches square being sufficient to stain a whole house.[34]

The "great man" now credited with inaugurating the bungalow of upright boards was not a single individual but a team, two brothers, fifteen months apart in age, Charles Sumner and Henry Mather Greene, who had come to California to visit their parents and stayed to open an office at Pasadena in 1894. Preparations for their vocation had begun at the Manual Training High School operated by Washington University in St. Louis, where they had lived during adolescence. Advanced study was pursued at the Massachusetts Institute of Technology, after which they obtained practical experience in several Boston architectural firms.[35] In southern California their early work was in revived colonial, "Queen Anne," Spanish mission, and Old English vernaculars, prior to 1903, when they were given a commission for the Arturo Bandini Bungalow. Bandini specified that his house was to reflect the patio plan of the homes of his ancestors in this locale, and the outcome was a U-shaped bungalow having a gallery around three sides of the court, with a pergola forming a screen across the open end (fig. 13).[36] Construction was in the simplest manner, of redwood boards set upright; the joints both inside and outside were covered with three-inch battens. The board walls were stained on the exterior and given a "thin light oil finish to prevent spotting of the wood and yet retain as nearly as possible its natural color" within. The interior provided "much room and comfort and artistic possibilities at comparatively small outlay."[37] The exposed cobblestones of the chimneys were brought into the rooms. Living and dining rooms were located at the base of the U-form (fig. 14). Both rooms were about twice as long as wide, and with folding doors opened back between them the effect was that of a single hall fifteen by sixty-five feet. Kitchen, pantries and service rooms, and a bath were in one corner, and there were three bedrooms in each wing. The arrangement may have been derived from Spanish colonial antecedents, but there was none of the enclosed feeling one gets from thick adobe walls. The lightness of construction came from Japan. The Greene brothers visited the Columbian Exposition at Chicago in 1893 and the Mid Winter Exposition at San Francisco the following year, and at both were impressed and delighted by the Japanese constructions conceived especially for

Figure 13. Arturo Bandini Bungalow, Pasadena, Calif., designed by Greene and Greene. (Restoration drawing by the author.)

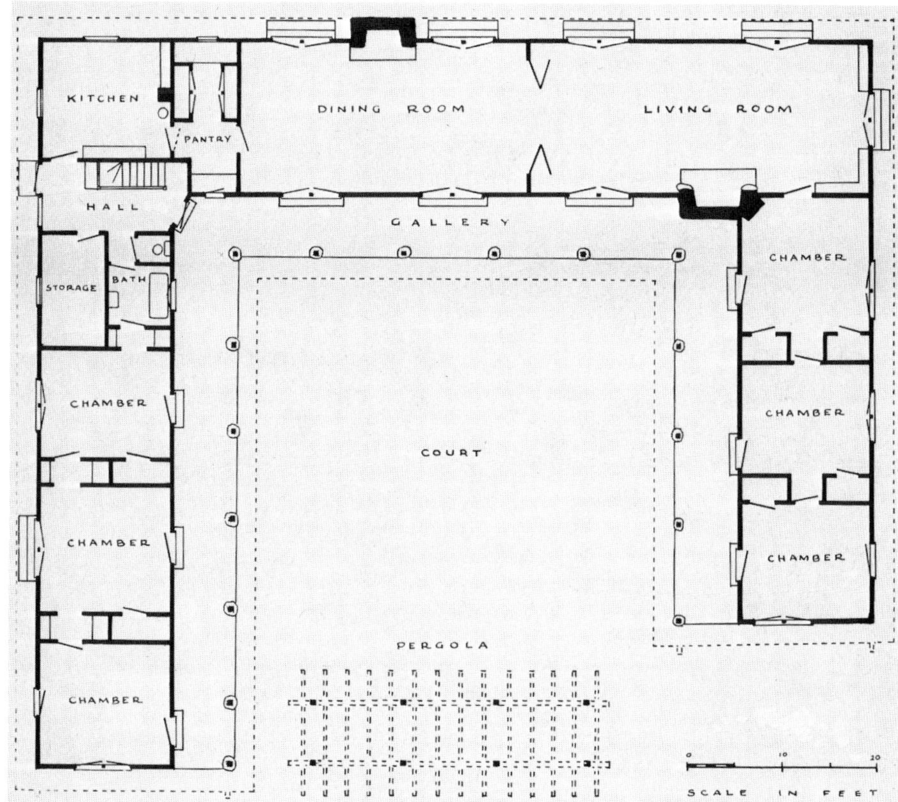

Figure 14. Plan of the Arturo Bandini Bungalow. (Drawing by the author.)

the fairs.[38] The one at Chicago was styled after Yorimichi's mid eleventh century villa at Uji, the Hōō-dō, later used as a temple; it is considered by the Japanese to be their first building in mature native style.[39] The Chicago version was brought in pieces from Nippon and assembled on the fair-grounds by Japanese workmen. At San Francisco the exhibit took the form of a Japanese hill-and-water garden, its architectural features including a two-story gateway and two-story house, a theater, tea house and another small pavilion, and an arched bridge and several stone lanterns. The brothers also collected photographs of Japanese buildings, many of which are preserved in the Carmel studio of the late Charles Sumner Greene. Unmistakably Japanese was the practice of resting the bases of posts upon rounded stones half sunk into the ground which function as supports in the Bandini bungalow gallery.

Japanese influence became most strongly pronounced in Greene and Greene's work beginning in 1906. Two outstanding residences begun that year were the Tichenor House of brick and wood at Long Beach (Ocean Boulevard and First Place), facing the sea, discussed and illustrated in Embury's *One Hundred Country Houses,* published three years later, and the shingled Theodore Irwin House in Pasadena, constructed on a corner lot separated from the Charles Sumner Greene property by the old covered reservoir, overlooking the beautiful Arroyo Valley, site of the later Rose Bowl.[40] The Irwin House was situated near the south line of the more or less trapezoidal lot, with only enough space for a walk between the building and the rustic lattice fence. Coming up the front walk from North Grand Avenue, one went around the huge eucalyptus tree and the arbored porch to a flight of steps ascending to the terrace and confronting a modest door to the stairhall; or else one mounted the long bank of steps arranged like a seat along the front walk and crossed the lawn to the living-room terrace, entering the far side of the reception room (figs. 15 and 16). The submergence of the entrances was not the most conspicuous Japanese feature in this irregular

Figure 15. Theodore Irwin House, Pasadena, Calif., designed by Greene and Greene. (Drawing by the author.)

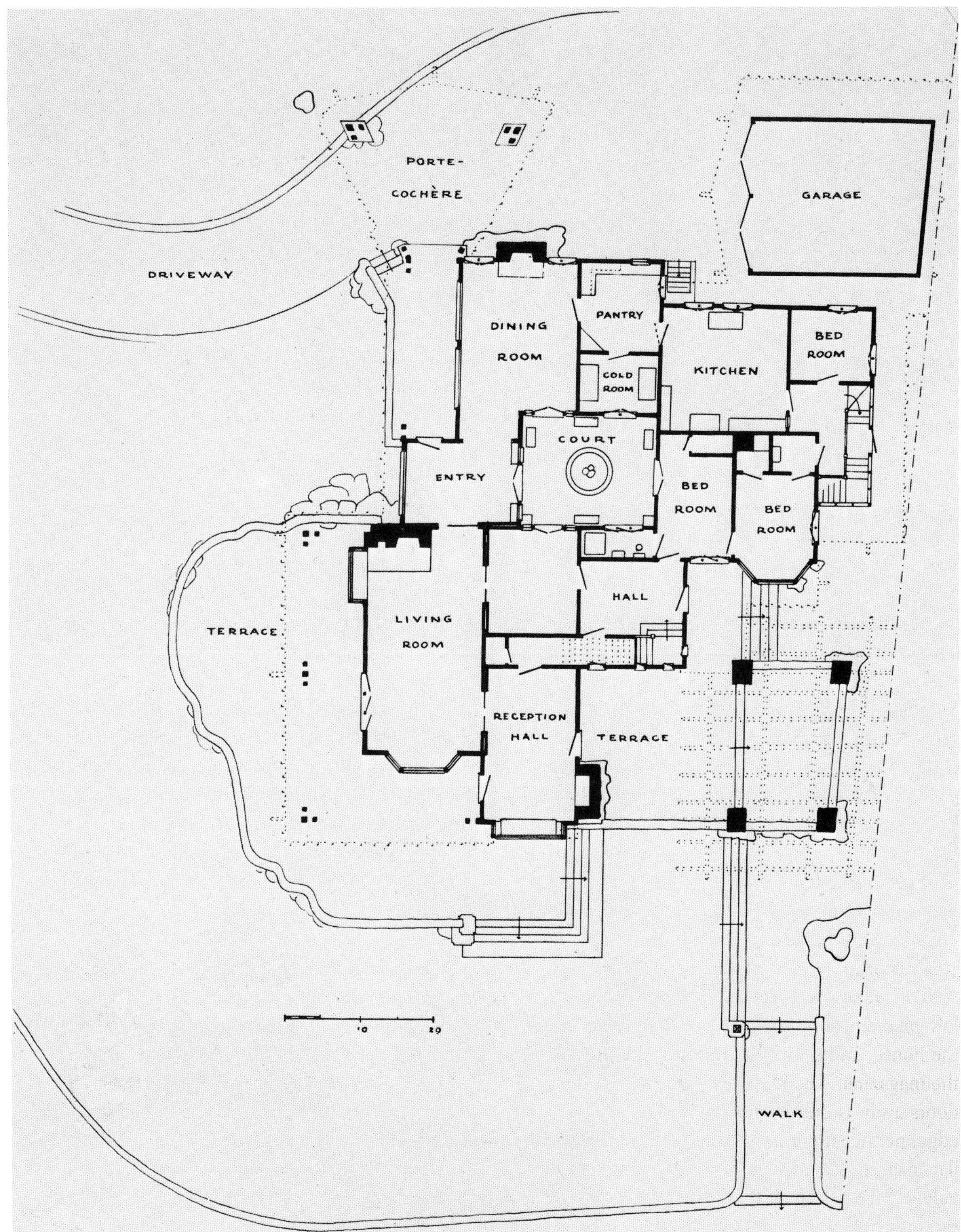

Figure 16. Restored plan of the Theodore Irwin House. (Drawing by the author.)

composition of so much open timberwork and deep eaves. The chimneys were somewhat pagoda-like, there being no authentic prototype for smoke conduits in Japan other than open gables in primitive farmhouses, hardly applicable here. Contemporary magazine articles listed the Irwin house prominently when speaking of "The Trail of Japanese Influence in our Modern American Architecture," or else outright called it a "Bungalow in Japanese Style" and "Japanesque Bungalow."[41] The numerous and relatively small rooms enclosed a paved court with pool and fountain in the center; a gallery, shaded by a trellis overhead, extended around three sides of the expanded upper level. The billiard room on the second floor, across one end of the court, was glazed on two sides and on part of a third, and opened onto a small roofed gallery adjoining the fan-shaped *porte cochere.* The chamber next to it had a tall ceiling lighted by a clerestory above the gallery roof. The curved-walled living room terrace spotted with bay trees recalls the treatment of the bungalow on the Lincoln estate by Schweinfurth (fig. 4). The living room was enlarged at a later date, and entrance steps were placed at the front of the projecting porch, the wall between the piers being removed for this alteration.

The Greene brothers and some of their prospective clients were pleased with the way the Irwin house turned out, and new commissions were given for other residences to be built along similar lines. Two were erected in the neighborhood during the next couple of years, these being numbers Two and Four Westmoreland Place. A photograph of the street front of number Two was reproduced in the April 1909 issue of *Western Architect.*[42] The broad, low-pitched roof provided a third story over part of the house, and yet it was inscribed a bungalow in the magazine. The David B. Gamble House, two doors away, is only slightly larger; but, to my knowledge, neither it nor any of the other houses of similar magnitude and style has been termed a bungalow.[43] The plans of these later buildings were more flexible and open than that of the Irwin House.

The finest Greene and Greene bungalow of the next few years is the Charles Pratt House (1909) on Foothill Road at Ojai, a low, crescent-shaped timber construction, of which only a part is two-storied.[44] The interplay of angles and casually placed planes show the ingenuity of the architects (fig. 17). They have achieved here a synthesis of house and landscaping perhaps unequaled elsewhere in America. The central room is a living hall, entered from a terrace of free form, several curved steps above the motor court.[45]

A variation of the Greene and Greene house, with Swiss rather than Japanese detailing, was otherwise undifferentiated in construction and effect. The Swiss style was utilized extensively by several other California architects, one of the most creative being Arthur R. Kelly, architect of the C. L. Frost Ranch House and the John T. Allen House, both dating from around 1910.[46] These two bungalows at Hollywood were built upon hill sites, the former having a wing turned at an irregular angle to coincide with the terrain, and the latter having the second floor uphill from the first. The rock used in terrace walls was excavated from the site. The Swiss style has been interpreted rather loosely, which places these examples in an entirely different category from that of the Burlingame Chalet of earlier date (fig. 3). The difference of interpretation is that between nineteenth- and twentieth-century attitudes. The affinity to the Japanese in the Kelly houses indicates the internationality of timber building in mountainous regions all over the world—in the Alps, Himalayas, and islands of Japan.

A second variation is represented by a bungalow on South Grand Avenue in Pasadena, locally attributed sometimes to Greene and Greene and at other times to Frank Lloyd Wright. The small house is unusual and attractive, consisting of a cubic form bound by exposed square timbers and capped by a projecting flat roof, and one little wonders that it has been ascribed to the well-known architects mentioned; but it was the work of a lesser builder, John C. Austin (fig. 18). A picture of the

Figure 17. Charles Pratt House, near Ojai, Calif., designed by Greene and Greene. (Photograph by Wayne Andrews.)

Figure 18. Bungalow, Pasadena, Calif., designed by John C. Austin. (From Western Architect *13, no. 6 [June 1909].)*

bungalow in *House and Garden* identifies the style of the house as Japanese.[47] It was more evidently inspired by the reconstruction of an ancient house at Lycia, Asia Minor, illustrated in *American Architect and Building News* a short while before the Pasadena house was built (fig. 19).

Other southern California architects working in a similar vein include Albert R. Walker and John Terrell Vawter, Sylvanus Marston (designer of St. Francis Court, Pasadena), Myron Hunt and Elmer Grey, George A. Clark and L. du P. Miller, J. F. Kavanaugh, and Arthur S. Heineman.[48] Amateur builders bitten by the craftsman bug produced a few notable bungalows, such as that of Frank Underhill near Santa Barbara, and the A. J. Eddy House at Pasadena.[49]

Figure 19. Restoration drawing of a Lycian house, Asia Minor. (From Charles de Kay, "Primitive Homes," American Architect and Building News *94, no. 1710 [September 30, 1908]: 106.)*

BUNGALOWS DIRECT FROM BUNGALOW LAND

Perfect Gems of Home Comfort and Attractiveness

My designs have been selected from the very best types of bungalows in Southern California, which have become so popular throughout America. They are *practical in any part of the country.* Special specifications are prepared by an expert familiar with all the details of eastern and northern localities.

Now is the time to build, as lumber and labor are 50 per cent cheaper than it was six months ago.

If You are Interested in Home Building—

Design No. 18 Built of Stained Rustic Siding and Shingles Cost $2,200

Take Advantage of My Special Offer

I will send my book containing exterior and interior views of typical one and a half and two-story California residences—also 24 California Bungalows—prepaid in one package for one dollar—post office or express money order. These houses range in price from $1,500 to $10,000, and are the very best examples of Southern California Architecture.

To all who order plans this dollar will be rebated.

My experience of over ten years in the East enables me to prepare specifications and make structural details suitable for building these houses in cold as well as in warm climates.

My terms, for making plans, etc., are stamped on the back of each photograph.

These designs are entirely different from anything that has been published along these lines.

F. G. BROWN, Architect

624-5 Security Bldg. LOS ANGELES, CAL.

Figure 20. Advertisement for bungalow designs. (From House Beautiful *23, no. 6 [May 1908]: 50.)*

Figure 21. Ralph N. Maxson Bungalow, Lexington, Ky. (Photograph by Jessie L. Maxson, ca. 1910.)

An overwhelming flood of literature on the bungalow was issued shortly after the turn of the century. Much of it was in the form of booklet catalogs of plans offered inexpensively as an agent for ordering sets of working drawings, which sold for five dollars upward. Many originated in California, especially in the Los Angeles vicinity. These were advertised in home and building magazines, and to them may be accounted the dissemination of the California bungalow throughout the country. As an example, a young professor at the University of Kentucky and his wife, Dr. and Mrs. Ralph N. Maxson, were attracted by the illustration publicizing a portfolio of two dozen bungalow schemes conceived by F. G. Brown of Los Angeles, advertised in the May 1908 issue of *House Beautiful* (fig. 20).[50] The portfolio sold for a dollar, which could be deducted later from the purchase price of plans. The Maxsons liked best the bungalow illustrated, design 18 in the portfolio, and proceeded to build this $2,200 house in Transylvania Park, Lexington, near the university (fig. 21).[51] The plan was reversed so that the porch would extend around the right instead of the left flank, and the living room, originally intended to span the whole front of the house (about thirty-three feet in length) was divided by a partition with sliding doors, making a small office at the fireplace end of the room, where the professor could interview students in temporary privacy. A dining room, connected to the pantry with kitchen and porch beyond, a stairhall in the center, and two chambers and bath also were on the first floor. Bedrooms were finished upstairs at a later date. This small house was unique in the community, where colonial bungalows were more fashionable. Its curving gables gave it some Japanese flavor. The side extension of the porch was subsequently removed to make way for a driveway. The architect stated that ten years' experience in the East enabled him "to prepare specifications and make structural details suitable for building these houses in cold as well as in warm climates," an important consideration in Kentucky, which gets more snow than New York City.

That the bungalow properly belonged to California was indicated in the F. G. Brown advertisement captioning the design as being "Direct from Bungalow Land." A Grand Rapids concern, following the trend, entitled its publication *California Bungalows: The Book of the Real Bungalow.*[52] Another, in Minneapolis, issuing *The Plan Shop Bungalow Book,* declared that the "designer is a Californian and knows the bungalow by heart."[53] The following year the "Californian" moved on to Boston.[54]

A periodical devoted to the small house, and called *Bungalow Magazine,* came out monthly from March 1909 through March 1918, at first in Los Angeles and later (beginning 1914) in Seattle. The price rose from a dime to a quarter per copy at the time of editorial change.[55] All bungalow styles were given space. A plan similar to the flat-roofed bungalow in Pasadena was discussed in the February 1910 issue and, as in *House and Garden,* identified as Japanese.[56] One of the most appealing examples presented during the nine years of publication was in the April 1910 edition (fig. 22). It was designed for a narrow lot at a street intersection, with the L-shaped house itself placed near the front inner corner, having a pergola flanking the side street and extending to the garage, a gate several bays below leading into the gardened area, where the planting centered on a circular motif including a pool with a lantern in the middle, adjoining an open summer house against the neighboring lot, which was masked by a thick screen of foliage. Here is an ideal integration of house and garden in a restricted area. The lines of the house recall somewhat those of Mr. Tudor's mid nineteenth-century cottage at Nahant (fig. 5), making the bungalow seem to belong more to the eastern side of the continent than to the West. The house, called a "Wilson bungalow," after the editor, contains five rooms, the living room in the projecting wing terminated by the chimney, a porch in front and dining room behind under the broad block, with two bedrooms connected by a passageway opening into a bath, a kitchen and back porch, and so forth, forming a suite along the far side.[57] The dining terrace in the angle between living and dining rooms is an exquisite bit of design.

Magazines having little to do with architecture as such often encouraged bungalow living. The Curtis Publishing Company presented two of Frank Lloyd Wright's domestic creations in the *Ladies' Home Journal* for February and June 1901. The first, the larger of the two, was a typical specimen of Wright's "prairie house" style, with low hipped roofs over a cruciform of unequal arm lengths. The later house had roofs extending into "Japanese" gables, that is, wide eaves pushed forward at the apex. The same motif was used on the Warren Hickox and neighboring B. Harley Bradley houses in Kankakee, Illinois, conceived at the same time as the Curtis Publishing Company projects (1900). The Hickox House, the smaller of the Kankakee pair, with its exposed light timbered walls, plastered between, thin raking roof planes, and predominance of horizontal lines, displays some indebtedness to the Japanese, though it remains an original composition (fig. 23). The reception hall and service rooms are on the left side of the house, with living room beyond the chimney, a demi-octagonal music room in front and dining room of the same shape to the rear, with broad openings making the three units into a single large interior.[58] The Bradley House, next door, is a more complex mass, with a covered gallery leading to the kennels-stable-garage behind the house. The Kankakee River, which flows to the side and back of the Bradley House, provides at once a frame for the property and view from the houses.

Frank Lloyd Wright, a protégé of and successor to Louis Sullivan as leader of the Chicago School, made an inestimable contribution to the bungalow vogue. Other outstanding examples are the W. A. Glasner House (1905) in Glencoe, Illinois, with its attached octagons, one of which was to have been used as a "tea room" across a *passerelle* (not built

Figure 22. Perspective sketch of a five-room bungalow. (From Bungalow Magazine *2, no. 2 [April 1910]: 46.)*

Figure 23. Warren Hickox House, Kankakee, Ill., designed by Frank Lloyd Wright. (From "Work of Frank Lloyd Wright and Its Influence," Architectural Record *18, no. 1 [July 1905]: 60.)*

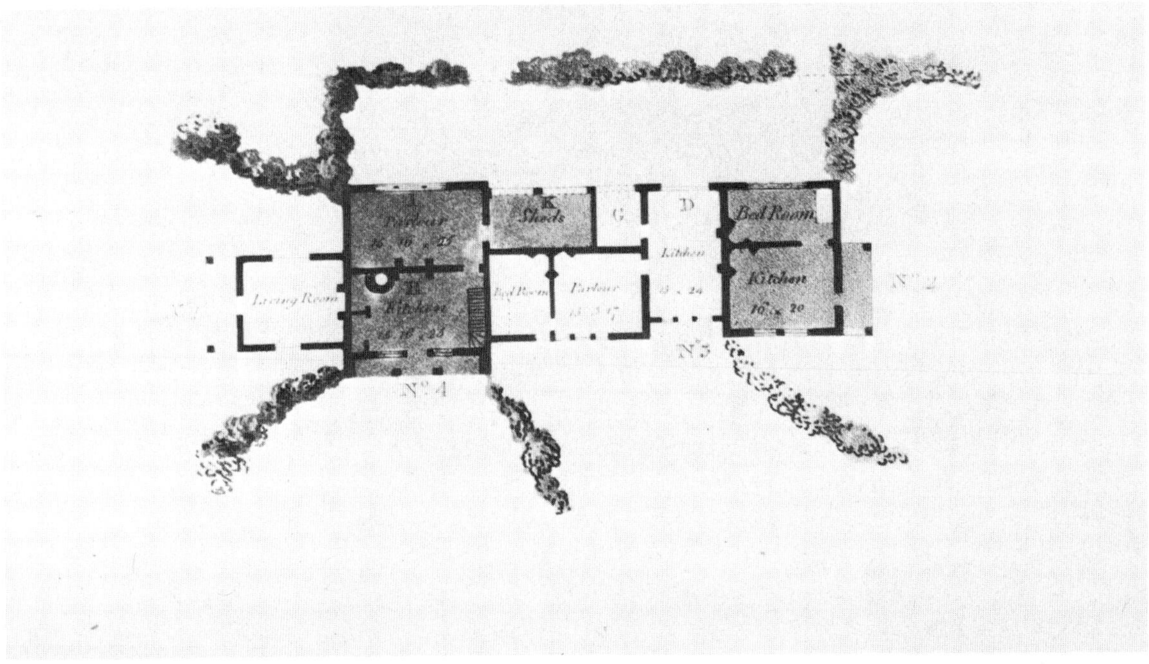

Figure 24. Rural house made up of "Four Cottages." (From Joseph Gandy, The Rural Architect *[London: J. Harding, 1805]: plate 23.)*

because of lot size restrictions), and the Isabel Roberts House (1908) at River Forest, with high-ceilinged living room at the center of an "aero-plane" plan.[59]

The clean-cut shapes and broad hipped roofs of Wright's bungalows known as prairie houses suggest influence from the work of an enigmatic British architect of the early nineteenth century, Joseph Michael Gandy, who, although he attempted to practice independently after 1800, made his best earnings producing renderings in the office of John Soane. Gandy published two books in 1805, *Designs for Cottages* and *The Rural Architect,* in which were illustrated schemes for country houses, or rather dependencies, built close to the ground, with horizontal banks of windows and other elements in common with Wright's constructions of a hundred years later (fig. 24). Gandy undoubtedly was influenced in the simple species of building he devised by plebeian Mediterranean housing of a type that survived with little change from Etruscan times, which he had examined in Italy during his sojourn there when a young man. Gandy's interest in the Orient may indicate a possible derivation from the East Indian bungalow: Oriental subjects appeared among compositions exhibited by him at the Royal Academy, and the divinity he professed to worship was "the Sacred Aum" of Hindustan.[60]

One of the freshest innovations produced by Chicago School architects is the "Bungalow on the Point" or "Seashore Bungalow"—so labeled on the original plans—built by William Gray Purcell and George Grant Elmslie on the Crane estate at Woods Hole, Massachusetts, in 1911 (fig. 25).[61] The structure incorporates the central chimney and shingled walls of the traditional Cape Cod dwelling, but in other respects departs from the local precedent. The horizontal fenestration of the curved end of the living room overlooking the sea that surrounds Juniper Point on three sides may be compared with the corresponding feature on the Schweinfurth Bungalow of 1895 (fig. 4). A long, rectangular mass forming a background to the lower

Figure 25. Seashore Bungalow, Crane Estate, Woods Hole, Mass., designed by W. G. Purcell and G. G. Elmslie. (Photograph by the author.)

semicircular projection has the upper story cantilevered out at the ends and very long roof overhang, achieving a buoyant and flightlike quality. The total plan is cruciform, or "aeroplane." This plan well may have been suggested to the Chicago School by the Hōō-den, or Phoenix Villa, the Japanese pavilion in the form of a bird at the World's Columbian Exposition of 1893, spoken of earlier.[62] William Gray Purcell called the Bungalow on the Point "the first building East of New York—and with a few exceptions the first building East of Chicago to be designed in indigenous, organic American form."[63]

The bungalow considered closest to an indigenous type of American construction was the rustic one, having walls made of logs laid horizontally. First introduced into this country by the Swedes settling along the Delaware River during the middle of the seventeenth century, the log house was used

Figure 26. Charles Basham Bungalow, White Bluffs, Tenn., designed by D. V. Stroop. (From Western Architect *10, no. 10 [October 1907].)*

by German, Irish, and finally by the English as a convenient, practical, and comfortable means of frontier housing. By the end of the nineteenth century the log cabin was looked upon, erroneously, as the earliest colonial habitation, and as such was given a niche in the bungalow movement, especially in mountainous settings.[64] D. V. Stroop built a number of log bungalows for clients in the vicinity of White Bluffs, Tennessee. The Charles Basham House was one of these intended only for summer use. Walls were of spruce logs, retaining the bark outside, and hand-scraped inside; some of the rooms were surfaced with plaster. The doors and roof shingles were of cedar (fig. 26). The square plan included a porch across the entire front and a recessed porch at the back flanked by a pantry and bath.[65] A long transverse dining and living hall (18′ × 28′) occupied the center of the building, with kitchen and three bedrooms surrounding it, and a large dormitory above lighted by dormers at front and back. This log bungalow differs from early log cabins in having a high basement, a more complex arrangement, and a hipped roof with curved, upturned eaves. The last, at least, is a characteristic of Far Eastern architecture, the Basham bungalow bearing a resemblance to the 1200-year-old log Shōsōin, famed art treasure house of the Tōdai-ji (temple) at Nara, Japan.[66]

Examples of the American bungalow that have been discussed above have hardly exceeded the first thirty-year period of the bungalow regime, or about half of its vital life's span. The bungalow had reached its zenith as an artistic form before the First World War and did not improve afterward. The boom following the war tended, if anything, to lower building standards, reducing the bungalow from an unassuming creative expression to an insignificant and cheap means of housing. During its heyday the bungalow completely captivated and held the public's attention. Not everybody, of course, was in sympathy with the bungalow idea. Some writers were amused by or even hostile to it. An article entitled "The Rampant Craze for the Bungle-oh," in *Country Life in America,* poked fun at the fashionable contemporary home.[67] Another writer registered a reflective mood in versification, calling his opus the "Bungal-Ode." One of his stanzas runs:

For I oft get bungalonely
  In the mingled human drove,
And I long for bungaloafing
  In some bungalotus grove,
In a cooling bung' location
  Where no troubling trails intrude,
'Neath some bungalowly rooftree
  In east bungalongitude.[68]

Interest in Southeast Asia was a sustaining factor throughout the bungalow era. Sometimes it overstepped its bounds and entered the realm of false attribution, as in the case of "An East Indian Bungalow" built on Buckingham Way near Prospect Park in Brooklyn, New York. The architect's perspective rendering for the bungalow was reproduced, prior to its construction, in the *Brooklyn Daily Eagle* in 1902, and the accompanying article characterized the house as one of the most original ever conceived in America, being "in the form of an East India bungalow as closely as the climatic conditions will allow"—a familiar label. The architect's drawing, one notes, despite descriptive claims to the contrary, is entirely Japanese in style (fig. 27). The house was designed by John J. Petit and James C. Green for Dean Alvord, a New York investor, who anticipated that the bungalow would "prove to be a good seller." As built, the Alvord House contained more usable space than was indicated by the published sketch; the roof between floor levels was exchanged for an encircling balcony, and the main gables were pushed out flush with the end walls of the house, while the fenestration in the gables was supplemented by dormers on either side of the sloping roof (fig. 28). To assure authenticity of finish in Japanese style, the work was entrusted to three Japanese artisans, Saburo Arai (contractor), Shunsi Ishikawa (decorator), and Chogoro Sugai (gardener).[69] A Japanese gateway and several lanterns embellished the garden on the south side of the house. The residence recently was redecorated and furnished largely with Grand Rapids Chinese-style pieces. Its originally rich exterior colors are now obliterated by a battleship gray.

Figure 28. Dean Alvord House, Brooklyn, N.Y., designed by John J. Petit and James C. Green following the design of Figure 27. (Photograph by the author.)

The term *bungalow* stood for the best and worst—and much that was in between—in American private housing during the last two decades of the nineteenth and first quarter or so of the twentieth centuries. Its examples range from the most imitative, confused, and sentimental, to the freshest, clearest, and most rational of designs. That the bungalow was a low, small house lay in the claims for it more than in application to buildings, as we have seen. Though it grew out of the American cottage tradition, the bungalow vogue made new and definite contributions to the evolution of home planning in the direction of informality and unpretentiousness, use of common, natural materials, integration of house and landscape setting, simplification of design that became closely allied to practical requirements, and concentration on livability. The bungalow movement differed from earlier revivals in the indefiniteness of its source of inspiration, which allowed the architect's imagination free play, thereby sanctioning originality in a roundabout way. The American house during the bungalow period became lighter in construction, more flexible and open of plan, and less fussy in its furnishings. These were all good qualities when held under control, and resulted in sloppiness when they got out of hand. A large percentage of contemporary

*Figure 27. Architect's rendering of an "East Indian bungalow," Brooklyn, N.Y. (*Brooklyn Daily Eagle, *June 7, 1902, p. 11.)*

Americans were brought up and still dwell in bungalows, and many others have built virtual bungalows recently, though they are called by other names. The bungalow, therefore, still is a factor in American life, through its role in American housing; and it may be said to form, together with the skyscraper, one of the characteristic building types of democratic America.

Notes

This article was originally published in the *Art Bulletin* (September 1958).

1. James H. Murray, ed., *A New English Dictionary on Historical Principles* (Oxford: Clarendon Press, 1888), 1: 1178; J. A. T., "A Bungalow Modified on a Swiss Chalet," *House Beautiful* 36, no. 8 (July 1914): 55.
2. Mary Martha Sherwood, *The Lady of the Manor* (Bridgeport: M. Sherman, 1818), 5:50. The first English edition, in seven volumes, was issued at Wellington between 1825 and 1829.
3. "Bungalows," *American Architect and Building News* 94, no. 1704 (August 19, 1908): 63.
4. "How to Build a Bungalow," *Craftsman* 5, no. 3 (December 1904): 253; Seymour E. Locke, "Bungalows, What They Really Are," *House and Garden* 12, no. 2 (August 1907): 45.
5. J. Lockwood Kipling, "The Origin of the Bungalow," *Country Life in America* 19, no. 8 (February 1911): 309.
6. "Bungalow at Monument Beach, Mass., by Mr. W. G. Preston, Architect, Boston," *American Architect and Building News* 7, no. 222 (March 27, 1880): 130.
7. Vincent J. Scully, Jr., "Romantic Rationalism and the Expression of Structure in Wood: Downing, Wheeler, Gardner, and the 'Stick Style,' 1840–1876," *Art Bulletin* 35, no. 2 (June 1953): 141.
8. Information courtesy of J. A. Schweinfurth II, interviewed September 2, 1954.
9. J. M. A. Dorrach attributes the low cost of the bungalow to its single story, which (1) eliminates construction expense of a stairway, (2) makes external decoration unnecessary, the low form being pleasing in itself, (3) cuts down on vertical plumbing extensions, (4) requires little hall space, (5) keeps framing at a minimum, (6) avoids heat waste up the stairwell, and (7) calls for plain interior trim. ("Why Not a Bungalow?" *Country Life in America* 10, no. 6 [October 1906]: 637–40).
10. "What is a Bungalow?" *Arts and Decoration* 1, no. 12 (October 1911): 487.
11. "How to Build a Bungalow," p. 253.
12. The house now serves as headquarters for the Thomson (Country) Club.
13. Andrew Jackson Downing, *Rural Essays* (New York: Leavitt and Allen, 1857), p. 188.
14. The Spanish, it will be remembered, held dominion over the western territory from 1762 until a short while before its acquisition by the United States government in the Louisiana Purchase Act of 1803.
15. See Buford L. Pickens, "Regional Aspects of Early Louisiana Architecture," *Journal of the Society of Architectural Historians* 7, nos. 1–2 (January–June 1948): 33–36; Charles E. Peterson, "French Landmarks along the Mississippi," *Antiques* 53, no. 4 (April 1948): 286–88.
16. Revived colonial became popular as a result of McKim, Mead, and White's "Colonial Tour" of 1877, and the buildings they—and others—designed in this idiom. Periodicals and books also did their share to further the trend toward the eighteenth-century style.
17. Illustrated in Hubert Howe Bancroft, *The Book of the Fair* (Chicago and San Francisco: Bancroft, 1893), 2:799.
18. "The damage wrought by the World's Fair will last for half a century from its date, if not longer" (quoted in Hugh Morrison, *Louis Sullivan* [New York: W. W. Norton, 1935], p. 184).
19. Publications have created some confusion over the authorship and identification of the buildings on the Sullivan and adjoining estates, the designs of which were evidently produced in the office of Adler and Sullivan. For instance, Henry-Russell Hitchcock attributes them to Frank Lloyd Wright (1890), while Wright was an apprentice in the Chicago office, and he notes that his accompanying illustration of the Sullivan bungalow is a photograph of a structure that does not correspond with early plans of it (see *In the Nature of Materials* [New York: Duell, Sloan and Pearce, 1942], p. 11, fig. 4). We await the appearance of a definitive study for the untangling of the Ocean Springs group. Meanwhile, the reader is referred to an article by Lyndon P. Smith, "The Home of an Artist-Architect," *Architectural Record* 17, no. 6 (June 1905): 471–90, which presents plans and views of the Sullivan estate, the much-shaded residence proper looking about the same as in the accompanying contemporary photograph, except for the removal of a couple of shed dormers from the front slope of the roof.

20. The W. C. Egan Bungalow is typical. See W. C. Egan, "Mistakes I Have Made," *Country Life in America* 2, no. 3 (July 1902): lxv; W. C. Egan, "Why and How I Made My Country Home," *Country Life in America* 3, no. 5 (March 1903): 211.
21. Also in the June 1907 issue of *House Beautiful* is a view of this house from the southeast, showing it to have had a low-pitched hipped roof, and minor variations with the plan, in the number and arrangement of gallery supports and fenestration.
22. Eva Scott Fényes and Isabel López de Fáges, *Thirty-Two Adobe Houses of Old California* (Los Angeles: Southwest Museum, 1950), p. 26; Donald R. Hannaford and Revel Edwards, *Spanish Colonial or Adobe Architecture of California, 1800–1850* (New York: Architectural Book Publishing, 1931), pp. 82–83.
23. Pictured among "Our Illustrations," *Inland Architect* 32, no. 6 (January 1899), are: "Winter House of D. R. Cameron" and "Residence of D. M. Smyth."
24. A series of articles on the western missions was published in the *Craftsman* in 1904 and in the *Inland Architect* in 1906. See George Wharton James's eight-part series entitled "The Spanish Missions of the Southwest" in the *Craftsman:* "The Franciscan Mission Buildings of California," 5, no. 4 (January 1904): 320–35; "The Influence of the 'Mission Style' upon the Civic and Domestic Architecture of Modern California," 5, no. 5 (February 1904): 458–69; "The Indians of the Franciscan Missions," 5, no. 6 (March 1904): 599–617; "The Founding of the Spanish Missions in California," 6, no. 1 (April 1904): 38–48; "The California Missions," 6, no. 2 (May 1904): 198–211; "The Franciscan Missions of the Southwest: Their Interior Decorations," 6, no. 4 (July 1904): 329–42; "The Franciscan Missions of the Southwest: Some Architectural Details," 6, no. 5 (August 1904): 446–64; "The Furniture and Other Woodwork," 6, no. 6 (September 1904): 541–55. See William Le Baron Jenney's articles in the *Inland Architect:* "The Old California Missions and Their Influence on Modern Design," 47, nos. 1–3 (February-April 1906): 70, 23, 35; "A Remarkable Dwelling," 47, no. 4 (May 1906): 57–60; "The Old California Missions, etc." 47, no. 5 (June 1906): 71–72; "Parks and Gardens of Southern California," 47, no. 6 (July 1906): 85. For typical details of "mission" furniture, see "Decorating and Furnishing the Country Home," *Architectural Record* 23, no. 6 (June 1908): 456.
25. The plan of this house consists of a central living room, with four bedrooms and bath off a corridor to the right and rear, a dining room, kitchen and pantry to the left and rear of the court in the narrow space between the two wings, and a den and porch in front extending into a *porte cochere* off the dining room (Charles Alma Byers, "A Ranch Bungalow Embodying Many Modern Ideas," *Craftsman* 22, no. 2 [May 1912]: 210).
26. George A. Clark, "Bungalow Architecture from a Layman's Viewpoint," *House Beautiful* 24, no. 5 (October 1908): 103.
27. "The Theory of Grosvenor Attebury . . . That Originality in Architecture Springs Only from the Direct Meeting of Material Conditions," *Craftsman* 16, no. 3 (June 1909): 300.
28. Peter B. Wight, "California Bungalows," *Western Architect* 27, no. 10 (October 1918): 97.
29. Waldon Fawcett, "Bungalows in Southern California," *Architects' and Builders' Magazine* 38 (July 1906): 419.
30. The East Indian bungalow often had a false ceiling of calcimined calico (Kipling, "The Origin of the Bungalow," p. 308).
31. M. H. Lazear, "The Evolution of the Bungalow," *House Beautiful* 36, no. 1 (June 1914): 2.
32. Mrs. B. W. McKenzie, "A Home in the Desert," *Country Life in America* 20, no. 3 (June 1, 1911): 76.
33. The Palm Springs bungalow, with its hipped roof, closely resembles another building, the "bungalow at Cawnpore," shown in Kipling's "The Origin of the Bungalow" (p. 309).
34. Lazear, "The Evolution of the Bungalow," pp. 2–3.
35. Jean Murray Bangs, "Greene and Greene," *Architectural Forum* 89, no. 4 (October 1948): 82; Clay Lancaster, "My Interviews with Greene and Greene," *Journal of the American Institute of Architects* 28, no. 3 (July 1957): 202–6.
36. The author is very much indebted to Mr. Donald L. Pray of Grossmont, California, for having located the Bandini House for him (1149 San Pasqual Street, Pasadena) and for supplying him with certain architectural details supplementing his material gathered earlier on the West Coast, making possible the completion of this restoration drawing.
37. Locke, "Bungalows, What They Really Are," p. 50.
38. Information related during an interview with the late Henry Mather Greene, April 1, 1954.
39. Clay Lancaster, "Japanese Buildings in the United States before 1900: Their Influence upon American Domestic Architecture," *Art Bulletin* 35, no. 3 (September 1953): 220–21, figs. 8, 9, 11.
40. Aymar Embury II, *One Hundred Country Houses: Modern American Examples* (New York: Century, 1909), pp. 215–21.

41. Henrietta P. Keith, "The Trail of Japanese Influence in Our Modern Domestic Architecture," *Craftsman* 12, no. 4 (July 1907): 449–50; "Bungalows," *House Beautiful* 29, no. 2 (January 1911): 49.
42. Reproduced as figure 20 in Lancaster, "Japanese Buildings," facing p. 224.
43. Such as the R. R. Blacker House, 1177 Hillcrest Avenue, Pasadena, and the William R. Thorsen House, 2307 Piedmont Avenue, Berkeley.
44. A rear perspective of the Pratt house appears in Lazear, "The Evolution of the Bungalow," p. 5.
45. Like the Gamble House, the Pratt House still contains much furniture designed and built by the Greene brothers.
46. Henry H. Saylor, *Bungalows: Their Design, Construction and Furnishing* (Philadelphia: John C. Winston, 1911), pp. 58–59, 82–83.
47. Charles de Kay, "Primitive Homes," *American Architect and Building News,* 94, no. 1710 (September 30, 1908): 106.
48. Lancaster, "Japanese Buildings," p. 224; Saylor, *Bungalows,* pp. 20–25, 57, 77, 114–15, 130, 142, 145, 151; "In the California Mountains: The House of Mrs. E. M. Neustadt of Altadena, Calif.," *House Beautiful* 38, no. 1 (June 1915): 27–29; Henry Higgins, "Homes of Well-Known Architects: The Home of Mr. Myron Hunt of Pasadena, California," *House Beautiful* 39, no. 4 (March 1916): 101–3, and "Homes of Well-Known Architects: The Home of Mr. Elmer Grey, Pasadena, California," *House Beautiful* 39, no. 5 (April 1916): 137–39; "Portfolio of Current Architecture," *Architectural Record* 39, no. 3 (March 1916): 280–81; Charles Alma Byers, "Attractive California Homes," *House Beautiful* 28, no. 4 (September 1910): 106; Louis Du P. Miller, "The Bungalow Courts of California: Bowen's Court. Arthur S. Heineman, Architect," *House Beautiful* 40, no. 12 (November 1916): 338–39; *Western Architect* 20, no. 8 (August 1914): unpaged.
49. "The Bungalow at Its Best," *Architectural Record* 20, no. 4 (October 1906): 296–305; Arthur R. Kelly, "California Bungalows," *Country Life in America* 26, no. 1 (May 1914): 44, 82; Henry H. Saylor, "The Best Twelve Country Houses in America: La Chiquita, the Home of Francis T. Underhill," *Country Life in America* 29, no. 1 (November 1915): 27–30, also picture on the cover of the September 1914 issue of *Country Life in America* (26, no. 5); Jenney, "A Remarkable Dwelling," pp. 57–60.
50. *House Beautiful* 23, no. 6 (May 1908): 50.
51. Photograph courtesy of the late Jessie L. Maxson, who told the author about seeing the design in *House Beautiful.*
52. J. H. Daverman and Son, *California Bungalows: The Book of the Real Bungalow* (Grand Rapids, Mich.: J. H. Daverman and Son, 1908).
53. Advertised in *House Beautiful* 31, no. 6 (May 1912): xv.
54. *House Beautiful* 33, no. 2 (January 1913): iv.
55. The original publisher of *Bungalow Magazine* was Henry L. Wilson; later editor was D. E. Hooker.
56. *Bungalow Magazine* (February 1910): 340–41.
57. Plan illustrated in *Bungalow Magazine* 2, no. 2 (April 1910): 50.
58. Hitchcock, *In the Nature of Materials,* fig. 54.
59. Ibid., figs. 110–11, 154–56.
60. John Summerson, *Heavenly Mansions and Other Essays on Architecture* (New York: Cresset Press, 1948), pp. 131, 116.
61. In the possession of the present owner, Mr. Gerard Swope. Facsimiles of the plans have been published in William Gray Purcell, George Feick, and George Grant Elmslie, "The Statics and Dynamics of Architecture," *Western Architect* 19, no. 1 (January 1913): unpaged; Talbot F. Hamlin, "George Grant Elmslie and the Chicago Scene," *Pencil Points* 22, no. 9 (September 1941): 577.
62. Lancaster, "Japanese Buildings," pp. 220–22.
63. Letter from William Gray Purcell to Mrs. Dorothy Norman, June 24, 1949. For further reading on the Chicago group, see Hamlin, "George Grant Elmslie," pp. 575–86.
64. Harold Robert Shurtleff, *The Log Cabin Myth: A Study of the Early Dwellings of the English Colonists in North America,* ed. Samuel Eliot Morison (Cambridge: Harvard University Press, 1939).
65. William Phillips Comstock, *Bungalows, Camps and Mountain Houses* (New York: W. T. Comstock, 1908), p. 110 (plan).
66. Illustrated in Arthur Drexler, *The Architecture of Japan* (New York: Museum of Modern Art, 1955), pp. 84–85.
67. L. D. Thomson, "The Rampant Craze for the Bungle-oh," *Country Life in America* 22, no. 6 (July 15, 1912): 20–21. This article is illustrated with photographs of specimens showing exotic influences and a Frank Lloyd Wright banded house.
68. Burgess Johnson, from *Good Housekeeping,* in Saylor, *Bungalows,* p. 3.
69. "Japanese House and Garden at Prospect Park South, Brooklyn," *Country Life in America* 4, no. 3 (July 1903): 169.

Eighteenth-Century Field Patterns as Vernacular Art

STEWART G. MCHENRY

If we expand our investigation of vernacular architecture to include the building's site, we are sure to encounter the plowed fields, gardens, and pastures that surround houses or barns. Even though such open spaces are commonly left to geographers as part of their scholarly domain, there is much that the student of architecture can learn from fields. Since it was the harvest from the field that provided the capital required to build, modify, or transform a farmhouse, it follows that the fate of a house is critically linked to its fields. But beyond this practical economic connection there are other equally significant, but less apparent, ties. Because the traditional values of folk society flow consistently through all of its expressive forms, the cultural statement made by a house is likely to be echoed in the design of its fields as well. Just as there is a German or British style of house, there will also be ethnic patterns for using tilled soil.

In this article cultural geographer Stewart G. McHenry analyzes the various field patterns of the Vermont countryside. Combining the study of historical maps and aerial photographs with site inspection, he develops a typology of field forms that he correlates with the ethnic backgrounds of the various populations who settled Vermont. McHenry thus stresses that fields embody more than man's relationship with the environment; they reflect a particular cultural consciousness. Shared patterns of field design allowed people to identify with one another. McHenry implies that a sense of community was forged by a group's use of the same field shape in much the same manner that their use of the same house form would. The local idea of field, an abstract concept of land pattern, was then as important as the uses to which the soil might be put. It is because of this conceptual content, argues McHenry, that fields should be considered not only as artifacts but as works of art.

Eighteenth-century field patterns are a unique type of vernacular art, bearing many similarities to vernacular architecture or building practices: they have a particular shape or form and are composed of specific materials; they have texture and color as well as regular variations of texture and color; pattern and design are clearly apparent in the rural landscape. Furthermore, field patterns, like vernacular architecture, can be associated with different culture groups who settled in America. This article is about the field patterns associated with and created by different settlement groups who entered Vermont during the eighteenth century. It will describe the roles that culture and environment played in creating the patterns and demonstrate how these patterns can be interpreted as vernacular art forms created by different settlement groups in Vermont.

The three culture groups are French-Canadians, Dutch settlers from New York, and Yankee settlers from southern New England.[1] The last group is divided into three subcultures, settlers from Massachusetts, New Hampshire, and Connecticut. French-Canadians settled in two different areas of Vermont, one during the eighteenth and the other during the nineteenth century. Both areas were studied because they are significantly different.[2]

Although eighteenth-century town planning has been treated in various publications,[3] field patterns have generally been documented by consulting original lot survey records with little or no ground inspection of what actually happened once settlement commenced.[4] The subtle interplay between culture and environment that affected the regular lot survey or metes and bounds survey system is thus scarcely commented upon.[5] Here, three sources have been used to describe the character of eighteenth-century fields: historical documents, ground inspection, and aerial photos. Historical documents, including early drawings and survey maps, can be used without ground inspection only in the rare instances when it is relatively certain that the original field survey systems were implemented and are unaltered. Ground inspection is usually necessary, to be certain that what was planned was actually implemented. In addition, aerial photos of townships settled at the time show the patterns lying beneath present-day usages that are probably of eighteenth-century origin (figs. 2, 4, 6, 8). These photographs need to be compared with early historical documents (figs. 1, 3, 5, 7), though, for several reasons. Remnants of early cadastral surveys are sometimes

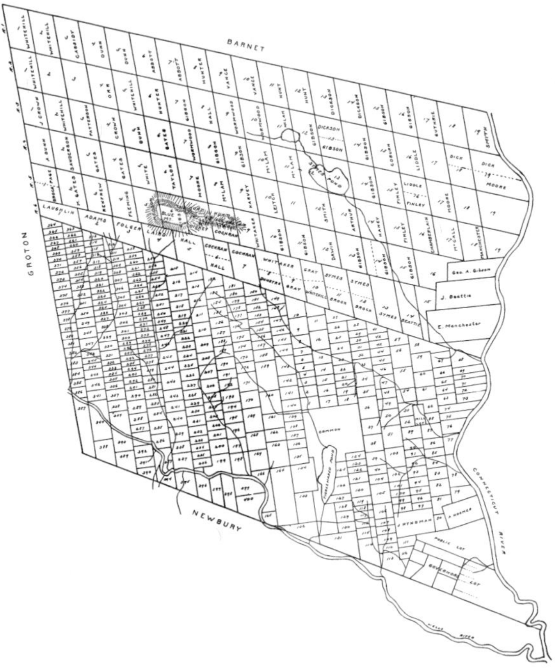

Figure 1. Town planning in Ryegate, Vt. (From Edward Miller and Frederick P. Wells, History of Ryegate, Vermont *[St. Johnsbury, Vt., 1913], p. 96.)*

Figure 2. Schema of relic field lines for the town of Ryegate, Vt., showing actual development. (From 1974 aerial photographs, State Highway Department, Montpelier, Vt.)

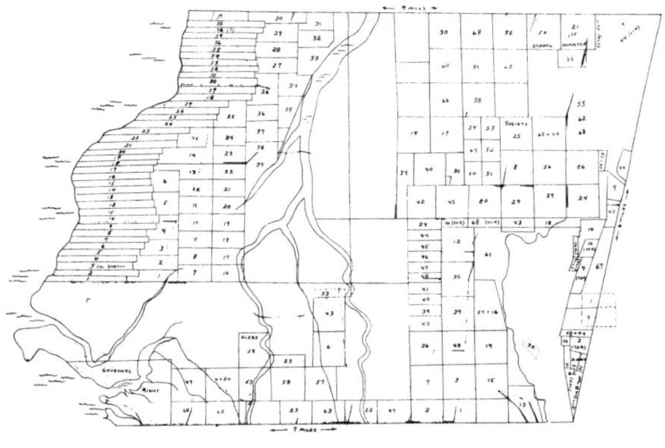

Figure 3. *Town planning in Addison, Vt. (From folder 1, State Highway Department, Montpelier, Vt.)*

Figure 4. Schema of relic field lines for the town of Addison, Vt., showing actual development. (From 1974 aerial photographs, Highway Department, Montpelier, Vt.)

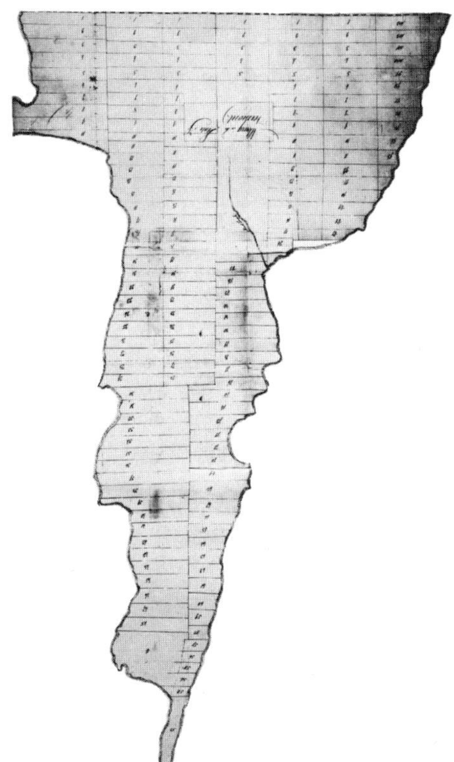

Figure 5. Town planning in Alburg, Vt. (From Surveyor General's Papers, *"Plans," p. 5, Henry Stevens Collection, State Papers, Montpelier, Vt.)*

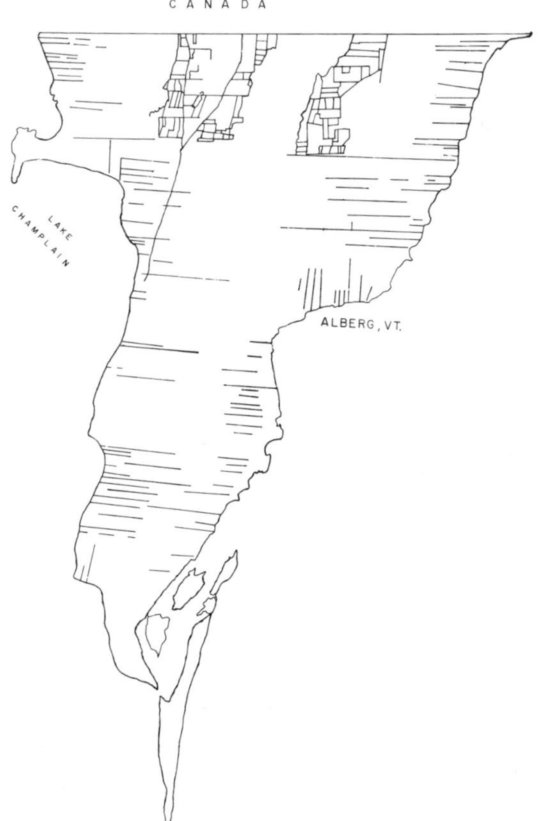

Figure 6. Schema of relic field lines for the town of Alburg, Vt., showing actual development. (From 1974 aerial photographs, State Highway Department, Montpelier, Vt.)

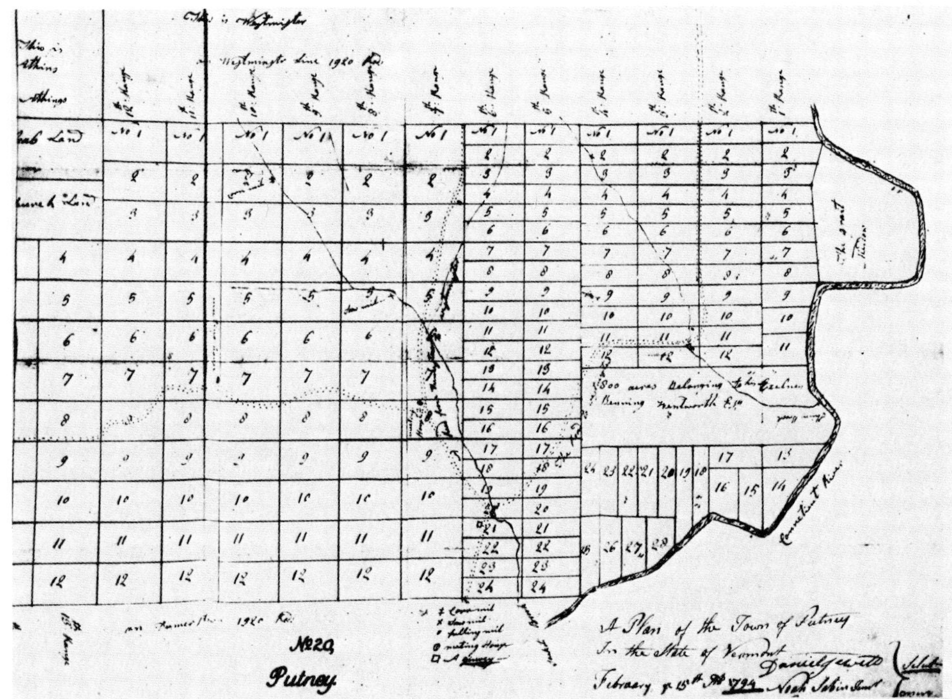

Figure 7. Town planning in Putney, Vt. (From Surveyor General's Papers *1794, 1:20, Whitelaw Plans and Papers, State Papers, Montpelier, Vt.)*

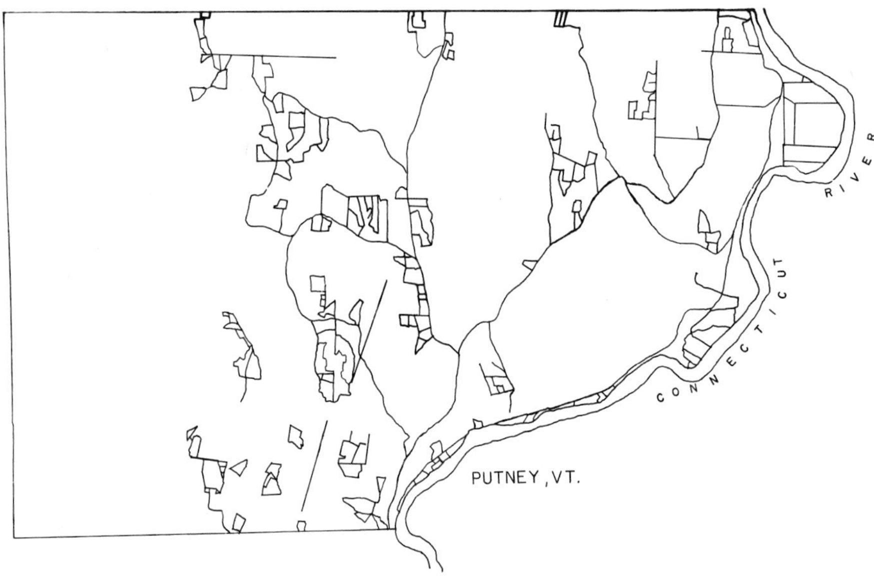

Figure 8. Schema of relic field lines for the town of Putney, Vt., showing actual development. (From 1974 aerial photographs, State Highway Department, Montpelier, Vt.)

very difficult to discern in photos, especially when an area has grown back into forest cover or when one is using large-scale imagery.

The first step in this identification of eighteenth-century field patterns has been to develop a typology of patterns found in six different physiographic regions in Vermont. Subsequently, a distinction has been made between physical and cultural contributions to those patterns. The patterns are related to five settlement groups for the purposes of demonstrating that a given culture group will produce an identifiable set of field characteristics which will result in unique agricultural landscapes that have distinctive forms, textures, patterns, and stylistic characters.

Several terms used in studying cultural landscapes of the past need to be explained. A *field* is defined here as a cleared piece of land used for crops or agricultural purposes. Fields are not distinguished from each other by their land or crop use or present-day ownership, but rather by the existence of semipermanent man-made or natural boundaries that may have originally been based on eighteenth-century land ownership.

The word *pattern* has a slightly different meaning in this article from that intended by artists and architects, to whom it often means the form, shape, and outline of an object that reveals an arrangement, or the composition that suggests a design. Here, pattern includes many other attributes besides form, shape, and outline. Field pattern refers to the generalized summary statements of traits that characterize the site and situation attributes of fields. To describe a particular field pattern both its general and particular field traits are enumerated. Field pattern may refer to a single field or fields in a particular area. For example, the field pattern found in Pawlet, Vermont, has seven characteristics: location, size, shape, edges, spatial arrangement, spatial orientation, and special features. These field characteristics are composed of specific traits: valley location, specific size (three acres), rectangular shape, an absence of tree lines at the edges, spatial arrangement as one of many fields in a cluster, spatial orientation to the river, and consolidation into a larger unit. (The particular traits compiled refer specifically to the Vermont scene and may need modification when applied elsewhere in New England or other parts of America.)

1

An historical-cultural criterion was used to determine which towns would be sampled (fig. 9). Culture groups were associated with certain areas by consulting historical documents that indicated the place of origin of the first settlers in each township. Making this kind of association between

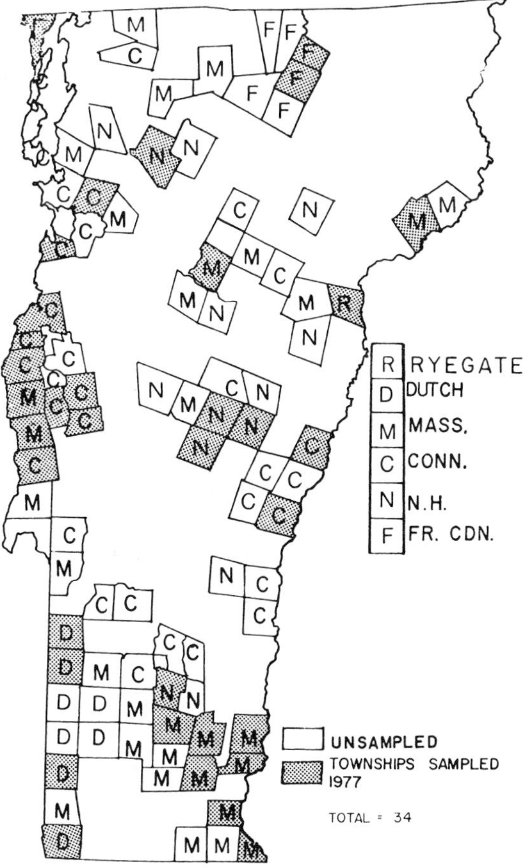

Figure 9. Photo imagery sample area in Vermont. Shaded areas denote townships sampled in 1977; blank areas remain unsampled.

culture group and culture area is valid and appropriate, for several reasons. Migration theory states that subsequent settlers would probably come from the same point of origin as the first settlers, because of restricted communications and lack of detailed knowledge of other possible areas in which to settle.[6] Other research using this method in Vermont was tested with an analysis of variance and chi square tests and received very positive results, thus demonstrating the validity of the association.[7]

Townships to be surveyed were selected primarily from the major concentrations of each culture group, so that the probability of external influences would be minimal. A preference was given to those concentrations located in the southern part of the state because the pattern of settlement in Vermont moved northward. Townships that had settlers from more than one out-of-state source or were settled by Vermonters were excluded from this study.

Black and white images at a scale of 1 to 20,000 were found to be the most useful for constructing a typology of colonial field patterns. A larger scale, such as 1 to 8,000, proved to be much too detailed and somewhat cumbersome to use in making photo mosaics. However, this scale was useful in making detailed checks on certain features. A smaller scale, such as found in Landsat and Erts images, lacked the detail necessary to easily make initial generalizations and construct a field typology. However, these scales are appropriate for wide application with an existing typology and will be used by the author in future research. Due to the expense and general unavailability of infrared images, they were used only sparingly to make detailed analyses of small groups of fields.

Sampling was carried out in three stages; the second and third steps acted as a check and refinement upon initial findings. In the first stage five towns were selected from the Massachusetts and Connecticut settlers' concentrations, while two towns were selected from the Dutch, French-Canadian and New Hampshire settlers' concentrations.

A second sample was randomly drawn from each of the concentrations identified with a culture group and served as a test of the model's reliability. Three towns were selected from the Massachusetts and Connecticut groups and one town was selected from the French-Canadian, New Hampshire, and Dutch groups.

A third and final sample was taken in order to distinguish between environmental and cultural factors as elements influencing the field patterns found in the different physiographic regions. Five towns, associated with two different subculture groups but located in the same or similar soil or relief regions, were compared with each other to check environmental and cultural influences. County soil and relief maps were consulted in order to determine which towns to select for sampling.

Detailed drawings of the field lines in each of the towns selected in the first and second sample were made for two reasons. The drawings acted as a perception filter that focused attention upon the individual fields and eliminated unnecessary detail contained in the photo images. Also, it was easier to count and measure individual traits on the drawings than on the photos.

These drawings generally show present-day field boundaries. Areas where there was either abandonment or consolidation were noted and studied with special care. Each drawing was then studied for attributes common to other towns within the same subculture area. Once the characteristics that were common or typical for the particular group were enumerated they were compared with the attributes of the different subculture areas. Those traits that were unique to one group were considered to be the primary indicators of that group. Secondary indicators were those traits that occurred in many different towns but were more frequently found in one subculture area than in another. Collectively, the primary and secondary indicators served as the basis for constructing a model of eighteenth-century field patterns (table 1 and fig. 10).

The aerial photo signatures that point to an eighteenth-century origin for a field pattern are: location with respect to the town center, evidence of being composed of small consolidated fields, and abandonment. In many New England communities

Table 1
Important Traits of Field Patterns

Characteristic	Trait
Location	Hillside
	In flood plain close to river
	In flood plain but back from river
	Plain
	Valley
Size	1–3 acres
	3–10 acres
	10–20 acres
	20+ acres
Shape	Square or rectangular
	Triangle
	Polyangle
	Curved
Edges	Acute angle
	Obtuse angle
	Ends at water
	Fronts road
	Tree lines
	Stone walls
	Irregular
	Straight
Spatial Arrangement	Large squares and grid lines
	Cells in squares
	Isolated
	Clusters
	String and bead
Spatial Orientation	To house
	To road
	To grid lines
	To stream or river
Special features	Rock piles in middle of field
	Consolidations (where)
	Abandonment (where)
	Stream not part of boundary

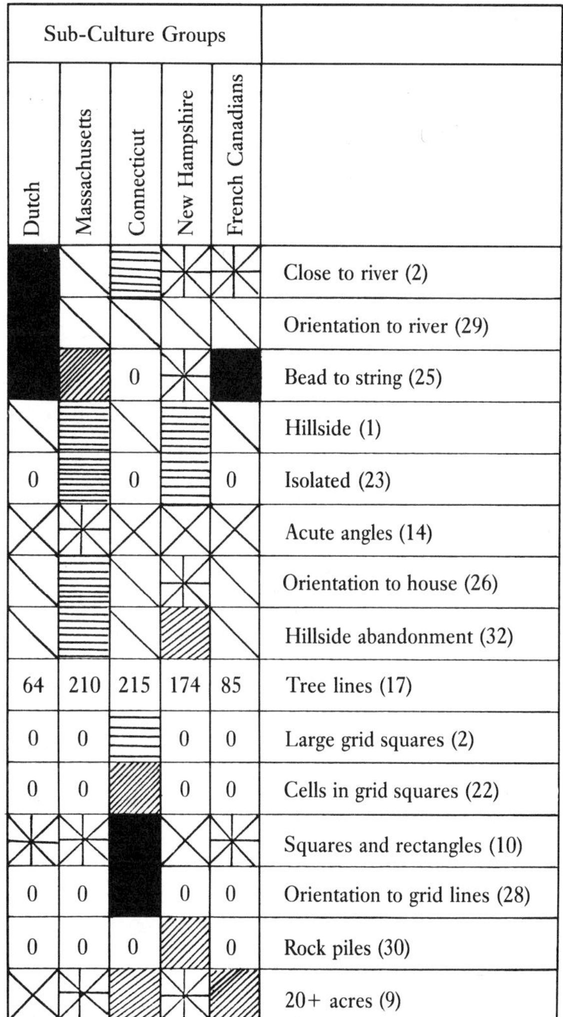

Sub-Culture Groups
Dutch
Massachusetts
Connecticut
New Hampshire
French Canadians
Close to river (2)
Orientation to river (29)
0
Bead to string (25)
Hillside (1)
0 0 0
Isolated (23)
Acute angles (14)
Orientation to house (26)
Hillside abandonment (32)
64 210 215 174 85
Tree lines (17)
0 0 0 0
Large grid squares (2)
0 0 0 0
Cells in grid squares (22)
Squares and rectangles (10)
0 0 0 0
Orientation to grid lines (28)
0 0 0 0
Rock piles (30)
20+ acres (9)

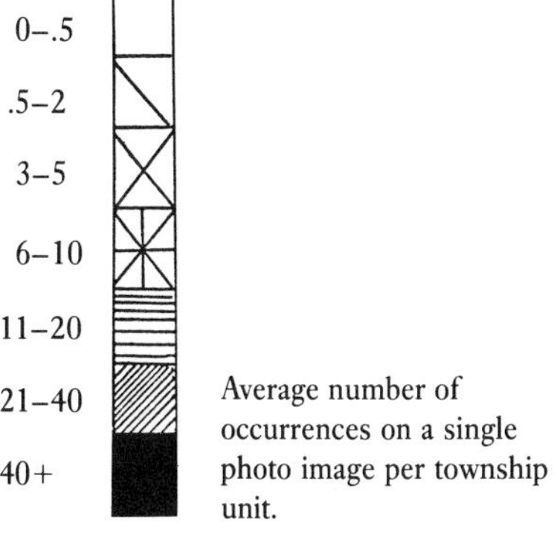

Figure 10. Major field pattern characteristics.

the town center was commonly the place of initial settlement. The town grew outward from the center and generally was not a later creation of dispersed settlers who sought a central location for religious, social, and commercial reasons. Therefore, the fields immediately surrounding the town center are very likely to be of eighteenth-century origin. Small fields (one to five acres) found in other parts of the township may also be eighteenth-century in origin, if they have been consolidated into larger fields that are more appropriate for contemporary mechanized

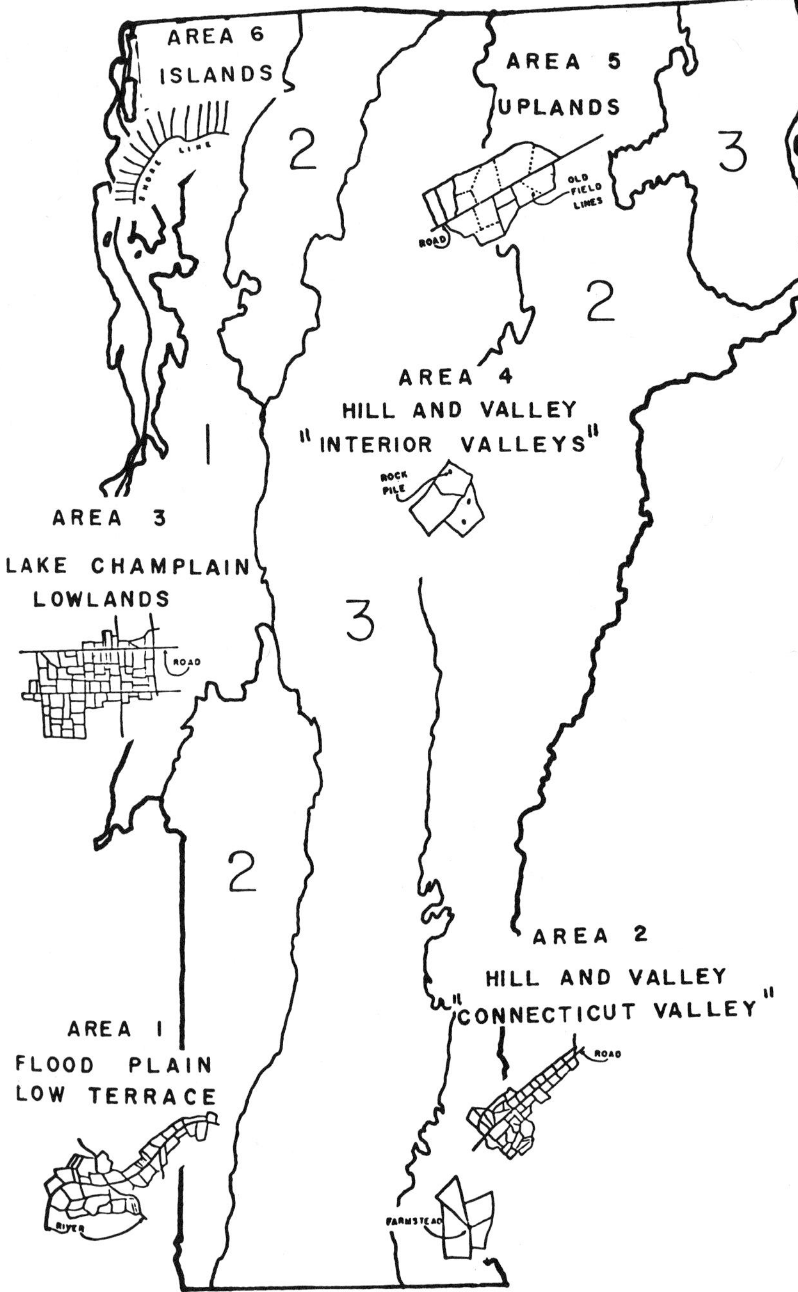

Figure 11. Soils, topography, and distribution of types of field patterns. (From field data compiled in 1977 by E. J. Miles.)

agriculture. Small fields located in diverse parts of the township that have been abandoned might also have originated in the same time period.

This study examined all fields near the town centers, as well as outlying fields that were abandoned or consolidated, in order to construct a typology of colonial field patterns, because urban growth had often obliterated earlier field lines near the town center. Some towns had experienced continuous agricultural expansion and there was little indication of abandonment.

Several field patterns exist in each of the townships besides the ones identified with certain colonial subculture groups. The signature field patterns differ from the other patterns in that the former are consistently repeated in townships identified with specific colonial subculture groups, while the other patterns occur randomly and are not consistently repeated in a distribution pattern associated with another presently identified culture group. Many of these patterns may be associated with diverse physical processes, such as erosion or fluvial deposition.

Figure 12. Area 1. Dutch fields hug the valley floor and are found next to water. Few tree lines bound the irregularly shaped fields. (Figures 12–17 are black-and-white reproductions of color aerial photographs by the author.)

2

The following paragraphs enumerate the most important field patterns associated with the six different physiographic areas that were derived from sample one and checked with samples two and three (fig. 11).

Area 1. Floodplain-low Terrace (fig. 12)

Location of these fields was invariably in sands, silts, and loams of the floodplain, close to water and rarely on the hillsides.[8] The size of most fields was between three and ten acres. In general most fields were irregularly-shaped polygons, though a number were long, narrow rectangles. Most fields did not have tree lines and only a very few had stone walls. Many of the fields ended at the river and a few had curved sides, due to the meandering nature of the tributary streams. There were occasional large concentrations of fields, but most were found strung out along the floodplain of the river. Some of the fields were definitely oriented to the river but it was often difficult to tell if the fields were oriented to a river or the roads that ran parallel to it. Some abandonment was found in the valleys; fields were very scarce on the hillsides. There was some consolidation evident in the floodplain.

Figure 13. Area 2. Tree lines bound the Massachusetts settlers' fields, which front on roads that run at irregular angles through the hillsides. Acute angles characterize many of the field corners.

Figure 14. Area 3. Connecticut settlers' fields are very similar in layout to their original lot survey. Tree-lined square and rectangular fields spread over the land to give a tartan plaid appearance.

Area 2. Hill and Valley (fig. 13)

Most fields were located in the Connecticut Valley on river terraces and secondarily on hillsides or in the floodplain, in the sands and loamy soils, but generally back from the river's edge. Many large new fields were found adjacent to the river but there was very little evidence of small fields being found adjacent to the river. Most fields were quite small (three to ten acres) and were irregularly-shaped polygons. The sides were most commonly straight lines and frequently met at right angles, though a number of fields exhibited variable, angled corners. Tree lines were common, as were stone walls. Some fields were isolated from the larger concentrations or clusters, and seemed to be oriented to roads or to each other. Extensive abandonment was apparent on the hillsides.

Area 3. Lake Champlain Lowlands (fig. 14)

Most fields were found on a plain or rolling hills in heavy soils such as lacrustrian clays. Square or rectangular in shape, they were oriented to grid lines. Where relief was encountered, fields were found on the lower hill slopes. Most fields in the lacrustrian sediments were small (three to ten acres), but some were slightly larger (ten to twenty acres). Most edges met at right angles and were straight lines. Tree lines were quite common but only a few stone walls were apparent. Fields were ubiquitous and not found in clusters or isolated. Large squares of grid lines were readily apparent. In a few cases it was possible to see small, square-shaped cells within a larger, square-shaped unit. There was very little abandonment apparent, and only a moderate amount of consolidation. Fields that were consolidated generally did not have tree lines.

Area 4. Hill and Valley Complex (fig. 15)

A high frequency of rock piles located in the middle of fields was found in every township in this area. Fields were found in both the valley bottom and on the gently-to-moderately-sloping hillsides. Most fields were quite small (three to ten acres) and commonly bounded with trees. The fields were irregularly-shaped polygons with many stone walls. Most of the fields, with their acid and shallow soils, were found on the valley floor, which is not surprising since the mountains rise rather steeply in this area.

Figure 15. Area 4. Vermont fields settled during the eighteenth century by migrants from New Hampshire invariably exhibit circular mounds, which are actually rock piles with vegetation growing out of them.

Orientation was unclear, since the road, river and fields were commonly crowded very close together. Abandonment on the hillside was more apparent than consolidation. Some fields located on the hillsides were isolated and seemed to be oriented to the farmstead.

Area 5. Uplands (fig. 16)

Most fields with their sandy loams and silt soils were located on the lower, gently-to-moderately rolling hills, though they were also found in the valleys and on the hillsides. The majority of fields

Figure 16. Area 5. Twentieth-century French-Canadian fields exhibit considerable consolidation and have very few tree lines.

were small, but one can discern outlines of a number of larger fields of ten to twenty acres and over. Most fields were irregularly-shaped polygons, but one can see square- and rectangular-shaped fields. Consolidation is quite evident and the small fields that have been aggregated into a new one invariably have had their tree lines removed. (The previous existence of tree lines is inferred from the presence of wide lines of soil disturbance. It almost appears as if tree lines were systematically removed.) Fields were evenly spread over the landscape and appeared, as often as not, oriented to the road.

Area 6. Island Lowlands (fig. 17)

The majority of fields were found in sandy soils associated with the island. Most fields were fairly regular in shape, either square or rectangular and relatively large in size (ten to twenty acres). A substantial number of fields were long, narrow rectangles that were clearly oriented to the shoreline. Tree lines were fairly common. Fields tended to be large by Vermont standards, over five acres in size. Many of the long, narrow fields were over ten acres in size.

The preceding paragraphs suggest that there are substantial differences between the field patterns found in the six different areas. All seven of the

Figure 17. Area 6. Eighteenth-century French-Canadian fields in Alburg are long and narrow and front on the water. Tree lines are found on many of the fields, which are much more irregular than their lot survey maps.

field characteristics (location, size, shape, edges, arrangement, orientation, and special features) can be used to distinguish the field patterns of one area from another. Area 4 seems to be least unique in that, with the exception of rock piles, its field traits are similar to those of some other areas. In Area 5 there are three field traits (extensive consolidation, large-sized fields, and tree line removal) that distinguish it from other areas. All other areas have at least five field traits that differ from other areas.

3

The floodplain lowlands, Area 1, is an area that was settled by both Yankee and Dutch settlers, a fact that adds to the complexity of making interpretations. Three of the towns, Pownal, Rupert, and Pawlet, have experienced little economic growth, making photo imagery of these towns relatively easy to interpret, but other towns in this area have experienced significant urban development that has substantially obliterated eighteenth-century field patterns.

According to town and state histories, all towns in this area were settled by Yankees. However, historical documents, local township tax and land records, suggest that in some cases Dutch settlement preceded Yankee settlement, while it was at least coincident in other cases.[9] For example, the Dutch are recorded as having settled in Pownal in 1724, almost forty years before Yankees entered the area. Historical documents served as the basis for considering this entire area to be Dutch-influenced (fig. 18). The presence of field patterns that differ significantly from Yankee-settled areas further justifies the designation of this area as being Dutch-influenced.

Cultural preference can be considered the explanation for many of the field traits in this area. The Dutch evidently preferred to locate their fields in the floodplain next to rivers instead of on the hillsides. They also seem not to have liked tree lines as field boundaries. The extent of field concentration in the valley bottom seems to correspond to the width of the valley bottom. The orientation of the fields to the river could indicate an intent to use the river as a transportation system. The curved and irregular shapes of fields would seem to be influenced by the meandering nature of rivers. Narrow rectangular fields would seem to be a cultural preference.

The hill and valley fields section, or Area 2, was primarily settled by Yankees from Massachusetts; two towns, however, were settled by people from Connecticut. In this area, unlike the Dutch area,

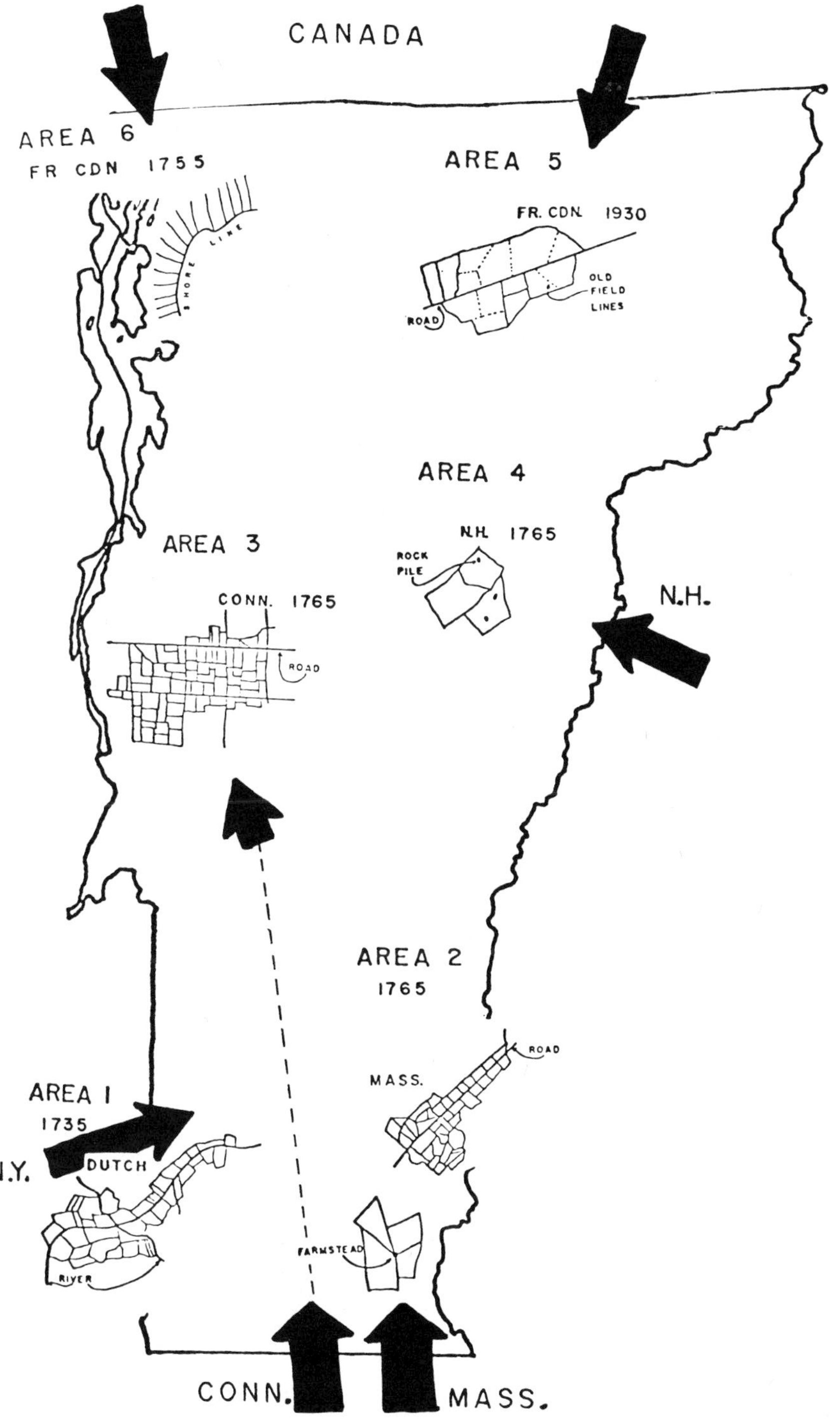

Figure 18. Source and distribution of types of field patterns. (From 1977 field data compiled for town records.)

one finds substantial abandonment on the hillsides, though some hill fields are still in use. Utilization of the floodplain is another point of contrast between Dutch and Yankee areas. In general, Yankees avoided the river, while the Dutch seemed to have been attracted to it. Tree lines are much more common in this Yankee area than in the Dutch area. Farmsteads in the Dutch area are rarely isolated, a trait that is fairly common in this Yankee area. The shapes of fields with their variable angles would seem to be the result of environmental rather than cultural influence. When aerial photographs are compared with the original lot survey it is possible to see the influence of this early cadastral system. However, it is impressive to note how little influence the survey system seems to have had on the overall field patterns. This is true not only for the floodplain but the terraces and hillsides as well. It would seem as if the lots and ranges were generally ignored with the onset of settlement, and a metes and bounds pattern quickly emerged.

Area 3 was settled primarily by Yankees from Connecticut, but two towns had Massachusetts origins. The influence of culture, under the direction of the original lot surveys, is clearly seen in this area. Six of the seven field characteristics are related to the widespread use of lot surveys. In areas where the relief becomes significant or where swamps exist, a metes and bounds pattern is found, while the original surveys seem to have been ignored. The widespread existence of the original lot surveys suggests that the flatness of the area lent itself to overall adoption of this survey system. This area stands in sharp contrast to the other Yankee-settled section, Area 2, where there was substantial relief, the original lot surveys seemed to have been ignored, and a metes and bounds cadastral pattern emerged.

Field patterns in Area 4, settled by Yankees from New Hampshire, seem to have been strongly influenced by a variety of environmental and cultural factors. Where culture seems to have played a part in influencing the field patterns it is difficult to say that this area is really unique and different from other areas, especially Area 2, another area of substantial relief. The extensive occurrence of rock piles in the middle of fields may be related to both cultural preference and environmental factors. Without further field investigations to compare the soil stoniness of Areas 2 and 4, an evaluation is difficult to make.

Area 5 is an area originally settled by Yankees and more recently occupied by French-Canadians, a fact that adds to the complexity of unravelling cultural and environmental influences contributing to the look of the land. The small size of consolidated fields is reminiscent of other Yankee-settled areas. Extensive consolidation and systematic removal of tree lines are cultural attributes that should be considered French-Canadian preferences, giving the landscape a Quebec-like appearance. The association of field consolidation and tree line removal with French-Canadians was made by this writer after driving all roads in Coventry, Irasburg, and Troy that appear on the state highway map, and making note of the names on the mailboxes. Location, shape, arrangement, and orientation of fields seem to be influenced by environment as much as culture.

The field patterns in Area 6 suggest two things: that cultural preference was a major element in shaping the character of the patterns, and that there are two patterns present, one superimposed on the other. The earliest pattern, that of long, narrow fields oriented to the waterfront, does not penetrate into the interior of the island but is found exclusively on the shore. This is probably the product of French-Canadian settlement in Alburg during the 1740s and bears a striking resemblance to the long lot system found in Quebec and southern Louisiana.[10] The second, more recent pattern reveals an attempt to take sections of the long, narrow fields and consolidate them into square-shaped fields that are larger in size. The irregularity of the second pattern is most pronounced in the center of the island away from the coast. Fields along the shore and inland commonly have tree lines bounding them. Since Yankees moved into the area as the French moved out after the French and Indian War, it is not surprising that tree lines were maintained and even extended over the whole island. The size of the narrow rectangular fields is substantially greater than fields found in Area 1.

It is clear from the preceding paragraphs that both culture and environment played a part in shaping the field patterns in Vermont. Eleven, and possibly fourteen, field traits can be attributed to cultural preference; each of the seven field categories demonstrates cultural influence. The following field characteristics and traits were found to be most important in showing such cultural preference: location (hillside or close to a river); size (large or small); shape (long, narrow, rectangular); edges (presence or absence of tree lines as boundary markers); arrangement (presence or absence of grid lines); orientation (to a river, to a farmstead, to other fields or grid lines, or to the shore); and special features (for example, consolidation, the presence of rock piles).

4

Several different field traits are characteristic of each of the physiographic areas; collectively they form a design which can be associated with the groups that settled in each area. While these patterns are not the only ones found in the settlement regions, they are the most characteristic of each area and are quite different from the patterns found in other areas.

Dutch

Fields in this area (fig. 12) flow like a multicolored ribbon that is confined to the valley floor. The texture and color of the hillsides of the valley are relatively uniform: it is forest-covered and shows no evidence of agricultural intrusion. The ribbon of fields in the valley floor has a flow that is generally uninterrupted by tree lines. The course of the river in the valley serves as a major seam to which the individual small patches or fields are sewn. The shape of most fields is like a detailed, irregular patchwork quilt, and the meandering of streams and rivers lends a curving shape to many of the fields. Fields are small, located in the floodplain close to, and frequently oriented to, rivers. Some fields are long, narrow rectangles. Tree lines are uncommon and fields are rarely found on the hillsides.

Massachusetts Yankee

The impression that one gets of fields in the Connecticut River Valley (fig. 13) is similar to that created by a gigantic patchwork quilt that has been draped across the valley. The texture of the hillsides is dominated by the forest cover but it is possible to see numerous intruding patches of fields and isolated farmsteads halfway up the hillsides. Even though forest cover is dominant, one can see seams or roads running irregularly through the woods. Irregularly-shaped, small-sized fields or patches are connected to each of these seams. The outline or edges of these fields are frequently bounded with tree lines that clearly demarcate the form and shape of each individual field. Moving down the hillsides one finds many patch fields that have sharp, acute-angled corners. Large, regularly shaped contemporary fields, instead of small irregularly shaped colonial fields, dominate the river's edge. Fields are small, commonly located on the hillsides away from major streams and rivers. Most fields are bounded with tree lines oriented to the farmstead, to each other, or to a road.

Connecticut Yankee

The rural agricultural landscape of this area (fig. 14) has the appearance of an enormous tartan plaid. Most fields are basically square or rectangular in form, a shape accentuated by the presence of tree lines. The rhythm of repeating squares and rectangles stems from an overall general adherence to the original lot surveys that were quite regular in pattern. Like a tartan plaid, one finds smaller squares and rectangles within larger units. Most of these small fields are oriented to grid lines. They are primarily square and rectangular in shape and bounded with tree lines.

New Hampshire Yankee

The most striking field design in this area (fig. 15) is the presence of circles, or rock piles, in the square- or rectangular-shaped fields.

French-Canadian Colonial

The fields on the island (fig. 17) have almost the appearance of a gigantic rib cage. They begin at the top and both sides of the island and are regularly spaced to the bottom of it. Tree lines accentuate the long, narrow-shaped fields that start at the water's edge. In part, the rib cage appearance of the fields stems from the fact that they are oriented to the water. Where the shoreline begins to curve a fanlike appearance is faintly seen because the fields tend to follow the shoreline and not a survey system. Fields are large (ten to twenty acres), located exclusively on the shore line, and have a long, narrow, rectangular shape. They are bounded with tree lines and are oriented to the water.

French-Canadian Modern

The field patterns in this area (fig. 16) show evidence of professional design, beginning with a vernacular form. Many of the patterns and outlines suggest the adoption of agricultural engineering practices. Shape, size, and outline of fields show an absence of tree lines and large, regularly shaped fields dominate the view. This pattern has generally been created by consolidating small, older fields into new units. The contour and curve of the land is very apparent since there are few tree lines to obstruct a panoramic view. Texture and color are defined more by crops than by forest cover, which characterized the vernacular patterns described previously. Some fields are fairly large (ten to twenty and over acres). There is evidence of extensive consolidation and removal of tree lines that at one time existed on the field lines.

In conclusion, it is possible to say that the rural agricultural landscape can be viewed as a unique vernacular art form. Field patterns have been shown to have shape, texture, form, pattern, design, and color, constituting a landscape mosaic that is not only man-made but may be identified with the different groups who settled in the Green Mountain State. Aerial photographs have been found to be very useful research documents and, when used in conjunction with original lot survey maps and field study, have made it possible to identify the field designs made by the major culture groups, Dutch, Yankee, and French-Canadian. Subcultural distinctions between Connecticut, New Hampshire and Massachusetts settlement patterns could also be identified.

Notes

This article was originally published in *Old-Time New England* (Summer–Fall 1978), the Bulletin of the Society for the Preservation of New England Antiquities.

1. Zadock Thompson, *History of Vermont, Natural Civil and Statistical* (Burlington, Vt.: Chauncey Goodrich, 1842).
2. Stewart G. McHenry, "Vermont Barns: A Cultural Landscape Analysis," *Proceedings of the New England–St. Lawrence Valley Geographical Society* 6 (1976): 19–21.
3. As, for example, in John Reps, *Town Planning in Frontier America* (Princeton, N.J.: Princeton University Press, 1965); Douglas R. McManis, *Colonial New England* (New York: Oxford University Press, 1975); John Fraser Hart, *The Look of the Land* (Englewood Cliffs, N.J.: Prentice-Hall, 1975); and Hildegard Binder Johnson, *Order upon the Land: The U.S. Rectangular Land Survey and the Upper Mississippi Country* (New York: Oxford University Press, 1976).
4. Norman J. W. Thrower, *Original Survey and Land Subdivision: A Comparative Study of the Form and Effect of Contrasting Cadastral Surveys* (Chicago: Rand McNally, 1966); N. Merton Burns, "A Summary of Vermont Lotting," *The Corner Post* 6, no. 2 (May 1976): 1–24.
5. Albert Brown, "Aerial Relationships between Land Use, Population, and Political Jurisdiction along a Segment of the Vermont/New York Boundary," Ph.D. diss., Syracuse University, 1952.

6. Everett S. Lee, "A Theory of Migration," *Demography* 3, no. 1 (1966): 47–59.
7. Stewart G. McHenry, "Vermont Barns: A Geographic Interpretation," manuscript in preparation for Dartmouth College geography publications.
8. E. J. Miles, *A Study of Vermont in Maps* (Burlington: University of Vermont, 1963), pp. 2–11.
9. Stewart G. McHenry, "Vermont's Sleepy Hollow: The Colonial Dutch Landscape Legacy," *Vermont History* 47, no. 4 (Fall 1979): 279–85.
10. Lewis Cass, *History of Franklin and Grand Isle Counties, Vermont* (Syracuse, N.Y.: D. Mason, 1891), p. 629.

The Central Courthouse Square in the American County Seat

EDWARD T. PRICE

Details of the biography of a vernacular building can be learned or inferred from evidence concerning the origin and development of town plans. Moreoever, given the probable dearth of documentation on any vernacular structure, a knowledge of the spatial contexts of a building—the spatial relationship of various buildings to each other, the pattern of streets and roads, the location of major services, and other such features—should prove most useful in developing an accurate interpretation of individual buildings and their residents. While the history of a town's form is much broader than the history of a single house, one can be reasonably confident that the cultural values that operate in a town's planning in some measure also influence the planning of its houses.

In this article Edward T. Price makes common cause with Fred B. Kniffen, confirming Kniffen's description of the regional patterns of folk housing in the United States. He sees the form of the central courthouse square as a convenient shorthand for the settlement sequences of the eighteenth and nineteenth centuries. For example, the Lancaster plan, a block intersected perpendicularly at the middle of each side, can be used as an index of the movement of Scotch-Irish settlers out of southeastern Pennsylvania into the Upland South and the Midwest. The Lancaster plan was but another item of cultural baggage which the Scotch-Irish carried with them along with other plans for houses and barns and other outbuildings. The so-called Shelbyville plan, a block bounded by four streets, was first used in central Tennessee from whence it was carried in all directions although it took hold most noticeably in the Midwest. This plan, unlike the former, which has its origins in northern Ireland, seems to have been an American development. Its distribution suggests that after the first push of settlement beyond the Appalachians new patterns began to replace some of the practices inherited from the Old World. The Shelbyville plan might then be interpreted as a progressive alternative to the more traditional Lancaster courthouse square in much the same way that the transverse-crib barn was eventually preferred over the double-crib barn. Price uses town plans to argue for the early dominance of Pennsylvania on American frontier building traditions to suggest that the Tennessee basin was an important secondary hearth area where new building customs were synthesized and developed.

American town plans derive their most characteristic form from the replication of the rectangular grid. In New England towns the familiar greens or commons provide a distinctive focus. More widespread, but less written about, are the courthouse squares that give stark shape to the centers of hundreds of county seats (fig. 1). A highway traveler in much of the Middle West and South must thread his way through a busy square every twenty or thirty miles. He is likely to carry in his memory a composite picture of these squares—a rectangular block surrounded by streets, with the courthouse, often the grandest and most ornate building in the county, standing alone in the middle of the square and the town's leading business houses enclosing the square symmetrically on all four sides. This ensemble is used here to define a central courthouse square; attention is given also to squares possessing only part of the three characteristics but achieving much the same visual effect. The names used to identify various central-courthouse-square plans are given in figure 2.

Local historians have left us no accounts of the debates that must have set forth the advantages and disadvantages of the different proposals for the town plan, nor are we often told who drew the plans that were finally adopted or what models they sought to match or overshadow. There seem to have been no manuals on how to form a new county that might have provided directions, and little evidence exists that there were professional planners of towns other than the surveyors who marked them off and the promoters who tried to gain from their growth. Innovation must have been infrequent: clearly, one town copied another. The pioneer leaders applied as best they could the experience gained in their former hometowns. To follow their tracks through the squares they left is the main purpose of this study.[1]

Distribution and Antecedents of Courthouse Squares

County courthouses in all parts of the country usually stand in, or face, some special open space. The heartland of central courthouse squares lies around the population center of the United States, in Tennessee, Kentucky, Indiana, Illinois, Iowa, and Missouri (figs. 3, 4, and 5).[2] But their frequency is equally high in Georgia on the southeast and Texas on the southwest. To the north and west—from Michigan west and south to Kansas—the courthouse is most often placed in the center of a block outside the business district. Central

Figure 1. The central courthouse square in Bloomington, Indiana, surrounded by prime business locations.

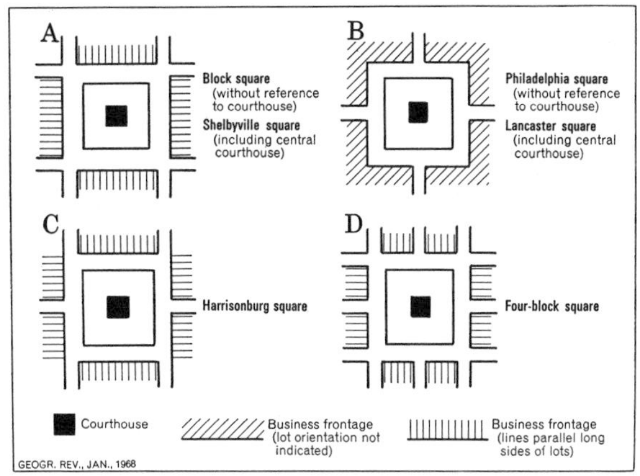

Figure 2. The most common types of central courthouse squares, with identifying terms used in the text.

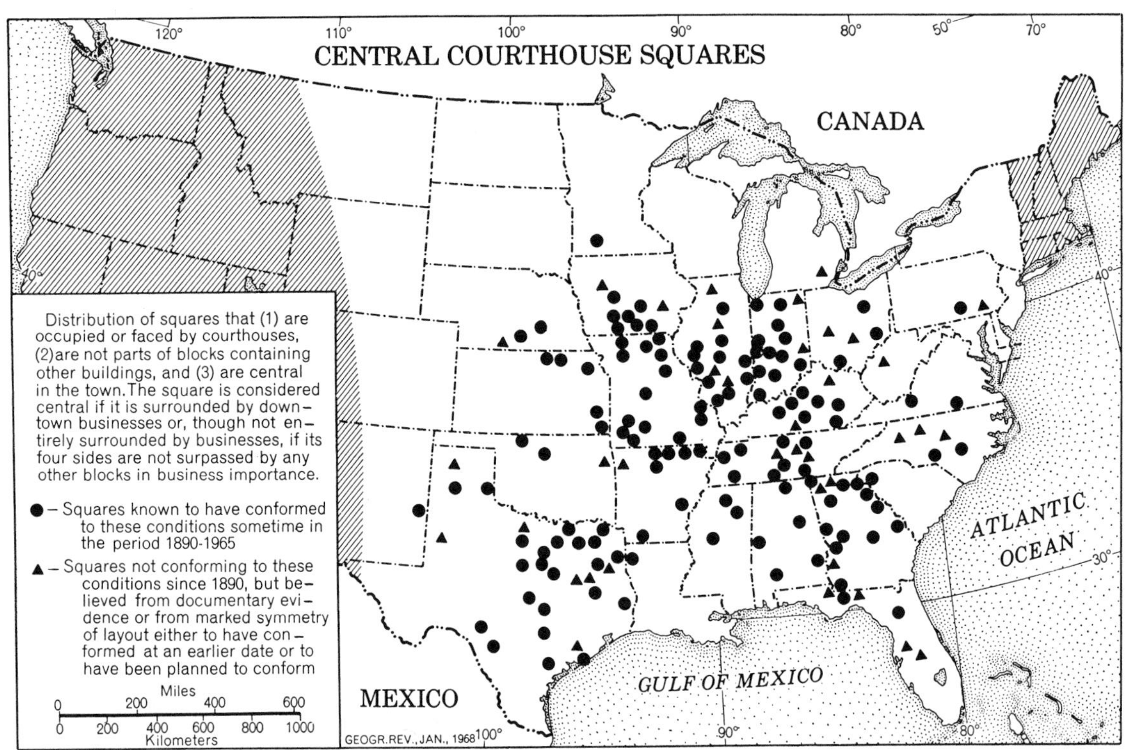

Figure 3

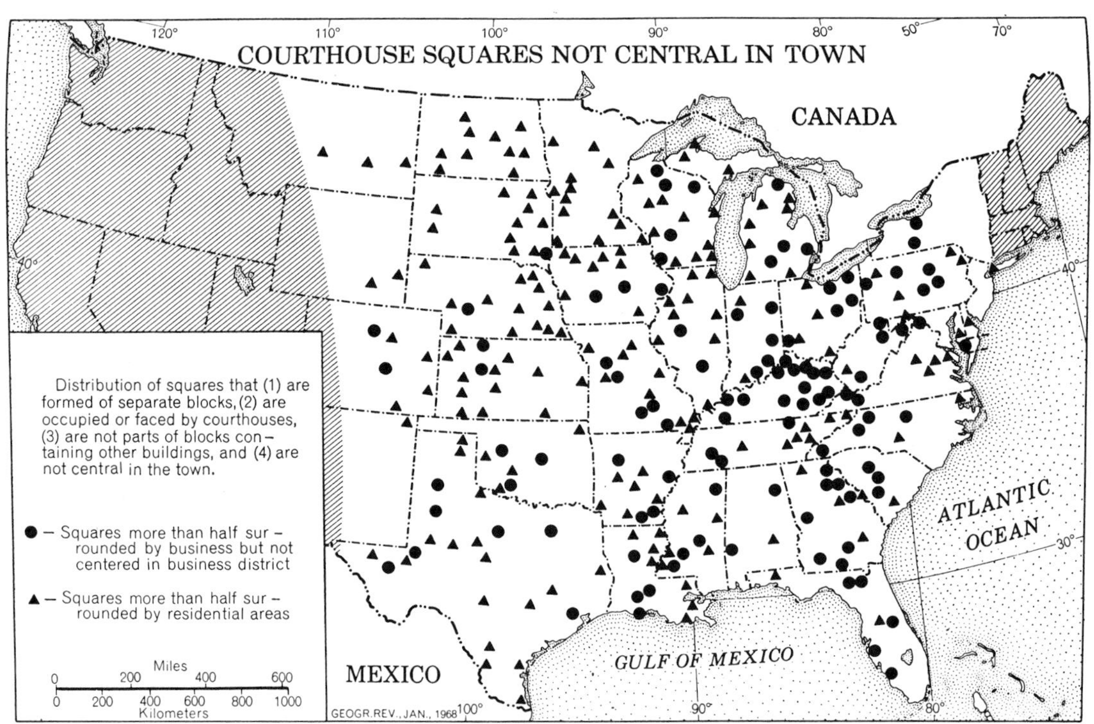

Figure 4

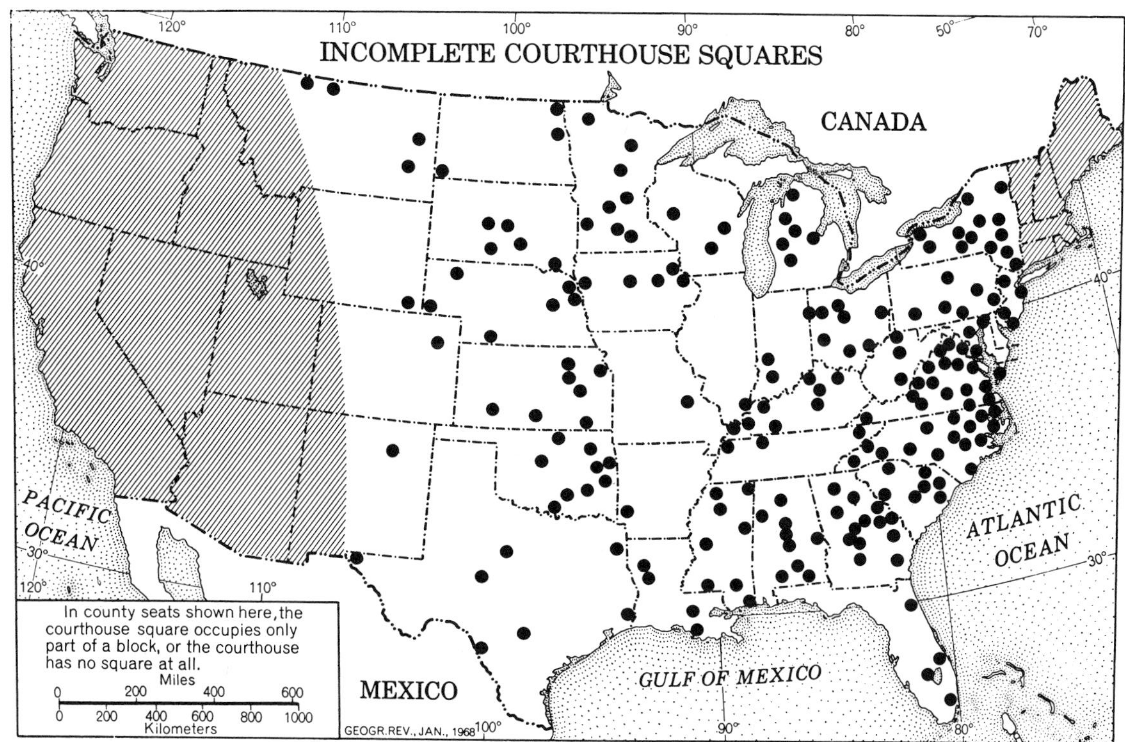

Figure 5

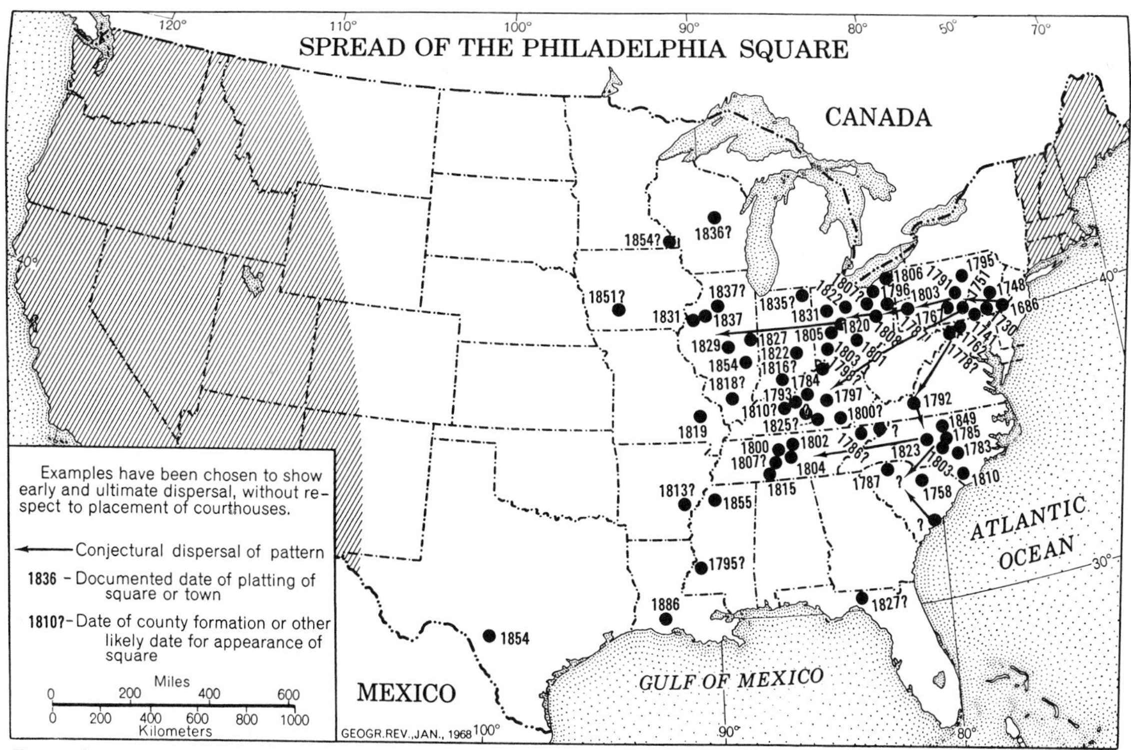

Figure 6

courthouse squares are almost absent in a wide band across the north of the country.

The idea of an open square in the town center is so widespread that it presents no problem in finding possible sources but gives us little help in selecting among them. Europe is full of town squares, usually with the major buildings on their edges. The open European square conduces to the view of the enclosing building facades from or across the square; the county-seat square, focused on the courthouse, emphasizes the view from edge to center.

The square with the town hall or market building in the center occurs in two parts of Europe where towns were planned. The more important is the medieval German-Polish border zone. Erstwhile German towns that have the principal building in the center of the square are Hammerstein (Czarne),[3] Breslau (Wroclaw),[4] and Prausnitz (Prusice).[5] The plan is also common in old Polish towns.[6] Silesia did contribute a small proportion of early German migrants to America.

The early seventeenth-century English towns of Northern Ireland were often planned with a central square.[7] Londonderry's "Town House" stood in the center of its square (Philadelphia plan) from 1622 until recently replaced by a war monument.[8] Coleraine has had a public building on its square or "diamond" (Harrisonburg plan) since 1743.[9] The Ulster towns, contemporary with the first American settlement, display a regularity without precedent in the towns of England, where, however, one may find public buildings in the middle of a widened street or in an old marketplace.

The Spanish colonial town plaza and the New England town green are frequently suggested as the models for the courthouse square. The plaza normally occupied a block of the grid and held a central position in the town. There are cases of specific inheritance, such as Santa Rosa, California, where Americans placed their courthouse in the center of the Spanish plaza. But in the Spanish plan the principal buildings, among which the church had first place, normally faced the plaza instead of standing within it. The New England green also differs from the courthouse square, and in the particular features with which we are concerned. It is seldom surrounded by the business establishments, is seldom symmetrical, and now, at least, is usually faced by the principal buildings. That county government is not important in New England and that the building emphasized was the church or meetinghouse are perhaps beside the point. There is no reason why the middle and southern colonies, which drew their people and traditions from rich transatlantic hearths, should have singled out the New England or Spanish colonial square for borrowing.

Establishment of a County and a County Seat

Counties were created by colonial and state lawmakers, most often by splitting off newly settled outlying parts of established counties whose residents sought a government more truly local.[10] Either the county court or a special committee was authorized to fix on a site for the seat of justice with its appurtenances—the jail, the whipping post, and the stocks—near the center of the new county. Elections to choose the county seat were more common west of the Mississippi.

Most typically the courthouse was erected on a new site, where it served as the nucleus of the county seat, which became the largest town and trade center in the county. Land for the public square, or even for the whole town, was often donated by a single landowner (sometimes a member of the site commission), who thus improved the location of his remaining property. If the site proved unsuitable, the seat could later be moved. West of the Mississippi, towns were often laid out by promoters, who used every kind of influence to have them selected as county seats. No wonder the number and intensity of county-seat wars increased westward! The mixture of individual and government enterprise in the making of the county seat changed with the times, but everywhere the county seat was a creature, if not a creation, of the county.

Courthouse Sites in the Southern Colonies

The first eight counties in the present United States were formed in Virginia in 1634. The courthouse and public square seem to have been identified by the early eighteenth century. The public square may have first been conceived as a market square. Instructions for the formation of Jamestown advised that the streets "be carried square about your marketplace."[11] However, the plat of Yorktown as "the towne belonging to Yorke County" shows no sign of a square; the courthouse today occupies the corner lot where the first courthouse was placed in 1691.[12] Williamsburg was founded at the end of the century with a baroque design that removed the main monumental buildings to the ends of the principal streets. Very likely the Market Square, central to the town but not to the present business district, was reserved at that time. The old courthouse of 1770 fronts on the north side of the main street where it cuts through the middle of the square. The 1715 courthouse had stood inconspicuously in the second block to the south, where the present courthouse stands.[13] A 1706 plat of Tappahannock reserved "for Publick use" a full block, where the courthouse was placed in 1728.[14] Today one end of the square has been turned over to business, and the old courthouse has been converted to a church. The greater part of the block is intact and contains the courthouse of 1848, with the clerk's office of 1808 and the debtor's prison of 1769, now the treasurer's office, on its flanks.

The early courthouses were, literally, court houses, containing only a courtroom and jury rooms. An office for the court clerk was soon provided in a separate building, and other record and administrative offices were added. These were architectural miniatures of the simple gabled buildings of the day, often of brick with slate roofs, suggesting the clustering of service buildings about the plantation house. The multibuilding county compound survives in many Virginia counties, perhaps most notably in Gloucester (ca. 1769), where the oval green contains six buildings facing a central walk, the whole surrounded by a low wall of (modern) colonial brick.[15] In other places the county offices use attached or breezeway-connected wings that leave the integrity of the original courthouse discernible.

Many Virginia courthouses remained rural in spite of efforts, beginning in the seventeenth century, to force the growth of towns. A tavern or ordinary was usually the first accessory to the courthouse,[16] and the county court determined its rates. The courthouse had a prime attraction for lawyers, who often set up their offices in a row across the street or even within the square; such a row survives in the square at Halifax. But early Virginia did not need many towns, and when, much later, they became necessary, the old courthouse settlements were not always the most convenient sites for them. Many a rural courthouse faces the main road through the community without being strikingly its focal center. Often the public square is not bounded by streets.

The Sauthier maps of the principal North Carolina cities of 1768–70 provide specific information on courthouse sites.[17] None shows even a hint of a modern courthouse square, but most give prominence to the courthouse itself. In Wilmington, Edenton, Salisbury, New Bern, and Hillsboro the courthouse was placed in or near an important road crossing. Greensboro was platted in 1808, with a space in the main intersection marked for the courthouse.[18] At least two courthouses occupied that spot successively, and two others stood on an adjoining corner before the courthouse was moved away from the center.[19]

South Carolina counties were not formed until 1785, though there were a few district courthouses before then; evidence of early courthouse squares is discussed in some detail below. Early Georgia towns were elaborately provided with squares, but the best known of these did not have a central focus.

The Central Square in Early Pennsylvania

The 1682 plan for Philadelphia shows at the crossing of Broad and High streets a square formed of rectangular corners cut out of the four adjoining blocks, a type identified with Philadelphia (fig. 2b), though somewhat modified in its execution there.[20] The Philadelphia-type square was regularly adopted in the early cities of southeastern Pennsylvania and occurs at least occasionally in nearly all parts of the United States.[21] More broadly, "the single open square in the center of the town became the typical expression of the Philadelphia plan as it was transplanted west."[22] If Philadelphia accounts for the idea of a central square, what about the building in the center of the square?

The original plan of Philadelphia called for "Houses for publick Affairs, as a Meeting-House, Assembly or State-House, Market-House, School-House" in the four "angles" of the square.[23] However, an early plan shows, in addition to the small building in each of the four corners, a prominent building in the center of the square, where it could be seen from any of the four directions along Broad and High streets.[24] The square did not actually contain a major building at any time in the colonial period; in fact, the urbanized area that formed along the Delaware had not even reached the square. An ornate pump house stood in the square from 1801 to 1827; the present city hall was begun there in 1872.

The central courthouse square appeared much earlier in Philadelphia's hinterland. Pennsylvania's original counties were Philadelphia, Bucks, and Chester. The seats of the last two have been moved, and I have little information on their early layouts.[25] The next four counties all placed the courthouse within the central square. Lancaster was laid out on the site chosen after formation of the county in 1729; its courthouse was completed in 1739 on the sixty-six-foot-square lot saved for it in the center of Centre Square (fig. 7).[26] The open square at York, laid out in 1741, was chosen for the courthouse when the county was formed in 1749; the site was

Figure 7. Lancaster, Pennsylvania, about 1790, showing the 1787 courthouse hemmed in by the buildings around the square. The courthouse was moved in 1854, and an elaborate Civil War monument now occupies the site.

changed in 1841.[27] Carlisle has an elaborate version of the square, divided into four separate blocks with diagonal streets entering its corners. The courthouse has occupied the southwest block since 1766; the Presbyterian and Episcopal churches and a market house occupy the other three.[28] Reading was platted in 1748, before the formation of Berks County, but had its courthouse by 1762 (fig. 8).[29]

Pennsylvania, then, appears to be the American source of a trait it scarcely possesses today. The central courthouse square must be added to the farm practices, rural and urban settlement patterns and house types, the Kentucky rifle and the Conestoga wagon, that settlers carried with them from southeastern Pennsylvania. The variety of people in eighteenth-century Pennsylvania and their subsequent dispersion south, southwest, and west provided the material and the vector for establishing the area as a major culture hearth of pioneer arts.

The influence of the Philadelphia square, even while still only a plan, is hard to deny. An additional conjecture can be offered as to why the square, with the courthouse in it, should appear at Lancaster. Scotch-Irish settlers in Lancaster County gave Donegal and Colerain townships names from their home localities. For the Donegal emigrants the principal trade center and most likely port of embarkation was Londonderry. Donegal Township was influential in the early county government. Its member on the commission for choosing the courthouse site was James Mitchell, a surveyor,[30] and it is likely that Mitchell was instrumental in the virtual duplication of the Londonderry square in Lancaster.[31] The restless Scotch-Irish, too, are the most likely carriers of the central square to other areas. Several bits of evidence suggest that the Lancaster square was spread by Pennsylvanians. Specifically, Lancaster gave its name and design to towns in other states.

Lancaster, South Carolina, in a county of the same name, was settled by Pennsylvanians in the 1750s. Though it cannot have been planned as a county seat, the courthouse and jail once occupied a widened principal street near its main intersection in a manner at least slightly suggestive of the Pennsylvania plan.[32]

Lancaster, Kentucky, was laid out in 1797 following the formation of Garrard County. No document explains its name, but Forrest Calico has traced the brother of one of the principal landowners to Lancaster, Pennsylvania.[33] The square followed the Lancaster style. The first courthouse was built in its center in 1799; since 1868 the courthouse has been on a lot facing the square.[34] The circular grassy plot occupying the original courthouse site was being removed in 1965 to speed passage through town on the two main highways that intersect there. Lancaster, Kentucky, also spawned a namesake, complete with an oblong Philadelphia square laid out by one of her emigrants, in Dallas County, Texas, in 1852.[35] Lancaster, Texas, however, has no courthouse.

Lancaster, Ohio (1800), was one of the towns founded by Ebenezer Zane on land granted him at river crossings in payment for the trace he cut across Ohio from Wheeling, (West) Virginia, to Limestone (Maysville), Kentucky. The articles of agreement with the purchasers of lots provided that four lots at the intersection of Broad and Main streets known as "the Center Square are given for the purpose of erecting public buildings."[36] The lots, each about twice as long as it was broad, combined to make an elongated Philadelphia square.[37] Lancaster was given its name in compliment to a number of settlers who had come from the Pennsylvania town. Since Zane himself was a Virginian, and since Wheeling and Zanesville, also platted under his auspices, and Chillicothe, founded across the Scioto from his property, do not have such squares, it is reasonable to suppose that the Pennsylvania settlers provided the idea. The courthouse stood for many years in the middle of Broad Street just north of Main and was matched by the market house just south of Main.[38]

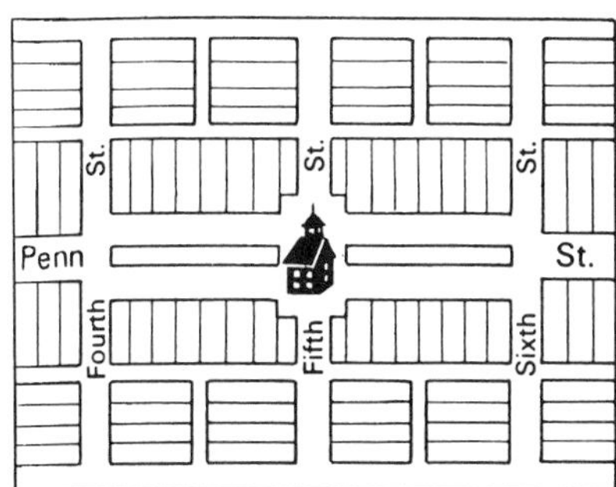

Figure 8. Part of Reading, Pennsylvania, redrawn from an 1804 copy of an early plat. The square is an elaboration of the Philadelphia plan, and the center strips were used for markets. The courthouse held the central spot until 1840.

Spread of Central Courthouse Squares of the Lancaster Pattern

About 1780 central courthouse squares began to appear in states to the south and west of Pennsylvania. The order they reflect is probably a logical growth beyond the cruder designs of earlier days and an expression of pride in the land's new independence. It may also evidence a growing tendency to put town platting in the hands of county authorities rather than of private landowners. The Lancaster plan showed up early in several states in nearly completed form, while the block-square plan was still evolving, only later to be laid out with clear intention as the starting point of new towns. In this contrast lies a major argument for tracing all central courthouse squares to the Pennsylvania source.

It is necessary to note that Charleston, South Carolina, was laid out after a "Grand Modell" that very likely included a Philadelphia-type square even before the Philadelphia plan came into being. An account of 1680 virtually implies a central courthouse placement in it: "The Court house which we are now building is to be erected in the middle of it, in a Square of two ackers of land upon which the four great streets of 60 foot wide doe center. . . ."[39] The square was not actually developed until sometime after 1717; the principal buildings were placed in the quadrants of the square, and the courthouse made its appearance there only about 1788.[40] A possible offshoot of the Charleston square is found in Camden, South Carolina, first surveyed in 1758. Its old center was a square of Philadelphia-Charleston design. The early district courthouses, the first in 1771, were somewhere in or near the square; the third courthouse building is near the square but does not face it.[41] Spartanburg was platted with a long, narrow square of similar design that once had the courthouse in the main crossing.[42] I have no evidence as to whether the Camden and Spartanburg squares followed Charleston or Pennsylvania, whose settlers had already reached the Carolina Piedmont. The almost complete absence of other such squares in South Carolina argues against any wide dispersal from Charleston.

The appearance of the Philadelphia square in county seats is summarized in figure 6. The square at the center of Hagerstown, Maryland, probably never held the courthouse. Christiansburg has the only such square I have identified in Virginia; its first two courthouses stood in the center, the later ones in one quarter of the square.[43]

The Philadelphia square had some currency in North Carolina. It may have been introduced by Moravians in the street village of Bethania (1759), which, though not a county seat, had a church or town hall in the center of its square.[44] Fayetteville (Cambleton) acquired two Philadelphia squares in

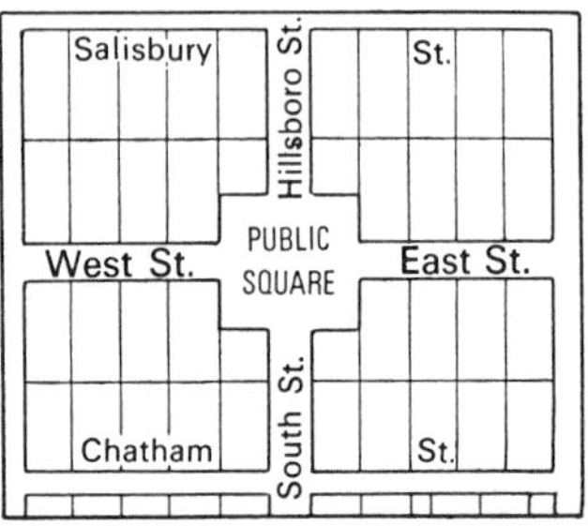

Figure 9. Part of Pittsboro, North Carolina, redrawn from an 1890 copy of a 1785 plat. Today most of the business is along Salisbury Street. The courthouse still occupies the center of the square, but when it first did so is not certain.

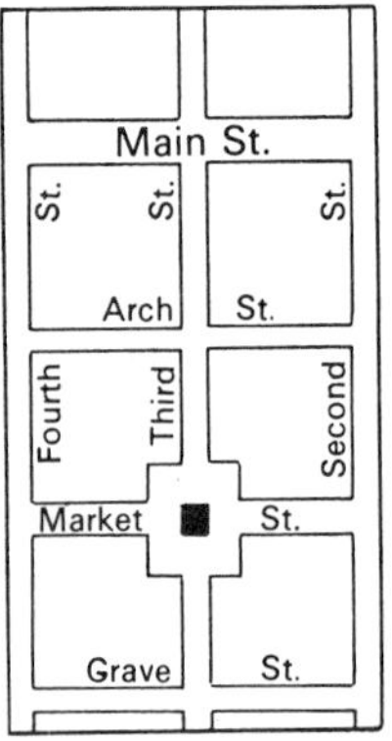

Figure 10. Part of Bardstown, Kentucky, redrawn from an 1807 plat that presumably was in accord with the plat of 1785. Bardstown was named for a Pennsylvania family who donated the land for the square and probably were responsible for the plat. Third Street, between the courthouse and Main Street, is now the business center. Main Street may have been the locus of a settlement that preceded the plat.

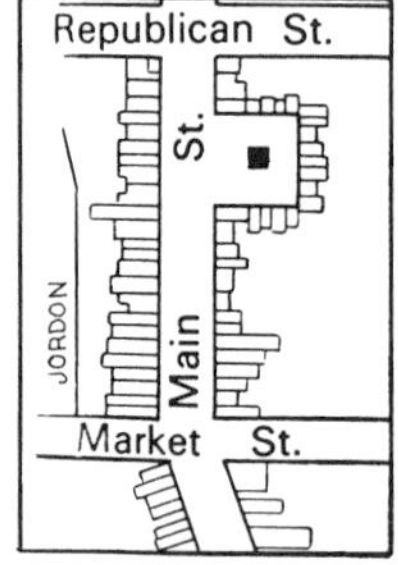

Figure 11. Lebanon, Kentucky, in 1863, redrawn from a map in the Lebanon Enterprise *(June 27, 1963). The layout has changed very little in the last hundred years. The buildings around the square may have started as a lawyers' row; they now contain a variety of businesses.*

1783 when the legislature, noting its destiny as an important town, appointed a commission to arrange as regular a plat as was consistent with minimizing injury to existing houses and lots.[45] The square at the town center still contains the market house and city hall of 1838; the other square, still irregular, once held the courthouse. Pittsboro followed in short order (fig. 9). Raleigh (1792) has a square at its center for the capitol and an additional square in each quadrant in detailed conformity with the Philadelphia model.[46]

Bardstown (fig. 10) probably had the first Lancaster-style square in Kentucky, where numerous examples are found (fig. 12).[47] It is less common in Tennessee; Elizabethton and Rogersville may be the earliest, but in neither is the square in the heart of town, and the dates are uncertain. The squares in the counties south of Nashville were originally central.[48]

Settlers took the Philadelphia square westward into Ohio, where it is often described, but with little justification, as a New England square. New England settlers may have found the Philadelphia square convenient for their purpose, but any New England character it developed must have been in the buildings and planting rather than in the ground plan. The map shows these squares not only in the Western Reserve but also in the United States and Virginia Military Tracts, in the Symmes Purchase, in old Scioto Company lands, and in Congressional lands in the northeastern and northwestern parts of the state. Cleveland (1796) may have had the first, a ten-acre square that held the 1813 courthouse in one of its quarters but only later became the city center.[49] Most of the Ohio squares do not now contain the courthouse, and some may never have done so.

Indiana has few of the Lancaster squares, but they were more numerous in Illinois. They seldom appeared anywhere after 1840 and are rare both in the Deep South and in the trans-Mississippi states.

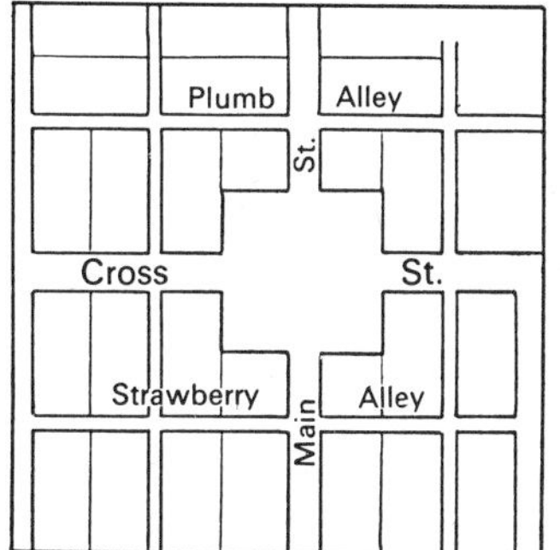

Figure 12. Part of Elizabethtown, Kentucky, redrawn from an 1835 copy of the original plat by Andrew Hynes. The 1805 courthouse stood in one quadrant of the square, but the 1872 courthouse, still extant, was sited in the middle of the square.

Development and Spread of the Block Square

The Shelbyville square (figs. 2a, 14, 15), so called from its prototype in Shelbyville, Tennessee, simply uses a block of the grid. It is simpler in concept than the Lancaster square and easier to lay out and is more frequently encountered. The earlier examples are tentative and unplanned. This cannot be because the plan of the square without the courthouse was radical or new. New Haven (1638) could have been the model; its huge square green, 825 feet on a side, central among nine blocks, was even dominated by a meetinghouse near the center.[50] The layout was almost duplicated in the unrealized plan of 1736 for the Swiss settlements of Eden in Virginia, but neither of these germs resulted in an epidemic.[51]

Powhatan, Virginia, was established under the name of Scottsville in 1777 by the General Assembly, which took the unique step of specifying its plan: six squares three hundred feet on a side, separated by one-hundred-foot-wide streets, one of the squares to be used for the public buildings.[52] Here is the block square, but no block can be central in a six-block town!

The block square sometimes developed even when no provision had been made for it. The public

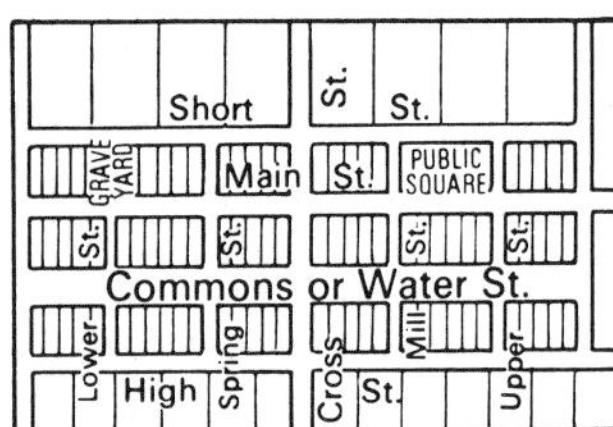

Figure 13. Part of Lexington, Kentucky, redrawn from a map of 1791 (reproduced as a frontispiece in Charles R. Staples, The History of Pioneer Lexington, 1779–1806 *[Lexington: Transylvania Press, 1939]). The town provided a corner lot for its first courthouse at Main Street and Main Cross; the 1788 courthouse was placed in the Public Square.*

square of Charlottesville, Virginia (1762), is described as having been originally outside the community and conceived as an English green with houses facing directly on it. By the 1820s it had been surrounded by streets, and business was collecting on its sides, but fifty years later business had concentrated on Main Street (a block removed from the square), where it is today.[53] Warrenton, North Carolina, platted in 1779 by the man who later planned Raleigh, gave the courthouse only a single lot across the end of a block.[54] The courthouse later received the place of honor in the center of the block, but business is all concentrated on the Main Street side of the square. The plan of Lexington, Kentucky (1780), was not at all symmetrical, but a traveler of 1796 could say, "A square is left at the central point, in the midst of which a court house is erected" (fig. 13).[55]

Nashville, Tennessee, was laid out on the bluff above the Cumberland River in 1784, but the original plan is missing. No marked symmetry seems ever to have characterized the arrangement of streets or buildings around its square, though this now has the city-county courthouse in its center. The South Carolina central squares tend to be irregular in shape and street plan. Although the visual effect of an irregular square is much like that of a regular one, the irregular squares must have developed by growth rather than from original plans. Laurens probably reflects more thoughtful planning than most of these squares.

In other towns the square was laid out as only part of a block, as little as a quarter or a sixth, and was later isolated as a separate block by cutting additional streets around its edges. Louisburg, North Carolina (1779); Washington, Georgia (1780); Winchester (1793), Georgetown (1796), and Cynthiana (1797), Kentucky; Springfield (1798) and Gallatin (1802), Tennessee; and Boydton, Virginia (1812), all seem to have had this history. Lebanon, Kentucky, has an unusual arrangement (fig. 11) that may be ancestral to some of these small squares.

Richmond, Kentucky, and West Union, Ohio, both platted in 1804, may have planned central courthouse squares, but these are marginal cases. The 1805 courthouse in West Union was placed on one lot of the square, hence probably not in the center, where the present courthouse is. The business district has grown around the square but is not large enough to enclose it. Corydon, Indiana (1808), for a time the state capital, approached the central plan but was probably not so conceived.

The first flowering of a group of planned central squares of the block type appears to have occurred

Figure 14. Central courthouse square of Princeton, Indiana, in 1969. (Courtesy of the Public Service Company of Indiana.)

Figure 15. Central courthouse square in Shelby, North Carolina. (Courtesy of the Willis Studio.)

in southern Middle Tennessee, following an 1806 cession of Indian lands (fig. 16). Shelbyville (figs. 17 and 18), Fayetteville, Pulaski, and Winchester (fig. 19), all laid out between 1810 and 1812, are today as nearly perfect examples of central courthouse squares as can be found. Huntsville, across the line in Alabama, is probably of about the same vintage. We must believe that local officials in these towns were exchanging ideas, perhaps through the mediation of legislators or surveyors.[56] The time to plan the already well-developed block square was ripe.

The Shelbyville square quickly became the most frequent county-seat plan in new counties in most states (figs. 20 and 21). The Lancaster type rarely appeared again except in Ohio, Indiana, and Illinois. Standardization and prosperity probably produced the Shelbyville square's greatest exuberance in Texas and the lower Middle West, with varying occurrence of larger squares, more massive courthouses, and more imposing store fronts. The fad eventually lost its momentum, but occasional county seats were laid out in the Shelbyville pattern up to at least 1900 (fig. 16).

Figure 16

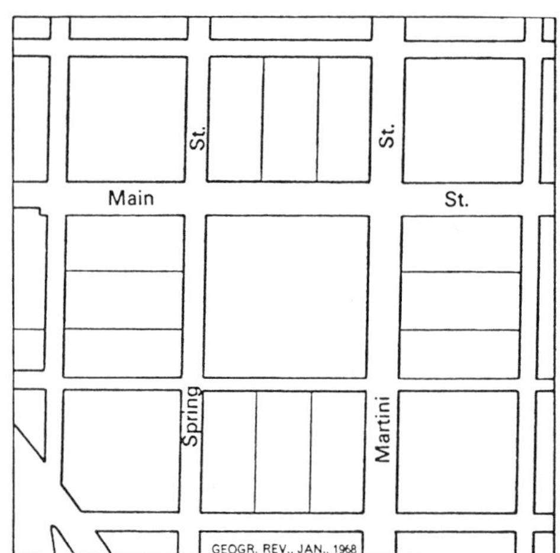

Figure 17. Part of Shelbyville, Tennessee, redrawn from an 1827 map of the original plat. Although the streets bounding the square are not uniform in width, the square is clearly the central focus.

Figure 18. The square and courthouse in Shelbyville, Tennessee.

Figure 19. The square and courthouse in Winchester, Tennessee.

Figure 20. This courthouse square in Lynchburg, Tennessee, dates from 1884. The town, much older, was rearranged after the county was formed in 1872.

Figure 21. Former Creek capitol in Okmulgee, Oklahoma, later the county courthouse, now a museum.

Other Central Courthouse Plans

Geometrically the Harrisonburg square lies halfway between the Lancaster and Shelbyville types (fig. 2c). The example at Harrisonburg, Virginia, may have been laid out in 1780.[57] If so, it precedes any planned block square and may be a variant of the Lancaster square. Other early examples are uncertain in date, often irregular in plan, and not always in the town centers. Possible appearances are Jefferson (1796) and Dublin (1812) in Georgia and Cambridge (1806), Chardon (1808), and Carrollton (1815) in Ohio. Later they are especially numerous in northern Georgia, where both the squares and the towns are usually small (Dahlonega, 1833; Ellijay, 1832). Examples occur in many other states, but with low frequency.

Perhaps the most lavish of the squares, combining features of both the block and the Philadelphia types, comprise four blocks (fig. 2d). A flurry of these appeared in the 1830s in county seats scattered from Georgia to Indiana and Texas. One town planner may have been involved in their dissemination.

Mention must be given the unusual example of Circleville, Ohio, laid out to conform with an ancient Indian earthwork. The circular "square," about four hundred feet in diameter, at the center of town was reached by eight radial streets, each

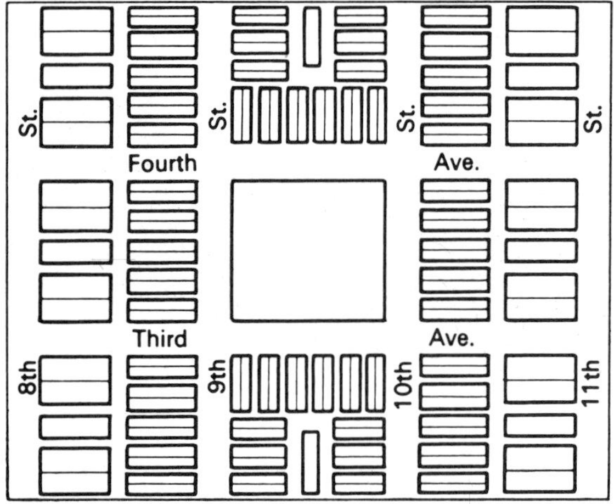

Figure 22. Part of Windom, Minnesota, redrawn from a plat of 1872. The courthouse did not reach the square until 1904, when merchants effected a swap of land between the county and the city, which formerly owned the square.

terminating opposite a side of the octagonal courthouse. Today, Circleville has a grid plan without a central square.[58]

One means of dramatizing the courthouse is a corner location at the town's principal intersection. Another is a position that blocks the view along the principal street, particularly effective when a hill site is available. The street-blocking square is convenient when a site is sought in an existing town.

The rarity of the central courthouse square in some regions is not readily explained. Restricted sites and slow or late development may account in part for scarcity in the mountain lands. For the dry plains north of Texas we may suggest the late date of settlement, sparse populations, and poor prospects. But the great void in the northern tier of states is a puzzle. If New York was a little early for the central square to be in style, and Montana a little late, what about the Upper Lake states and the Dakotas? Is this the sphere of New England, rather than Middle Colony, influence? Yes, but why were central squares rejected while the major features of county government and other settlement forms that went with it were accepted? In fact, the block square with the courthouse in its center was widely accepted in the western part of the north; only its placement in the center of town was rejected. Perhaps the towns were established before the counties? This often happened, especially when the county seat was moved, but the common hope for a new town was to make it a county seat. There are other possibilities. The town built to face a railroad could not well focus on a square. Severe winters gave greater advantage to a compact shopping district than to a central square, but if such reasoning motivated the planners, why did they not design the whole town on a more compact scale? All the conjectures seem insufficient to explain the failure of the central courthouse square to be accepted in the north—with rare exceptions, such as Windom, Minnesota (fig. 22), laid out by a railroad company. The problem is only shifted in time by evidence that a few towns began with central squares but later gave them up or changed them.

Change on the Square: Plan and Elevation

Original town plats that survive for our scrutiny are gaunt two-dimensional projections of elaborate three-dimensional dreams, which could be made real only by those who built the town. We are not told what townscapes the planner visualized as he drew out streets, blocks, and lots. Central courthouse squares formed as they became fixed in the minds of the townspeople as the proper arrangement of the town center.

The usual plat of a county seat specified the location neither of the courthouse nor of the business establishments. Often the first courthouse was constructed on a corner of the square or on a lot across the street. I believe the central place was thus saved for the permanent building that was to follow. The courthouse was often moved when an old courthouse had to be replaced; there are clear advantages in completing a new building before tearing down the old one. When a courthouse burns, it is more likely that the new courthouse will be erected on the same spot.

The subdivision of blocks into lots sometimes

gives a hint of the plans for the square. Early plats in the eastern colonies usually divided the block into four lots by bisecting it each way.[59] Trans-Appalachian plans usually divided the block into two rows of elongated lots separated by an alley. Only after 1850 was it common to identify the planned business center by laying off lots narrower than those provided in residential areas (fig. 22). Often the central square was given special deference by orienting the lots in the four bordering blocks to face it (figs. 17 and 22), even when all the other lots in the town ran in one direction, either north–south or east–west. In the original sale of lots those facing the square were tagged with the highest prices and were the first to sell.

Given the usual ability of a business district to develop and grow in the places most desirable for it, what determined whether it grew around the square? The courthouse was a magnet that attracted many people, and first businesses obviously gained from being near it. As the number of businesses grew, the business community itself became a magnet, and the importance of location near the courthouse declined. Each merchant, banker, or restaurant owner had to choose among the sites available. If a site on the square met the popular idea of a desirable location, then we should expect the stores to spread around the four sides of the square. If Main Street or a pair of main cross streets accorded with the community image, then we should expect the square to be off-center. A favorable town plat was a great help in the development of a central square, but it was neither sufficient nor necessary for that development. In many county seats today we can see the main street and courthouse square in a continuing struggle, two town concepts competing for stores and customers.[60] No doubt the automobile encouraged the main street development in towns where the highway ran along one side of the square. It may have reversed an older tendency of business to expand around the square.

An earlier competitor of the square was, of course, the railroad. Whiteville, North Carolina, has its downtown on Main Street, which runs beside the Atlantic Coast Line tracks; a mile away is an uptown with a few stores facing a courthouse on a Lancaster square, whose radiating streets—Washington, Jefferson, Madison, and Pinckney—name the statesmen heroes of the town's founders in 1810.

The original plat of a square did not determine its subsequent landscaping. Many early squares were not cleared of trees for decades. Some cleared squares presented a bare unpaved surface without curbs or other markers of the edges of the traffic ways. Then, as the courthouse was surrounded with a picket fence, trees were replanted, either parklike in the courthouse yard or in neat rows bordering the sides of the street. Soldiers on pedestals commemorated successive wars. Paving the streets and sidewalks and edging them with stone or concrete curbs gave the square a clearer geometry. Depending on the placement of curbs, a square of the Philadelphia type may appear as an undifferentiated rectangular open space, a square block surrounded by streets, a round block surrounded by streets, four small blocks surrounded by streets, or a simple street intersection with grassy lots at its four corners.

The store buildings, originally of wood, were small and separated. Gradually they crowded together to enclose the square with their composite facade. The typical buildings surrounding the square are still late nineteenth-century, two-story, flat-roof brick structures, distinguished by the repetitive Victorian trim of the windows and cornices, somber reflections of the grandeur sought in the courthouse opposite. Many of these old buildings, by controlling the discordant commercial signs that now cover them, could be tidied up as witnesses of their time.

The eclectic courthouse architecture far exceeds the design of the square in variety and complexity. The figure of the county was expressed by a professional city architect especially chosen (by laymen!) for the purpose. Unhappily the maintenance of the grand structure often testifies to the dingy parsimony considered appropriate in the expenditure of current tax dollars. Harrisonburg, Virginia, epitomizes the changing courthouse modes over most of the country. The 1784 courthouse was "of square Logs with diamond Corners Thirty feet long by 20 feet Wide." The 1833 courthouse was a modest rectangular brick building with a hipped roof and a simple louvered wooden cupola at its crest. In 1874 came a rectangular building with gabled ends, in front a pronaos with Greek columns and a cupola provided with a clock. The 1897 courthouse was more massive and ornate, typical of many baroque or Victorian styles that survive to the present.[61] As courthouses are replaced, the new buildings tend to more modern styles (fig. 19). Courthouse architecture often matches the symmetry of the central square with facades and entrances impartially placed on four sides, or at least on two opposite sides.[62]

Perhaps the newest county seat in the country is Eddyville, Kentucky, recently relocated in expectation of the rising waters behind the Barkley Dam. It preserves some of the traditional elements of the courthouse town (fig. 23).

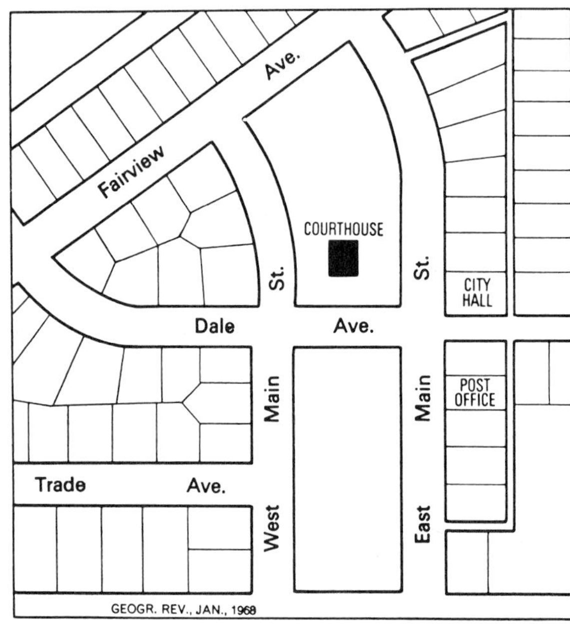

Figure 23. Plan of Eddyville, Kentucky, redrawn from original design by Barge, Waggoner, Sumner, 1959. The square, flat-roofed, one-story courthouse occupies a high point.

Change on the Square: Function

Taverns, stores, workshops, dwellings, and churches occupied almost indiscriminately the lots facing the log courthouse of the pioneer county seat. The square itself long welcomed informal marketing. Farmers sold their produce, horses and mules were traded, and itinerant salesmen set up their stands. The business today is almost entirely in the hands of permanent establishments. The larger the town, the more specialized will be the business on the square, but the square seldom survives as the center of a town that has grown beyond twenty-five thousand. Grocery stores have been leaving crowded squares for a long time, seeking convenient neighborhood locations with room for parking. More surprising is the recent move of many banks from their pillared strongholds on the square to more spacious drive-in quarters.

The early square was the terminus of roads coming in from the county and a parking space for the clumsy horse-drawn conveyances then in use. The automobile greatly increased the traffic that the same roads brought through the square. Today bypass routes are rapidly separating the through traffic from the county traffic. The open space of the square is more and more utilized for parking, often with four rows of cars on each side, even if the courthouse grounds have had to be trimmed to make room. If the courthouse has been removed, even more parking space is available.

Automobile congestion is one reason for some decline in the role of the square as a social center. The square brings together those who work there, those who come to do business, and those who come merely to visit and loaf. The square provides more room for socializing and a more attractive setting than a downtown devoted only to business and traffic. And it belongs to everybody. Different sides of the square often became the meeting places for different social groups on court and market days. The courthouse was once the only meetinghouse in the town, and its grounds were the scene of the county fair and the Fourth of July celebration. Even now, on a Sunday or in the evening the younger crowd may hang around the drugstore or, on a drive, make a loop around the square on the chance of finding another group in the same maneuver.

The central courthouse square is still widely accepted as the proper order of things. "We wouldn't want our town any other way" is a common evaluation. But impetus for change arises when the square becomes congested, most often when its dimensions are small. Many squares on the Lancaster design were formed by cutting very small corners out of the adjoining blocks. The square is left with inadequate room for the town's business, and the press of traffic makes the pedestrian's progress slow and frustrating. Congestion can lead to migration of business, to opening of self-contained shopping centers elsewhere, to decay of buildings that the owners hesitate to repair or replace, and even to removal of the courthouse.

I have seen only one recent effort to recapture some of the old use of the space reserved in the square. In Canton, Ohio, the square is a two-block widened main street; the courthouse faces this square at its principal intersection. The city has recently paved and planted a central strip of the square in colorful modern style and provided an indoor-outdoor cafe, an exhibit hall, and outdoor assembly space. Central placement of the courthouse would put some obstacles in the way of similar developments elsewhere, but they may not be more difficult than the problem in Canton.

The Meaning of the Square

The place of the courthouse square in American consciousness still awaits its interpreter. Two novels of the 1930s were titled *Court House Square,* but like Sinclair Lewis's *Main Street* before them, the square was only a symbol for the town with which the book really dealt.[63] The square is often taken for granted in American novels as simply a place where things happen. Friend meets friend. A mob gathers. A plot is hatched. Gossip is exchanged. Goods are purchased. Vehicles approach their destinations.

A few writers have given the square more consideration. William Faulkner's characters frequent the square of Jefferson: "A Square, the courthouse in its grove the center; quadrangular around it, the stores, two-storey, the offices of the lawyers and doctors . . . each in its ordered place; the four broad diverging avenues . . . becoming the network of roads and by-roads . . . . But above all the courthouse: the center, the focus, the hub; sitting looming in the center of the county's circumference . . . protector of the weak, judiciate and curb of the passions and lusts, repository and guardian of the aspirations and hopes."[64]

In *Raintree County,* Ross Lockridge writes of Freehaven: "The four walls of the Square were holed with a hundred immutable doors to a hundred immutable desires. The old pomps and prohibitions of Raintree County were enacted into the shapes of this enclosure. . . . In the years when there was no courthouse in the middle of the Square, Esther and everyone else had felt as if a sacred object containing the innermost meaning of life in Raintree County had lost its tabernacle. But as the New Court House had begun to rise, slowly the feeling of security returned. . . . Somewhere in these odorous, secret rooms reposed the State."[65]

Conrad Arensberg, an anthropologist, sees the county seat in the South as the rural counterpart of the baroque capital, where "assembled planter and field- or house-hand from the fat plantations, free poor white or Negro from the lean hills and swamps, for the pageantry and drama of Saturdays around the courthouse . . . cynosure of all eyes, seat and power of decision, repository of land grants and commercial debt-bonds."[66]

Faulkner, Lockridge, and Arensberg agree on the primary importance of the courthouse in the ensemble of the square, but they attribute to it different, and really antithetical, meanings. They also attribute different meanings to the square, but here the different qualities are complementary. Variety is the genius of the square, in an interweaving of form, meaning, and function.

The square seems to violate the rule that a downtown devote its prime space to only certain kinds of business.[67] The returns of the square are not only from private profit but also from government and government services placed in a spot of maximum accessibility, esteem, and scrutiny; from its aesthetic charms, even caught in the midst of mundane errands; from its promotion of social contact; and from an increased sense of civic pride for residents of town and county alike. The true intensiveness of the land use is the whole made up of all the economic, political, aesthetic, and social gains, each evaluated in its own currency. In its multivalue system the central courthouse square may give priority to location-sensitive, high-return activities. A courthouse conceived in the ways suggested can conform to this theory of location, no matter how monopolistic and small its business may be. If this square design makes the community a better place to live, there are benefits for the individual citizen. We need not draw on the special community interest and fetishism rooted in the past that Firey emphasizes in his explanation of the survival of Boston Common in a high-value area.[68] The appeal of the square lies in its meaning of many things to everybody.[69]

The geometry of the square is not merely symbolic. It governs the access to the various stores and offices in their places around it. Their clustering or scattering guides the steps of those who seek their goods. He who wishes to reach the square must follow the course of its streets, north and south, east and west. The courthouse is entered by its gates and doors, lined up with the center of the square. The square recapitulates the history of the town. The courthouse was its reason for being, its first central function, the seat of its creator. Even had no town been laid off, a community of businesses and residents would have gathered around it.

What deeper human demands the form of the square satisfies through its symmetry and symbolism I cannot tell. The cozy enclosure may suggest security from a variety of threats. The edifice of government in a cavity surrounded by business may be given its own meaning. The nuclear functions of town and county are embodied in a nuclear frame: in the center the cupolated tower with its four-faced clock striking the hours; then the courthouse building; the unbuilt void with its park, fence, and circulation lines; the town's business district; the residential part of the town; finally the rural county. All these are linked together, not least by the "four broad diverging avenues."

Arensberg is at least partly right in his interpretation of the central courthouse square in the South as serving the power of the planters. But the origin of the form in Pennsylvania and its eventual spread into the Middle West suggest that it can equally serve other societies. If one man sees in it the power of his wealthy superiors, another in a more democratic society can see in it his own power. Work of art or natural resource—the beholder and user complete its meaning!

Like the Spanish-American plaza, the central courthouse square is a design uncommon in the mother countries from which the settlers came. Unlike the plaza, it was not the product of bureaucratic order, but an expression of pioneer pride on the frontier of a burgeoning civilization. It withstood the preemption of the town center on the part of business, which for a time found the square a tool it could use. We find a satisfying order in comparing the dispersal of central squares and their subtypes with the main routes of settlers.[70]

Notes

This article was originally published in the *Geographical Review* (January 1968).

1. Altogether, data on more than a thousand county seats have been compiled. About three hundred were visited during the summers of 1964 and 1965, some in all the states of the study area except New York, New Jersey, Delaware, West Virginia, Michigan, and Florida. Libraries and local historians were consulted

in many of the places visited. County and state records and numerous county histories and county atlases were also consulted. Leon E. Seltzer, ed., *The Columbia Lippincott Gazetteer of the World* (New York: Columbia University Press, 1952), proved a rich, if spotty, source of dates on town foundings. Joseph Nathan Kane, *The American Counties* (New York: Scarecrow Press, 1960), has useful data on county origins.

At best the topographic history of most towns is difficult to reconstruct, and analysis of most squares has to be based partly on inference. Although this process may have led to an occasional error in individual towns, the main conclusions of the study seem statistically safe. But information from counties not tapped in the present sample could modify conclusions about origins of particular traits. More intensive, state-by-state study is to be encouraged as the way to greater refinement of knowledge on the subject.

2. Figures 3, 4, and 5 show courthouse squares, graded in accordance with their conformity to the definition of "central courthouse squares," for a sample of about 25 percent of the counties in each state between New England and the Rocky Mountains. The sample is random with respect to type of square, stratified to obtain reasonably uniform areal coverage, and biased by unevenness of available information and by some scarcity of very small and very large towns. The data are taken primarily from insurance maps of the Sanborn Map Company, usually the latest edition available at the Library of Congress. Their dates differ but most typically belong to the 1920s and 1930s. The Sanborn maps usually do not cover the very small towns.
3. Paul Zucker, *Town and Square* (New York: Columbia University Press, 1959). The picture of Hammerstein, plate 19b, closely duplicates the block-square plan as it must have appeared in many an American county seat between 1820 and 1860.
4. Ibid., p. 79.
5. Herbert Schlenger, "Schlesiens Kulturlandschaften," in Karl Pagel, ed., *Deutsche Heimat in Osten* (Berlin: K. Lemmer, 1951), pp. 103–17; photograph of Prausnitz on p. 113.
6. Conversation with Andrzej Wrobel, 1965.
7. Gilbert Camblin, *The Town in Ulster* (Belfast: W. Mullan, 1951), pp. 17, 31.
8. Ibid., plate 5; Robert Common, ed., *Northern Ireland from the Air* (Belfast: Queen's University, 1964), pp. 48–49; Samuel Lewis, *A Topographical Dictionary of Ireland,* 2 vols. (London: S. Lewis, 1846), 2:265.
9. Camblin, *The Town in Ulster,* plates 4, 37; Lewis, *A Topographical Dictionary of Ireland,* 1:373.
10. The reasons are detailed in one petition: "That by reason of their great distance from ye County Town, where Courts are held; Offices are kept and annual elections made, they lie under very great Inconveniences being obliged in the recovery of their just Debts to travel near One Hundred Miles to obtain a Writ; that for want of a sufficient number of Justices, Constables, and other Officers in those parts, no care is taken of ye highways; Townships are not laid out nor bridges built when there is an apparent Necessity for them; and, further, that for want of a Gaol there several Vagabonds and other Dissolute people harbor among them, thinking themselves safe from Justice in so remote a Place." Quoted in Franklin Ellis and Samuel Evans, *History of Lancaster County, Pennsylvania* (Philadelphia: Everts and Peck, 1883), p. 24.
11. Quoted in Alexander Brown, *The Genesis of the United States,* 2 vols. (Boston: Houghton Mifflin: 1890), 1:84.
12. John W. Reps, *The Making of Urban America* (Princeton: Princeton University Press, 1965), p. 96. In this monumental history of American city planning Reps has brought together much background material useful for the present study.
13. "The Frenchman's Map of Williamsburg, Virginia" (facsimile edition, Williamsburg, 1945; original believed to be 1781–82); *The Official Guidebook of Colonial Williamsburg* (Williamsburg: Colonial Williamsburg, 1951), pp. 48, 92.
14. *Old Homes of Essex County* (Fredericksburg, Va.: Essex County Woman's Club, 1940), p. 6.
15. Mary Wiatt Gray, *Gloucester County* (Richmond, Va.: Cottrell and Cooke, 1936), p. 86.
16. Sometimes the landowner who donated the public square operated the tavern. This practice parallels that in eastern Germany in which the *Lokator* received the right to operate the tavern in the new village; see Ervin A. Gutkind, *International History of City Development* (New York: Free Press, 1964), p. 103.
17. Maps by Claude Joseph Sauthier, examined in the University of North Carolina Library, Chapel Hill.
18. Copy of plat from Deed Book 9, pp. 345–46, displayed in the Public Library, Greensboro.
19. Ethel Stephens Arnett, *Greensboro, North Carolina* (Chapel Hill: University of North Carolina Press, 1955), pp. 51–56.
20. Reps, *The Making of Urban America,* p. 162.

21. Ibid., p. 174; Wilbur Zelinsky, "Research Memorandum on the Settlement Geography of Older Anglo-America," unpublished manuscript, pp. 54–55.
22. Reps, *The Making of Urban America,* p. 174.
23. William Penn, "Letter from William Penn to the Committee of the Free Society of Traders, 1683," in Albert Cook Myers, ed., *Narratives of Early Pennsylvania, West New Jersey, and Delaware, 1630–1707* (New York: C. Scribner's Sons, 1912), p. 243.
24. Reps, *The Making of Urban America,* p. 166. The plan was apparently done ca. 1720.
25. Chester, laid out in 1686, has a Philadelphia square, but the 1724 courthouse is neither in nor on it. W.P.A. Writers' Program, *Pennsylvania: A Guide to the Keystone State* (New York: Oxford University Press, 1940), p. 205.
26. Ellis and Evans, *History of Lancaster County,* pp. 24, 203–6.
27. George R. Prowell, *History of York County, Pennsylvania* (Chicago: J. H. Beers, 1907), pp. 291, 577.
28. *Pennsylvania: A Guide to the Keystone State,* p. 198.
29. Morton L. Montgomery, *Historical and Biographical Annals of Berks County, Pennsylvania,* 2 vols. (Chicago: J. H. Beers, 1909), 1:86–87, 153.
30. Ellis and Evans, *History of Lancaster County,* pp. 27, 764.
31. Use of the term *diamond* for *square* in Pennsylvania, first pointed out to me by Wilbur Zelinsky, further knits the ties with Ulster. Outside Pennsylvania and Ulster the only occurrence of *diamond* of which I am aware is on the original plat of Cleveland, Ohio.
32. Viola C. Floyd, *Lancaster County Tours* (Lancaster, S.C.: Lancaster County Historical Commission, 1956), p. 15.
33. Personal conversation with Forrest Calico, July 1965.
34. Forrest Calico, *History of Garrard County, Kentucky* (New York: Hobson Book Press, 1947), pp. 61–63.
35. H. E. Rawlins, *History of the City of Lancaster (Texas)* (mimeographed, 1945).
36. Charles C. Miller, *History of Fairfield, Ohio* (Chicago: Richmond-Arnold Publishing, 1912), pp. 102–4.
37. Plat of Lancaster, Ohio, Deed Book A, item 24 (1801).
38. A. A. Graham, *History of Fairfield and Perry Counties, Ohio* (Chicago: W. H. Beers, 1883), pp. 77, 135.
39. Quoted in Maurice Mathews, "A Contemporary View of Carolina in 1680," *South Carolina Historical Magazine* 55, no. 3 (July 1954): 154.
40. Frederic R. Stevenson, "Charleston and Savannah," *Journal of the Society of Architectural Historians* 10, no. 4 (December 1951): 3–9.
41. Edward Boltwodd Hull, *Guide-Book of Camden* (Camden, S.C.: E. B. Hull, 1918), pp. 10, 25, 31. The present business center of Camden is about six blocks from the old square. Fires were one reason for the move.
42. W.P.A. Writers' Program, *A History of Spartanburg County* (Spartanburg, S.C.: Band and White, 1940); 1802 shown on front endpaper. The present plan of Spartanburg is less regular.
43. Charles W. Crush, *The Montgomery County Story, 1776–1957* (n.p., 1957), pp. 145, 147.
44. Reps, *The Making of Urban America,* pp. 444, 448.
45. Walter Clark, ed., *The State Records of North Carolina,* 26 vols. (Raleigh: P. M. Hale, 1905), 24:513, 695.
46. Reps, *The Making of Urban America,* p. 174.
47. Nora L. McGee, *Tales of Old Bardstown* (Bardstown Woman's Club, ca. 1920), pp. 5, 8; Matt Spalding, *Bardstown: Town of Tradition* (Louisville, Ky.: M. Spalding, 1942), p. 2.
48. Lebanon, Tennessee, and Lebanon, Ohio, very likely have affinities with Lebanon, Pennsylvania, though the Philadelphia square of the last has not held the courthouse and is unusually narrow, the corners cut out of the four blocks, measuring 200 by 15 feet.
49. Edmund H. Chapman, *Cleveland: Village to Metropolis* (Cleveland: Western Reserve Historical Society, 1964), pp. 4, 11, 13.
50. Reps, *The Making of Urban America,* pp. 128–29.
51. Ibid., p. 102.
52. William Waller Hening, *Statutes at Large (Laws of Virginia),* 13 vols. (Richmond and Philadelphia: J. and G. Cochran, 1823), 9:322.
53. Mary Rawlings, *Ante-Bellum Albemarle* (Charlottesville, Va.: Peoples National Bank, 1935), p. 34; James Alexander, *Early Charlottesville: Recollections of James Alexander, 1828–1874,* ed. Mary Rawlings (Charlottesville: Michie, 1942), pp. 1, 24–25.
54. Original plat of Warrenton, in possession of Miss Miriam Boyd; Lizzie Wilson Montgomery, *Sketches of Old Warrenton* (Raleigh: Edwards and Broughton, 1924), p. 7.
55. Victor Collot, *A Journey in North America, 1826,* quoted in Charles R. Staples, *The History of Pioneer Lexington, 1779–1806* (Lexington: Transylvania Press, 1939), p. 124.
56. The law establishing Lincoln County (Fayetteville) gave the commissioners power to "procure" 100 acres of land and to "cause a town to be laid off thereon, reserving *near the center* thereof a public square of two acres, on which the courthouse and stocks shall be built, likewise reserving a lot in any *other* portion of said town for purposes of erecting a

jail . . ." (emphasis added), quoted in W. A. Goodspeed, et al., *History of Tennessee (with sketches of Lincoln and other counties)* (Nashville: Goodspeed Publishing, 1886), p. 770. Thus the legislators seemed to envision a central square with a courthouse on it and to recognize the square as a place unsuitable for a jail, which detracts from the charm of the squares in many other states. In early Nashville citizens had petitioned to have the jail removed from the square for reasons of sanitation. In the case of Pulaski the legislation specified an auction of the town lots, the proceeds to be used for the construction of the courthouse.

57. John W. Wayland, *A History of Rockingham County* (Dayton, Va.: Ruebush-Elkins, 1912), pp. 74–75.
58. Reps, *The Making of Urban America,* pp. 484–90.
59. The same plan of lots was common in the early Argentine towns (information from manuscript prepared by Melvin Droubay, University of Oregon, 1966).
60. Lewis Atherton suggested in *Main Street on the Middle Border* (Bloomington: Indiana University Press, 1954), p. 29, that "if the dream of becoming a county seat failed, the central square became . . . an unsightly weed patch and dumping ground, and the disappointed town straggled off along a Main Street as if to hide from its former ambitions."
61. Wayland, *A History of Rockingham County,* pp. 64, 79.
62. The original courthouse in Shelbyville, Indiana, was provided with only one door, on the west side. A few years later a newly elected sheriff had a door cut on the north side at county expense to give convenient access to his business property. Still later another faction provided, at its own expense, a door on the south side to reach the property of some of its members.
63. Hamilton Basso, *Court House Square* (New York: C. Scribner's Sons, 1936), and Phil LaMar Anderson, *Court House Square* (Minneapolis: Augsburg Publishing, 1934).
64. William Faulkner, *Requiem for a Nun* (New York: Random House, 1951), pp. 39–40.
65. Ross Lockridge, *Raintree County* (Boston: Houghton Mifflin, 1948), pp. 118, 380–81.
66. "American Communities," *American Anthropologist* 57, no. 6 (December 1955): 1151–52.
67. Everett G. Smith points out the question of the business district versus the multifunctional downtown in *Downtown Change in Three Middle-Sized Cities* (Urbana: University of Illinois Press, 1964), pp. 1, 84.
68. Walter Firey, *Land Use in Central Boston* (Cambridge: Harvard University Press, 1947), pp. 138–54.
69. Edward T. Hall, *The Hidden Dimension* (New York: Doubleday, 1966), p. 163, suggests, however, that the American prefers one thing at a time rather than mixing several activities (polychronism): "The Spanish plaza and the Italian piazza serve both involvement and polychronic functions, whereas the strung-out Main Street so characteristic of the United States reflects not only our structuring of time, but our lack of involvement with others." If he is right that the square does not serve the American style, we should not be surprised that squares are not fully utilized, and we should not expect them to be defended if they interfere with traffic and trade.
70. See the maps showing the dispersal of certain house types and building techniques in Fred B. Kniffen, "Folk Housing: Key to Diffusion," *Annals of the Association of American Geographers* 55, no. 4 (December 1965): 560, fig. 11 (reprinted in this volume); and Fred B. Kniffen and Henry Glassie, "Building in Wood in the Eastern United States: A Time-Place Perspective," *Geographical Review* 56, no. 1 (January 1966): 60, fig. 27 (reprinted in this volume). The maps could be used, with only some changes in detail, to show the main flow of ideas of the design of courthouse squares.

Part Two Construction

Early Rhode Island Houses

NORMAN MORRISON ISHAM AND
ALBERT F. BROWN

Although recent students of vernacular architecture have considered the formal qualities of buildings to be their most significant ones, interest in vernacular building technologies is as old as the study of vernacular architecture itself. Building systems are intrinsically interesting and they are important tools for understanding the changes in plan and elevation that individual buildings have undergone as well, as the following excerpts from Norman Morrison Isham and Albert F. Brown's classic Early Rhode Island Houses: An Historical and Architectural Study *(1895) show.*

Most of the earliest houses in Rhode Island had been heavily altered by the late nineteenth century, and Isham and Brown had to do considerable detective work to establish the buildings' seventeenth-century plans and elevations. Many of their conclusions were based on the meticulous examination of the framing of the houses. From the careful observation of tell tale mortises and peg holes and other evidence of missing parts, they were able to understand how buildings went together. They were consequently able to determine what were and what were not plausible early forms for each building.

From their technological observations, Isham and Brown compiled a descriptive chronology of early Rhode Island building. They assumed a gradual evolution from small houses to larger ones, paralleling Rhode Island's economic growth. They were particularly interested in a peculiar kind of late seventeenth-century house known locally as a "stone ender," in recognition of its most striking visual feature. Isham and Brown saw this distinctive house type as evidence of Rhode Island's seventeenth-century isolation, and they interpreted its eighteenth-century abandonment as a sign of growing prosperity and integration into New England society. Yet the architects were careful not to let any grand scheme obscure what they observed in the buildings. Their summary chart (fig. 1) is not "logical" because Rhode Island's seventeenth-century architectural history was not logical.

Early Rhode Island Houses *was the first scholarly work on American vernacular architecture. While contemporary scholars may disagree with some details of Isham and Brown's account—no one now believes that the first Rhode Island colonists lived in log houses, for example—their work has not been surpassed in its field methodology, its attempt to describe a larger pattern of historical change, its careful consideration of building technology, or its use of measured plans and drawings. Reprinted below are an excerpt from the preface that outlines the authors' methods, a description of the chronology of seventeenth-century Rhode Island architecture, and analyses of two houses. One, the Eleazer Arnold House in Lincoln, is a museum of the Society for the Preservation of New England Antiquities.*

Scope and Method of the Work

This essay is the result of much observation and study of the early colonial work in Rhode Island. Yet it can hardly be said to have exhausted even so small a subject as this would seem to be; however, we claim for it considerable accuracy, and whatever may be the reader's opinion of the theories put forth in the text, he may rest assured that the drawings are veritable historical data. Every plan, elevation and section is based upon measurements of the house it illustrates; and the perspectives are made—two from pencil sketches made on the spot, the rest of the number from photographs.

We have thus personally examined, sometimes from garret to cellar, every house described, and our thanks are most heartily tendered to the courteous owners and occupants who allowed us to explore, measure and sketch at our leisure, and often shared our enthusiasm.

We hope that this essay will be a help to the future historians of New England and that it will promote the collection of scientific data about the oldest houses in the original New England colonies, so that the vague descriptions of too many of our town histories may be supplemented by accurate measured drawings.

The Early History of Rhode Island's Architecture

The obscurity of early Rhode Island history is well known. There was no historian, not even a diarist of any account, and the separation of church and state deprives us of church records. The public records are rather brief and fragmentary, and are full of gaps; and the meagreness of their references to building—for the probate inventories do not begin till comparatively late—makes it difficult to gather from contemporary evidence of what kind were the houses of the earliest settlers. When we say of any house now standing that it was built before King Philip's War, we cannot stand prepared to prove our statement with documents signed, sealed, and witnessed. Nevertheless it is fairly well known of what sort these early houses were, and we shall make the First Period of the three into which we intend to divide the chronology of the subject extend to 1675, the date of the Indian War. The Second Period extends from 1675 to 1700. The Third Period, the last of our divisions, brings us down to 1725–30, when the old forms of construction were abandoned, or rather were transformed, and the pre-Revolutionary style began—a style more easily recognized as "Colonial," and closely akin to that of the great houses which from 1750 to the end of the century gave its peculiar architectural character to the Atlantic seaboard.

These periods are not so arbitrary as they look. The war with King Philip was one of extermination on both sides. Its successful end marked a great step in colonial progress. Security was assured; the Indian question was settled in Eastern New England. From now on the outlying settlements in the Plantations grew stronger. Again, it was about the beginning of the eighteenth century that occurred the significant change in the habits of the good towns-people which turned them from agriculture to sea-traffic and brought in the wealth and the wider ideas which, acting with the weakening of the old traditions under successive apprentices, destroyed the almost medieval types of the old craftsmen, and substituted, not all at once, of course, work akin to the classic models with which Chambers afterward made men so familiar.

The first houses of Providence, built around the spring near where St. John's Church now stands, were no doubt of logs halved together at the corners, and contained but one room roofed with other logs, or with bark or thatch on poles. The chimney, if there was one—for the settlement was made in the early summer when cooking could be done out of doors—was probably also of logs, on the outside of the house, at one end, and like the house was plastered with clay. But these huts were only temporary. The news of the founding of a new settlement soon attracted those who through tenderness of conscience or through contumacious disposition could no longer dwell with peace and comfort in the Colony of the Bay. With the immigrants came craftsmen, if indeed they were not among the original few; and perhaps as winter came on the new plantation of Providence began to have more substantial dwellings, akin to what Roger Williams called an "English house."[1]

The houses which succeeded log huts did not differ from them in plan. They contained only a single room, the "Fire Room," one end of which was almost entirely taken up by a huge stone chimney with its cavernous fireplace.[2] Beside the fireplace, in the corner of the room was the staircase—little, if anything, better than a ladder—which led to the "chamber" above; for few of these houses were more than a story and a half high. A glance at figure 1a will show this arrangement, and also will give in 1b, the plan in vogue in the colony of Connecticut, and in 1e, that common in Salem. It will be noticed that a Rhode Island plan is just the half of one of those in vogue among our early neighbors of Connecticut, and so it remained until nearly 1730. Nor did this earlier form, which we have just described, undergo, as far as can be seen, any modifications except the lean-to, before King Philip's War. More than that, it lived on for some years side by side with a later form, which we shall next describe.

After the close of the Indian War some of the burned houses were rebuilt on the same primitive lines, but in a few years the increased sense of security and the greater wealth which now prevailed brought about a change. The older houses were added to, partly by the lean-to, partly by lengthening at the end away from the chimney. This probably took place very early, and was not confined to any one time. But the main characteristic of the second period is the construction, under one roof, with a lean-to and with or without additions at the end away from the chimney, of houses whose plan is given at fig. 1c; and the difference which marks the third period, which sometimes contains houses of the plan of the first, but mostly of the second, is that the houses are often of two full stories and the chimneys are partly or wholly of brick.

Beyond the third period, or beyond 1725, the transition is rapid, but it takes two directions. From 1c, which with brick chimney is practically the plan of the old Crawford house at the corner of North Main and Mill streets, the step is easy to the plan at 1d, which is that of the Brown house, all of brick, on the grounds of Butler Hospital. It is also a very common disposition of an end-chimney, when an old house has been lengthened, as mentioned above, at the end opposite the original chimney. But this form seems never to have been developed further. Another, and a more convenient, supplanted it, and it was only after many years that it reappears, and then it does not have its original form; it is rather a fresh discovery.

In figure 1f, we have this supplanting form. The chimney is now in the middle or nearly so, as for a time at least the original single room is larger than the room which was added at *R*. In many old houses, notably in the Tillinghast House on South Main Street, built probably about 1730, the "great room," the descendant of the single room in the ancient houses, as they were the descendants of the old English "hall," has two windows, while that on the opposite side of the chimney has but one. The staircase, it will be noted, has not changed its place—it is still next to the chimney in the same

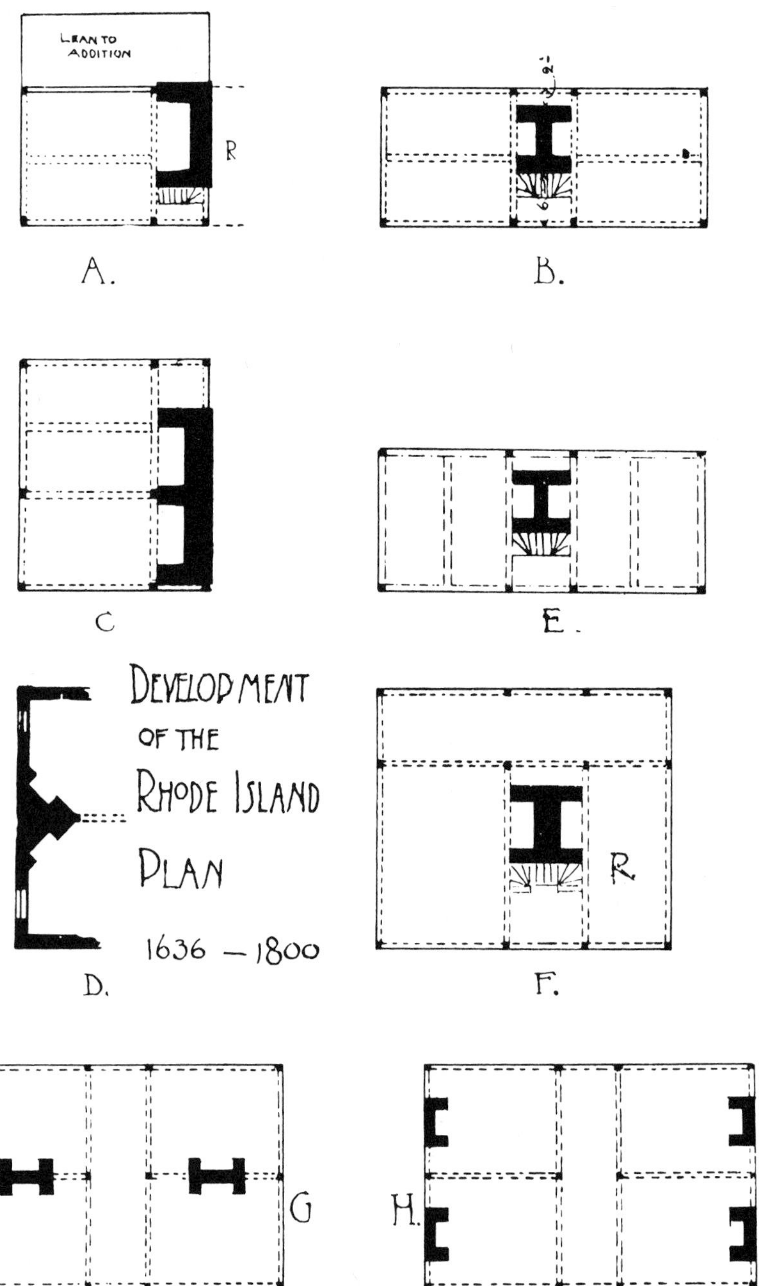

Figure 1. Development of the Rhode Island plan, 1636–1800.

relation to the old room as before; and the door, which in some old houses opened upon the stairs, has been brought naturally into the centre of the new front, without changing its old location.

Soon the two rooms became equal, with the chimney still in the centre, and now nothing except detail distinguishes the Rhode Island house from those of the neighboring colonies. Next, each room had its chimney (fig. 1g) and the hall ran through the house. Finally, at the end of the eighteenth and the beginning of the nineteenth century, each of the four rooms has its fireplace (fig. 1h) and these are in the wall again.

This broad classification generalizes the architectural history of Rhode Island. With its later forms this essay has nothing to do, except incidentally.

Figure 2. The Roger Mowry House, Providence, Rhode Island.

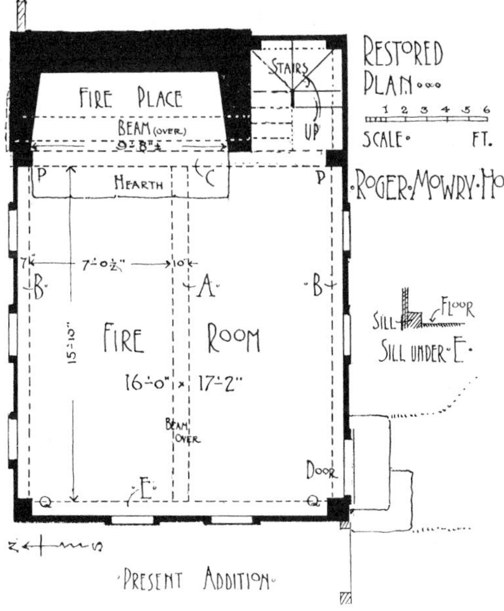

Figure 3. Restored plan of the Roger Mowry House.

Two Rhode Island Houses

THE ROGER MOWRY HOUSE

When we turn to the existing house and remnant of a house which claim the long descent from the middle of the seventeenth century, we find that the houses of that date were, as far as these examples show, all single-roomed, story-and-a-half structures with a huge stone chimney at one end. We have only two examples to appeal to, and of these only one is now standing. In the case of this one, however—the so-called Whipple or Abbott House on Abbott Street near the North Burying Ground in Providence—tradition, the documents, and the testimony of the house itself seem to unite in the statement that it was built as early as 1653, perhaps earlier. It belonged undoubtedly to Roger Mowry, and as his tavern played a very prominent part in the affairs of the early colony.[3] We shall therefore refer to it hereafter as the Roger Mowry House.

This house as the visitor approaches it along Abbott street, up the hill from North Main, gives no impression of its age. From above it, looking back, we see the old stone chimney (fig. 2), which though topped out with brick is almost exactly in its ancient condition, and which shows, on its sides, the shoulders or slopes which mark the position of the rafters of the original roof. It is inside the building, however, that its age can best be appreciated. The plan (fig. 3) indicates the difference between the old and the new portions of the house, which like all these old homesteads has been greatly altered. It originally consisted of the single "Fire Room" shown in black on the plan, which gives the additions in cross-hatching; and in that room the original fram-

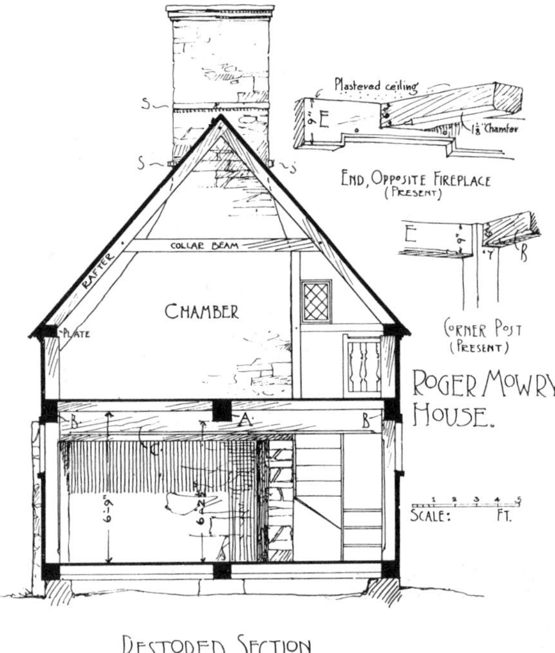

Figure 4. Restored section of the Roger Mowry House.

ing is almost intact. The four corner posts *PP, QQ,* the *side girts BB,* which connected each pair of them at the level of the second floor, and the "summer"[4] or large middle beam *A,* which spanned the room lengthwise from the *chimney girt C,* connecting the two posts *PP,* to the *end girt E,* connecting *QQ,* are all in place; and those of them which are not cased show their ancient chamfers with their medieval stops.

The end girt *E* is cut out curiously under the end of the "summer," as is shown in the sketch on the restored section (fig. 4). This cutting away, which is quite common as an afterthought, is here probably original—a view which is favored by the holes for the pins which held the tenons of studs or posts at the sides. These posts could hardly have been put in after the sill and girt were in place, for it was the custom to tenon them at top and bottom. The framing of the girts into the corner posts is also shown in a sketch on the section (fig. 4), while on the plan will be found a note of the manner in which the old sill projected into the room.

The present arrangement of the room would not lead the visitor to suspect the size or even the existence of the old stone fireplace. There is a fire-board behind the stove, and on each side of the fire-board a closet. Opening one of the closet doors, however, will reveal the stone cavern wherein, when the Town Council met, Roger Mowry burnt the logs of "this daies fireing," for which, and for the "house roome," we read the Town Treasurer was ordered, on January 27, 1657, to pay him one shilling and sixpence.[5] Some idea of the size of this ancient heating apparatus may be gained from the plan and from the section, which shows that it was nearly as high as the underside of the chimney girt. It will be seen that one side of the chimney is out of doors, while the other did not, and does not now, reach the outer wall of the house. It was in this space between chimney and outer wall that the stairs, or the ladder which served instead, were placed. This is abundantly proved in other houses, some of which still retain a flight of stairs in that very location.

Upstairs, in what the old inventories call the "Chamber," there is at present a large high room. None of this framing can be original above three feet or so from the floor where the original posts stop, as can be proved by sounding the casing of the posts as they show in the room. The shoulders, also, on the chimney, shown in figure 2, and the positions of the old shelves or water-tables *SSS* (fig. 4), which were made to project a couple of inches to prevent the rain-water from running down the chimney face into the house, leave no doubt of the original position of the rafters. Their evidence may always be relied on, whatever the position of the modern roof. The original house, then (fig. 5), was no doubt such as the restoration shows.

An examination of the perspective view of the framing of this type of house given in figure 6 will help the reader to understand the more technically drawn plan and elevation. A little patience spent in studying these first figures will be of much value in the later chapters, as the names "sill," "plate," "summer," "side girt," "end girt," "chimney girt," "floor joist," "rafter," "collar beam," and "post" will constantly recur, and a glance at figure 6 will explain what they are, better than many words of definition.

From this description, with a study of the drawings which accompany it, the reader can form a clear idea of the original house of the settlers of Providence. With such houses as these, with their gables toward the street and their chimneys toward the hill, the old "Towne Street" was more or less thickly fringed.[6] And of all the old dwellings, this veteran—this old tavern—an eyewitness of the town's history, a sharer in all its early struggles, almost an embodiment of its early life—alone remains.

THE ELEAZER ARNOLD HOUSE

This picturesque dwelling—built in 1687 by Eleazer Arnold—stands on the old North Road, half a mile this side of the Butterfly Factory, and about a mile west of Lonsdale. It is very well placed on rising ground, near a brook, and not far from the bank of the Moshassuck river. The house differs from any we have thus far studied. It was originally built, as the old slope of the chimney shows (fig. 7), with a lean-to like the Field House. But here the lean-to is not a sleeping-room or a mere storeroom. The chimney, as can be seen from the perspective (fig. 7) and the plan (fig. 8), extended across the whole end of the house on the outside; the lean-to became the kitchen and had its own

Figure 5. Restored view of the Roger Mowry House.

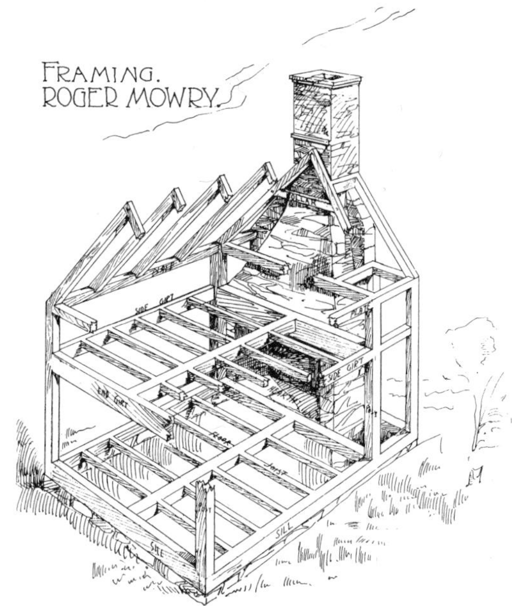

Figure 6. Perspective of framing for the Roger Mowry House.

Figure 7. The Eleazer Arnold House, Lincoln, Rhode Island.

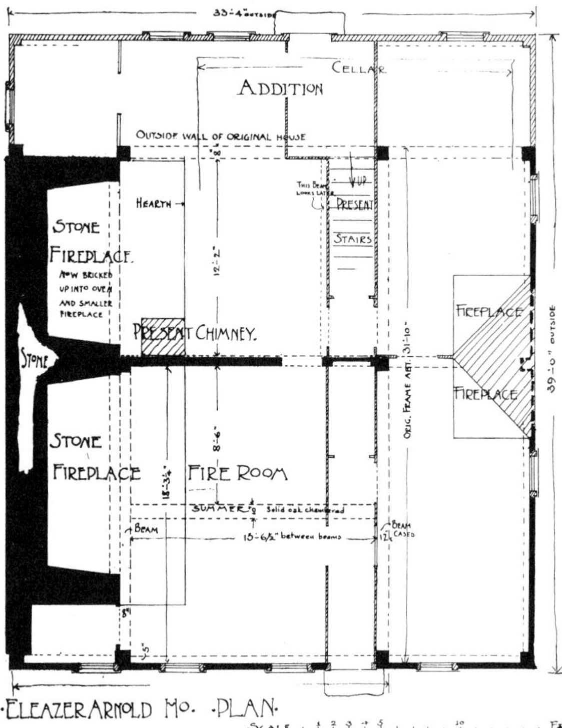

Figure 8. Plan of the Eleazer Arnold House.

Figure 9. Restored view of the Eleazer Arnold House.

fireplace like its more aristocratic neighbor, the old fire-room. Here, then, we have the plan which is characteristic of the second period—that of two fireplaces side by side in two different rooms of the same house. In this house the lengthening shown on the plan (fig. 8) at the end opposite the chimney was not an addition, but was, like the lean-to, a part of the original building; and, a marked peculiarity in a Providence house, there was a gable on the side which now faces the road.[7]

Figure 9, which gives a restoration of the original building, will explain these statements, while the sections (figs. 10 and 11) will show the transition from the ancient framing to the construction of the present roof. The house, which is the oldest example we have of a two-story house built with a lean-to, was originally framed, as the section shows, with the ordinary two-story construction in the front room, while on the rear the framing stopped with the level of the new side-girt. What would be the side-girt in a one-room-deep house here is a sort of second summer (fig. 10). The plate on the front carries the rafters of that side of the roof. The second story chimney girt *X*, the second story end girt *Y*, the additional end girt *Z* and the second story summer, which here, as in the Thomas Fenner house, runs across the house, are notched down upon the plate over the second summer (corresponding to the plate on that side in the Fenner house), and, projecting beyond, are tenoned into the rafters in the rear of the roof, which run down and frame into the lower plate (marked *W* in fig. 10). We have thus four trusses united by purlins, which are framed into the principal rafters *P* and *Q*.[8] These trusses are all original, and the absence of any stud mortises in that over the girt which usually formed the end of the house, prove that the present length was that of the original building.

When the modern roof was put on, the rear of the house was built up and a new plate put on at the level of the third floor, as the section shows. The old tie beams were taken out and replaced by others spanning the second story rooms and supporting the old rafters, or were spliced so as to accomplish the

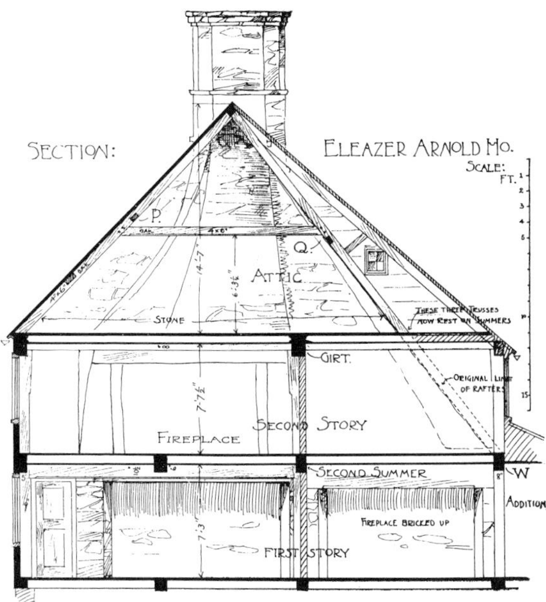

Figure 10. Section of the Eleazer Arnold House.

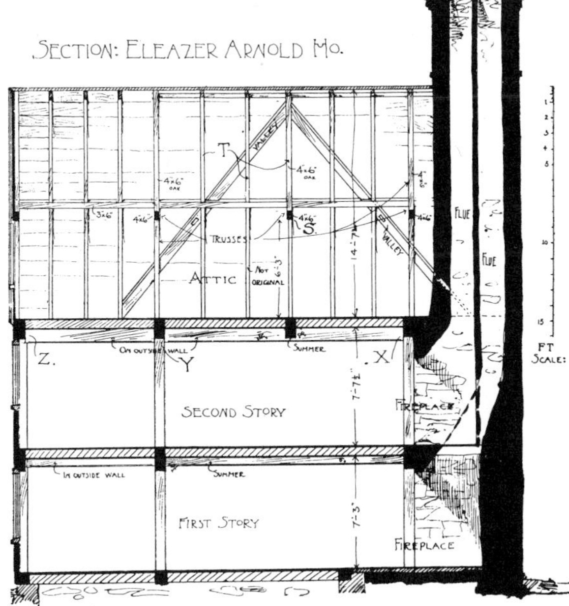

Figure 11. Section of the Eleazer Arnold House.

same purpose, and the new rafters were sustained in the middle by struts from the old trusses.

In the longitudinal section (fig. 11) can be seen two slanting beams cutting across the trusses, and interrupting the common rafters (*T*) supported by their purlins. These are the valley rafters of the old gable which once existed on the front of the house. The fact that the rafter on which they meet does not run down to the plate, and never did run down, is proof of this. We know it never ran down because the collar beams (fig. 11) run through to the roof and the rafter is tenoned into the collar, not the collar into the rafter. Further, the rafters (fig. 11, *T*) now filling in the space between the two valleys are newer, and are nailed to them, a thing not dreamed of by the ancient carpenters. Finally, the mortises for the gable purlins still exist in the valley rafters—which are laid flatwise and halved into the truss rafters—and, by the angle they make with the face of the valley, bear invincible testimony to their character, and to the existence of the gable.[9]

How common an occurrence this gable on the front of a house was we have no means of knowing. Though this is the only instance of it in Providence, we know from the work in Newport and in the other colonies that it cannot have been unfamiliar.

By the time the Eleazer Arnold House was built, the dwelling-house in the Providence Plantations had passed through several steps, which may be roughly indicated as follows: First, the single-roomed, story-and-a-half structure with one fireplace; second, the two-story house with one room on each floor, still with a single fireplace; third, the story-and-a-half house with a lean-to, but with only one fireplace; fourth, the story-and-a-half house with the lean-to and two fireplaces, like the building we have just considered.[10] Though these steps did not follow each other chronologically—for all these types appeared together in the second period—they still showed progress toward a larger dwelling. In the third period houses of two full stories appeared.

Notes

This article was originally published in Isham and Brown's *Early Rhode Island Houses* (1895). All illustrations in this article were drawn by Norman Morrison Isham.

1. Rhode Island Historical Society, *Collections*, 34 vols. (Providence: Rhode Island Historical Society, 1827–1947), 3:166.
2. Henry Crawford Dorr, *Planting and Growth of Providence* (Providence: S. S. Rider, 1882), p. 24. We reached our conclusion, however, before seeing his work.
3. The town council met here, and tradition says Williams held prayer meetings in it.
4. Derived from the French *sommier*, Latin *sagmarius*, a pack-horse.
5. Horatio Rogers, ed., *The Early Records of the Town of Providence*, 21 vols. (Providence: Snow and Farnham, 1892–1915), 1:110.
6. Dorr, *Planting and Growth of Providence*, p. 24.
7. The chimney in this addition is new.
8. The purlin is the horizontal beam framed between the trusses (see fig. 11) to carry the small rafters on which the roof boards are nailed.
9. Note the distinction in the section (fig. 11) between the principal rafter, which is part of the truss, and the common rafter which the truss carries by means of the purlins. The truss consists of these principal rafters—one on each side—the collar beam which is a tie, and of the tie beam formed by the summer in the attic floor.
10. During the first period all lean-tos were probably additions.

Building in Wood in the Eastern United States: A Time-Place Perspective

FRED B. KNIFFEN AND
HENRY GLASSIE

Noting that wood was by far the most dominant building material used in American construction, Fred B. Kniffen and Henry Glassie attempt to resolve the conflicting interpretations of the terms used for describing building processes and to refute the facile assumption that American houses were fashioned by methods newly invented out of the American experience. The main purpose of this article is then to set the record straight so that a dependable history of vernacular architecture might be written.

The various technologies discussed here can be grouped into two main categories: joined framing and horizontal log construction. A number of framing techniques are labeled and described but it is log construction that is treated most extensively. Kniffen and Glassie not only establish a typology of log-notching forms but plot their geographical distribution. The patterns that they present suggest that the major tradition of American log construction had its origins in the cultural hearth zone of the Mid-Atlantic region, namely in southeastern Pennsylvania. In the 1730s when German and Scotch-Irish settlers began to move out of Pennsylvania into Maryland and Virginia, they extended the regional distribution of particular forms of log construction. Their descendants, argue Kniffen and Glassie, would eventually spread log-building techniques throughout the Upland and Lowland South while another migration moving west from Pennsylvania would bring German-derived log construction into the Midwest. The mid eighteenth to the mid nineteenth century is presented as the great period of American log construction, the period of westward expansion in the eastern half of the United States. Log houses are then to be taken as a key indicator of how the land was peopled and notching types are their particular regional or ethnic signature.

If the geography of settlement is ever to reach its full potential as the interpretable record of the historical events and cultural processes imprinted on the land, the components of settlements of all kinds must be systematically reduced to types and quantities before they are set against the revealing vagaries of reality.

It is the purpose of this study to examine a basic aspect of settlements—the methods of constructing buildings. In the timber-rich eastern United States other materials in common use in Europe declined in importance as the frontier moved westward. New Englanders never built extensively in anything but wood, and the stone construction of eastern Pennsylvania and the brick of Tidewater Virginia disappeared rapidly away from these nuclear areas.[1]

European America has known three general methods of building in wood: with framed walls; with walls of closely set vertical timbers; and with walls of horizontal timbers. Framing, typologically the youngest, begins with a skeletal structure of horizontal, vertical, and diagonal squared timbers, which is then covered in one of several ways. In this study framing is given less emphasis because it is already amply and expertly documented. It is the older building with timbers or logs, round or faced, vertical or horizontal, about which there is a lack of accurate information and little agreement on concept and nomenclature, and it is here that this study aspires to make its major contribution. However, with respect to areal distribution framing is of course of equal or even greater concern.

This article is the first part of an undertaking to describe and interpret the first settlements resulting from the westward movement out of established seaboard nuclei, roughly between 1790 and 1850, or between the opening of the trans-Appalachian West and the invasion of the grasslands. We propose to consider, in order, methods of building construction, types of buildings, fences and fencing practices, field forms and agricultural practices, and other aspects of settlements. In treating methods of construction no initial time limit can be set, for their antecedents reach back at least to the European Neolithic.

The procedure consists in the synthesizing of published materials with the results of extensive field observation. All too frequently there are no ready-made generic groupings. Every effort has been made to discover and adapt existing concepts and terms, and to reconcile conflicting usages. Definitions and nomenclature are proposed where they are nonexistent.

A strong emphasis on folk practices will be evident throughout. This is because they better serve the ultimate purposes of the undertaking to find origins and to trace diffusions and changes. Folkways are comparatively the simplest and most direct expression of fundamental needs and urges. They conform to type with a minimum of individual deviation, and thus attest to the innate conservatism of their practitioners. They are often areally, even when not numerically, dominant. Further, folk practices with respect to material things have been badly neglected in comparison with, say, traditional music and tales. Architects, for example, have largely disregarded the simpler folk methods and forms of construction in favor of more sophisticated methods and more pretentious structures. Finally, the new attack on rural poverty will surely accelerate the destruction of unchronicled folk structures and practices to the point where their record is beyond recovery.

Fully aware of the inability of two persons to familiarize themselves with all the details of building in wood, we proffer an open invitation to correct and extend the observations and conclusions of this presentation.

Antecedents of American Construction in Wood

It seems safe to assert that no significant method of wood construction employed in America before 1850 was developed here. Techniques were modified, and even perverted, but their European ancestry is certain. Seventeenth-century Europe provided half-timbering;[2] weatherboarding over heavy frame; vertical log, paling, and plank construction; and horizontal logs, planks, and timbers with various corner joinings. The wattle-daub and thatched huts, and even the more primitive "wigwams" of branches, rushes, and turf that appeared early in Massachusetts had their counterparts in contemporary England.[3]

Frame Construction

Framing is so old in Europe that it became the dominant method of building in the English seaboard settlements. It is typologically more advanced than the vertical construction from which it is derived. The frames were built of very heavy timbers (fig. 1), with a safety factor far in excess of any possible demand. This is a major reason why so many of the older houses have survived. It was not until about 1830 that so-called balloon framing was devised, using much smaller and lighter timbers set closely together (fig. 2). Balloon framing for dwellings began to be important only after 1850; barns continued to be heavily framed well into the twentieth century.

To the extent, then, that wood was used in the English and Dutch seaboard colonies framing was almost the sole method of construction. Except in the upland South and its culturally dominated periphery, frame construction was transmitted westward and became the near-universal form, quickly replacing the pioneer log house. The significant changes were from heavy to balloon framing and, much earlier, from half-timbering to an almost exclusive sheathing and weatherboarding.

Figure 1. Heavy Framing, Indiana. (Photograph by L. Jones, courtesy of the Library of Congress.)

Figure 2. Balloon framing, Louisiana.

Half-Timbering

Half-timbering—a heavy framing of squared timbers with a filling, or nogging, between them—was part of the cultural heritage of most Europeans in America at the time of the Revolution. Half-timbering was practiced in Britain, France, and Germany, and northward into southern Sweden, to mention only the important source areas. The nogging was sometimes brick (fig. 3), sometimes clay clinging to rods, or "cats," set vertically or horizontally between the timbers (fig. 4). Occasionally the filling was stone, or plastered wattle or lath. This skeletal construction eliminated the need for a large amount of lumber, presumably a reason for its wide use in Europe.

Half-timbering was common in the early seaboard settlements, but the timbers were frequently covered with siding, a not unexpected consequence of an abundance of cheap wood, just as the Old World thatch roof gave way to wooden shingles. Eventually the use of nogging was discontinued (but not, as has sometimes been suggested, exclusively because of the low lime content of American clays). This stage of constructional evolution was practiced by early New England settlers who came from heavily wooded southeastern England, the one area where heavy framing was clapboarded without the use of nogging.[4]

Figure 3. Brick nogging in heavy frame, New Orleans.

Figure 4. Clay in heavy frame, Louisiana. (Courtesy of the Library of Congress.)

Figure 5. German half-timbering, Ohio. (Courtesy of the Library of Congress.)

Although surviving examples of half-timbering are fairly common in the easternmost states, notably in Virginia and in German areas of Pennsylvania, the method was not carried westward to any great extent. However, nineteenth-century German immigrants from Europe introduced half-timbering in Ohio (fig. 5), Wisconsin, Missouri, and Texas, and perhaps elsewhere,[5] and the French in the Mississippi Valley (fig. 6) have continued the practice virtually to the present.[6] Vestiges of half-timbering are occasionally seen in brick nogging within the light balloon framing of the latter nineteenth century (fig. 7).

Figure 6. Half-timbering and clay nogging, Louisiana. (Courtesy of W. Knipmeyer.)

Vertical Posts, Planks, and Timbers

Building with closely set vertical members is so widespread, and so varied in detail, as to suggest that any common origin must lie in a remote European concept. Indeed, vertical post construction seems to have originated in the Near East in the Neolithic and to have spread across Europe as a major element in the Neolithic complex. By the late Neolithic it was a dominant form of construction in all of Europe except the far north, the western Mediterranean, and the Atlantic area of England, in the last two of which stone was of greater importance. Initially, the posts were driven into the ground a foot or so apart, and the spaces between them were woven in wattle or filled with clay and straw. During the late Neolithic, in the area of Jutland, the posts were set without interstices for added warmth, perhaps through influence from the palisades known throughout Europe. This type of close-set vertical timber construction spread slowly; it did not reach Russia until the third century before Christ, and England until Anglo-Saxon time.[7]

Vertical construction survives in an old Saxon church in Essex, composed of vertical half logs between sill and plate, tongued and grooved on adjoining edges to produce a tight fit.[8] Numerous examples of vertical construction have been noted in France, especially in Normandy.[9] Construction using vertical logs and timbers is cited for early New England,[10] and the medieval "puncheoning"—wattle-daub on upright posts—for Virginia.[11] The use of vertical oak planking (fig. 9) to provide structural support in place of studding, which extended into the nineteenth century, has been traced from England.[12] Vertical board-and-batten construction has been postulated for Spanish Florida,[13] and Spanish records show that settlers in St. Augustine built houses "palisado" style before 1597.[14] Another example of vertical log construction is a twentieth-century Scandinavian barn in Wisconsin.[15]

Figure 7. Brick nogging in balloon framing, New Orleans.

But it was the French in America who employed

Figure 8. Poteaux sur sole *construction, Cahokia Courthouse. (Courtesy of the Library of Congress.)*

Figure 9. Vertical plank construction.

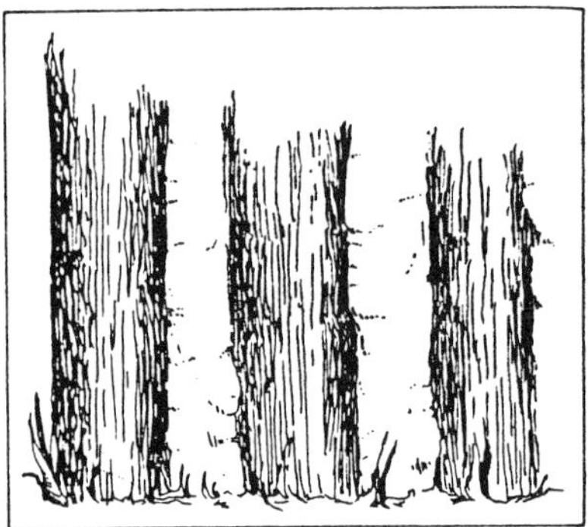

Figure 10. Poteaux en terre *construction.*

vertical construction most extensively. *Poteaux en terre* (fig. 10) or *pieux en terre* (a variant term is *pièces en terre*) was the earliest method used throughout the great arc of French colonial settlement extending from Acadia westward to the Great Lakes and southward to the lower Mississippi Valley.[16] Poteaux en terre consisted of close-set vertical posts tamped into a trench, pieux en terre of sharp stakes driven into the ground; the interstices, about as wide as the diameter of a post, were filled with clay and grass or with stones and mortar, sometimes plastered over or even covered with planks. Peterson distinguishes poteaux as squared above ground, pieux as round posts.[17] Here again usage has varied with time and place.

A variant, one might say an improvement, is the placement of the vertical members *sur sole* (on a sill) rather than *en terre*; from pictures, the old courthouse at Cahokia, Illinois, appears to be a surviving example (fig. 8). The old term surely was *poteaux sur sole,* employed concurrently with *poteaux en terre*[18] and *colombage,*[19] a term used at least on the upper Mississippi and in Canada to designate half-timbering. The two *poteaux* terms, then, referred to closely set, unbraced vertical timbers, *colombage* to more widely spaced, normally braced, vertical, squared timbers, the spaces between filled with various materials. At least two writers have used *poteaux sur sole* to designate horizontal construction, which is surely a perversion, even if it is popular modern usage.[20]

In French America, only among the Mississippi and Great Lakes settlements did vertical construction long remain popular. In Canada it gave way generally to horizontal timber construction or stone, and Dumont records the change to brick or half-brick and half-wood (half-timber) structures in New Orleans in the early eighteenth century.[21] In rural Louisiana poteaux en terre persisted well into the nineteenth century. To this day pieux en terre remains faintly alive in Louisiana in the form of a tight paling yard fence (fig. 11), *barrière en pieux debouts,* in the original form of which cypress palings are driven into the ground.

Figure 11. Barrière en pieux debouts, *Louisiana.*

In the attempt to account for the prevalence of vertical construction among the French in America it has been suggested that it was inspired by Indian vertical post stockades or palisades and buildings or was borrowed from the Gulf Coast Spaniards. Neither suggestion seems tenable in view of the fact that the earliest form of construction in French Canada was poteaux en terre,[22] which was introduced into Louisiana by the Canadian Iberville.[23] Moreover, since conclusive evidence indicates that vertical post construction of palisades and buildings reaches back to the European Neolithic, it would seem unnecessary to seek further for explanation of its American incidence. It is in keeping with the evidence to assume for the present that a method of construction which was very old and largely vestigial in western Europe experienced a brief rejuvenation in timber-rich colonial America.

Horizontal Logs, Timbers, and Planks

Construction in which the individual members are placed horizontally, close together, and one above the other has been used nearly everywhere in the New World. It appeared most widely in the upland South, only slightly less so in the timber houses of French Canada. Every form of horizontal construction employed in America has ample European precedent, and again it is unnecessary to invoke either local borrowing from the Indians or independent invention.

The fundamental distinction is the manner in which the horizontal members are joined at the corners. The variety of techniques employed is considerable. A basic difference distinguishes two all-inclusive groups—the utilization or nonutilization of corner posts or supports to which the horizontal timbers are attached. To the second group belongs the method commonly used in American log houses, in which the timbers are so notched at the ends that they become immovable when locked to the timbers above and below. In some marginal areas, however, the original and effective type of corner-timbering has deteriorated to the point where the timbers no longer lock and must be secured by some other means.

All horizontal construction may be descriptively classed as having either even tiers or alternating tiers (fig. 12). In the first group the timbers of the corresponding tiers of the four walls lie even with one another; in the second the timbers in one wall

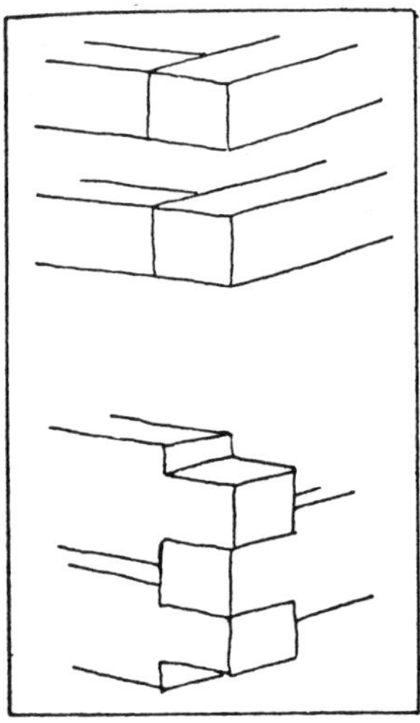

Figure 12. Even tiers (above) and alternating tiers (below).

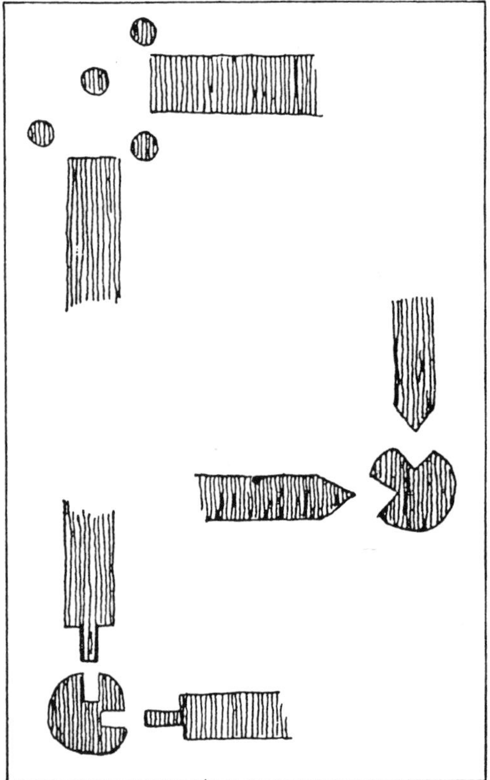

Figure 13. Methods of corner-post construction. (After Richard W. Hale, Jr., "The French Side of the 'Log Cabin Myth,'" Proceedings of the Massachusetts Historical Society *72 [October 1957–December 1960]: 121.)*

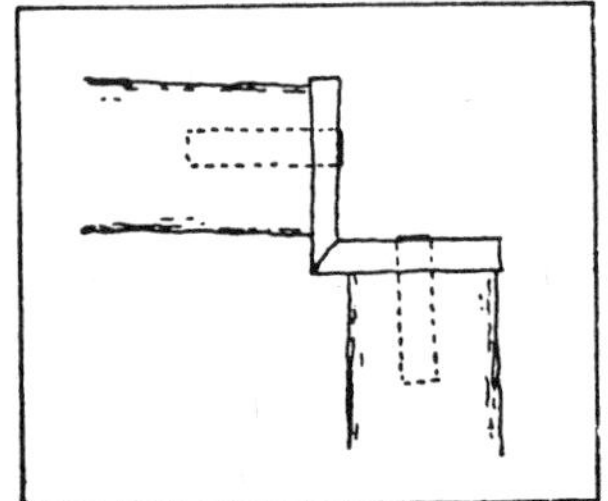

Figure 14. Hog-trough corner construction.

lie half a thickness above or below those of the corresponding tiers in the adjoining walls. This latter relative position is inherent in all "true" corner timbering.

There are several methods of providing corner support for even-tiered horizontal timbers. One consists of a vertical post with continuous grooves from top to bottom, into which the tapered ends of the horizontal logs are dropped. In another the vertical post is mortised to receive the tenoned ends of the horizontal pieces. A third utilizes four posts driven into the ground at each corner ("Canuck" style), so arranged that the horizontal timbers are held in place (fig. 13). A possibly related form is a "hog trough" of heavy planks, the apex set into the corner, the wings abutting the ends of the horizontal logs, to which they are spiked or pegged (fig. 14).

The support of horizontal timbers by corner posts is an old form of construction in Europe. It was apparently carried across much of the continent from Silesia by the Lausitz urnfield culture in the late Bronze Age.[24] Examples persist in southern Sweden, in the Alps, and probably elsewhere.[25] In French America horizontal timber construction came early but was later than poteaux en terre to be widely practiced.[26] *Pièce sur pièce,* as the method is commonly called, was used, at least sparingly, throughout French America.[27] Although it has been impossible to localize the European source of pièce sur pièce construction as carried by the French to America, its ancient appearance in Europe and its present-day survival there militate against an independent New World origin.

Figure 15. Pièce-sur-pièce *construction, Brown's Valley, Minnesota. Originally built at Fort Wadsworth, Dakota Territory, ca. 1863. (Photograph by C. E. Peterson, courtesy of the Library of Congress.)*

Pièce sur pièce was the prevailing method of wood construction in early French Canada. The old Hudson's Bay Company buildings and remote police posts are overwhelmingly of this type. The American practice of notching the ends of the logs has invaded Canada in some parts fairly recently, but it has by no means displaced the older method, which is still very much alive.[28] One of the merits of the Canadian method is that construction with corner (and intermediate) posts, unlike the American corner-timbering, permits the utilization of short logs and at the same time puts no restrictions on the size of the building (fig. 15).[29]

Horizontal construction with corner posts has generously invaded the areas of the United States peripheral to Canada—New England, New York, the Upper Lakes region, and the northern Great Plains states.[30] It occurs also in areas as remote from Canada as Pennsylvania, Virginia (fig. 16), and Tennessee, in these last surely a direct importation from Europe by Germans. Also non-French in origin, and hence evidence of the once-widespread European practice, are timbers tenoned into corner posts, found in seventeenth-century garrison houses of the New England frontier.[31] There are rather frequent later references to this method of construction for northern New England.

Types of Corner-Timbering

There are several methods without corner posts, all of European origin, in which horizontal timbers are notched and fitted in alternating tiers in a manner to lock them continuously from bottom to top. In what might be termed "false" corner-timbering the tiers are even and the interlocking, if present, is

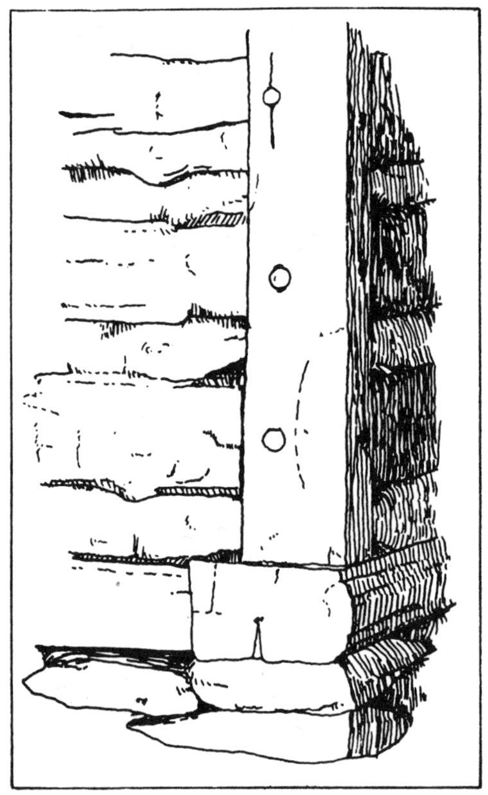

Figure 16. Corner-post construction, northern valley of Virginia.

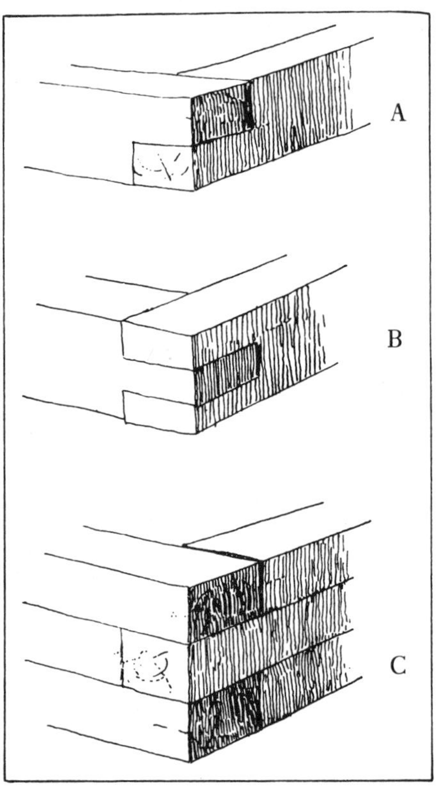

Figure 17. False corner-timbering: a, lap or rebated joint; b, tongue and groove; c, butt joint.

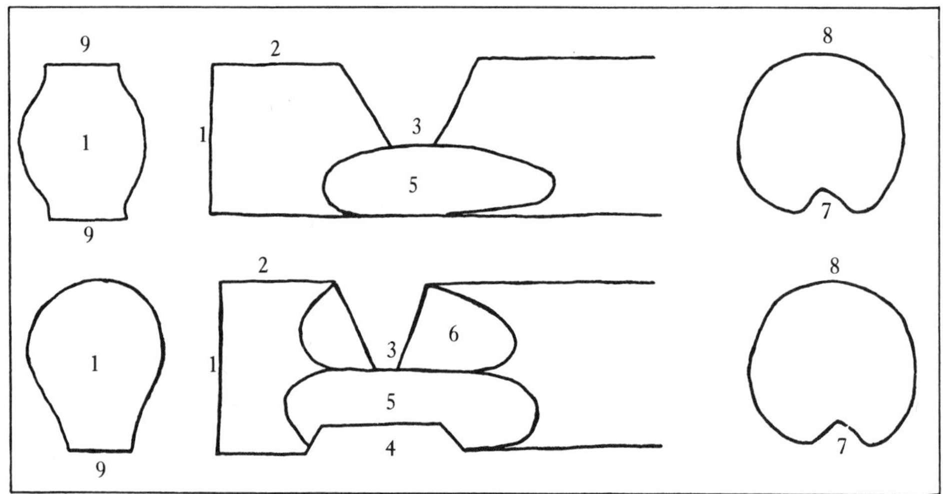

Figure 18. Terminology for log ends of corner joints: 1, crown; 2, head; 3, top notch; 4, bottom notch; 5, lower necking; 6, upper necking; 7, long groove; 8, the back of the log; 9, butt end. (Terminology from Sigurd Erixon, "The North-European Technique of Corner Timbering," Folkliv *1 [1937].)*

restricted to one tier (fig. 17). False corner-timbering had appeared in the New England garrison houses by the middle of the seventeenth century, not long after the arrival of the log-using Swedes on the Delaware.[32] Although later examples might suggest by their nature and location a stimulus diffusion from the areas of true corner-timbering to the south, false corner-timbering is more likely to have originated as a product of English carpentry than as an indirect inspiration from Swedish settlers. From New England false corner-timbering spread through upstate New York and as far west as Michigan, but it never attained any great areal or numerical importance.

In the eastern United States six methods of producing a truly corner-timbered joint are employed: saddle notching, V-notching, diamond notching, full dovetailing, half dovetailing, and square notching.[33] In all but the last each log is locked into the ones above and below it, and the necessity of nailing or pegging is eliminated.

Saddle notching is the simplest method and is usually used on logs left in the round. For the corner to be tight the logs must extend somewhat beyond the plane of the wall, and the application of siding is difficult. Although in modern rustic cabins and in frontier structures the end of the log may extend a foot or more beyond the plane of the wall, in traditional American practice the end rarely extends more than a few inches. There are three forms of saddle notching: double notching, in which the notches are on both sides of the log; and single notching, in which the notch may be either on the top or on the bottom (fig. 19).

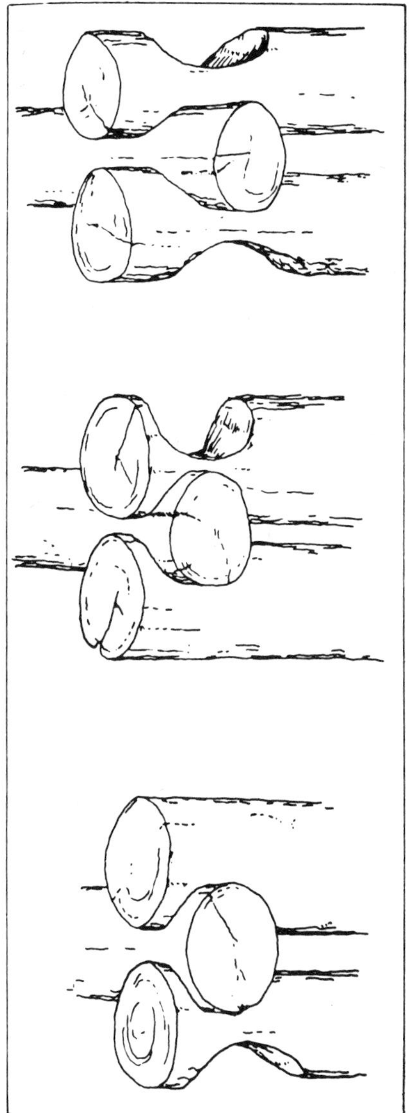

Figure 19. Saddle notches.

The V-notch seems to have developed directly from the saddle notch on the bottom of the log only. Instead of being rounded, the notch is cut sharply in a V, into which the chamfered head of the lower log fits (fig. 20). If the log is left in the round the crown is pear-shaped; if the log is hewn the crown is shaped like the gable end of a house—indeed, it is often referred to as "roof topping." In V-notching the ends of the log are cut off flush; the square or box corner thus produced permits the addition of board siding or, rarely, brick veneer.

In the diamond notch (fig. 21) both the top and the bottom of the end of the log are chamfered to produce a diamond-shaped crown. Diamond notching, which bears a superficial and probably accidental similarity in the shape of the crown to some Scandinavian types, seems to have been developed from V-notching.[34]

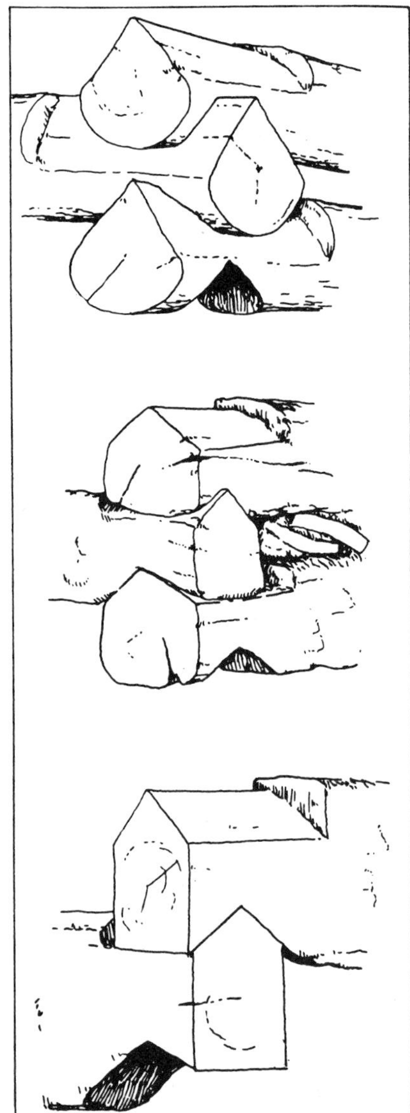

Figure 20. V-notches.

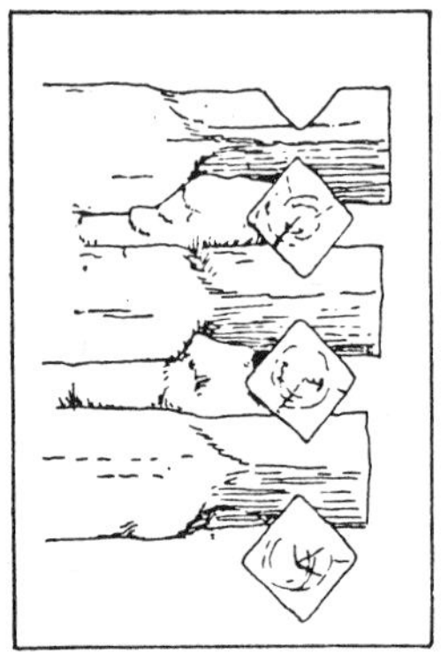

Figure 21. Diamond notch.

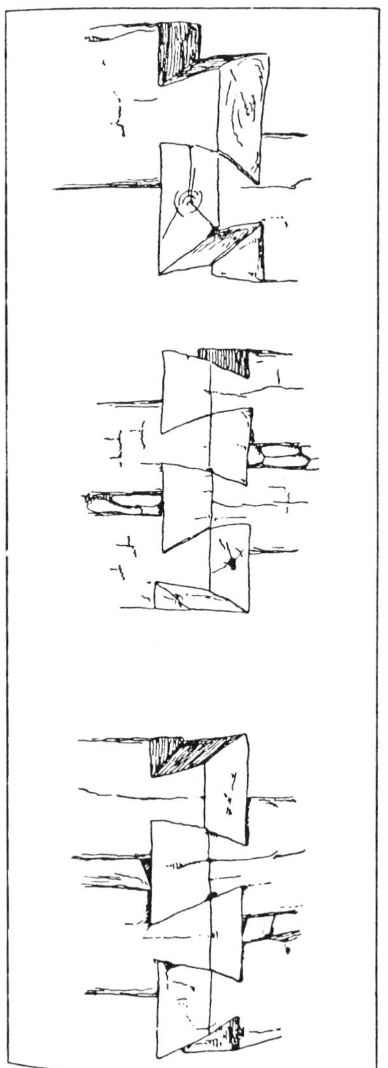

Figure 22. Full-dovetail notches.

Full dovetailing is the most complicated of the methods commonly used in American corner-timbering, and the most difficult to execute. It effectively locks the logs in both directions, produces a box corner, slopes downward on every face (so that water drains out), and is employed both on hewn and, though rarely, on round logs (fig. 22). The dovetail is familiar to every joiner of timber, yet many who could apply it in framing a house did not use it when corner-timbering logs. For example, in New England dovetailing was used in the early garrison houses but was seldom, if ever, used in the log construction of ordinary houses.[35] Elsewhere, in areas of log construction, dovetailing was applied to all kinds of buildings.

In half dovetailing, also known to all woodworkers, the head of the notch slopes upward but the bottom is flat (fig. 23). It is, in effect, half of a V-notch, yet it seems to have been developed from a full dovetail. The top angle of a full-dovetail notch is more acute than the bottom angle, and the bottom angle was easily straightened to produce the half dovetail, which is no less effective than the full dovetail but much easier to make.

The square notch is simple, and familiar as a tenon to a woodworker (fig. 24). It lacks the structure to lock the logs, a deficiency sometimes remedied by drilling and pegging through two squares or more. The square notch degenerated in different areas from both the V-notch and the half dovetail. The two forms are distinguishable by the shape of the log: the V-notch and its derivative square notch are found on logs square or rectangular in section (that is, about eight by twelve inches); the half dovetail and its derivative square notch are usually found on planked logs (that is, logs hewn to some six inches in thickness and about fourteen to thirty-six inches in width).

What is probably a variant of the square notch is the half notch (fig. 25). It is only occasionally used exclusively but frequently appears with the square notch as a means of adjusting the position of a particular timber.[36]

No other method of corner-timbering has signifi-

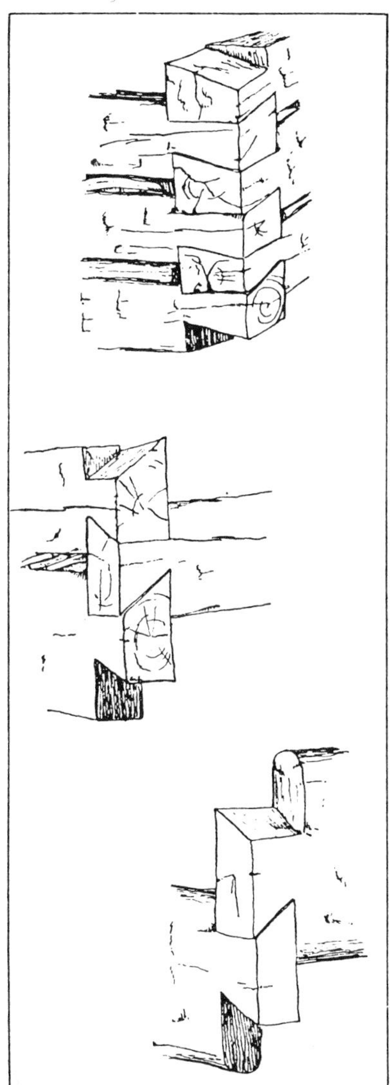

Figure 23. Half-dovetail notches.

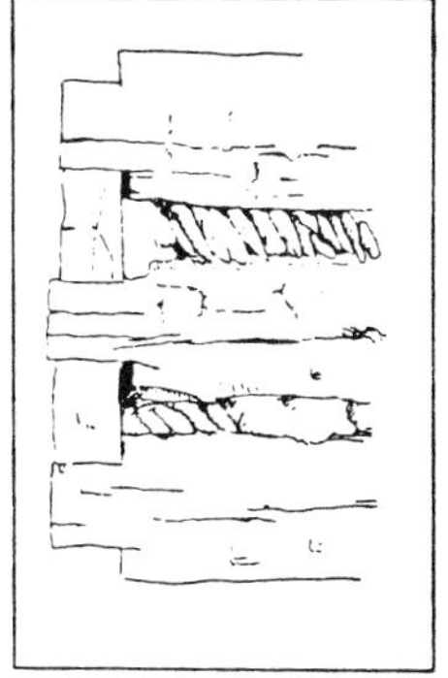

Figure 24. Square notch.

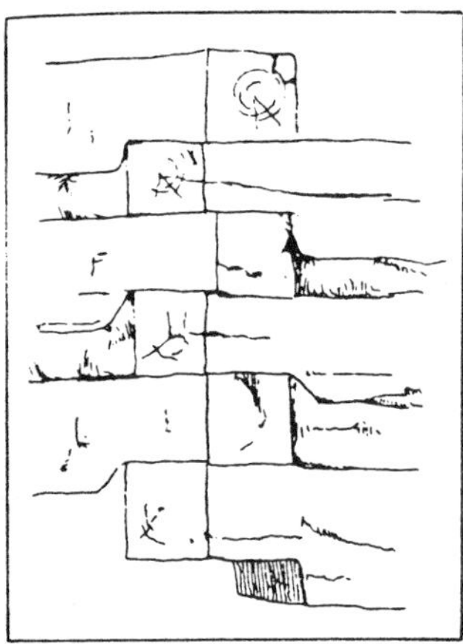

Figure 25. Half notch.

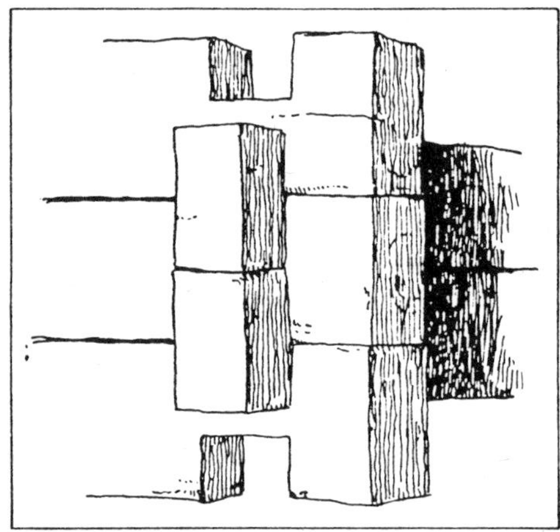

Figure 26. Double-notch joint.

cant distribution in the eastern United States, but odd methods are occasionally encountered, especially in the areas settled relatively recently by Scandinavians and Finns. One such is the double-notch joint (fig. 26), named by Erixon as the form most commonly used in Sweden.[37] In the United States it is encountered commonly in the Upper Lakes states—and in Hollywood movie sets ranging in locale from Wounded Knee, South Dakota, to Charleston, South Carolina. A popular brand of toy logs is of this type. In both the movies and the toys the use is an unfortunate and unnecessary violation of the verities of time and place.

The double-notch joint seems to have been widely distributed in Europe at one time; outside Fennoscandia surviving examples are known in the Spreewald, near Berlin, in Poland, in Switzerland, and in southwestern France. Its more recent popularity in northern Europe was apparently not matched in the source areas, for it did not have an effective early introduction into America.

Distribution and Development of Corner-Timbering

Horizontal log construction employing true corner-timbering originated in the Mesolithic with the Maglemosian culture, which was centered in Denmark, southern Sweden, and northern Germany.[38] By the Bronze Age horizontal logs had replaced vertical posts as the commonest method of construction from France to Russia and from Norway to Czechoslovakia.[39] Prehistoric horizontal log construction was universally characterized by round logs notched on the top or on both sides, a foot or more from the end of the log.

Horizontal log construction was not part of the cultural equipment of the Dutch, English, or French emigrants to the New World,[40] since it had receded during the early medieval period into the wooded mountainous sections of an area bounded on the west by an arc reaching from Scandinavia through Germany into the Alps, and possibly into the Pyrenees. The Swedes who settled on the Delaware in 1638 were the first to employ horizontal log construction in what is now the eastern United States. The log work of Scandinavia was similar to that found throughout Europe in the Bronze Age: the logs were generally left in the round; the notches were on the top or both sides of the log about a foot from the end, producing a characteristic overhang; and each log was grooved along the entire length of its bottom to fit tightly with the log below it. Although log houses were certainly built in New Sweden, references to them are strangely few. The first mention of log houses outside New Sweden is in 1669 for Maryland, in 1680 for North Carolina, but there is no evidence that the houses were truly corner-timbered, or that they were inspired by Swedish sources.[41] The Swedes had little contact with their English neighbors, and their log work did not spread beyond New Sweden; in fact, they soon abandoned it for stone and brick.[42] Even their normally conservative religious architecture was English or American rather than Swedish.[43]

Beginning in the late seventeenth century, and reaching a peak in the early eighteenth, great numbers of Scotch-Irish and Germans arrived in Pennsylvania and settled just west of the English.[44] The Pennsylvania Germans used horizontal log construction of the type which they had known in Europe, and which may still be found there, particularly in Bohemia, Moravia, and Silesia.[45] The previously stone- or mud-using Scotch-Irish quickly adopted Pennsylvania German log construction, primarily because of its practicality in timber-rich America. Pennsylvania German log work, and subsequent American log work, were characterized by logs notched near the end, a method that eliminated the overhang and produced a box corner. Spaces between the logs were filled—"chinked"—with clay, stones, poles, or shingles. The logs were usually squared, split and faced, or planked. Logs were hewn for a variety of reasons. A large log could be handled more easily when reduced in size; and a large round log took up interior space and produced an irregular wall that was hard to utilize. Primarily, however, hewn logs were thought to produce a tighter building, more finished in appearance.

In the German areas of southeastern Pennsylvania three forms of corner-timbering are found: saddle notching, V-notching, and full dovetailing. In the saddle notching, in contrast with that of prehistoric Germany and modern Scandinavia, the notch is usually only on the bottom of the log, and as close to the end as possible. Saddle notching was used primarily for barns and other outbuildings, and for temporary structures, which were less carefully constructed than houses. Pennsylvania German houses and the better-built barns and outbuildings were either V-notched or, less often, full-dovetailed.

The Pennsylvania German forms of corner-timbering were carried from southeastern Pennsylvania in all directions by the Germans and the Scotch-Irish (fig. 27). The earliest movement, beginning about 1732, led into central Maryland and the Valley of Virginia. All three corner-timbering forms may be found in the northern Shenandoah Valley, but during the movement east into the Blue Ridge and south through the Valley of Virginia V-notching came to predominate (fig. 28) to the virtual exclusion of the other forms. Although barns and outbuildings were often constructed as carefully as houses in the Valley and Blue Ridge of Virginia, the corner-timbering was frequently of lower quality than that used in houses, and occasionally the logs were left in the round.

The English east of the Blue Ridge received the concept of horizontal log construction more by diffusion than by direct migration. Although they employed the Pennsylvania German handling of the logs, they developed new corner-timbering types from V-notching instead of reproducing it. The square notch is the commonest form of corner-timbering east of the Blue Ridge, particularly in the Virginia Piedmont, where also a few buildings use the half notch exclusively. The diamond notch is found only rarely outside the general area of the North Carolina–Virginia border from the Tidewater to the Piedmont. The saddle notch is commonly found east of the Blue Ridge and well into the Tidewater, but it is restricted to smaller outbuildings; the Tidewater English retained rived cypress shakes or clapboards over timber framing as the prevailing method of folk construction (fig. 29).

The movement from eastern Pennsylvania down the western Appalachian valleys began later than that down the Valley of Virginia, yet the same three forms of corner-timbering—saddle notching, V-notching, and full dovetailing—may be found in the Alleghenies along the northern section of the Virginia–West Virginia border. In this area, where half dovetailing, which was probably brought to America

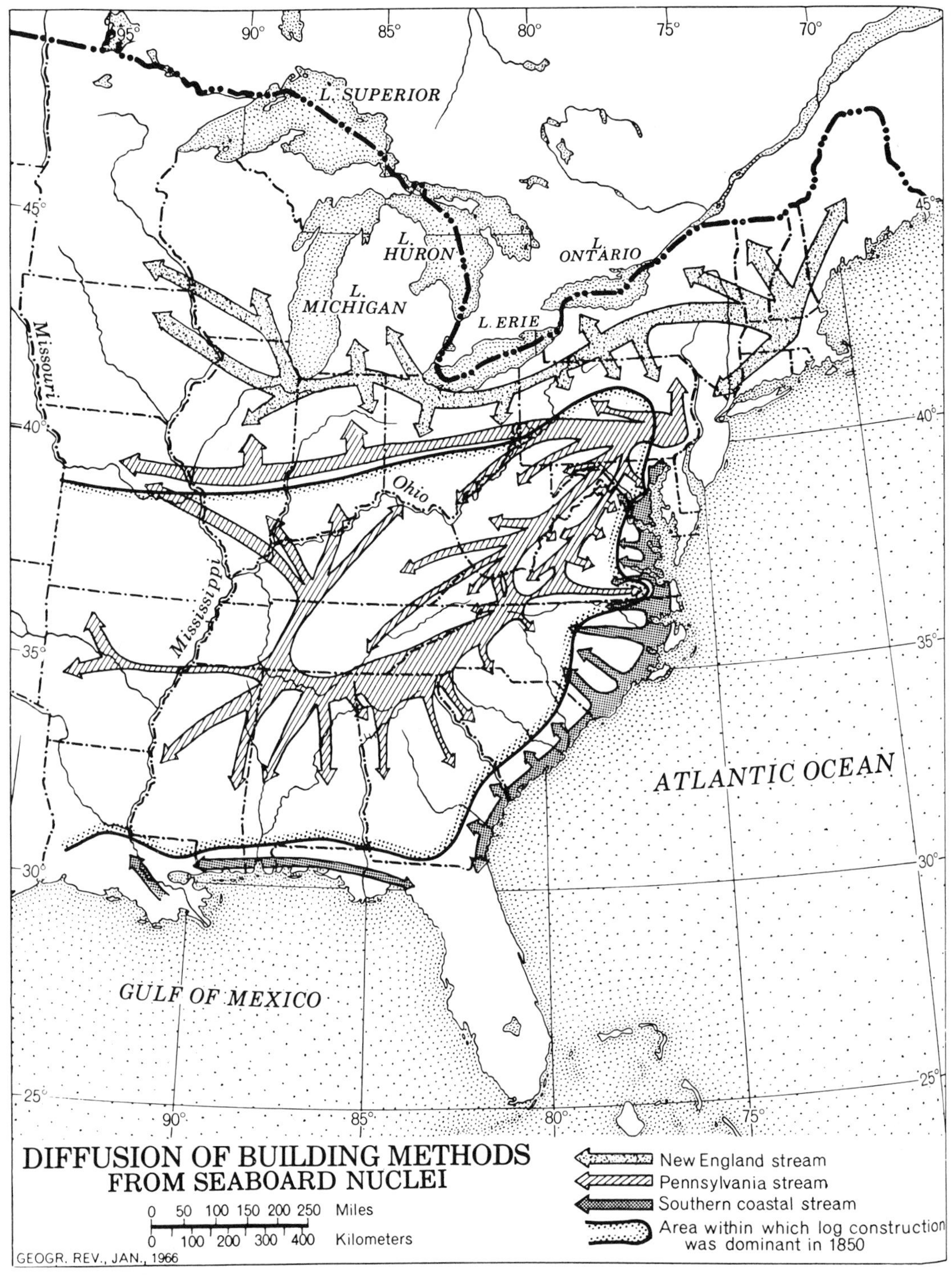

Figure 27. Diffusion of building methods from seaboard nuclei and areas of predominantly log and frame construction as of 1850. Routes are diagrammatic. Variation in width of streams suggests strength of diffusion.

Figure 28. Distribution and dominance of methods of horizontal log construction, based on approximately one thousand examples. Differences in weight of terms are indicative of relative importance.

Figure 29. Clapboarded frame house, Mississippi. (Courtesy of the Library of Congress.)

from Europe as a dormant aspect of full dovetailing, first became commonly employed, are farms where the houses are full dovetail and the outbuildings half dovetail; farther south in the Alleghenies, however, into southeastern West Virginia and Kentucky and adjacent Virginia, and down the Cumberlands, half dovetailing predominates on buildings of all kinds, though a few have V-notching, and numerous outbuildings and barns have saddle notching.

The two Appalachian streams, one coming down the Valley of Virginia bordering the Blue Ridge and the other down the Allegheny Front, met in southwestern Virginia, northwestern North Carolina, and northeastern Tennessee, and here saddle notching, V-notching, and half dovetailing all commonly appear, even on the same building. In this southern Appalachian region, corresponding roughly to the early settlement areas of Watauga, Holston, and Nolichucky, half dovetailing came to prevail on houses and on carefully made barns and outbuildings, and saddle notching—usually with the notch only on the bottom, occasionally with the notch only on the top—became dominant on temporary cabins, or "pole shacks," and on less carefully made barns and outbuildings. However, V-notching was still used, rarely on houses but frequently on barns. In the southwestern Appalachian region half dovetailing degenerated into square notching as V-notching had done in the Virginia Piedmont.

Saddle notching, V-notching, square notching, and half dovetailing, the last strongly predominant, were carried through the Tennessee Valley, and thence southeast into Georgia, south into Alabama, southwest into Mississippi and Louisiana, and west into Arkansas and Missouri. Although the log work of the mountainous areas of Arkansas and Missouri is comparable in quality with that of the Tennessee Valley, in the Deep South the quality declined with distance. Here, where horizontal log construction is still very much alive, saddle notching is strongly dominant on barns and outbuildings, and square notching and half dovetailing are frequently encountered on older houses. In some southern areas where the pines were so small that they could not be used if hewn, the logs were split, and the half-round section was used with the flat side facing inward. Half-round logs usually were half-dovetailed but sometimes were square-notched or notched only on the bottom, to produce a semilunate crown approximating the full dovetail (fig. 31).

A stream of log construction in which half dovetailing greatly predominated but square notching, saddle notching, and V-notching were also employed flowed northward through the Tennessee Valley and central Kentucky into southern Illinois, Indiana, and Ohio, where it encountered a stream in which V-notching was strongly dominant moving westward from Pennsylvania (fig. 27).

Only the northward flow of Pennsylvania corner-timbering into the westward-moving New England stream was largely ineffectual. Here it encountered false corner-timbering and the conceptually different French method of setting horizontal timbers into corner posts, and was overlain by more-recent exotic, but excellent, log construction techniques introduced from Fennoscandia directly into the Great Lakes region. The predominance of the simpler methods of corner-timbering—square and saddle notching—over V-notching and dovetailing in the northern tier of states tends to support the conclusion that the migrating New Englanders, like the English of the Tidewater, regarded log construction

Figure 30. Stovewood construction, Wisconsin. (Courtesy of William H. Tishler.)

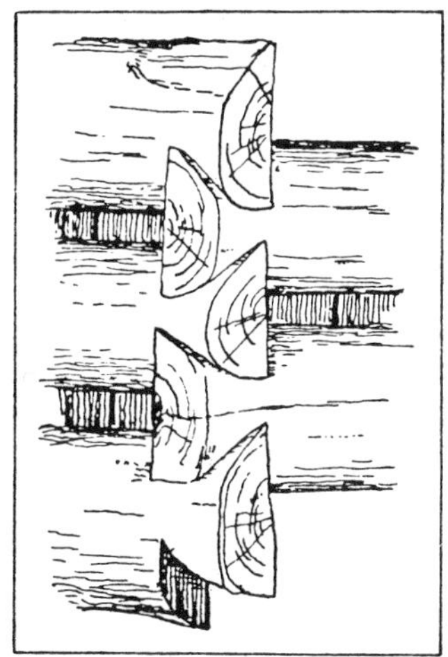

Figure 31. Semilunate crown on half-round logs.

as so temporary as to be unworthy of the skills they undoubtedly possessed as workers in wood.

The horizontal log construction with true corner-timbering that came to characterize the American frontier was, then, not a New World adaptation to environment, nor was it a Scandinavian introduction; rather, it was introduced by the Pennsylvania Germans and carried by them and by the Scotch-Irish in all directions from southeastern Pennsylvania (figs. 27 and 28).

For completeness, "stovewood" construction, found most abundantly in Wisconsin but also in Michigan and Quebec, should be mentioned.[46] In some half-timber structures stovewood-length logs form the nogging. In others they are laid horizontally in lime mortar to form unbraced walls (fig. 30). Barns, sheds, two-story buildings, and lumbermen's shanties with stovewood construction have all been observed.

Summary

In the American westward expansion between 1790 and 1850 wood became even more important as a building material than it had been on the seaboard. Nevertheless, every significant method of construction employed had its European antecedents. In the exuberance fostered by an endless supply of wood, construction methods were revived that were no more than vestigial in much of western Europe, if indeed they were even traditional. This is true of construction using closely set vertical or horizontal timbers.

During the early colonial period wood-saving half-timbering, then widely practiced in western Europe, was fairly common. It died out rapidly in favor of siding over the framing and thus was insignificant in the westward movement. Only the Louisiana French held steadfastly to half-timbering. In this and other respects construction practices in the French pockets stood in strong contrast with those of incoming frontier Americans. These had no equivalent of the French poteaux en terre, poteaux sur sole, and pièce sur pièce. In complement, the French rarely adopted American log construction.

In the New England stream the heavily framed, clapboarded house was dominant until the substitution of light balloon framing in the latter half of the nineteenth century. This was true also of the western projection of the Middle Atlantic States and of that of the Tidewater South. Where their influences prevailed, the log house was regarded as a temporary structure, to be replaced by traditional forms as soon as circumstances permitted. Only in the upland South was log construction the accepted practice.

Great changes have taken place in the construction, materials, and forms of buildings since 1850. Still, a survey of farm housing published in 1939 revealed that some 97 percent of the rural dwellings sampled were built of wood (frame, 93.2 percent; log, 3.7); 1.8 percent of brick; 0.5 percent of stone; 0.4 percent of earth; and 0.4 percent of concrete.[47] Thus, true to the tradition strengthened during the westward movement, wood was the overwhelmingly dominant building material, at least for the humbler dwellings.

Log houses, though of course far fewer than in 1850, conformed in their relative abundance to the old pattern. From the seaboard westward along the New England route log houses were few. This was true also of New Jersey (for some reason Pennsylvania and New York were not sampled) and the Tidewater counties of the South. Percentages climbed sharply in the upland South, even into the southern parts of Ohio, Indiana, and Illinois. In Halifax County, Virginia, well out in the Piedmont, the percentage of rural log dwellings rose to 42. In the more recent "frontier" sections of the Upper Lakes and the wooded West log construction was well represented.[48]

The next stage of our work should shed greater light on the cultural meaning of the several methods of timber construction, on their associations with different groups of peoples, on their place in the westward movement, and on their relative importance during the change from frontier to settled community. The first step will be to relate specific methods of wood construction to specific types and forms of folk housing. It should then be possible to match the idealized results of a systematic approach against the revealing vagaries of reality.

Notes

This article was originally published in the *Geographical Review* (January 1966).

1. The brick- and stone-using Dutch on the Hudson are not considered here because they were insignificant as a cultural source.
2. The term *half-timbering* is employed here in the full realization that its use is discouraged by architectural historians as misleading and confusing. However, we know of no substitute term to apply to heavy framing, commonly with horizontal, vertical, and diagonal squared members spaced as much as several feet apart, and with the interstices filled with various materials.

3. Fiske Kimball, *Domestic Architecture of the American Colonies and of the Early Republic* (New York: C. Scribner's Sons, 1922), p. 4.
4. Martin Shaw Briggs, *The Homes of the Pilgrim Fathers in England and America, 1620–1685* (London: Oxford University Press, 1932), p. 56.
5. For illustrations of half-timbering in Wisconsin, see Richard W. Perrin, *Historic Wisconsin Buildings: A Survey of Pioneer Architecture, 1835–1870,* Milwaukee Public Museum Publications in History, no. 4 (1962), pp. 14–25. Zoar, Ohio, has a number of examples of German half-timbering, and so have the German settlements between San Antonio and Austin, Texas, though in the examples observed there the half-timbering was hidden by siding.
6. French half-timbering in Louisiana uses both brick and clay cats as nogging. The brick nogging is referred to as *briquette entre poteaux,* the clay simply as *bousillage.* Plastered brick nogging appears in New Orleans, but more-rural bousillage is now invariably weatherboarded except, occasionally, for the front wall, which is protected by a broad roof overhang. Here the bousillage may be whitewashed and the wood framing left exposed, or the whole may be plastered over. This old practice explains the frequent appearance today of small rural frame houses with only the fronts painted white or whitewashed. The clay-wrapped rods, or "rabbits," of Louisiana bousillage are horizontally set, whereas in Europe they are more commonly vertical.
7. S. J. de Laet, *The Low Countries* (New York: Praeger, 1958), pp. 62–88; Marija Gimbutas, *The Balts* (New York: Praeger, 1963), pp. 103–4.
8. Briggs, *Homes of the Pilgrim Fathers,* pp. 56–57. Recent research indicates that the vertical logs were originally set in the ground and that the sill was introduced to preserve them; see H. L. Edlin, *Woodland Crafts in Britain* (London: B. T. Batsford, 1949), p. 137.
9. See Antonio di Nardo, *Farm Houses, Small Chateaux and Country Churches in France* (Cleveland: J. H. Jansen, 1924), esp. pp. 18, 75, 82. Note that in contrast with half-timbering the vertical members are close together and lack diagonal or horizontal bracing.
10. Kimball, *Domestic Architecture of the American Colonies,* p. 6.
11. Henry Chandlee Forman, *Virginia Architecture in the Seventeenth Century* (Williamsburg: Virginia 350th Anniversary Corp.: 1957), p. 30.
12. Kimball, *Domestic Architecture of the American Colonies,* p. 6. See also John Frederick Kelly's description of "plank-frame" houses in Connecticut as early as 1690 in *Early Domestic Architecture of Connecticut* (New Haven: Yale University Press, 1924), pp. 40–41.
13. "Evolution of the Oldest House," *Notes in Anthropology,* Department Anthropology, Florida State University, Tallahassee 7 (1962): 7.
14. Henry C. Mercer, "The Origin of Log Houses in the United States: A Paper Read . . . at Doylestown, Pa., Jan. 19, 1924," *Collection of Papers Read before the Bucks County Historical Society* 5 (1926): 572.
15. Perrin, *Historic Wisconsin Buildings,* p. 12.
16. See, for example, George-Marie Butel-Dumont, *Memoires historiques sur la Louisiane,* 2 vols. (Paris, C. J. B. Bauche, 1753), 1:50, 20:50; and for Quebec, see Reuben Gold Thwaites, ed., *The Jesuit Relations and Allied Documents,* 73 vols. (Cleveland: Burrows Brothers, 1897), 7:281.
17. Charles E. Peterson, "Early Ste. Genevieve and Its Architecture," *Missouri Historical Review* 35, no. 2 (January 1941):217.
18. Rexford Newcomb, *Architecture of the Old Northwest Territory* (Chicago: University of Chicago Press, 1950), p. 21.
19. In modern French *colombage* refers to frame construction.
20. Richard W. Hale, Jr., "The French Side of the 'Log Cabin Myth,'" *Proceedings of the Massachusetts Historical Society* 72 (October 1957–December 1960): 118–25; and Marius Barbeau, "The House That Mac Built," *The Beaver: A Magazine of the North,* outfit 276 (Dec. 1945):10–13.
21. Butel-Dumont, *Memoires,* 2:50.
22. In addition to the *Jesuit Relations,* see Richard Colebrook Harris, "A Geography of the Seigneurial System in Canada during the French Regime," Ph.D. diss., University of Wisconsin, 1964, pp. 147, 278.
23. See Butel-Dumont, *Memoires,* 2:7.
24. V. Gordon Childe, *The Bronze Age* (New York: Macmillan, 1930), pp. 206–8.
25. Sigurd Erixon, "The North-European Technique of Corner Timbering," *Folkliv* 1 (1937): 13–60, esp. fig. 25 and plate 14.
26. Harris, "Geography of the Seigneurial System."
27. Hale, "The French Side of the 'Log Cabin Myth,'" p. 121, cites the use of *pièce sur pièce* for the "notch and saddle" construction that found its way into Canada from the United States. Again, this may be a modern usage, but it is a perversion of the term used for corner-post construction before American notching was introduced into Canada, probably about 1740 (see Mercer, "The Origin of Log Houses," p. 571). Incidentally, Mercer's citation, for 1727, clarified a misunderstanding sometimes expressed that Canadian French laws opposed the use of timber construc-

tion in towns where stone was available. Surely this measure was directed against the fire hazard inherent in closely set wooden buildings, rather than against log or timber construction as such.

28. In his citation for 1664 Mercer ("The Origin of Log Houses," p. 571) refers to a church constructed of "round wood dovetailed at the corners," which sounds much like an American-style structure. Dovetailing, however, was known to every joiner; the logs may have been dovetailed into a corner post. If this was a case of alternating tiers and true corner-timbering, it must have been an isolated freak.
29. A limit to the size of a corner-timbered building is imposed by the very weight of the timber and by the tapering of tree trunks to an unusable disparity in dimension between the two ends; twenty-four to thirty-six feet has been advanced as the average maximum practicable length. There is no widely practiced means of enlarging a corner-timbered house except by adding a story; for the logs are not commonly spliced, and building a new structure poses the problem of how to connect it with the old.
30. Philip W. Sultz, in "From Sagebrush to Hay and Back Again," *American West* 1, no. 1 (Winter 1964): 20–30, shows a number of pictures of buildings, chiefly, one may surmise, in western Wyoming. On pages 26, 27, and 30 are shown respectively a house, a jail, and a church, all of which appear to have corner-post construction. The other buildings are corner-timbered.
31. Stuart Bartlett, "Garrison Houses along the New England Frontier," *Pencil Points* 14, no. 6 (June 1933): 255.
32. Ibid., p. 254.
33. The nomenclature proposed by Erixon ("The North-European Technique of Corner Timbering," p. 14) for the constituent parts of corner-timbering is used here and is illustrated in figure 18.
34. In support of his theory that the American log cabin is of Swedish origin, Mercer ("The Origin of Log Houses," p. 582) states that the "notch and chamfer" (V-notch) corner-timbering is Scandanavian. Further, the log house in America as pictured in many books and labeled seventeenth-century Swedish is roughly V-notched and has wide, chinked interstices; see, for example, Ernest Pickering, *The Homes of America* (New York: Crowell, 1951), p. 9, fig. P-1. However Mercer (pp. 577–79) quotes Dutch visitors who, traveling in 1670–80, contrasted the English frame house with the Swedish log house in which the logs are notched a foot from the end. Two things are learned from this description: first, by 1680, only five years before large numbers of Germans began arriving in eastern Pennsylvania, the English colonists had not adopted Swedish construction; second, authentic seventeenth-century Swedish log houses were corner-timbered like those found today in Sweden and not like those in America labeled seventeenth-century Swedish. Mercer (p. 579) states also that he knows of no definitely Swedish or seventeenth-century log houses that were extant in America in the early twentieth century. It seems, therefore, that the so-called seventeenth-century Swedish houses in America are more recent than that and, although conceivably built by Swedes, reflect Pennsylvania German log-construction techniques rather than Swedish. See also Henry Glassie, "Eighteenth-Century Cultural Process in Delaware Valley Folk Building," n. 50 (reprinted in this volume).
35. Bartlett, "Garrison Houses along the New England Frontier," p. 255.
36. Our attempt to compile a synonymy of terms for corner-timbering has yielded nothing worthwhile. The only usage that might conceivably prove confusing is the apparent employment of "halved" for our "square" notch by Mercer, "The Origin of Log Houses," p. 80.
37. Erixon, "The North-European Technique of Corner Timbering," p. 30.
38. Karl Schuchhardt, *Vorgeschichte von Deutschland* (Berlin: R. Oldenburg, 1934), p. 29.
39. Childe, *The Bronze Age,* p. 206; Gimbutas, *The Balts,* p. 74.
40. C. F. Innocent, *The Development of English Building Construction* (Cambridge: Cambridge University Press, 1916), p. 109, finds no evidence that log construction was ever practiced in England. Pierre Deffontaines in *Les hommes and leur travaux dans les pays de la moyenne Garonne* (Lille: S.I.L.I.C., 1932), plate 26, shows what is unquestionably corner-timbering in an old abandoned structure in southwestern France, but this seems to possess no significance with respect to French practice in America.
41. Kimball, *Domestic Architecture of the American Colonies,* p. 7.
42. C. A. Weslager, "Log Structures in New Sweden during the Seventeenth Century," *Delaware History* 5, no. 2 (September 1952): 92.
43. Thomas Jefferson Wertenbaker, *The Founding of American Civilization: The Middle Colonies* (New York: C. Scribner's Sons, 1938), p. 241.
44. The Scotch-Irish were primarily Lowland Scots who had emigrated to Ulster. The Pennsylvania Germans, also known as the Pennsylvania Dutch, were pri-

marily from the Rhenish Palatinate and Switzerland, but were also from Bohemia, Silesia, Moravia, Württenberg, and Hesse.

45. Moravian log work is much like that introduced by the Germans into Pennsylvania; see *Ethnographica,* vols. 3–4 (Brno, Czechosiovakia: Moravské Museum v Brně, 1962). Polish log work, on the other hand, more nearly resembles Swedish practice; see H. Grisebach, *Das polniche Bauernhaus,* Beiträge zur polnischen Landeskunde, ser. B, vol. 3 (Berlin, 1917). It now begins to appear that the primary source of log construction in America not only was not Swedish, but neither was it Rhenish German or Swiss. More likely conveyers were the Germans who came from Moravia, Bohemia, and Silesia. To this day it is the local tradition that the Schwenkfelders who arrived from Silesia in 1734 brought V-notching to Pennsylvania.
46. Richard W. E. Perrin, "Wisconsin 'Stovewood' Wall: Ingenious Forms of Early Log Construction," *Wisconsin Magazine of History* 46, no. 3 (Spring 1963): 215–19.
47. *The Farm-Housing Survey,* U.S. Department of Agriculture Miscellaneous Publication no. 323 (Washington, D.C., 1939), table 2.
48. The figures are 48.8 percent for Albany County, Wyoming, and 25.4 percent for San Miguel County, New Mexico, but the New Mexican log house is possibly not entirely of Anglo-American provenance.

The Tools Used in Building Log Houses in Indiana

WARREN E. ROBERTS

If the notion that log cabins are the oldest structures built by American colonists is the most persistent misconception about folk architecture, then surely its most persistent corollary is that log cabins were built with but a single tool—the axe. The longstanding image of the axe-wielding cabin builder, who with brawn and courageous will transformed standing forests into snug shelters, is attractive but is nonetheless an exaggeration. In this article Warren E. Roberts sets forth modestly to examine the tools used to build nineteenth-century log houses. From a careful analysis of extant log buildings in Indiana, he creates an account of the work of the carpenters who built those houses. These men, he argues, must have been highly skilled and must have possessed considerable expertise because their task required them to use knowledgeably no fewer than seventy-six tools.

Clearly then the substantial log houses that dot the landscape today were not simply carved out of the wilderness by a lone, rugged pioneer with a flintlock in one hand and an axe in the other. Rather log house builders were carpenters with chests full of tools and equipment, a large burden of civilizing machinery. The log house, Roberts suggests, should be appreciated as a refined statement of rural society and should no longer be seen as the meager or crude response of pioneers to the threatening wilderness. He reads marks on wooden timbers as signs of tool use, as telltale clues that can provide answers to the mysteries of the building process. The repeated occurrence of square corners and level foundations is interpreted not as the result of luck but as the results of the deliberate use of measuring devices like squares, rulers, straight edges, and levels.

After having studied for several years the log houses that still stand in southern Indiana, I made a list of the tools used to build these houses, restricting myself to those built in the first half of the nineteenth century. Such a list will help our understanding of how the houses were built and will show the number and kind of tools that were commonly to be had in the area at that time. By studying histories and visiting museums that portray life in the area in that era, I had become aware of a general belief that life at that time was generally simple and crude and that people had only a very few tools.

Trying to discover what tools were used in building the log houses that still stand in southern Indiana revealed that the available accounts are inadequate. One of the two kinds of written sources comprises the reminiscences of people who actually lived in Indiana in the early nineteenth century and who described log buildings. But these accounts describe the construction of the round-log *cabins* that were hastily built, temporary dwellings; no building of this type survives in southern Indiana. Although these writers often mention much more carefully built, hewn-log houses for the same period as the round-log cabins, they do not describe the building of hewn-log houses, the type that survives in southern Indiana. The accounts of the building of round-log cabins are often confusing and contradictory with regard to the tools used. While one writer says that these cabins were built with "an axe and a frow" another mentions "sawing" blocks from a white oak log and "boring holes," tasks requiring a saw and an auger.[1]

Another kind of source is recent writing describing log buildings. C. A. Weslager's *The Log Cabin in America* covers the entire United States, but concentrates on the eastern part of the country for historical reasons, while Donald and Jean Hutslar's "The Log Architecture of Ohio" concentrates on one state.[2] Both studies recognize the difference between the hastily constructed, temporary, round-log cabins and the more carefully built, hewn-log buildings intended as permanent. Cabins, they believe, were built by the earliest settlers in a region, whereas the log houses came later. Because most of the cabins have disappeared in their areas, these writers know of them through historic accounts. For illustrating extant log houses, they mainly restrict themselves to hewn-log buildings. The tools that they list, very few in number, are those that might have served to build an extremely crude, round-log cabin without, for instance, windows or much of a door. The extant hewn-log buildings that they illustrate, however, could not have been built with the four or five tools that they list. Despite distinguishing between the round-log cabin and the hewn-log house, these authors lump them together as regards the tools needed to build them.

Methods and Rationale

I have, therefore, relied mainly on fieldwork, examining over four hundred log houses, most of them built in the first half of the nineteenth century. Many were tumbling down, making it possible to examine almost every detail of their construction. I have helped take apart five log houses, noting the details of their construction. My list of tools is based upon this experience.

Tools often leave characteristic marks, such as those left by an axe, a plane, or saw teeth. More often, I had to rely on a general knowledge of how tools are used and of the tools demanded by specific tasks. This general knowledge came from several sources, beyond my own craft experience. I interviewed older craftsmen who still use older tools or who learned about them from their fathers. I also examined collections of old tools, many in private hands. I have used works that describe older tools and their use, especially Henry C. Mercer's whose research began, as he says, "in the carpenter's tool chest of one hundred years ago."[3]

To illustrate how a general knowledge of the use of tools leads to inescapable conclusions, I give one example. Every log house that I have examined had wooden floors. True enough, accounts of round-log cabins mention dirt floors, but it is inconceivable that a hewn-log house be built with a dirt floor and later have a wooden floor added. Hewn-log houses in southern Indiana always sit well up off the ground, upon stones at each corner. Without a wooden floor, they would have been uninhabitable. In every case, an original first-story floor was made of boards six to eight inches wide and about one and a quarter inches thick. The top surfaces of the boards had been planed smooth. The hidden bottom surfaces still showed the marks left by the saw that cut them from the log. The boards were always jointed to one another by tongue-and-groove joints, and the boards were held down by nails driven diagonally through the tongue edge of one board so that the nailheads were hidden by the groove edge of the next board.

From field examination of floors, I can state positively that a sawmill cut the boards, that a jack plane smoothed the surfaces of the boards, that a tongue plane and a plow plane made the joints, and that nails held the boards down. Several other tools were certainly used in making such a floor, tools whose marks are not obvious on the finished floor, but whose use can be safely assumed from a general knowledge of how work had to have been done.

The use of planes raises the question of how a board is held while being planed. A board cannot be planed while lying flat on the ground without extreme discomfort. A board cannot conveniently be placed across sawhorses and planed, for the thrust of the plane will push the board off the horses or knock them over. Some kind of workbench, no matter how crude and simple, is required to support the board while it is being planed, and the workbench must be supplied with some device, such as a vise, to hold the board to the bench. A plane that is used constantly soon becomes dull. The bit of the iron must be honed fairly often on a whetstone and occasionally sharpened on a grindstone.

The boards that come from a sawmill must be cut to length at the building site, so that a handsaw certainly was used. Moreover, a square and a marking device, either a scratch awl or a pencil, is needed to make a mark for the saw to follow. Some boards in a floor had to be narrower than the rest to fit the space exactly. To cut a board lengthwise requires a rip saw, a handsaw and a rip saw not being interchangeable. The mark on the board for a rip saw to follow was probably made with a marking gauge. Saws that are used constantly must have their teeth sharpened and reset from time to time, implying saw files, a saw set, and a saw vise. Finally, a hammer drives the nails into the floorboards, and a nail set is needed to sink the head of the nail below the surface of the wood.

One could use any of several approaches to the tools used in building a hewn-log house. The most satisfactory way might be to describe in detail how a log house was built and to treat the tools and their uses in this context. Because the primary purpose of this brief paper is to emphasize the large number and wide variety of tools needed, I will, instead, simply list the tools and comment briefly on how they were used. I will confine myself to tools that were probably used in the first half of the nineteenth century, even though hewn-log houses were built in southern Indiana throughout the nineteenth century and well into the twentieth century. Many aspects of American life during the second half of the nineteenth century saw many changes, and that is true of tools. Woodworking tools that had changed little for centuries were still being used in the early nineteenth century, but shortly after the Civil War, factory-made tools began to supplant the older forms. The fairly common practice for the early nineteenth-century craftsman was to procure the metal parts of his tools from a blacksmith and to make the wooden parts himself. If he needed an axe, for example, the craftsman got the handmade head from the blacksmith and made the handle to suit himself. After the Civil War, however, factories produced more and more of the tools and tool parts, and many parts that had previously been made of wood were made of metal, even though the basic tool shapes remained largely unchanged. Many patents for factory-made tools were issued in the late nineteenth century.[4] Many of the older types of tools continued, however, to be made and used in the late nineteenth and twentieth centuries. Older types of tools continued in use because they were still in good condition, because many craftsmen preferred the older forms of tools, and because it was still often cheaper for a craftsman to make a tool for himself.

I can vouch only for the tools used in building the hewn-log houses of southern Indiana. Those who are familiar with the log houses of other parts of the country can judge for themselves whether the same features and marks are present in the houses familiar to them. If they are, the same tools were used. Some tools have different names in other parts of the country. The tool commonly called a "drawshave" in New England is called a "drawknife" in Indiana. The same holds true for some building terms. Horizontal, overlapping siding used on the exterior of a house is called "clapboards" in New England; in Indiana, it is called "weatherboards." Insofar as possible, I have used the names and terms common among older craftsmen in Indiana.

The Tools

TOOLS FOR FELLING, SPLITTING, AND SAWING LOGS

1. The FELLING AXE, so familiar as scarcely to need general description, felled the trees used to build a log house and was used in a number of other tasks, such as supplementing the work of the broadaxe when the logs were hewed and to shape the corner notches that held the horizontal logs together in the walls of the house. I have never seen a hewn-log building of any kind in southern Indiana where any tool other than an axe was used to shape the notches. When a log building is dismantled, one can closely examine the notches, and the marks left by tools are especially obvious. Even in parts of the notch where a modern carpenter would almost certainly use a handsaw, the nineteenth-century builder used only an axe.

A century and a half ago, axe heads were generally made by local smiths from wrought iron with inserted steel bits. The owner made the handle, or helve, to suit himself. Axes made elsewhere in the country were also available in southern Indiana. In Bloomington, Indiana, in the 1830s, a local smith made axes that "brought in real cash, one dollar beyond any patent flashy affairs from New England, done up in pine boxes and painted half black, while their edge-part was polished and shiney as a new razor."[5] Even today, several patterns of axes are made, usually named for some locality or part of the country: for example, Michigan pattern and Western pattern. In turn-of-the-century hardware catalogs, I have found twenty-four pattern names, not brand names but names of specific shapes. Several different companies made Michigan-pattern axes, for example. No writer has, to the best of my knowledge, explored the origins, significance, and ages of these names. A recent book on the American axe ignores the question altogether.[6] At any rate, a Hoosier pattern axe was made and sold for a number of years by a large hardware firm in Louisville, Kentucky.[7] In the light of what is known about other tools and implements, I assume that local smiths in southern Indiana developed an axe of a special size and shape adapted to the kind of tree to be felled and the kind of work to be done in the area and that, when factories began to produce axes in quantity, they retained this special shape.

2. The FROE is a heavy, thick, dull-edged knife, usually at least a foot long and two inches wide, with a short handle rising at a right angle through an eye at one end of the blade; the cutting edge is *froe,* or away from, the handle. The froe served in carefully controlled splitting, or riving. Splitting that requires no great accuracy can be done with wedges as in making rails for a worm fence or in splitting firewood. Very small pieces can be split with such a tool as a pocket knife, but the froe served when most of the materials for a log house were rove out (*rove out* seems to be the most commonly used term in southern Indiana). When making shingles, an appropriate length of oak log was cut with a cross-cut saw. This section was roughly split into smaller pieces, or billets, with wedges and a maul. The sap wood, which is found just under the bark of the tree and which decays more rapidly than the heart wood, was then split off. Then a billet was stood on end in a froe horse, and the froe was beaten down with a froe club into the top end of the billet. When the blade was buried in the wood, the handle protruded on one side and part of the blade protruded on the other. By clubbing the end of the blade and prying the handle back and forth, a slab about the size of a shingle was riven off. The froe also served in riving

1
3
7
2
6
4
9
10

out the lath to be nailed to the interior walls to hold plaster, and it seems that pieces of wood riven to the appropriate size served as the basis for the chinking between the logs.

Compared to other tools, the froe must have presented a relatively simple task for a blacksmith. The blade should not be particularly sharp ("dull as a froe"), for it is meant to split, not to cut. Many a froe that I have seen has for a handle only a short length cut from a branch of appropriate size. The tool often appears to be clumsy and crude, but in the hands of a good workman, it was very effective.

3. The FROE CLUB drives the froe into the billet. It is frequently nothing more than a section of a branch about four inches in diameter and eighteen inches long with one end whittled down to a comfortable size for the hand. Some especially hard and tough wood, such as hickory, would be used if possible, but clubs soon became so battered that they were discarded and new ones made.

4. The FROE HORSE, which holds the billet upright while the froe is driven into it, usually consists of a large forked branch. It may be raised off the ground by legs, or it may be supported at a comfortable working height by a stump.

5. The SHINGLE CUTTER consists of a large, sharp blade that can move up and down in a heavy frame. It looks like a small guillotine, except that the shingle-cutter blade is forced down by a long lever. The block of wood from which the shingle is cut is held under the knife against a swiveling fence so that the operator can cut shingles that are thicker at one end. In addition to the man who holds the block under the knife, one or two men pull the long lever. While woods that split easily, such as oak, were used in making shingles with a froe, woods which are softer and cut more easily, such as yellow poplar, were used with the shingle cutter. The shingles could be cut much more readily and evenly if the blocks from which they were to be made had been steamed for some hours in a tank before being used. Shingle cutters were being used in southern Indiana in the late nineteenth century. Whether they were used in the first half, I have been unable to determine. Making the large blade was not beyond the skill of a good blacksmith, and most of the rest of the machine was made of wood. A shingle cutter could, therefore, have been made by a craftsman, just as he made other woodworking tools.

6. WEDGES were used for various kinds of rough splitting, such as preparing the billets from which shingles were either rove or cut. An iron wedge was usually used to start the split, and a wooden wedge, a GLUT, was used to finish it. I have never found any evidence that wedges were used to split or otherwise work the logs used in the walls of a house, for these were hewn with a broadaxe.

7. The MAUL, a large wooden hammer, drove the wedges; a hammer with an iron head would soon have battered the top of the wedge so badly as to make it useless. Mauls served other purposes, such as driving large wooden pins into their holes or driving two timbers together. Mauls were made in several ways, but the continued currency of *knot maul* in southern Indiana indicates that the heads were often made from a knotty piece of wood or one with intertwined fiber, such as a burl.

8. The SAWMILL, driven mostly by water power, must have been in wide use in early nineteenth-century southern Indiana because I have never seen a house of log or of any other type in the area from that period that failed to include many boards sawed by a water-driven sawmill. The blade in such a mill was long and narrow, something like a two-man cross-cut saw, and moved up and down while the log was moved against it and left vertical, straight scratch marks quite unlike the curved marks left by the steam-powered, circular saws of the later nineteenth and twentieth centuries. Although carpenters planed away any saw marks that would have been exposed to view, they often left the saw marks in such hidden places as the undersides of floor boards on the ground floor. Strange though it may seem at first to term a sawmill a tool, it is one in the broadest sense and was used to produce the boards that made the floors, staircase, mantelpieces, doors, windows, purlins, siding, trim, and fre-

quently such smaller timbers as rafters and the joists that supported the floor for the sleeping loft or second floor.

9. The PIT SAW, or WHIP SAW, consists of a long, narrow blade like that in a water-driven sawmill, but with a handle at each end. A log having been rolled over a pit or raised on trestles, two men, one above and one below the log, sawed boards from it. Such saws were certainly used in southern Indiana at one time, for some examples have been found in the area and are displayed in museums, such as that at Spring Mill State Park near Mitchell, Indiana. How common they were is impossible to say. I have never seen a board in any early house that I can say with certainty was sawed with a pit saw, but its mark is straight, slanting saw scratches.

10. The CROSS-CUT SAW has a long, narrow blade, but is used to cut a log or large timber to length, rather than to cut it into boards. Such saws may be one-man saws, relatively short, with a handle on only one end or two-man saws, longer, with a handle on each end. Cross-cut saws seem not to have been used to fell trees in the early nineteenth century, the felling axe alone being used in that task. The logs used in the walls of most log houses were cut to length with a cross-cut saw, for the ends of such logs do not show axe marks. The smaller handsaw may have been used for this purpose because cross-cut saws would have been costly. The manufacture of the blades for pit and cross-cut saws and for sawmills required facilities not available to most local blacksmiths.

TOOLS FOR MOVING AND MEASURING

11. CHAINS and HOOKS of some sort must have been used to drag logs from the woods to the site of the house or to the mill and to move them about generally. I have been unable to discover exactly what types of chain were in use in the era under consideration, but the chains and hooks would have been forged by local smiths. Oxen, supposedly common at the time, were probably used more for this type of work than were horses.

12. A SLED may have been used to support the front end of a large log as it was hauled, and smaller logs may have been piled on a sled. Sleds were probably used more than wagons because it is far easier to load logs onto a sled, and there is far less danger of the sled's tipping over on uneven ground. Sleds of relatively simple construction were often home-made with runners of some very hard, smooth wood, such as dogwood.

13. The CANT HOOK has a sturdy wooden handle four or five feet long, about one foot from the lower end of which a curved, iron arm with a spur is hinged so that it can move freely. With this device, a log can be rolled over with relative ease by one or two men.

14. The CROW BAR, a metal rod three or more feet long, with one end either pointed or flattened, served in prying up heavy timbers and logs and in shifting them a few inches at a time. A wooden pry bar might have been used in its place, but the greater size of a wooden bar made it more awkward and restricted its use.

15. The CHALK LINE is simply a length of stout string rolled for convenience in carrying on a reel or spool. When the string is pulled over a lump of chalk and held firmly at two points on a board or log, if it is pulled up vertically at its center and allowed to snap back, it will mark a straight line in chalk between the two points. I have seen in a few old barns the 150-year-old mark left by a string that was probably soaked in a reddish-purple fluid, such as pokeberry juice, rather than rubbed with chalk. The chalk line, used especially to mark straight lines on logs before they were hewed, would have served in a variety of ways in building a log house.

16. The PLUMB LINE is a heavy weight (the PLUMB BOB) at the end of a string used to establish a truly vertical line or to test whether a wall is vertical. The weight was often a piece of lead.

17. The SQUARE is used continually in marking boards to be cut square, in testing whether timbers meet at a right angle, and in other ways. Several types of square were used in the first half of the nineteenth century. In building a log house, probably at least one large FRAMING SQUARE and a small

TRY SQUARE would have been indispensable. Some squares of the period are home-made of wood, while some are iron, both probably used in southern Indiana.

18. The MITER SQUARE is so constructed that a forty-five-degree angle, or miter, can be marked on a board, permitting the craftsman to make matching cuts on two boards in a right-angle joint. Although a miter square is used far less frequently than a square, it is hard to imagine how without one a mantelpiece could be made or how trim could be fitted around doors and windows.

19. The BEVEL somewhat resembles a miter square, except that the two arms can be set at a chosen angle and the ends of a number of rafters, for instance, marked at the same angle. During the era that we consider, bevels were often simply constructed by riveting two strips of wood together so that they could be moved but would remain in position once set.

20. The DIVIDERS consists of two sharply pointed legs that may be set at appropriate distances apart by means of a quadrant wing projecting from one leg and passing through the other or passing through both. Some dividers have set screws to hold the leg position by friction on the wing. They may be made of metal, but in early nineteenth-century southern Indiana were more probably made of wood. They can, of course, be used to lay off circles and arcs, but they have another important use. When the edge of a board is to be fitted up against an irregular surface, the board is held close to the surface. The dividers are opened an appropriate distance and drawn along so that one leg follows the irregular surface while the other leg scribes a matching line on the board. When cut along the scribed line, the board will fit against the irregular surface.

21. The MARKING GAUGE consists of a bar of wood with one or more metal points set in it; the bar passes through a block of wood, or head, that can be set at any distance along the bar from the metal point. The head may be set with a wedge or a thumb screw of wood or metal. The purpose of the marking gauge is to scribe a line on a board, the line being parallel to one edge of the board. As the head is slid along the edge of the board, the metal point in the bar scribes the line. Marking gauges are of many different sizes and shapes. Some having two metal points and used to lay out mortises are MORTISE GAUGES. Those eighteen or more inches long are PANEL GAUGES. A carpenter who needed to lay off many lines always the same distance from an edge could have made a nonadjustable gauge of the right size so that he would always have it ready to hand.

22. The SCRATCH AWL, a thin metal rod with a convenient handle on one end and a sharpened point on the other end, is used for many sorts of marking, but especially to draw along the arm of a square to mark where a board is to be cut. Pencils, though expensive, were available at this time. When old buildings are torn down, boards occasionally show pencil marks, such as simple arithmetical computations, but the scratch awl, which once sharpened rarely needs resharpening, has an important advantage over a pencil, namely greater accuracy.

23. The RULE was constantly used for measuring, and rules of many kinds were available in the first half of the nineteenth century. Let us assume, however, that our builder of a log house had only the simplest of instruments, a foot-long wooden rule with one-eighth of an inch as the smallest division and numbered from right to left, rather than from left to right as in modern rules. With this rule he could construct a ten-foot rule, or ten-foot pole, from a suitable strip of wood notched or pencil-marked at needed intervals. We sometimes hear that an axe handle was a frequently used measuring device in earlier days, and it may well be that an axe handle was used roughly to gauge the length of logs or for similar tasks, but a more precise rule was certainly needed for many measurements in building a log house.

24. The LEVEL is, of course, a tool used to establish a true horizontal line. Spirit levels with a bubble in a curved tube were available in the early

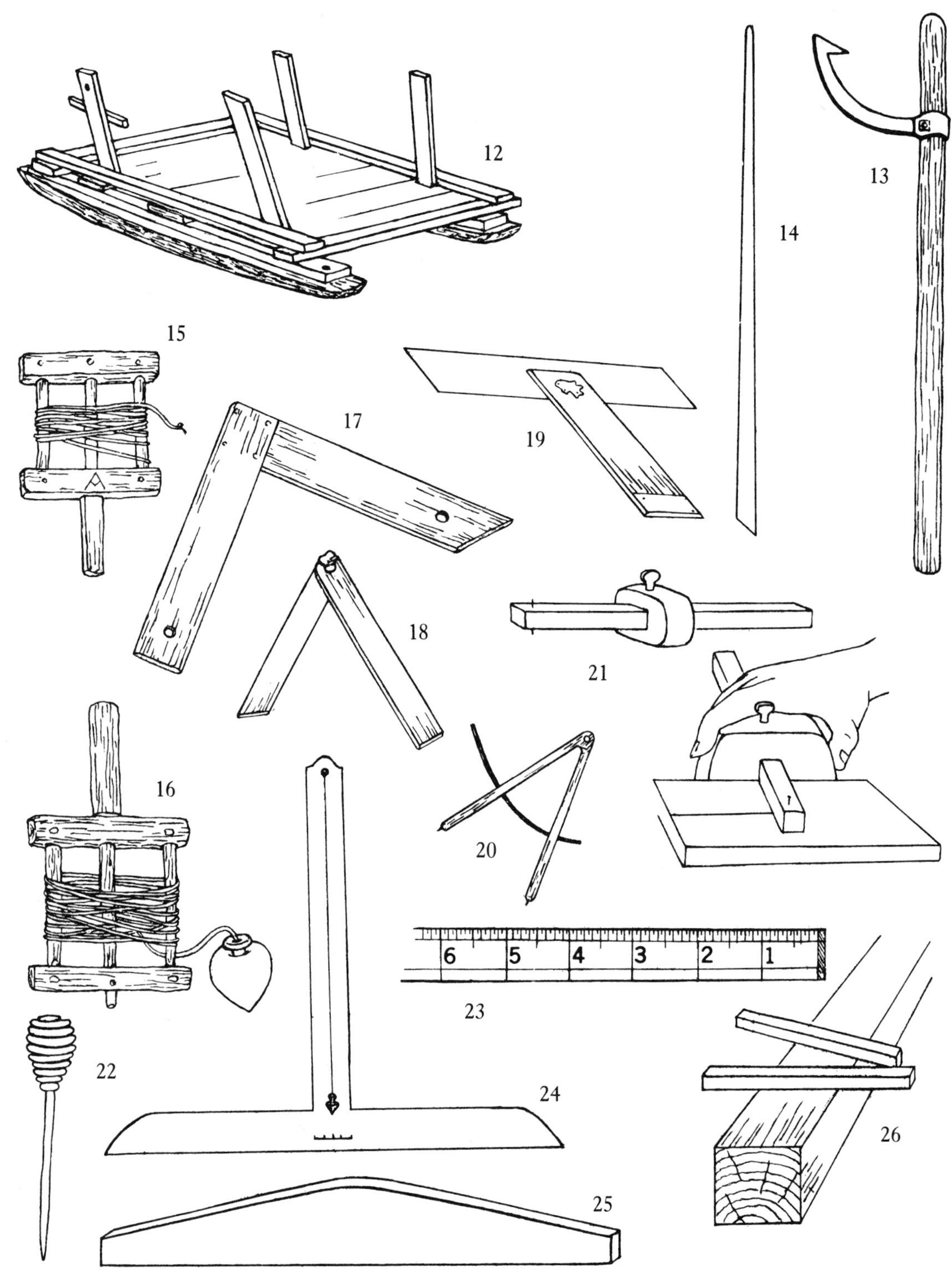
12
13
14
15
17
19
18
21
16
20
6
5
4
3
2
1
23
22
24
26
25

nineteenth century, but were probably uncommon and expensive. Much more likely to have been used was a device consisting of a straight strip of wood two or more feet long with an arm extending upward from the middle of it, at a right angle, so that a small plumb bob attached at the top of the arm could dangle down. When the string coincided with a line scribed on the arm or when the point of the bob rested over a mark on the base, the strip of wood was level. Levels of this sort could be constructed in a number of ways as far as the shape of the arm is concerned, but the basic principle was always the same.

25. The STRAIGHT EDGE is any object known to have a truly straight-line edge. It may be several feet long with one straight side and a back edge of greater width at the center to keep it from bending. A straight edge may also be a narrow board planed so as to have two straight parallel edges. It was used in many ways, such as to extend the line established by a level or a square or to test the surface of a board or timber to detect irregularities.

26. TRY STICKS, TRYING STICKS, or WIND STICKS are two short straight edges. When the craftsman sets the sticks across a timber at some distance from each other, he can sight over the tops of the sticks and tell whether the timber is plane and true or whether it has a wind (twist) in it. They are especially useful when a board that is being planed is clamped flat on the workbench.

TOOLS FOR HOLDING AND GRIPPING

27. The WORKBENCH is a multi-purpose tool, using the word in a broad sense, for holding and supporting work in a number of ways. It is, however, almost indispensable in holding boards for planing, and great numbers of planed boards were used in a log house. Workbenches can be of many kinds, but a craftsman building a log house surely had a bench to use, no matter how simple and crude it might have been, together with most of the devices used with a workbench.

28. The VISE that was attached to, or built into, the workbench, was almost entirely of wood in the first half of the nineteenth century, including the vital wooden bench screw. Although the vise is very convenient, a board could be held on the bench with other devices.

29. The HOLDFAST is a stout, L-shaped iron device with one long, round arm and one short arm flattened at least on the under side of its outer end. When a board is laid on the bench and the long arm of the holdfast is driven down through a round hole in the bench top, the short arm pressing down on the board binds the long arm in the hole so that the board is held firmly to the bench top. The hold of the holdfast is released by pounding the lower end of the long arm upward. The holdfast could easily have been made by a blacksmith.

30. The CATCH, or BENCH STOP, is a short, rectangular iron plug with a projecting, notched tip on its upper end. When driven into a hole in the top of the workbench so that the lip is a short distance above the surface, it can snag a board forced against it. When the surface of the board is planed, the catch will hold the board steady, yet leave the surface of the board unobstructed. A wooden plug can also be used.

31. SAWHORSES are simply made wooden trestles, generally used in pairs, to support boards or small timbers that are being sawed. Sawhorses can be quickly moved from place to place in and around a house that is being built. Moreover, a plank laid between a pair of sawhorses provides a platform on which the craftsman can stand.

32. CLAMPS come in various kinds. The HAND SCREW, commonly made entirely of wood and using wooden screws, is very convenient for holding small pieces of work. A BAR CLAMP, or DOOR CLAMP, is almost indispensable when a mitered door or window sash is being assembled.

33. The HOOK, or HOOK PIN, is shaped like the number 4. The shank can be driven into the previously bored hole of the joint where two timbers, such as rafters, are fitted together to test the fit of the joint. The pin can be removed by prying up or

hammering up on the underside of its protruding head.

34. DOGS are large iron staples. When a small timber is being hewed, one end of the dog can be driven into the timber and the other end into the block of wood on which the timber rests in order to hold the timber steady.

35. The MITER BOX is made of three boards forming a bottom and two sides. The sides have accurate forty-five-degree saw cuts (kerfs) in them so that if a piece of molding is held firmly against the inside of the box, a saw worked in the kerfs will cut the molding at a forty-five-degree angle. Two such mitered pieces fit so as to let them form a right-angle joint.

TOOLS FOR SURFACING, CHOPPING, AND PARING

36. The BROADAXE is the tool rightly associated by most people with the hewn-log house, for it is the main hewing tool. Most of the broadaxes at farm sales in southern Indiana have blades that are ten or twelve inches wide at the bit. One side of the head is completely flat. If the flat side of the head is laid on a plane surface, the bent handle curves upward. These features allow the axe head to slide along the flattened face of a log, removing irregularities, without the workman's fingers being scraped against the work.

A log to be hewn is dogged onto two timbers to hold it at a convenient height. Some bark is removed so that a chalk line can mark straight lines for the top and bottom of the surface to be flattened. Then a series of notches is cut with a felling axe into the part to be removed, the notches penetrating almost to the marked lines. The wood between the notches is split away in big chunks with either the felling axe or the broadaxe. Shallow cuts at an angle into the resulting surface are made with the felling axe. Finally, the broadaxe is used to pare the surface down to the level established by the chalk marks ("hew to the line"). Cuts made with a felling axe enable the broadaxe to pare away shavings. The chipmarks that are so obvious on hewn logs that have not been disfigured by decay, usually said to be the marks of the broadaxe, are actually the marks left by the felling axe.

37. The BROAD HATCHET, or HEWING HATCHET, a small version of the broadaxe, has a bit about five or six inches wide. The hatchet, used with one hand, is especially useful in working on smaller timbers or for removing wood from a timber already in place in a house where using the ponderous broadaxe would be awkward.

38. The SHINGLING HATCHET is actually a multipurpose tool very convenient for the workman who is shingling the roof and who finds it awkward to carry several single-purpose tools. With the shingling hatchet, he can drive nails into the shingles, for one end of the head is shaped like a hammer; he can split or pare down shingles to fit certain spots, for the other end is a sharp hatchet, and he can pull misdirected nails because a nail slot is cut into the side of the hatchet face. Frequently, too, the handle is marked with a notch letting the shingler measure the correct distance between courses of shingles.

39. The LATHING HATCHET resembles the shingling hatchet, except that it is flat across the entire top so that it can be used to nail lath along the top of a wall, near the ceiling. Many log houses had one or more plastered walls. The laths that I have examined from log houses of the first half of the nineteenth century have almost always been split, undoubtedly with a froe, from larger blocks of wood. They are, like modern lath, about three-eighths of an inch thick, about one and a quarter inches wide, and of various lengths. The ends of the laths have never been sawed, but have been cut with a hatchet.

40. The FOOT, or CARPENTER'S, ADZE is shaped somewhat like an old-fashioned garden hoe, except that the head is much heavier, the blade longer and much sharper, and the handle shorter. Unlike the axe, the cutting edge of the blade is at a right angle to the handle. The foot adze was probably used to true the surfaces of floor joists and timbers once they were in place. I have never seen marks on the logs in the walls of houses that could be identified

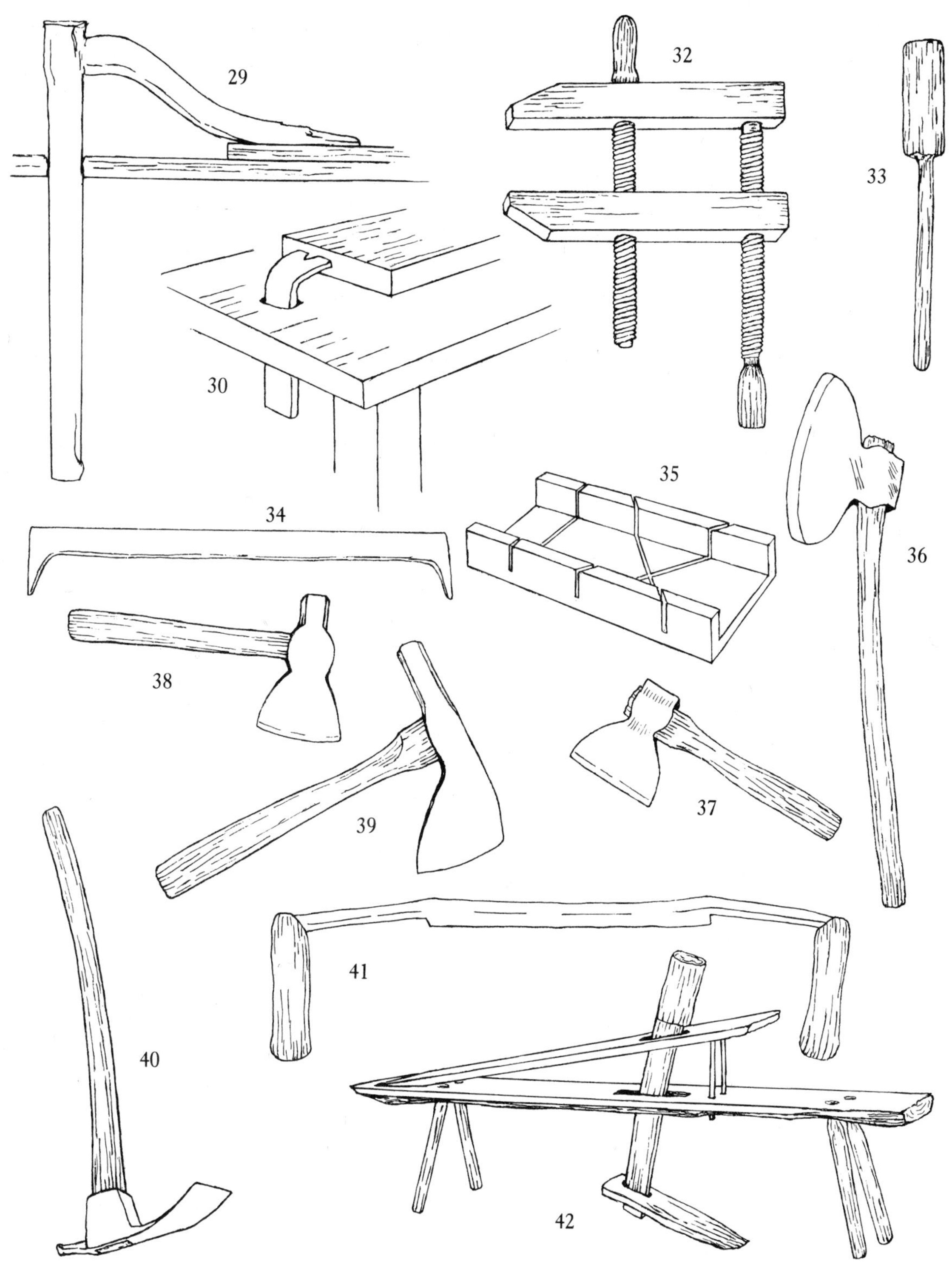

TOOLS USED IN BUILDING LOG HOUSES

with certainty as adze marks, and no older craftsman has told me of using the adze for finishing house logs. Nonetheless, because old examples seem very common at farm sales in southern Indiana, foot adzes were available and used. Although neither the early catalogs nor the reference works that I have consulted use it, the term *foot adze* is most common among older men in southern Indiana.

41. The DRAWKNIFE is a sharp, straight, knifelike blade, from eight to twelve inches long, with a wooden, right-angle handle at each end placed such that the tool cuts as the blade is drawn toward the craftsman. Drawknives may also have longer, shorter, or curved blades. The drawknife serves well where there is more material to be removed than can be done conveniently with a plane, but not enough to warrant using a broadaxe or adze. One important use was thinning the upper end of a shingle after it had been rove out with a froe.

42. The SHAVING HORSE is built in such a way that a workman sitting astride it can clamp a shingle on a surface before him by pushing down with his foot on a lever under the bench. He can then shave thin with a drawknife the end closest to him. The shaving horse was used almost exclusively with a drawknife.

43. The JACK PLANE of the era that we consider is a rectangular block of wood about sixteen inches long, three inches wide and three inches high. Near the center of the block, a slot pierces it, tapering from top to bottom and sloping down toward the front in such a way that with a wooden wedge a steel-tipped blade, or iron, can be wedged into the slot. Such a plane iron is about two and a half inches wide, six inches long, and one-eighth of an inch thick. When set for work, the iron's bit protrudes slightly from the bottom of the block of wood, and the entire iron inclines at about a forty-five-degree angle toward the back of the block. A handle is fastened on top of the back of the body of the plane.

Because each of the several kinds of plane has its specific purpose, a craftsman building a log house would have needed a number of different planes. Each kind of plane usually leaves its characteristic mark so that one can tell with reasonable certainty what planes were used. The jack plane removes relatively large amounts of wood as the first step in planing a board to remove the sawmill's marks and to bring the board down quickly to near the finish size. The jack plane's iron is slightly convex so that it protrudes most in the center and cuts a slight trough into the surface of the board. With other planes, the ridges between these grooves are removed from surfaces exposed to view, but they were sometimes left on the backs of boards, such as those used in mantelpieces, that were wanted to be straight and true, but which would not be exposed.

A craftsman in southern Indiana in the early nineteenth century could well have made the wooden parts of his planes himself and gotten the irons from the blacksmith. Planes were specifically mentioned as produced by the Bloomington smith, Austin Seward, during the 1820s.

44. The SMOOTH, or SMOOTHING, PLANE is about half as long as the jack plane (that is, about eight inches long). Some versions are narrower at the front and rear than in the middle, and the most common type has no handle. The bit of its iron is straight across, unlike the jack plane, and it is used mostly to remove the ridges left by the jack plane.

45. The JOINTER PLANE is twenty-eight inches or more in length. Its iron is straight across, and the plane has a handle. The jointer plane makes an especially straight surface and the edges of boards, such as floor boards, so finished can fit closely together. Other long planes include the TRYING PLANE (22 to 24 inches) and the FORE PLANE (18 inches). The jack plane can serve as a jointer plane if its iron is exchanged for a straight one.

46. The RABBET, or REBATE, PLANE, narrower and shorter than a jack plane, is so constructed that its iron cuts a notch along one edge of a board. Rabbet planes would have been especially useful in building the window frames into which the sash fit and the door frames.

47. TONGUE AND PLOW, or MATCH, PLANES were usually made in pairs that made tongue-and-groove cuts that fit together, or match. They are

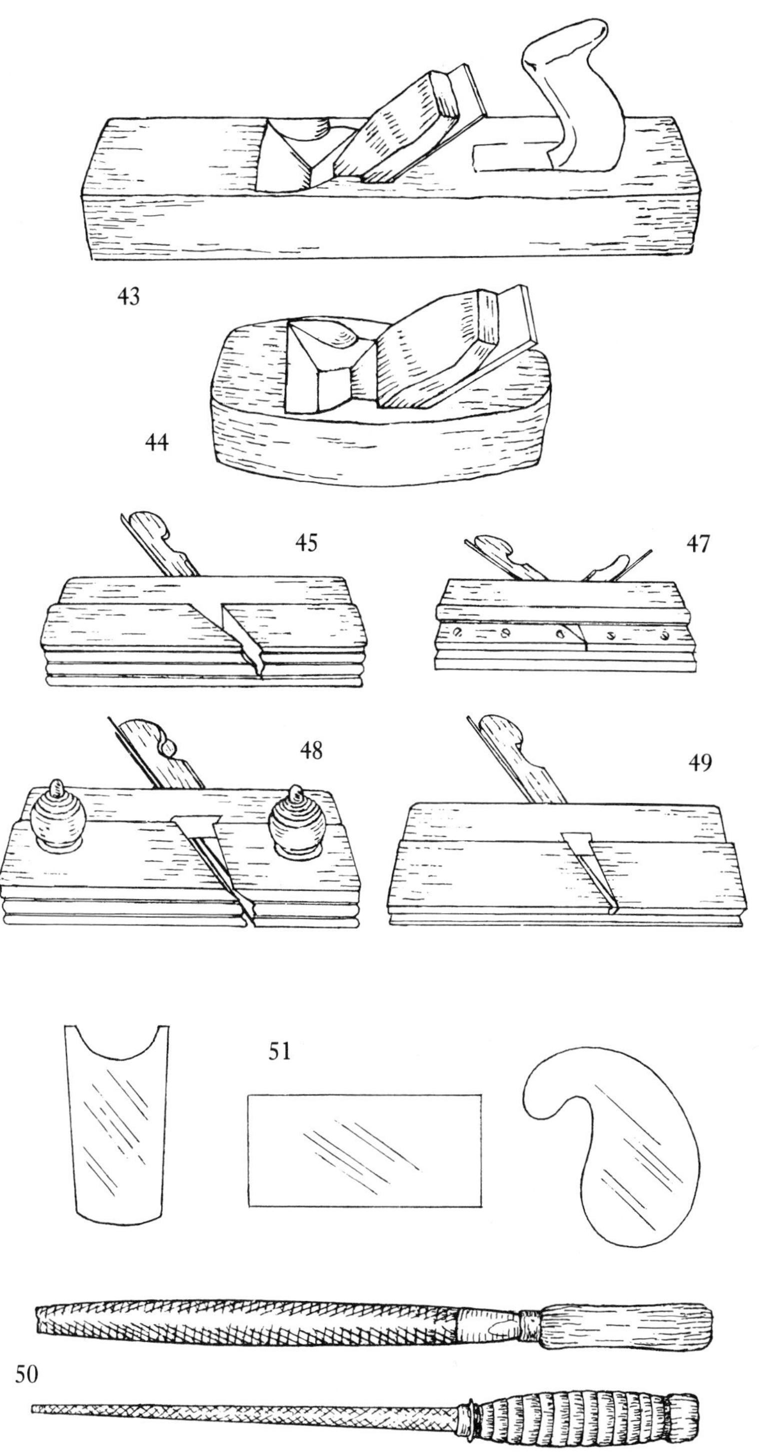
43
44
45
47
48
49
51
50

shorter and narrower than a jack plane. The tongue plane's iron has a notched bit that cuts in one operation the familiar tongue of a tongue-and-groove joint. The plow plane's iron has a narrower bit that cuts the groove. Every log house that I have seen had tongue-and-groove flooring. If the flooring was made in the first half of the nineteenth century, the joints were almost certainly made with tongue and plow planes, for no other tools could very well have made them.

48. The SASH PLANE is another specialized plane used to shape the wooden parts of a sash that actually hold the glass panes. Although the work can be done with a rabbet plane and a molding plane, a sash plane is more convenient. The early nineteenth-century log houses that I have seen as they were being disassembled or that were falling into decay, seem to have had windows in them since they were first built.

All of my evidence points to the making of window sash at or near the site of the house. The same may be said for doors, mantelpieces, and other finish items. Even though these items are today commonly made in specially equipped mills, I have never found any documentation that mills of this sort operated in the area in the era that we consider. Long distance shipping of a fragile piece, such as a window sash, or a bulky piece, such as a door, would have been prohibitively expensive. Panes of glass could have been properly packed and shipped. They were very early stocked by stores in southern Indiana.[8] I have closely examined sashes, mantelpieces, and doors from early houses and have carefully disassembled doors to see how they were made and what tools were used. They were all made with hand tools and, I am convinced, by local craftsmen.

49. MOLDING PLANES are of many different sizes and make many different shapes of molding. One plane normally makes one size and shape of molding, though complicated moldings result from combining the shapes formed by different planes. In some log houses, several different planes were used to make fairly elaborate mantelpieces, doors, baseboards, and the like, while in other log houses very few molding planes were used. One molding shape, however, in almost every log house is *bead molding,* which is in cross section one-quarter or one-half of a circle. The edges of boards and timbers that can be seen in the inside of the finished house almost never have sharp edges, but have bead moldings of different sizes worked upon them.

50. The WOOD RASP is a file-shaped, metal tool with coarser teeth than a file. It was used to smooth the cut ends of boards and to remove small amounts of wood in fitting joints together.

51. The SCRAPER is a piece of thin steel, usually rectangular in shape and not much larger than four by six inches. Scrapers were often cut out of worn-out saw blades. When properly sharpened and drawn with the grain, a scraper will remove a tiny amount of wood and leave a smooth surface. Scrapers were often used for the same sort of task for which a modern carpenter uses sandpaper, but sandpaper would have been scarce and expensive.

TOOLS FOR SHAPING AND FITTING

52. The HANDSAW used during the first half of the nineteenth century was very similar in shape and size to contemporary ones. It was in constant use to cut boards and small timbers to length, that is, across the grain. The handsaw commonly has twenty-six pointed teeth per inch.

53. The RIP SAW looks very much like the handsaw. Close inspection reveals that its teeth are slightly larger and chisel-shaped. The rip saw is used to cut boards lengthwise, with the grain. Forging the blade of a saw would have been a difficult task for a blacksmith. Most handsaws and rip saws were probably imported into southern Indiana.

54. The COMPASS SAW has a much narrower and shorter blade than the handsaw. The walls of a hewn-log house were commonly built up of solid logs and openings for doors, windows, and the fireplace cut only later, using a saw with a narrow blade in the gap between two logs. Once a narrow-bladed saw, perhaps the compass saw, had begun the cut, a handsaw could finish it.

55. The TENON, or DOVETAIL, SAW, a smaller variety of the handsaw, has a blade made of such thin steel that the blade must be stiffened with a thick brass or steel rib along its top. Consequently, it cannot make a deep cut, but its smaller size, finer teeth, and thinner blade fit it for such fine work as shaping the tenons for the joints that held window sash together.

56. The FIRMER CHISEL, a long, narrow blade sharpened on one end and with a wooden handle on the other end, is a general purpose chisel used to cut, pare, and trim in a number of ways. It may be pushed by hand or driven with a mallet. A craftsman building a log house probably had several firmer chisels of different sizes.

57. The PARING CHISEL is usually longer and of lighter construction than the firmer chisel, being pushed by hand pressure only. It is kept very sharp and used for light paring in fitting joints and similar work. A very large paring chisel with a blade two and a half inches or more in width is a SLICK, or CARPENTER'S SLICK.

58. The MORTISE CHISEL has a much thicker blade than the firmer chisel and is driven with a mallet. In making mortises, chisels of several different sizes were used, depending on the size of the mortise. A special type of mortise chisel that is L-shaped in cross section is a CORNER CHISEL. It was used especially to square-cut the corners of mortises.

59. The MALLET is a lump of wood with a handle of convenient size, usually about a foot long. They were made in a number of shapes. Sometimes the head and the handle are made from one piece of wood. They are used especially to drive chisels because the wooden head of the mallet will not destroy the chisel handle as would the metal head of a hammer.

60. The BRAD AWL is a small steel rod flattened and sharpened on one end with a wooden handle on the other end. By pushing the sharpened end into the wood and turning it back and forth, the brad awl makes a small hole into which a nail may be driven. If a nail is driven in near the end of the board without this preliminary hole, the board may split.

61. The AUGER, or GIMLET, is a metal rod with one end shaped so as to cut a round hole in wood and with a wooden handle attached to the other end at right angles to the axis of the rod; turning the handle turns the shaft of the auger, making it cut the hole. Augers were made in a number of ways in the early nineteenth century. The TWISTED AUGER with spiral flutes was just coming into use at the beginning of the century; but because its manufacture demanded equipment not available to the average smith, it was probably not widely used in southern Indiana in the first half of the century.

Even though the twisted auger bores a deep hole rapidly across the grain of a piece of wood because the flutes carry the chips up and out of the hole, it cannot bore a hole lengthwise, with the grain, into the end of a timber. In building a log house, many holes were bored into the ends of logs where openings were cut through the walls for doors, windows, and fireplaces. At these openings, a heavy plank was set against the cut ends of the logs, a hole an inch or more in diameter bored through the plank and several inches into the end of the log, and a wooden pin was driven through the plank and into the log. Augers (other than spiral twist augers) must have been used for this task, but their exact form is unknown. The most likely form is the POD AUGER in which the cutting end of the rod is shaped into a short, cylindrical trough that tapers, thins, and curls to the right. A blacksmith can make a pod auger.

Augers were used to bore large holes from one inch to three inches in diameter, but the largest bored holes usually made in a log house were the two-inch holes bored through the plate and into the log supporting it at each outside corner of the house so that a large wooden pin could hold the plate in place.

62. The BRACE AND BIT makes holes smaller than those of the auger and larger than those of the broad awl, roughly diameters between one-quarter

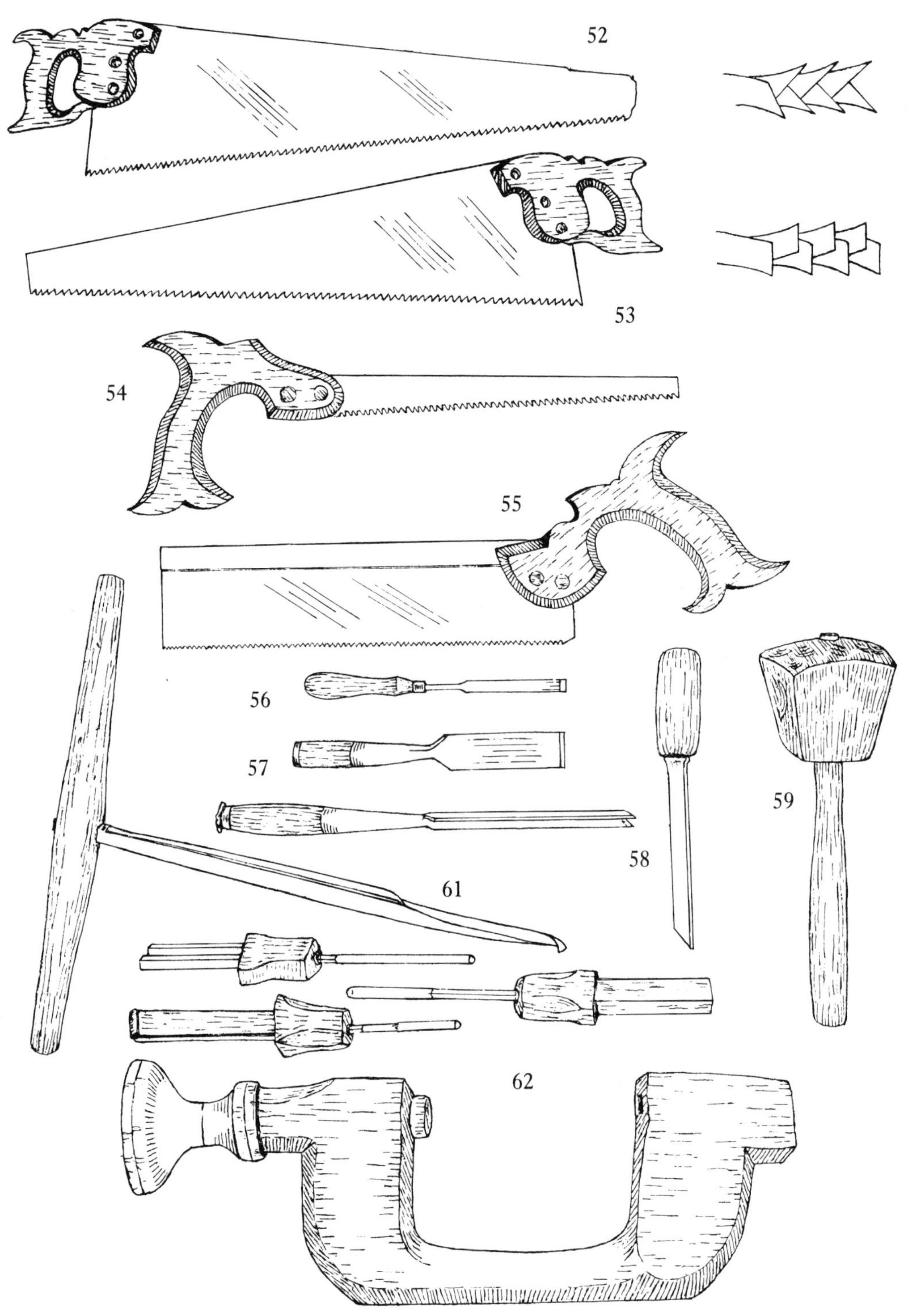
52
53
54
55
56
57
58
59
61
62

inch and one inch. The brace commonly used in the early nineteenth century, while having generally the shape of the familiar modern tool, was made of wood. Bits of several different types and in a variety of sizes could be made by smiths, but the spiral bit was probably not common.

TOOLS FOR FASTENING AND UNFASTENING

63. NAILS were used in large numbers in a hewn-log house, and although I may seem to extend the meaning of the term to classify them as tools, I follow Mercer.[9] The handmade WROUGHT NAIL, laboriously produced one by one by the smith at the forge, was superseded about 1800 by the CUT NAIL that was quickly stamped by machine from a thin sheet of iron and that had its head formed by another machine. It is very unusual in my experience to find any wrought nails in an early nineteenth-century, southern Indiana hewn-log house. The machine-made cut nail, which is rectangular in cross section and today often called a "square" nail, was used throughout the log house. Some are headless or nearly so in order that they can be driven beneath the surface of a board, such as floor boards or baseboards; others have noticeable heads; and some are large spikes and some tiny brads; even so, they are essentially alike. Hundreds of nails were used to shingle the roof, and the log houses that I have seen were originally roofed with wooden shingles nailed on. Hundreds more were used elsewhere in the house. Whether there were nail-making machines in southern Indiana or whether the nails were imported ready-made, I cannot say.

64. The CLAW HAMMER, used both to drive and to pull nails, hardly needs to be described, for the early nineteenth-century claw hammer looks very much like the modern one, except that the head of the early hammer does not have the deepened eye (the hole that the handle fits in) of the modern hammer. The heads of claw hammers were probably made by local smiths in earlier times, and the owner made the wooden handle.

65. The NAIL PUNCH, or SET, is a short, steel rod tapering at one end to a blunt point. It is used to sink the heads of nails below the surface of the wood in floor boards, baseboards, and the like.

66. The WOOD SCREW was used in a log house to hold door hinges, latches, and such. Those that I have been able to remove from their places in early nineteenth-century log houses usually appear to be machine-made; but, unlike modern screws, they are blunt-ended. A machine to make pointed wood screws was patented in 1846, and pointed screws quickly superseded the blunt ones.[10]

67. The SCREWDRIVERS of the early nineteenth century were often made by blacksmiths from worn-out files, hence the most common early screwdrivers resemble modern ones, except that their shanks are flat.

68. The WOODEN PEG, PIN, or TRUNNEL was widely used in log houses of the first half of the nineteenth century. Logs notched to interlock at the corners were held in place by their own weight and needed no fasteners, but pegs were used to secure planks against the cut ends of logs at window and door openings, to hold the plate at each corner to the log beneath, to hold the butt ends of rafters to the plate, and elsewhere. As time went on, more spikes and fewer pegs were used so that, in later houses, the butt ends of rafters were spiked to the plate. Even in late log houses, however, the plates are nearly always held to the logs beneath them by pegs a foot or more in length and two inches in diameter. Iron spikes large enough for this task seem not to have been available. Every peg that I have seen removed for examination from its hole was handmade, whether a tiny peg from a window sash or a large trunnel from a plate. They seem first to have been rove out from a straight-grained piece of wood, usually oak, and then trimmed, the small ones probably with a knife, the large ones with a drawknife, to a roughly cylindrical shape. Many are more or less octagonal in cross section while some are nearly square, but none is smooth and round in cross section as if machine-made or turned in a lathe. The rough shape insured that the peg would

stay tight in the bored hole into which it was driven. The word *peg* seems to be in wide use in southern Indiana, and the barns with heavy frames are often called "pegged barns."

69. The CLAW, or WRECKING BAR (as it is often called today) is an iron rod perhaps an inch in diameter and two feet long. At least one end of the rod is flattened, tapered, and notched so that it can be slipped under a nail-head, around the nail shank, and pry out the nail. The rod is usually bent near one end, sometimes into a half circle, to provide more leverage. Even though the claw hammer pulls nails effectively, the common early nineteenth-century type had a much shorter eye than the modern one, and the head could not be so strongly affixed to the handle. Frequent nail pulling with the claw hammer would have loosened the head, and pulling a large nail might well have broken the handle. A claw, commonly kept on hand to pull large nails, could easily be made by blacksmiths.

70. PINCERS are a plierlike tool having wide, sharply tapered jaws. Pincers can be used to pull headless nails and brads where a claw hammer or claw cannot be used. They were frequently made by blacksmiths.

TOOLS FOR SHARPENING

71. The GRINDSTONE is a thick disc of carefully selected sandstone. It is pierced by a horizontal axle that is set in a frame so that the stone can rotate when the axle is turned by a crank. Some arrangement, such as a container above it from which water drips, keeps the surface of the stone wet while it is being used. Almost all edged woodworking tools require rough sharpening from time to time. The whetstone and the file will produce a finer edge and can touch up the edge between grindings, but they could not fully take the place of the grindstone, especially for sharpening axes.

We might pause to wonder how the pioneer, so frequently described in historical accounts as moving into a heavily forested area with not much more than an axe, managed to survive.[11] On the one hand, he had constantly to use his axe to clear trees from his land and to build all sorts of things, including a log cabin, so that his axe would need continually to be sharpened. On the other hand, a grindstone large enough to be of any use would have been very difficult to bring with him. It seems unlikely that the average pioneer could count on finding suitable stone or have had the skill to make a grindstone even if he had found suitable raw material, because a grindstone that is not round and that does not run true is nearly useless. If he used his neighbor's, where did his neighbor get one? It seems that the average pioneer was better provided with tools and equipment than many have believed.

72. The WHETSTONE is a small piece of fine-grained sandstone with at least one flat surface. When this surface is moistened with water or oil, it can put a fine edge on chisels, plane irons, axes, and the like. Very small or specially shaped stones were needed to sharpen some tools, such as augers. Frequently used stones often sat in lidded wooden boxes to protect them from being chipped and to keep them clean.

73. The FILE is needed to sharpen the teeth of saws. While other shapes might be used on the large teeth of the cross-cut saw, only a file which is triangular in cross section can be used on the smaller teeth of handsaws, rip saws, compass saws, and tenon saws. Files were probably imported into southern Indiana because making them was a highly specialized craft.

74. The SAW SET, or WREST, is a thin metal blade having notches of various size in it. For a saw to cut properly without binding, the teeth must be bent out to each side, one to the left and the next to the right. The teeth then cut a groove, or kerf, in the wood, which is wider than the blade and which keeps the blade from binding. During use, the teeth of the saw tend to lose their outward bend, and from time to time, they must be rebent, or set, with the saw set.

75. The SAW VISE, or CLAMP, holds the saw with the teeth uppermost while the saw is filed and set. The vise can be made in a number of ways and may be of wood, but it must be made to hold the blade

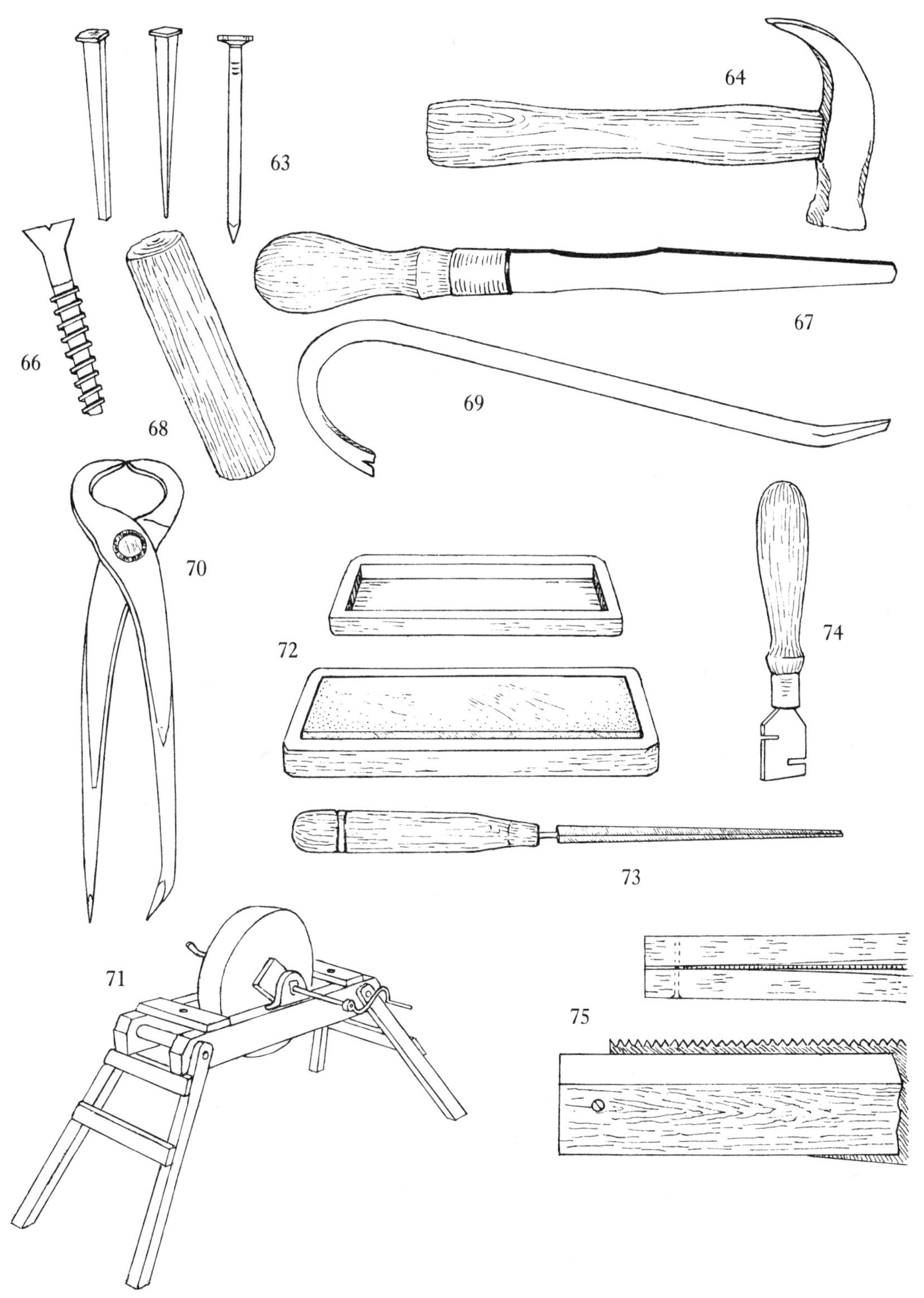
63
64
66
67
68
69
70
72
74
73
71
75

firmly just below the teeth, else the saw will chatter, or vibrate, and quickly dull the file.

OTHER TOOLS

76. The LADDER, while Mercer does not mention it, would certainly have been used in building a log house, and probably several ladders of different lengths, at that.

Conclusion

In building a hewn-log house during the first half of the nineteenth century, a large number of tools were used, far more than most writers lead us to believe. Some of these tools, admittedly, were of the kind that might have been made just for the job of building the one house and might have been discarded when that job was completed. Disposable tools include the long measuring stick and the trying sticks. Most of the tools, however, were of the permanent type which would be used on job after job. It seems unlikely that the average farmer owned all of the tools needed to construct a house. He certainly owned axes, hatchets, saws, hammers, wedges, and other tools because he would often have needed them about the farm. The more specialized tools, such as molding planes, however, probably would have been owned by only a few men in any community or comparable rural area. These men were carpenters, as well as farmers. In any early nineteenth-century rural area, there was a variety of craftsmen who farmed, in addition to practicing their craft, and who helped their neighbors when their special skills were needed. In return, their neighbors helped them at harvesting, hog-butchering, or maple sugaring. It was these carpenters who made the sash, mantelpieces, and other house parts that required special tools and skills and who, aided by the owner of the house and perhaps other neighbors, built the rest of the house. It also was a common practice in earlier times to lend tools and implements. At any rate, the tools and the skill to use them must have been readily available in earlier times because a large number of solid, well-built log houses was constructed in southern Indiana in the first half of the nineteenth century, and while many have disappeared from neglect or destruction, many are still in use today.

The belief that the tools needed to build a log house were simple and few may be the result of two factors. First, the simple, round-log *cabin* intended for temporary shelter has been confused with the hewn-log *house* intended as a permanent dwelling. In southern Indiana, at least, the cabins all seem to have disappeared if they were, indeed, as common as historical accounts would lead us to believe. The hewn-log houses remain in fair numbers. The average person thinks of them as "pioneer log cabins," and, recalling the accounts in history books, assumes that they were built with a few simple tools. Writers on log buildings have, for the most part, helped to perpetuate this idea, which for southern Indiana, at least, is a misconception. The second factor is the general notion that life in "pioneer times" was very simple and crude. Life in the first half of the nineteenth century was certainly different from what it is today, but a close inspection of log houses shows that far more tools were available and used than is generally believed and that life was perhaps not so crude as we have been led to believe.

Notes

This article was originally published in *Pioneer America* (July 1977). The author gratefully acknowledges the fine illustrations by Ada L. K. Newton.

1. Logan Esarey, *The Indiana Home* (Crawfordsville, Ind.: R. E. Banta, 1947), p. 29; S. W. Widney, *Pioneer Sketches; Containing Facts and Incidents of the Early History of Dekalb County* (Auburn, Ind.: W. T. and H. M. Kimsey, 1859), p. 5.
2. C. A. Weslager, *The Log Cabin in America* (New Brunswick, N.J.: Rutgers University Press, 1969); Donald Hutslar and Jean Hutslar, "The Log Archi-

tecture of Ohio," *Ohio History* 80, nos. 3–4 (Summer–Autumn 1971): 171–271.
3. Henry C. Mercer, *Ancient Carpenters' Tools* (Doylestown, Pa.: Bucks County Historical Society, 1929), p. 300.
4. Peter C. Welsh, *Woodworking Tools, 1600–1900,* Smithsonian Institution, Contributions from the Museum of History and Technology, no. 241 (Washington, D.C., 1966), pp. 178–228.
5. Baynard Rush Hall, *The New Purchase* (Princeton: Princeton University Press, 1916), p. 278.
6. Henry J. Kauffman, *American Axes* (Brattleboro, Vt.: S. Greene Press, 1972).
7. Belknap Hardware and Manufacturing, *Catalog No. 86* (1932), p. 15; *Catalog No. 88* (1937), p. 13.
8. Hall, *The New Purchase,* p. 215.
9. Mercer, *Ancient Carpenters' Tools,* p. 247.
10. Ibid., p. 256.
11. Esarey, *The Indiana Home,* p. 17.

The Dutch Barn in America: Survival of a Medieval Structural Frame

THEODORE H. M. PRUDON

Dutch architecture in the United States has been celebrated more often than it has been investigated, consequently the Netherlandish character of Dutch colonial buildings has usually been assumed rather than demonstrated. Theodore H. M. Prudon's article is an attempt to remedy this defect through a precise comparative investigation of Dutch structural traditions in the Old and New Worlds. As such, it is a rare example of a study of an ethnic building tradition that did not enter mainstream American vernacular practice.

Prudon builds on the work of European scholars and on John Fitchen's pioneering study of The New World Dutch Barn *(1968). Though the formal qualities of buildings in old and New Netherlands differed, Prudon argues, building construction is innately conservative and transcends stylistic and formal change. Thus, Prudon assumes that one ought to find structural similarities between Dutch buildings on the two continents. He begins with a precise four-point description of the characteristics of the New World Dutch barn, then goes on to locate each of those characteristics in a single, clearly defined framing tradition that crosses national boundaries in the Low Countries and Germany. Next, he shows that this kind of framing dates from the Middle Ages. Finally, he suggests that the method of manufacturing and assembling the frame as well as the four-bay length of the standard American Dutch barn are further links with the Netherlandish tradition.*

Where Fitchen chose to emphasize the differences between European and American practice, Prudon stresses the continuities. Given his careful specification of what, exactly, is Dutch *about the New World Dutch barn, one could then go on to investigate the forces that acted on it in America and the reasons for its failure to be built after the early nineteenth century, thus raising questions about the* New World *qualities of the barn.*

During the years the term *Dutch Colonial* has become well-accepted and widely used. While it is generally used to describe some examples of eighteenth-century residential architecture, which has a number of clearly identifiable features, it is a very ill-defined term. Extensive and well-founded research hardly exists and that typical phenomenon, the so-called Dutch barn, is not included.

Interest in vernacular architecture has more recently increased. The resulting studies are in most instances not very systematic or methodological and as a result the published studies are not conclusive. The Dutch barn has, of course, received more attention and is mentioned now in most general surveys. Most of these publications are aesthetic or appreciative in nature.

In 1929, Helen Wilkinson Reynolds in her book on Dutch Colonial architecture in the Hudson Valley illustrated only one example of a Dutch barn, the Verplanck–Van Wyck barn.[1] Articles such as Mary Mix Foley's "The American Barn" or Amos Rapoport and Henry Sarnoff's "Our Unpretentious Past," both of more recent date, are still general surveys.[2] Publications by Eric Sloane and others do recognize the uniqueness of this barn type but provide mostly inaccurate or misunderstood information.[3] The recent book by Eric Arthur and Dudley Witney, although a survey, is more precise than most others.[4] John Fitchen's *The New World Dutch Barn* is probably the first attempt to analyze this type of barn more systematically and in-depth including the possible origins of this type of structure.[5]

Because the purpose here is to explore European precedents in greater depth, it is useful to develop a sort of prototype as an architectural form, which combines all the typical characteristics. This approach is possible because as is clear from Fitchen's survey a great consistency exists. Moreover, a comparative analysis based upon the structure is possible because building technology is essentially a very conservative art. In spite of rapid changes in style that only affect the surface appearance of the building, the structure remains the same for an extended period of time. For instance, when comparing an eighteenth-century Georgian church spire in America with a late medieval European example, it is apparent that the structural appearance remained the same in spite of the separation in time and place. Seen in this light and especially for buildings where the stylistic appearance of the structure was of no concern, a comparative study of structural elements offers a valid approach to identifying possible origins.

On this basis a number of characteristics of the Dutch barn in America have been identified and compared with European prototypes and practices. To illustrate these features a Dutch barn that once stood along Route 20 in Sharon, New York, has been selected (fig. 1).[6]

1. The structural frame consists primarily of H-shaped bents, which are lined up in a longitudinal direction. The bents are formed by two posts, which are connected horizontally by a large cross beam with mortise and tenon. Very distinctive is the tenon, which extends beyond the post and is securely wedged to increase the stiffness of the bent (fig. 2). To increase the rigidity of the bent, diagonal braces are installed. This type is usually described as "anchor beam" construction, an awkward translation of the German and Dutch word *Ankerbalk,* a term probably used for the first time by F. Ostendorf in his 1908 book *Geschichte des Dachwerks.*[7] On the ground the various bents are placed on continuous sills, which increase further the stability of the H-bent system and the sidewalls.

2. The secondary posts, which are placed on

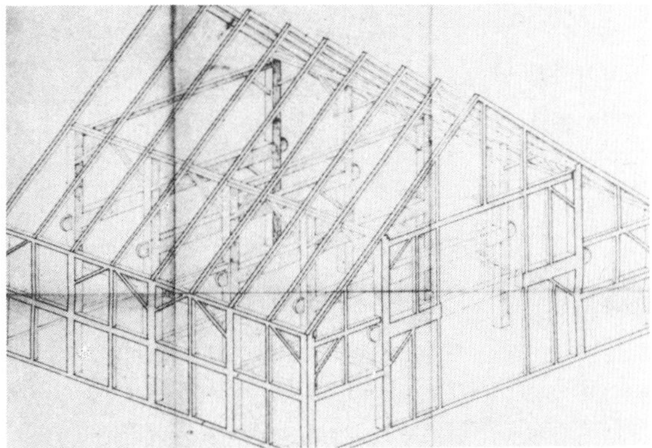

Figure 1. Isometric reconstruction drawing of a barn originally along Route 20 in Sharon, N.Y. This barn is an excellent example of the type of Dutch barn found in the United States. The barn was dismantled and moved to Bethpage, Long Island. (Drawing by Michael Emrick and the author.)

Figure 2. Typical mortise and tenon joint for the anchorbent. (From John Fitchen, The New World Dutch Barn *[Syracuse: Syracuse University Press, 1968].)*

continuous sills and which form the exterior sidewalls, are connected to the bents by transverse struts. The result is generally a four-bay-long barn with three aisles, nearly square in plan.

3. The roof consists originally of widely spaced rafters, which are tied at the top and rest at the bottom on the plate, which runs atop the posts of the main H-bents. This plate is stiffened by diagonal braces.

4. Access to the building is mostly through large double doors, which are located at either side in the gable ends. The center aisle, accessible in this manner, was used for unloading large wagons, while storage could take place in the side aisles or on top of the bents where a loft area is created by placing widely spaced poles on top of the cross pieces.

If these characteristics can be considered prototypical, then it will be possible to compare the structural form found in this country with European developments. This development is, compared with America, quite well-known as a result of the work of R. C. Hekker, R. Meischke, F. Ostendorf, H. Zantkuyl, Adelhart Zippelius and others.[8]

In figure 3 the evolution of the three-aisled house or barn in Europe is illustrated.[9] In the first phase of the *Einhaus* or *Hallehaus,* the roof is supported by posts individually. The posts of this prehistoric structure are driven independently in the ground, giving sufficient rigidity to the structure. By the beginning of our era the posts appear to be interconnected by transverse members. At the end of the first millennium the bents are stiffened by the installation of diagonal braces (fig. 4). This improvement had two advantages; first, it facilitated an increase in the span and, second, it was necessary to provide sufficient rigidity because the posts no longer were driven in the ground but placed on sills or masonry piers. To counter the increased shear at the ends of the anchor beams the dimensions of the beam sometimes were increased at the end by adding a corbel (fig. 5).[10] As illustrated in the fourth phase, the evolution was essentially complete. When exactly the posts were extended to create a large loft space is not clear, but according to Zippelius this development in the Rhineland region took place at the end of the Middle Ages because of the need for larger storage facilities (fig. 6).[11]

Although the basic form of the structure seems to have been fully developed by the end of the Middle Ages, later alterations are of some importance. While the one-bay type developed simultaneously with the three-bay type, the latter subsequently was reduced again by removing one or both side aisles, but with the H-shaped anchorbeam bents retained. This type was frequently used for smaller town or farm houses and can be found in Holland as well as in the United States, for instance, in the Schenck House, now in the Brooklyn Museum (figs. 7, 8).[12]

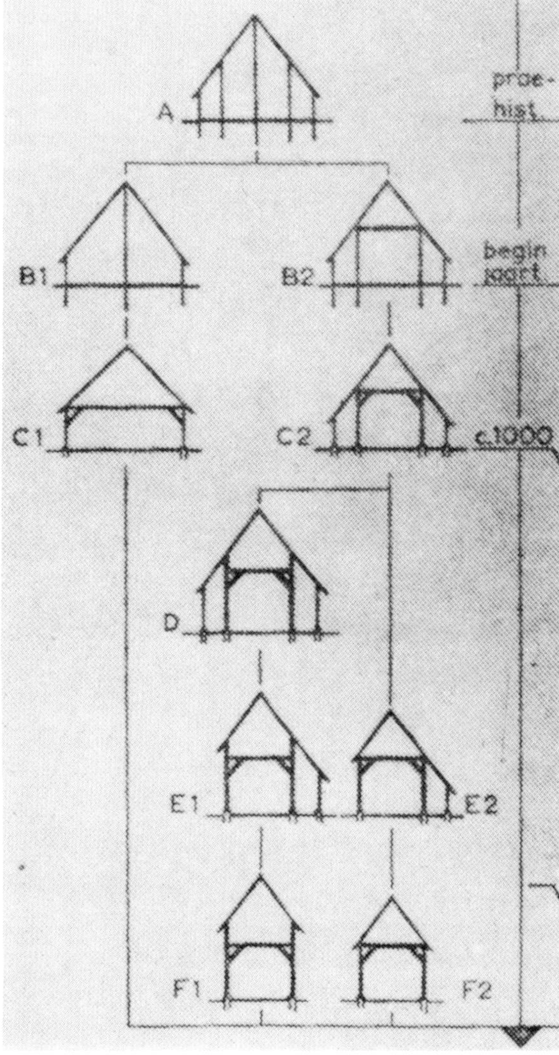

Figure 3. Schematic development of the wooden frame in northwestern Europe from prehistoric times to the seventeenth and eighteenth centuries. The prehistoric frame consists of stakes in the ground (a) that are initially not interconnected horizontally but later develop some horizontal ties (b). By the year 1000 A.D. the posts are placed on separate foundations, while the anchorbent has diagonal cross bracing to give it sufficient rigidity (c). At that time two basic types exist, with either three aisles or one. Subsequently the three-aisle type (d) is found with three, two, or even one aisle by simply omitting one or both side aisles (e and f). In addition, the proportions of the anchorbent itself can vary. By extending the post substantially above the anchorbeam, a second story is created, which was an adaptation useful in more urban environments. Both the types e and f are encountered more or less simultaneously. (Drawing by Michael Emrick, after H. Zantkuyl, Bouwen in Amsterdam *[Amsterdam, n.d.].)*

Figure 4. Barn under reconstruction in Orvelte, the Netherlands. The anchorbents with the typical mortise and tenon joints and its dowels are clearly visible and essentially similar to the connections found in the Dutch barns of the United States. (Courtesy of the Provincial Museum, Drenthe.)

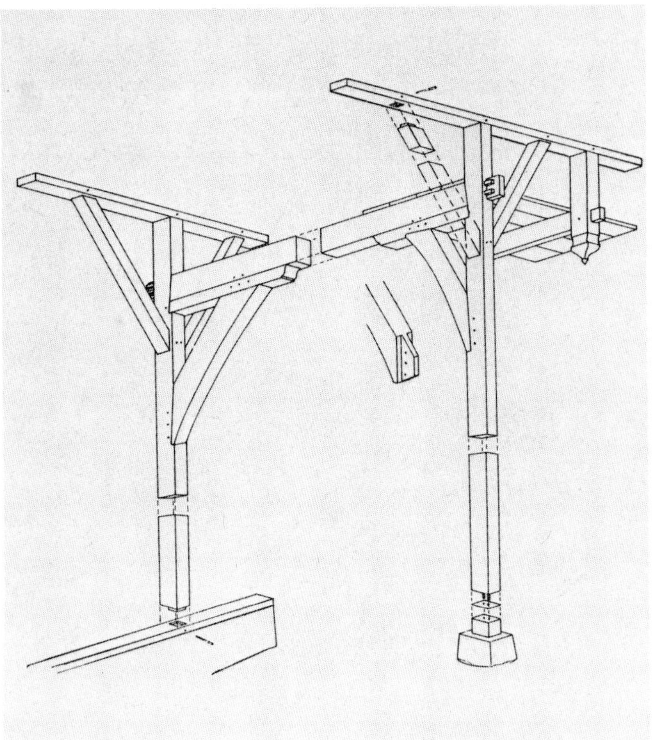

Figure 5. Isometric drawings of typical anchorbent connections found in the Netherlands. In some cases the post is placed on a separate footing, while in some instances a sill beam resting on a continuous foundation is found. Mortise and tenon joints are identical as are the diagonal cross braces. A curious detail, which is probably unknown in the United States, is the smaller intermediate beam suspended from the main girder. (Drawing by Michael Emrick, after H. Zantkuyl, Bouwen in Amsterdam *[Amsterdam, n.d.].)*

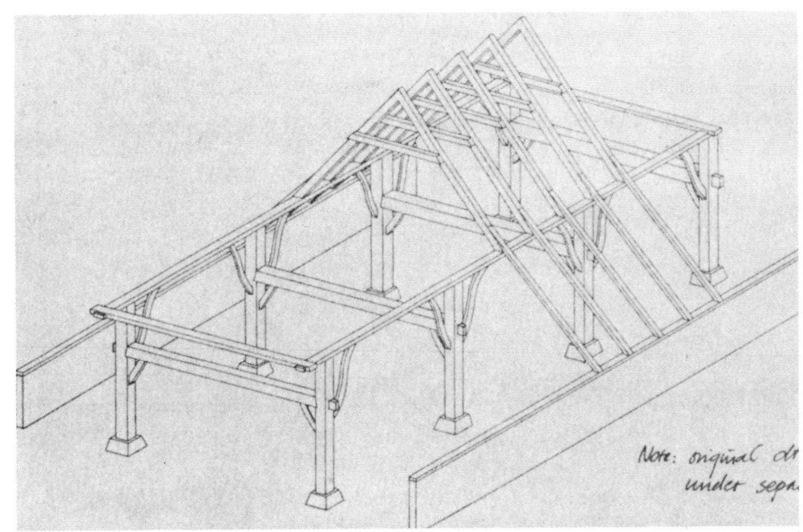

Figure 6. Isometric drawing of a typical frame found in farm and vernacular structures in the Rhineland region of Germany. While the side walls are quite low and made of masonry (wood had become scarce), the frame is essentially the same as the ones found in the American examples. The rafters are interconnected by collarbeams but customarily no ridgepole is found. (Drawing by Michael Emrick, after Adelhart Zippelius, Das Bauernhaus am unteren deutschen Niederrhein *[Wuppertal, W. Germany: A. Martini and Grüttefien, 1957], p. 21.)*

Figure 7. Typical medieval wooden frame of a small house in Amsterdam. While the building has only one aisle, it is four bays deep with the typical anchorbents. See also figure 3, type e1. (From H. Zantkuyl, Bouwen in Amsterdam *[Amsterdam, n.d.].)*

The isometric drawing of a segment of a bent is a typical example of how such constructions appeared in northwest Europe at the end of the Middle Ages (fig. 5). The continuous sill as observed in this example was not unusual as is sometimes implied.[13] Both sills as well as separate footings do occur in the Rhineland region as in Holland.[14] Certainly it is apparent from a comparison of the structural frame of the Dutch barn in the United States that it is quite similar to the one found in the Rhineland region (figs. 1 and 6).

From the developmental outline presented and the characteristics of the barn in North America, the late medieval origin of the latter is unmistakable. This form of the *Hallehaus* has since been modified and altered in Europe.[15] This makes a careful comparison of existing examples difficult and inconclusive; certainly most European structures lack this consistency and clarity of type.[16] Some of these differences can easily be attributed to the separation in time and place.

The type of *Hallehaus* described was initially quite widespread over the European continent.[17] Depending upon the region, and the geographic and economic conditions, the basic form was altered, modified, and adapted to the specific needs of agriculture and to the available materials (fig. 9). Changes of this sort had already begun to take place in the seventeenth century, resulting in the present complex and composite form of these farm structures.[18] A good indication that this development in Europe was completed by the end of the eighteenth century is a surviving group of drawings of farm buildings erected around 1800.[19] In this extensive collection only a few illustrate a farm close to the American examples of the same period. These few structures are small in scale and intended for very small farms (fig. 10).[20] Some of these smaller exam-

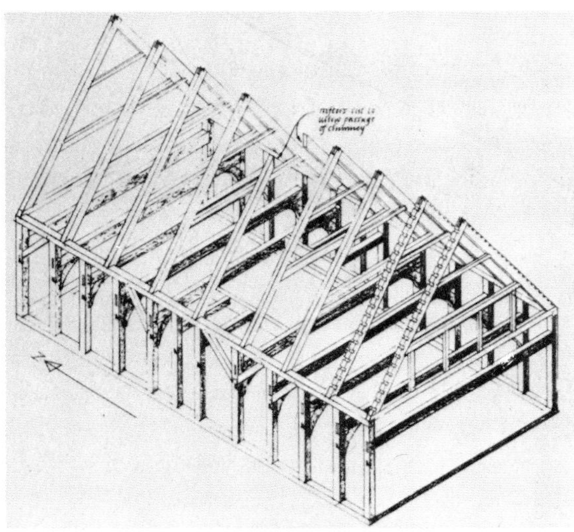

Figure 8. Reconstruction of the anchorbent frame of the seventeenth-century Schenck House presently exhibited in the Brooklyn Museum. The house is one aisle wide (see figure 3, type f2) and has collar beams connecting the rafters. (Courtesy of the Brooklyn Museum.)

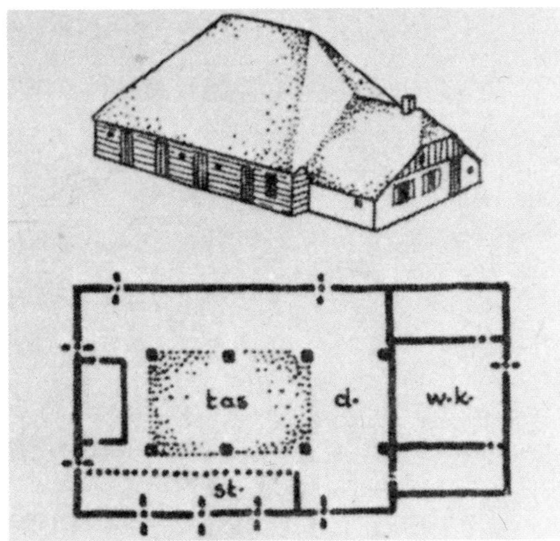

Figure 9. Schematic drawing of an example of modifications that occurred in the basic anchorbent frame when adapted to the needs of a particular agricultural environment. Note that, while the house is attached directly to the large barn, the barn itself forms structurally and visually a totally independent entity. (From R. C. Hekker, "De Ontwikkeling van de Boerderij-vormen in Nederland," Duizend Jaar Bouwen in Nederland *[Amsterdam: Allert de Lange, 1957].)*

ples survive today. Combining living and storage space under one roof with no separation, in true *Einhaus* fashion, their smoke escaped through a hole in the roof (fig. 11). By 1800 these were considered unhealthy, although some appear to have been in use as late as 1942.[21] Traditionally, this house type is called Saxon in the early literature, but this has to be considered a misnomer.[22] While most of the surviving examples are located in the same area today, this is more a result of poverty and lack of materials making changes less likely to occur than a reflection at their original distribution. The type was initially widespread. At the same time, the few examples still existing in the eastern part of Holland, although much smaller in scale than American examples, are frequently considered the most likely sources for the Dutch barns in America (fig. 12).[23] However, it seems hardly likely that this small and quite sparsely inhabited area would form the sole origin.

While the combination of living and storage needs in one large space was never encountered in this country, the concept of separate storage structures was not uncommon on the late medieval European farm, especially in view of the increase of farming and subsequently of material wealth taking place at that time. Large barns attached to monastic structures were, of course, not unusual, although they were generally of a different construction type; the barn in Ter Doest is a good example.[24] On farms smaller separate storage structures could be found, in Holland as well as in the Rhineland region, many of which have disappeared (fig. 13).[25]

In Fitchen's survey of Dutch barns in Upstate New York, he not only emphasizes the complexity of presently existing European examples but also that

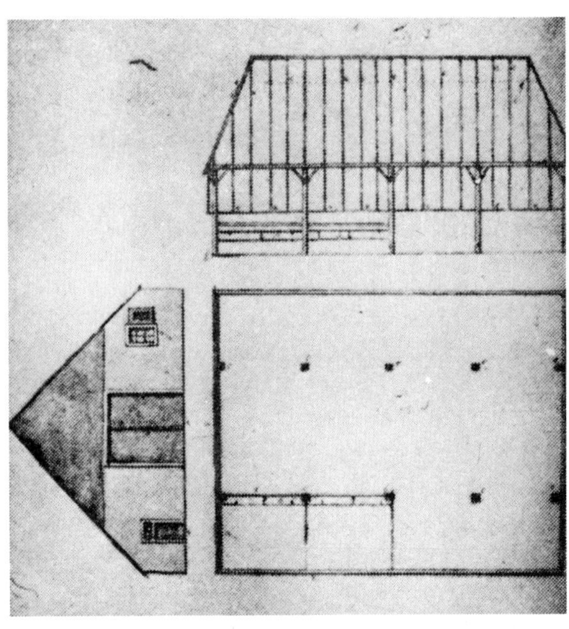

Figure 10. Early nineteenth-century drawing of a carriage barn in the Netherlands. In spite of its late date the structural frame has essentially retained its medieval character and is four bays long. The outside walls are made of masonry and some changes in the gable ends have occurred. Large double doors are located in the gable ends as is found in the American prototypes. (From R. C. Hekker, De Nederlandsboerderij in het begin der 19 de eeuw *[Arnhem: Stichting Historisch Boerderij-onderzoek, 1967].)*

the Dutch barn in the United States is generally four bays long.[26] This preference for a length of four bays is probably an even stronger indication of the late medieval origin of the structure. Many of the farm structures found in the Rhineland region frequently evolved around a four-bay nucleus.[27] Documentary evidence contained in medieval privileges seems to support this. In the eastern part of

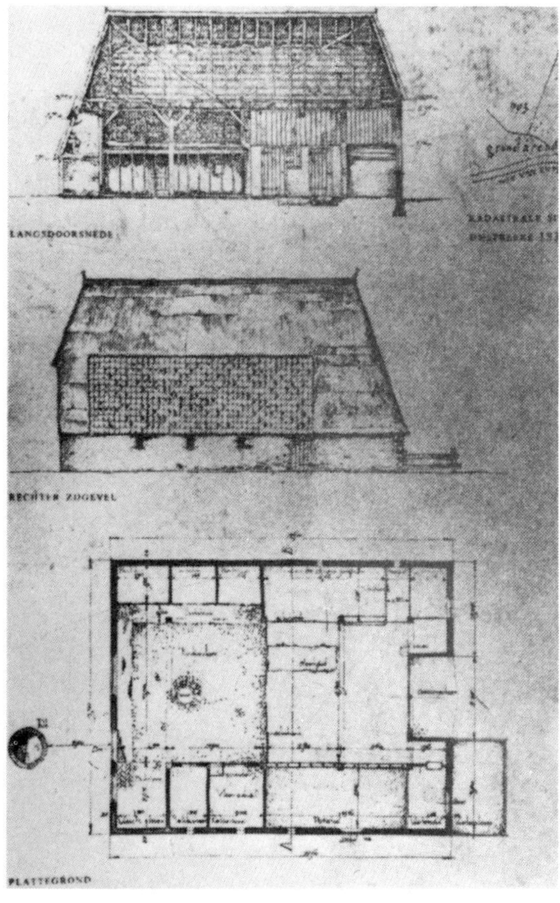

Figure 11. Typical example of Los Hoes *or* Einhaus, *Enter, the Netherlands. This basically medieval building was one open space with no division between human habitat and animals. Fire was kept in the center aisle with the smoke escaping through a hole in the roof. The wooden frame consists of anchorbents. The sidewalls are made of masonry but are probably nineteenth-century replacements. Long diagonal braces in the roof provide the necessary rigidity for the rafter roof. Recorded in 1942, demolished in 1945. (Courtesy of the Stichting Historisch Boerderij-onderzoek.)*

Figure 12. Los Hoes *or* Einhaus, *Enter, the Netherlands. (Courtesy of the Stichting Historisch Boerderij-onderzoek.)*

Holland it is recorded that a person whose house was destroyed by fire was allowed to collect enough timber in the common lands to erect a four-bay house.[28] A similar provision existed for common walls, which were built on the property boundary. The neighbors acquired the right to insert their joints into the wall while having to contribute to the cost of building the wall only for the first four bays, each of some 3.75 meters.[29] Naturally this does not preclude the possibility of building larger houses. Even some of the storage structures like the *Speichers* might be four bays long.[30]

That a close relationship existed between medieval practice and the Dutch barn in this country can also be perceived from other elements. Frequently the members of a wood-frame structure were made and fitted on the ground. To assure proper assem-

Figure 13. Small secondary storage structure with typical anchorbent frame, Orvelte, the Netherlands. (Courtesy of the Provincial Museum, Drenthe.)

bly, the various elements were marked in Roman numerals, a standard medieval practice that also can be found on most Dutch barns in this country. Also the peculiar overhang in the gable end of the Verplanck–Van Wyck barn, although not considered typical, is quite similar to overhangs found in some examples of medieval architecture, like the buildings illustrated in the sixteenth-century altarpiece in the Dom of Xanten or like some urban architecture in Holland (figs. 14, 15, 16).[31]

Although at present the hipped roof appears to be the most common one used in North European barn structures, it is a recent development. As noted above, regular gable ends were not uncommon and can still be found today. Frequently these gable ends were covered with vertical boards, which was essentially a survival from an earlier time. Even the sidewalls once had vertical boards, but because of the change from oak to pine and the resulting production of longer boards, horizontal boarding was quite common as in most Dutch barns in New York State (fig. 17).[32] Building with brick or wattle and daub can be attributed more to lack of materials than to a specific aesthetic or structural need.

If the basic structural form is clearly identifiable as late medieval in origin, the roof structures are somewhat more complex.[33] Originally both the medieval frame structure and the Dutch barn in the United States had a simple roof construction consisting of widely spaced rafters. These rafters, made from one piece of timber, were connected at the top and supported at the bottom on the plate of the exterior wall. The plate on top of the posts of the H-bents provided additional support (fig. 18). In the medieval structure, smaller additional rafters would

Figure 14. Gable end of Verplanck-Van Wyck barn, Dutchess County, N.Y. (From John Fitchen, New World Dutch Barn: A Study of Its Characteristics, Its Structural System, and Its Probable Erectional Procedures *[Syracuse: Syracuse University Press, 1968], plate 14.)*

Figure 15. Barn structure as depicted in a fifteenth-century altarpiece in the Dom of Xanten, Germany. Note the overhang in the gable end, which is not unlike the overhang found in the Verplanck-Van Wyck Barn.

Figure 16. Medieval house in the Netherlands. (From R. Meischke and H. Zantkuyl, Het Nederlandse Woonhuis van 1300–1800 *[Haarlem: H. D. Tjeenk Willink, 1969].)*

Figure 17. Typical example of a one-aisle anchorbent frame, Zaandam, the Netherlands. The exterior walls have clapboards but the frame itself is essentially the same as found in the Schenck House or the house in figure 16 with a brick-filled anchorbeam frame.

Figure 18. Detail of an anchorbent frame in Zeddam, the Netherlands, that has retained all typical features but also has the modifications that are found in later examples of the anchorbent frame in the Netherlands. The sidewalls have become masonry, while the rafters and purlins are not sawed or planed. Different also are the diagonal braces that are supporting the purlins, which are giving additional support to the rafter roof. Part of the modifications can be attributed to the relative scarcity of wood. Note that all the parts of the frame are marked with Roman numerals to make assembly possible, a method that is found in most medieval barns and wooden frame structures. (Courtesy of the Stichting Historisch Boerderij-onderzoek.)

sometimes be attached to create a sufficient overhang to throw water far off the wall. This practice might also be partly responsible for the two-piece rafters so frequently found today in North European farm structures.[34] The rafters themselves would be tied together at the top similar to the American examples. If the ends were narrow, a ridge pole would appear in the North European farm structure, but if the rafters were square and substantial enough in size, the ridge pole would be omitted.[35] That both traditions occur is also confirmed by the evidence found in the Rhineland region.[36] With the increase in span and changes in structural principles and materials, the roof structures became more complex, a development that can be noted in both the North European and New York State examples.

It is clear that the frame construction of the Dutch barn in North America is essentially late medieval in origin, a conclusion that can be confirmed further by the analysis of other minor elements. This framing system, in spite of various later modifications, is of extreme importance because it represents a thus far hardly recognized example of survival. While in North Europe the structure was modified beyond recognition at the end of the eighteenth century, it could be found in the United States virtually intact, an even more remarkable phenomenon because the influx of Dutch or Rhineland immigrants had then long since ceased. However, it raises a number of interesting questions regarding the residential architecture frequently designated *Dutch Colonial.* Many of these houses were erected simultaneously with these barns and possibly a similar late medieval origin could be observed in their structural frames. As already indicated, the one-bay, H-bent frame house was a common-enough North European type. This points out the need for a more extensive and intensive study of these various examples to establish clearly their relationship to the frame of the Dutch barn in America on the one hand and to residential prototypes in North Europe on the other.

Notes

This article was originally published in *New York Folklore* (1976).

1. Helen Wilkinson Reynolds, *Dutch Houses in the Hudson Valley before 1776* (New York: Payson and Clark, 1929), p. 43, plate 9 and fig. 14.
2. Mary Mix Foley, "The American Barn," *Architectural Forum* 95, no. 2 (August 1951): 170–77; Amos Rapoport and Henry Sarnoff, "Our Unpretentious Past," *AIA Journal* 44, no. 5 (November 1965): 37–40.
3. Eric Sloane, *American Barns and Covered Bridges* (New York: Wilfred Funk, 1956). See also Eric Sloane, *An Age of Barns* (New York: Funk and Wagnalls, 1966).
4. Eric Arthur and Dudley Witney, *The Barn: A Vanishing Landmark in North America* (Greenwich, Conn.: New York Graphic Society, 1972), pp. 36–49.
5. John Fitchen, *The New World Dutch Barn: A Study of Its Characteristics, Its Structural System, and Its Probable Erectional Procedures* (Syracuse: Syracuse University Press, 1968).
6. This drawing was prepared from basic measurements provided by the staff of Old Bethpage Village in 1970.
7. F. Ostendorf, *Geschichte des Dachwerks* (Leipzig-Berlin: B. G. Teubner, 1908).
8. R. C. Hekker, "De Ontwikkeling van de Boerderijvormen in Nederland," in S. J. Fockema Andreae, E. H. ter Kuile, and R. C. Hekker, *Duizend Jaar Bouwen in Nederland,* vol. 2, *De Bouwkunst na de Middelleeuwen* (Amsterdam: Allert de Lange, 1957), pp. 195–316; R. Meischke and H. Zantkuyl, *Het Nederlandse Woonhuis van 1300–1800* (Haarlem, The Netherlands: H. D. Tjeenk Willink, 1969); Ostendorf, *Geschichte des Dachwerks;* H. J. Zantkuyl, *Bouwen in Amsterdam* (Amsterdam, n.d.), a continuing series of pamphlets dealing with the development of the house and its various components; Adelhart Zippelius, *Das Bauernhaus am unteren deutschen Niederrhein* (Wuppertal, West Germany: A. Martini and Gruttefein Gmbh., 1957).
9. The chart is from Zantkuyl's *Bouwen in Amsterdam,* vol. 3, *De Vroegste Vormen van het Stadshuis,* p. 23.
10. Zantkuyl, *Bouwen in Amsterdam,* vol. 1, *Het landelijke houten huis als voorloper van het stadshuis,* p. 7.
11. Zippelius, *Das Bauernhaus,* pp. 50–53.
12. Meischke and Zantkuyl, *Het Nederlandse Woonhuis,* pp. 35–37; Zantkuyl, *Bouwen in Amsterdam,* vol. 1; H. J. Zantkuyl, "Het Jan Martense Schenckhuis te Brooklyn," *Bulletin van de Koninklijke Nederlanse Oudheidkundige Bond,* 6th ser., 7 (1964): 58ff.

13. Fitchen, *New World Dutch Barn,* p. 15.
14. Zippelius, *Das Bauernhaus,* pp. 140–50; letter of H. J. Zantkuyl to author, May 9, 1975.
15. For an analysis, see Gerhard Eitzen, "Die alteren Hallenhausgefugen in Niedersachsen," *Zeitschrift für Volkskunde* 51 (1954): 37–76. For the Mecklenburg region see Karl Baumgarten, "Probleme der Mecklenburgisches Hausforschung," *Deutsches Jahrbuch für Volkskunde* 1, nos. 1–2 (1955): 169–82; Karl Baumgarten, *Zimmermanswerk in Mecklenburg: Die Scheune* (Berlin: Akademie-Verlag, 1961).
16. Foley compares it with the Frisian barns, while Fitchen uses several European types for comparison (Foley, "The American Barn," p. 173; Fitchen, *New World Dutch Barn,* p. 77).
17. Eitzen, "Die alteren Hallenhausgefugen," pp. 37–76; Adelhart Zippelius, "Das vormittelalterliche dreischiffige Hallenhaus in Mitteleuropa," *Bonner Jahrbuch,* no. 153 (1953): 24–45.
18. Hekker, "De Ontwikkeling van de Boerderijvormen," pp. 195–316.
19. R. C. Hekker and J. M. G. van der Poel, *De Nederlandse Boerderij in het begin der 19 de eeuw* (Arnhem: Stichting Historisch Boerderij-onderzoek, 1967).
20. Jan Jans, *Landelijke Bouwkunst in Oost-Nederland* (Enschede: Van der Loeff, 1967), pp. 153–55 and figs. 15–18.
21. Hekker and van der Poel, *De Nederlandse Boerderij,* p. 47, which discusses a report of 1826; Jans, *Landelijke Bouwkunst,* p. 14.
22. Henry Glassie derives the type from the Saxon house (*Pattern in the Material Folk Culture of the Eastern United States* [Philadelphia: University of Pennsylvania Press, 1968], p. 146, no. 204). This is an older and somewhat erroneous interpretation initially suggested by W. Pessler, who attempted to identify this house type with the ethnic and linguistic boundaries of the Saxon people (*Das altersachsische Bauernhaus in seiner geographischen Verbreitung* [Braunschweig: Vieweg, 1906]). For more recent interpretations, see Eitzen, "Die alteren Hallenhausgefugen," pp. 37–76, or Zippelius, "Das vormittelalterliche dreischiffige Hallenhaus," pp. 13–45.
23. Jans, *Landelijke Bouwkunst,* p. 29.
24. Clemens V. Trefois, *Ontwikkelingsgeschiedenis van onze Landelijke Bouwkunst* (Antwerpen: Sikkel, 1950), pp. 200–210; H. Janse, "De Abdyschuur van Ter Doest," *Bulletin van de Koninklijke Nederlandse Oudheidkundige Bond,* 6th ser., 6 (1964): 190–202.
25. Trefois, *Ontwikkelingsgeschiedenis,* p. 27; Zippelius, *Das Bauernhaus.*
26. Fitchen, *New World Dutch Barn,* p. 77.
27. Zippelius, *Das Bauernhaus,* pp. 24–26.
28. For an example of a four-bay unit, see Fitchen, *New World Dutch Barn,* p. 77. The archival evidence is first mentioned in J. H. Gallée, *Het Boerenhuis in Nederland en zijn bewoners* (Utrecht: Oosthoek, 1907), p. 50. The charter, Lukter Markt Recht 89, states that a person whose house is burnt is allowed to haul timber from the Markt to build a house of four bays. See also Zippelius, *Das Bauernhaus,* pp. 24–26.
29. Zantkuyl to author, May 9, 1975.
30. C. A. van Swigchem, *Afbraak of Restauratie* (Bussum: Van Dishoeck, 1966), p. 31; Trefois, *Ontwikkelingsgeschiedenis,* p. 211, fig. 203.
31. Fitchen, *New World Dutch Barn,* p. 149; Zippelius, *Das Bauernhaus,* p. 176, fig. 21; Meischke and Zantkuyl, *Het Nederlandse Woonhuis,* p. 78.
32. Fitchen, *New World Dutch Barn,* p. 15.
33. Zantkuyl, *Bouwen in Amsterdam,* vol. 6, *Van Sporenkap tot Mansarde;* letter from John R. Stevens to author, December 27, 1974.
34. Zantkuyl, *Bouwen in Amsterdam,* 6.
35. Zantkuyl to author, May 9, 1975.
36. Zippelius, *Das Bauernhaus,* p. 28, fig. 11; Zippelius, "Das vormittelalterliche dreischiffige Hallenhaus," pp. 24–25.

Part Three Function

Inside the Massachusetts House

ABBOTT LOWELL CUMMINGS

While formal and technological descriptions can capture the physical essence of a building or a landscape, it is in being used that the artifact comes alive. People build partly to create appropriate settings for their day-to-day activities and personal interactions. Usually builders and users of vernacular buildings employ a limited repertoire of kinds of spaces, which they conceive of as having certain appropriate furnishings and uses. To each cluster of space, furnishings, and use, a customary name—such as parlor, hall, chamber, kitchen, or passage—is attached.

Few old buildings retain their original furnishings, and of course it is impossible to question their original occupants about names, furnishings, or uses. But in most western European societies it has been customary since the Middle Ages for church or secular authorities to appoint appraisers to make probate inventories of the possessions of deceased people, as a way of insuring a fair and legal division of the estate. Sometimes the appraisers organized their list according to the room in which each group of items was found. Since the late nineteenth century, these "room-by-room inventories" have been a major tool of the vernacular architecture scholar.

Abbott Lowell Cummings's essay, which was first published as the introduction to his Rural Household Inventories: Establishing the Names, Uses and Furnishings of Rooms in the Colonial New England Home, 1675–1775, *illustrates some of the uses probate inventories can serve in vernacular architecture studies. Cummings extracts from his documents the range of traditional room names and typical contents for decedents of a variety of economic conditions, and from this information he extrapolates the uses to which each space was put. By looking at inventories as a group rather than restricting himself to applying individual inventories to standing buildings, as is often done, he is able to correct misconceptions about the relative sumptuousness of household goods and the uses of rooms that have crept into scholarly and museum practice since the late nineteenth century.*

The three sample inventories that follow the essay illustrate the differences in number and quality of possessions and in size of houses that might be encountered in eastern Massachusetts during the century preceding the Revolution. Of the three houses represented here one,

William Boardman's, survives in Saugus as a museum of the Society for the Preservation of New England Antiquities.

THE invention of the camera in the mid nineteenth century made possible for the first time an exact record of how people furnish their houses. For earlier periods the student of social history must rely upon a number of scattered (and imperfect) sources, one of the most helpful being the room-by-room inventory of household possessions taken soon after an owner's death.

For the most part these inventories reflect plausible patterns of living, yet once in a while a curious mélange of items will be listed which do not imply any reasonable use for a given room (other than perhaps pure storage). One suspects, too, that certain objects were at times withheld from an inventory when they belonged to someone else, or were moved about for ease of appraisal. This is especially true of silverware or "plate," the individual pieces of which are invariably lumped together in the inventories. In other respects, however, the consistent similarity of entries in any sampling would suggest that the appraisers were apt to take things pretty much as they found them.

As a group the inventories should speak for themselves. We must examine these documents in light of the life and thought of the seventeenth and eighteenth centuries and not from a present-day point of view. The uses for rooms, as well as fashions in style, change with new ideas and with inventions. Consider, for example, the alteration in our habits which the furnace has produced. Now we comfortably occupy a whole house throughout the winter. In the colonial period family life was very much restricted within doors during these months. In one room, probably the keeping-room or kitchen, a fire would have burned continually during the coldest days of the year, but elsewhere fires were made only when a room was needed for some special purpose. This was true even among the well-to-do, as Samuel Sewall's vastly illuminating diary makes repeatedly clear. "Mr. Sewall the Minister comes hither p.m̃," he noted for example on February 17, 1719; "I have a fire made in his Mother's Chamber, and there we pray together." For fully six months of the year the use of rooms and arrangement of furnishings in the Colonial home were governed by this confining factor—one which we can scarcely appreciate in our steam-heated houses of today. In midwinter of 1716, Sewall recorded on the evening of January 15: "At six a-clock my ink freezes so that I can hardly write by a good fire in my Wive's Chamber."[1]

In some of the early inventories the rooms of a given house are called simply the *front room* and *back room* or *eastern room* and *western room,* or again, the *lower room* and *chamber over the lower room.* But we do find more descriptive names for the rooms in those houses whose arrangements were typical of the colonial era. The developed seventeenth-century house plan was that of two rooms, one usually a little larger than the other, on either side of a central chimney. Often there would be a lean-to at the rear, and sometimes the small entry with its staircase in front of the chimney was projected to provide a two-story enclosed *porch,* as it was called.

Normally, the two principal ground-floor rooms were referred to in the inventories as the *parlor* or *best room* and the *hall* or *keeping room* (sometimes *lodging room, fire room* or *kitchen*). The rooms above them were called *parlor chamber* and *hall chamber,* and the main room in the lean-to, when it existed, was the *kitchen.* To one side of the lean-to kitchen, usually at the cooler end, depending upon the orientation of the house, was a *buttery* or *dairy.* At the other end was a small warm *bed room* as it was invariably called (in contrast to those rooms on the second floor which were always designated as chambers).[2] The room above the projecting porch was called the *porch chamber.*

Neither the words *parlor* nor *hall* meant then what they do today. The term *hall,* brought over by the first colonists, recalled the large open room of the English manor house in which much of the daily life was centered, and which was, loosely speaking, the ancestor of our modern living room.

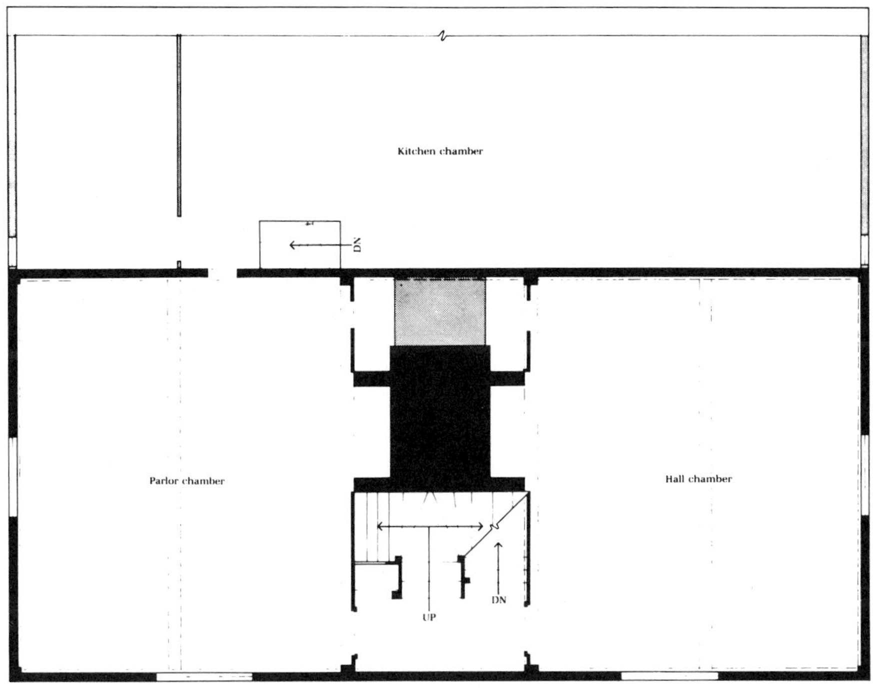

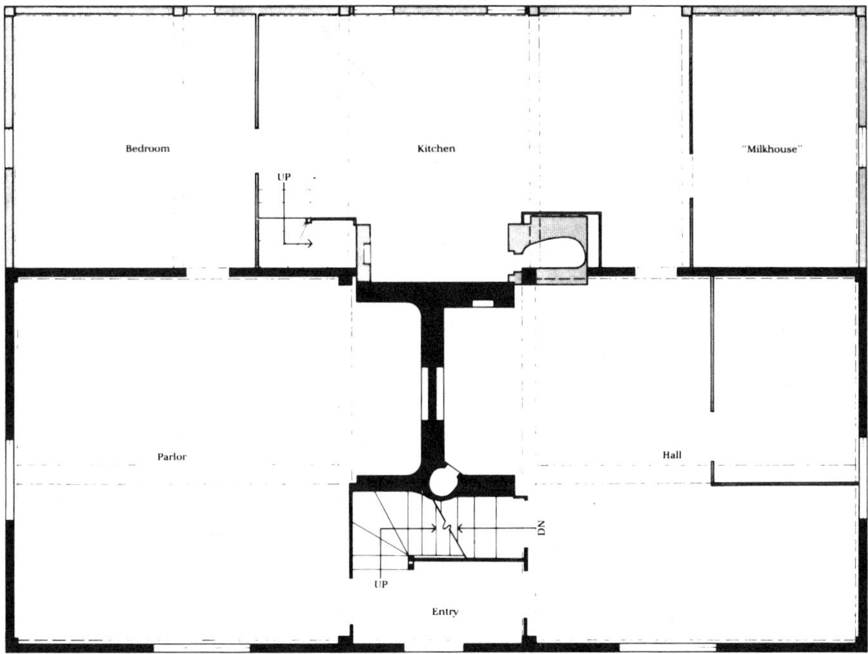

Figure 1. First- and second-floor plans of the "Scotch"-Boardman House, Saugus, Massachusetts. Built ca. 1687; lean-to built before 1696. (From Abbott Lowell Cummings, The Framed Houses of Massachusetts Bay, 1625–1725 *[Cambridge: Harvard University Press, 1979], p. 24.)*

The seventeenth-century parlor, however, has no exact parallel in the twentieth-century house. Nor was it the formal room of the Victorian era, to be entered only on special occasions. Actually, it had multiple uses, all related to its character as the best room. Here was the best furniture; here important company was entertained and dined; and at the same time wills and inventories show that it was the room in which the parents slept.[3]

For the furnishings of the parlor there were the parents' best bed, often with curtains and valances, a trundle bed, and fine cupboard, probably the court cupboard as we call it today. This was apt to be covered with a cushion or cupboard cloth, or both, a "cushen & cubbard cloth on the Cubbards head" being itemized in one typical inventory of 1676 (John Kitchen, Salem, Massachusetts). A variety of materials for these coverings are suggested in the inventories: "two callico cupboard cloathes" (Thomas Woodbridge, Newbury, Massachusetts, 1681), "2 linen cubert cloathes" (Jonathan Browne, Salem, 1667), "one cubberd cloath rought with needleworke" and "one cubberd cloath with fringe" (George Burrill, Sr., Lynn, Massachusetts, 1654). European prints of the seventeenth century indicate that these came well down over the front, falling halfway to the floor. The cushion was perhaps a protection for fine ceramics or glassware, or its use may have been rooted in customs peculiar to the period. John Osgood of Andover, Massachusetts, in 1650 bequeathed "to the meeting hous off newbery 18 shillings to Buie a Chushion for the minister to lay his *Book* Vpon," and it is of passing interest that Samuel Sewall under date of January 13, 1696, mentions a book of law "on the Cup-board's head."

Invariably there was a table in the parlor, and while there were virtually no floor coverings in the seventeenth century, carpets did at least exist, but were placed on the table rather than on the floor. One Samuel Haines, for example, testified at a court hearing in December of 1676 concerning one of the Cogswells who had settled earlier in what is now Essex, Massachusetts, "that my master had a Turkey worked carpet in Old England, which he commonly used to lay upon his parlour table, and this carpet was put aboard among my master's goods [bound for New England], and came safe ashore."[4] Seventeenth-century Dutch paintings often show these colorful table carpets, and two New England pictorial examples are known, John Smibert's group portrait of Bishop Berkeley and his entourage (1729) and Robert Feke's portrait of the Isaac Royall family of Medford, Massachusetts (1741), showing that the custom persisted here into the eighteenth century.

A variety of tables are described in seventeenth-century inventories, including the square table, round table, "fall table," chair-table and long table. The long table could have been a refectory table, so-called, though often there is mention of a table board and frame, referring to the long, narrow table top which rested separately upon a trestle and could be removed when its space was needed.

In nearly every room one would have found chests and boxes. These filled a vital need in houses which had little or nothing comparable to the roomy storage closets of today. In the "Parlor" of Daniel Ringe's house in Ipswich, Massachusetts, in 1662, there were a total of four chests, including "One chest with Apparell," and three boxes. The chests and boxes to which higher values were assigned in the appraisals were almost certainly among the more handsomely decorated examples which have survived.

Inventories show that these seventeenth-century rooms were often over-furnished according to our standards. "13 Leather chairs," "6 Turkey work chaires," and "4 Stools wth: needle work covers" along with other furniture in the "Parlour" of John Bowles's house in Roxbury, Massachusetts, in 1691 seem curiously plentiful to us today. European prints indicate that these many chairs were often lined up against the wall. On the other hand, candlesticks are seldom mentioned in any room but the hall or kitchen where they were kept, and from which they were carried into other rooms as needed. Candlestands are not mentioned at all in the seventeenth century. Madam Sarah Knight of Boston, traveling to New York in 1704, stopped overnight at the Havens House near Kingston, Rhode Island, and recorded in her diary after supper that "I then betook me to my Apartment, wch was a little Room parted from the Kitchen by a single bord partition. . . . I set my Candle on a Chest by the bed side, and setting up, fell to my old way of composing my Resentments."[5]

The hall is the easiest seventeenth-century room to reconstruct in terms of furnishings, especially today when we are returning in some of our homes to the concept of an all-purpose living area. There were many and varied utensils used in the preparation and consumption of food. In addition to chairs, tables, and cupboards there was also apt to be a bed in the hall, of less value than the parents' best bed in the parlor, a settle, and quite commonly some tools and light farm equipment. In the "Hall" of Daniel Ringe's house, for example, were "Carpenters tooles . . . Other tooles & two bottles . . . Two Axes," and so forth.

It is interesting to compare the contents of a seventeenth-century hall and kitchen when both are found in the same house, for often the lean-to kitchen was a later addition to a house in which the hall had served for some time as the only "kitchen" area. Generally there is a tendency for the hall to contain the eating utensils and some occasional lightweight cooking equipment, with the heavy-duty cooking gear relegated to the kitchen.

The colonial housewife seems to have taken some care in the arrangement of her kitchen equipment—the pots and pans, skillets and toasters, skimmers and ladles—which in so many of our historic house museums today are strewn about, making of the hearth a culinary obstacle course. Some of the smaller objects were designed to be hung as loops or holes in the handles will prove. A row of hand-wrought nails can often be found in the wooden sleeper, just beneath the great oaken lintel which spanned the seventeenth-century fireplace opening. Running back into the fireplace on either side these projecting nails were obviously designed as hooks for the smaller implements. For larger items, and for the pewter, ceramics, and wooden ware, there were dressers and shelves as both the inventories and construction of our earliest houses reveal. In the "kitchin" of Rev. James Noyes's house in Newbury, in 1656, there were "on one shelfe, one Charger, 5 pewter platters and a bason and a salt seller," and "on another shelfe, 9 pewter platters, small and great."

In the buttery or dairy were all those items associated with the milk room and the processing of dairy products, for example, "severall trayes & boulles & keellers about ye dairy" (Mrs. Abigail Pearce, Ipswich, 1680), while the principal items of furnishing for the bedroom at the other end of the lean-to were the bedstead and bedding which made this small, warm room opening from the kitchen ideal for the care and oversight of sick or bedridden persons, or for a confinement.

There was not in the seventeenth century any one fixed area for dining. Family meals were taken, apparently, in the hall or kitchen with the head of the family occupying a great chair and the children seated on joint stools or forms. For the smallest there was sometimes "a childs chayre" (Rev. James Noyes, Newbury, 1656). More formal dining was either in the parlor or in one of the chambers. "Mr. Willard and I visit loansom Mr. Torrey," writes Sewall on October 7, 1692; "Din'd in his Kitchin Chamber." This custom of dining in a chamber, which may seem unusual to us today, is reflected also in the inventories. In the "Parlor Chamber" of the home of Isaac Little, Esq., Marshfield, Massachusetts, in 1699, there were a bed and "Linnen Curtains & Valians," "three Tables" and "6 Chairs & Eight wrought Cushions" together with "Diaper Table Cloaths & Napkins," "12 Glass bottles & some Earthen ware," "more Earthen & Glass ware," and "a Case of Knives."

The inventories of the simple houses make it clear from the furnishings described that these upper rooms were often set up in dormitory fashion, with more than a single bed in each chamber. They were also used, especially in rural areas, for the storage of miscellaneous staples and foodstuffs, for example, "all the wool that was in the chamber, about one or two hundred pounds" (John Proctor,

Sr., Ipswich, 1672), and "Corne, meate, aples and other lumber in the Chamber, with a firkin of butter" (Benjamin Auger, Salem, 1671). Some of the seventeenth-century houses, moreover, like the Fairbanks House in Dedham, Massachusetts, had an unfinished chamber for which a fireplace was never planned. Yet in many of the substantial houses of the period one finds the chamber more elaborately appointed. In these upper rooms there is also apt to be greater refinement of architectural detail offering a more attractive setting for polite entertainment or formal events. "Mr. James Sherman Married Richard Fifield and Mary Thirston . . . in our Bed-Chamber, about 9. at night," Sewall recorded on August 6, 1688.

And here it should be noted that our modern concept of the attic as a storage area was not widely held in the seventeenth century. Even in its relatively unfinished state the attic was often occupied, as we learn from the inventories. The "East Garret" of Isaac Little's house in Marshfield in 1699, for example, contained "One Feather Bed & ffurniture," "another ffeather Bed & ffurniture" and "Cesars bed & Beding," while in the "West Garret" there occurs the single entry "Dicks Bed & Beding." In the Capt. Matthew Perkins House, built in Ipswich soon after 1701, the eastern end of the attic was partially finished off at the very start, and was furnished with a fireplace of its own, a condition found even more commonly later in the eighteenth century.

Without pictures we know very little about the exact arrangement of furnishings in the seventeenth-century New England room. It is impossible, however, to think of the hall with its spinning wheels, tools, tables, stools, and cooking utensils in constant use, serving the needs of a large family, arranged as fastidiously as they often are in many period rooms and museum houses. The hall in the seventeenth-century farm house must have presented an undisciplined appearance much of the time! The parlor and best chamber, on the other hand, were apparently furnished with some concern for the niceties of life. Cushions are mentioned at times, for example, "4 silke Cushions" (Mrs. Rebecca Bacon, Salem, 1655), "velvet cushin" (Mrs. Elizabeth Stacey, Ipswich, 1670), "3 turkie work cushins" (William Symonds, Ipswich, 1679), and "leather Cushin" (William Woodcock, Salem, 1669). And the beds, especially the best bed in the parlor, could be colorfully decked out with "yellow Curtaines & vallens" (Thomas Antrum, Salem, 1662), "greene say Curtaines" (Francis Lawes, Salem, 1665), and a "tapestre Coverlit" (Mrs. Margaret Lake, Ipswich, 1672). One inventory in 1656, however, mentions "a bare's skin" with the furniture of the bed (Thomas Wickes, Salem), an excellent reminder that seventeenth-century New England houses were never far from the frontier. It should be stressed, in fact, that this period was at one and the same time more richly elaborate and more starkly primitive than we realize. From the very start, there were prosperous men whose parlor chambers, like that of John Bowles's of Roxbury, could boast in 1691 "a Down bed and bolster . . . greenserge Silke fringed Curtains & Vallains with the bedstead & cord, and green curtains to the Windows. . . ." Yet, at the other end of the scale, there was a peasantlike closeness to nature. The English visitor, John Josselyn, reports of one house in Boston which he visited in 1663, that "the poultry had their breakfast usually in cold weather in the kitchin."[6]

The housewife then, as now, had convictions and goals, whatever the circumstances. Mrs. Mary Rowlandson, returning to Boston in 1676 after her Indian captivity, "thought it somewhat strange to set up House-keeping with bare walls; but as *Solomon* sayes, *Mony answers all things*; and that we had through the benevolence of Christian-friends."[7] Boston and Salem merchants offered a wide variety of goods by the late seventeenth century, and it is not surprising to find window curtains in the inventories though they were by no means common even in the coastal towns. Maps are mentioned at times, but pictures rarely. What few there were appear in the homes of the more well-to-do, and were confined to an occasional portrait and a sprinkling of prints. There were "Seven Framed pictures" in the "best roome" of William Hollingsworth's house in Salem in 1677, and Thomas Wells of Ipswich, in 1666, bequeathed to his son "the new pictures, viz. of the Kinge and Queene & of the five senccees," probably among those items listed as "maps & papar pictures" in the inventory of his estate taken the same year. On March 28, 1688, Sewall tells us that "Mr. Randolph . . . had me to his House to see the Landscips of Oxford Colledges and Halls," and the inventory of the Boston bookseller Michael Perry, in 1700, mentions "1 large picture [&] 1 d^{o} of Jerusalem."

An interesting glimpse of seventeenth-century rooms which survived until the end of the eighteenth century with very little change is given us by Rev. William Bentley of Salem, writing on February 5, 1796:

> This day was buried Mr John Symonds, a Batchelor, from his House near the ferry. With the loss of this man the appearance of the last & the beginning of this Century is lost. His father died a few years since at 100, & John died at 74. The children all lived in single life till they were advanced, & only one ever entered into married life & she after 70. The windows of this house are of the small glass with lead in diamonds & open upon hinges. The Doors open with wooden latches. The Chairs are the upright high arm chairs, & the common chairs are the short backed. The tables small & oval, the chest of drawers with knobs, & short swelled legs. The large fire places, & the iron for the lamp. . . . The Press for pewter plates with round holes over the door of it: . . . Old Dutch maps & map mondes highly coloured above a Century old. The Beds very low, & the curtains hung upon the walls.

The last comment is of particular interest. Many of the "low" beds of the seventeenth-century farm house must have had their curtains suspended from the exposed joists overhead, as one sees occasionally in European prints.

The central chimney lean-to house continued as a form throughout the eighteenth century, especially in rural areas, and the uses for its various rooms remained largely unchanged. Thus within such houses one would still have found the parents' best bed downstairs in the parlor and the meal and grain in the chambers until the time of the Revolution—and even later. In the meantime, however, the four-room plan with central passage spread widely during the early years of the eighteenth century as an expression of the new academic style in which functionalism was exchanged for an expansive formality. With higher ceilings and larger windows, the rooms themselves acquired a new sense of spaciousness, and those structural elements which had been frankly exposed in the seventeenth century were now almost entirely masked with plaster and finely molded trim. The entry—which had been no more than the minimum amount of space needed for circulation in the seventeenth century—was transformed into a wide passage, occupying in some cases nearly a third of the total floor space. Though dignified by a broad paneled staircase, this area was called simply the *entry* or *entry way* or sometimes the *great entry* when there was a *little entry* or side passage as well. The Englishwoman Mrs. Anne Grant, who visited the Schuyler House in Albany, New York, in the 1760s, recalled later that "Through the middle of the house was a very wide passage, with opposite front and back doors, which in summer admitted a stream of air peculiarly grateful to the languid senses. It was furnished with chairs and pictures like a summer parlour. Here the family usually sat in hot weather, when there were no ceremonious strangers."[8]

Of the four principal rooms on the ground floor, at least two in the Colonial eighteenth-century house served as parlors. They were variously described as the "First Parlour" and "Second Parlour" (Samuel Wentworth House, Boston, 1767), "Little Parlour" and "Great Parlour" (John Baydell House, Boston, 1740), or "East Parlour" and "West Parlour" (Johnson Jackson House, Boston, 1774), and their exact location varied. Both the "Best Parlour" and "great Parlour" of Mr. Charles Apthorp's house in Boston in 1759 appear to have been at the front of the house. Often, however, the two parlors were located at the front and back of the house respectively, either in opposite corners or lined up one in front of the other. Such was the case with the house on Beacon Hill in Boston which the colonial artist John Singleton Copley remodeled in 1771–72. Here the "best Parlour" and "great Room" were on the left side with the "best Parlour" in front. John Crunden, on the other hand, whose *Original Designs,* published in London in 1767, circulated in the Colonies, illustrates a floor plan with a small "common parlour" at the front of the house and a larger "best parlour" at the back, which he calls the "back front"—an amusing reminder that orientation in the eighteenth century was not exclusively toward the street, and that the garden front had an importance of its own.

The best parlor, as its name implies, was reserved for best affairs. Samuel Sewall recorded on October 14, 1720, a dinner party which he gave for several friends, including "His Excellency," in the "best Room" of his Boston home. A year earlier, on October 29, 1719, "Thanks-giving-day," his second marriage to the Widow Abigail Tilley took place "in the best room below stairs." Copley, writing to his half brother in 1771 about the plan of his house on Beacon Hill, mentions in passing that "your Mamma will never make fire in the Best room," which suggests that like the later Victorian parlor it may have been opened only for ceremonious occasions.

The second, or common, parlor was obviously designed for somewhat less formal use. The use of the term dining room, incidentally, did not become widespread until after the Revolution. Mr. Charles Apthorp's inventory in 1759 mentions a "great Parlour," "Best Parlour" and "Back Lower Room" as well as a "Dining Room up Stairs," and a "Dining Roome" can be found as early as 1681 in an inventory of the estate of Jeremiah Cushing of Boston. Generally speaking, however, these were exceptions and no one room in the colonial period seems to have been used as an exclusive dining area. Mrs. Grant says of the "eating-room" in the Schuyler House in Albany that it was "rarely used for that purpose."[9]

Of the two remaining principal rooms on the ground floor one was called the hall or keeping room and the other the kitchen. That room which Copley calls a "keeping Room" in 1771 is referred to by his half brother as the "Sitting Room," a term which became much more common after the Revolution. It was, as pointed out earlier, the ancestor of our modern living room, and combined functions of living, dining, and occasionally, especially in rural areas, sleeping. Copley's was at the front of the house with the kitchen behind it. His "Chinea Clossit" was to open directly into this "Keeping Room," suggesting at least one use to which it would be put, but curiously enough he instructs his half brother to "make no Door from the Keeping Room Directly into the kitchen."

The kitchen, undisputed area for the preparation of food, was almost invariably located at the rear of the house or occasionally in the cellar. The inventory in 1735 of the estate of John Hayes, mariner, of Boston, mentions both a "Kitchen" with equipment for light housekeeping and a "Kitchen Cellar" with all the pots and pans and other fireplace equipment necessary for heavy-duty cooking. It is not unusual to find a detached kitchen in Boston during the eighteenth century, as both inventories and deeds and building permits in timber make clear, but one rarely finds a detached kitchen in rural New England.

The second floor and third, when it existed, were almost entirely given over to bed chambers. These were normally named in relation to the rooms below with which they lined up, for example, hall chamber, parlor chamber, kitchen chamber or entry chamber (that small room over the front entrance which we would call a hall bedroom today). Often, however, the names for these rooms took their cue from the color scheme of the woodwork. The Henry Vassall House in Cambridge, Massachusetts, for instance, inventoried in 1769, had a "Best Room," "Blue Room," "Keeping Room," "Little Room," and "Kitchen." On the second floor were a "Marble Chamber," "Green Chamber," "Cader Chamber," "Little Chamber," and "Kitchen Chamber." Both the "Marble" and "Cader," of course, referred to painted decoration in imitation of marble and cedar wood. Occasionally some other unusual feature would determine the name of a room or chamber, for example, the "Paper Room" found in an inventory of 1737 for the home of the Boston distiller Capt. John Welland.

The chamber continued to serve a number of functions. While spinning and weaving activities were sometimes carried on in the attic, a chamber could also serve this purpose. In the "east Chamber" of the Peter Tufts House in Medford, Massachusetts, according to an inventory of 1750, there were "a Flax comb," "2 woollen whee[l]s 2 linnen wheels and Real," while the early eighteenth-century James Bradley House in North Haven, Connecticut, contained a loom which had actually been built in as a part of the exposed frame of one chamber. On a more formal level Samuel Sewall noted, December 24, 1706, "My wife and I execute a Lease to Mr. Seth Dwight, for 21. years, of the House he dwells in. . . . Twas transacted in our Bedchamber." On September 15, 1702, the diarist had been married to Mrs. Rebekah Dudley "in the Dining Room Chamber about 8 aclock," and on November 24, 1708, he recorded, "Dine in my wives Chamber at the great Oval Table. . . . Eleven in all." One will occasionally find shelves with grooves for plates in chamber closets of the eighteenth century, and both dishes and table linen continued to be inventoried upstairs during this period. In the simpler houses the chamber remained a semistorage area for foodstuffs as it had been in the seventeenth century, and as late as July 22, 1791, the Rev. William Bentley of Salem, recording a conversation on this subject, observed "that the effluvia from the human body by fair experiment did render cheese, butter, &c. rancid, & that the custom of lodging in chambers with cheese, &c. was detrimental to the cheese, &c."

In the first-floor plan of his house on Beacon Hill, sketched shortly before the Revolution, John Singleton Copley included a "Chinea Clossit"—apparently a closet in our modern sense of the word, that is, a fairly small and windowless storage area. Such closets, furnished with shelves, can be found in our Colonial houses, often next to the chimney. The term *closet,* however, could also mean a small room with a window of its own in the eighteenth century. Generally the closet in this sense opened directly from one of the larger rooms or chambers. When located on the ground floor such an area could serve as a little "office" or study. There is one such ground-floor closet, measuring about six by seven feet, with a single window, in the Jonathan Cogswell House in Essex, Massachusetts, built about 1733. Here the original shelves for books and ledgers have survived, and below them is a writing shelf which pulls out for the convenience of anyone wishing to use this space.

Those closets on the second floor were perhaps sometimes dressing rooms, although Sewall indicates clearly that that which opened from his chamber was used as a study. An account of a fire in this little room gives a clear picture of the eighteenth-century closet and its contents. "Last night, between 2 or 3 hours after midnight," he writes on July 13, 1709, "my wife complain'd of Smoak; I presently went out of Bed, and saw and felt the Chamber very full of Smoak to my great Consternation. . . . I felt the partition of my Bed-Chamber Closet warm; which made me with fear to unlock it, and going in I found the Deal-Box of Wafers all afire, burning livelily; yet not blazing. I drew away the papers nearest to it, and call'd for a Bucket of Water. By that time it came, I had much adoe to recover the Closet agen: But I did, and threw my Water on it, and so more, and quench'd it thorowly. . . . And it seems admirable, that the opening the Closet-Door did not cause the Fire to burst forth into an Unquenchable Flame. The Box was 18 inches over, Closet full of loose papers, boxes, Cases, some Powder. The Window-Curtain was of Stubborn Woolen and refus'd to burn though the Iron-Bars were hot with the fire. Had that burnt it would have fired the pine-shelves and files of Papers and Flask and Bandaliers of powder. . . . We imagine a Mouse might take our lighted Candle out of the Candlestick on the hearth and dragg it under my closet-door behind the Box of Wafers."

When we consider the furnishings of the individual eighteenth-century Colonial rooms it is perhaps the color scheme which must receive first attention. The woodwork was not white, as we have long mistakenly believed, but of varied and rich colors. This is amply borne out by scraping original woodwork and by documents as well. The *Boston Gazette* on September 18, 1753, advertised for sale a house on Pleasant Street in Boston which was "handsomely painted throughout, one of the Rooms is painted Green, another Blue, one Cedar and one Marble; the other four a Lead colour." The dominant room color, in fact, usually controlled the color of the furnishings which were often *en suite* as far as the upholstery was concerned. An interesting case in point can be found in one of the larger chambers of the Moffatt-Ladd House in Portsmouth, New Hampshire. The original color of this room, as determined by scraping through layers of later paint, was a strong mustard yellow with the door painted a rich chocolate brown. A sample of the original wallpaper has survived, revealing a pattern of black and gray upon a yellow ground. It is thus not at all surprising to find in an inventory taken in 1768 that this room was called the "Yellow Cham:" Among its furnishings were "1 Yellow Damask Bed & Curtains & fluted Black Walnut Bedstead," "6 Yellow Damask Cover'd Chairs," "1 Yellow Damask Cover'd Easy Chair," and "3 Window Curtains Yellow Damask."[10]

Looking at the disposition of furniture in the individual rooms of the eighteenth-century Colonial house one would find in the entry both fire-fighting equipment and the ceremonial (or actual) armor belonging to the head of the household, together with a lantern. In the "Entry" of Edward Pell's house in Boston, for example, in 1737, were "2 Half Pikes, Silver Spears, &c, 1 Glass Lanthorne, 2 Leather Fire Buckets & Baggs," with no mention of other furniture. This may have been a house with a narrow entry in the seventeenth-century tradition, but in houses with wider entries as well there is, curiously, little mention of case furniture. In the "Entry" of Thomas Hutchinson's fine mansion in Garden-Court Street, Boston, there were at the time the house was sacked in 1765 "a dozen very good cane chairs & great chair," "a large walnut table," "a large hanging lanthorn & small lanthorn," while the "upper entry" contained "1 large table," "1 Oval ditto," and "1 faneered side board table."[11] In the more modest home of Capt. John Crowninshield of Salem there was also "a Walnut Table in the Entry" (1762), and in keeping with a tradition made popular later by the poet Longfellow we find "On the Stair Case" of James Townsend's house in Boston in 1738 "1 Clock." The lantern, incidentally, seems to have been an almost standard piece of equipment for the entry, as many inventories show. The *Boston News-Letter* for August 17–24, 1719, advertised "fine Glass Lamps and Lanthorns well gilt and painted, both convex and plain; being suitable for Halls, Stair-cases, or other Passageways."

For a comparison of the furnishings in the different ground-floor rooms of a fine eighteenth-century central passage house it is interesting to examine the contents of the well-known Royall House in Medford as revealed in an inventory of the first Isaac Royall's estate in 1739. In the "Best Room," as one might expect, were the finer pieces of furniture commensurate with formal occasions. In addition to the smaller items there were:

1 peer Looking Glass	[£] 55:0:0
1 p: Large Sconsces	60:0:0
a marvel [marble] table w:th Iron frames	35:0:0
2 p: brass Armes . . .	4:0:0
a Jappaned tea table	7:0:0
a Sett of Cheney for the Same	13:0:0
a Large mahogeney table	10:0:0
a Small Ditto	7:0:0
a Doz of wallnut Chares w:th Leather bottomes	30:0:0
. . .	
a Turkey Carpitt	40:0:0

together with the usual fireplace equipment. The "peer Looking Glass" and "p: Large Sconsces" suggest the very elegant arrangements found in fashionable eighteenth-century parlors. In Charles Apthorp's "Best Parlour" in Boston in 1759 there were "1 Large looking glass & a Chimney glass & 2 p: brass branches." The "Chimney [looking] glass," of course, was designed for the space above the fireplace, and the brass branches, or sconces, would have projected from the mirror itself or from the woodwork, as was the case in the parlor of Thomas Hutchinson's house in Boston in 1765 where there were "2 Glass sconces at ye side of the mantle piece."[12]

The contents of Isaac Royall's "Front Room Next to medford" were not radically different from those of the "Best Room," though differences in quality are suggested by somewhat lower valuations:

1 peer Looking Glass	[£] 55:0:0
1 Sconce	15:0:0
1 mahogeny tea table	3:0:0
a parcell of Cheney for the Same	3:0:0
a Black wallnut Desk	6:0:0
an Easey Chear Covered wth Blew	7:0:0
a Green Cheney Bead [Bed]	30:0:0
1 wallnut Cheare	2:10:0

together with a large number of China plates, dishes, bowls, custard cups, and glassware. The boffat or cupboard, built into a corner of the room or into the fireplace wall in many eighteenth-century houses, was a normal repository for china and glassware, although miscellaneous other items are sometimes found. "In the Beaufet" of John Smith's "Keeping Room" in Boston in 1768 there were "7 China Mugs, 2 China Bowls crackd, 15 China plates & Dishes $diff^t$ sorts, 1 broken Turene & Dish, 6 China Bowls, 23 Syllabub, Jelly, Orange & Wine Glasses, 3 glass Salvers, 6 glass Basketts."

The variety of tables mentioned in the eighteenth century was extensive, and their exact location in a room cannot always be suggested. The "marble Side-Table" advertised in the *Boston Gazette* on October 10, 1752, describes itself. The card table by its very form was designed to be placed against a wall until needed, when it could be pulled out into the room. The tea table was presumably free standing, and note that there was full tea equipage in both the "Best Room" and "Front Room" of the Royall House. Inventories make it clear that the tea sets normally sat upon the tea tables at all times. The appraisers of William Welstead's estate in Boston, for example, found in the "front Lower Room," in 1729, "1 Tea Table wth a set of China upon it wth spoons a Bell &c." For many of the other tables, whether round or square, there were apt to be fabric covers. Benjamin Pratt, Esq., in a Boston inventory of 1763, had a "small old pine Table with green Covering," and judging from both English and American pictures of the period these coverings very often fell to the floor.

In addition to the kitchen, "Best Room" and "Front Room," there was also on the first floor of the Royall House a "Dineing Room"—though as we have noted the term was by no means common before the Revolution. Interestingly enough, only "1 doz of burnt Cheney plats," "1 Glass Decanter," "2 Glass Salts," and "1 Tubler" are listed in this room, in contrast to a much larger assortment of glass and tableware in the "Front Room." In the way of furniture there were:

a Large Sconce	£ 30:0:0
a Mahogoney table	8:0:0
1 Smal $Ditt^o$	5:0:0
8 Leather Chears . . .	10:0:0
a wooden Arm Chear	10:0

in addition to the usual fireplace equipment, "2 p^r brass arms," "2 fowling pieces" and "1 p^r of tobacco tongs."

One of the rooms in the Royall House must have contained a handsome collection of books which are catalogued separately in the inventory. Normally the desk alone or the secretary (the "desk and bookcase" as it is called in the inventories) was apt to be in the back parlor or hall of the eighteenth-century house. Here also could be found whatever there was in the way of a library. In the "Back Room" of Rev. Samuel Checkley's house in Boston, for example (which contained in addition a "Parlour," "Hall," and "Kitchen"), there were in 1770 among other items "a parcel of Books and pamphlets," "pine desk & table," "oval table," "Case of draws," "pine Table," "5 Book Cases," "a ℘ Spectacles" and "a small stand."

One can pass over without comment the furnishings of the eighteenth-century kitchen, except to note that as in the seventeenth century the supply of lighting devices for the whole house was usually kept in this room. There were "Two Large Brass Candlesticks," "Four old Iron Candlesticks" and "Two Small Brass Candlesticks" in the "new Kitchin" of Jonathan Cogswell's house in Essex, Massachusetts, in 1752. No other lighting devices are mentioned, though occasionally in eighteenth-century inventories one will find a "standing candlestick" in one of the principal rooms at the front of the house.

As in the seventeenth century, much of the tableware continued to be arranged on shelves. In the eighteenth-century kitchen the shelves or dresser were often built into the room, as is the case at the Coffin House in Newbury. Several shelves and their contents are mentioned in the "Kitchen" of William Young's house in Boston in 1750: "Sundry Small Articles upon the Shelf over the Desk, Sundry Pewter Dishes on the upper Shelf over the Dresser 10 in Number weighing 37^{lb}, on the 2^{d} & 3^{d} Shelves 21 Plates w^{t} 19^{lb}."

Turning to the chambers, we find first the continuing presence of equipage necessary for dining. In the "Closet" of the "best Chamber" of Rev. Joshua Gee's house in Boston in 1748 there were "12 China Dishes," "12 Enamild plates," "2 Ditto," "10 Enameld plates & 1 Dish mended," "3 Tea pots," "6 Cups Saucer & Sund^{y} odd peices of China," and "1 beer Glass." In the "Hall Chamber" of John Welland's house in Boston, in 1737, there were "55 p^{s} small coarse China on ye Draws," and for the number of people which these implied at table there were "12 Chairs [&] 1 Elbow D^{o}." The bedstead in this same room was furnished with "a Suit Camblet Curtains & vallens" and the fireplace was equipped with "a p^{r} flow^{r} De Luce Doggs."

The chamber appointments were often lavish, and included certain items which seem to have been considered chamber furniture almost exclusively. Two of these were the "highboy" and "lowboy"—so-called. The highboy as a receptacle for clothing and linens and the lowboy as a dressing table seldom seem to have descended to the first floor. In Mr. Welland's "N. E. Corner Chamber over the Paper Room" were a "Case Draws & Table" (a typical entry), while the inventory of Thomas Fayrweather of Boston in 1734 mentions "1 Jappan'd Chest of Drawers & Steps for China and Dressing Table." Similarly, the "wing chair," or easy chair as described in the inventories, despite its appearance in Isaac Royall's "Front Room" in 1739, is mentioned more frequently as a part of the furnishings of the chamber. Looking again at John Welland's "Hall Chamber" there was "One Easy Chair with Callico Covering." The lesser chambers were naturally more simply furnished. Often there would be two or three beds in a room and little else—understandable when we recall the size of the average colonial family.

Throughout the eighteenth century variety in color and texture seems to have been very much the fashion. Yet it is clear that every window was not invariably curtained, nor was every floor, particularly in the farm house, furnished with some form of covering. The brilliant imported oriental carpets were not as common as we might like to think. They are mentioned often in the seventeenth and early eighteenth centuries as table coverings, as we have seen, but appear only occasionally, even among the well-to-do, as a covering for the floor. Thomas Hutchinson of Boston had a "large turkey carpet" valued at £8 in his parlor in 1765, and the Moffatt-Ladd House in Portsmouth, New Hampshire, was even more resplendent.[13] In nearly every principal room of the house there was a "Persia Carpett" while the staircase was furnished with a "Stair Carpet," as we are informed in an inventory of 1768.[14] European manufactures also appear in the probate records, for example "1 English Carpet" (Capt. James Hornby, mariner, Boston, 1766) and "One small Scotch Carpet" (Benjamin Pratt, Esq., Milton, 1763), and "Three very beautiful rich Wilton carpets, three yards square each," were advertised for sale in the *Boston News-Letter* on Dec. 21, 1769. There is reference as well to "1 large Homespun Carpet" (Thomas Greene, Boston, 1766), but the painted floor cloth seems to have been the more popular floor covering—in even the finer houses. Governor William Burnet, who occupied the Province House in Boston, had "a Large painted Canvas square as the Room" and "Two old Checquered Canvass's to Lay under a Table" (1729), and the inventory of Peter Faneuil's fine mansion on Tremont Street in Boston included "Painted Canvis for Flours of Rooms & Entry" (1743).

The materials in use for window curtains, when they occur, parallel those of the bed furniture for the same period. Woolens led the field before the Revolution, for example "Searge window curtains" (Duncan Campbel, Boston, 1703), "Green Cheney Wid^{o} Curtains & Vallans Laced with Scarlett & white" (Thomas Selby, Boston, 1727), "Scarlet Callamanco Win: Curtains" (Estes Hatch, Roxbury, 1760), and "6 window Curtains strip't Camblett" (Samuel Kelling, Esq., Boston, 1730), though we find cotton calicoes and linens as well: "Two Window Curtains & Vallins of fine Chints & 2 Cushions for Windows" (Gov. William Burnet, Boston, 1729), "2 p^{r} Check window Curtains" (Mrs. Elizabeth Hutchinson, Boston, 1766), and "4 Copp^{r} plate Window Curtains" (Nathaniel Rogers, Boston, 1770). The curtain rods, incidentally, whenever material is specified, were of iron.

The always popular crewel work embroideries which involved so much patient labor and are found seldom enough in the inventories in connection with bed hangings (in contrast to numberless yards of material which had merely been purchased) do not seem to have been used for window curtains at all in New England. A single reference has been found in the Suffolk County probate records before the Revolution: "1 Work'd Bed & Window Curtains," appraised at £60 (Capt. John Hubbart, feltmaker, Boston, 1734). Even if the wording of this entry was not open to question, it could still serve only as the exception which proves the rule. Inasmuch as the fabric furnishings of a given room in the eighteenth-century house were apt to match, one may well then ask how this problem was solved. Since the curtaining of windows was not an invariable rule, the simplest expedient seems to have been that of omission, which can be found in more than one of the references to the use of needlework bed hangings or upholstery. In the "Best Chamber" of the Stephen Clap House in Boston, in 1750, there were "8 Workt Black Walnut Chairs Compas Seats" and "1 Workt Bed"—with no mention of window curtains. In the "Drawing room" of the Loring-Greenough House in Jamaica Plain, Massachusetts, on the other hand, there were, just before the Revolution, "8 Chairs, very handsome with work'd bottoms," and in the same room "4 dammask Curtains yellow."[15]

If we have been overambitious in the use of embroidered fabrics in many of our period rooms we have erred in the opposite direction when it comes to the matter of pictures and wall decorations. In restored houses of both the seventeenth and eighteenth centuries in New England, the standard solution has been to adorn the walls with looking glasses, portraits, and here and there a print. Carefully located in order that the single item (or pair) might make a charming abstract pattern against the white of the wall in conjunction with other pieces of furniture, these decorations give only a hint of how the walls of the Colonial home were embellished.

Judging from the inventories there must have been many a simple farm house whose walls were bare of any other decoration than perhaps a looking glass or whatever utilitarian objects might have been hung upon them. Well before the middle of the seventeenth century, however, we find very occasional references to fabric wall hangings. In 1641 there is record of a sale of the "dwelinge Howse" of Walter Blackborne in Boston "wth the appurteinances and the hangings of the parler."[16] By 1730 Henry Guionneau of Boston had relegated to his "Garrett" "a Turkey tapestry for room," while Mrs. Mary Henderson's "1 sett of painted Hangings" were still apparently in use in her Boston home in 1762. Fragments of a painted tapestry hanging from the old Thaxter House in Hingham, Massachusetts, have survived to the present day. The material is a pure, coarse linen, and the design, quite simply painted with some block-printed details, would suggest a date in the early 1700s.

Throughout the eighteenth century the painted portrait came to appear on many more walls than it had in the seventeenth century. Hanging in the home of Francis Wells, Esq., of Boston, for example, in 1767, at the time of his death, were a "Picture of Capt. Wells," "do. his Wife," "do. his Grandfathers," "do. his Grandmother" and "do. his Uncle." Often there would be some representation as well of their sovereigns. In the "Front Lower Room" of the home of Capt. John Ballantine, merchant, of Boston, were "2 oval Pictures of King William & Queen Mary" (1729). Both coats of arms and ship pictures were also popular, for example, "a Family arms in Gilt Frame" in the "Front Room" (Thomas Smith, Esq., Boston, 1742) and "a large draft of a ship" (Capt. John Ventiman, mariner, Boston, 1724).

Of telling importance, however, were the smaller pictures which existed in what now seem like incredible numbers. "7 Copper plate Pictures" (Mrs. Elizabeth Hutchinson, Boston, 1766) seems a reasonable number, but Dr. Thomas Bulfinch, grandfather of the architect, Charles, had "38 pictures on ye. stair Case" in the "Great Entry" of his house on Bowdoin Square in Boston in 1761. Were these hung in groups or in superimposed layers, as we find in later Victorian interiors? Mr. Henry Vassall had an even greater number "On the Stair Case" of his house in Cambridge: "33 Great & small Glass pictures" and "51 Great & small pictures" (1769). Similarly, Mrs. Sarah Dennie of Boston in 1750 had "27 large Pictures painted on Glass" and "12 smaller Ditto," yet much of what is mentioned in the inventories was more apt to be representative of the graphic arts. That many of these prints were not simply portfolio collections is demonstrated in such entries as the following: "16 Metzitinto Pictures fram'd & Glaz'd" (John Indicott, Boston, 1749). While the entry of the Colonial eighteenth-century house held the lead in the number of pictures on the walls, there were large numbers in other rooms as well. An inventory taken in 1742 of the famous "House of Seven Gables" in Salem, home of John Turner, mentions "20 Pictures Lachered Frames" in the "great Chamber," while in the "Best room" below were "19 Metzitintoes Cover'd with Glass."

Of these many prints, maps, and "prospects" accounted for some of the bulk. Alexander Hunt, shipwright, for example, had "4 Maps fram'd" (Boston, 1765), and the following localities are represented in the inventories: Europe, the Holy Land, the English Channel, London, Dublin, Glasgow, Rotterdam, as well as Virginia, Maryland, Boston, and New York. The Honorable Benjamin Pratt of Boston and New York had "Mitchel's large Map of North America pasted on a Green board" (1763). In addition there are frequent references to "Prospects" or "Draughts" of Boston, New York, and London, and Capt. Peter De Jersey of Boston possessed at the time of his death "A Draft of Chelsea Hospital" (1751).

There was seemingly no limit in interest to the subject matter, as we find it reflected in the inventories, with special emphasis upon sets: "10 Massatinto Pictures with Glass & frames of ye. Royal Family" in the "Parlour" (Arthur Savage, merchant, Boston, 1735); "6 stain'd peices of Duke Marlbrough's Battles" together with "29 Pictures of the Cathedrl. Churchs. in England" in the "Entry" of the merchant Thomas Fayrweather's house in Boston (1734); "12 Roman Emperours & Stage Man" (Mrs. Mary Walker, Boston, 1735); "12 Pictures being 12 Apostles" in the "Back Room" (Henry Guionneau, merchant, Boston, 1730); "The Ten Commandments" (Daniel Willard, ship chandler, Boston, 1728); "4 Indian Kings" "In the front Room" (Theodore Wheelwright, upholsterer, Boston, 1750); "6 large Gravings of Alexander's Battles Fram'd" (Mrs. Miriam Tyler, Boston, 1766); "8 Pictures, Call'd Raphals Cartoons" (Andrew Oliver, Esq., Boston, 1774); "The 5 Sciences" and "4 Hunting pieces" (John Simpson, merchant, Boston, 1764); and "Twelve pictures of the months" and "four pictures of the seasons" (Abiah Holbrook, Boston, 1769). Single subjects are mentioned also but by no means as often as sets: "a picture of Duke Boltons Horse" (Mrs. Sarah Dol-

Figure 2. The "Scotch"-Boardman House. (Photograph by Dell Upton.)

bear, Boston, 1745) and "One Picture by Hogarth colourd & gilt frame" (Benjamin Pratt, Esq., Boston, 1763). Those mezzotint portraits of the leading local lights of the day which have survived in a number of private and public collections can also be found, for example "Doct[r] Cotton Mathers [picture] . . . in Misitintue" in the "Front Room" of the Reverend Joshua Gee's house in Boston in 1748.

Large painted subjects are mentioned in the inventories, but not as commonly as engraved pictures. Nathaniel Rogers, Esq., of Boston, had "1 picture painted on Board" (1770), and Thomas Fayrweather had "2 painted Sea peices" in the "Entry" of his Boston home in 1734. Finally, there were the embroidered pictures. In the "front East Room" of John Simpson's house in Boston were "1 large work picture & 7 small ditto" (1764), and Gov. William Burnet's inventory in 1729 included "a fine peice of Needle work Representing a Rustick." Perhaps one of the best-known examples of all, the Bourne heirloom, so-called, owned by the Boston Museum of Fine Arts, was described in the will of Mrs. Mercy Bourne, dated July 10, 1781, as a "chimny-piece."

The chimney breast does indeed seem to have been considered the logical place for pictures of horizontal rectangular dimensions. These included landscapes, and occasionally, as we know, the overmantel panel itself was made the ground for a landscape painting directly upon the woodwork.

Sometimes, however, a number of prints were hung in this location, for example "6 Views of the River St Lawrince of [over] the fireplace" (Joshua Loring, Jamaica Plain, Massachusetts, 1785, but referring to the contents of the house before the Revolution).[17] Fascinating evidence of such an arrangement has survived in Deerfield, Massachusetts, in the Joseph Barnard House or "Old Manse." When many later layers of paint were removed from the overmantel in the south front parlor clear indications of discoloration were found where a series of six pictures had hung upon the woodwork in the earliest years. The inventory of the first owner's estate, incidentally, taken in 1790, mentions "5 pict^{rs} Kings & Queens" "8 D^{o} wth Glasses" and "2 small D^{o} Yellow frames." We do not find record of vertical portraits hanging above the fireplace as is the popular custom today. These were hung, apparently, upon the other wall surfaces, and Gov. William Burnet's inventory in 1729 mentions "a Ladys Picture over the door." In this connection it is interesting to note that pictures were commonly hung at higher levels than might seem normal to us today. The *Boston News-Letter* on June 20, 1745, tells us that lightning struck the house of Jacob Wendell in Boston, and "scorch'd the Cieling and some Pictures that hung up near it."

The chimney breast suggests another problem in furnishings, that of the mantelpiece which has been a familiar feature from the Federal period onward. Some kind of a shelf above the fireplace can be found in various periods, but not consistently so. The seventeenth-century New England fireplace was totally lacking in any such refinement, with occasional exceptions towards the very end of the period. The lintels of the chamber fireplaces of the "Scotch"-Boardman House in Saugus, Massachusetts, for example, built about 1686, are sheathed, and the masonry construction above them set back to provide a mantel ledge. This was the beginning of a trend which reached its height in the early eighteenth century. Typical examples of such mantels in this period can be found in the kitchen chamber and in the kitchen as well of the Jonathan Cogswell House in Essex, Massachusetts, ca. 1733. Those early eighteenth-century fireplaces which were surrounded with heavy bolection moldings were often furnished with a similarly heavy bed of moldings above, which provided a mantel shelf of bold projection. An excellent example of both bolection and mantel can be seen in the chamber of the Crowninshield-Bentley House in Salem, ca. 1727, which was occupied by the celebrated Dr. William Bentley, and a similar shelf, with a much simpler fireplace enframement survives in the ell chamber of the Ebenezer Clough House at Twenty-One Unity Street in Boston, about 1715. The front chamber of this same house has no mantel, however, and after 1725–30, with the exception of the kitchen fireplace, the mantel in many cases disappears in favor of the paneled chimney breast without mantel projection of any kind. As one might expect, this architectural development is reflected in the records. References in Colonial Boston inventories to things on mantelpieces are confined almost entirely to the period 1700 to 1735, and tea sets are among the more common entries. In the "Eastern Chamber" of the home of William Young, distiller, of Boston, for example, there was "A parcell of Tea Cups, a Tea pott, Saucers & other Appũrces on the Mantle peice" (1750). Capt. Peter Papillon, merchant, of Boston had "16 small peices coarse China on the Mantle tree" of his "Parlour" (1733) while in the "back long Chamber" there were "1 p^{r} small Decanters on the mantle p^{s}" and "13 p^{s} of Glass on Ditto." These items must have been functional, but the inventory of John Elzey of Boston, 1703, specifies "Baubles for a Mantletree p^{s}, and that of John Dixwell of Boston, goldsmith, records the presence of "Images and Glasses on the Mantle Tree" in the "Hall" (1725). When a mantel shelf existed in those finer houses built before the Revolution it was apt to be furnished with a garniture. In Thomas Hutchinson's "parlour" in Boston in 1765 there were "Gilt Jarrs &c^{r} being a set for the mantle piece,"[18] and in the hall of the Loring-Greenough House in Jamaica Plain, Massachusetts, there was "ornamental China over the mantle piece."[19]

The custom of a flower container on the hearth or inside the fireplace during the warm months when it was not in use, is reflected in the following entries: "N. East Chamber," "Chimney flower pot" ("Capt. Joseph Domett, Boston, 1762), and "2 Flowered Chimney Potts," "Front Lower Rome" (Jacob Wendell, Jr., merchant, Boston, 1754).

In conclusion, one should emphasize in matters of interpretation the need for awareness of both social and economic differences. Because a certain wealthy merchant of Boston might have had a brass or crystal chandelier before the Revolution (a fact, by the way, which would be hard to prove from the inventories) does not mean that every farmer owned one! The furnishing of our simpler New England farm houses, which are open to the public, with Aubusson carpets, crystal chandeliers and damask window curtains is perhaps the greatest disservice we can perform in building up a correct picture of life in early America.

The household inventories of the wealthier colonial families do indeed conjure up an elegance which is a fit complement to the fine architectural detail of those great houses built during the period before the Revolution. But rural inventories paint quite another picture—to which color is added by such occasional glimpses as that of the caustic Madam Sarah Knight who stopped overnight at an "ordinary" in Rye, Connecticut, on the night of December 7, 1704: "being shewd the way up a pair of stairs wch had such a narrow passage that I had almost stopt by the Bulk of my Body, But arriving at my apartment found it to be a little Lento Chamber furnisht amongst other Rubbish with a High Bedd and a Low one, a Long Table, a Bench and a Bottomless chair,—Little Miss went to scratch up my Kennell wch Russelled as if shee'd bin in the Barn amongst the Husks, and supose such was the contents of the tickin—nevertheless being exceeding weary, down I laid my poor Carkes (never more tired) and found my Covering as scanty as my Bed was hard. Annon I heard another Russelling noise in Y^{e} Room—called to know the matter—Little miss said shee was making a bed for the men; who, when they were in Bed, complained their leggs lay out of it by reason of its shortness—my poor bones complained bitterly not being used to such Lodgings, and so did the man who was with us."[20]

Ultimately the most important single fact about the inventories for rural Suffolk County, in comparison with those of the same period for nearby Boston, is their simplicity. While it may have reflected palely some of the grander urban fashions, the village and country farm house, as opposed to the town house or "country seat," was unpretentious and geared to the outdoor pursuits of the husbandman. Aside from other values, these inventories show what the average rural yeoman's house was really like during the colonial period.

An Inventory of the Estate of William Bordman Dečed belonging to [Rumney Marsh in the Township of] Boston [Joyner]. [Figs 1, 2.] Apprized by us the Subscribers May 25th 1696.

The particulars are as follow:

Imp^{rs} Wearing Cloaths 16^{lb} Bookes 1^{lb} Armes 6^{lb}	£ 23.—.—
It. 1 Cupboard. 2 tables. 6 Leather Chairs wth all y^{t} belongs *to ye best room*	10.—.—
It. 2 Featherbeds and bedsteads with all the furniture belonging to them that stand *in the Parlour*	12.10.—
It. 11 p^{r} of Sheets and 4 p^{r} of pillowbeers	8.12.—
It. 2 doz^{n} of Napkins and Table Linnen	3.—.—
It. 1 table. 1 chest. 1 p^{r} of andirons & warmingpan with all that belongs to the parlour	3. 5.—
It. 1 featherbed and bedstead with the furniture belonging to it with 1 table, 1 chest. halfe a dozen Chaires with all that belongs *to the Hall Chamber*	10.10.—
It. 1 flockbed and the furniture belonging to it, with 1 table 6 chaires standing *in the Parlour Chamber*	5.—.—
It. 1 bed with the furniture to it *in the Kitchen Chamber*	2.10.—
It. Pewter 3^{lb} 5^{s} Brass 4^{lb} 1 p^{r} of Stilliards 12/	7.17.—
It. 2 Iron pots. 2 kettles. 2 tram̃els. 1 p^{r} of Andirons. 1 p^{r} of tongs 1 Shovel fire. 1 gridiron. A chafingdish & some old Iron	2.16.—
It. 1 Churn, 3 Seives with ye Wooden Lumber *in the Milkhouse*	1.—.—
It. 12 old barrels and other Lumber *in the Cellar*	1.—.—
It. 2 Saddles and Bridle & 1 old pillion	1. 5.—
It. 2 Linnen Wheeles and 1 Woollen Wheel	—.10.—
It. The Joyners tooles 2^{lb} 10^{s} 1 grind stone 8^{s} Cart & Wheeles 2^{lb} 10^{s}	5. 8.—

It. Yoakes. Chains, ploughs. ploughshares — 3. 5.—
It. Axes, hoes, beetle and wedges, Iron Crow & some old Iron — 1.10.—
It. Plate 3^{lb} 3 old Scythes and 2 old Sickles 12^{s} — 3.12.—
It. 6 Oxen 21^{lb} 4 Cows 12^{lb} 2 two year old 4^{lb} 4 year old 4^{lb} 10^{s} 1 horse 2^{lb} 10^{s} 14 Sheep & 3 Lambs 4^{lb} 10^{s} 3 Swine 3^{lb} — 51.10.—
It. Housing. Upland and fresh Meadow belonging to ye Farme with 6 acres of Salt Marsh bought with s^{d} Farme — 291.—.—
It. 6 acres of Salt Marsh bought of Mr Doolittle — 24.—.—
It. Halfe of Squires Meadow so called — 17.—.—
It. A Wood Lot at Spot pond — 10.—.—

Sum̃ Total	£500.—.—
Personal Estate	£158.—.—
Real Estate	342.—.—
	£500.—.—

Henry Green Joseph Hasey Jno Burrill

A true & perfect Inventory of all & Singular the Goods Chattles Lands Debts & Credits of Thomas Jones Yeoman late of Hingham Deceased prized at Hingham aforesaid 1724 [presented Oct. 21]. by us the Subscribers as follows Viz^{t}

Imp^{rs} His Purse Apparel & Books — £ 12.10.—

In the Bed Roome, Bed Bedstead Curtains & Bedcloaths — 10.—.—
To a Looking Glass 50/ Sword & Cane 30/ — 4.—.—
Two Boxes & a Table 10/ Glass & Earthenware on the mantletree 6/ — —.16.—

In the Great Chamber, Bed Bedstead & Furniture — 8.—.—
A Trundle Bed Bedstead & Bedding — 8.—.—
1 Chest 6/ Cradle & Box 6/ one Rug 25/ Blanket 10/ a Table 1/ — 1.16.—

In the Bed Roome at the End of the Great Roome
One Bed Bedstead Sheets & Coverlit £7.
One Chest & the Linnen in it 48/ — 9. 8.—

In the Great Roome, Arms & Ammunition — 3.—.—
Warming pan 10/ 11 Chairs 22/ Trammel 6/ Gridiron 2/ Fender 2/ — 2. 2.—
Lanthorn 3/ Candlestick 1/6 Tubs 6/ 3 Seives 3/ — —.13. 6
2 p^{r} Cards 5/ Choping knife & Rowling pin 1/ Mortar 4/ — —.10.—
Spit 5/ hammer & awls 2/ Box Iron & heaters 3/ — —.10.—
Fire Shovel & Tongs 10/ Flax 8/ Sythes & Staves 25/ — 2. 3.—
Leather aprons 2/ Looking Glass 5/ — —. 7.—

In the Garret old Iron & other Lumber — 2.15.—
Meal bags 4/ Rule & files 3/ Combs 1/ Gimblet 1/ — —. 9.—

Tubs *in the Lento Chamber* — —. 6.—

In the Dary Roome Cheespress Meat trough Churn & Milk pans — 1. 4.—
2 Skillets 14/ brass kittle 26/ Iron pot & kettle 30/ — 3.10.—
Pewter 31 Glass bottles 7/ Earthen ware knives & forks 13/ — 2.11.—
Frying pan 5/ Greas Tubs &c — —.17.—

In the Cellar Hogsheads 16/ 3 Meal Tubs 20/ — 1.16.—
1 Marsh Tub 5/ half a Barrel Pork 2/10 half a Barrel beef 15/ — 5.—.—
Candles & Hogs Suit 2/6 Tallow & grease 2/ Bear Vessels & rundlets — —. 7.—
Butter Tubs & Brooms 3/8 Pails & other wooden ware — 1.13.—
20^{lb} Sheeps wool 30/ *In the old House,* Loome & Weaving Tacklin 4^{lb} — 5.10.—
Barrels & Tubs 38/ 2 wheels 12/ — 2.10.—
Corn £17. 10/ Syder £3 — 20.10.—

Moveables Out Doors Cart & wheels £9. Yokes & Chains £4. 5/ — 13. 5.—
Horse Tackling 16/ Plow 10/ Axes & hoes Axes & hoes 20/ 2 bells 10/ — 2.16.—
Bridle Sadle Pillion & Fetters £2. 19/ Rakes Pitchforks &c 10/ Shave 5/ — 3.14.—
Led 10/ Timber 5/ Hurdles 32/ Cart rope 12/ — 2.19.—
Iron Crow 16/ Sheep Shears 2/ Corn fat 10/ Grindstone 10/ — 1.18.—
Quick Stock, 4 Oxen £26. 4 Cows £20. 2 Stears £8. 4 yearlings £7 — 61.—.—
40 Sheep £16. 3 Swine £3. Bees 30/ Mare & Colt £12 — 32.10.—
Real Estate House & Homestead — 350.—.—

Land in the 3d Division Est. 40. Acres — 300.—.—
one peice of Meadow called the [blank] Meadow — 30.—.—
Another peice called the Run Meadow — 25.—.—
2 Acres of Salt Marsh at Cohasit — 160.—.—
half an acre of Salt Marsh at the Ware River — 15.—.—
6 Shares of the Undivided Land — 18.—.—
£1128.15. 6

Israel Tazel Josiah Sprague Adam Cushing

Dorchester Jan^{ry} 11th 1763.

Inventory of what Estates Real & Personall, belonging to $Coll^{o}$ Robert Oliver [Esquire] late of Dorchester Deceased, that has been Exhibited to us the Subscribers, for Apprizement, Viz^{t}

In the Setting Parlour Viz^{tt}

a looking Glass — £ 4.—.—
a Small Ditto — 0. 6. 0
12 Metzitens pictures Glaz'd @ 6/ — 3.12.—

8 Cartoons Dº Ditto		4.—.—
11 small Pictures		—. 4.—
4 Maps		—.10.—
1 Prospect Glass		—.10.—
2 Escutchons Glaz'd		—. 4.—
1 pair small hand Irons		—. 6.—
1 Shovel & Tongs		—. 8.—
1 Tobacco Tongs		—. 1.—
1 pair Bellowes		—. 2.—
1 Tea Chest		—. 2.—
2 Small Waters [waiters?]		—. 1.—
1 Mehogony Tea Table		1.—.—
8 China Cups & Saucers		—. 2.—
1 Earthen Cream Pott		—.—. 1
1 Ditto. Sugar Dish		—.—. 4
1 Black Walnut Table		1.—.—
1 Black Ditto Smaller		0. 6.—
1 Round painted Table		0. 1.—
7 Leather Bottom Chairs	@ 6/	2. 2.—
1 Arm^{d} Chair Common		0. 3.—
1 Black Walnut Desk		1.12.—
1 pair Candlesticks snuffers & Stand Base Mettle		—. 4.—
6 Wine Glasses 1 Water Glass		—. 1.—
2 parcell of Books		1.—.—
2 Case with Small Bottles		0. 4.—
		22. 1. 5

In the Marble Chamber Viz^{t}

1 Bedstead & Curtains Compleat		£ 8.—.—
1 feather Bed, Bolster & 2 pillows		8.—.—
1 Chest of Drawers		2. 8.—
1 Buroe Table		1.—.—
6 Chairs Leather'd Bottoms	@ 6/	1.16.—
1 Small dressing Glass		—. 6.—
1 Small Carpett		1.—.—
1 White Cotton Counterpin		—.18.—
1 pair Blanketts		1.12.—
1 pair holland Sheets		1. 4.—
3 pair Dowlases Dº New	12^{s}/p^{r}	1.16.—
3 pair & 1 Ditto Coarser	4/	0.14.—
3 pair Cotton & Linnen Dº	3/	0. 9.—
4 pair Servants Ditto	2/	0. 8.—
4 Coarse Table Cloths	1/	0. 4.—
10 Ditto Kitchen Towels	1	—. 1.—
5 Diaper Table Cloths	12/	3.—.—
6 Damask Table Cloths	@ 18/	5. 8.—
4 N: England Diaper Dº	3/	0.12.—
4 pair Linnen pillow Cases	2/	0. 8.—
5 Coarser Ditto	1/	0. 5.—
6 Diaper Towels	6^{d}	0. 3.—
7 Damask Ditto	2/	0.14.—
2 doz^{n} & 9 Damask Napkins	@ 24/ ℘ doz^{n}	3. 6.—
1 Gauze Tea Table Cover		0. 1.—
		43.13. 0

In the Entry & Stair Case Viz^{t}

17 Pictures		£ 0.10.—
		0.10. 0

In the Blue Chamber Viz^{t}

a Bedstead & Curtains Compleat		£ 5.—.—
a Bed Bolster & pillows		8.—.—
1 White Counterpin		0.18.—
3 Blanketts	13/4	2.—.—
1 Callico Quilt		1.—.—
3 Corded Bedsteads	6/	0.18.—
1 feild Bedstead		0. 6.—
1 Couch		1.10.—
2 Trunks	6/	0.12.—
1 Looking Glass		1.—.—
1 Table		0. 2.—
a pine Table		0. 6.—
1 pair Brass and Irons		0.18.—
3 Glass Pictures	6/	0.18.—
3 pictures		0. 1.—
1 Easy Chair Coverd		0.12.—
7 Bass Bottom Chairs	1/	0. 7.—
3 feather Beds 2 Bolsters 2 pillows	@ 100^{s}/℘ p^{s}	15.—.—
1 Straw Bed		0. 1.—
6 Coarse Rugs	6/	1.16.—
1 Coarser Ditto		0. 4.—
3 Cloths Basketts with Iron Cloth		0. 3.—
1 Small Desk		0. 1.—
Sundry Cloathing & Linnen belonging to the Deseas'd		10.—.—
		50.13. 0

In the Kitchen Chamber Viz^{t}

a Bedstead & Curtains Compleat		£ 4.—.—
a Bed Bolster & 2 pillows		5.—.—
a Under Bed & 1 Chair		0. 1.—
2 Rugs & 1 Blankett	@ 6/	0.18.—
		09.19. 0

In the Dining Room Viz^{t}

1 pair and Irons		£ 0. 3.—
7 Bass Bottoms Chairs	1/	0. 7.—
1 Large Wooden Table		0. 3.—
1 Small Ditto Oak		0. 1.—
1 Small looking Glass		0. 6.—
1 Old Desk		0. 6.—
1 Case with 2 Bottles		0. 2.—
1 Warming pan		0.12.—
		2. 0. 0

In the front parlour Viz^{t}

6 Bass Bottom Chairs		£ 0. 2.—
1 Childs Chair		0. 1.—
a Baskett with 11 white Stone plates & 3 White Dishes		0.12.—
4 Burn China Dishes & 1 doz^{n} Plates with flower Pott in the middle		1. 8.—
1 doz^{n} & 11 ditto plates		1.12.—
6 Burnt China Bowls		1. 8.—
Blue & w^{t} China		
2 Dishes & 7 Plates		0. 8.—
2 Burnt China Bowls Broke		0. 8.—

Item	Rate		£ s d
2 Ditto Cract	@ 6/		0.12.—
1 Ditto Small Bowl			0.10.—
2 Mustard Pots. Dº	@ 3/		0. 6.—
5 Ditto Butter Plates	8/		0.15.—
A Sett Burnt China Coffees Sugar Dishes a Dish & Tea Pott & a Bowl some Broke			3.—.—
A parcell of Cract & Broken China & Earthen			0. 8.—
6 China Patty Pans & 6 Coffees & 1 plate			0.14.—
2 Dishes & 5 plates a Decanter a Cream Pott & a Salt			0. 6.—
a looking Glass			8.—.—
16 Landskip Pictures Glaz'd.wth the Camera Obscura Glass			10.—.—
Empty Glass Bottles			1.12.—
5 Bottom leather Chairs	6/		1.10.—
a saddle & Bridle & Straps			2.—.—
a Close stool & a Bed pans			0.12.—
a flasket Voider & knife Baskett & 3 Matts			0.18.—
a Cloths Horse foldg Board & a leaf			0. 8.—
Sad Irons Irong Boxes heaters & Grate			0.15.—
1 Glass Lanthorn			0. 6.—
a parcell of Gardening Seeds			2. 8.—
a Case of Instruments			1.—.—
a Shaveing Box & Raisors			0. 6.—
Old Earthen plates for Kitchen			0. 2.—
a Gun & 3 Swords			1.16.—
1 Lingum Vitae Morter			0. 6.—
1 Marble Ditto			1.—.—
1 Warming pan			0. 1.—
1 pair Stylyards			0. 4.—
a Cleaver a Choping knife & a hatchet			0. 8.—
a pair large Shears			0. 3.—
Scails & wts			0. 7.—
a Stone Stove			0. 1.—
a Copper Sauce pan			0.12.—
a Broaken Skillet			0. 1.—
a Compass			0. 1.—
2 Iron potts & 2 Skillets			0.10.—
a pr of Andirons Shovel & Tongs			0. 5.—
2 pair Brass Candlesticks 4/ the 4			0. 4.—
Sundry Tin Ware	6/		0. 6.—
1 Copper Stew pan			0.12.—
Sundrys in a Box			0.12.—
Sundry Old Trumpery Iron &c			1.—.—
1 Small Sauce pan			0. 6.—
8 pewter water Plates	3/	£ 1. 4.—	
2 dozn New plates pewter 1 dozn Soop Ditto		4.—.—	
2 dozn old Ditto	18/	1.16.—	
1 Cullindar		0. 3.—	
10 New Dishes	6/	3.—.—	
3 old Ditto	2/	0. 6.—	
1 Can 1/ 1 Coffee Pott 2/ 1 Sett. of 6 midg Dishes 24 is		1. 7.—	11.16.—
a Boats Anchor			0. 3.—
			63. 1. 0

In the Kitchen Viz!

Item	£ s d
2 Iron Potts, Dish Kittle, Tea Kittle & flesh fork	1.—.—
1 Jack	0. 4.—
1 Gridiron 1/ 1 frying pan 2/	0. 3.—
a Copper Kittle	2.—.—
a Small Brass Ditto	0.12.—
Trammells	0.12.—
Andirons Shovel & Tongs	0.18.—
	5. 9. 0

In the Cellars Vizt!

Item	£ s d
4 Hogsheads Syder	£ 3.—.—
½ Barrells Soap	1. 4.—
1 Barrell Pork	3. 6.—
Barrells &c	1.—.—
	8.10. 0

Stock & Farm Utensells Vizt!

Item	£ s d
2 yoake of Oxen	£ 25. 6. 8
1 Cow	4.—.—
3 Shotes	3. 6.—
1 Old Horse	3.—.—
a Mare	5.—.—
1 Chaise & Harnass	12.—.—
1 pair Runners	0.12.—
1 Cart	4.—.—
1 Slead	0.10.—
a plow & Chains	1. 4.—
a Cyder Mill	0.14.—
a Wheel Barrow & 3 Ladders	0.6.—
Hay in the Barn Exclusive of what must be kept for the use of the Stock 2 Tons English & 2 Ton Salt Hay	17. 6. 8
	77. 5. 4

Item	£ s d
A Negrow Man Named Cato	53. 6. 8
A Negrow Man Named Buff	60. 0. 0
A Negrow Boy Named Jack	46.13. 4
An Old Negrow Woman Named Lucey	13. 6. 8
An Old Negrow Woman Named Miber[?]	13. 6. 8
A Negrow Woman Named Mirah	20. 0. 0
A Negrow Girl Named Jude	40. 0. 0
	246.13. 4

Sundry Peices of Plate Viz!

Item	£ s d
2 Chaffin Dishes wt 51 oz a Sett Castars wt 45 oz 96 oz @ 7/4	£ 35.14. 0
a large Tankard wt 31 oz 16 pwt	
a Midg ditto wt 25 oz 13	
a small dº wt 19:3	
a Cann wt 11:19	
a large Salver wt 10:16	
a small dº wt 4:5	
a small Bowl wt 6.17.	

a Soop Spoon wt 4:0	
a Punch Strainer wt 5:7	
6 Table Spoons & 1 do wt 12:9	
6 Tea spoons Tongss & Strainr wt 4:7	
a Fork wt 1:6	
1 pr Salts wt 2:18	
a pepper Box wt 2:1	
a Tobacco Box wt 1:3	
a Sett Buckls & a pipe Stopr wt 2:0 146, oz 1dwt @ 6/8	£ 48.13. 8
A Gold Neck Buckle wt 11dwt 16av	2.19. 2
2 ditto Ring 4dwt £1.0.3½ a Gold Ring £1.6.8	2. 6.11½
Cash in the House Vizt 78 Dollars' @ 6/.	23. 8. 0
10 do gave Gloves & expended £3.18.11 11 Crowns @ 6/8. £3.13.4	7.12. 3
20 Johanne's @ 48/.£48. 1 Maidore (short wt) £1.14.8½	49.14.11½
New England shilling 1/. A Silver Watch £6	6. 1. 0
A Pew at the Revd Mr Hoopers Church	13. 6. 8
A Pew at the Revd Mr Boardman's Church	3. 0. 0
A Farm at Dorchester Contg 36½ Acres of Pasture; Marsh & Mowing & Pasture Land Gardens & Orchards included @ £13.6.8 pr are	486.13. 4
Mantion House, two Barn's & all the Out Houses on said Farm included Valued at	666.13. 4
A Small House & Land in Boston	33. 6. 8
A Tract abot 74 Acres of Waste Land in Worcester @ 8/.	29.12. 0
	£ 1948.16.10

Edward Davis Christopher Minot

Notes

This article was originally published as the Introduction and part of the inventories included in *Rural Household Inventories: Establishing the Names, Uses and Furnishings of Rooms in the Colonial New England Home, 1675–1775*, edited by Cummings (1964). The author gratefully acknowledges the Harvard University Press for permission to use figure 27, first- and second-floor plans of the Boardman House, Saugus, Massachusetts, from Cummings's *Framed House of Massachusetts Bay, 1625–1725* (Cambridge: Harvard University Press, 1979), p. 24.

1. Quotations that can be located easily in public records and published documents have not been noted. Full citations for those sources appearing in the text are as follows: The Letters and Papers of John Singleton Copley, *Collections of the Massachusetts Historical Society,* 83 vols. (Boston: Massachusetts Historical Society, 1914), vol. 71; *The Diary of William Bentley, D. D.* (Salem, Mass.: Essex Institute, 1905–14); The Diary of Samuel Sewall, *Collections of the Massachusetts Historical Society,* 10 vols. (Boston: Massachusetts Historical Society, 1878–82), 5: 5–7; and the Registries of Probate for Essex County (Salem, Mass.), Hampshire County (Northampton, Mass.), Middlesex County (East Cambridge, Mass.), Plymouth County (Plymouth, Mass.), and Suffolk County (Boston, Mass.).
2. The term *borning room* is never found in our early records, and must be considered a nineteenth-century invention.
3. For a more detailed discussion of beds and bedding in the colonial period see Abbott Lowell Cummings, ed., *Bed Hangings: A Treatise on Fabrics and Styles in the Curtaining of Beds, 1650–1850* (Boston: Society for the Preservation of New England Antiquities, 1961).
4. E. O. Jameson, *The Cogswells in America* (Boston: A. Mudge and Son, 1884), p. 11, in which this deposition, quoted in full, is credited to an Essex County court case that in turn was appealed and heard in Suffolk County. A routine search of the court files in both counties has failed to discover the original document.
5. Sarah Kemble Knight, *The Private Journal of a Journey from Boston to New York, in the year 1704. Kept by Madam Knight* (Albany: F. H. Little, 1865), pp. 33–35.
6. John Josselyn, *An Account of Two Voyages to New-England* [1638, 1663] (Boston: W. Veazie, 1865), p. 148.
7. *Narrative of the Captivity and Restauration of Mrs. Mary Rowlandson* (Cambridge, Mass., 1682), p. 70.
8. [Anne Grant], *Memoirs of an American Lady,* 2 vols. (London: Longman, Hurst, Rees and Orm, 1808), 1:165.
9. Ibid., 1:172.
10. New Hampshire Archives, Court Files, case no. 25135.
11. Massachusetts Archives, 6:301, 302.
12. Ibid., 6:301.
13. Ibid.
14. New Hampshire Archives, Court Files, case no. 25135.
15. Public Records Office, London, A.O. 13/47.
16. Suffolk County Deeds, 1:20.
17. Public Records Office, London, A.O. 13/47.
18. Massachusetts Archives, 6:309.
19. Public Records Office, London, A.O. 13/47.
20. Knight, *Private Journal,* pp. 62, 63.

Meaning in Artifacts: Hall Furnishings in Victorian America

KENNETH L. AMES

Like Abbott Lowell Cummings, Kenneth L. Ames is interested in "peopling" architectural spaces. His choice of late nineteenth-century middle-class houses offers him different source materials and the possibility of asking different questions. Considerably more information is available about nineteenth-century American material culture than about earlier periods; it no longer requires an exhaustive effort merely to identify house spaces and their contents. Ames thus turns his attention to a close examination of one aspect of the Victorian house—the entrance hall and three common items of hall furniture—and to a particular social ritual—the reception of social callers. His major primary sources are contemporary illustrations, architectural handbooks and furniture manufacturers' catalogs for the objects, and etiquette books for behavior. All of these represent kinds of sources that did not exist before the nineteenth century. At the same time, they convey normative values: they inform us of their creators' ideas of how buildings should *look, how people* ought *to behave, rather than providing glimpses of the real lives of individuals, as probate inventories, for example, do. Ames thus uses his sources to ask about the values that were shared by middle-class nineteenth-century urban and suburban Americans. Halls and their furnishings are revealed to have been devices for "attaining elegance and personal nobility" in a mass industrial society through the maintenance of elaborate social ceremonies in everyday life. Though many of the same phenomena that worried the Victorians continue to vex us, the social world the hall furnishings represent is as dead as that of Cummings's colonial New Englanders. Without an analysis such as Ames offers, the hall chair, the hallstand, and the card receiver might appear to us simply as characteristically "Victorian" over-elaborate responses to simple technological functions, as quaint as bedwarmers.*

Most people agree that Independence Hall, the Statue of Liberty, and the Brooklyn Bridge are important. Unique and heroic artifacts known to millions, they can be viewed as material culture counterparts of great individuals like George Washington, Abraham Lincoln, and Thomas Edison. There is probably less agreement about the significance of Victorian hallstands, hall chairs, and card receivers. Yet the commonplace artifacts of everyday life mirror a society's values as accurately as its great monuments.[1] This article extends our understanding of Victorian America by analyzing hall furnishings typical of that era. By examining artifacts such as these one can gain insights into the past not readily accessible by conventional verbal approaches.

Hall furnishings have usually been outside the scope of historical inquiry. So have the majority of their users. Today, however, many historians are looking at ordinary people rather than traditional heroes and asking new sets of questions. By concentrating less on the unique and more on the typical they hope to compile an account of the past which is more responsive to contemporary needs. Reflecting both this changing orientation of history and the growing intellectual prestige of the social sciences, material culture studies are becoming more varied, rigorous, and suggestive.[2] Once dominated by historians of art and technology, the field is being invaded by scholars from many different disciplines. Students of folk and popular material culture are beginning to explore categories of objects usually ignored in their search for fuller understanding of the culture and values of people who lived apart from elite society. Anthropologists, psychologists, sociologists, educators, and philosophers are studying material culture for what it reveals about the social and psychological realities of the past and present and for insights into the processes of cognition and communication. The diversity of questions being asked and the variety of disciplines generating them indicate that material culture is currently perceived as a new frontier for scholarship likely to yield particularly rich data about what Howard Gardner calls man's systems for making, perceiving, and feeling.[3]

The student of material culture requires some basis for isolating groups of artifacts closely enough related to be discussed intelligibly yet limited enough in number to be encompassed mentally. For reducing artifacts to manageable groups, classifications based on form, function, material, date, school or maker, or style are frequently employed. More subtle models may incorporate several of these factors. George Kubler suggests dividing the pool of artifacts into formal sequences composed of prime objects and their replications. Some archaeologists employ the polar concepts of tradition and horizon. Because both models involve form, function, style, and duration they may be synthesized. One can, then, designate as traditional objects those that belong to long formal sequences and are produced with minimal change over considerable time. Horizonal objects belong to short formal sequences and are produced for only a brief while before being eliminated or substantially altered. One can also speak of horizonal constellations or clusters of objects in interlocking sequences. As with celestial constellations, artifact constellations yield a larger picture when read as a whole. Horizonal constellations serve as indices of attitudes, values, and patterns of behavior of relatively limited duration.[4]

Hall furnishings in Victorian America form a horizonal constellation. Hallstands, hall chairs, and card receivers became popular around the middle of the nineteenth century, declined by the early years of this century and are largely obsolete today. Although they survive in museums and in private hands across the country, the culture that produced them, the people who first used them, and the meanings they once had have faded, died, or been forgotten. By studying these objects, one can locate and analyze certain features of the Victorian age. Because these furnishings were commonplace they can be useful for working toward a definition of Victorian culture and for documenting subdivisions within that culture.[5] Furthermore, it is appropriate to investigate objects that were prominent parts of Victorian everyday life precisely because the Victorians themselves were fascinated with material culture. By studying the things that surrounded them we can not only better comprehend their physical environment but come closer to understanding their mentality as well.[6]

The emphasis of this article is on artifacts used by the upper middle class in urban and urban-oriented areas of the North in the second half of the nineteenth century. The objects are factory-made, mass-produced examples of Victorian popular culture of the sort found in the more expensive homes in cities and in houses of the villa class in towns and suburbs. The North was selected because of its relative homogeneity; it was dominated and unified by a Yankee culture formulated on the east coast and carried westward to the Mississippi River and beyond. The geographical configuration of this Yankee culture can be seen with remarkable clarity on maps recording urban growth, industrialization, and rail transportation. These maps indicate that the South was, as it remains, a distinctive subculture; for that reason it is not dealt with here. Lastly, the time span treated was dictated by the objects themselves. The discussion that follows includes observations on the nature and availability of materials for research on household artifacts, and hall furnishings in particular, analysis of three major types of hall furnishings, and suggestions for their interpretation.[7]

It may seem like putting the cart before the horse to discuss research materials before the objects themselves but the nature of the resources has a significant bearing on how one approaches the objects and also explains some of the difficulties encountered in trying to interpret them.

The ideal situation for a scholar interested in the nature and meaning of the hall and its furnishings in Victorian America would be to discover a large number of halls distributed over time, space, and social class, with all original artifacts wholly intact, fully documented, and accompanied by extensive written records of conscious as well as subconscious reponses to the space and its objects. In fact, resources are scattered and of varying value. Written documents are among the least useful, at least at the outset, because considerable prior knowledge of the artifacts is necessary to make sense of them. Conventional records like wills, inventories, bills, and receipts list furnishings and place a dollar value on individual pieces but, until large numbers of such documents are tabulated and the results correlated, few conclusions can be drawn.[8]

Literature constitutes an exceptionally rich resource for the study of cultural history. However, it may be rather more fruitfully seen as a manifestation parallel to material culture, responding to or recording related cultural tendencies in a different medium, than as a direct path to the interpretation of the material world. Most of the occasional specific references to objects which appear in novels—"on one occasion, when my brother was visiting me, his overcoat was taken from the hatstand in the hall," or " 'Then I must wait til she returns,' and Ben quietly placed his hat on the hatstand"—do little more than confirm the existence of the objects and describe their most obvious functions. Sometimes authors go further and record the mood of a space in some detail, as Hay did.[9] Although occasional passages may be illuminating, finding them is not easy; investigating literature is an inefficient way to learn about artifacts of the past. Even when lucid verbal accounts are uncovered, they must always be weighed against other forms of evidence.[10]

Combinations of verbal and pictorial materials occur in architectural and home furnishing books but these, too, are of limited value. Even Andrew Jackson Downing's *Architecture of Country Houses* (1850), notable in so many ways, is of little use for studying hall furnishings. It contains nearly 150 illustrations of furniture appropriate for mid nineteenth-century homes but only six are of hall pieces and the discussion of them is minimal. Samuel Sloan's *Homestead Architecture* (1861 and 1867), another major volume of this genre, illustrates no hall furniture and contains only one deprecating reference.[11]

Beginning in the late 1870s, a flurry of books appeared expressing design reform sentiments formulated in England a decade earlier. These works illustrated and discussed halls and their furnishings but the views that they set forth belonged to a vocal if growing minority with new attitudes toward style, the home, and furnishings. These publications are related to a distinct phase in the history of Victorian furnishings of which more will be said later. Here it is sufficient to note that this phase was characterized by a degree of verbal activity absent in the previous phase. Although the latter made its primary appeal through the artifacts themselves, the reform phase relied heavily on rhetoric. As a result, the written testimony is strongly biased in favor of the reform movement and against its immediate antecedents.[12] A typical book, *A Domestic Cyclopoedia of Practical Information* (1877), demonstrates the strong Anglophile stance of this reform phase and its manner of proselytizing for furniture still relatively unknown. Another work from the same year, Clarence Cook's *The House Beautiful,* disparages most mass-produced furnishings in favor of antiques and pieces in the English reform style sensitively combined. Books such as these are valuable as long as their crusading purpose is understood. American historians of the decorative arts, however, have often accepted these polemics at face value without attempting to view the arguments in their original social context. They have also failed to acknowledge that reform sentiments and artifacts belonged only to a small segment of a larger American society which, although unified in a general sense, was nevertheless highly pluralistic in object preference, as it remains today.[13] The reformers represented neither the only point of view nor, in the 1870s, the dominant one. In a rough analogy we could say that their publications reflect conventional Victorian hall furnishings about as accurately as today's professional architectural journals do suburban tract housing.

From these verbal and published sources we still have little idea of the appearance or placement of the most typical objects in Victorian halls, especially for the period before 1880. Here more strictly pictorial materials, paintings, prints, photographs, and trade catalogs, can be helpful. Painted or printed views of American interiors survive in considerable number but many are nostalgic, mythologizing images of rural life rather than reliable records of the real appearance of middle- or upper-middle-class interiors in the cities and suburbs. Within the class of presumably reliable interior views, paintings or prints showing the hall are scarce. The long, narrow, dark space was difficult to delineate and beyond the recording capabilities of the early camera. Photographs of halls grow more common in the last two decades of the century when the performance of the camera and the space of the hall were both altered, the latter under the impact of the English reform movement mentioned before.[14]

For pictorial records of individual objects, trade catalogs are the most valuable resource. They survive in great numbers from the late 1860s. Hall furniture, lighting, card receivers, cards, wall and floor materials, hardware, and nearly every other element of furnishing needed for the hall or any other room in the house can be found lithographed or sometimes photographed. Trade catalogs are important for providing incontrovertible evidence of objects in production or available on order. They can be used by scholars seeking answers to a variety of questions: How long were certain articles made? Were they manufactured in one location, a few places, or nationwide? How did design and cost change over time? How and to what extent were certain styles reflected in given classes of objects? How was price reflected in the design and construction of the object? How were production and marketing organized within a given industry? Trade catalogs can also be of great help in identifying and dating extant artifacts. Perhaps most significant of all, they can provide a scholar with more images of thoroughly documented artifacts of certain kinds than he could hope to gather in years of scouring museums, historical societies, and private collections.[15]

The drawback of trade catalogs is that the images are only reminders of the objects. To appreciate scale, volume, color, and surface, one must turn to the objects themselves, which is where all artifact study should begin. Working directly with objects is a difficult task, however, and the historian should be willing to utilize all the conventional tools of his trade, including intuition and his own subjective feelings. But, as John Demos noted in *A Little Commonwealth,* it is not easy to judge the meanings of objects in people's lives or how they felt about a certain artifact. Not only did those meanings and feelings go unrecorded but they often existed below the level of consciousness. This article, then, can serve to point out to scholars the nature of and problems attached to the various kinds of documents relevant to the study of artifacts. And if it is not an account which resolves major historical problems or contradictions, it may at least be useful, to paraphrase Willie Lee Rose's goal for *A Documentary History of Slavery in North America,* in helping historians to think about ways hall furnishings or other categories of artifacts may profitably be introduced into their own studies.[16]

To understand hall furniture one needs to know something about the hall, for this space and its relationship to other spaces in the home had an influence on the objects placed within it. Domestic building in America is more notable for continuity than lack of it. A few basic ideas, altered occasionally by ideological, economic, or other factors, underlie the spatial organization of most homes. Thus it is possible to separate middle- and upper-middle-class homes of the nineteenth century into two types on the basis of the form of hall employed. The first chronologically was a relatively narrow passage leading from the outside of the house to its interior spaces. Up to about 1880 this was the dominant mode. It was based on late Renaissance ideas introduced to this country in the eighteenth century with the Georgian style. Although the fact is frequently obscured by an overlay of complicated ornament or a degree of asymmetry, Georgian concepts of spatial organization were perpetuated in Victorian houses; some nineteenth-century plans are nearly identical to eighteenth-century examples. A characteristic feature of these houses of the Georgian-Victorian continuum was the use of a hall as a passage.[17]

The other type of hall was a passage expanded into a large living space. It derived from medieval great halls and the multifunction rooms of pre-Georgian dwellings in colonial America. This type was associated with the reform movement, was widely published and illustrated in the last quarter of the century, and became a prominent feature of many architect-designed homes. These two hall alternatives can be related to two very different models for the domestic structure in the nineteenth century. The first is the home as palace; the second the home as hereditary estate or old homestead. The emphasis here is on the prereform model of the home as a palace and the hall as a passage.[18]

A typical upper-middle-class house plan illustrates the characteristic of this concept of hall (fig. 1). The space was usually six to eight feet wide and twelve to twenty feet long, or considerably longer if it ran all the way from the front of the house to the back, as it does here. Its chief architectural embellishments were the framed doorways to parlor, drawing room, library, or dining room and the stair and its ornamented newel post. No communal activity took place in the hall; its shape, dimensions, and placement emphasized its function as both a connector and separator of rooms. In most homes of this class, one did not enter directly from the outside into one of the formal rooms but into the hall instead. Although it was possible to move from some rooms to others without entering the hall, it was also possible to enter each room from the hall without passing through any other, thus preserving privacy and the specialized function of each space. By this arrangement social peers of the homeowner could visit in the formal spaces of the home, while social inferiors remained in the hall or were directed elsewhere and kept from intruding upon the family or its guests.[19]

The hall just described might be identified more accurately as a front hall. Many homes also had a back hall, which was sometimes an extension of the front hall, sometimes another smaller corridor adjacent to it. It was not necessarily a discrete space; in some cases its function was incorporated within another room, as it is in the kitchen here. To divide the front hall from the back and formal space from functional there was usually some real or symbolic barrier—a door, lower ceiling, narrower passage, or change in wall or floor materials or finish. There was also a rear stair, usually narrower and steeper than the front stair and free of architectural pretense. This creation of separate and unequal halls and stairs reflects the segregation of ceremonial and utilitarian functions within the home and the division of nineteenth-century society into the two nations described by Disraeli. This same inclination toward stratification is seen in the way the plans of upper-middle-class homes are conceptually divisible into two units. The first, larger than the other, is the formal or ceremonial portion of the house. Behind it, to fulfill the vulgar requirements that make the former possible, is the service section of kitchen, pantry, and laundry room. The significant difference in the way the two areas were conceived is reflected in their decorative treatment. The front section was architecture as Ruskin understood it; the rear was only building. Designs for facades appeared in architectural books in great numbers but backs were rarely shown, for the front belonged to ceremony and the rear to utility. The front stair was for dramatic descent to meet family and guests; the back stair for servants carrying slop buckets and dirty laundry. Today when household servants are unknown to most Americans living in the North, it is easy to forget the social realities of the nineteenth century. Victorian homes document a way of life which has largely disappeared.[20]

In these homes, the front hall was usually too small for much furniture. It sometimes contained a table, stand, or pedestal, and two chairs or a settee or both. In most cases it contained at least a hallstand. The hallstand is a nineteenth-century invention. Unlike most furniture of that age, it has no clearly discernible antecedents. The hallstand appeared around the time of Victoria's accession and its life cycle parallels the course of the Victorian way of life in America. After the middle of the century it grew more popular and became the focus of considerable design attention. The form reached its greatest prominence in the 1870s, then declined in scale and importance, undergoing significant alteration in the late nineteenth and early twentieth century and largely passing out of production by 1920.[21]

The appearance of the hallstand in the late 1870s can be seen in the examples illustrated here (fig. 2). One was manufactured in Grand Rapids, Michigan, noted for producing quality furniture for the middle- and upper-middle class markets.[22] The others were made in New York City at about the same time. Taken together, all four indicate that although there was considerable diversity in the details of design, a high degree of consistency prevailed in the overall concept of the object. Four functional components were generally repeated: (1) provisions for umbrellas; (2) hooks or pegs for hats and coats; (3) a looking glass; and (4) a small table, often with a drawer and a marble top. Each of these is conceptually separable from the others but the synthesis of the four (or sometimes only the first three) into an architecturally conceived whole is what constitutes a hallstand: the nineteenth-century innovation consists of combining these elements in precisely this manner.

The provisions for umbrellas normally follow the arrangement shown here. Crook-shaped or armlike devices were mounted on each side of the stand at a height of about twenty-five to thirty inches above the floor. These held the upper ends of the umbrellas. In the base of the hallstand were usually one or two dished receptacles. Their function was twofold: to terminate the implied cylinders in which the umbrellas were placed, and to catch and contain water that might drip from them. Cast iron pans were the most common material for these. Some less expensive hallstands had thin sheet metal boxes but expensive hallstands, particularly those built as part of the woodwork, had concave marble slabs. Regardless of material, all served the same utilitarian functions of protecting the floor and carpet and keeping the umbrellas accessible.

That such an impressive piece of furniture should be designed for umbrellas indicates something about the status of the latter which, from the vantage point of the twentieth century, might be called the insignia of the Victorian age. The umbrella has a long, eventful history which has been recorded by several artifact historians. It was well known in antiquity in both the Orient and the Occi-

Figure 1. Elevation and plan of a conventional Victorian house, similar to thousands built in the third quarter of the nineteenth century. (From John Riddell, Architectural Designs for Model Country Residences *[Philadelphia: John Riddell, J. B. Lippincott, 1864].)*

15'
WASH HOUSE
14 × 11' 6"
12'
C. D.
RANGE
KITCHEN
14' 10" × 14' 6"
20'
PORCH
DOOR
STORE ROOM
CLOSET
DINING ROOM
13' 7" × 18' 6"
PARLOR
13' 7" × 30' 2"
33'
HALL
7
LIBRARY
13' 7" × 11' 6"
38 FT
VERANDA
FIRST STORY
ROOF
NURSERY
14' 10" × 11' 5"
BATH ROOM
8' 2" × 6"
ROOF
PASSAGE
B. TUB.
CHAMBER
13' 7" × 13' 6"
CHAMBER
13' 7" × 13' 6"
PASSAGE
CHAMBER
13' 7" × 15'
D. ROOM
7' × 10' 6"
CHAMBER
13' 7" × 15
ROOF
SECOND STORY
SCALE 8 ft. to an Inch

Figure 2. Hallstands produced in the 1870s. (Photograph from Nelson, Matter, and Company sales catalog, ca. 1878, Grand Rapids Library. Lithographs from J. Wayland Kimball, Book of Designs, Furniture and Drapery *[Boston, 1876], plate 22, illustrating products of Conrad Eckhardt of New York City.)*

dent but its modern history stems from contacts between the East and West during the Renaissance. It came by sea to Portugal and by land to Italy, spreading from there to other areas. At the outset the umbrella was associated with high status; servants held them over their masters when they walked in public. By the eighteenth century the umbrella and a related form, the parasol, had become relatively common; they were depicted frequently in paintings and prints of that period and mentioned in written documents. The parasol served largely a cosmetic function by protecting female skin from the harsh rays of the sun; although its use spread through many levels of society, it remained the mark of a woman of leisure. The umbrella performed a

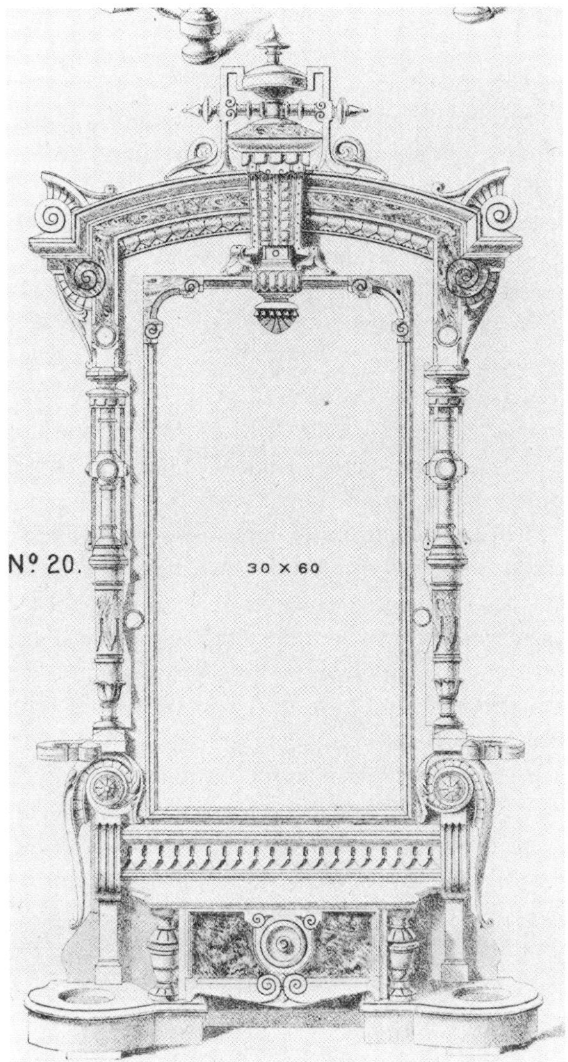

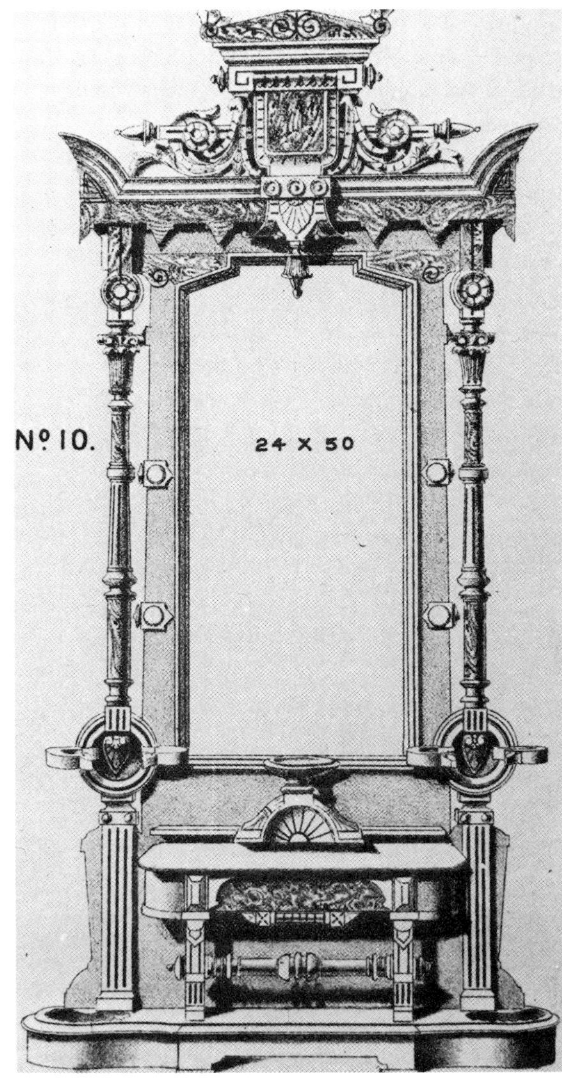

more utilitarian function and was carried by men only after the middle of the eighteenth century. Perhaps because the very wealthy owned carriages to protect them from the weather, carrying one's own umbrella came to be associated with lesser affluence and republican sentiments. In the nineteenth century it became a bourgeois attribute, a portable emblem of respectability, and its prominence reflects a culture dominated by middle-class values.[23]

The second set of functional components of the hallstand, the provisions for hats and coats, reiterates the nineteenth-century emphasis on attire and appearance. The peak of popularity for the hallstand coincides with that of the top hat, which in its most extreme form became the "stove-pipe" hat of Lincoln and his generation. Laver has argued that the top hat was what we would call *macho* today, an assertion of masculinity most extreme at the time of greatest role differentiation between the sexes. Its gradual decline he associated with that of male-dominated society.[24]

Hats and coats were usually hung on turned wooden pegs on less expensive hallstands and on small bronzed or gilt metal hooks on more costly pieces. These rarely projected more than six or eight inches from the surface of the hallstand and were generally only six or eight in number and were arranged symmetrically around the mirror. The relatively few attachments for hats, coats, cloaks, or other outer garments, make it clear that the hallstand was not intended as open storage. Only a limited number of objects could be placed on it; examination of old photographs may help in determining the rules governing the selection. Some homes had storage closets near the hall; some had closets behind the stair, easily accessible from the hall, yet they still had a hallstand in the front hall.[25] When large numbers of people came, to a party, for instance, coats were placed on the beds in the chambers, as they are today. Therefore, there were reasons other than storage for placing these garments on the hallstand. We will suggest what these reasons might be after discussing the two other functional components.

The third element, the mirror, emphasizes again the Victorian fixation with personal appearance but has other ramifications as well. Mirrors were a Victorian convention. They appeared where they still do in twentieth-century interiors, on walls in bedrooms and dressing rooms, on chests of drawers, dressing tables, and wardrobes, and adjacent to facilities for washing and shaving. They also appeared, however, on hallstands, *étagères,* cabinets, and sideboards, over mantels, and extending from floor to ceiling between pairs of windows in formal rooms. The functions of glass were not limited to the obvious utilitarian goal of reflecting an image. Behind the glass in parlors and halls of the 1870s lay the example of the *Galerie des Glaces* at Versailles of two centuries earlier. Plate glass was still expensive in the nineteenth century and its prominent display was a sign of wealth and, as Thorstein Veblen argued, high social standing. Glass was significant, too, for its ability to reflect forms and light and so expand and illuminate a space. Large glasses were normally on axis with lighting fixtures so that illumination was increased. The mirror also caused certain visual effects which people enjoyed. When a glass is viewed from an angle, it reflects segments of the interior which change as the viewer moves, a kinetic phenomenon exploited as a novelty a few years ago on the art scene but once commonplace in Victorian interiors.[26] The glass in the hallstand was also a mirror in the ordinary sense, a dressing glass in front of which to adjust clothing or hair, brush off dust, or otherwise prepare either to leave the house or to enter one of the formal rooms.

The last component of the hallstand, the table, was optional and not included in less expensive examples. It was a convenient resting place for packages, books, gloves, or other small objects. In some instances a decorative object was placed on it; in others it held a card receiver. The drawer was also a place for a variety of small objects, including brushes and whiskbrooms for cleaning garments. The presence of the table can further be explained as providing an occasion for the perpetuation of the "marble-mania" characteristic of the age. The use of marble tops on tables and case pieces is an instance of what Siegfried Giedion called the devaluation of symbols.[27] Marble tops, used in antiquity, were revived during the Renaissance for use on luxury pieces of furniture. By the nineteenth century what had been confined to the very wealthy became commonplace, as the vast number of surviving examples indicates. Although marble was heavier, more expensive, and more dangerous to fragile objects than wood, it was very popular. It is possible that the marble on hallstands might have helped stabilize the great weight of the mirror but there were other less expensive ways of achieving this end. It is more likely that this marble, like the clearly disfunctional pieces of sideboards, chests of drawers, dressing cases, washstands, cabinets, tables, and stands, was largely a matter of conspicuous consumption.

All four functional components were combined into a single object by people now as forgotten as any of America's minorities. Indeed, there is no need to turn to what is called folk art to find unsung artisans in the American past; they worked for American industry in the nineteenth century. Their charge was not to express themselves in an uninhibited personal manner but to create a saleable product much like others available at the same time. Surviving artifacts and illustrations in trade catalogs show how these unknown people produced scores of varied designs, yet adhered to shared notions about symmetry, placement of the functional components, projection into space, and consumption of wall area. Because of the limited space of the hall, the components were combined in a spatially efficient way. Hallstands rarely project far into the space of the hall, usually only twelve or fifteen inches. But if practical considerations inhibited the consumption of space, there were no such strictures on the use of area. Most hallstands, including those illustrated here, spread expansively along the wall to create a major focal point in the hall and indicate their own significance. In fact, the large size of the hallstand is the most obvious clue that it was intended to represent more than the mere total of its utilitarian functions. The Victorians must have felt that the purposes of the hallstand and the concepts and feelings associated with it were important to their lives, for they enshrined it in grandeur.

People do not make objects large if they wish to hide them and hallstands are usually large. The smallest, usually of cast iron rather than wood, are normally about the height of an adult. The wooden examples are more often between six and a half and eight feet tall and some of the most costly are ten feet. This great size was not inexpensive; the hallstand rarely appeared in lower-class homes. It served, then, as a tool for social differentiation, since its mere possession was a mark of some social standing. The willingness of people to pay significant sums for hallstands, and the obvious expenditure of energy on the design, construction, and finish of the objects, all reaffirm their significance.[28]

The placement of the functional and decorative features of the object is of consequence. The former are placed in a balanced and symmetrical arrangement, augmented and emphasized by the latter, which confer importance and elevate the status of the object. The recurring symmetry has already been mentioned and deserves a few words. Symmetry is such a common feature of man-made objects that it may seem inconsequential, yet one also can argue that it is this very persistence that gives it importance. As common as it is, symmetry has nevertheless not been adequately explained. One of the usual arguments is that man makes symmetrical objects because he is himself symmetrical. Others have argued that symmetry is restful and mentally satisfying, fulfilling the search of the mind for equilibrium. Symmetry is also a way creative man can demonstrate control of his tools and material. A form created once may be an accident; its exact duplication is not likely to be.[29]

The ornamentation of the hallstand suggests that the piece met more than utilitarian necessity. Much of the wooden frame and all the veneer panels, paterae, pilasters, and other applied and incised decoration are functionally superficial, the more so in the more expensive examples. The glass is usually larger than needed and the sections above it are in every case beyond physical need. This top part of the hallstand performs an honorific function in direct relationship to the cost of the object. The ornament of the upper section is also honorific in another less direct, more symbolic way. Most of these examples are capped by an architectural element—an arch, a pediment, a cartouche, or some combination of these devices. Each has a long tradition of playing a status-conferring role in architectural contexts and may have retained a residuum of this meaning in the nineteenth century. It is also worth observing that the architectural quality of these pieces of furniture, the more expensive examples especially, calls to mind the facades of temples, churches, and other monumental and meaning-laden architecture, again suggesting that there was more significance in these objects than their utilitarian functions would indicate.[30]

Figure 3. View of a hall furnished according to reform ideas of the 1870s. (From Clarence Cook, The House Beautiful *[New York: Scribner, Armstrong, 1878], p. 27.)*

A final argument for the importance to the Victorians of the hallstand and the activities associated with it is the critical matter of placement. The hallstand stood prominently in the front hall, immediately visible upon entering the house. If people believed that "the hall determines the first impression on entering the house," and that in some cases it might be advisable to economize elsewhere in order to create a good effect there, they must have depended heavily on the hallstand to help achieve the effect that they sought.[31] The hallstand was the major piece of furniture in the hall and one of the most important visual elements. Visitors could not avoid seeing it, nor could they avoid seeing the hats, coats, canes, or umbrellas on it. Today we use closets to keep garments out of sight because they violate our sense of propriety. A century ago, halls were furnished with immense, unavoidable wooden objects which loomed prominently in the semidarkness of the hall and were decked out with articles of personal costume. For some, the scale and stern design were awesome and intimidating; for others, there was a more approachable, human quality about the piece. To all, the hallstand conveyed something of the spirit or mood of the household and was useful as well. It helped with details of grooming. It communicated nonverbally about who was or was not at home by the objects on or missing from the hallstand. It ceremonialized the coming and going, the entry and exit of the members of the household and their guests. And it served as a setting, a theatrical backdrop for the ritual of card leaving, which also took place in the hall.

Cook, an Anglophile writer of the 1870s, called hallstands like those illustrated here "ugly things made of tiresome walnut."[32] Although he rejected its form, he did not reject the hallstand's function. An illustration from his book (fig. 3) shows the functions discussed previously performed by objects which are nearly devoid of the conspicuous consumption and symbolic meaning suggested above.[33] Yet the image and the caption—"She'll be down in a minute, sir"—are potent reminders of physical and social realities, including, once again, the harsh fact of a servant class. They also indicate how artifacts were deliberately used in the nineteenth century as props for the drama of life. The self-conscious quality evident here and the suggestions of an emotional response to artifacts based on the functions that they perform and the associations connected with them remind us that hallstands are a creation of the age of romanticism. The concept of romanticism is employed by historians of the arts and literature but often ignored by others. Like all such broad terms, it has to be used with caution but the attitudes and values conventionally associated with it help us understand the creation of the hallstand, for those elements of the object defined as beyond necessity—and in fact, the entire object itself—worked to appeal to the senses and the emotions. It may seem a superficial job of labeling to call the hallstand a product of the romantic age, but precisely because that term is usually limited to the so-called fine arts, it is important to recognize its relevance to another class of artifacts.

The other usual objects of furniture in the hall were for seating. The wealthy sometimes had leather upholstered settees and matching chairs. The typical middle-class hall seat looked much like those illustrated here, which were probably made in the 1870s (fig. 4). Certain features were characteristic. First, there was the unupholstered plank seat, which was otherwise unknown in the formal rooms of the middle-class home. The plank seat was normally hinged, as it is here, so that it could be raised to give access to a shallow compartment underneath for gloves, brushes, and other small items. Front legs were usually turned, stretchers were rare, and the backs were elaborate and expansive so that, like hallstands, they commanded and controlled considerable wall area. The design of the chairs indicates that they were not intended for prolonged sitting, at least not for members of the household or their social peers, for the qualities that they embodied were visual appeal and utility, not comfort. The plank seat was employed in lieu of upholstery because it would not be ruined by contact with wet or soiled outer garments, because it contributed to the stern, somewhat intimidating grandeur of the hall, and possibly because it was uncomfortable. Peers or superiors were shown into one of the formal rooms of the home. The people kept waiting in the hall were socially inferior to the residents of the house, like the "messenger-boys, book-agents, . . . census-man and . . . [the] bereaved lady who offers us soap" condescendingly listed by Cook, who went on to argue that "as visitors of this class are the only ones who will sit in

Figure 4. Walnut hall chairs, 1870–1880. (Top: Collection of William J. Wiesand, Sr.; bottom, Stowe-Day Foundation, Hartford, Conn.)

the hall, considerations of comfort may be allowed to yield to picturesqueness." When hall chairs were used by people of higher status, they served only as perching places for pulling on overshoes or some similar chore. This utilitarian purpose, however, seems to have been secondary to their potential for social and psychological manipulation.[34]

The last important part of this horizonal constellation of hall furnishings was a card receiver. Like the other objects discussed, the card receiver is also an obsolete form, intimately tied to a ritual of card leaving little practiced today. Its early history is obscure but it was much in vogue by the time of the Civil War. On the grandest scale, card receivers were elaborate cast metal stands, often made in France, which rested directly on the floor. More typical was a smaller model, ranging from a few inches to over a foot in height, which was placed on a table or stand. In all cases, the concept of the card receiver was of a dish or tray on a stand which stabilized it and gave it prominence.

From card receivers one turns logically to the cards themselves and the ritual of calling. Again, it is difficult to fix the point at which cards or the ceremony first became part of middle-class life in the last century. The phenomenon probably derives from royal examples of earlier times, for the dual purpose of preserving social status and distinctions and ritualizing interactions recalls courtly protocol for audiences or interviews. As with so many other adaptations of earlier conventions, certain alterations were made in the nineteenth century which we now think of as typical of that era.

The entire card system was well-codified by the middle of the last century and remained largely intact well into the twentieth. The card ritual fitted neatly into the patterns of conspicuous consumption outlined by Veblen, for the task of leaving cards fell to the woman of the household. If she were at all genteel, she was presumed to have the time to devote to this activity. The card ritual, then, was evidence of conspicuous leisure and an instance of nonproductive, if gracious, labor.[35]

It is always difficult to know how much credence to give to the normative arguments of etiquette books. In the case of the ritual of the cards, the existence of the props or tools—hallstand, card receivers, and cards—lends support to the testimony of those books. And since there is general agreement about most aspects of card leaving from the earliest books up to those of only a few years ago, we can assume that many who used cards did so in the same way.[36]

Most of the etiquette books stressed the importance of leaving cards. "Leaving cards is one of the most important of social observances, as it is the groundwork or nucleus in society of all acquaintanceship." Card leaving was a way of entering society, of designating changes in status or address, of issuing invitations and responding to them, of sending sentiments of happiness or condolence, and, in general, of carrying on all the communication associated with social life. Not to participate in this ritual, with its strict rules, was to risk being considered what was termed ill-bred, a euphemism for lower class.[37]

It was important that cards be left in person. Some books equivocated on this point and indicated that cards could be sent with a messenger or by post. Others took a hard line and maintained that it was a breach of etiquette to do anything but deliver them oneself. Certainly it was in violation of the concept of conspicuous leisure not to deliver them, for to mail them or send them with a servant suggested that one had household responsibilities or an activity one valued higher. Related to emphasis upon leisure was the requirement that cards be left between three and five o'clock in the afternoon. Since these were normal business hours, it is clear that men could not be expected to leave cards. They were at work to support these women of conspicuous leisure.

The card ritual was part of a larger ritual of calling. In this framework, we might speak of primary calling and secondary calling or perhaps human interaction and artifact interaction. When individuals were not present, their cards were their surrogates. Since husbands did not normally accompany their wives when they paid calls, the wife left her husband's card where she visited. If the lady of the house being visited was at home, the guest left two of her husbands's cards, one for the lady visited and the other for her husband. She did not leave her own card, for it would be redundant since she had already seen the lady of the house.

If a woman were paying calls and the woman she intended to visit was not home, she left three cards, one of her own and two of her husband's. The latter were to be distributed as before, but her card would be left for the mistress of the house; "a lady leaves a card for a lady only." This cult of protecting the virtue of matrons extended to that of maidens too, for in some circles it was not considered appropriate for a young lady to have visiting cards of her own. Her name was printed beneath that of her mother on the latter's card. The use of Miss on a card was reserved for older unmarried women.[38] With this situation, we come closer to the more formalistic aspects of a ritual which was in many ways a social perpetual motion machine which, once set going among equals, could not with propriety be stopped unless one party moved away. In the case of social unequals it could be halted when the superior ignored the inferior. When there was no intention to visit, a woman merely handed three cards to a servant, who presumably placed them in the card receiver, the contents of which were later sorted and evaluated. Whatever the intention of the individual—to pay a visit or only a surrogate visit by way of the card, a kind of social code of Hammurabi obtained—a card for a card, a call for a call, and the person visited or called on was obliged to reciprocate.

Rules were also spelled out about how and when people of different social status might interact. Calling or only leaving a card signified different degrees of intimacy. Among social equals, the law cited before was normally in operation. In cases of obvious social distinction, the situation was different. If a woman of higher social position returned a card with a call, it was considered a compliment. If the opposite took place, it was brash and presumptive.

The use of cards and servants as barriers was extensive in the last century. For example, a man wishing to make the acquaintance of a young woman could arrange to have his card left at her home by a female friend. If the young woman had no interest in meeting him, the solution was simple; his card was not noticed. Similarly, an intended visit could be reduced to the level of a call through the expedient of having the servant announce that one was "not at home."

Today much of this activity takes place in business rather than private life. Telephone calls are our cards and secretaries the servants who announce that the important person is at a meeting or cannot be reached. Yet even if some aspects of these rituals survive today, contemporary American society no longer cherishes the same values the Victorians did nor expresses itself in the same way. The Victorians believed in the ceremony of daily life as a way of attaining elegance and personal nobility. Their world emphasized social competition and the artifacts that they made were often designed as tools for that activity. Yet there was more behind hall furnishings of the nineteenth century than conspicuous consumption and invidious comparison, for the emphasis on personal possessions—hats, coats, umbrellas, and cards—suggests a sentimental or emotional attachment to objects of the kind commemorated in well-known songs and poems like "The Old Arm Chair," "The Old Oaken Bucket," and most of all, "Home, Sweet Home."[39]

If the people who owned the objects we have been discussing could vigorously defend social station and privilege, they could also be moved by associations and relationships with their friends and relatives.[40] The objects that they placed in their halls reflected not only these competing facets of the Victorian personality but the very nature of the hall itself. For it was a space which was neither wholly interior nor exterior but a sheltered testing zone which some passed through with ease and others never went beyond.

Notes

This article was originally published in the *Journal of Interdisciplinary History* (Summer 1978).

1. Among America's best-known artifacts, Independence Hall is widely illustrated, especially in studies of colonial architecture and history; the Brooklyn Bridge and the Statue of Liberty are the subjects of recent monographs: Alan Trachtenberg, *Brooklyn Bridge, Fact and Symbol* (New York: Oxford University Press, 1965); Marvin Trachtenberg, *The Statue of Liberty* (New York: Viking Press, 1976). For a defense of monuments, see Theo Crosby, *The Necessary Monument: Its Future in the Civilized City* (Greenwich, Conn.: New York Graphic Society, 1970).
2. For succinct comments on elitism in history and the need to use artifacts, see Henry Glassie, *Folk Housing in Middle Virginia: A Structural Analysis of Historic Artifacts* (Knoxville: University of Tennessee Press, 1975), pp. 8–12. Comments on the impact of sociology appear in Dwight Macdonald, *Against the American Grain* (New York: Random House, 1962).
3. Most art historians still seem constrained to work only with those artifacts defined as art. Their unwillingness to go beyond this artificial barrier makes it unlikely that art history, among the earliest disciplines to develop and refine tools for the study of material culture, will make further significant contribution(s) to artifact study. For appraisals of art history practices and paradigms, see James S. Ackerman and Rhys Carpenter, *Art and Archaeology* (Englewood Cliffs, N.J.: Prentice-Hall, 1963), pp. 196–229; W. Eugene Kleinbauer, *Modern Perspectives in Western Art History* (New York: Holt, Rinehart and Winston, 1971), pp. 1–105; Michael Owen Jones, *The Hand Made Object and Its Maker* (Berkeley and Los Angeles: University of California Press, 1975), esp. chs. 1 and 7. For observations on the usefulness of art to historians, see Theodore K. Rabb, "The Historian and the Art Historian," *Journal of Interdisciplinary History* 4, no. 1 (Summer 1973): 107–17. On folk material culture, see Kenneth L. Ames, *Beyond Necessity: Art in the Folk Tradition* (Winterthur, Del.: Winterthur Museum, 1977); Glassie, *Folk Housing;* Henry Glassie, *Pattern in the Material Folk Culture of the Eastern United States* (Philadelphia: University of Pennsylvania Press, 1969); Jones, *Hand Made Object;* Robert F. Trent, *Hearts and Crowns: Folk Chairs of the Connecticut Coast, 1720–1840* (New Haven: New Haven Colony Historical Society, 1977). Works suggesting avenues to understanding artifacts from social or psychological perspectives include Edward T. Hall, *The Hidden Dimension* (Garden City, N.Y.: Anchor Books, 1973); Albert F. Scheflen, *How Behavior Means* (New York: Jacob Aronson, 1974); Robert Sommer, *Personal Space: The Behavioral Basis of Design* (Englewood Cliffs, N.J.: Prentice-Hall, 1969). Cognition and communication are discussed in Howard Gardner, *The Arts and Human Development* (New York: Wiley, 1973), esp. p. 37; D. E. Berlyne, *Aesthetics and Psychobiology* (New York: Appleton-Century-Crofts, 1971); David Perkins and Barbara Leondar, eds., *The Arts and Cognition* (Baltimore: Johns Hopkins University Press, 1977).
4. George Kubler, *The Shape of Time: Remarks on the History of Things* (New Haven: Yale University Press, 1962). In archaeological use tradition refers to phenomena of relatively long temporal duration but narrow geographic range. Horizon is the opposite: broad geographic range but limited temporary duration. See Gordon R. Willey and Philip Phillips, *Method and Theory in American Archaeology* (Chicago: University of Chicago Press, 1958), pp. 11–43.
5. By plotting the life span of objects like hall furnishings and many others as well, and then looking for correlations in functions, design elements, materials and other measurable phenomena, we may be able to see (literally, perhaps) the extent of Victorianism. One way to extract elements that might be quantified and seriated is through structuralism. For some general comments on its application to objects, see James Deetz, *Invitation to Archaeology* (Garden City, N.Y.: Natural History Press, 1967), pp. 83–101. For an example, see Glassie, *Folk Housing,* pp. 19–113.
6. The Victorian fascination with the material world can be noted first and most impressively in the rich physical remains of that era. This fascination was institutionalized with the world's fairs held from 1851 onward. Some of the period's most perceptive authors, among them Marx, Veblen, and Twain, wrote in response to contemporary enthusiasm for what Mumford called "the goods life" (Lewis Mumford, *Technics and Civilization* [New York: Harcourt, Brace and World, 1934], p. 105).
7. The generalizations about Victorian culture are from Daniel Walker Howe, "American Victorianism as a Culture," *American Quarterly* 27, no. 5 (December 1975): 507–32. For the geographical aspect, see David Ward, *Cities and Immigrants: A Geography of Change in Nineteenth-Century America* (New York: Oxford University Press, 1971), pp. 11–49.
8. Quantitative studies of earlier periods include Barbara and Cary Carson, "Styles and Standards of Living

in Southern Maryland, 1670–1752," a paper delivered to the Southern Historical Association, Atlanta, Ga., November, 1976; Susan Prendergast Schoelwer, "Form, Function, and Meaning in the Use of Fabric Furnishings: A Philadelphia Case Study," *Winterthur Portfolio* 14, no. 1 (Spring 1979): 25–40.

9. Horatio Alger, *The Store Boy or the Fortunes of Ben Barclay,* in *Strive and Succeed* (New York: Holt, Rinehart and Winston, 1967), pp. 114, 155; John Hay, *The Bread-Winners; A Social Study* (New York: Harper and Brothers, 1884).
10. Nor do artifacts normally provide a useful approach to literature. The two realms are distinct and often very different aspects of human creativity. Older attempts at synthesis include two books by Wylie Sypher, *Four Stages of Renaissance Style: Transformations in Art and Literature* (Garden City, N.Y.: Doubleday, 1955), and *Rococo to Cubism in Art and Literature* (New York: Random House, 1960). A more recent attempt to find correspondences in the arts is David Burrows, "Style in Culture: Vivaldi, Zeon, and Ricci," *Journal of Interdisciplinary History* 4, no. 1 (Summer 1973): 1–24. A somewhat different approach is used by Gaston Bachelard, *The Poetics of Space* (New York: Orion Press, 1964).
11. Andrew Jackson Downing, *The Architecture of Country Houses* (1850; reprint, New York: Dover Publications 1969), pp. 441–42, 459–60; Samuel Sloan, *Sloan's Domestic Architecture* (Philadelphia: J. B. Lippincott, 1867), p. 328.
12. In art historical parlance, this phenomenon is usually referred to as the Arts and Crafts movement and seen as the beginning of modern design. See Nikolaus Pevsner, *Pioneers of Modern Design: From William Morris to Walter Gropius* (Harmondsworth: Penguin Books, 1966), pp. 19–67; Gillian Naylor, *The Arts and Crafts Movement: A Study of Its Sources, Ideals and Influence on Design Theory* (Cambridge: MIT Press, 1971). Succinct analyses of the social aspects of the movement appear in Robert W. Winter, "The Arts and Crafts Movement as a Social Movement," and Carl E. Schorske, "Observations on Style and Society in the Arts and Crafts Movement," in *Aspects of the Arts and Crafts Movement in America,* ed. Robert Judson Clark, *Record of the Art Museum, Princeton University* 34, no. 2 (1975): 36–40, 41–42.
13. Todd S. Goodholme, ed., *A Domestic Cyclopaedia of Practical Information* (New York: Henry Holt, 1877), pp. 222–36; Clarence Cook, *The House Beautiful* (New York: Scribner, Armstrong, 1878); Robert Judson Clark, ed., *The Arts and Crafts Movement in America, 1876–1916* (Princeton: Princeton University Press, 1972), pp. 9, 94; Mary Jean Smith Madigan, "The Influence of Charles Locke Eastlake on American Furniture Manufacture, 1870–1890," *Winterthur Portfolio 10,* ed. Ian M. G. Quimby (Charlottesville: University Press of Virginia, 1975), pp. 1–22. The difficulty of sorting ideology from reality is constantly faced by historians who deal with verbal, especially literary, sources. Compare, for example, the interpretation of the nineteenth-century home in Kirk Jeffrey, "The Family as Utopian Retreat from the City," *Soundings* 55, no. 1 (Spring 1972): 21–41, with that in Thorstein Veblen, *The Theory of the Leisure Class* (New York: Macmillan, 1912).

    The question of cultural heterogeneity or homogeneity is related to the ideology of the melting pot, debunked in recent years. See Nathan Glazer and Daniel Patrick Moynihan, *Beyond the Melting Pot: The Negroes, Puerto Ricans, Jews, Italians and Irish of New York City* (Cambridge: MIT Press and Harvard University Press, 1963), pp. 1–23, 288–315; Charles Keil, *Urban Blues* (Chicago: University of Chicago Press, 1966).
14. Important collections of photographs of nineteenth-century interiors have been assembled in William Seale, *The Tasteful Interlude,* 2d ed., rev. and enl. (Nashville: American Association for State and Local History, 1981); George Talbot, *At Home: Domestic Life in the Post-Centennial Era, 1876–1920* (Madison: State Historical Society of Wisconsin, 1977). Halls of the wealthy, usually bearing the impress of English reform taste, appear frequently in *Artistic Houses: Being a Series of Interior Views of a Number of the Most Beautiful and Celebrated Houses in the United States* (New York: D. Appleton, 1883–84). The photograph has recently come into its own as a collectible artifact, as art, and as a tool for historians. Two recent controversial but compelling historical studies emphasizing photographs are by Michael Lesy: *Wisconsin Death Trip* (New York: Pantheon Books, 1973); *Real Life: Louisville in the Twenties* (New York: Pantheon Books, 1976).
15. Extensive collections of nineteenth-century trade catalogs of household furnishings can be found at the following institutions: Chicago Historical Society; Eleutherian Mills Historical Library, Greenville, Del.; Henry Ford Museum, Dearborn, Mich.; Metropolitan Museum of Art; National Museum of American History; Margaret Woodbury Strong Museum, Rochester, N.Y.; Winterthur Museum, Winterthur, Del. Most state libraries and larger historical societies also have holdings in this area. Although out of date, the best introduction to trade catalog holdings in America is Lawrence B. Romaine, *A Guide to*

American Trade Catalogs, 1744–1900 (New York: R. R. Bowker, 1969).

16. For comments on subjective history and scientific measurement, see Glassie, *Folk Housing,* pp. 41–42; Peter L. Berger, *Invitation to Sociology* (Garden City, N.Y.: Natural History Press, 1963), p. 141; John Demos, *A Little Commonwealth: Family Life in Plymouth Colony* (New York: Oxford University Press, 1970), pp. 20–23; Willie Lee Rose, ed., *A Documentary History of Slavery in North America* (New York: Oxford University Press, 1976), p. 3.
17. On eighteenth-century house plans, see George B. Tatum, *Philadelphia Georgian: The City House of Samuel Powel and Some of Its Eighteenth-Century Neighbors* (Middletown, Conn.: Wesleyan University Press, 1976), pp. 55–61.
18. Vincent J. Scully, Jr., *The Shingle Style and the Stick Style* (New Haven: Yale University Press, 1971), pp. 3–7. Hundreds of house plans can be found in the many nineteenth-century architectural manuals aimed at the lay public. For an extensive listing of these, see Henry-Russell Hitchcock, *American Architectural Books: A List of Books, Portfolios, and Pamphlets on Architecture and Related Subjects Published in America before 1895,* new expanded ed. (New York: Da Capo Press, 1976). A brief bibliography of twentieth-century titles on domestic architecture is in Clifford E. Clark, Jr., "Domestic Architecture as an Index to Social History: The Romantic Revival and the Cult of Domesticity in America, 1840–1870," *Journal of Interdisciplinary History* 7, no. 1 (Summer 1976): 34. Clark's article might be read in conjunction with this one, for it presents the ideology behind the architecture, its style and its form. A more cynical view might be that the elaborate religious and moral arguments Clark records disguised middle-class emulation of the upper class, as compellingly described by Veblen in *The Theory of the Leisure Class.* One might add to Clark's comments on specialization of household spaces that such division was already typical of the homes of the wealthy in the eighteenth century, where the services were often located in outbuildings symmetrically deployed around the main block of the house.
19. In some more costly homes the hall was preceded by a vestibule that can be considered as an insulating area. The vestibule also heightened the sense of drama of moving into the house by adding another stage to the process.
20. A discussion of front and back zones is skillfully developed in Erving Goffman, *The Presentation of Self in Everyday Life* (Garden City, N.Y.: Anchor Books, 1959). Benjamin Disraeli, *Sybil; or, The Two Nations* (London: Henry Colburn, 1850). Evidence of stratification in types of domestic structures is found in Downing, *Architecture of Country Houses,* p. 257, where he argues that a cottage is appropriate for a family with no more than two servants, but three or more servants entitles one to a villa. Much of Downing's approach can be traced to John Claudius Loudon, *Encyclopaedia of Cottage, Farm, and Villa Architecture and Furniture* (London: Longman, Rees, Orme, Brown, Green and Longman, 1833). Comments on Downing's debt to Loudon appear in J. Stewart Johnson's introduction to the Dover edition of *Architecture of Country Houses,* pp. ix–x. John Ruskin, *The Seven Lamps of Architecture* (New York: John Wiley, 1854), pp. 7–8.
21. Comments about hallstands appear in Christopher Gilbert, *Loudon Furniture Designs* (East Ardsley: S. R. Publishers, 1970), pp. 56–57; Thomas Webster, *An Encyclopaedia of Domestic Economy* (New York: Harper and Brothers, 1845), pp. 287–88; Rudolph Ackermann, ed., *The Repository of Arts, Literature, Commerce, Manufacture, Fashions, and Politics* (London: R. Ackermann, 1822); Charles F. Montgomery, *American Furniture: The Federal Period* (New York: Viking Press, 1966), p. 435; Henry Havard, *Dictionnaire de l'ameublement et de la décoration,* 4 vols. (Paris: Maison Quantin, 1887–90), 4:515–18. Despite its prominence and extensive production, the hallstand has not held much appeal for enthusiasts of elegant furniture: "As a piece of furniture it was seldom designed; it merely occurred" (John Gloag, *A Short Dictionary of Furniture* [New York: Holt, Rinehart and Winston, 1965], p. 282). On the 1870s as the visual high point of Victorian style, see the provocative concept of picturesque electicism in Carroll L. V. Meeks, *The Railroad Station* (New Haven: Yale University Press, 1964), pp. 1–25.
22. For more on Grand Rapids furniture in the 1870s, see Kenneth L. Ames, "Grand Rapids Furniture at the Time of the Centennial," *Winterthur Portfolio 10,* ed. Ian M. G. Quimby (Charlottesville: University Press of Virginia, 1975), pp. 23–50.
23. On umbrellas, see Louis Octave Uzanne, *Les ornements de la femme* (Paris: Librairies-imprimeries réunies, 1892); A. Varron, "The Umbrella," *Ciba Review* 42 (February 1942): 1510–48; T. S. Crawford, *A History of the Umbrella* (Newton Abbot: David and Charles, 1970). Canes were also placed on hallstands. For a classic analysis of this object in nineteenth-century society, see Veblen, *The Theory of*

the Leisure Class, p. 265. There is a notable distinction between the connotations of the umbrella and the cane or walking stick. In nineteenth-century imagery the umbrella was often associated with the country parson, the cane with the dandy or rake.

24. James Laver, *Modesty in Dress: An Inquiry into the Fundamentals of Fashion* (Boston: Houghton Mifflin, 1969), pp. 121–23.
25. Closets were known in eighteenth-century halls, often also under the stair.
26. *Glass: History, Manufacture and its Universal Application* (Pittsburgh: Pittsburgh Plate Glass Co., 1923), p. 31; Sloan, *Sloan's Homestead Architecture,* p. 321; Veblen, *The Theory of the Leisure Class,* pp. 33–40. The use of similar visual effects is found most notably in the work of Michelangelo Pistoletto. See Edward Lucie-Smith, *Late Modern: The Visual Arts since 1945* (New York: Frederick A. Praeger, 1969), p. 132; Aldo Pellegrini, *New Tendencies in Art,* trans. Robin Carson (New York: Crown Publishers, 1966), pp. 244, 247.
27. Siegfried Giedion, *Mechanization Takes Command: A Contribution to Anonymous History* (New York: Oxford University Press, 1948), pp. 329–32.
28. It was possible to purchase the various components of the hallstand individually and in this case the units themselves were small; cast iron umbrella stands and wooden hat and coat racks with mirrors designed to be hung on the wall are the most common. These were less expensive than the combination of models discussed here.
29. Ray Faulkner and Edwin Ziegfield, *Art Today: An Introduction to the Visual Arts* (New York: Holt, Rinehart and Winston, 1969), pp. 373–75; Glassie, *Folk Housing,* pp. 170–75; Henry Glassie, "Folk Art," in *Folklore and Folklife: An Introduction,* ed. Richard M. Dorson (Chicago: University of Chicago Press, 1972), pp. 272–79.
30. An important aspect of meaning in artifacts is style. The social function of style has yet to be suitably analyzed; see Hanna Deinhard, "Reflections on Art History and Sociology of Art," *Art Journal* 35, no. 1 (Fall 1975): 30. A summary of some of the theories about the style of the later nineteenth century is in James D. Kornwolf, "High Victorian Gothic; or, The Dilemma of Style in Modern Architecture," *Journal of the Society of Architectural Historians* 34, no. 1 (March 1975): 37–47. Most of the hallstands illustrated here are examples of what was known as the *néo-grec* style in the 1870s. For comments on this style, see Kenneth L. Ames, "What is the *néo-grec*?" *Nineteenth Century* 2, no. 2 (Summer 1976): 12–21; Kenneth L. Ames, "Sitting in (*Néo-Grec*) Style," *Nineteenth Century* 2, nos. 3–4 (Autumn 1976): 50–58. For hallstands in the Gothic style, see Katherine S. Howe and David B. Warren, *The Gothic Revival Style in America, 1830–1870* (Houston: Museum of Fine Arts, 1976), pp. 59–60. Studies of the meaning of these architectural elements and related forms include Karl Lehmann, "The Dome of Heaven," in *Modern Perspectives,* ed. Kleinbauer, pp. 227–70; Earl Baldwin Smith, *The Dome: A Study in the History of Ideas* (Princeton: Princeton University Press, 1970); John Summerson, *Heavenly Mansions* (New York: W. W. Norton, 1963), pp. 1–28.
31. Goodholme, *Domestic Cyclopaedia,* p. 223.
32. Cook, *House Beautiful,* p. 31. Goodholme agrees: "Probably the worst possible step is to buy the stereotyped hat and umbrella rack. No matter how elaborate, they are always the same thing over again, and generally very ugly" (*Domestic Cyclopaedia,* p. 223).
33. If the ideology surrounding domestic architecture around the middle of the century deserves to be called a reform movement (Clark, "Domestic Architecture," pp. 33–34), it needs to be reconciled with the reform movement of the 1870s. Perhaps the best way to see these two manifestations is as stages of the same movement. Despite Clark's claims, I see little evidence that the midcentury ideology had a marked effect on material culture. I would agree that the publications of the earlier period helped to set the stage for the reform movement, which left a much stronger imprint on the artifactual world. Both stages are part of the transition from palace to old homestead.
34. Plank seat chairs were inexpensive but durable forms of seating, normally used by the poor or in utilitarian contexts where upholstery was not appropriate. Unlike hallstands, hall chairs can be traced to the early eighteenth century in England and have Continental cognates and antecedents. They were especially useful in the great Palladian houses of the eighteenth century and occasionally were adorned with the family crest. The history of this form may suggest that it was another attribute of the wealthy democratized, but to an undemocratic purpose. The quotation is from Cook, *House Beautiful,* p. 33.
35. Veblen, *The Theory of the Leisure Class,* pp. 41–60; Abba Goold Woolson, *Woman in American Society* (Boston: Roberts Brothers, 1873), passim.
36. The rules for card etiquette can be found in the following volumes, among others: Mrs. E. B. Duffey, *The Ladies' and Gentlemen's Etiquette* (Philadelphia: Porter and Coates, 1877), pp. 50–62, 174–77; John A. Ruth, comp., *A Practical Treatise on the Etiquette and Dress of the Best American Society* (Chicago: C. L.

Snyder, 1878), pp. 70–90; George D. Carroll, *Diamonds from Brilliant Minds* (New York: Dempsey and Carroll, 1881), books 5 and 6. For a survey of these books, see Arthur M. Schlesinger, *Learning How to Behave* (New York: Macmillan, 1947).

37. Carroll, *Diamonds from Brilliant Minds,* 5:3. On the social uses of etiquette, see Berger, *Invitation to Sociology,* p. 140.
38. Carroll, *Diamonds from Brilliant Minds,* 5:7. There is some disagreement in these works about the appropriate use of "Miss."
39. The card ritual may still be practiced in some circles. Sophia C. Hadida begins her sections on cards by noting, "When you call at a private home and the door is opened by a maid, ask for the person whom you wish to see. If the home is conducted with style, the maid extends her card tray. . . ." She went on to note that "in simple homes where there is no attempt at formality, the maid may have no card receiver." It is not likely that many of the millions referred to in Hadida's title lived in homes with maids in 1959. (*Manners for Millions* [1932; reprint, New York: Barnes and Noble, 1959], pp. 85–87.) See also Howe, "American Victorianism as a Culture," p. 522.
40. On what is called segregated consciousness, see Berger, *Invitation to Sociology,* p. 108.

Embellishing a Life of Labor: An Interpretation of the Material Culture of American Working-Class Homes, 1885–1915

LIZABETH A. COHEN

Lizabeth A. Cohen's essay shows us what happened when the middle-class domestic practices that Kenneth Ames discusses were put forth as universal ideals. Cohen begins by examining the prescriptive literature that Ames also uses to discover what the middle classes themselves believed in the closing years of the nineteenth century and the opening years of the twentieth. She ties domestic ideals not only to professed social aims but to broader conflicts that were perhaps less consciously, though no less forcefully, embodied in domestic theories. Then she describes the middle-class campaign to carry their domestic ideals and attendant social values directly into the lives of manual workers.

Both to middle-class reformers and to their working-class clients, the house and its furnishings were icons of cherished ways of life, and tools for change. Cohen depicts a complex material environment in which the artifacts of commercial American consumerism were used by workers and especially by immigrants to construct "a creative compromise . . . between two very different social and economic worlds." They were interested in the material goods that American capitalism offered, but they wished to use them to create in their homes environments evocative of comfort and success as defined by their own experience and by values often forged in Europe.

Cohen's method might be described as a kind of visual archaeology, in which photographs are used to resurrect real physical environments that once existed, but no longer do. As such it bridges the gap between Cummings's probate inventories and Ames's normative literature. Cohen's article enables us to understand something of the living spaces of people whose homes are otherwise unrecoverable, and it reflects as well on the notions of placemaking and symbolic process.

The material life of American urban workers from 1885 to 1915, as revealed in patterns of home furnishings and organizations of domestic space, provides a new way of understanding the historical development of working-class culture. While in recent years historians have pursued the often elusive lives of working people, they have almost totally ignored domestic settings, and the material culture within them, as sources. Instead, historical investigation has focused on the workplace and local community. Only a few sociologists have examined home environments for evidence of the values and social identities of workers.[1]

Historians have examined working-class homes primarily in the context of the Progressive Era housing reform movement. The keen interest that these early twentieth-century social reformers displayed in workers' home environment, however, should alert us to the significance of the home, the most private and independent world of the worker, in expressing the working-class family's social identity and interaction with middle-class culture.

Studies of the material culture of the working-class home have much to contribute to our understanding of workers' experience beyond the outlines sketched by social historians who have quantified occupations and family events such as births, marriages and deaths. Although workers were often constrained in their household activities and consumption by low incomes and scarcity in housing options, they still made revealing choices in the process of ordering their personal environments.

This essay explores developments in the consumption preferences of urban working-class families from 1885 to 1915 and interprets how these choices reflected and affected worker social identity. My investigation of working-class homes places them in the context of the material standards of the larger society in which the workers lived. Only a comparison between working-class and middle-class homes can elucidate the degree to which working-class material culture was distinctive or part of a larger cultural system.

During the period 1885–1915 new people joined the ranks of the American working class as industry expanded.[2] Foreign-born and native American workers commonly shared the experience of having recently left rural, small town settings for the urban industrial workplace. This study examines the homes both immigrant and native American workers made within the city environment.

I will first trace the development of interior styles among the middle class during this period, probing particularly how aesthetic trends reflected middle-class social attitudes. While the middle class was by no means a clear-cut group with uniform tastes, still its trend setters and reflectors, such as popular magazines and home decoration advice books, articulated a consistent set of standards. Second, I will examine efforts by reformers and institutions to influence the tastes of workers toward these middle-class norms. Finally, I will analyze working-class homes in the light of workers' experiences and values and in relation to middle-class society.

Herbert Gutman urged at the close of his seminal essay on the integration of pre-industrial peoples into nineteenth-century and early twentieth-century America that "much remains to be learned about the transition of native and foreign-born American men and women to industrial society, and how that transition affected such persons and the society in which they entered."[3] The study of the material life of American working people as expressed in consumption patterns and the arrangement of domestic interiors may offer some new insights toward that goal. Workers who left no private written records may speak to us through the artifacts of their homes.

The Changing Look of the Middle-Class Home

American homes from the 1840s through the 1880s mirrored the nation's transformation from an agricultural to an industrial society. Just as industrialization affected people and places in the country in different ways and at various rates, so too homes reflected an individual's or family's degree of integration into the industrial economy. Location, occupation and financial status all affected the quantity and quality of consumption. The middle classes, with a status and income often attributable to an expanded economy and the mechanized means of production, were the most enthusiastic purchasers of mass-produced objects for their homes.[4] Meanwhile, technologically advanced products were less abundant in the houses of those who lived more self-sufficient economic lives.

The home served as an accurate indicator of one's relationship to the industrial economy not by accident but as a result of the Victorians' contradictory attitude toward economic and technological change. Enthusiasm for, as well as anxiety toward, industrialization provoked both an appetite for new products and a need to incorporate them carefully into private life. At the same time that new kinds of objects transformed the home, the Victorians loudly proclaimed the sanctity of the family refuge in a menacing, changing world. As John Ruskin wrote: "This is the true nature of home—it is the place of peace; the shelter, not only from injury, but from all terror, doubt and division. In so far as it is not this, it is not home; so far as the anxieties of the outer life penetrate into it, and the inconsistently-minded, unloved, or hostile society of the outer world is allowed by either husband or wife to cross the threshold, it ceases to be a home."[5] The home embodied a contradiction as both the arena for and refuge from technological penetration. Insofar as people could tolerate this contradictory domestic environment, the home provided a setting for gradual adaptation to a technological and commercial world.

The parlor best represented this accommodation to industrial life. As the room reserved for greeting and entertaining those beyond the family circle, the parlor permitted controlled interaction with the outside world. Similarly, a typical parlor overflowed with store-bought mass-produced objects, carefully arranged by family members: wall-to-wall carpeting enclosed by papered and bordered walls and ceilings; upholstered furniture topped with antimacassars; shawl-draped center tables displaying carefully arranged souvenir albums and alabaster sculptures; shelves and small stands overloaded with bric-a-brac and purchased mementos. Technology made much of this decor possible: carpeting, wallpaper, and textiles were ever cheaper and more elaborate, and the invention of the spiral spring encouraged the mass distribution of upholstered furniture. Artificial covering of surfaces and structural frames thus replaced the painted walls and floors and the hard wood furniture of an earlier era.[6]

After about 1885, popular magazines, home decoration manuals and architectural journals revealed a gradual but dramatic rejection of the cluttered spaces of the Victorian home in favor of two stylistic trends unified around a common concern for traditional American symbols. The Colonial Revival and the Arts and Crafts Movement both sought an American esthetic to replace European-inspired and technologically sophisticated styles. In the early twentieth century, an up-to-date middle-class family almost anywhere in America most likely lived in a Colonial Revival house, perhaps along newly extended trolley lines, or in a craftsman-style bungalow, often in a recently developed housing tract.[7]

The Colonial Revival had its debut at the Philadelphia Centennial Exposition in 1876 amid the salute to American technological progress; the style reached full maturity in the 1920s with the opening of the American Wing of the Metropolitan Museum of Art in New York and the restoration of Williamsburg.[8] Middle-class Americans encountered the Colonial Revival style more intimately, however, not at these public sites, but within their own homes and neighborhoods. Just as house construction had dominated colonial American building, the domestic setting most engaged the attention of the revival style. While for some people Colonial Revival meant "accurately" recreating early American interiors replete with spinning wheels and antique furniture, for most middle-class Americans, adoption entailed purchasing new, usually mass-produced items in the colonial style, such as a house or parlor set.

The Arts and Crafts Movement, also referred to at the time as the "craftsman" or "mission" style, evolved concurrently with the Colonial Revival. Exteriors and interiors boasted natural materials such as wood, shingle and greenery, exposed structural elements and surfaces, and open, flexible spaces. Elbert Hubbard's Roycroft Industries, Henry L. Wilson's Bungalow House Plan business, and similar firms popularized on a mass level the unique work of such artists as furniture-maker Gustav Stickley and architects Greene and Greene.

This craftsman style, justified in contradictory terms, responded to varied concerns of the era. On the one hand, the style depended on technological innovations in heating, lighting and windowglass and was merchandised as a solution to the household problems of dust, germs and inefficiency.[9] On the other hand, the Arts and Crafts Movement invoked and sought to replicate such traditional American symbols as the farm house and its furnishings. In the Hingham, Massachusetts, Arts and Crafts Society, as elsewhere in the country, "bits of old needlework and embroidery were brought down from dusty attics for admiration and imitation. Chairs and tables, of exquisite design and honest purpose, took the place of flimsy and overdecorated furniture."[10]

Middle-class people's attraction to the Colonial Revival and Arts and Crafts Movement corresponded to prevailing social attitudes, particularly toward workers and immigrants. Nativism, anti-industrialism, and a propensity toward environmental solutions for social problems were values incorporated into the new esthetic. Patriotic organizations such as the Daughters of the American Revolution and the National Society of Colonial Dames, both formed in the early 1890s, frequently encouraged the preservation of colonial artifacts and buildings.[11] Architects and client congregations found in the Colonial Revival an appropriate architecture for Protestant churches to replace the Catholic-associated Gothic style.[12] Founders of the Society for the Preservation of New England Antiquities blamed immigrant residents for the destruction of historical areas like Boston's North End.[13] Outspoken xenophobes like Henry Ford, Abbott Lawrence Lowell, and Henry Cabot Lodge were important patrons of the preservation and Colonial Revival movements.[14]

The Arts and Crafts style satisfied the anti-industrial instincts of many middle-class Americans. Montgomery Schuyler, organizer of an arts and crafts production studio outside Philadelphia, argued that this new style was not only wholesome, but it revived the accomplishment of the colonial craftsman, "an educated and thinking being" who loved his work without demanding a wage or labor union membership.[15] Instruction manuals for making mission furniture at home encouraged the demechanization of furniture-making. Earlier, middle-class Victorians had handled ambivalence toward industrialism by monitoring, while increasing, their interaction with industrial products within the home. Now, the next generation was employing technological advances to restrain and deny the extent to which industrialism affected private life.

Supporters of the craftsman and Colonial Revival styles had confidence in the moral effect of this new physical environment. Stickley's *Craftsman* magazine declared in a 1903 issue: "Luxurious surroundings . . . suggest and induce idleness. Complex forms and costly materials have an influence upon life which tells a sad story in history. On the other hand, chasteness and restraint in form, simple, but artistic materials are equally expressive of the character of the people who use them."[16] The new domestic ideal represented a search for a truly American environment, in Stickley's words, "American homes exclusively for American needs."[17]

Spreading the Middle-Class Message

Progressive Era reformers seized upon this new American domestic esthetic, contributing to its popularity and using it to assist in their campaigns to "uplift," "modernize," and "Americanize." Though social reform efforts in this period were broad in scope, a surprising range of reformers made use of the new styles as they sought to transform people's home environments in order to promote social improvement and cultural homogeneity. Often behind their pleas for cleaner, simpler, more sanitary homes for working people lay a desire to encourage more middle-class American environments. In a twist that would have shocked any colonial farmer, the "early American look" became linked with a dust-, germ-, and disease-free scientific ideal. Reformers and associated organizations made efforts to influence workers in their homes, their neighborhoods, and their workplaces through promulgating domestic models; elsewhere, workers encountered these new middle-class style standards more indirectly.

Both public institutions and privately-funded organizations conveyed the new aesthetic to working-class girls within model classrooms created for housekeeping instruction. By the 1890s, particularly in urban areas, domestic science classes in public schools promoted ideal domestic environments. Similarly, settlement houses in workers' neighborhoods fostered middle-class home standards through "Housekeeping Centers."

In a guide to planning Housekeeping Centers, *Housekeeping Notes: How to Furnish and Keep House in a Tenement Flat: A Series of Lessons Prepared for Use in the Association of Practical Housekeeping Centers of New York,* reformer Mabel Kittredge perfectly stated the new esthetic. The section "Suitable Furnishing for a Model Housekeeping Flat or Home for Five People" recommended wood-stained and uncluttered furniture surfaces, iron beds with mattresses, and un-upholstered chairs. Walls must be painted, not papered; floors should be oak stained; window seats must be built in for storage; shelves should replace bulky sideboards ("the latter being too large for an ordinary tenement room; cheap sideboards are also very ugly"); screens provide privacy in bedrooms; a few good pictures should grace the walls, but only in the living room.[18] One settlement worker who gave domestic science instruction observed, "The purpose in our work is to help those in our classes to learn what is the true American home ideal, and then do what we can to make it possible for them to realize it for themselves" (fig. 1).[19]

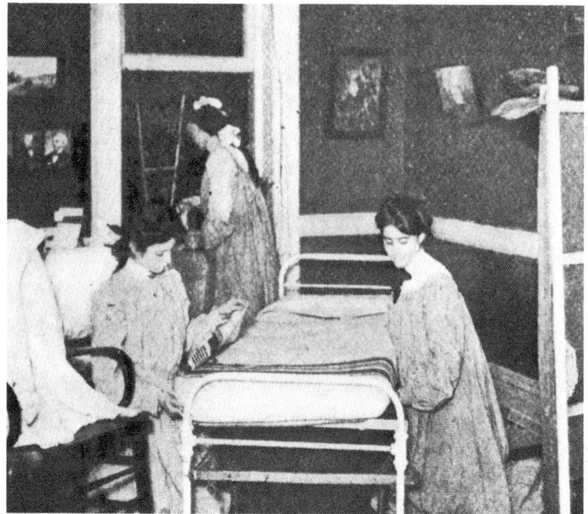

Figure 1. "Homemaking in a Model Flat." (From Mabel Kittredge, "Homemaking in a Model Flat," Charities and the Commons *(Nov. 4, 1905), p. 176.)*

Settlement workers further promoted middle-class styles through the didactic power of the house itself. Furnishing the settlement house interior became a self-conscious process for its residents. In a letter to her sister, a young Jane Addams exclaimed, "Madame Mason gave us an elegant old oak sideboard . . . and we indulged in a set of heavy leather covered chairs and a 16″ cut oak table. Our antique oak book case and my writing desk completes it."[20] Esther Barrows, a settlement worker in Boston's South End House, recorded in her diary, "The pretty green sitting-room with its crackling fire and gay rugs and simple early American furniture is a good setting for all that transpires. I find that it has a spiritual and, I think, almost a physical reaction in the neighborhood."[21] Settlement workers hoped that community patrons would incorporate the styles observed at the house into the furnishing of their own homes (fig. 2).

Figure 2. Interior of Hull House, Chicago, 1895. (From Hull House Maps and Papers *[New York: Crowell, 1895].)*

Industries were also involved in the business of setting standards for workers' homes through company housing, welfare programs and the creation of domestic-like spaces in the factory.

Companies sought to communicate middle-class values through housing provided for workers. Frequently, individual entrances, even in multiple or attached dwellings, sought to reinforce nuclear family privacy.[22] Interiors promoted the specialization of rooms in an effort to discourage the taking in of boarders and to enforce a middle-class pattern of living revolving around parlor, kitchen, dining room, and bedrooms.

Some companies offered employees welfare programs which also affirmed middle-class domestic standards. Amoskeag Mills' employee benefits, for example, included a Textile Club (established to compete with ethnic organizations), a Textile School, a Cooking School, and a Home Nursing Service.[23]

Within the factory, workers were frequently treated to domestic-like environments deliberately planned along middle-class esthetic lines. Employee lounges and lunchrooms were an innovation in the early twentieth century and frequently provided models for light, airy rooms with hardwood floors and simple furniture (fig. 3). Thus, McCormick Harvesting Machine Company hired a social worker to survey factories nationwide and recommend proper recreation, education, luncheon, and lounge facilities, which they proceeded to install.[24]

In the minds of the reformers, simple, mission-style furniture and colonial objects, associated with the agrarian world of the pre-industrial craftsman, seemed the obvious—and most appropriate—material arrangement for all Americans, particularly for industrial workers newly arrived from rural areas. And they tried with a vengeance to impose it.

Despite the missionary zeal of middle-class reformers, however, they did not succeed very well in communicating new standards for domestic interiors to workers. In part, they were responsible for their own failure through ineffective organizational techniques and flawed programs.[25] Yet these shortcomings notwithstanding, workers seem to have actively rejected the means and messages of the reformers.

Although working-class people patronized settlement houses, employee lounges and other model environments, many did so on their own terms, partaking of the recreational facilities and resources without taking the social message to heart.[26]

Some working-class people did make objections known directly to the reformers. Miss Jane E. Robbins, M.D., reported that during her first year at the College Settlement another resident encountered a patient on a home visit who said "that she had had her breakfast, that she did not want anything, and that she did not like strange people poking around in her bureau drawer anyway."[27] Others used more tact but rejected the attentions of reformers nonetheless. A Boston settlement worker recalled her neighbors' response to a circulating collection of photographs of famous paintings:

> South End House had a loan collection of photographs of paintings which were given to the House to use in acquainting our friends with great works of art. These were sent from tenement to tenement to stay for a period of time and then removed while others took their place. The "Holy Pictures," as all of the Madonnas were called, were always mildly welcomed, but the lack of color made them unattractive, and the "unholy" pictures were usually tucked away to await the visitor's return. Some of our earliest calls became very informal . . . when the visitor joined the whole family in a hunt, often ending by finding us all on our knees when the missing photographs were drawn from beneath the bed or bureau.[28]

More than working-class rejection of middle-class tastes, however, separated the worlds of the worker and the reformer. Workers' homes themselves hold the key to the nature and sources of

Figure 3. Recreation room in the McCreary Store, Pittsburgh, ca. 1907. (Photograph by Lewis Hine, from Elizabeth Beardsley Butler, Women and the Trades *[New York: Russell Sage Foundation, 1909], p. 322.)*

their material preferences, apparently at odds with those held by the middle class. This conflict of value systems was powerfully perceived by a young participant in settlement house programs when she was faced with furnishing her own home at marriage.

> We had many opportunities to talk quite naturally of some of the problems of home-making and house-furnishing [wrote settlement worker Esther Barrows]. . . . The lack of plush and stuffed furniture [in our house] was a surprise to many, whose first thought would have been just that. One of our club girls who was about to be married sat down to discuss the matter in relation to her own new home. She seemed convinced by all the arguments brought forward to prove its undesirability from the point of view of hygiene and cleanliness. Months afterward she invited us to her home, much later than would have seemed natural, and as she greeted us rather fearfully she said, "Here it is, but you must remember you have had your plush days." Her small livingroom was overfilled by the inevitable "parlor set," while plush curtains hung at the windows and on either side of the door. The lesson learned by us from this incident was never to be forgotten.[29]

A commitment to a classless America, achievable through educational and environmental solutions to social problems, blinded settlement workers like Esther Barrows to the strength of workers' own culture. Reformers had little conception of how deeply rooted these material values were in working-class life.[30]

The Working Class Becomes "At Home" in Urban America

Workers in this period had few options in selecting their housing. Whether home was an urban slum or a model tenement block, a milltown shack settlement or a company town, families frequently lived in substandard housing far below the quality that middle-class residents enjoyed, and had few alternatives. Furthermore, workers found themselves forced into low-rent districts separated from middle-class residential neighborhoods. Proximity to other working-class people of similar job and income status typified workers' experience more than the ethnic isolation we commonly associate with working-class life. Often, ethnic enclaves were no more than islands of a few blocks within a working-class community.[31] Limitations of housing choices, however, may have encouraged workers to value interior spaces even more.

Within these working-class neighborhoods and homes, workers expressed a distinctive set of material values. An examination of attitudes toward home ownership; space allocation within the house or flat; the covering of the structural shell—floors, walls and windows; furniture selection; and decorative details illuminates the meanings workers attached to the artifacts of their homes.

The view that workers should own their homes provided a rare convergence of opinion between reformers and working people, though each group advocated home ownership for different reasons. Some reformers felt that a home-owning working class would be more dependable and less radical, and thus America would be "preserved" as a classless society. Others hoped that meeting mortgage payments in America might discourage immigrants from sending money home, and hence stem the tide of further immigration.[32] In short, reformers saw home ownership as a strategy for directing worker ambition along acceptable middle-class lines.

Workers, on the other hand, sought to purchase homes for reasons more consistent with their previous cultural experience than with American middle-class values.[33] In Russia, even poor Jews often had owned the rooms in which they lived.[34] Jews in many cases left Eastern Europe in response to Tsarist regulations prohibiting their ownership of property and interfering in their livelihoods as artisans, merchants and businessmen.[35] For these immigrants, the flight to America was a way of resisting "peasantizing" forces. Recent work on Italian immigrants has shown that they likewise came to America hoping to preserve their traditional society and to resist efforts at making them laborers.[36] They viewed a sojourn in the States as a way of subsidizing the purchase of a home upon return to Italy.[37] Many Italians both in Europe and America sacrificed in order to leave their children a legacy of land, which supports David Riesman's theory that pre-industrial families trained and encouraged their children to "succeed them" rather than to "succeed" by rising in the social system.[38] In America, owning a home allowed Italians to uphold traditional community ties by renting apartments to their relatives or paesani, and in less urban areas, to grow the fresh vegetables necessary to maintain a traditional diet.[39] Furthermore, Slavic immigrants, propertyless peasants in the old country, eagerly sought homes in America to satisfy long-standing ambitions.[40] Native American workers, moreover, descended from a tradition that equated private property ownership with full citizenship and promised all deserving, hardworking persons a piece of land. Thus, working-class people of many backgrounds sent mother and children to work, took in boarders, made the home a workshop, and sacrificed proper diet in order to save and buy a house, compromises too severe to substantiate some historians' claims that workers were merely pursuing upward social mobility toward middle-class goals.[41]

Once workers occupied purchased homes or

rented flats their attitudes toward the utilization of interior space diverged markedly from those of the middle class. Reformers advocated a careful allocation of domestic space to create sharp divisions between public and family interactions and to separate family members from one another within the house. Reformers often blamed working-class people for contributing to unnecessary overcrowding and violations of privacy by huddling in the kitchen, for example, while other rooms were left vacant.[42]

While the middle classes were better equipped with, and could more easily afford, housewide heating and lighting than the working classes, a difference of attitudes toward home living was more at issue. Many people from rural backgrounds were used to sharing a bedroom—and sometimes even a bed—with other family members.[43] And for those working people whose homes were also their workplaces, the middle-class ethos of the home as an environment detached from the economic world was particularly inappropriate. Jewish, Irish, Italian, and Slavic women frequently took in boarders and laundry, did homework, and assisted in family stores often adjoining their living quarters. For former farmers and self-employed artisans and merchants, this integration of home and work seemed normal.[44] Among southern Italian women, doing tenement homework in groups sustained "cortile" (shared housekeeping) relationships endangered in the American environment of more isolated homes.[45]

The reformer ideal of the kitchen as an efficient laboratory servicing other parts of the house found little acceptance among workers. Even when workers had a parlor, they often preferred to socialize in their kitchens. Mary Antin fondly recalled frequent visits in her married sister's kitchen in East Boston where after dinner dishes were washed: "Frieda took out her sewing, and I took a book; and the lamp was between us, shining on the table, on the large brown roses on the wall, on the green and brown diamonds of the oil cloth on the floor . . . on the shining stove in the corner. It was such a pleasant kitchen—such a cosy, friendly room—that when Frieda and I were left alone I was perfectly happy just to sit there. Frieda had a beautiful parlor, with plush chairs and a velvet carpet and gilt picture frames; but we preferred the homely, homelike kitchen."[46] When investigators surveyed working-class people for their housing preferences in 1920, most still rejected small kitchens or kitchenettes in favor of ones large enough for dining.[47] Workers kept their Old World hearths burning bright in their new American homes.[48]

Reformers applauded all attempts by workers to create parlors in their homes. They viewed such spaces as evidence of civilization, self-respect, and acceptance of American middle-class standards.[49] A home with a parlor was more likely, they felt, to instill the middle-class image of the family as an emotional, sentimental unit. Margaret Byington's investigation of Homestead workers' homes reflected this bias: "It has been said that the first evidence of the growth of the social instinct in any family is the desire to have a parlor. In Homestead this ambition has in many cases been attained. Not every family, it is true, can afford one, yet among my English-speaking acquaintances even the six families each of whom lived in three rooms attempted to have at least the semblance of a room devoted to sociability."[50]

Worker interest in creating parlor space at home varied, though often it correlated with occupational status. People who did little income-producing work at home, such as Jews and native Americans, most often established sitting rooms. Among Italians and Slavs, where men frequently had low status jobs and women brought work into the home, the combination living room–kitchen, so similar to their European homes, survived the longest. When George Kracha left the Homestead steel mills and established his own butcher business, his home soon reflected his change in status in a way that his neighbors all recognized:

> They still lived in Cherry Alley and much as they had always lived, though Elena no longer kept boarders. . . . Kracha had bought new furniture and the room adjoining the kitchen, where the girls had slept, was now a parlor. Its chief glories were a tasseled

> couch, a matching chair with an ingenious footrest that slid out like a drawer from inside the chair itself, and an immense oil lamp suspended from the ceiling by gilt chains. The lampshade was made of pieces of colored glass leaded together like a church window; it seemed to fill the room and was one of the most impressive objects Cherry Lane had ever seen. On the walls were colored lithographs in elaborate gilt frames of the Holy Family and of the Virgin with a dagger through her exposed heart. Drying ribbons of Easter palm were stuck behind them. On the floor was flowered oilcloth.[51]

Kracha's adoption of a parlor, however, did not entail acceptance of middle-class modes of furnishing. Rather, his parlor presented an elaborate collage of traditional and technological symbols.

Nevertheless, reformers were not mistaken in recognizing a relationship between the presence of a parlor and some acculturation to middle-class ways. The expression of sentiment toward family and community through consumption involved in "parlorization" could indicate a favorable nod to middle-class values. For many workers, though, their usage of kitchen and parlor still respected long-established patterns of sociability. As Mary Antin's comment indicated, people with parlors did not necessarily abandon a preference for the kitchen. Likewise, workers' parlors frequently doubled as sleeping rooms at night.[52] Often when workers accommodated middle-class concepts of space in their homes, they imbued them with different social expectations. For example, Byington noted that even when a native American worker in Homestead had a dining room, "it did not live up to its name." "In five-room houses we find an anomaly known as the 'dining room.' Though a full set of dining room furniture, sideboard, table and dining chairs, are usually in evidence, they are rarely used at meals. The family sewing is frequently done there, the machine standing in the corner by the window; and sometimes, too, the ironing, to escape the heat of the kitchen; but rarely is the room used for breakfast, dinner or supper. The kitchen is the important room of the house."[53]

Whereas the middle-class home provided a setting for a wide range of complex interactions related to work, family and community, and therefore required distinctions between private and public space, workers conceived of home as a private realm distinct from the public world. Because workers only invited close friends and family inside, the kitchen provided an appropriate setting for most exchange. Relationships with more distant acquaintances took place in the neighborhood—on the street or within shops, saloons, or churches. The transference of these traditional patterns of socializing from an intimate pre-industrial community to the city had the impact of increasing the isolation of the working-class home. It is not surprising, therefore, that historians have noted that among many immigrant groups, the American home became a haven as it had never been in the Old World.[54]

When addressing working-class people, reformers justified the new aesthetic primarily in terms of cleanliness; specifically they promoted a simple house shell free of "dust-collecting" carpets, drapes and wallpaper. For most working-class people, however, these decorative treatments were signs of taste and status that they hated to forsake. In almost all European rural societies, as in comparable places in America, only upper-class people had carpets and curtains.[55] Workers embraced the accessibility of these products in urban America with delight.[56] In her autobiography, Mary Antin significantly remarked, "We had *achieved* a carpet since Chelsea days."[57] Given alien and institutional-looking housing facades, curtained windows were often a family's only way to make a personal statement to the world passing by.[58] Wallpaper—the worst demon of all to reformers—was for workers a privilege possible with prosperity and a relief from otherwise dull home walls. The behavior of one family occupying company housing which prohibited wallpaper near U.S. Steel's Gary, Indiana, plant spoke for many others: " 'If you'll give us the colors we want, Sophie will do the painting herself.' This broken up into foreign-sounding English, ended the parley with the company decorator. . . . And in the 'box' occupied by her family she had her way. Outside it remained like all the rest in the row, but indoors,

Figure 4. "Where Some of the Surplus Goes," 1907. (Photograph by Lewis Hine, from Margaret Byington, Homestead: Households of a Mill Town *[New York: Russell Sage Foundation, 1910], facing p. 85.)*

with stencil designs, such as she had learned to make at school, she painted the walls with borders at the top and panels running down to the floor."[59] This young girl replicated in paint the borders and backgrounds of wallpaper design; though learned in school, this long-standing form of rural folk art satisfied the aesthetic tastes and status needs of her family (fig. 4).

Workers' selection of furniture perhaps best demonstrates their struggle to satisfy both traditional and new expectations with products available on the mass market. The middle-class preference for colonial-inspired natural and wood furniture, built-ins and antiseptic iron bedsteads satisfied neither of these needs.

As indicated earlier by Mabel Kittredge's despair in her *Housekeeping Notes* at "cheap" and "ugly" sideboards, workers valued case pieces like bureaus, chiffoniers, and buffets. This preference evolved out of a long tradition of dowry chests and precious wardrobes, often the only substantial furniture in rural homes. Workers, however, did not necessarily consider their acquisition of such furnishings in urban America a conscious perpetuation of traditional material values. An uncomprehending settlement worker noted that "there were the Dipskis, who displayed a buffet among other new possessions, and on the top of it rested a large cut-glass punch bowl. Mrs. Dipski said proudly, 'And so I become American,' as she waved her hand toward the huge piece of furniture, which took an inordinately large place in her small room."[60]

While reformers counseled against unhealthy wood bed frames as vermin-infested and expensive, feather bedding for causing overheating of the body, and fancy lines as unsanitary, working-class people sought to bring all three items into their homes.[61] Byington found a "large puffy bed with one feather tick to sleep on and another to cover" typical of native American homes in Homestead.[62] An observer in Lawrence, Massachusetts, in 1912 described the interior of an Italian mill-worker's home as boasting "pleasant vistas of spotless beds rising high to enormous heights and crowned with crochet-edged pillows" (fig. 5).[63]

Immigrants carried feather bedding with them on the long trek to America more frequently than any other single item.[64] Antin recalled her Russian neighbor's warnings before the family departed for the United States: "In America they sleep on hard mattresses, even in winter. Haveh Mirel, Yachne the dressmaker's daughter, who emigrated to New York two years ago, wrote her mother that she got up from childbed with sore sides, because she had no featherbed."[65] Jews, Italians, Slavs, and most other groups shared a native experience which prized feather bedding and viewed "the bed"—unveiled at marriage—as an emotional symbol of future family happiness.[66] The bed was the dominant feature of most peasant homes, often overpowering all other furniture, which usually was very minimal. Elizabeth Hasonovitz nostalgically remembered her mother in Russia, "bending over a boxful of goose feather, separating the down, preparing pillows for her daughters' future homes."[67] Italian marriage rituals prescribed that the bride's trousseau would provide hand-sewn, heavily embroidered linens along with the marital bed. Pride often produced beds so high that a stool was needed to climb into them.[68]

At least for Italians, the bed played a part in the rituals of death as well. While in Italian villages an elaborate funeral bed commonly was carried into the public square, in America, Italian families laid out their dead ceremoniously at home.[69]

The embellished bed, then, was an important family symbol of birth, marriage and death, not an object to abandon easily.

We have seen throughout this essay that workers' homes were crowded with plush upholstered furniture, a taste which may have emerged out of valuing fluffy, elaborately decorated beds. As the parlor appeared on the home scene, workers brought traditional bed-associated standards to their newly acquired and prized possessions. Well aware of this working-class market for Victorian style furniture, Grand Rapids furniture factories produced their cheapest lines in styles no longer fashionable among middle-class consumers.[70]

Since domestic reformers were promoting a simpler esthetic at the turn of the century, they denounced workers' taste for ornamentation. Photographs of working-class homes nevertheless reveal the persistence of abundant images on the walls (if only cheap prints, torn-out magazine illustrations and free merchant calendars), objects on tabletops, and layering in fabric and fancy paper of surface areas such as mantels, furniture and cabinet shelves.

The fabric valance which appears in almost every photograph of a working-class interior demonstrates how a traditional symbol took on new applications in the American environment of industrial textile manufacture (fig. 6). In cultures such as the Italian, for example, where people treasured the elaborate bed, they adorned it with as much decorative detailing as possible. In fact, it was often the only object warranting such art and expense in the home. A visitor to Sicily in 1905 shared with his travelogue readers a peek into a typical home where "you are greeted by a bed, good enough for a person with a thousand a year, of full double-width, with ends of handsomely carved walnut wood or massive brass. The counterpane which sweeps down to the floor is either hand-knitted, of enormous weight, or made of strips of linen joined together with valuable lace, over which is thrown the yellow quilt so handy for decoration. The show pillows are even finer, being smaller."[71] Under this spread, women fastened a piece of embroidered linen in a deep frill to cover any part of the bed's frame which might show. Even when families could afford attractive, wood frame bedsteads, they still used this "turnialettu," or valance, its original purpose forgotten.[72] In America, where fabric was cheap, the valance of gathered fabric found even more applications, adorning every possible surface and exposed area; in the 1930s Phyllis Williams even discovered valances over washing machines in second-generation Italian-American homes.[73] Fabric was draped and deco-

Figure 5. "Finishing Pants," ca. 1900. (From the Jacob A. Riis Collection, courtesy of the Museum of the City of New York.)

ratively placed in a multitude of other ways as well. Thus a French-Canadian woman who ran a boarding house for shoe factory workers in Lynn inappropriately adorned the inexpensive craftsman-style Morris chairs in her cluttered parlor with antimacassars, an affront to any Arts and Crafts devotee (fig. 7).

While workers brought distinctive cultural heritages to bear on the furnishing of their urban-American homes, much less variety in material preferences resulted than one might have expected. Common pre-industrial small town experience, limits to the preferred and affordable merchandise available for purchase, and mixed ethnic worker communities seem to have encouraged a surprisingly consistent American working-class material ethos that was distinct from that of the middle class. The speed with which a particular working-class family forged a material transition to industrial life depended on numerous factors, among them the intent and length of the family's stay in urban America, prior economic and social experience, and financial resources.

Once workers achieved a certain basic level of economic stability, their homes began to reflect this distinctive material ethos. While working-class people at the time may not have viewed their choices in reified terms, their set of preferences seems not arbitrary but a recurrent, symbolic pattern; not a

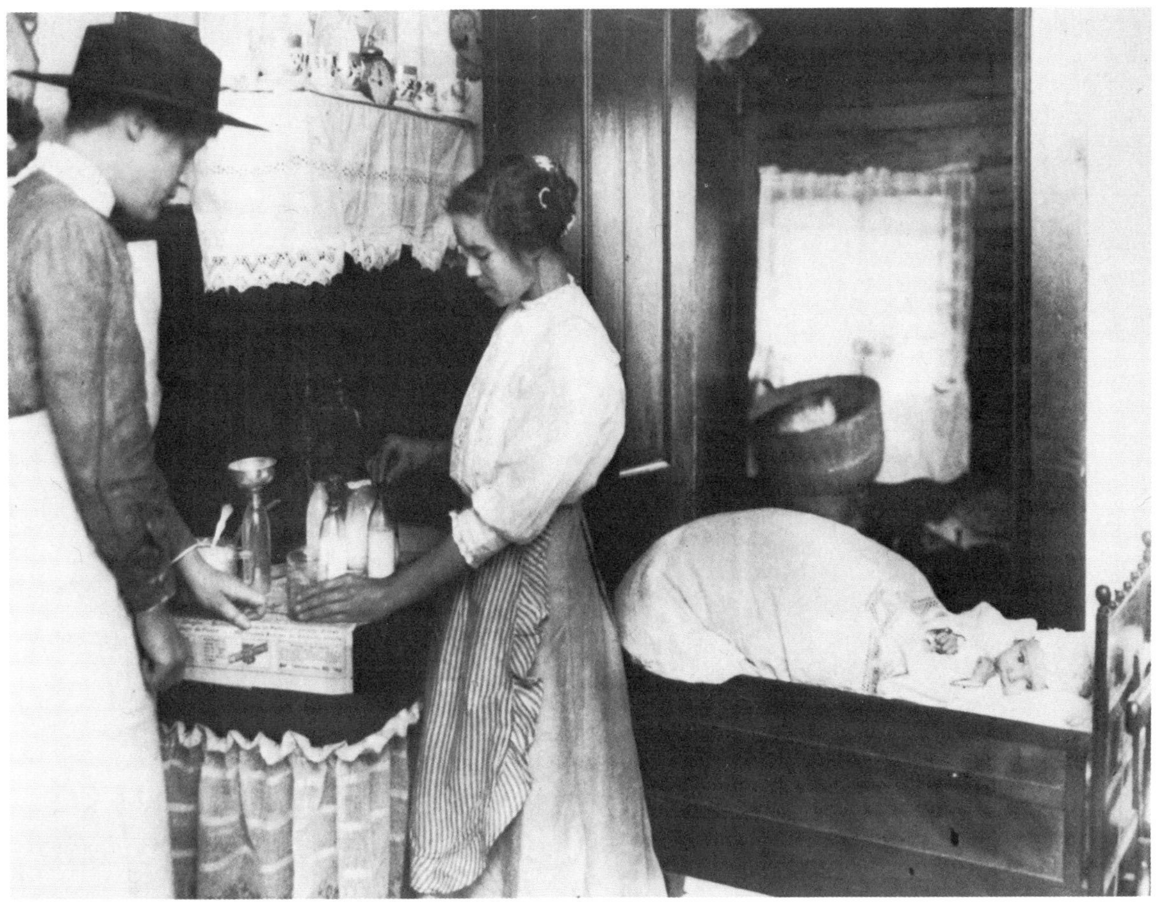

Figure 6. Infant Welfare Society nurse with Polish immigrant mother and baby, 1910–20. (Courtesy of the Chicago Historical Society.)

simple emulation of middle-class Victorian standards with a time lag due to delayed prosperity, but rather a creative compromise forged in making a transition between two very different social and economic worlds. This working-class ethos of material values, inspired by rural values and reinforced within the urban neighborhood, departed in almost every way from aesthetics favored by the middle class and promoted by the domestic reformers. Ironically, while middle-class people viewed the appearance of working-class homes as unsanitary, tasteless, and un-American, workers in fact felt that their new material world represented acculturation to American urban ways. Through the purchase of mass-produced objects, they struggled to come to terms with this industrial society.

Material acculturation occurred as an individual or family made peace between traditional and New World needs. While many workers must have realized their home decor differed from the styles promoted by the middle class, they still felt they had adapted to their new environment and had advanced far beyond their former conditions. While the middle-class person and reformer could not see it, the working-class homes steeped in comfort and covers stood as a symbol of being at home in industrial America.

At the turn of the century, the homes of both the middle class and the working class reflected the

Figure 7. "The Window Side of Miss K's Parlour at Lynn, Mass.," ca. 1903. (From Mrs. John [Bessie] Van Vorst and Marie Van Vorst, The Woman Who Toils: Being the Experiences of Two Gentlewomen as Factory Girls *[New York: Doubleday, Page, 1903].)*

transitions in their respective social experience. On the one hand, middle-class people rejected Victorian decor for a simpler, more "American" aesthetic, which they tried to impose on workers. On the other hand, the working class found in the ornate Victorian furnishing style an appropriate transition to industrial life. The "Victorian solution" was not an inevitable stage working people had to pass through, but a circumstance of need finding available product. Furniture in the Victorian style persisted even as the Colonial Revival and Arts and Crafts dominated middle-class tastes. The old style well suited workers' rural based material values, while satisfying their desire to adapt to mass produced goods, just as it had for the middle class several generations earlier. The contrast in middle-class and working-class tastes in this period suggests that working-class culture indeed had an integrity of its own.

Further historical research may explain the recent findings of sociologists studying contemporary working-class material life. Lee Rainwater and David Coplovitz, for example, have discovered distinctive patterns in working-class domestic values: a preference for plush and new furnishings over used ones; a taste for modern products such as appliances; the valuing of the interior over the exterior appearance of the house; and a common conception of home as a private haven for the working-class family.[74] While these sociologists do not attempt to explain the historical development of material choices, connections to workers' homes in the 1885–1915 period are striking and warrant investigation.

The decades discussed in this essay, when waves of new workers were integrated into an expanding industrial society, may have served as the formative stage for the development of a working-class culture. We have seen how the transitional interior created by workers during this period, as they adjusted to twentieth-century American life, satisfied some ambivalence toward the urban, industrial world. Within this material compromise, traditional cultural values and new consumer benefits could coexist. If workers' homes throughout the twentieth century continued to reflect the attributes of this initial transition, as Rainwater's and Coplovitz's studies tentatively suggest, we may have evidence that contradictions still lie at the core of the American working-class identity. Workers may have reified and passed down this transitional style, or a contradictory attitude toward industrial society may continue to inform their domestic selections. In either case, working-class material values have emerged through both resistance and adaptation to the social environment and have remained distinct from those of the middle class. The chief legacy of this contradiction may be a worker population which on the one hand boasts a unique and discernible material culture and on the other hand does not identify itself forthrightly as a working class.

Notes

This article was originally published in the *Journal of American Culture* (Winter 1980).

1. See Lee Rainwater, *Workingman's Wife: Her Personality, World and Life Style* (New York: Oceana Publications, 1959); Lee Rainwater, "Fear and the House as Haven in the Lower Class," *Journal of the American Institute of Planners* 32, no. 1 (January 1966): 23–31; Dennis Chapman, *The Home and Social Status* (New York: Grove Press, 1955); Marc Fried, *The World of the Urban Working Class* (Cambridge: Harvard University Press, 1973); Michael Young and Peter Willmott, *The Symmetrical Family: A Study of Work and Leisure in the London Region* (London: Routledge and Kegan Paul, 1973).
2. All historians who study "the working class" struggle to define it. While I am convinced that the experience of class is complex, I will adopt a simple definition for the purposes of this essay and use "working class" to refer to skilled and unskilled workers. This essay will explore the extent to which people in the manual trades developed a distinctive material culture.
3. Herbert Gutman, *Work, Culture and Society in Industrializing America* (New York: Vintage Books, 1977), pp. 3–78.
4. Siegfried Giedion, *Mechanization Takes Command: A Contribution to Anonymous History* (New York: W. W. Norton, 1969), p. 365.
5. John Ruskin, "Of Queen's Gardens," in *Sesame and Lilies* (London: Smith, Elder, 1865), quoted in Gwendolyn Wright, "Making the Model Home: Domestic Architecture and Cultural Conflict in Chicago, 1873–1913," Ph.D. diss., University of California, Berkeley, 1978, p. 21.
6. Giedion, *Mechanization,* p. 384.
7. See Sam Bass Warner, Jr., *Streetcar Suburbs: The Process of Growth in Boston 1870–1900* (Cambridge: Harvard University Press), and photographs of newly developed areas in almost any town or city in America during this period.
8. William B. Rhoads, *The Colonial Revival* (New York: Garland Publishing, 1977).
9. Barbara Ehrenreich and Dierdre English, "The Manufacture of Housework," *Socialist Revolution 26* 5, no. 4 (October–December 1975): 5–40.
10. C. Chester Lane, "Hingham Arts and Crafts: Their Aims and Objectives," *Craftsman* 5, no. 3 (December 1903): 276–81, quoted in Rhoads, *Colonial Revival,* p. 367. Even though American Arts and Crafts designers like Gustav Stickley were inspired by William Morris's English Arts and Crafts Movement, their debt to this source did not receive much attention in America. Stickley conveniently equated the American colonial experience with the medieval heritage being revived by the British.
11. Rhoads, *Colonial Revival,* p. 416.
12. Ibid., p. 207.
13. Ibid., p. 517.
14. Ibid., p. 524. See also Barbara Solomon, *Ancestors and Immigrants: A Changing New England Tradition* (Cambridge: Harvard University Press, 1956), on the restrictionist ideology of these Colonial Revival patrons.
15. Rhoads, *Colonial Revival,* p. 390.
16. "A Child's Bedroom," *Craftsman* 4, no. 4 (July 1903): 285, quoted in Rhoads, *Colonial Revival,* p. 285. See also Rhoads, *Colonial Revival,* pp. 412, 832.
17. Gustav Stickley, "Als Ik Kan: 'Made in America,'" *Craftsman* 27, no. 1 (October 1914): 109.

18. Mabel Kittredge, *Housekeeping Notes* (Boston: Whitcomb and Barrows, 1911), pp. 1–13.
19. College Settlement Association, *Annual Report 1902* (New York: College Settlement Association, 1902), p. 37.
20. Jane Addams, Letter to Sarah Alice Addams Haldeman, September 13, 1889, courtesy of Jane Addams Papers Project, Hull House, Chicago, Ill.
21. Esther Barrows, *Neighbors All: A Settlement Notebook* (Boston: Houghton Mifflin, 1929), p. 37.
22. Roy Lubove, *The Progressives and the Slums: Tenement House Reform in New York City, 1890–1917* (Pittsburgh: University of Pittsburgh Press, 1962), p. 163.
23. Tamara Hareven and Randolph Langenbach, *Amoskeag: Life and Work in an American Factory City* (New York: Pantheon Books, 1978), p. 22.
24. Gerd Korman, *Industrialization, Immigrants and Americanization* (Madison: University of Wisconsin Press, 1967), p. 88.
25. See Maxine Seller, "The Education of the Immigrant Woman, 1900 to 1935," *Journal of Urban History* 4, no. 3 (May 1978): 307–30; John Daniels, *Americanization via the Neighborhood* (New York: Harper and Brothers, 1920), pp. 174–222; Sophonisba Breckenridge, *New Homes for Old* (New York: Harper and Brothers, 1921), pp. 280–98.
26. Herbert Gans, *The Urban Villagers: Group and Class in the Life of Italian Americans* (New York: Free Press, 1962), pp. 152–53.
27. Jane E. Robbins, "The First Year at the College Settlement," *The Survey* 27, no. 21 (February 24, 1912): 1801.
28. Barrows, *Neighbors All,* pp. 7–8.
29. Ibid., pp. 40–41.
30. Here and elsewhere in this paper, *material values* refers to preferences in the selection and arrangement of objects of material culture.
31. See Stephen Thernstrom and Peter R. Knights, "Men in Motion: Some Data and Speculations about Urban Population Mobility in Nineteenth-Century America," *Journal of Interdisciplinary History* 1, no. 1 (Autumn 1970): 7–35; Humbert S. Nelli, *Italians in Chicago, 1880–1930* (New York: Oxford University Press, 1970), p. 25; Madelon Powers, "Faces along the Bar: The Saloon in Working-Class Life, 1890–1920," unpublished paper, Department of History, University of California, Berkeley, 1979. Madelon Powers has found that "neighborhood saloons" drew together mixed ethnic groups living in the same residential areas.
32. Rhoads, *Colonial Revival,* p. 716; Lubove, *Progressives and the Slums,* pp. 23–24.
33. James Henretta, "The Study of Social Mobility," *Labor History* 18, no. 2 (Spring 1977): 165–78.
34. Philip Cowen, *Memories of an American Jew* (New York: International Press, 1932), p. 231.
35. See Moses Rischin, *The Promised City* (Cambridge: Harvard University Press, 1962), p. 22; Eli Ginzberg and Hyman Berman, eds., *The American Worker in the Twentieth Century: A History through Autobiographies* (New York: Free Press, 1963), p. 12.
36. John Briggs, *An Italian Passage: Italians in Three American Cities, 1890–1930* (New Haven: Yale University Press, 1978), pp. 11, 272.
37. Pascal D'Angelo, *Son of Italy* (New York: Macmillan, 1924), p. 50.
38. David Riesman, *The Lonely Crowd: A Study of the Changing American Character* (New Haven: Yale University Press, 1950), pp. 40, 17–18, quoted in James Henretta, "Families and Farms: *Mentalité* in Pre-Industrial America," *William and Mary Quarterly,* 3d ser., 35, no. 1 (January 1978): 30.
39. Phyllis Williams, *South Italian Folkways in Europe and America* (New Haven: Yale University Press, 1938), p. 50.
40. Peter Roberts, *The Anthracite Coal Communities* (New York: Macmillan, 1904), p. 43.
41. See Stephen Thernstrom, *Poverty and Progress: Social Mobility in a Nineteenth-Century City* (New York: Atheneum, 1971), pp. 136–37, 155–56; John Modell, "Patterns of Consumption, Acculturation, and Family Income Strategies in Late Nineteenth-Century America," in *Family and Population in Nineteenth-Century America,* ed. Tamara Hareven and Maris Vinovskis (Princeton: Princeton University Press, 1978), pp. 206–40; Virginia Yans-McLaughlin, *Family and Community: Italian Immigrants in Buffalo, 1880–1930* (Ithaca: Cornell University Press, 1977), pp. 47–48, 175–77, for sacrifices made toward buying a house.
42. Edith Abbott and Sophonisba Breckenridge, *The Tenements of Chicago, 1908–1935* (Chicago: University of Chicago Press, 1936), pp. 263–64.
43. D'Angelo, *Son of Italy,* p. 5.
44. See Sydelle Kramer and Jenny Masur, eds., *Jewish Grandmothers* (Boston: Beacon Press, 1976); Mary Antin, *Promised Land* (Boston: Houghton Mifflin Sentry Editions, 1969), p. 195.
45. Donna Gabaccia, "Housing and Household Work in Sicily and New York, 1890–1910," unpublished paper, Department of History, University of Michigan, Ann Arbor, n.d., p. 18.
46. Antin, *Promised Land,* p. 337.
47. Morris Knowles, *Industrial Housing* (New York: McGraw-Hill, 1920), p. 295.

48. Donald Cole, *Immigrant City: Lawrence, Massachusetts, 1845–1921* (Chapel Hill: University of North Carolina Press, 1963), p. 107.
49. Robert Woods, *The City Wilderness* (New York: Arno Press, 1970), p. 102.
50. Margaret Byington, *Homestead: The Households of a Mill Town* (New York: Russell Sage Foundation, 1910), p. 55.
51. Thomas Bell, *Out of This Furnace* (Boston: Little, Brown, 1941), p. 62.
52. See Rose Cohen, *Out of the Shadow* (New York: n.p., 1918), pp. 196–97, quoted in Judith Smith, "Our Own Kind: Family and Community Networks in Providence," *Radical History Review,* no. 17 (Spring 1978): 113; William Elsing, "Life in New York Tenement Houses," in Robert Woods, *Poor in Great Cities* (New York: Charles Scribner's Sons, 1895), p. 50.
53. Byington, *Homestead,* p. 56.
54. Williams, *South Italian Folkways,* p. 17; Yans-McLaughlin, *Family and Community,* p. 223; Nelli, *Italians in Chicago,* p. 6.
55. Probate inventory research at Old Sturbridge Village on western Massachusetts houses, 1790–1840, revealed a similar pattern: carpets and curtains were rare and precious (Research Department, Old Sturbridge Village, Sturbridge, Mass.).
56. Carla Bianco, *The Two Rosetos* (Bloomington: Indiana University Press, 1974), p. 14; Williams, *South Italian Folkways,* p. 43.
57. Antin, *Promised Land,* p. 274 (emphasis mine).
58. Robert Roberts, *The Classic Slum* (Harmondsworth: Penguin Books, 1971), p. 33.
59. Graham Taylor, *Satellite Cities* (New York: Arno Press, 1970), p. 194.
60. Barrows, *Neighbors All,* p. 70.
61. *Reports of the President's Homes Commission* (Washington: Government Printing Office, 1909), p. 117.
62. Byington, *Homestead,* p. 145.
63. Cole, *Immigrant City,* p. 107.
64. See Thomas Wheeler, ed., *The Immigrant Experience* (New York: Dial Press, 1971), pp. 20, 155; Cowen, *Memories,* p. 233.
65. Antin, *Promised Land,* p. 164.
66. Williams, *South Italian Folkways,* p. 86.
67. Elizabeth Hasonovitz, *One of Them* (Boston: Houghton Mifflin, 1918), p. 6.
68. Williams, *South Italian Folkways,* p. 42.
69. Bianco, *Two Rosetos,* p. 124.
70. Kenneth L. Ames, "Grand Rapids Furniture at the Time of the Centennial," *Winterthur Portfolio 10,* ed. Ian M. G. Quimby (Charlottesville: University Press of Virginia, 1975), p. 42.
71. Douglas Sladen and Norma Latimer, *Queer Things about Sicily* (London: Anthony Traherne, 1905), p. 85.
72. Williams, *South Italian Folkways,* pp. 42–43.
73. Ibid., p. 47.
74. Rainwater, *Workingman's Wife* and "House as Haven"; David Coplovitz, "The Problems of Blue-Collar Consumers," in *Blue Collar World: Studies of the American Worker,* ed. Arthur B. Shostak and William Gomberg (Englewood Cliffs, N.J.: Prentice-Hall, 1964), pp. 110–20.

Part Four History

Alley Landscapes of Washington

JAMES BORCHERT

It is with some misgivings that one leaves the well lighted outer streets with their impressive residences and turns into a narrow passageway where he must walk by faith, not sight. Noises which faintly recall those of the Midway Plaisance at the world's fair, grow louder as the explorer approaches the wider inside alleys. Night with its dark shadows accentuates the strangeness of the scene. Near a gas light on one of the inner corners a group of people are seen playing together roughly. A cheap phonograph near by rasps out a merry ditty. The shrill cries of children pierce the air as . . . youngsters dart about among their elders. Two lads skillfully dance while a . . . woman picks at her guitar. . . . Older folks, crowded around their doorways, are complaining of the sultry, oppressive August air and some are arranging ironing boards and rocking chairs on which they will sleep all night outside their houses. They call back and forth to each other across the alley street.

—Charles Weller, *Neglected Neighbors*, 1909

In the heart of Washington, D.C., literally in the shadow of the Capitol Building, there was a "second city" built in the alleys. Beginning in the 1850s, rural southern migrants, almost all of them black, were funneled into thousands of houses set around closed courts in the middle of many of the city's blocks. While they were separated from the main thoroughfares by only a few yards, these settlements were nevertheless cut off visually from the outside world. But the way these spaces were used and interpreted varied with different occupants. This is what social historian James Borchert illustrates very clearly in his portrait of the alley dwellings of Washington, D.C. A change of residents was accompanied by a revised perception of the alleys.

The first alley folk did much of their living outside regardless of the weather and thus the alley street itself became a communal living space. It was filled with all manner of "furniture" and the doors and windows of the small houses were generally left open. This served to promote social interaction among alley dwellers by reducing the distinction between inside and outside. During the summer some people even slept in the alley and in winter men gathered there around open fires to swap tales. People passing on the street, expecting the worst from alley dwellers, no doubt found their negative expectations fulfilled by what they perceived as dangerous and unwholesome commotion.

While many of the alley house clusters were demolished in the 1940s, as late as the 1970s at least twenty alley settlements still survived, only now they were populated by relatively affluent whites. For them the alley street was generally a neutral zone. Each dwelling was treated as a separate residence so that there was little interaction via the alley. Ironically the same alley that was once thought of as dangerous and unsafe came to be regarded as the best place to park one's car; the public street now being thought of as the most likely place for a crime. Thus a landscape that once provided blacks with a basis for communal interaction was converted into an environment of personal security and privacy.

Winston Churchill once observed that "we shape our buildings and afterwards our buildings shape us." Although this may be true, it presumes an environmental determinism that needs tempering. A built environment imposes limits on the activities of residents and users, but residents also can mold the environment. The results are striking when two groups of people with different cultural backgrounds take the same environment and, with little change in the physical layout or structure, transform that landscape in radically different ways to fit the needs and values of each group.

Nowhere is this transformation of an environment more apparent than in the uses made of Washington alleys and alley dwellings. Two quite different groups are involved in this story. The first were black migrants from the Virginia and Maryland countryside who dominated alley housing almost from its inception in the 1850s until the restoration movement of the 1940s and 1950s. At that time while-collar and especially professional workers, many of whom were white, began to replace working-class blacks. The contrasting uses of space and the different landscapes each developed with the same containers and layout suggest not only the strength and persistence of human will, but also the inadequacies of strict environmental determinism.

Alley Origins

Alley housing in Washington began on a small scale in the 1850s as the city started the transformation from a southern town to one of the larger cities in the country. Most alley houses were constructed in the last quarter of the nineteenth century by absentee owner-developers—residents of the city but not the immediate neighborhood—on land that had been subdivided and sold separately from street-front land. In many cases the developer of a set of alley houses sold off the newly constructed two-story brick or frame row houses, each about twelve feet wide and thirty feet deep, as soon as they were completed to new owners who were also likely to be nonresidents.

The construction and sale was usually a highly speculative and profitable venture. It was based on what appeared to be an insatiable demand for cheap rental housing that resulted from a continuing migration of blacks from the surrounding countryside as well as racial restrictions on existing housing. Because the city lacked a quick, cheap transportation system that would permit dispersal of new residents to the countryside, alley construction took place in or near the most built-up parts of the city, often at the same time as street-front housing. Nevertheless, Washington's population pressures never equalled those of cities such as New York, where separate development of street and alley property was quickly abandoned for the more space-efficient tenement.

The number and size of inhabited alleys continued to grow in the last quarter of the century. By the peak in 1900 about 3,500 houses existed in nearly 250 alley blocks throughout the city. The alley population was just over 19,000 people, of whom more than 90 percent were black. Several forces, however, began to threaten alley housing just before the turn of the century. Construction of a trolley in the 1890s permitted the beginnings of population dispersal, while a ban on alley house construction stopped further building. Moreover, housing reformers, business encroachments on alley land, and the need for automobile garages increasingly diminished the number of alley houses. By 1970 just over twenty inhabited alleys housed about two hundred households. At least half of these alleys, especially on Capitol Hill and in "Foggy Bottom," had been restored and housed professional people.

Alley Form and Structure

Although wide variation existed in the 1800s, a typical block was lined on the outside by middle-class housing of three-story brick row houses, usually with only a small front yard separating the houses from the street. Much here resembles Wilbur Zelinsky's "Pennsylvania Town," which also had ex-

Figure 1. "Alley Dwellings in Logan Court, Northwest." (Photograph by Carl Mydans, November 1935, Farm Security Administration Collection, Library of Congress.)

tensive alley development. This pattern left long, narrow backyards that were originally intended for gardens. These were usually fenced on both sides and enclosed at the back by a shed that ensured privacy. An alley network provided service access to the rear of these lots.

The first part of this network was a narrow, twelve-to-fifteen-foot-wide alley that bisected the block. In the center of the block this narrow alley opened at right angles onto a larger, thirty-foot-wide H-shaped alley that touched the rear of every street-front lot and was wide enough for a wagon to turn around. On this alley, on subdivided land, the tiny alley houses were placed with their fronts immediately on the alley. In the early years small backyards of varying sizes contained water hydrants, privies, clotheslines, and assortments of junk, as well as household items and wash buckets that could not be stored in the small houses. This yard was enclosed by a board fence and a small shed at the back, thus obscuring the view of street-front houses.

The result of this physical pattern, with one set of houses facing outward, fortified at the rear by sheds and fences, and the inward-facing alley houses equally protected at the rear, was considerable isolation of the two worlds from each other. Even more marked was the isolation of the alley world from the rest of the city. Once inside the block via one of the narrow entrance-exit alleys, the sensation was that of a maze in a quadrangle. In contrast to the visual experience of the "canyon" street in American cities, where, despite the height of buildings you can

Figure 2. "Logan Place," September 26, 1935. Residents who sought to avoid the constant interaction of the alley drew their shades or closed their shutters. Ethel Waters, who lived with her grandmother in several alley houses in Philadelphia while she was growing up, remembered that her grandmother sought to block out the "evil alley influences" by keeping the shades tightly drawn and the windows closed. As a result, Ethel could play outside her home with "evil alley children" without being caught by her grandmother (Ethel Waters, His Eye Is on the Sparrow *[Garden City, N.Y.: Doubleday, 1950]). (Courtesy of the Alley Dwelling Authority Collection, Library, Department of Housing and Community Development, Washington, D.C.)*

see miles in four directions, the alleys present a visual maze enclosed all around with little basis for orientation. All visual contact with the rest of the city is limited to the tops of the three-story row houses that rim the block, and even city sounds are kept out of the interior by the same red brick wall.

Although the two-story alley row houses are relatively low-density housing, within the alley the impression is one of great concentration, with two rows of nearly identical houses only thirty feet apart on the main interior alley and enclosed at both ends by similar rows of houses. Unlike the tree-lined streets not far away, the alleys had no physical barriers to break or partially obscure the open alley or the continuous line of alley dwellings. The alley house and environs clearly were constructed in the early years to provide for the worst-paid workers the least in space and amenities. This was a stripped-down economy environment that minimized everything except profits.

The Making of a Working-Class Environment

Reformers who studied the alleys around 1900 concluded, à la Churchill, that the environment was responsible for a wide variety of social ills ranging from illegitimacy and broken families to delinquency and crime. Certainly this environment was cramped and frequently overcrowded, not to mention often unsanitary because of malfunctioning outhouses or the proximity of stables. Nevertheless, migrants from the countryside took this minimal environment and transformed it socially into a landscape that provided for their needs and protection. This was not done by substantial change to the physical fabric but through the behavioral and symbolic use made of the space.

Alley dwellers were often recent black migrants who had to confront a series of extremely difficult tasks if they were to survive in the new environment. In the first place, there was the nearly daily search for work, because racism limited many black Washingtonians to the most dangerous, least paid, and least secure occupations. This required finding ways to survive on inadequate incomes. In addition, the constant danger of overt hostility from whites haunted them.

What alley dwellers did was construct a series of interrelated and integrated social worlds, based on previous experiences, that made survival possible. Extended kinship networks that pooled their resources acted as the first level of support, and the alley community became a second level of organization that provided a wide range of services for its members. These varied from the exchange of information on jobs and where to shop and fish, to where to find discarded lumber or coal for fuel, and how and where to junk. (Junking involved collecting discarded glass, rags, paper, clothing, and metals and keeping them in the disorderly backyard until circumstances required cashing them in to salvage operators.) The alley community also took care of sick and needy families, maintained social order, and served as a focal point for entertaining and neighboring.

Figure 3. "Aerial View: Logan Court," October 6, 1939. Logan Court appears in the foreground of this photograph. Note the long, narrow lots with houses on the interior of the block. (Courtesy of the Alley Dwelling Authority Collection, Library, Department of Housing and Community Development, Washington, D.C.)

To maintain the extended kinship networks, neighboring, and community on which survival was based, intense face-to-face contact and interaction were necessary. In order to facilitate contact alley dwellers used natural advantages offered by the alley landscape. Because the alley was isolated from street-front neighbors and the alley entrance was unobtrusive from the street, there was little likelihood that nonresidents would enter the alley. The single-exit alley also increased the potential for face-to-face meetings among residents. Moreover, density of alley houses and their inward focus meant that much that went on, whether in the alley or alley houses, was common knowledge, unless residents made an effort to maintain their privacy. Finally, the hot, humid summers of Washington encouraged residents to spend as much time as possible in front of their small, crowded homes. The tiny, cluttered backyards with malodorous privies must have discouraged many from moving in that direction.

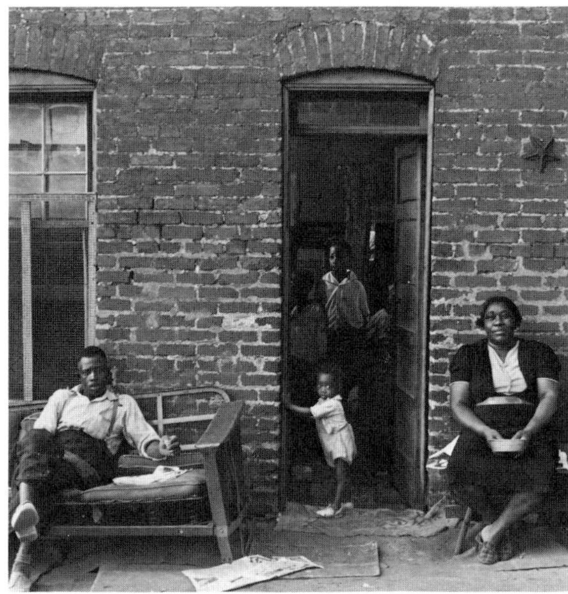

Figure 4. "Family and their home in an alley dwelling area." (Photograph by Edwin Rosskam, July 1941, Farm Security Administration Collection, Library of Congress.)

Using these alley features and transforming others, alley dwellers changed the environment to one that permitted, encouraged, and advanced the social patterns of their community. One of the key aspects of this transformation involved the use of the alley itself. Although builders conceived of the alley only as a path for movement in and out of the interior of the block, residents converted the alley into a multipurpose commons and community center.

Alley dwellers turned their home inside out by projecting part of it into the alley and opening the rest to the alley. This meant moving furniture into the alley, although virtually anything could be used for sitting or lounging—from chairs and benches to stoops, stairs, and boxes. The use of the alley for neighboring was nearly universal by all alley residents and seemingly continuous throughout the day and well into the night, save for the worst weather.

Although builders had installed small doors and windows in the facade, alley dwellers figuratively punched out these tentative openings. As a result it was not unusual to find heads sticking out of doors and windows or heads pushed into first-story doors and windows. Despite occasional screens on doors and windows, the overall impression of the alley was one of open doors and windows, with curtains pulled back and shades raised.

Neighbors moved back and forth from house to alley to neighbor's house unimpeded by the physical or social barriers. Household sounds and smells mingled with those of the alley, and both reverberated off the enclosing walls. It was difficult to know where the alley house ended and the alley commons began and vice versa.

Not everyone who lived in the alley wanted to be part of this community. They set themselves off from neighbors by avoiding contact and protecting their privacy. These households could be identified easily by their drawn shades and closed doors, windows, and shutters.

At the same time the open alley house facilitated social interaction, neighboring, and community, it also served as a symbol of the interdependence of the residents. Moreover, the openness made the maintenance of social order within the alley much easier. This was true not only of the immediate alley

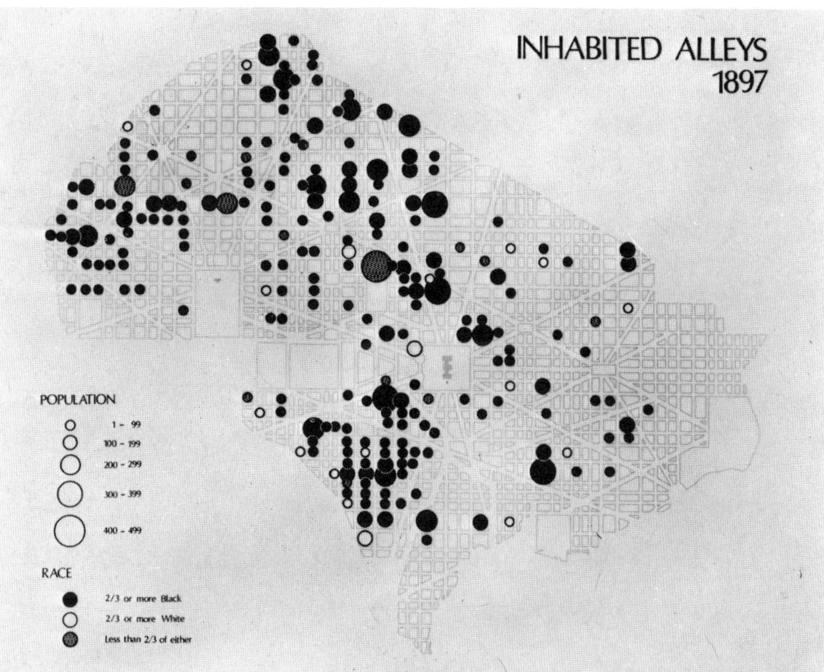

Figure 5. Total population of inhabited alleys by race in 1897. The size of the circle indicates the number of people living in the alley, and the shading of the circle signifies the race of the inhabitants. (Map by Judith Rood; based on Commissioners of the District of Columbia, Annual Report, 1897 *[Washington, 1897], pp. 195–202; reprinted with permission of the University of Illinois Press.)*

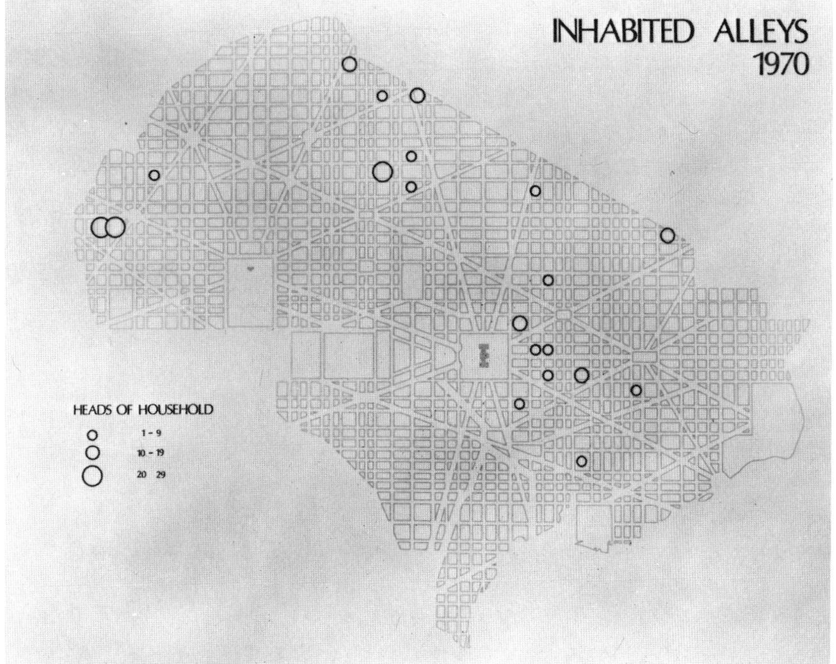

Figure 6. Number of households living in alleys in 1970. The number of people living in alleys has declined dramatically from a peak at the turn of the century. (Map by Judith Rood; based on R. L. Polk, Polk's Washington, D.C. Directory, 1970 *[Washington, 1970]; reprinted with the permission of the University of Illinois Press.)*

community, but extended to the maintenance of "alley turf."

The intensity of interaction in the alleys ensured that any outsiders would be recognized immediately because the physical layout aided in the development of defensible space, and the interaction also discouraged entry. This was especially true for outsiders, usually middle class, whose sense of space and use of the alley only as a path made entry into an apparently seething mass of humanity as frightening as the opening quote suggests. Alley residents encouraged this by confronting intruders and demanding to know the reason for their presence, as well as by using occasional physical attacks to reinforce the message. The success of these efforts can be seen in the extensive folklore that existed in the city about the dangers of inhabited alleys and the need for police patrols to go in pairs with their guns ready.

This was the landscape created by working-class alley residents to fit the urban culture they developed for survival. It involved little change in the physical form and few additional artifacts, virtually all temporary. This landscape was more behavioral than physical, but it was as loaded with social, psychological, and symbolic meaning as any physical landscape could be.

The Making of a White-Collar Environment

The new landscape developed by alley dwellers beginning in the 1940s contrasts sharply with the earlier one. The restoration movement that led to the white-collar takeover did bring changes to the environment. The major ones were the inclusion of electricity, plumbing, telephones, air conditioning and central heating, as well as a general renovation of the structures. None significantly altered the alley layout or the physical containers, although they did remove several factors that had encouraged earlier residents to use the alley. Air conditioning turned

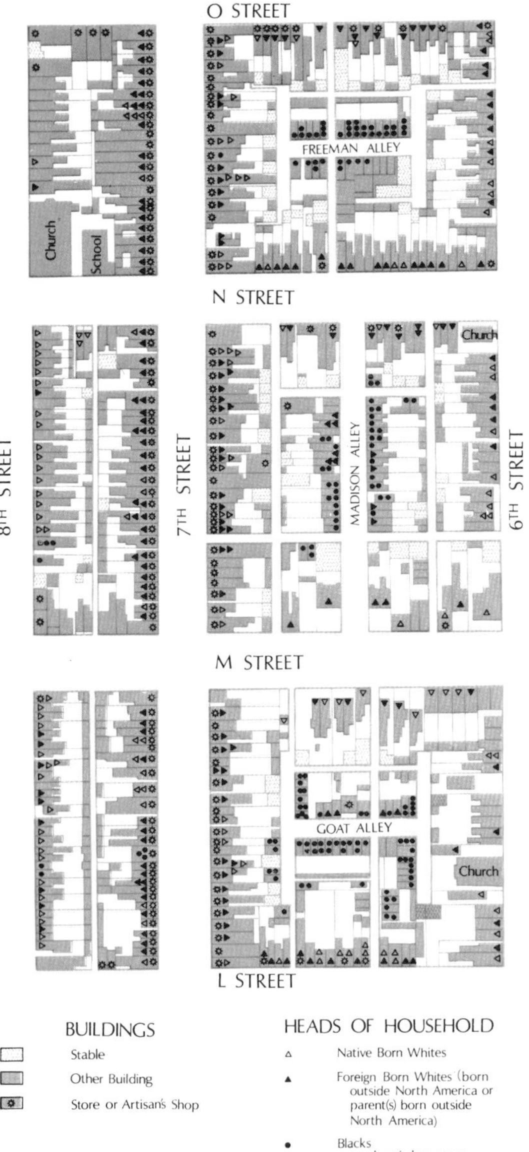

Figure 7. Physical and demographic map of sample blocks in Washington. The map shows the types of buildings on a block, as well as the population mix. Blacks dominate the interior alley housing. (Map by Judith Rood; based on Sanborn Map Publishing Company, Insurance Maps of Washington, D.C. *[New York, 1888], and Federal Population Census Schedules, 1880, Washington, D.C., vol. 2, pt. 2, Record Group 29, National Archives; reprinted with the permission of the University of Illinois Press).*

the hot, breezeless houses into more attractive retreats in the summer, and removing the privy from the backyard eliminated a key deterrent to using that area.

The inclusion of one particular new artifact has had further impacts on the use of alley space. The automobile, which had not been commonly available for earlier residents, has become central to the lives of new residents. As a result they devote much of the alley space to parking. This adds a series of temporary, movable barriers that break up alley space and vistas. It also means that many residents go directly from their homes to their cars rather than walking in the alleys, thus reducing personal contact.

The new alley dwellers tend to be single individuals or couples without children. They perceive themselves to be self-sufficient, they are much better paid, and have far greater job security than previous residents. They are engrossed in their occupations as well as the cultural life of the city. Unlike earlier residents they are cosmopolitan and have wide-ranging contacts throughout the city and suburbs. Their automobiles provide the mobility to maintain that network.

Given this professional culture, it is not surprising that the new residents have drastically altered the alley landscape in terms of their use. The need for maintaining neighboring and community has vanished, save for immediate, local issues. Survival depends on links outside the alley maintained by telephone and automobile. The new alley dwellers have converted the alley back to its original function as path, as well as adding a new use, a place to park automobiles. The proximity of car to house improves the access of residents to their far-flung contacts. This conversion of the alley to a neutral path has encouraged others in search of parking to venture into the now seemingly safe alleys, with the consequence that at some hours of the day the houses look like outcroppings in a field of automobiles.

Because the professional world is largely outside the alley and neighbors are not necessary for survival, as well as because the professional home is a retreat, the new residents altered the relationship of the house to the alley. In contrast to the open alley house of earlier years, the restored house has been turned around and boarded up to protect the privacy, independence, and anonymity of its residents. In many respects these new residents have sought to establish the physical features often found in suburban housing or in the houses on the outside of the block. Suburban dwellers have large front yards in which plantings can be used as barriers and screens to protect the residents from unwanted intrusion, while Washington street-front houses with smaller front yards are often set off by wrought-iron fences. But the new alley dwellers have much less space to use because their houses front directly on the alley.

To solve this problem, the initial restorers of alley housing installed various architectural features to create the same effect. They began by introducing a porch wherever possible to provide a mediating space between the public alley and the private house. In some cases the porch is no more than an expanded step made out of bricks or a concrete slab. More often the porch and steps run the width

Figure 8. Terrace Court, Northeast, restored alley houses, with small porches and "yards" extended out into the alley. Windows filled with air conditioners and drawn venetian blinds. (Photograph by the author, July 1972.)

of the house and are accentuated by a sharp black iron railing that marks them off as private. Entry to the working-class alley house was direct with only a couple of wooden steps in front of the door, but entry to the white-collar house requires a more circuitous path with more obstacles. Some restorers have made their steps and porch quite formal as in the case of the neo-Baroque ones in Marks Court Southeast. These additions have severely restricted potential sitting space, and the use of hard, sharp materials in place of wood has further discouraged lounging.

Individual residents have carried mediating space several steps further. In contrast to the earlier landscape in which the only living parts were human, the new alley environment, although devoid of human presence, has been naturalized by the inclusion of plants. Although these are meant for decoration, they also expand a buffer zone into the alley. This encroachment of the private alley house onto the public alley ranges from the subtle, unobtrusive ivy of Terrace Court to the more massive evergreens in Gessford Court. In other alleys hedges and shrubs placed in front of the steps, railings, and porch further obscure the entrance into the house. In alleys where plantings are less feasible, residents seem to use their cars as a barrier.

Residents have turned the facade into an unobtrusive, yet substantial, fortress as a second line of defense against potential intrusion. Renewed exteriors look far more aesthetically pleasing, but their pristine appearance makes them colder than the dark red brick of earlier years. More significant, however, are iron bars that protect many first-story windows. Front doors and first-floor windows are always kept shut while second-story windows are only occasionally open. Window blinds, shades, or curtains are tightly drawn. Only when the privacy of the second story is uncompromised by surrounding buildings is this rule broken. In the unusual case of a set of houses in Brown's Court Southeast, where the brick front was replaced by a glass wall to provide a splendid view of the alley, the curtains are almost always kept closed. Where central air conditioning has not been installed, window units fill much of the small opening and provide the only alley sounds save for those of automobiles. The automobiles also produce the only smells.

Unlike the working-class alley, which promoted constant interaction, the white-collar landscape restricts and controls the number and extent of interactions. Spontaneous visits by neighbors and friends are far less common. Visitors enter the new alley house only by invitation at agreed times. The same facade and layout that once encouraged interaction has now been converted to discourage such behavior.

The older alley house was projected into the alley, but the focal point of the restored home has been drawn inside. There is, however, a new orientation to the backyard. Here privacy has been established even more strongly by high, board fences around the perimeter, occasionally reinforced by tall plants just inside the fence. Where this protective barrier has been installed, residents move outside, at least in good weather. Outdoor furniture and occasionally household furniture add confort to the secured area where professionals read, relax, entertain friends, or work without interruptions from neighbors or passersby.

Middle-class alley dwellers have privatized their alley homes to protect the nuclear family. Save for the buffer area in front, they have relinquished any claim to the alley and returned it to public use. This act of turning the alley back to path supports the desired isolation, protection, and anonymity of residents by encouraging movement through the alley. Working-class alley residents discouraged outsiders from encroaching on their turf by physically dominating their environment, but their white-collar counterparts use camouflage and misdirection.

Although physical forms and layouts influence human behavior, the physical fabric is, at least partly, neutral. It offers a variety of possible uses and adaptations. Human groups, however, come to an environment with specific needs, concerns, and perceptions. Although some physical environments facilitate a group's behavior better than others, what is often overlooked is the power of a group to transform and transcend an environment.

We find that alley residents, working class and white collar, have taken the same physical layout and structures and have altered them behaviorally and symbolically to facilitate the life and culture that each group wanted, within the constraints of the larger society. They have done so without altering that layout or structure in significant ways. This suggests that each social group has its own constraints, needs, and perceptions about the appropriate ways to order a landscape and that these ideas are consistent with the *zeitgeist* of the group. Physical landscapes are transformed by the collective behavior of a group, with each person working as a craftsperson in a guild to reconstruct the environment to fit the needs of the group. Thus, the completed landscape is the result of changes in the physical fabric made by residents and the behavioral uses made of the spaces that inject social and symbolic meaning into the environment.

Further Reading

James Borchert. "Alley Life in Washington: Analysis of 600 Photographs." Columbia Historical Society *Records* 49 (1973–74): 244–59.

———. *Alley Life in Washington: Family, Community, Religion and Folklife in the City, 1850–1970.* Urbana: University of Illinois Press, 1980.

———. "The Rise and Fall of Washington's Inhabited Alleys, 1852–1972." Columbia Historical Society *Records* 48 (1971–72): 267–88.

Philippe Boudon. *Lived-in Architecture: Le Corbusier's Pessac Revisited.* Cambridge: MIT Press, 1972.

Grady Clay. *Alleys: A Hidden Resource.* Louisville: Grady Clay and Co., 1978.

Leon Festinger, Stanley Schacter, and Kurt Back. *Social Pressures in Informal Groups: A Study of Human Factors in Housing.* Stanford: Stanford University Press, 1950.

Marc Fried and Peggy Gleicher. "Some Sources of Residential Satisfaction in an Urban Slum." *Journal of the American Institute of Planners* 27, no. 4 (November 1961): 305–15.

Paul A. Groves. "The 'Hidden' Population: Washington Alley Dwellers in the Late Nineteenth Century." *The Professional Geographer* 26, no. 3 (August 1974): 270–76.

Robert L. Vickery, Jr. *Anthrophysical Form: Two Families and Their Urban Environments.* Charlottesville: University Press of Virginia, 1972.

Ethel Waters. *His Eye Is on the Sparrow.* Garden City, N.J.: Doubleday, 1950.

Charles F. Weller. *Neglected Neighbors in the National Capital.* Philadelphia: John C. Winston, 1909.

William H. Whyte, Jr. *The Organization Man.* Garden City, N.J.: Doubleday, 1957.

Wilbur Zelinsky. "The Pennsylvania Town: An Overdue Geographical Account." *Geographical Review* 67, no. 2 (April 1977): 127–47.

This article was originally published in *Landscape* (Spring 1979).

Domestic Architecture at the Clifts Plantation: The Social Context of Early Virginia Building

FRASER D. NEIMAN

Students of pre-twentieth-century vernacular architecture tend to be interested in long-lasting traditions and sometimes treat changes as unwelcome and unexpected intruders. Fraser Neiman's article reminds us that even the most traditional of forms can change rapidly when their builders find it expedient. Neiman chronicles the radical transformations that English architectural traditions underwent in seventeenth-century Virginia, concentrating on two important aspects of seventeenth-century Chesapeake building that had been lost to architectural historians before the onset of intensive archaeological excavations in the late 1960s: the dominance of post construction and the initial use and subsequent abandonment of the English vernacular three-room house plan.

Post building, the practice of setting wooden buildings directly on or into the earth without the use of masonry foundations, was introduced into Virginia in the first years of settlements, and was the major structural system employed in the colony until the early eighteenth century. As with the log-building traditions discussed by Kniffen and Glassie, post building represented the transformation of a minor European building technology to a dominant American one under new economic and social conditions. Neiman is interested in the elaboration of post building techniques over time within a relatively small area, and in using these technological changes as indicators of social history and the world views of seventeenth-century Virginians.

The analysis is enriched by Neiman's discussion of the three-room, through-passage or lobby-entry English vernacular houses built by Virginians until late in the seventeenth century. He explains the significance of three-room houses in Anglo-American social history and then sketches the social changes that resulted in their abandonment in favor of the one-story, two-room, hall-parlor-plan houses that architectural historians, hampered by knowledge only of surviving buildings, have traditionally presented as the characteristic houses of seventeenth-century Virginia. Neiman emphasizes that this became true only at the end of the century.

Neiman's article demonstrates the possibilities for using archaeological and documentary evidence to construct an account of vernacular traditions even when no examples survive. Using his own archaeological site as the central example, Neiman draws on evidence as diverse as the reports of other excavations, statistical studies of county records, and passing remarks by seventeenth-century observers that offer insight into the uses and meanings of buildings otherwise too ordinary to merit literary comment by their builders and users.

Since the 1930s, when the matter was first given serious attention, popular and most scholarly awareness of the architecture of colonial Virginia has begun and ended with the great mansions of the Tidewater. This state of affairs is not surprising, for these houses, with their Renaissance-inspired balanced facades and symmetrical plans arranged around an axial hall (attributes that are for convenience called Georgian), comprise a remarkably impressive and homogenous group. Since the sudden appearance of the earliest of them in the second quarter of the eighteenth century, they have remained for many an architectural high water in the Old Dominion. While the Stratfords and Westovers have loomed large in many accounts of the colonial period, their true importance, their potential for elucidating the world of their builders, has for the most part gone unrecognized. Rather the attention they have received has been a product of the near idolatrous reverence with which we often view the aristocracy that created them.

This infatuation with the eighteenth century has a long tradition in Virginia, dating from the 1830s when economic decline and social change convinced many Virginians that Sir Thomas Browne's famous description of another defunct way of life might have application close to home: "Egypt is now become a land of obliviousness and doteth. Her ancient civility is gone; her glory hath vanished as a phantasma. Her youthful days are over and her face has become wrinkled and tetrick. She poreth not upon the heavens, astronomy is dead unto her and knowledge maketh other cycles."[1]

The malaise, a growing sense that the center of things had moved elsewhere, brought with it a romantic nostalgia that has persisted ever since. Latter-day Virginians apotheosized the "ancient cavaliers." As early as 1824, George Tucker wistfully characterized the last of the surviving eighteenth-century gentry as "remarkable for their urbanity, frankness and ease; great epicures of the table, great lovers of Madeira wine, of horses and dogs, free at jest."[2] In the mansions of the Tidewater, Virginians soon found powerful metaphors for this vanished, elegant way of life. For many of us the houses evoke the gentility of our predecessors and have become symbols of our own historical legitimacy. Just as a genealogist chooses as recognized ancestors a couple of illustrious individuals from scores of possible candidates, we dote upon and restore old houses not from an altruistic sense of what we can do for the buildings themselves, but because of what the buildings, seen through our eyes, can do for us. The need for roots, satisfied by linking ourselves with old buildings or with people of long ago, is reasonable in itself. Yet the constructions of the past that it engenders often tell more about ourselves than our forebears.

While houses are our most visible link with the past, they do not speak for themselves. Special care, therefore, needs to be taken to ensure that the meanings that we supply them—our interpretations—approximate as closely as possible the meanings they had for the individuals who built and used them. This is a particularly difficult task. Traditionally treatments of Virginia's colonial houses have been little more than superficial descriptions of individual buildings accompanied by a few allusions to specific English precedents that, we are to believe, somehow seamlessly influenced their design. Commenting on the general inutility of this approach, the French anthropologist Claude Lévi-Strauss once noted that "such studies deceive us for they teach us nothing about the conscious or unconscious processes in concrete individuals or collective experiences by means of which men who did not possess a certain institution went about acquiring it."[3] While it is obvious that the elements which comprised Virginia houses had their immediate sources in England, there was nothing automatic about their appearance on this side of the Atlantic.

To use a familiar example, no matter how long we spend trying to run down specific English precedents of the H-shaped plan of Stratford Hall, Westmoreland County, Virginia (there are many and they are easily found), we shall never get any closer to understanding why this element appeared in Virginia when it did. The answer to this question lies on this side of the Atlantic. The elements to be found in Virginia houses were the product of the architectural needs of Virginians.

If many of our notions about Virginia houses are uniquely our own, it is because we have considered the buildings apart from a wider context. Those old houses are silent because our treatments of them are inventories of unconnected details. Details, considered in isolation, are as meaningless as the isolated letters in alphabet soup. We need to recognize that every detail is part of a greater complex, that everything is meshed with everything else. In addition, we need to view the houses not as objects in themselves, but as the products of ideas in the minds of their builders, which to a large extent are shared by the members of the social group under consideration. Of course ideas about architecture are only part of a larger shared corpus of ideas that we call culture. The guiding assumption in this approach is that culture is man's unique way of parsing and making sense of a potentially infinite variety of experience. Culture imparts pattern and meaning to our basic perceptions and allows us to deal effectively with the world around us. Culture can be conceived as a complexly networked adaptive system whose components, arbitrarily divided under familiar headings like society, economy, religion, and architecture, are linked in such a way that changes in one area will produce adaptive shifts in the others. It follows that understanding houses, or anything else for that matter, requires puzzling out the relationships between a group's ideas about architecture and their ideas about the rest of the world. In fact the very existence of these relationships can allow us to learn about things other than architecture by studying old houses.[4] To take Stratford as an example once again, the essence of the enterprise is to divorce our object of study from the immediate, immaculate context in which we find it today and which is of our own making, and to attempt to connect the ideas embodied in it to the rest of the dynamic system of which they were originally a part. Since the forms that Thomas Lee used in constructing Stratford in 1730 were new to Virginia, their use was evidently prompted by rather recent developments in the colony. Getting the meaning of Stratford right entails getting at these changes and why they occurred. This problem has been one of the major foci of recent archaeological work at the Clifts Plantation site at Stratford (fig. 1). By studying architectural change at a plantation that was occupied for sixty years prior to the construction of the mansion which stands today, we hope to arrive at a better understanding of cultural change during that watershed period in Virginia's history and of the new conditions that underlay the construction of Stratford itself.

The land on which the Clifts Plantation was situated was first patented in 1651 by Nathaniel Pope, shortly after the Northern Neck was first opened to white settlement (fig. 1). Pope was one of a relatively small group of men who through connections with provincial government managed to obtain huge tracts of land in what was then a wilderness. These men and their descendants would rule Westmoreland County throughout the colonial period. Although he arrived in the New World as an illiterate yeoman, Pope was one of the richest men in Westmoreland County, a justice of the peace, and a colonel in the county militia when he died in 1660. Nathaniel Pope willed the Clifts Plantation to his son Thomas, during whose ownership it was first occupied circa 1670.

Thomas Pope seems to have divided his time between Virginia and England. Like many members of the county elite he was able to make money at both ends of the tobacco trade, growing the crop and shipping it to England and in turn shipping retail goods to Virginia for sale to his poorer neighbors. Thomas owned two tobacco farms on his twenty-four-hundred-odd acres on the Potomac. His residence was on the western edge of this property on

Figure 1. The Clifts Plantation site, Westmoreland County, Virginia, after excavation.

Pope's Creek and the Clifts Plantation was on the eastern edge. We conclude from the documentary record that during these years the Clifts was a tenancy. Yet the archaeological evidence demonstrates that the tenants were far from poor. From the beginning the Clifts had a separate servant's quarter, a feature that in the Westmoreland County probate inventories only appears in the households of individuals comprising the wealthiest 20 percent of the population during the late seventeenth century.

Thomas Pope died in 1685 and the plantation passed to his wife, Joanna, who for the rest of her days lived in Bristol, England. Tenants continued to occupy the Clifts. Shortly after 1705 her son Nathaniel and his wife Elizabeth also became involved in management of the plantation. Nathaniel apparently followed his father's pattern of close association with both ends of the tobacco trade, for we find him referred to in the Westmoreland County records as a "mariner of London." It is clear from references to his personal appearances in the county court that he was a frequent visitor in Westmoreland County. There is no concrete evidence, however, that Nathaniel lived at the Clifts.

In 1716 Nathaniel and his mother began the legal procedures necessary to transfer title of the land to Thomas Lee, a young and prominent member of another of the county's handful of ruling families. The Lees' political success extended beyond the borders of Westmoreland County to the provincial level. In 1718 Thomas Lee finally received the deed of sale for the eleven hundred acres and the buildings that comprised the Clifts Plantation, including "the manner house on the second clift." Lee, how-

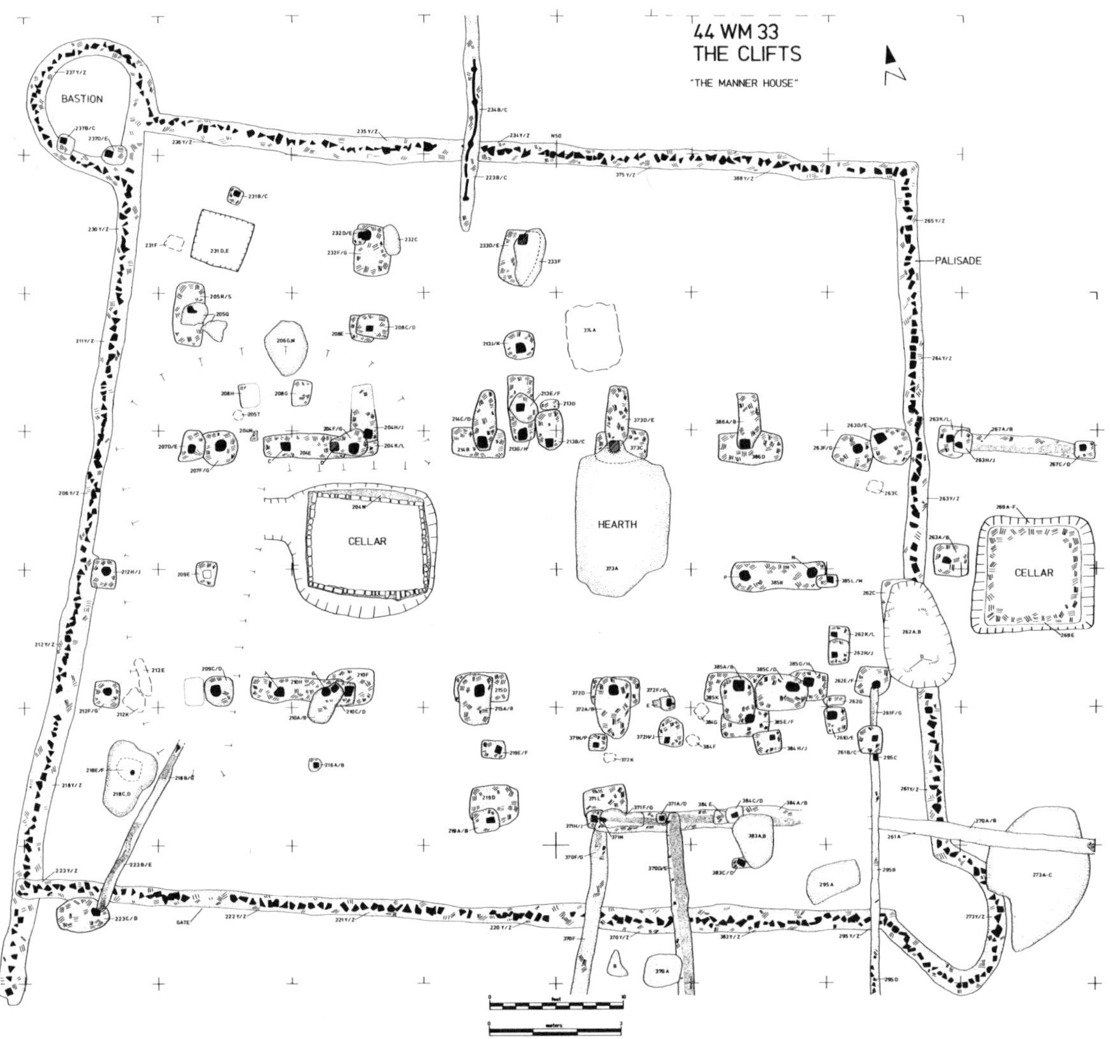

Figure 2. Archaeological plan of the "manner house" and palisade at the Clifts Plantation. The palisade was erected in 1675 in response to the depredations of the Susquehannock Indians, provoked by the English, which helped to precipitate Bacon's Rebellion. It was dismantled soon afterward.

ever, continued to live at his family seat at Machodoc, several miles down river. During this period the occupants of the Clifts seem once again to have been tenants whose means far excelled those of the majority of Virginians at that time. Lee's house at Machodoc was burned to the ground by arsonists in 1729. Sometime early in the next decade he completed construction of what to his contemporaries must have been an awesomely impressive brick mansion on the Clifts tract. The old "manner house" was torn down, because it obstructed access from the new Georgian complex to the river landing, the outlet on the commercial world around which much of the Lees' fortune was based. The Clifts tract itself thus became the core of Lee's six-thousand-acre Stratford Plantation. The Clifts Plantation and the world of which it was a part were forgotten, victims of history's selective memory of the colonial past.[5]

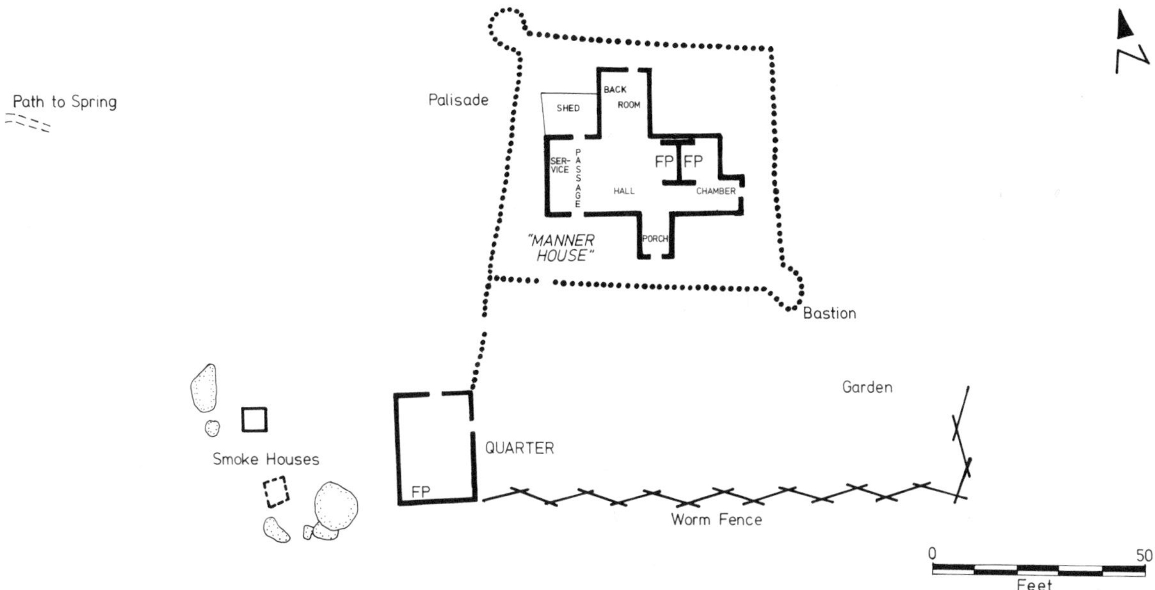

Figure 3. Schematic plan of the Clifts Plantation as it appeared ca. 1675.

Although it was referred to in 1718 as a "manner house"—an appellation suggesting that nearly fifty years after its construction it was still one of the most commodious buildings in the neighborhood—the principal dwelling at the Clifts was a surprisingly modest structure, a single-story frame house (figs. 2, 3). Its three-cell core, subsequently altered and enlarged, originally measured 18.5′ × 41′. Its walls and roof were probably covered with clapboards, which were given a coating of watery tar to provide a degree of weatherproofing.[6] At least a portion of its interior was plastered, typical of the houses of better-off Virginians during the period. In 1687 a visitor observed: "Some people in this country are comfortably housed; The farmers' houses are built entirely of wood, the roofs being made of small boards of chesnut as are the walls. Those who have some means cover them inside with a coating of mortar in which they use oyster shells for lime."[7]

The description of Virginians' houses as built "entirely of wood" was not exaggerated. The only brick employed in the "manner house" and on the entire site was that used to line a root cellar installed beneath the building about 1725, near the end of its existence. In lieu of masonry foundations the walls of the "manner house" were framed around vertical wooden posts, roughly nine inches square and set at ten-foot intervals. These were seated in large, flat-bottomed post holes dug originally to a depth of about three feet below grade. A central hearth heated the two principal rooms of the core, the hall and the chamber, and was comprised of ferrous sandstone rubble (bog iron) set in clay to form a low platform on which the fire burned. A firehood or canopy of wattle-and-daub channeled the smoke up through the roof and out of the house.

If the "manner house" was an unusually fine building for its day, the other domestic structure that also dates to the initial occupation of the Clifts may have been more representative of the accommodations of ordinary seventeenth-century Virginia planters. Measuring 18.5′ × 25′, the early servants' quarter, like the "manner house," was framed around hole-set posts (figs. 3, 4). Again tarred clapboards probably served as exterior covering. The interior of the quarter was not plastered, and it may well have been entirely unfinished. A small pit dug into the ground in the west gable end may have

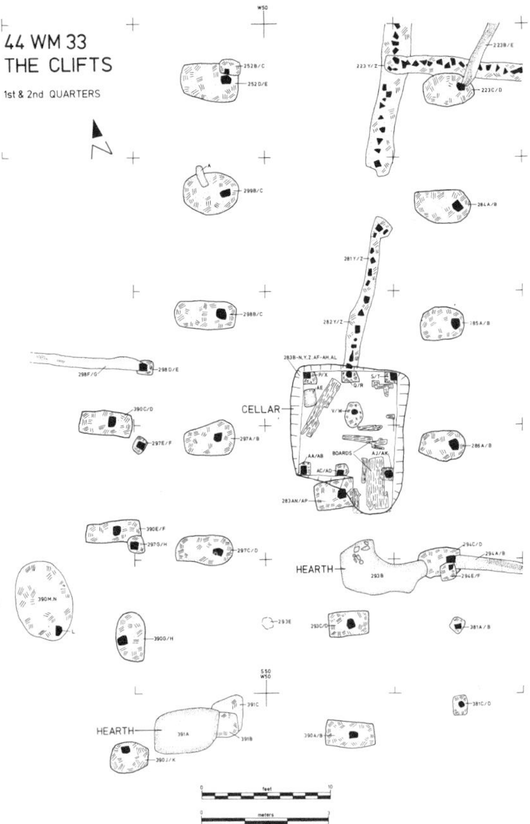

Figure 4. Archaeological plan of the early and later servants' quarters at the Clifts Plantation.

heated the building. The absence in the pit of daub from a firehood indicates that smoke simply floated into the roof where it trickled out a hole in the peak of the gable. The servants and slaves who lived in this building had at least this in common with most medieval Englishmen and Chaucer's widow in particular: "Full sooty was hir bour, and eek her halle, / In which she eet ful many a sclendere meel."[8]

The structure that replaced the early servants' quarter about 1685 was slightly more elaborate (figs. 4, 5). A two-cell, 19′ × 36′ building, it had an exterior chimney on its western gable end. The stack was comprised of a wood frame, covered with lath and plastered with mud. It stood over a hearth of bog iron laid in clay, as in the "manner house." Like its predecessor, the later quarter was not plastered. It too was framed around regularly spaced posts set in the ground. Unlike the "manner house," neither quarter had a tight floor.

It is not difficult to see even from this brief description that the architectural technology employed at the Clifts differed vastly from that used in the eighteenth century by members of the provincial elite, including Thomas Lee at Stratford, or for that matter by members of the county elites in less pretentious surviving houses scattered across the Tidewater. Perhaps the most intriguing difference lies in the fact that the vertical framing members of all the domestic buildings at the Clifts were set in the ground and not on sills resting on a brick foundation. In this the houses at the Clifts were not unique. If nothing else, the past decade of archaeological work on seventeenth-century domestic sites in Virginia has demonstrated that *post building* (a term that subsumes several distinct technologies) was employed even by wealthy individuals in the colony during that period.

Examples of post building are not hard to find. In Westmoreland County, excavations at the sites of two prosperous seventeenth-century plantations have revealed dwellings of post construction. The house at the Hallowes site at Currioman was a three-cell post building with an axial chimney. It was apparently the residence of Restitute Whistone, whose marriage in 1674 to Matthew Steel caused something of a scandal in the county. Rev. John Waugh, who was officially responsible for the misalliance, was fined the hefty sum of ten thousand pounds of tobacco by the county court because he had married an heiress "to a person of no estate."[9] While no doubt deemed unfortunate by contemporaries, the incident provides a good indication of their appraisal of Restitute Whistone's social position. The house of John Washington on Bridges Creek was a two-cell post building with an exterior end chimney.[10] Before his death in 1677, Washington, the founder of one of the county's leading gentry families, was a justice of the peace, lieutenant colonel in the militia, and member of the House

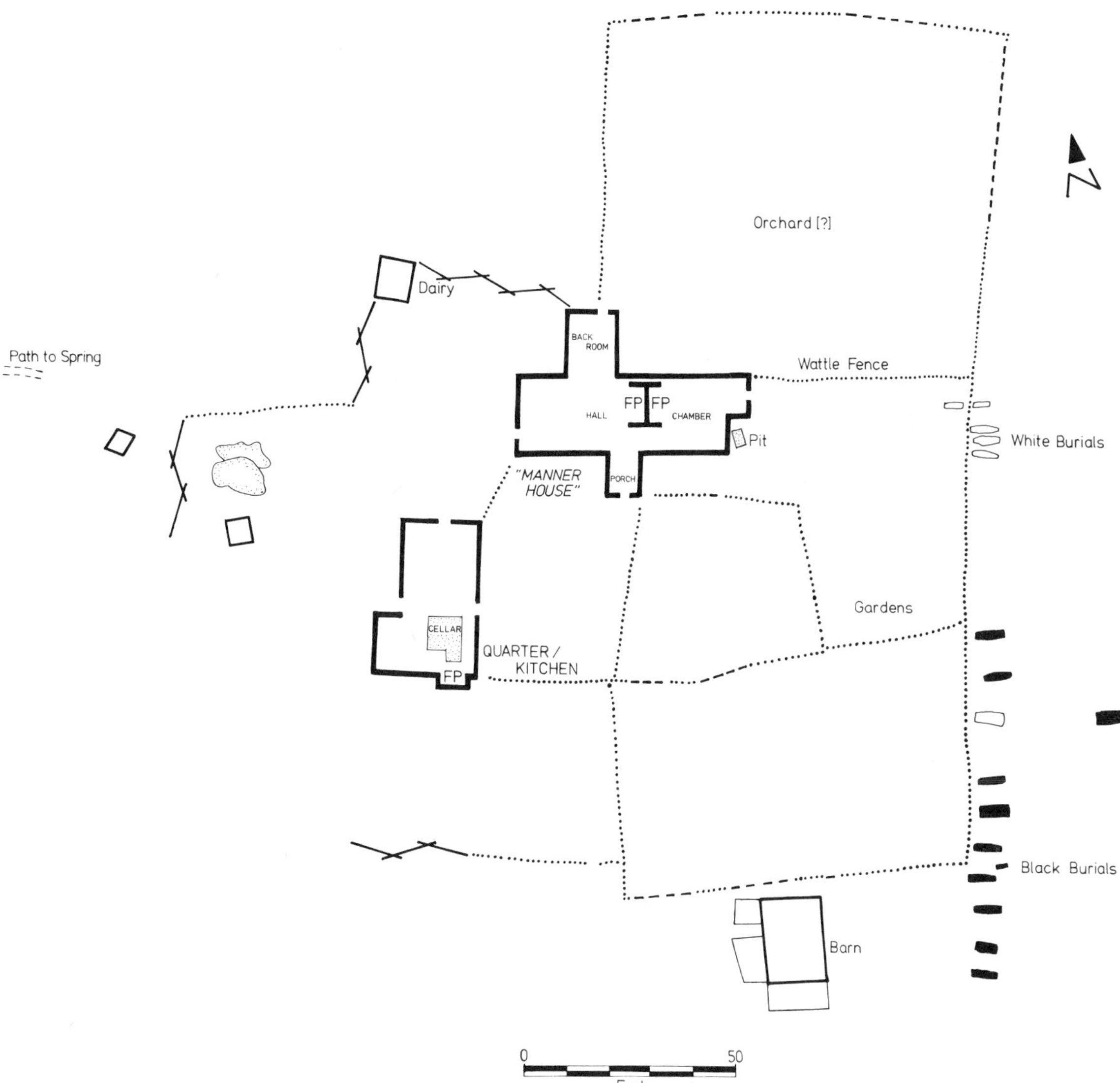

Figure 5. Schematic plan of the Clifts Plantation as it appeared ca. 1710.

of Burgesses.[11] If post construction was to be found in the houses of seventeenth-century Westmoreland's upper crust, it was equally prevalent in the dwellings of some of the richest and most powerful men in the colony. Col. Thomas Pettus, a member of the Governor's Council and a vestryman in Harrop Parish in James City who patented large tracts of land throughout the colony before his death in 1669, lived in a post house on the James River at Kingsmill very similar to the building at the Hallowes site.[12] A bit further up river, just outside Jamestown, a dwelling of the same sort has proved to have been the residence of William Drummond, an early favorite of Governor Berkeley and onetime governor of North Carolina, whose initiatives on the wrong side during Bacon's Rebellion resulted in his execution.[13] The paucity of extant seventeenth-century houses in Virginia underscores the fact that post construction was not only used by Virginians of all ranks, but employed almost to the exclusion of other methods.

This reliance on post building technology seems to have been unique to the Chesapeake area. Today only two seventeenth-century houses survive in Virginia, yet there are hundreds in New England and thousands in England.[14] Apparently Virginia building practices were sharply at odds with those in the other two areas. The reason for the striking discrepancies in the number of surviving houses is not hard to uncover. In post building Virginians had selected a technology whose products could not survive nearly three hundred years of exposure to the ravages of rot and termites. At the same time, men in England and New England were often building houses with masonry foundations, which were considerably more resistant in this respect. In fact, in the sixteenth and seventeenth centuries, many areas of England had witnessed campaigns of building in which for the first time a substantial number of yeomen and husbandmen, farmers of the "middling sort," were able to erect houses substantial enough to survive to the present.[15] While post houses were undoubtedly built in the seventeenth century in England and her northern American colonies, only in the Chesapeake were they erected in significant numbers by members of the gentry.

The overwhelming prevalence of post building, unique to the seventeenth-century Chesapeake, wants an explanation. But before we can proceed in that direction, we need to distinguish several varieties of post technology employed in colonial Virginia in different contexts. Two major categories can be recognized at the outset: puncheon construction and post-in-the-ground construction. The second of these can be further divided into three distinct subtypes: ground-to-plate, interrupted-sill, and block construction. While these distinctions may at first seem trifling and pedantic, they are absolutely essential if we are to fully understand the phenomenon at hand.

The most primitive form of building that involved placing vertical posts in the ground was puncheon construction. Lacking a regular structural skeleton of principal posts jointed together, the walls of puncheon buildings were simply comprised of "punches" or vertical members of slight dimension set closely together in the ground. The carcass of the house thus resembled a palisade more than it did carpenter's work. There were obviously no sills and quite possibly no plate. Horizontal stiffening was provided by the exterior covering of boards nailed to the outside of the punches. The remains of hovels of this kind have been excavated recently along the James River at the Maine site on the Governor's Land and at the Littletown Quarter site at Kingsmill. The houses there are typically single-cell structures. Their wall lines are defined by rather carelessly dug, shallow post holes, closely and somewhat irregularly spaced on roughly two-foot intervals. Both sites apparently date to the Virginia Company period (before 1626).[16]

Post-in-the-ground construction has also been identified on sites dating to the earliest decades of settlement, but unlike puncheon construction it is found on later seventeenth-century sites as well. Buildings of post-in-the-ground construction, of which the houses at the Clifts are typical, are archaeologically defined by sets of regularly shaped post holes that display vertical side walls and flat bottoms. These holes were prepared with more care than those associated with puncheon buildings. The vertical posts that the holes contained were set at regular bay intervals, ten feet being a commonly used module. Such characteristics are the natural result of the use of a regular skeletal frame of some sort, comprised in some cases of precut and preassembled units. Unfortunately for the archaeologist, there are a number of different types of framing systems that are compatible with such regular post holes. Three subtypes of post-in-the-ground construction can be distinguished: ground-to-plate post construction in which the wall frame is comprised of vertical posts whose bottoms rest in the ground and whose tops are joined to a horizontal member (a plate or tie beam), but which lack any sill; interrupted-sill post construction in which the frame is again comprised of posts running from ground to plate or tie beam but in which sills are mortised between the posts; and block construction in which the carcass of the building is a standard box frame (that is, one possessing continuous sills on which sit principal posts which in turn carry the plate) set off the ground on top of hole-set posts or blocks.

Puncheon construction and post-in-the-ground construction are readily distinguishable utilizing archaeological evidence alone. A cursory review of that evidence quickly establishes the fact that all the seventeenth-century post houses excavated to date in Virginia, save those at the Maine and Littletown Quarter sites, were of post-in-the-ground construction. However, the archaeological data do not allow the identification of the type of post-in-the-ground construction employed in the great majority of cases. The difficulties encountered in determining which kind of frame rested over the regularly spaced post holes at various sites are particularly troublesome if we are interested in understanding the factors that lay behind post-in-the-ground construction's popularity in the Chesapeake. Obviously we need to know which of the three kinds of post-in-the-ground technology was most widely used during the period and how the types were both temporally and conceptually related. Although the evidence is all too meager, some tentative answers to these questions can be framed utilizing a combination of archaeological and documentary sources.

On a handful of sites the evidence from the ground indicates that the houses were of ground-to-plate construction. Excavations at Kingsmill Tenement, a site on the James River just east of Williamsburg occupied in the second quarter of the seventeenth century, revealed a complex of three major domestic structures. One of them, measuring roughly 20′ × 50′, was framed around hole-set principal posts set at ten-foot intervals. Between each pair of posts in the side walls were found the remains of three studs driven into the ground.[17] If interrupted-sill or block construction had been employed, the studs would have been mortised into sills. Since the studs extended into the ground, the building apparently lacked sills of any sort. Ground-to-plate construction is therefore indicated. A slightly smaller building with the same characteristics has been excavated recently on the south side of the James River at Flowerdew Hundred.[18] The associated complex probably dates to the second decade of English settlement. At the Clifts, although the evidence is slightly less conclusive, the fact that the pairs of door posts which framed two entrances to the "manner house" were set into the ground seems to indicate ground-to-plate construction for similar reasons. Taken together, these archaeological data suggest that ground-to-plate construction appeared in Virginia with the first settlers and continued to be employed at least until the last quarter of the seventeenth century. However, unlike the Kingsmill and Flowerdew structures, post-in-the-ground buildings excavated at other seventeenth-century sites lack the evidence of stud impressions that alone conclusively indicates ground-to-plate construction. This state of affairs could be an indication that the buildings on these sites had sills, either interrupted or continuous. It could also mean that, while the buildings were of ground-to-plate construction, their studs were simply not seated deep enough in the ground for their impressions to have survived several hundred years of plowing. From this perspective, it may not be accidental that the two excavated houses for which stud impressions survive are of such an early date. As they became more familiar with the technology, Virginians may have abandoned the practice of seating the studs so deeply in the ground as structurally unnecessary in ordinary situations (see below).

Data for the other two kinds of post-in-the-ground technology are certainly no better. The use of interrupted-sill construction in the Chesapeake is known from a single example: Cedar Park, an extant house in Anne Arundel County, Maryland. Probably erected in the last decade of the seventeenth century, Cedar Park was originally a two-cell house with end chimneys. It is the only known surviving post house. Its walls were carried on hole-set posts spaced on approximate ten-foot centers. Interrupted sills were carefully mortised between each pair of posts and the wall studs were in turn mortised into the sills. Roughly in the middle of the eighteenth century the house was encased and underpinned with brick, an improvement that was responsible for its survival today.

Although it is quite possible that block construction was employed in the Chesapeake at least by the end of the seventeenth century, the only evidence for it comes from eighteenth-century sources. To date only one excavated dwelling can convincingly be demonstrated to have been built in this manner, the house of Capt. John Hicks in St. Mary's City, Maryland. Hicks was a wealthy merchant who arrived in St. Mary's in 1723. The building in question, a 16′ × 40′ structure with end chimneys of brick, was built not long after. The excavation revealed that the bottoms of the posts which had originally supported it had been set in the ground at substantially different depths, a strong indication that immediately after the holes were filled the upper ends of the posts protruded unevenly from the ground. Only then were they sawn level to accept a continuous sill on which the remainder of the building was framed.[19] In this respect, Hick's house was not unique. Earlier in the century, the same kind of post-in-the-ground technology was being employed in Gloucester County, Virginia. In 1704 the vestry of Petsworth Parish contracted the construction of a new glebe house "to be framed on good white oak sills and to stand upon blocks."[20]

Houses on blocks apparently continued to be built, at least in the lower margins of society, into the late eighteenth century. In 1784 an English traveler, J. F. D. Smyth, was forced to spend the night in one, along with the six slaves and their overseer who inhabited it. He wrote that it was a "miserable shell . . . which as it stood on blocks about a foot off the ground, the hogs lay constantly under the floor, which made it swarm with flies."[21]

Reviewing this scanty evidence we can tentatively conclude that puncheon construction was confined to the earliest period of settlement, that ground-to-plate construction was employed throughout the century, and that both interrupted-sill and block construction appeared on the scene with the approach of the eighteenth century. It would therefore seem that, on temporal considerations alone, ground-to-plate construction was the reigning post construction method in seventeenth-century Virginia, at least after initial settlement. Since the vast majority of houses in the Chesapeake at all social levels were post buildings, it also appears to have been the dominant architectural technology in the region. While quantitative evidence in support of this hypothesis is certainly desirable, the data currently available cannot provide it. Fortunately, some corroboration is forthcoming from a different avenue of approach: the examination of the way in which the colonists themselves perceived and categorized their architecture.

Chesapeake colonists were apparently quite aware that their houses were typically different from English farm houses and occasionally this perception was recorded, expressed in phrases like "Virginia style" and "Virginia house."[22] For example, writing to an English friend in 1687, William Fitzhugh contrasted two kinds of building: an "ordinary Virginia house" on the one hand and an "English framed house" on the other.[23] This way of looking at things was not unique to Fitzhugh. Similar terminology appears in a 1692 civil suit between two carpenters, William Barker and Thomas Dutton, in Charles County, Maryland. Barker and Dutton had entered a partnership and agreed to split the profits from their carpenter's work "except in framed or English built houses only." They worked together for three months and earned eighty-seven hundred pounds of tobacco, a sum that by the terms of the contract was to be divided equally between them since there was "noe framed nor English built worke by the sd. parties done" during that period. Barker claimed he had not received his fair share.[24]

Both Fitzhugh and the Maryland carpenters were using terms that are no longer a part of our language. If we are to penetrate that code, a word about meaning in general is in order. Human beings use linguistic categories derived from their culture to cut up a vast and continuous reality into recognizable objects and to relate these objects to one another in meaningful ways. Since meaning may be found in the relationships that we construct and perceive between objects, it is natural that the categories we use in dealing with the world around us and the symbols we use to represent them very often come in contrasting or opposing pairs.[25] In our own experience, the color opposition red-green has a very definite meaning when the terms are contrasted in the proper context at a traffic light. The color opposition is homologous to a linguistic one: stop-go. The terms on the same side of the two pairs signify the same thing. Fitzhugh's use of the terms *Virginia house* and *English house* is an opposition of just this sort. Fortunately, we find in both Fitzhugh's and the Maryland carpenter's categorizations one term of what looks very much like a second pair of terms homologous to the first. In both sources the term *framed* is paired with the term *English.* In fact, in the Maryland case the equation is explicit ("framed *or* English built"). We find ourselves then with a pair of homologous oppositions: Virginia house–English house and unframed-framed. Just as for us today, red means stop and green means go, for seventeenth-century Virginians, Virginia house meant unframed and English house meant framed. However, as we have seen, all three types of post-in-the-ground construction involve a regular skeletal frame of some sort. For Fitzhugh and the Maryland carpenters, then, the distinction was apparently based on their perception that Virginia-style houses lacked something that to their way of thinking made the skeleton of a house a *true* frame.

Interestingly enough, the Virginia House of Burgesses seems to have recognized a deficiency of a similar sort earlier in the century. In 1647 the Burgesses, realizing that "much damage hath arisen to the several sherriffs . . . for want of interpretation of what shall be accompted a sufficient prison," decreed that prisons were to be considered sufficient even if they were "built according to the form of Virginia houses."[26] Some people evidently felt the Virginia way of building was not suited for this rather specialized purpose. Prisons are, of course, designed to keep people from getting out. Even though the Burgesses decided that Virginia-style building could do the job, there seems initially to have been doubt. The inference is that there was something about Virginia building that made it appear less secure than other (that is, English) varieties.

A clue as to just what the deficiency might have been is to be found in a 1692 court order issued in Stafford County for the construction of a prison, presumably one built in the manner that the House of Burgesses "accompted sufficient" in 1647. Capt. George Mason, the county sheriff, was ordered to erect a prison "of twelve foot square Eight foot Pitch with Locust posts Twelve Inches Square Studded with Locust Stoods three foot in the ground . . . with a good Plank doore of Two inch Plank with a good and substantial lock and key. One window with three Iron Barrs made very strong. . . ."[27] The fact that the wall studs extended into the ground precludes the possibility of a sill of any sort. In fact, it seems very likely that the lack of a sill was precisely the characteristic that had caused the suitability of "the forme of Virginia houses" for prisons to be called into question earlier in the century. With no sill into which a tight floor could be framed, Virginia style prisons were not as escape-proof as they might otherwise have been. It was precisely this defect that a portion of the Stafford specifications was designed to correct. Even the most industrious prisoners would have had a hard time digging under studs whose ends were buried three feet in the earth.

Thus when Fitzhugh wrote about an "ordinary Virginia house" and the Burgesses enacted legislation dealing with "the forme of Virginia houses," they were alluding to Virginians' wholehearted acceptance of ground-to-plate construction and its pervasiveness in the colony (and in Maryland). The frames of houses built in this manner lacked sills, a feature that distinguished them both from the other two kinds of post-in-the-ground technology as well as standard English framing methods which rely on masonry foundations. However, one might also be tempted to argue that the term *Virginia house* referred to any dwelling in which hole-set posts were used, that the phrase actually denoted all three kinds of post-in-the-ground construction. But this hypothesis does not square with the explicit equation of "framed" with "English built" and the implied equation of "unframed" with "Virginia built." A frame with interrupted sills was still a complete frame even if its principal posts sat in the ground in Virginia and not on a masonry foundation in the Vale of York across the Atlantic. Similarly, a box frame was no less a true frame for being supported by wooden blocks or pilings set in Tidewater clay and not by a masonry foundation in Essex.

A final possible objection to this interpretation needs to be addressed. It might be argued that if ground-to-plate construction (without sills) had been the norm in the seventeenth century, one would expect eighteenth-century Virginia carpentry to be characterized by arch bracing in which the braces that provide lateral stability run diagonally from the posts up to the plate. However, the wall frames of nearly all extant eighteenth-century (box-frame) houses in Virginia are tension braced. That is, the braces run from the posts down to the sills. It is proposed that the prevalence of this form of bracing in the eighteenth century must have had its origins in seventeenth-century Virginia carpentry. The inference is that there must have been a strong and widespread tradition of post-in-the-ground construction involving sills to which the bottoms of tension braces were attached in the earlier period.

The (incorrect) assumption on which this line of reasoning is based is that ground-to-plate post buildings had to have angle bracing. Angle bracing is structurally essential only to certain kinds of framed construction. From an evolutionary perspective, it is only when all timberwork is removed from the ground that some sort of stiffening becomes desirable.[28] Before that stage is reached, the requisite lateral stability is provided by the depth of the holes in which the principal posts are seated. In the Chesapeake the nearly universal use of riven clapboards for wall covering provided additional rigidity. It is therefore likely that angle bracing became prevalent in Virginia only when a substantial number of box-frame buildings began to be built in the early eighteenth century. When their buildings first required bracing, Virginians may have chosen tension bracing over arch bracing because, like a post hole, it provided stability at the lower end of the post, or because they thought it appropriate to join this novelty, the diagonal brace, to another novelty, the sill.

What then are we to make of the pervasiveness of ground-to-plate post construction in the Chesapeake throughout the seventeenth century? Several avenues of approach are available but none by itself is satisfactory. The first of these takes the fact that post buildings were impermanent as its point of departure. The suggestion is, in Edmund Morgan's words, that "permanent buildings were some how inappropriate" in a Virginia context because "permanent buildings were for permanent places like England."[29] From this perspective seventeenth-century Virginia is seem as a place of short sojourning from which even its wealthiest inhabitants, having made a killing in tobacco, hoped to escape. Given this expectation, there was little point in erecting substantial houses. Virginians built as cheaply as they could, looking to the day they would be able to return to England. This argument may indeed adequately describe an important aspect of life in the Chesapeake during the first few decades of settlement. In 1626 the Council admitted as much: Virginians looked only for "a present cropp and their hastie retourne."[30] Thus the argument may go a long way toward explaining the prevalence of puncheon construction during this early period. Puncheon buildings were impermanent by almost anybody's standards. In 1626 the Virginia Company's tenants at the Governor's Land petitioned that they be allowed to vacate their holdings because of the "badness of their utterly decayed houses."[31] At the time less than a decade had passed since their construction.

Nevertheless, the adequacy of this portrayal of Virginians' attitudes toward life in the colony during the rest of the century and thus its utility as an explanation of post building in general is questionable. If nothing else, the political machinations of the local elite in the 1630s, which resulted in the "thrusting out" of Governor Harvey, evidence a certain commitment to residence in the colony on the part of the instigators. Similarly, however else we may choose to interpret their actions, the participants in Bacon's Rebellion thought enough of residence in the colony to risk at the very least place and purse. William Drummond's attachment to Virginia and his attempt, by siding with Bacon, to obtain a larger share of social and political clout lost him his life. Yet Drummond lived in a post-in-the-ground building.

The second problem with this interpretation lies in the notion of architectural impermanence on which it is based. Certainly the post-in-the-ground buildings that were built across the Chesapeake in the seventeenth century were impermanent in the sense that, with one exception, none of them survives today. But is this idea of impermanence meaningful in a cultural context? While the "miserable paillisadoed cottages" of the early settlers indeed seemed impermanent to contemporaries, can the same be said for a post-in-the-ground building like the "manner house" at the Clifts? The "manner house" stood for almost three generations, as did Pettus's and Drummond's houses on the James River. One wonders whether the majority of tract houses that spring up around us today will fare as well, yet certainly their owners would not consider them impermanent. In calling post buildings impermanent, we are applying standards that seem inappropriate even for our own stable culture. How appropriate can they be when applied to seventeenth-century Virginia? The argument then, at least in its application to most of the period under consideration, falls down on two counts, for neither seventeenth-century Virginians' ideas about residence in the colony nor their post houses were so temporary.

The second perspective on the post building phenomenon is an economic one. The seventeenth-century Chesapeake, like all frontiers, suffered a chronic shortage of labor, which in this case was exacerbated by a labor-intensive staple economy. The more laborers a planter possessed, the more tobacco he could produce. Larger crops produced more profits, which in turn allowed the purchase of more labor. In such a situation servants were in great demand. Planters "rushed to stake out claims on men, stole them, lured them, and bought and sold them, bidding the prices to four, five and six times the initial cost."[32] Labor was, therefore, expensive, a state of affairs that affected, among other things, building costs. William Fitzhugh perceptively detailed the result in a letter to an English friend contemplating establishing a plantation in Virginia:

> [I] should not advise to build either a great or English framed house, for labor is so intolerably dear, & workmen so idle and negligent that the building of a good house, to you there will seem unsupportable, for this I can assure you when I built my own house & agreed as cheap as I could with workmen & as diligently took care that they followed their work notwithstanding we have timber for nothing, but felling and getting in place, the frame of my house stood me in more money in Tobo @ 8 sh p Cent than a frame of the same dimensions would cost in London, by a third at least where everything is bought, & near three times as long preparing.
>
> Your brother Joseph's building that Shell of a house without chimneys or partition, & not one tittle of workmanship about it more than a Tobacco house work, carry'd him into those arrears with your self, & his other Employers as you found by his Accots. at his death.[33]

Note that Fitzhugh complains that it was the frame of his house that cost him so much money and time. It was precisely this problem for which ground-to-plate construction provided a partial remedy. With no sills of any sort, there were fewer timbers to dress and fewer joints to cut.[34]

From this same perspective, early Virginians' fondness for "Welsh" or wooden chimneys also becomes understandable. A surprising number of excavated houses that once belonged to members of the gentry had chimneys of wood plastered with mud, occasionally set on the slightest of brick footings (the Hallowes and Washington sites in Westmoreland County are examples). If the cost of labor made carpentry expensive, the same was true of brick masonry.

Thus several aspects of Chesapeake architectural technology can rightly be read as a response to prevailing economic conditions. But economic problems were only a necessary condition for these architectural developments. They were not in themselves sufficient. Unfortunately, this important point is often ignored and it is argued that economic constraints *forced* Virginians to build post houses and that only when these constraints were loosened, that is, when the problem of labor shortage was solved by the massive importation of black slaves, were Virginians finally able to build houses with brick foundations. But it is difficult to believe that the richest gentlemen in the entire colony, men like Col. Thomas Pettus and William Drummond, built post-in-the-ground houses because they could not afford bricks or sills. The problem with this part of the argument lies in its ethnocentric and uniformitarian assumptions, implicit in much historiography, about people's ideas and aspirations. Taking their own expectations as a point of departure, proponents of this view assume that individuals in other cultural contexts will want to behave in a manner acceptable to them. If they fail to do so, some force beyond their control must constrain them. We are here being asked to believe that the things we value, our standards, architectural or otherwise, are necessarily things of importance to people in other eras or places. As a rather homely counterexample, consider the great popularity that four-wheel-drive pickup trucks currently enjoy in rural America. On noting their absence on the streets of New York City, it would be foolish indeed to conclude that no New Yorkers could afford them. If ideas about desirable means of transportation differ in rural and urban areas of the United States, it should hardly be surprising that ideas about desirable building technologies differ over three centuries.

The architectural standards of the seventeenth-century Chesapeake gentry were from our jaundiced perspective rather modest, as the following 1653 building contract suggests:

> I Thomas Wilford of the County of Northumberland Gent. for a valuable consideration received of Paul Sympson Gent. . . . [agree] when nails and a Carpenter can be had to build him a fifteen foot house Square with a welsh chimney, the house to be floored and lofted with Deale boards, and lined with Riven Boards on the inside with a handsome Joined Bedstead, one small joined table and six joined stools and three wainscot chaires, and to furnish the said room with bedding curtaines and ballance chamber linnen and all things fitting and convenient. . . .[35]

As befitted the social standing of Paul Sympson, Gentleman, his house was to be handsomely furnished. But the building itself was to measure only fifteen feet square, have a wooden chimney, and be finished inside not with "wainscot" paneling, as were his chairs, nor even plaster, but with split clapboards. Elaborate architectural technology was simply not a matter of importance for Sympson and his peers.

The essential consideration without which the economic argument falls flat is that the way people respond to a new situation is conditioned not only by the nature of the immediate situation but by the rest of their experience. It is only when seventeenth-century Virginians' attitude toward architectural technology in general is explicitly acknowledged that their acceptance of ground-to-plate post construction as a solution to a particular problem becomes understandable.

With the acceptance of ground-to-plate construction, the idea of using hole-set posts to support a house frame entered the domestic architectural repertoire and became fair game for experimentation. By the end of the century, Virginians were naturally taking advantage of this situation. By incorporating the idea of hole-set posts with the English systems of box and interrupted-sill framing, which in an English context were associated with masonry foundations, Virginians were able to "invent" two additional technological forms: block and interrupted-sill post construction. As the meager dating evidence suggests, these two variants of post-in-the-ground technology are best seen as conceptual derivatives of ground-to-plate construction. With the dawn of the eighteenth century, as Cedar Park and the Petsworth Parish glebe house attest, the Chesapeake gentry had at their disposal post-in-the-ground technologies that involved the use of sills. Considered as a related whole, the three post-in-the-ground construction methods made post building a genre that was adaptable to a wide variety of needs and circumstances. Yet by the second quarter of the eighteenth century, wealthy colonists in the Chesapeake had for the most part given it up.[36]

The reasons for the sudden and nearly universal rejection in a domestic context of a form that had been accepted so widely and for so long require examination. Clearly the lack of sills, which had made post building attractive in the first place, was not what the gentry found objectionable. The problem with post building lay elsewhere. Foundations, walls, and chimneys of brick replaced those of wood in the houses of the rich. The change did not go unobserved by contemporaries. Robert Beverley noted in 1705, "The private buildings are of late very much improved; several Gentlemen of late having built themselves large Brick Houses."[37] As Beverley implied, in the early eighteenth century brick was a rarity even in gentry houses because of the vagaries of Virginia's environment, her economy, and the architectural attitudes of her residents. When these attitudes began to change, when gentlemen became interested in displaying their social eminence before the world at large, brick became a handy tool to that end, a tool that was all the more valuable because of its previously infrequent employment. Post building survived in the upper reaches of Virginia society only as long as gentlemen felt little need to distinguish themselves physically from their neighbors.

The social developments that underlay this shift in attitude are complex and not fully understood, yet they need to be dealt with if we are to appreciate the experience of our colonial forebears in general and a house like Stratford in particular. The change appears to have involved a dramatic restructuring on the basis of social relations, of the way in which men ordered and conducted their dealings with one another on a day-to-day basis. In historian Peter Laslett's phrase, it separates us today from "the world we have lost."[38] Some insight into the problem can be had from a brief consideration of changes that occurred in the plan of the "manner house" and in the spatial configuration of the Clifts during its sixty-year occupation.

The "manner house" began life about 1670 with what is known as a cross-passage plan, a form universal in England at the farm house level during the late medieval period (figs. 2, 3). The plan is characterized by a narrow passage running through one end of the house, perpendicular to the axis of the ridge, and separating a small service room on one side from a hall and chamber beyond it on the other. The passage, which opened directly into the hall, and the resulting disposition of architectural space allowed the hall to function in a myriad of ways as the base of agricultural operations for the planter and his laborers and as the common center of the house where the plantation's occupants spent most of their time indoors.[39] The impression that the house was the center of farmwork is reinforced by the existence of an open work shed tacked onto the side of the building during the early period. The cross-passage plan thus seems to have been well-suited to social situations in which the relations between its users could be described in John Norden's phrase as "knit [with] . . . a knot of collateral amytie," in which masters and men saw themselves as part of the same corporate community, a society characterized by coherently defined social roles upheld by mutually felt rights and responsibilities.[40]

Englishmen brought this organic conception of society to the Chesapeake where they attempted to reproduce in a frontier context both the idea and the forms that went with it. They were not entirely successful in the beginning, and ultimately, of course, they failed. Their community was a new one, lacking the old elites and old buildings of England. Separated from king, nobles, and gentry, their society was bound to have been less stable.[41] Yet this does seem to be the model of society that informed many of their dealings with one another during most of the seventeenth century. Thus early Virginians would have assented to John Norden's question, posed in 1607, "Is not every manor a little commonwealth whereof the tenants are the members, the land the body and the lord the head?"[42] Initially, white indentured servants and black slaves were integrated into the old order. We find some documentary confirmation for this suggestion in depositions taken in county court during the period. These indicate that life was shared by masters and men to a far greater extent than our own predilections, or those of the eighteenth century, might lead us to expect. John Birt, a servant to John Washington, swore the following in Westmoreland Court in 1659:

> Being at Mr. Thomas Blagg's House he was stripping off tobacco with Mr. Blagg and his servants and about noon they all went to dinner and after they had all dined Mr. Blagg and Edward Pickery and myself [went] . . . down to ye tobacco house and Mr. Blagg told us that Mr. Hutt's Tarrs had marked and received two hogsheads of Tobacco there and ye said Blagg said I have some ground leaves and I will pull out some good tobacco and put in ye ground leaves in ye room for thay have cozened me in ye salt and I will cozen them in their tobacco.[43]

The important insight to glean here is not that seventeenth-century Westmoreland County gentlemen stole from one another, but that Mr. Blagg and his servants all worked and ate dinner together. A comparable situation is depicted in a 1681 deposition from York County: "It happened that Mcarty and Burley came down the next day to speak with Mrs. Vaulx into the parlour and being there a drinking the Negroe Frank inveigles Peter Wells to go to them to pick a quarrel."[44] Once again the point is not that laborers were fond of fighting, but that a black slave might be found in the parlor socializing with his mistress. Servants and slaves were apparently a part of that old community.

As the argument here implies, cross-passage houses were far more common in the seventeenth-century Virginia than the small and somewhat biased sample of excavated structures might by itself suggest. Ivor Noël Hume has recently excavated a post house whose internal arrangement looks very similar to that of the "manner house" at the Clifts.[45] It is located on an important site at Carter's Grove dating from the second quarter of the seventeenth century, where the artifactual evidence indicates that its residents were of considerable means. Rev. John Clayton, in a letter to the Royal Society describing the weather in Virginia, implied in 1688 that such houses were commonplace: "These things are remarkable; that it generally breaks in at the Gavel End of Houses, and often kills persons in or near the Chimneys Range, darting most fiercely down the Funnel of the Chimney; more especially if there be a Fire, (I speak here confusedly of Thunder and Lightning). . . . It is dangerous when it thunders standing in a narrow Passage, where there's a thorough Passage, or in a room between two Windows."[46] Apparently then the old ideas about relations between masters and men were prevalent in the upper reaches of Virginia society not long after initial settlement. That they persisted into the last quarter of the seventeenth century is suggested both by the "manner house" at the Clifts and by Clayton's account. The facility of access to a shared hall that the cross passage provided remained unobjectionable to wealthy Virginians as long as clearly defined and mutually upheld role categories implicitly structured the course of social interaction. By the late seventeenth century, however, the days were numbered in which Virginians of different ranks could share important aspects of their lives with one another.

Roughly a decade or two after construction of the "manner house," the cross passage at the Clifts was blocked up and henceforth the main entry to the house was through the porch situated opposite the

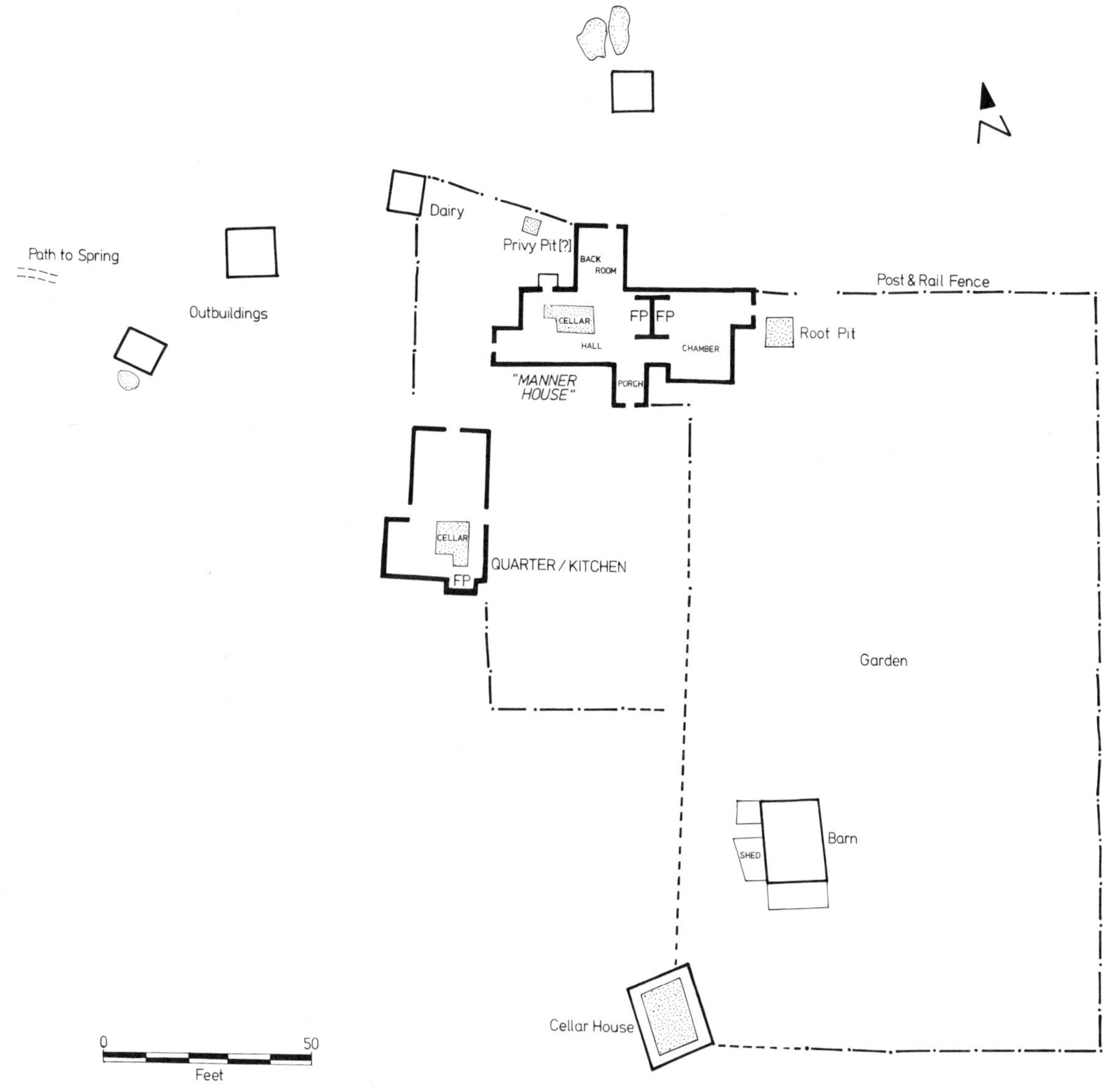

Figure 6. Schematic plan of the Clifts Plantation as it appeared ca. 1725.

hearth. Thus the house achieved the lobby entrance plan it was to retain until its destruction circa 1730. The blocking of the passage can be read as an attempt to exclude what was newly perceived as an increasingly threatening mass of laborers from the house, to preclude common usage of the hall by masters and men. Other manifestations of this trend can be discerned in architectural change at the Clifts. The work shed that had stood against the house was torn off and not replaced. In addition, the distributions of different kinds of ceramics across the site in the later phases of occupation indicate that the later quarter, erected circa 1700, was also used as a kitchen. The large hearth and the storage cellar beneath the new building seem to support this conclusion (figs. 4, 5, 6). The ceramic distributions also suggest that a small outbuilding west of the "manner house" was being used as a dairy. By the beginning of the eighteenth century, these service-related activities were going on outside the principal dwelling, a situation that they shared with the people who performed them. The hall was now being used primarily for dining, perhaps exclusively by the planter and his family. This picture of the later use of architectural space contrasts sharply with what we know about room functions during the initial phase of occupation (fig. 3). In the early period the only outbuilding at the Clifts was a small smokehouse. Dairying, therefore, seems to have been done in the "manner house" itself, probably in the small service room next to the passage. Although the early quarter had a hearth of sorts, it was hardly large enough to have served as a kitchen fireplace. Cooking, too, apparently went on in the hall of the "manner house." The subsequent removal of these activities from the dwelling is again a reflection of the planter's new need for increased physical separation from his social inferiors, in this case his work force. The "manner house" and the hall within it were becoming less the shared center of everyday life on the plantation for the planter and his laborers and more the isolated domain of the planter and his family.

The tenor of labor relations was not the only aspect of social life affected. Shifts also seem to have occurred in the way that planters dealt with one another. Once the passage was blocked, the porch and the small lobby beyond it provided a kind of no-man's-land in which visitors could be received. Having crossed the threshold, one's neighbor was in the house, but not in any of its living areas.[47] About 1685 the chamber, the room beyond the hall, was lengthened by the addition of a ten-foot bay, nearly doubling its size (fig. 5). Roughly thirty-five years later, a 4′ × 16′ addition was erected along its southern side (fig. 6). The chamber was clearly becoming a more important room, taking over some of the old functions of the hall. If in the early period, as its small size indicates, the chamber was being primarily used for sleeping, it later became a private sitting room as well.[48] The enlargement of the chamber can be seen as a product of the need to remove family life from the hall. This trend would eventually result in the division of the house into public and private areas, with the hall assuming the role of the former. Accordingly, the hall, stripped of its old functions, was reserved for ritualized dining and increasingly formal encounters between the planter and his social inferiors, men no longer regarded as integral parts of the social organism, men with whom the old sense of community was no longer felt. As the most public room in the house, the hall became progressively devoid of the objects connected with day-to-day living and was filled with objects that were designed to reinforce in the minds of visitors the social position of their owners. Thus in the inventory of Col. George Eskridge, a Westmoreland gentleman who died in 1735, we find six mezzotints, portraits of Eskridge and his wife, and "sundry glasses on the mantle piece" displayed prominently in the hall along with two tables, eighteen chairs, a fancy escritoire, and nothing else.[49]

If these developments left their mark at the Clifts in the first quarter of the eighteenth century, they are equally visible in the extant houses of the county and provincial gentry, which were built slightly later in the century and which survive today. In 1687 the traveler Durand de Dauphiné remarked that Virginians, "whatever their rank, and I know not why, . . . build only two rooms with some closets on the ground floor and two rooms in the attic above."[50] In the next century some gentlemen, primarily members of the county elites, continued to build two-room, hall-and-parlor houses "with some closets," houses that in those respects were similar to houses both the Frenchman and archaeologists have observed at all levels of society in the earlier period. But there were important differences. The evidence of excavated houses indicates that the lobby-entrance plan with a central chimney was one of the most widely used forms in gentry circles during the seventeenth century. Yet it disappeared from the architectural repertoire in the eighteenth century. Those members of the gentry who were still building hall-and-parlor houses built them with exterior chimneys of brick. In doing so they gave up the buffer between inside and outside, between themselves and others, which the lobby entrance itself could provide, in favor of publicly displayed brick stacks.[51] But the direct entry into the hall that the two-cell, end-chimney plan provided was not objectionable by this time. The hall had already become the public space in the house, contrived for the reception of others. On the other hand, richer men who could afford it no longer contented themselves with two-cell houses, even ones with impressive brick chimneys. Prodded by the same needs, they turned to the nontraditional, so-called Georgian forms that had already been in use in some sectors of English society for at least half a century.[52] At its simplest the plan with which they worked provided four rooms on a floor divided by a large central passage or hall. The multiplicity of rooms made possible a more exact correspondence between rooms and activities. The central hall, with its typically elaborate paneling and ornate stair, created a particularly effective and affecting receptacle for outsiders. Service related activities were of course relegated to symmetrically arranged outbuildings. In this context, Thomas Lee built Stratford (fig. 7).

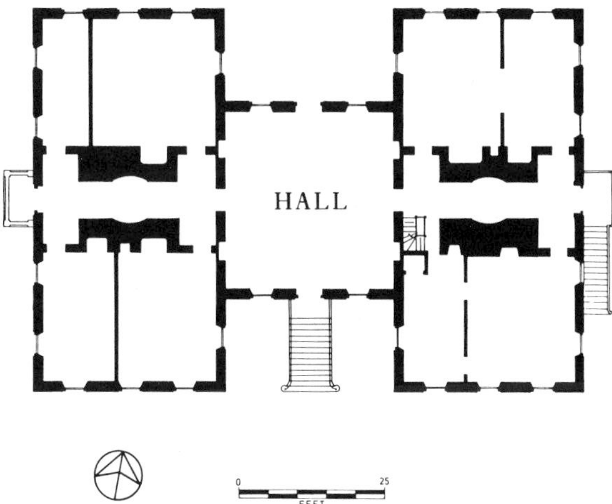

Figure 7. Plan of Stratford Hall, Westmoreland County, Virginia, before restoration.

Stratford is perhaps the most artfully and brilliantly contrived Georgian house in Virginia. A haha wall stretching across the forecourt permitted only humbling pedestrian access. Up an imposing flight of exterior steps, the front door opens into a cavernous unheated hall, the most highly decorated room in the house. Living areas are separated from the visitor not only by this room but by central passages leading off it on either side. Where his wealthy contemporaries—William Byrd, for example—contented themselves with a *single*, two-room-deep, central-hall house, Lee went further: he built *two*, linked by an elegantly finished hall.

The essential point to be grasped in all these developments is not that they were a response to a widening economic gap between social groups. The rich were always rich and the poor always poor. Rather they were the product of a loss of definition in social categories and the attendant decay of mutually felt obligations that had upheld them. Meaningful social intercourse requires structure, that is, prescriptions defining both social roles and acceptable behavior for individuals who occupy them. Men increasingly relied on their physical world to provide it. This happened in two ways. First, when the shared backcloth of assumptions about who belonged where in social space came apart, men looked to artifacts to communicate both to themselves and to others their place in society and their identity with other men whom they counted as their peers. Thus in the architectural sphere, bricks, symmetrical Georgian elevations, and interior paneling, among other things, assumed important roles to these twin ends. Such items identified their owner as a gentleman. For the gentry, symbolic forms served to distinguish "them" from "us." Second, with the demise of mutually felt duties or reciprocal standards of conduct, objects became essential in ordering and controlling the course of everyday encounters between men of different social status. Thus as the plan changes at the Clifts and the plan of Stratford Hall suggest, the spaces defined by architectural barriers became more functionally specific, progressively separating masters from laborers, superiors from inferiors, private from public, and finally the self from others.[53]

About the time the Clifts Plantation was being hacked out of the wilderness, Sir Thomas Browne wrote an archaeological treatise on a group of recently discovered Romano-British burial urns. He observed: "The treasures of time lie high, in Urnes, Coynes, and Monuments, scarce below the roots of some vegetables. Time hath endless rarities and shows of all varieties."[54] The present essay began with a similar proposition, that artifacts, whether they lie above or below ground, can elucidate the rarities and varieties of past experience and not simply serve as props to be manipulated in latter-day wish fulfillment. A few tentative connections between houses and the people who lived in them have been offered. Many more need to be made. A large part of our past "is still in the Urne to us."[55]

Notes

This article was originally published in the *Northern Neck of Virginia Historical Magazine* (December 1978). All illustrations in this article are by the author.

1. Quoted in Glyn Daniel, ed., *The Origins and Growth of Archaeology* (New York: Crowell, 1967), p. 118.
2. For the reference and a discussion of this matter, see Robert P. Sutton, "Nostalgia, Pessimism and Malaise: The Doomed Aristocrat in Late Jeffersonian Virginia," *Virginia Magazine of History and Biography* 76, no. 1 (January 1968): 44.
3. Claude Lévi-Strauss, *Structural Anthropology*, trans. Claire Jacobson and Brooke Grundfest Schoepf (New York: Anchor Books, 1967), p. 6.
4. For a rigorous and far more sophisticated approach of this sort, see Henry Glassie, *Folk Housing in Middle Virginia: A Structural Analysis of Historic Artifacts* (Knoxville: University of Tennessee Press, 1975). A scholarly and very readable treatment is to be found in James Deetz, *In Small Things Forgotten: The Archaeology of Early American Life* (Garden City: N.Y.: Anchor Books, 1977).
5. This synoptic account of the documentation of the Clifts Plantation is drawn from a report now in progress on the excavation.
6. The use of tarred clapboards is discussed in Dell Upton, "Board Roofing in Tidewater Virginia," *APT Bulletin* 8, no. 4 (1976): 22–43. On the Northern Neck, Linden Farm in Richmond County retains a portion of its original very early eighteenth-century tarred clapboard covering.
7. Durand de Dauphiné, *A Huguenot Exile in Virginia; or, Voyages of a Frenchman Exiled for His Religion*, trans. and ed. Gilbert Chinard (New York: Press of the Pioneers, 1934), pp. 119–20.
8. Quoted in Carl Bridenbaugh, *Vexed and Troubled Englishmen, 1590–1642* (New York: Oxford University Press, 1967), p. 72.
9. William T. Buchanan, Jr., and Edward F. Heite, "The Hallowes Site: A Seventeenth-Century Yeoman's Cottage in Virginia," *Historical Archaeology* 5 (1971): 41. Although it was a "yeoman's cottage" by the standards of the more prosperous areas of England during its day, the Hallowes house was not by any means ordinary in Virginia.
10. Brook Blades, "Archaeological Excavations at the Henry Brook and John Washington Sites, George Washington Birthplace National Monument, Virginia," manuscript, National Park Service.
11. Douglas Southall Freeman, *George Washington: A Biography*, 7 vols. (New York: Scribner's, 1947), 1:15–47.
12. William M. Kelso, "An Interim Report, Historical Archaeology at Kingsmill: The 1973 Season," manuscript, Virginia Research Center for Archaeology, Yorktown, Va., 1974.
13. Alain C. Outlaw, "Governor's Land Archaeological District Excavations: The 1976 Season," manuscript, Virginia Research Center for Archaeology, Yorktown, Va.
14. Among surviving Virginia houses, only Bacon's Castle, Surry County, and the Adam Thoroughgood House, Virginia Beach, can convincingly be shown to date to the seventeenth century. The latter barely slips under the wire.
15. W. G. Hoskins, "The Rebuilding of Rural England, 1570–1640," *Past and Present*, no. 4 (November 1953): 45–57.
16. Kelso, "Historical Archaeology at Kingsmill: The 1973 Season"; Outlaw, "Governor's Land Archaeological District Excavations."
17. William M. Kelso, "An Interim Report, Historical Archaeology at Kingsmill: The 1974 Season," manuscript, Virginia Research Center for Archaeology, Yorktown, Va., 1975.
18. Norman F. Barka, "Early Seventeenth-Century Architecture at Flowerdew Hundred Plantation: The Enclosed Settlement," manuscript, Flowerdew Hundred Foundation, Hopewell, Va.
19. Garry Wheeler Stone, J. Glenn Little III, and Stephen Israel, "Ceramics from the John Hicks Site, 1723–1743: The Material Culture," in *Ceramics in*

America, ed. Ian M. G. Quimby (Charlottesville: University of Virginia Press, 1973), pp. 103–39.

20. G. C. Chamberlayne, ed., *The Vestry Book of Petsworth Parish, Gloucester County, Virginia, 1677–1793* (Richmond: Library Board, 1933), p. 85.
21. Quoted in Gerald Mullin, *Flight and Rebellion: Slave Resistance in Eighteenth Century Virginia* (New York: Oxford University Press, 1972), p. 51.
22. For an interpretation of these terms at odds with this one see Cary Carson, "The 'Virginia House' in Maryland," *Maryland Historical Magazine* 69, no. 2 (Summer 1974): 185–95.
23. William Fitzhugh, *William Fitzhugh and His Chesapeake World, 1676–1701: The Fitzhugh Letters and Other Documents,* ed. Richard Beale Davis (Chapel Hill: University of North Carolina Press, 1963), p. 202.
24. Charles County Court and Land Records, Hall of Records, Annapolis, Reel no. 1, folio 513 (consulted in St. Mary's City Commission Chesapeake Area File).
25. For a concise discussion see Edmund Leach, *Culture and Communication: The Logic by Which Symbols Are Connected* (Cambridge: Cambridge University Press, 1976).
26. W. W. Hening, ed., *The Statutes at Large,* 10 vols. (New York: R., W. and G. Bartow, 1809–23), 1:340.
27. Stafford County Records, Stafford, Va., 1: folio 210.
28. J. T. Smith, "Timber-Framed Building in England," in *Medieval Domestic Architecture,* ed. M. J. Swanton (Leeds, Eng.: Royal Archaeological Institute, 1975), p. 14.
29. Edmund S. Morgan, *American Slavery, American Freedom: The Ordeal of Colonial Virginia* (New York: Norton, 1975), pp. 367–68.
30. Quoted in Morgan, *American Slavery, American Freedom,* p. 112.
31. Quoted in Outlaw, "Governor's Land Archaeological District Excavations," p. 11.
32. Edmund S. Morgan, "The First American Boom: Virginia, 1618 to 1630," *William and Mary Quarterly,* 3d ser., vol. 28, no. 2 (April 1971): 183.
33. Fitzhugh, *William Fitzhugh,* pp. 202–3.
34. Seventeenth-century Virginians' desires for economies in framing also found expression in carpentry techniques that are not archaeologically recoverable but that continued to be used in the following century in houses that are extant. The frames of all but the largest eighteenth-century Virginia houses display remarkable simplicity. One typical and particularly striking example is to be found in the ways Virginians cleverly avoided using the complicated joints that were standard in New England in favor of only lap and mortise-and-tenon joints. (My thinking on this matter, which cannot be treated in depth here, has been shaped by conversations with Dell Upton.)
35. William H. Browne, et al., eds., *Archives of Maryland,* 72 vols. (Baltimore: Maryland Historical Society, 1891), 10:302; in St. Mary's City Commission, Chesapeake Area File.
36. If the gentry ceased to build post houses in the second quarter of the eighteenth century, most Virginians continued the practice. In the Northern Neck, ordinary farmers were not able to erect houses substantial enough to survive to the present until the second quarter of the nineteenth century. As the nineteenth-century reformer Cassius Clay pointed out, large plantations staffed with enslaved blacks led to the persistent poverty of the yeomanry. Slaves were not consumers. Geographical accident, the proximity of the Northern Neck to rapidly industrializing areas to the north like Baltimore, which needed grain, may have been responsible for the belated "rebuilding" of this area.
37. Robert Beverley, *The History and Present State of Virginia,* ed. Louis B. Wright (Chapel Hill: University of North Carolina Press, 1947), p. 289.
38. Peter Laslett, *The World We Have Lost* (New York: Scribner's, 1971), pp. 3–4.
39. Eric Mercer, *English Vernacular Houses: A Study of Traditional Farmhouses and Cottages* (London: Her Majesty's Stationery Office, 1975), pp. 50–59.
40. Quoted in R. H. Tawney, *The Agrarian Problem in the Sixteenth Century* (New York: Burt Franklin, 1961), p. 349.
41. See Michael Zuckerman, "The Fabrication of Identity in Early America," *William and Mary Quarterly,* 3d ser., vol. 34, no. 2 (April 1977): 183–214.
42. Quoted in Tawney, *Agrarian Problem,* p. 350.
43. Westmoreland County Records, Montross, Va., Deeds and Wills, 1653–1659, folio 136.
44. York County Records, Yorktown, Va., 6: folio 362.
45. Ivor Noël Hume, *Martin's Hundred* (New York: Knopf, 1982), pp. 68–69.
46. John Clayton, *A Letter from Mr. John Clayton . . . to the Royal Society, May 1688. Giving an Account of Certain Observables,* in *Tracts and Other Papers,* ed. Peter Force, 4 vols. (Washington, D.C.: Peter Force, 1844), 3:7.
47. See Glassie, *Folk Housing,* p. 168.
48. M. W. Barley, *The English Farmhouse and Cottage* (London: Routledge and Kegan Paul, 1961), p. 142.
49. Westmoreland County Records, Inventories, 1: folio 159.
50. Durand de Dauphiné, *Huguenot Exile,* pp. 119–20.

51. A standing house in which this change occurred is Emerson's Ordinary, in Tappahannock, Essex County, Virginia. Erected soon after 1720, the house originally had a lobby-entrance plan with a centrally located chimney. About midcentury, if not before, this original stack was dismantled and replaced with two brick chimneys on the opposite gable ends of the house. The traditional explanation for the popularity of end chimneys in eighteenth-century Virginia is an example of environmental determinism at its worst. It is often claimed that Virginians built houses with end chimneys the better to dissipate the heat in a temperate climate, whereas New Englanders built houses with axial stacks to warm themselves more effectively in the frigid north. Given the preponderance of lobby-entrance houses revealed by excavations in the Chesapeake, proponents of this theory are committed to the unattractive idea that Virginia was in the midst of an ice age of sorts during the seventeenth century. In addition the Virginia gentry, that is, men who could afford to build two-cell houses with brick stacks in the first place, had already relegated cooking to outbuildings. Thus there was no need to burn fires in warm weather. End chimneys of masonry were not the rage in eighteenth-century New England primarily because masonry chimneys were very common in the seventeenth century. The materials to build them were to be had in every farmer's field and those farmers were not growing a labor-intensive staple crop.
52. See, for example, the plans of Thorpe Hall and Coleshill illustrated in John Summerson, *Architecture in Britain, 1530 to 1830* (New York: Penguin Books, 1977), pp. 151, 167.
53. The model of social relations used here is adapted from Mary Douglas, *Natural Symbols* (New York: Vintage Books, 1971), pp. 77–92.
54. Sir Thomas Browne, *Hydriotaphia. Urne Burial; or, A Discourse of the Sepulchrall Urnes Lately Found in Norfolk,* in *The Religio Medici and Other Writings of Sir Thomas Browne,* ed. C. H. Herford (London: J. M. Dent, 1911), p. 95.
55. Browne, *Hydriotaphia,* p. 95.

Vernacular Domestic Architecture in Eighteenth-Century Virginia

DELL UPTON

The following essay by Dell Upton implicitly challenges the old notion that vernacular buildings represent the reproduction of enduring architectural forms. Many of the buildings discussed here have unique plans, not found in any other standing eighteenth-century house in Virginia; most of the other plans illustrated in the article are uncommon. We are forced to ask what unique and rare examples have to do with "ordinary" architecture, and as a consequence to confront, in yet another guise, the issue of change in vernacular architecture.

Change is assumed in this essay. Upton calls into question the common beliefs that vernacular architecture (in the sense of traditional rural building) disappeared in the face of commercial and industrial developments in the eighteenth century, and casts in doubt as well the idea that novel or high-style architectural ideas were irresistible and fatal to vernacular traditions.

Virginia's eighteenth-century builders had to reconcile a variety of factors, including old and new architectural traditions, abstract concepts of social relations as suggested by the names Virginians gave to rooms, and the actual uses that individuals made of architectural spaces. Apparently simple ideas of "form" and "function" come to seem impossibly fragmented, and indeed some builders like the vestrymen of Lunenburg Parish, who figure in the article, were unable to solve their particular architectural problem successfully on the first try. While many eighteenth-century Virginia houses, not discussed here, were based on conventional hall-parlor, I-, and Georgian forms, what is remarkable is the number of Virginia builders who were willing to confront their tasks freshly, using traditional concepts and new ideas to devise a novel architectural solution. What ties them to the more conventional builders are a common underlying architectural vocabulary, common ends, and a common process *of design brought to bear on the new planning problems.*

Vernacular architecture is regional architecture. The vernacular buildings of any area display a mixture of indigenous forms and more broadly distributed folk and academic ones that are combined in a distinctive local manner. During the eighteenth and nineteenth centuries, powerful new popular and academic architectural ideas significantly affected regional architectures and are sometimes thought to have challenged them so severely that vernacular building was eradicated.[1] Yet a careful analysis of the local design process that examines the reasons for choosing new forms in any area and, most important, the system into which they were fitted demonstrates that local builders took the new ideas into account but were not overwhelmed by them. In eighteenth-century eastern Virginia, the subject of this article, builders systematically dismembered the new architectural concepts and fit them into traditional Virginia ones in ways that illustrate the close interdependence of local and extralocal impulses in vernacular building.[2]

While similar cultural impulses affected all of the colonies and the mother country, the peculiar history of each area determined the shape of its response to them. As with many other aspects of Anglo-American life, the shift from an agrarian to a capitalist society in England, marked by the late seventeenth-century triumph of what J. H. Plumb called "the Whig oligarchy," introduced changes in building practices in both England and America.[3] First was the restructuring of architectural authority. Architecture increasingly became the province of experts who could claim their position on the basis of superior knowledge and proved success in the field rather than from ascribed social status. Although this transition from traditional to professional authority outlasted the eighteenth century, the architectural expert became a force to be reckoned with then.[4]

The increased production of architectural treatises beginning in the early eighteenth century further extended the professional designers' influence. The rapid and widespread distribution of architects' wares could spread their ideas far beyond the network of personal contacts that had confined them earlier. Relatively inexpensive style and pattern books offered the architects' arcane knowledge to the "builder," the "youth," and the "workman."[5] But, we must ask, were the experts' claims accepted? To what extent did the specific forms and the general ideas that they promoted affect Virginia's architecture?

Historians of both vernacular and academic architecture have assumed that the progress of new ideas, especially after their dissemination in books, was rational, regular, even inevitable. In part this view derives from the common working assumptions of art historians of architecture and in part from the parallel historical view that the eighteenth century in England and America was a time of political and social consensus, when conflicts were less the result of differences of opinion than of personal interests.[6]

The architectural historiography of eighteenth-century America, and particularly that of Virginia, consequently places great emphasis on tracing the impact of books on American builders. Vingboons, Palladio, and Serlio as well as their English followers have been searched for every possible precedent, and buildings judged for the degree to which they conform to published norms. While such influences are undeniable, it is my argument that the use of international models in Virginia was closely controlled by local intention. The controlled mixture of local and extralocal features in turn conditioned the nature and extent of future penetration of academic architectural ideas. This complex process can best be understood by examining the reception of the "Georgian," or detached, house form in Virginia.

Recent archaeological and documentary research has demonstrated that while the first emigrants to Virginia built a wide variety of traditional English house plans, and continued to do so throughout the seventeenth century, a process of social winnowing resulted in the development by the end of the century of characteristic Virginia vernacular house forms that were recognized by contemporaries as characteristic and appropriate. These were one-and-a-half-story frame structures with one or two rooms on each floor.[7] Even wealthy planters lived in them. The pervasiveness of these houses was a recent phenomenon when French traveler Durand de Dauphiné reported in 1687 that "Whatever their rank, & I know not why, they build only two rooms with some closets on the ground floor, & two rooms in the attic above; but they build several like this, according to their means. They build also a separate kitchen, a separate house for the Christian slaves, [and] one for the negro slaves."[8] The choice of this small house type by prosperous planters who earlier in the century had built large three-cell English vernacular houses and tagged rambling additions to their dwellings was a reflection of the growing social separation of servant and master in late seventeenth-century Virginia. The labor-intensive nature of tobacco planting had combined with the pressures of a declining market to encourage an instrumental view of one's laborers that was aggravated in the third quarter of the seventeenth century by an influx of white indentured servants. Their rapid turnover made for anonymity, and their numbers made them seem threatening to Virginia's elite, whose position was itself questionable in terms of seventeenth-century social ideology. Increasingly in the period 1660–80, planters moved servants and slaves to separate buildings, creating a definite spatial division where no clear social one existed, and built smaller houses for themselves.[9]

In the early eighteenth century, small houses of this general character served even the wealthiest segments of the population. According to surviving room-by-room probate inventories taken between 1721 and 1730, twenty-seven of thirty-four of Virginia's wealthiest decedents had lived in houses with two ground-floor rooms, while two lived in houses with only one main room.[10] The predominant house plan was a traditional British one, with a large principal room, known as the hall, entered directly from the outside, and a small inner room, known as the chamber or the parlor, entered from the hall (fig. 1).[11]

Within twenty-five years many of the vernacular houses of the colony had incorporated new features—central passages, two-room depth, and symmetrical facade (fig. 2). Architectural historians have often associated these changes with the introduction of a prestigious "detached house" type imported into the colony through publications in the early years of the century (fig. 3). The detached house,

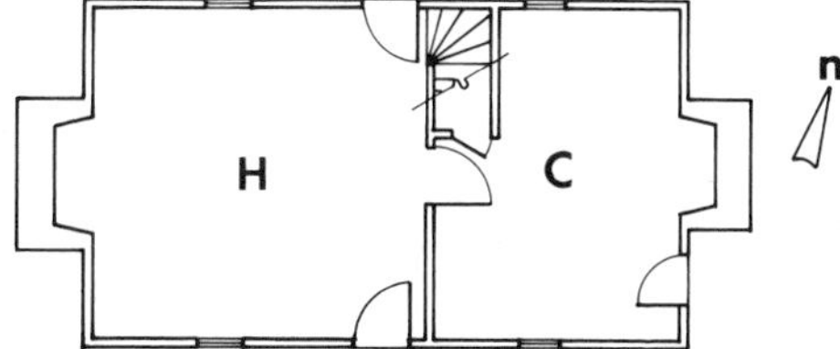

Figure 1. First-floor plan of the Stratman House, Surry County. Built in the late eighteenth century.

Key for all drawings: B = back room; BR = bedroom; C = chamber; Cl = closet; DR = dining room; E = entry; H = hall; K = kitchen; NH = new hall; OH = old hall; Pa = parlor; Ps = passage. Stippling indicates added wall or room; dashed line indicates wall removed; hatching indicates fireplace or opening filled. Only pre–Civil War additions are illustrated except where noted.

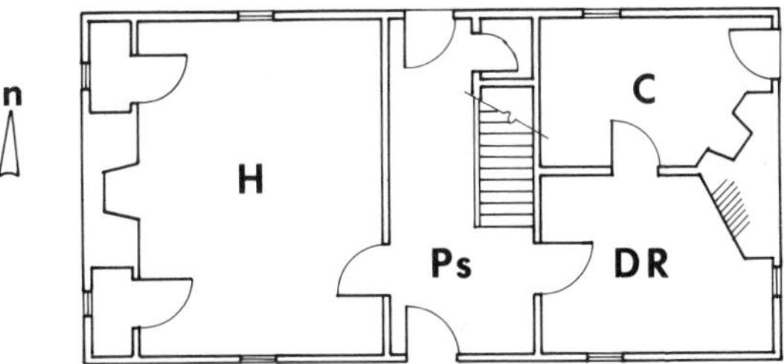

Figure 2. First-floor plan of the Billups House, Mathews County. Built ca. 1790.

developed in England in the late seventeenth century to accommodate minor rural gentry and urban merchants, was two stories tall with a roughly cubical mass, a symmetrical facade, and a hipped roof, and typically it had a central-entry, double-pile (two-room-deep) plan. Large by Virginian if not by European standards, these houses distilled many of the ideas of seventeenth-century academic architecture into what William H. Pierson has called "a major contribution of English middle-class society to the history of Western architecture."[12]

It is possible to see the small vernacular houses of eighteenth-century eastern Virginia as direct derivatives of this Georgian large-house model.[13] Whether resulting from the predictable emulation of the elite by middling social groups, from the acceptance of the new architectural experts, or from a transforming "Georgian mindset," builders at many levels of society adapted the detached house

Figure 3. North elevation of main block of Westover, Charles City County. Built in the mid eighteenth century. The hipped-roof, central-entry block with its seven bays of repetitive openings and classical doorway make this an outstanding example of the detached, or Georgian-plan, house in America.

type to their smaller dwellings.[14] For example, one of the most common house forms among surviving eighteenth-century Virginia dwellings is a one-and-a-half-story building with a single room on either side of a central passage (figs. 4, 5). These Virginia houses might be thought of as a quarter of the ideal type.

Although some nineteenth-century Virginia houses were, indeed, designed by geometrical manipulation of the plan, most pre-Revolutionary plans exhibited a complexity of layout and an interrelation of spaces that made simple expansion and contraction difficult (figs. 6, 7, 28). Eighteenth-century planning was a painstaking operation that involved the careful correlation of space and social function. No surviving eighteenth-century house, whether built in one campaign or in several, has four equal-sized rooms. In most, every single room has different dimensions. At the glebe house of Hungar's Parish, Northampton County, for example, a characteristically offset central passage is combined with staggered longitudinal brick bearing walls to create four unequal rooms.[15]

To relate large Georgian-plan houses and the smaller Virginia vernacular dwellings according to their geometrical similarities helps to explain how the new house type was compatible with Virginia's tradition. Such an approach is much more satisfying than that of architectural historians who see Virginia's smaller houses simply as mimetic of England's larger ones. But to describe the relationship adequately it is necessary to see Virginia houses in their own terms: as solutions that local builders formulated to solve planning problems of their own. Changing social habits among the colony's well-to-do planters in the eighteenth century left many of them wanting more spaces than the traditional two-room house offered. The example of the Georgian-plan house provided suggestions to the traditional builder about how to incorporate new spaces into the traditional house and how to control interior circulation. Rather than perceiving the Georgian house as a fixed and unalterable model to be imitated or ignored, Virginia's vernacular builders considered each of the elements of the detached house discretely, as a possible architectural response to a specific social requirement. The process of change involved the integration of some of these new elements in a distinctive new entity. We can best understand this process by looking first at the new social forms that needed to be incorporated into the vernacular house, then at the traditional principles of design, and, finally, at how the new architectural forms were used in Virginia vernacular building.

A first step toward analyzing the history of eighteenth-century Virginia vernacular housing is to understand room-naming patterns and how they were changed. Anthropologists have shown that naming systems are one of the chief methods people use to impose order on their experience.[16] As in any society, the particular experience of Virginians in the

Figure 4. First-floor plan of Kempsville, Gloucester County. Built in the third quarter of the eighteenth century. Not drawn is the mid nineteenth-century north wing visible in figure 5.

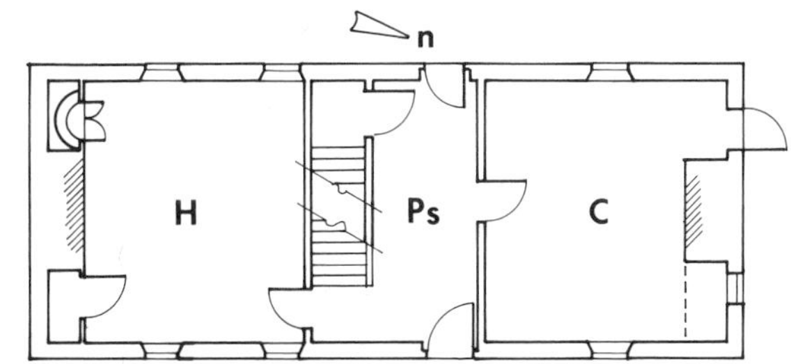

Figure 5. East elevation of Kempsville, Gloucester County.

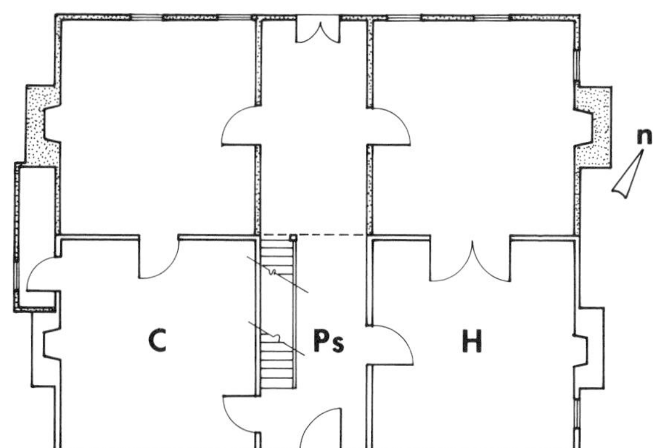

Figure 6. First-floor plan of Chippokes, Surry County. The south half was built in the early nineteenth century; the north half was built in the mid nineteenth century. The initial uses of the north rooms are uncertain.

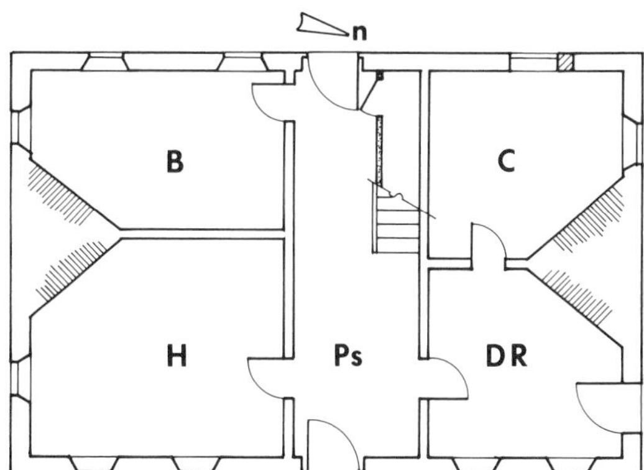

Figure 7. First-floor plan of the glebe house of Hungar's Parish, Northampton County. Built in the second quarter of the eighteenth century. The stair was moved from the hall to the passage in 1767.

seventeenth and eighteenth centuries created a system of social categories—habitual ways of grouping and classifying daily activities and personal relations—that underlay the physical forms of their houses. These categories were ordered in architectural terms by room names—labels that crystallized the intersection between physical spaces and social categories in a single term.

If we assume that to have a name for a space indicates that it fits into a conceptual pattern and that to use it regularly is a clue to local practice, then the pattern of name use in seventeenth- and eighteenth-century Virginia is revealing. Virginians inherited a large number of room names from English and Anglo-American traditions, but an examination of the room-by-room inventories shows that they used very few of them often. In the seventeenth century, inventory makers regularly used only *hall,* with its customary synonyms *great room* and *outer room,* and *the chamber,* with its equivalents *parlor* and *inner room.*[17] These were also the names applied to the major spaces of the standard early eighteenth-century two-room house. Of the room names that were introduced into the eighteenth-century Virginia inventories, only two were common: *passage* and *dining room.* The use of *passage* grew throughout the second and third quarters of the century, and that of *dining room* kept pace with it. The addition of new rooms reflected an analytical desire for order and separation that grew out of and amplified the seventeenth-century division of servant and served spaces.[18] This motive is obvious in virtually everything that Virginians wrote about buildings. For example, in 1705 Robert Beverley commented, "All their Drudgeries of Cookery, washing, Daries, &c. are perform'd in Offices detacht from their Dwelling-Houses, which by this means are kept more cool and Sweet." And building contracts continually stressed neatness and "decency" more than elegance and elaboration.[19]

Virginians also looked for neatness and order in their social lives. Their houses were part of a complex landscape defining and vitalizing that order, and changes in interior spaces can only be understood in the context of that whole landscape. The large planter set himself at the center of a private community that replicated in form and appearance the civic order of public society. Durand described the plantations he saw as resembling "a fairly large village," a simile that occurred to several eighteenth-century commentators as well.[20] Each part of the plantation reflected the hierarchy, with the planter at its pinnacle. The domestic buildings that served him were closest to the house, which was often set above them on a high basement. The farm buildings were carefully ordered, and in some parts of Virginia they were set in parallel rows as a street with the main house on axis.[21] Slave houses were also arranged in streets, often a quarter mile or more away from the main house. These communities had their own lives, at once bound to but independent of the planter's. On very large plantations, the property might be subdivided into quarters—subordinate farms on which the necessary slaves and overseers lived in self-contained settlements.[22] In these cases, the imitation of the civic order for personal benefit was even more pronounced, with the "home house" functioning as a kind of county seat to a far-flung group of small communities. The semipublic nature of the planter's house is evident, as is the extent to which he viewed it as an emblem of himself and his order. A passage from the diary of Landon Carter, the neurotically sensitive owner of Sabine Hall in Richmond County, is revealing. In inspecting his house, Carter found "my Sills to my posts in my communication Passage to my Kitching, though of oak, to be rotten and loose, and the posts of sweet Gum to be sound yet much cut to Pieces by these knife triflers," and therefore requiring replacement.[23] A man with a strong sense of possession—note the number of *mys* in the quote—Carter was nevertheless unable to prevent the random vandalism that infuriated him but that occurs in any public place. The social fact and the personal attitude together epitomized the nature of the planter's controlled order.

The heart of the planter's order was his hall. As they had in the seventeenth century, Virginians thought of the hall as the center of their world, as the meeting point between inside and outside. What had in the seventeenth century been a general-purpose living and working space became in the eighteenth century the focus of an institutionalized conviviality that compensated for the isolation of plantation life.[24] The new role of the hall was acknowledged by the Truro Parish vestry when it contracted with William Berkeley to erect a new glebe house complex in 1737. The vestrymen specified a square house with a 14′ × 16′ "hall or entertaining room" and three "other rooms" on the first floor. Furthermore, the visual character embodied the new social function. The planter furnished his hall as elegantly and as formally as circumstances allowed. His hospitality was genuine, but it was tightly restricted to specific channels. The elegance and formality of the entertaining room set the tone for sociability at the same time that it made the participants aware of the limits. Visually, everything about the planter's hall said "this far but no farther."[25]

While the planter's house was a public building in this sense, it was a residence as well. As the hall was given over to conviviality in the second quarter of the eighteenth century, beds and other personal goods disappeared from it in all but the smallest houses. Consequently, intermediate areas were needed between the hall and the private chambers on the one hand, and between the hall and the outside on the other. In the first instance, this led to the addition of a new room whose contents—tables, chairs, benches, beds, and hoes—often resembled those of the seventeenth-century hall. Although this new room was the scene of some communal events, it was on the same end of the house as the private chamber and was set in front of the chamber, communicating directly with it.[26] *Dining room* was the name eventually given to the new space, but it served multiple purposes. Maj. Traverse Trapley of Richmond County kept his hoes in the dining room along with several tables and his china. In 1727 Mr. Christopher Robinson's dining room contained, besides ten chairs and an old table, two bedsteads.[27]

By midcentury the term *dining room* had become fixed in the appraisers' vocabulary as the appropriate name for a secondary front room on the first floor, no matter what the function of that room might be. In 1750 Jeduthun Ball's appraisers used generic names, listing the second-floor rooms as being "over the hall," "over the dining room," "over the little room," and "over the bed chamber"—spaces that on the first floor they had called the "hall," "Betty Doxeman's room," "the little room," and "the taylor's room" respectively.[28]

The adoption of the name *dining room* was neither immediate nor inevitable. At first this new intermediate space retained the name *chamber,* as with a two-unit house, and the third space was called the back room, indicative of the usual physical arrangement. By the 1750s, however, the new nomenclature was firmly established; the term *chamber* was shifted to *back room,* and the old chamber space was then called the dining room (compare figs. 2, 4, 14).

The addition, in the second quarter of the eighteenth century, of a passage shielding the family and its visitors from the outside accompanied the insertion of the dining room (figs. 2, 4). Accordingly, no room was directly accessible through the formal entrance, and the planter could directly and individually control circulation to every room of the house.[29]

Passages were one solution to a problem that Virginians had been working on since the seventeenth century and represent the reinterpretation of a feature familiar from several sources, none of which was exactly analogous to the eighteenth-century Virginia central passage. Large seventeenth-century postmedieval English vernacular houses (and a few Virginia ones) incorporated a through passage that separated the service spaces from the living rooms and provided independent access to both.[30] In Virginia, most planters housed those spaces in separate buildings by the end of the seventeenth century. But some eighteenth-century Virginia builders must have remembered the circulation function of that postmedieval through passage, and a few Virginia

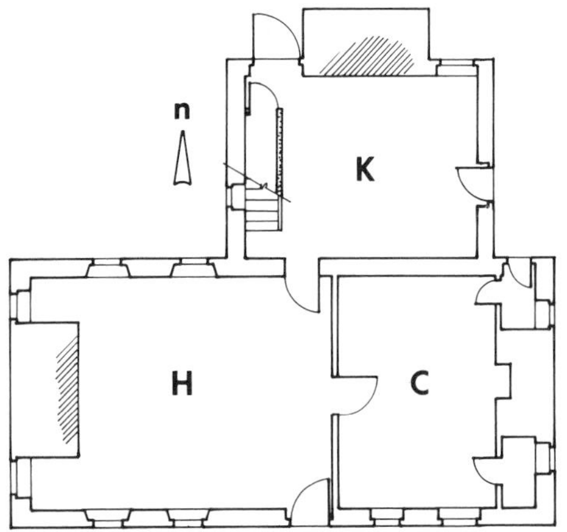

Figure 8. First-floor plan of Sweet Hall, King William County. Built in the early eighteenth century. The original stairs were replaced in the 1920s.

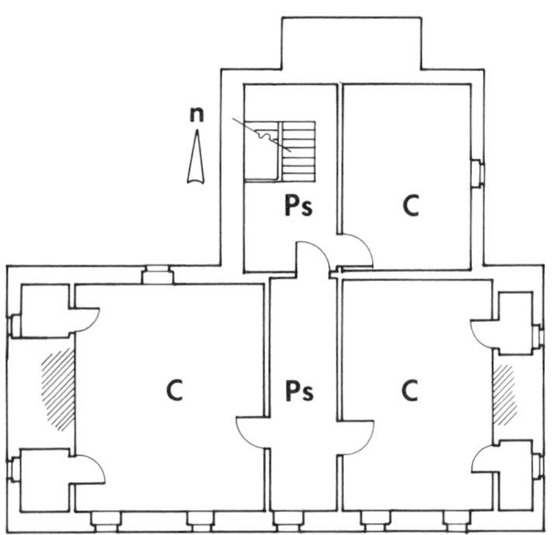

Figure 9. Second-floor plan of Sweet Hall, King William County.

houses with through passages reinforced the memory.

The passage in the large Georgian-plan house, like that in the postmedieval through-passage house, may have offered Virginians some help in solving the problem of circulation, but other sources were more relevant. For instance, Virginia's early hall-chamber houses, although lacking a passage on the first floor, often had one on the second floor to separate the sleeping chambers from the stair landing (figs. 8, 9).

In the minds of eighteenth-century Virginians, passages were most closely linked with the porches and entries of the seventeenth century than they were with the pretense of Georgian-plan mansions. From the earliest years of settlement, large planters had employed porches—either projecting in towers or set inside the body of the house as a vestibule or lobby—and by the end of the seventeenth century they were relatively common.[31] In some cases these porches contained the stairs and thus served another function in common with the central passage of later houses. That is, they were spaces that provided access to several first- and second-floor rooms without the necessity of passing through any of them to get to another. This may have been the case in Capt. Thomas Barber's Richmond County house; his 1754 inventory listed a "Stair Room."[32] Other houses—Bacon's Castle in Surry County is a well-known example—had a porch tower on the front and a separate stair tower on the rear, although this eliminated the advantage of having both entry and stairs in the same location (fig. 10).

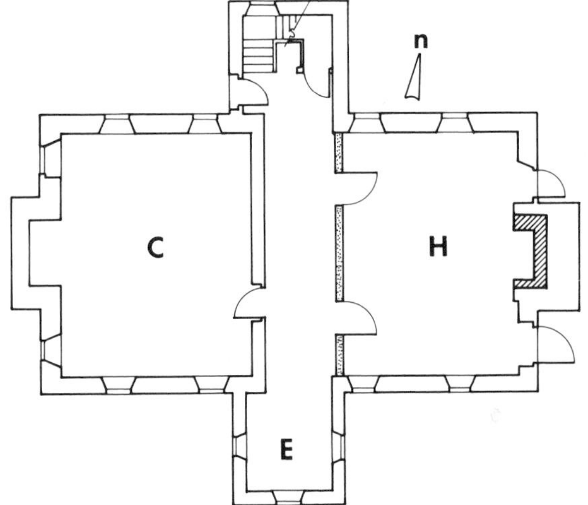

Figure 10. First-floor plan of Bacon's Castle, Surry County. Built in 1665. The east passage wall was added in the eighteenth century, and the original front door into the south side of the entry was replaced by a window in the 1850s. The room names were taken from the probate inventory of Maj. Arthur Allen (1711), the second owner (Surry County Deeds, etc., no. 5, 1709–15, pp. 84–88).

Eighteenth-century Virginia builders combined the projecting towers and the internal lobbies of earlier houses—both called porches or entries interchangeably—and drew them into the body of the house, creating the central-passage plan. That the two were viewed as analogous solutions to a single problem is apparent from the probate inventories. The number of houses with either a passage or a porch/entry rose rapidly in the second quarter of the eighteenth century, as Virginians worked to isolate themselves from outsiders to a greater and greater degree. Porches/entries ultimately ceased to be satisfactory solutions. More and more Virginians preferred passages instead, and some added passages to their hall-chamber houses even where, as at Bacon's Castle, there was already a porch (fig. 10). The terms *porch* and *entry* were no longer used in the inventories taken after 1760. Passages, which until that time had been less frequently mentioned, overtook them in significance (table 1). The transformation from one to the other was made explicit in the will of Col. Thomas Jones, recorded in Williamsburg in 1732. His house was equipped with an "entry or passage."[33]

The developed social structure of the mid eighteenth-century house, then, consisted first of a hall, a formal, public room set off from direct access to any other room of the house. Next was a dining room, a semipublic space that mediated between outside and inside. It was directly accessible from the formal passage and from the private chamber

Table 1
Frequency of Houses with a Porch/Entry and a Passage, 1721–80

Decade	Number of room-by-room inventories	Percentage with a porch/entry	Percentage with a passage
1721–30	32	14.7	12.5
1731–40	13	38.5	15.4
1741–50	32	25.1	21.8
1751–60	20	30.0	45.0
1761–70	13	0.0	38.5
1771–80	10	0.0	40.0

Source: Dell Upton, "Early Vernacular Architecture in Southeastern Virginia" (Ph.D. diss., Brown University, 1980), pp. 273–76.

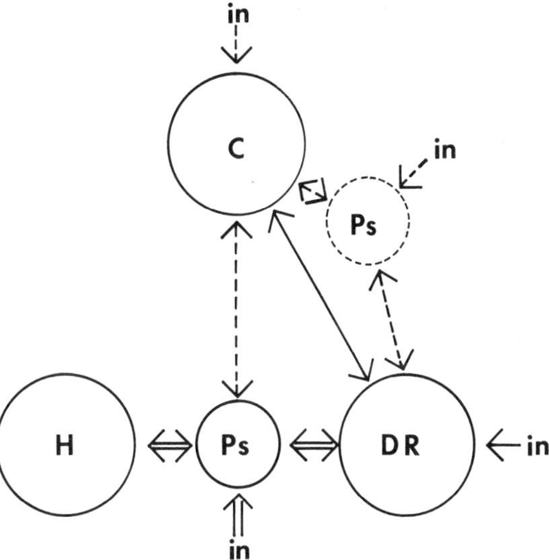

Figure 11. The "social molecule" or structure of social space in eighteenth-century eastern Virginia houses. The four principal spaces are represented by the balloons, and obligatory direct connections among them are indicated by double arrows. Single arrows indicate direct connections found in most houses, and the broken arrows and balloon depict optional arrangements. Note that what is depicted here is not physical space, but social categories and the customary relationships among them, as codified in the system of room names. The naming system keys the transition from social practice to house plan, that is, it suggests ways that spaces might be related to allow the social habits to operate.

and often had an exterior door facing the kitchen outbuilding, thus connecting it to the service system of the household as well. In this sense, the dining room was the heart of the family's house, as opposed to the hall which was the center of the family's social landscape. The most private first-floor room was the chamber, often only accessible through the dining room. The fourth space, the central passage, or entry, controlled circulation. These social relationships can be diagrammed in what we might call the molecule of the Virginia vernacular house (fig. 11).

The changes discussed above created the underlying social structure of the Virginia house, but the builder and client then had to translate the abstract concept into physical spaces enclosed by bricks and boards. Here the traditional rules of architectural composition were in effect. These were something quite different from the social rules, and considerable skill and experience were needed to produce a design that satisfied the requirements of both.

If the core of the Virginia house, socially, was the hall, its geometrical core was the square. The builder began with a square, and through a series of geometrical operations he produced a plan which, ideally, arranged the parts in a manner acceptable to him and to his client.[34] He then employed his craft to translate the abstract plan into traditional modular units, but the important relationships had less to do with geometry and dimensions than with ideas of propriety, relative privacy, convenience, and tradition.

A revealing incident illuminates the complex interaction of formal and social systems in design, even in the employment of a tried-and-true plan. In 1761, the vestry of Cumberland Parish, Lunenburg County, ordered the construction of a new glebe house 50′ × 18′ with "inside chimneys to be four foot deep, the Hall 18 foot square, the passage 10 foot wide, the Chamber 18 foot by 14 with a Dutch [gambrel] roof, and two rooms and passage above." A year later they reported, perhaps with some embarrassment, that "it is found by consultation with workmen of good judgment that the former plan of 50′ × 18′ is defective."[35] The problem lay in the dimensions given in the original specifications. The vestry had called for a 50′ × 18′ house, but their figures added up to only 42 feet. They wanted inside chimneys but had then added the depth of the chimneys to the total length of the building. Clearly they equated the hall with a square space and thought of it as a "pure" square, unconsciously pushing the chimneys out (fig. 12). Their very specifications revealed the ways that they related social and geometrical concepts. As laymen, they had combined many parts of house planning—the social divisions, the proxemic qualities, the physical dimensions that the carpenters needed—into a single confused document. The ineptitude reveals their thinking to us. The "workmen of good judgment" corrected the vestry's error and helped write new specifications that consisted of nothing more than a physical description of an object. The social and proxemic qualities that made the object a house, but were irrelevant to the physical act of construction, were eliminated.

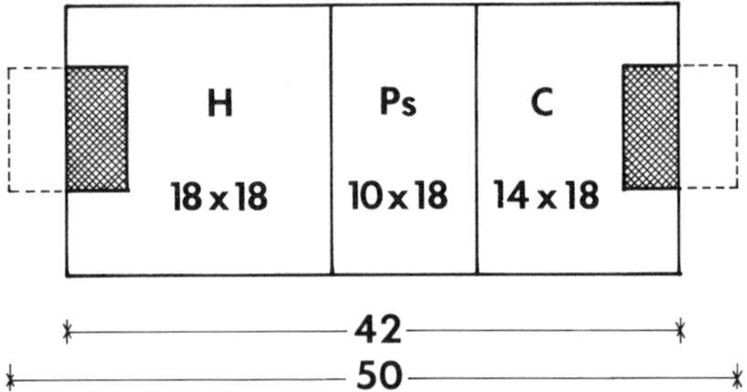

Figure 12. Schematic first-floor plan of a projected glebe house, Cumberland Parish, Lunenburg County, 1761.

Given this potentially confusing set of requirements for house design, the easy thing to do would have been to choose a ready-made "package" for the social molecule. The closest available model was the four-room, central-passage Georgian plan. Some Virginians did use this form, but when they did they found that they had no ready name for the fourth room. There was no place for it in their local social pattern, for the four-room plan did not fit the molecule exactly. Most often the term *back room* was given to the superfluous space (as it had been to the third space during the time that the molecule was being developed). William Bell's house in Lancaster County, for instance, contained a hall, a chamber, a dining room, and a back room in 1750. It was apparently a house with what was then called a lean-to, or shed, at the rear for there were only two upstairs rooms, and they were located over the hall and over the dining room. (The latter confirms that the dining room was a front room.) Similar room-name problems occurred at Col. John Allen's house in Surry County in 1742. His first floor contained a hall, a parlor, a chamber, a passage, and a back room as well as a porch. The appraisers of the estate of George Washington's father, Augustine, were content in 1743 with the labels *hall, hall back room, parlor, back room,* and *passage* for his first-floor rooms.[36]

The lack of a clear sense of the identity of the fourth room was as much a problem for the owners as for the appraisers. When Colonel Jones wrote his will, he left his house and many of its contents to his wife. His bequest included "a room of the dwelling house of the said Thomas Jones called the Hall and most of them [the contents] are part of the usual furniture of the hall," including five tables, chairs, china, pictures, glasses, and a cupboard. After that, he identified the other first-floor rooms as the "entry or passage," "a room called the back Porch," "a room called the chamber," "the New Room," "a small room behind the hall" (containing a chest, a bureau, and Negro clothes), and "a room of the house upon right coming into the back porch" (containing china and glass).[37] The form of these references indicates that customary terminology failed Jones at certain places in his house. That inventory makers found appraisable goods in these extra rooms of Georgian-plan houses shows that the rooms were used. To speak of owners and appraisers "not knowing" what to call them is merely to point out that the rooms had no social meaning, regardless of how intensely they were used.

The telling evidence of the power of the social over the formal framework is the number of ways that Virginians found to incorporate the essential elements of the molecule while minimizing the ambiguous spaces. While a standardized plan might have been easier to produce, mid eighteenth-century Virginians were willing to experiment to try to find a closer fit for their social molecule. The Moore House, York County, renowned as the site of Lord Cornwallis's surrender after the seige of Yorktown, is technically a Georgian-plan house (fig. 13). On one side of a central passage are two equal-sized rooms. The will of Lucy Moore, an original resident of the house, implies that these were the dining room and the chamber, as we might expect.[38] Across the passage were the other two rooms, one a large hall and the other reduced to a 5-foot-deep closet serving the hall.

In numerous houses builders designing around the social pattern devised plans that eliminated the troublesome fourth room entirely. While these varied and novel plans shared some features with Georgian-plan houses, their meanings and their logic were the products of local builders, not Europe's architectural experts.

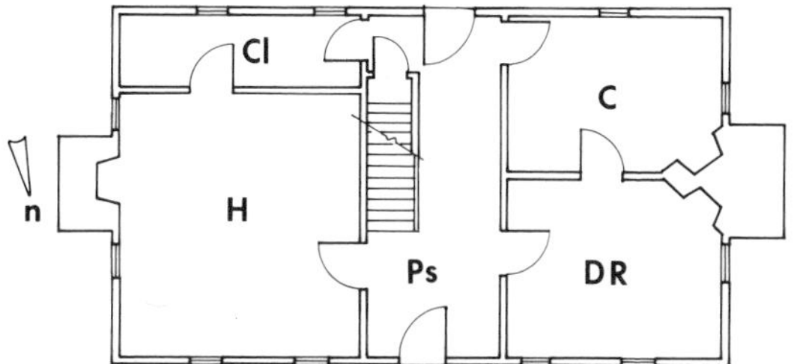

Figure 13. First-floor plan of the Moore House, York County. Built in the mid eighteenth century.

Rear ells—full-height additions—were the location of added "new rooms" that were usually bed chambers, but occasionally kitchens (fig. 8). It is not surprising, therefore, to find that the first eighteenth-century builders of houses with dining rooms often constructed original bed-chamber ells to accommodate a third space. These ells are the back rooms of the second quarter eighteenth-century inventories. In York County, Matthew Pierce's 1737 inventory described this sort of building, as did Samuel Timson's, made in 1739.[39] Timson's house had a hall, a porch, a parlor, and a back room, with upper chambers over only the first two spaces.

As the use of three major rooms spread, along with the regular use of the term *dining room,* there was a trend toward incorporating the rear chamber more fully into the plan. Indian Banks, a large two-story brick house built by the Glascock family, is among the earliest surviving examples of these three-room houses (fig. 14). The third room, still set in an ell, could be entered from the passage, since it protruded into the area of the main rectangle.

Related plans were used in three later, very dissimilar houses built south of the James River. Clements, Southampton County, is a one-and-a-half-story brick house with original stucco rendering

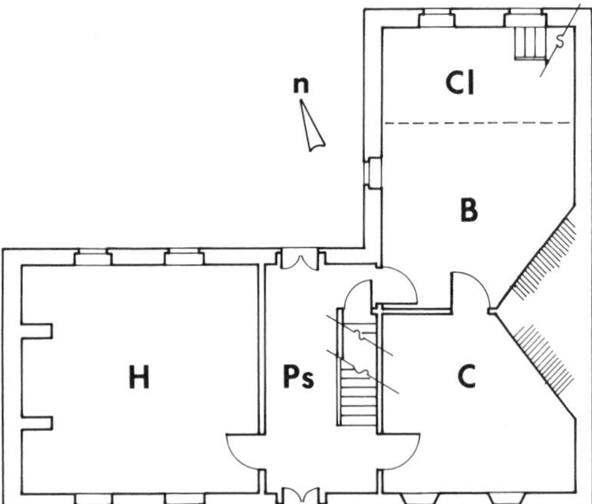

Figure 14. First-floor plan of Indian Banks, Richmond County. Built in the second quarter of the eighteenth century. The back stair is a modern replacement. The room names were found in the inventory of an early resident, John Glascock, who died in 1756 (Richmond County Will Book, no. 6, 1753–67, pp. 89–90).

Figure 15. Northeast view of Clements, Southampton County. Built ca. 1820–30. The large eastern projection is the closet, and the smaller one is a cellar entry.

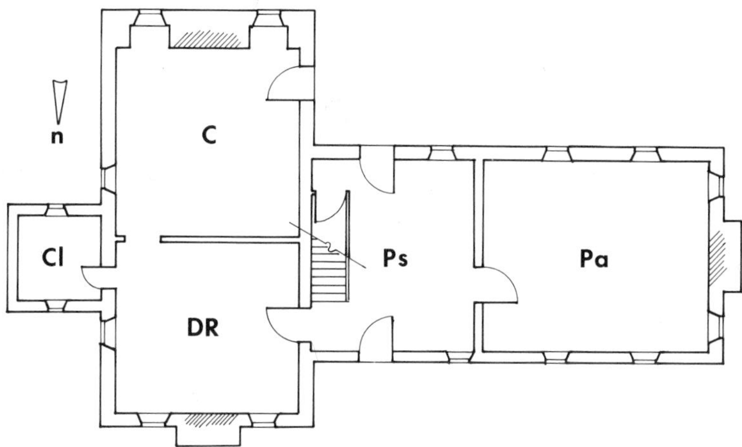

Figure 16. First-floor plan of Clements, Southampton County.

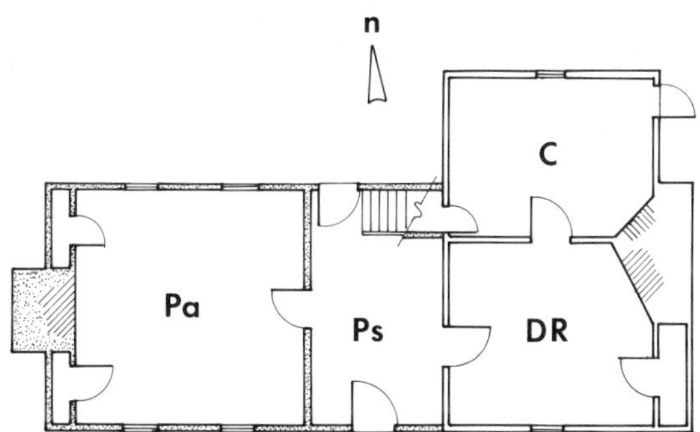

Figure 17. First-floor plan of the Hatcher House, Chesterfield County. Built in the late eighteenth century with an early nineteenth-century addition.

(figs. 15, 16). Its T-shaped plan consists of a parlor (hall) and a large passage in one section and two other rooms and a closet in a wing set perpendicular to it. The plaster quoins, in relief on the north corners but only incised on the southern ones, indicate that the building was meant to be approached directly from the north.

In contrast to the pretentiousness of Clements are two smaller dwellings in Chesterfield County. The Hatcher House, like Clements, employs a single large room on one side of the passage and two smaller ones on the other side. The floor plan in figure 17 represents two stages of construction.[40] The narrow, double-pile plan of the original section was a popular alternative to the more familiar hall-chamber plan among some builders of small houses in the late eighteenth century, and its large end chimney and corner fireplaces are characteristic of this (compare with fig. 1). The single-pile section is long and narrow and equally characteristic of its early nineteenth-century construction date. The addition created a three-room plan similar to those at the more sophisticated Indian Banks and Clements.

Related to the Hatcher House is a tiny house called Perkinsons, which began its existence in the last half of the eighteenth century as a single-cell dwelling (figs. 18, 19). Its original section is one of the smallest extant eighteenth-century houses in Virginia. Indeed, it remains unusually small despite the addition of a lean-to chamber and a slightly larger square wing around 1800. Despite its lack of a passage, this minuscule house employs the same three-room arrangement as its larger cousins.[41]

Clements, the Hatcher House, and Perkinsons offer a conceptual link between Indian Banks, the original three-room example, and a popular large house form of the early nineteenth century in which

Figure 18. Southeast view of Perkinsons, Chesterfield County. Built in the late eighteenth century with an addition ca. 1800.

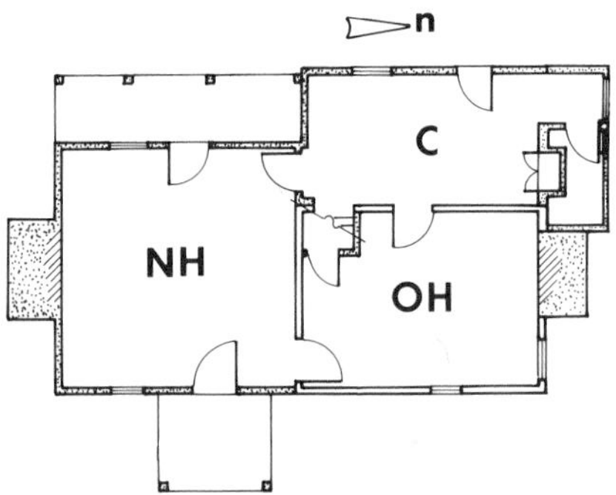

Figure 19. First-floor plan of Perkinsons, Chesterfield County. The original stair was in the southeast corner of the old hall.

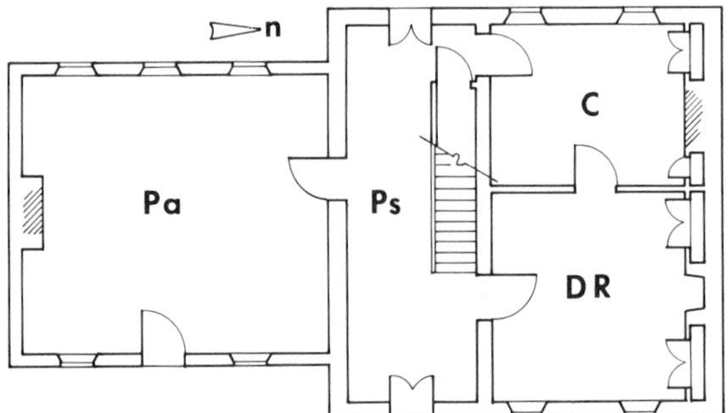

Figure 20. First-floor plan of Little Town, Sussex County. Built in 1811.

a double-pile, side-passage block, usually two stories tall, abutted an original one- or two-story parlor wing (fig. 20). As such, it is a main-block-with-rear-ell structure reformulated as a main block with lateral wing, but the arrangement of spaces is the same.

Indian Banks serves as the formal mediator of several alternative packages for the molecule. Some builders of large houses extruded the third room completely from the main block. In most cases it was set off by an additional back passage so that the underlying pattern of circulation was preserved, but no room was connected directly with another (fig. 21). First used in the third quarter of the eighteenth century, this floor plan remained popular through the first quarter of the nineteenth century.

A more compact solution, favored in the third and fourth quarters of the eighteenth century, collapsed the back room of the Indian Banks–type plan into the body of the house, presenting to passersby the simple rectangular shape of a single-pile building, as at the Billups House (figs. 2, 22). In these houses, the smaller rooms were served by corner fireplaces sharing a single chimney, which increased the visual single-pile illusion. Normally houses with this plan were one-and-a-half stories, but several two-story versions were built in Fredericksburg during the 1780s.

Finally, there are some three-room houses that show no direct relation to the central-passage, Georgian-plan form. At Seven Springs, King William County, the four spaces—hall, chamber, dining room, and entry—are grouped around a central stack. Three of the four rooms have exterior doors (figs. 23, 24).[42] Virtually the same plan, but with end chimneys, was used in the original portion of Timberneck Hall, Gloucester County, an early nineteenth-century house (figs. 25, 26).

Examined solely with reference to their plans and external appearance, the several houses just described appear disparate and unconnected. Understood in the light of the social molecule, however, they can be recognized as versions of the same house. They are alternative solutions to the same problem of integrating a particular group of hier-

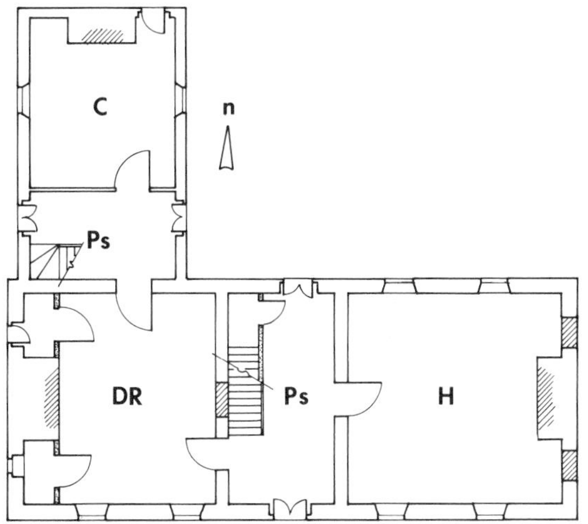

Figure 21. First-floor plan of Hewick, Middlesex County. Built in the mid eighteenth century. The main stair is a late nineteenth-century alteration.

Figure 22. Southeast view of the Billups House. The chamber door leads to a twentieth-century addition to the right, omitted in the plan in figure 2.

Figure 23. Southeast view of Seven Springs, King William County. Built in the mid eighteenth century.

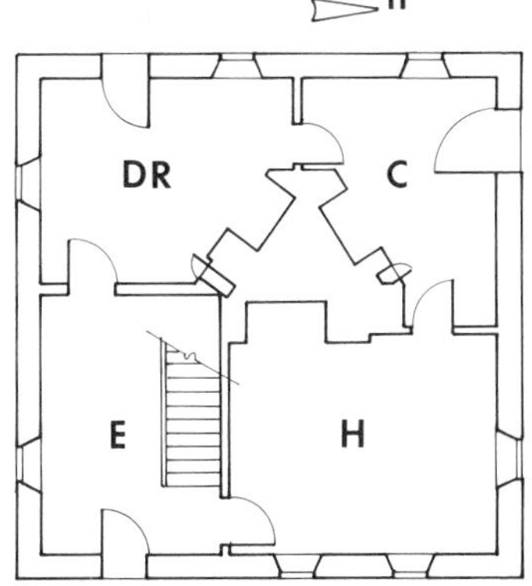

Figure 24. First-floor plan of Seven Springs, King William County.

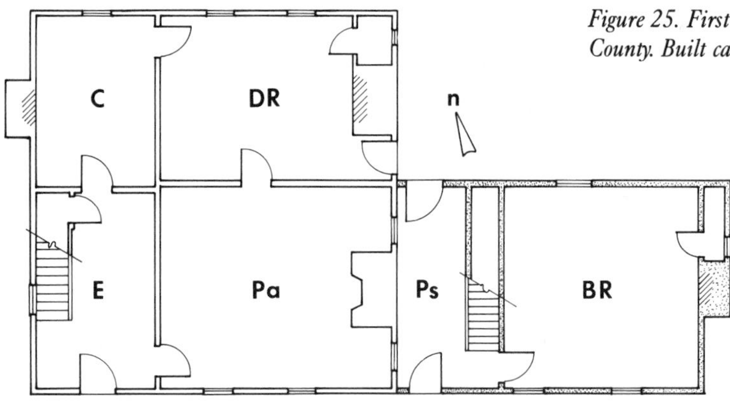

Figure 25. First-floor plan of Timberneck Hall, Gloucester County. Built ca. 1806; addition built ca. 1855.

Figure 26. South elevation of Timberneck Hall, Gloucester County. Note the double chimneys on the original section which reveal the double-pile plan. Compare these to the plan and the exterior of the Billups House (figs. 2, 22).

archical spaces into a coherent house. Although international architectural models, such as the Georgian-plan house, were one source of ideas for formal solutions, they became an increasingly less popular source than the three-room vernacular plan during the eighteenth century. Instead, Virginia's builders started with a traditional architecture forged in the hard years of the seventeenth century and altered and refined it to meet the more complex social and economic structures of the eighteenth.

The exteriors of these buildings reveal the same process at work (see figs. 5, 22, 23, 26; compare with fig. 3). In some ways, they do bear a general resemblance to the Georgian house form. However, they are plainer than most Georgian houses, and their classical decoration is used differently. It defines the house as one composed of a few simple shapes, decisively bounded at the edges. In intent these houses are aesthetically closer to Virginia's seventeenth-century houses, also treated as simple masses, than to those houses illustrated in eighteenth-century architectural treatises. Yet each of the Virginia houses, with the possible exception of Perkinsons, was the residence of a well-to-do or wealthy planter, and all show the kind of precision and careful workmanship that suggests that their plainness is deliberate rather than the result of penury or lack of skill. In addition, by strong monaxial massing, chimney placement, and fenestration,

Figure 27. Northeast view of the Judkins House, Surry County. Built in the late eighteenth century. Originally this was a three-room-plan house with a configuration similar to that at Timberneck Hall but with corner fireplaces and a single chimney stack. As such, it conformed to the traditions discussed in the text. Around 1840 the plan was altered to a side-passage, double-pile configuration by the removal of a partition, and the two-room depth was acknowledged by a new double chimney.

Figure 28. First-floor plan of Marmion, King George County. Built in the mid eighteenth century. Although the traditional front-back orientation of main and secondary rooms was reversed by the builder to create a dramatic entry, the circulation pattern among the rooms is standard.

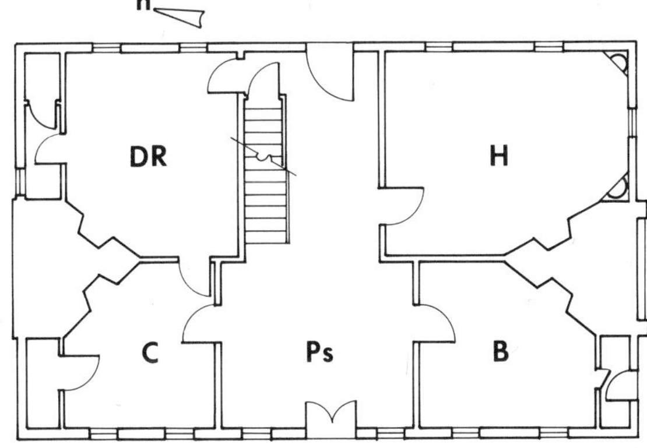

many of the three-room houses are disguised to look like single-pile houses even when they are in fact two rooms deep (fig. 22). A willingness to admit the appearance of double-pile planning to the exterior design of houses through the disposition of chimneys and window openings came slowly to Virginians, for the traditional single-pile aesthetic was still powerful. It was not until the early nineteenth century that a frank admission of double-pile depth was common (figs. 26, 27).

What was absorbed from European academic architecture was a taste for regularity that accorded well with Virginians' preference for "neatness" and decency. Although Virginia's upper-class vernacular buildings show little formulaic reproduction of the cubical house model, they do show an ordering of elements according to a strict, repetitive system. This gives them all an external similarity of appearance.[43]

It is possible to identify specific pattern-book models for some large Virginia houses. Mt. Airy, Richmond County, its exterior form derived from James Gibbs's 1728 *Book of Architecture,* is a famous example. Closer to the buildings discussed here is Marmion, a mid eighteenth-century house in King George County. A plan similar to that used at Marmion was published several times in eighteenth-century books like Abraham Swan's *Collection of Designs in Architecture* (fig. 28).[44] The significance of

Marmion is that this academic plan (which contained one extremely elaborate room now displayed in the Metropolitan Museum of Art) was enclosed in a framed exterior that looks like a farm house. Seven bays long and weatherboarded, it has a clipped-gable roof and asymmetrically shaped end chimneys that, in Virginia vernacular fashion, give the house a single-pile appearance.

Thus, close examination suggests that the answer to our opening query must be that the claims of published experts in the eighteenth century did not overwhelm vernacular building in Virginia. Rather, they were bypassed as the colony's builders helped themselves to specific design elements, reformulating them in the context of Virginia society, and particularly of the distancing and control in local social relations that had been developing since the mid seventeenth century.

Wealthy Virginians in the seventeenth century struggled to define their right to dominate their neighbors for political and economic advantage, only to find their domination limited in the eighteenth century by the need of English politics for American posts as rewards for its own faithful.[45] The architecture of mid eighteenth-century Virginia embodied social formality as an assertion of local social and political control where Virginia's elite could hope for little more. This architectural statement was novel only in its refinement. The social forms of control were encapsulated in a variety of house that employed to differing degrees, from a molding to a facade or a plan, the vocabulary of European classical architecture. But the emphasis remained local; it was the local context that allowed for the reception of academic forms. Change in the Anglo-American world had made available for Virginia use an architectural language that reinforced its values and amplified its peculiar meanings. Over the local social system it cast a unifying cloak, suggesting that Virginians rightfully belonged to a larger world, that theirs was a legitimate order even if a limited one.

Notes

This article was originally published in the *Winterthur Portfolio* (Summer–Autumn 1982). All illustrations in this article are by the author.

1. M. W. Barley, *The English Farmhouse and Cottage* (London: Routledge and Kegan Paul, 1961), p. 269.
2. Henry Glassie has offered a theoretical model for this process in *Folk Housing in Middle Virginia: A Structural Analysis of Historic Artifacts* (Knoxville: University of Tennessee Press, 1975), pp. 19–40, 66–113.
3. J. H. Plumb, *The Growth of Political Stability in England, 1675–1725* (Baltimore: Penguin Books, 1964).
4. John Wilton-Ely, "The Rise of the Professional Architect in England," in *The Architect: Chapters in the History of the Profession,* ed. Spiro Kostof (New York: Oxford University Press, 1977), pp. 180–208.
5. Batty Langley and Thomas Langley, *The Builder's Jewel; or, The Youth's Instructor and the Workman's Remembrancer* (1746; reprint, New York: Benjamin Blom, 1970).
6. This view has been challenged for social history in E. P. Thompson, *Whigs and Hunters: The Origin of the Black Act* (New York: Pantheon Books, 1975); and in Douglas Hay, et al., *Albion's Fatal Tree: Crime and Society in Eighteenth-Century England* (New York: Pantheon Books, 1975).
7. Cary Carson, "The 'Virginia House' in Maryland," *Maryland Historical Magazine* 69, no. 2 (Summer 1974): 186; Dell Upton, "Early Vernacular Architecture in Southeastern Virginia" (Ph.D. diss., Brown University, 1980), pp. 221, 232. In modern Virginia usage, a one-and-a-half-story building is one with a full-height ground floor and a loft that is finished or at least regularly used. After the early eighteenth century, these spaces were usually lighted by dormers.
8. Durand de Dauphiné, *A Huguenot Exile in Virginia; or, Voyages of a Frenchman Exiled for His Religion, with a Description of Virginia and Maryland,* trans. and ed. Gilbert Chinard (New York: Press of the Pioneers, 1934), pp. 119–20.
9. Dell Upton, "The Origins of Chesapeake Architecture," in *Three Centuries of Maryland Architecture* (Annapolis: Maryland Historical Trust, 1982), pp. 44–57; Upton, "Early Vernacular Architecture," pp. 154–64, 170–74. The influx of servants in the mid seventeenth century is treated in Wesley Frank Craven, *White, Red and Black: The Seventeenth-Century Virginian* (New York: W. W. Norton, 1977), pp. 1–

37. The political and social estrangement of master and servant is discussed in Bernard Bailyn, "Politics and Social Structure in Virginia," in *Seventeenth-Century America: Essays in Colonial History,* ed. James Morton Smith (Chapel Hill: University of North Carolina Press, 1959), pp. 90–115; and in greater detail in Russell R. Menard, "From Servant to Freeholder: Status Mobility and Property Accumulation in Seventeenth-Century Maryland," *William and Mary Quarterly,* 3d ser., 30, no. 1 (January 1973): 37–64; and Russell R. Menard, P. M. G. Harris, and Lois Green Carr, "Opportunity and Inequality: The Distribution of Wealth on the Lower Western Shore of Maryland, 1638–1705," *Maryland Historical Magazine* 69, no. 2 (Summer 1974): 169–84. For examples of seventeenth-century three-cell houses in Virginia, see Norman F. Barka, *Archaeology of Flowerdew Hundred: Stone House Foundation Site* (Williamsburg: Southside Historical Sites, 1976); Fraser D. Neiman, "Domestic Architecture at the Clifts Plantation: The Social Context of Early Virginia Building," *Northern Neck Historical Magazine* 28 (1978): 3096–3128 (reprinted in this volume); and Fraser D. Neiman, *The "Manner House" before Stratford (Discovering the Clifts Plantation)* (Stratford: Robert E. Lee Memorial Association, 1980). The alteration of one house to reflect the growing social division is described in Neiman, *"Manner House,"* pp. 31–35.

10. Upton, "Early Vernacular Architecture," pp. 221, 232. The categorization of a decedent's goods by the rooms that they were found in is a feature of some English and American probate inventories. This was a convenience to the appraisers, a way for them to keep track of what they had done in the case of an individual who had many possessions. Estates recorded in this manner constitute a very small proportion of Virginia probate inventories and are weighted overwhelmingly toward the upper end of the economic scale.

11. For representative English precedents of Virginia plans, see Raymond B. Wood-Jones, *Traditional Domestic Architecture in the Banbury Region* (Manchester: Manchester University Press, 1963), p. 108. All of the room terms used here are traditional Anglo-American names found in the room-by-room inventories of any English or American locality (F. W. Steer, *Farm and Cottage Inventories of Mid-Essex, 1635–1749* [Chelmsford: Essex County Council, 1950]; and Abbott Lowell Cummings, *Rural Household Inventories: Establishing Names, Uses and Furnishings of Rooms in the Colonial New England Home, 1675–1775* [Boston: Society for the Preservation of New England Antiquities, 1964] [introduction reprinted in this volume]). Nevertheless, meanings of the names varied over time and place (M. W. Barley, "A Glossary of Names for Rooms in Houses of the Sixteenth and Seventeenth Centuries," in *Culture and Environment: Essays in Honor of Sir Cyril Fox,* ed. I. Ll. Foster and L. Alcock [London: Routledge and Kegan Paul, 1963], pp. 479–501). For example, the term *parlor* had an erratic career in eighteenth-century Virginia. In most cases it was used as I have used it here, as a synonym for *the chamber,* meaning the principal ground-floor sleeping room. After the mid eighteenth century it was often used to designate the second most important room of an exceptionally large house, with the principal room still called the hall. In the early nineteenth century, *parlor* was often used instead of *hall* to identify the principal living room, and the word *hall* gradually was applied to the passage, the circulation corridor that ran through the house from front to rear.

12. Fiske Kimball, *Domestic Architecture of the American Colonies and of the Early Republic* (New York: Scribner's, 1922), pp. 40, 70, 72–75; William H. Pierson, *American Buildings and Their Architects: The Colonial and Neo-Classical Styles* (Garden City, N.Y.: Anchor Books, 1976), p. 66. The history of the "detached house" and its origins in Italian and Netherlandish Renaissance architecture are conveniently summarized in John Summerson, *Architecture in Britain, 1530–1830,* 5th ed. (Baltimore: Penguin Books, 1969), pp. 149–52, 189–92; and Pierson, *American Buildings,* pp. 61–68. A direct connection between the Dutch and the Virginian examples through the medium of design books is demonstrated in Nancy Halverson Schless, "Dutch Influence on the Governor's Palace, Williamsburg," *Journal of the Society of Architectural Historians* 28, no. 4 (December 1969): 254–70.

13. Henry Glassie, *Pattern in the Material Folk Culture of the Eastern United States* (Philadelphia: University of Pennsylvania Press, 1969), pp. 49, 54–55; Glassie, *Folk Housing,* pp. 88–113. The Georgian type is best described from the perspective of vernacular architecture studies in Henry Glassie, "Eighteenth-Century Cultural Process in Delaware Valley Folk Building," in *Winterthur Portfolio 7,* ed. Ian M. G. Quimby (Charlottesville: University Press of Virginia, 1972), pp. 35–38 (reprinted in this volume).

14. Marcus Whiffen, "Some Virginian House Plans Reconsidered," *Journal of the Society of Architectural Historians* 16, no. 2 (May 1957): 17; Glassie, "Cultural

Process," pp. 37–38; Pierson, *American Buildings*, p. 66; James Deetz, "Ceramics from Plymouth, 1620–1835: The Archaeological Evidence," in *Ceramics in America*, ed. Ian M. G. Quimby (Charlottesville: University Press of Virginia, 1972), p. 18; Glassie, *Folk Housing*, pp. 89–91.

15. Dell Upton, "Towards a Performance Theory of Vernacular Architecture in Tidewater Virginia," *Folklore Forum* 12, nos. 2–3 (1979): 173–96. For analogous English examples, see M. W. Barley, "The Double-Pile House," *Archaeological Journal* 136 (1979): 253–64.
16. Stephen A. Tyler, ed., *Cognitive Anthropology* (New York: Holt, Rinehart and Winston, 1969), p. 6.
17. In 365 Virginia room-by-room inventories dating 1646–1805, there were thirty-two basic categories used. These were combined with descriptive terms into 384 *different* room designations (Upton, "Early Vernacular Architecture," pp. 129–30). Significantly, *the chamber* was used in contrast to *a chamber*, a general term. Also used regularly, although not as often in the seventeenth century, were names of service spaces—kitchens and dairies—that were removed from the house by the late seventeenth century.
18. Cary Carson, "Doing History with Material Culture," in *Material Culture and the Study of American Life*, ed. Ian M. G. Quimby (New York: W. W. Norton, 1978), pp. 52–54.
19. Robert Beverley, *The History and Present State of Virginia*, ed. Louis B. Wright (Chapel Hill: University of North Carolina Press, 1947), pp. 289–90; the Truro Parish glebe house of 1737 was to have "a neat cornish" and a stair with "a neat rail"; the Essex County courthouse of 1702 was to be "decently Railed and Banistered" and "decently Glased" (Truro Parish, *Minutes of the Vestry: Truro Parish, Virginia, 1732–1785* [Lorton: Pohick Church, 1974], pp. 15, 32; Beverley Fleet, comp., *Colonial Virginia Abstracts, 14, King and Queen County: Records Concerning Eighteenth Century Persons,* 5th coll. [Richmond: Privately printed, 1942], p. 6).
20. Durand, *Huguenot Exile,* p. 120.
21. This was particularly true of the counties south of James River, in which many of the houses described later are located.
22. Gerald W. Mullin, *Flight and Rebellion: Slave Resistance in Eighteenth-Century Virginia* (New York: Oxford University Press, 1974), p. 6; Dell Upton, "Slave Housing in Eighteenth-Century Virginia: A Report to the Department of Social and Cultural History, National Museum of American History," manuscript, Smithsonian Institution, 1982, pp. 2–4, 35–37a.
23. Landon Carter, *The Diary of Colonel Landon Carter of Sabine Hall, 1752–1778,* ed. Jack P. Greene (Charlottesville: University Press of Virginia, 1965), p. 1090.
24. Edmund S. Morgan, *Virginians at Home: Family Life in the Eighteenth Century* (Williamsburg: Colonial Williamsburg Foundation, 1952), chap. 4; Jane Carson, *Colonial Virginians at Play* (Williamsburg: Colonial Williamsburg Foundation, 1965), pp. 1–8. As Michael Zuckerman has demonstrated, the "thinness" of Virginia social life led some planters to invest large portions of their energy in the creation of a network of conviviality that surpassed that of the English gentry circles in extent and emotional importance (Michael Zuckerman, "William Byrd's Family," in *Perspectives in American History,* vol. 12, ed. Donald Fleming [Cambridge, Mass.: Charles Warren Center for Studies in American History, 1979], pp. 290–95, 299–311).
25. Truro Parish, *Minutes,* p. 15. Again, for an amusing glimpse of the dichotomy between the social and the practical aspects of the Virginia plantation house, we can turn to Carter. Of the decoration at Sabine Hall, he noted that "wainscoted rooms have their [in]conveniencies. A dead rat has been stinking behind mine in the hall at least 6 days and is now intolerable in spite of burning tar" (*Diary,* p. 1100).
26. Where there was a fourth room behind the hall, however, there was normally no such direct connection (see fig. 7).
27. Richmond County Will Book, no. 7, 1767–87, pp. 13–16; Middlesex County Will Book, 1713–34, pp. 317–24. All citations of county records are from photostatic copies of the originals in the Archives of the Virginia State Library, Richmond. Titles are listed as they are on the spines of those volumes.
28. King George County Deed Book, no. 6 (Inventories, 1745–65), pp. 65–66.
29. Glassie, *Folk Housing,* p. 121. As my drawings show, service entrances into dining rooms and chambers were common.
30. For an illustration of a postmedieval through-passage house, see Eric Mercer, *English Vernacular Houses: A Study of Traditional Farmhouses and Cottages* (London: Her Majesty's Stationery Office, 1975), p. 57. Through-passage houses can be discovered in Virginia records and in several of the seventeenth-century archaeological sites recently excavated in the state (York County Deeds, Orders, Wills, no. 8, pp. 362–63; York County Records, no. 15, pp. 529–32; Neiman, *"Manner House,"* pp. 12–15).
31. An early example is the porch that was specified for the Accomack County parsonage of 1635 (Susie M. Ames, ed., *County Court Records for Accomack-North-*

ampton, Virginia, 1640–1645 [Charlottesville: University Press of Virginia, 1973], p. 43).

32. Richmond County Will Book, no. 6, 1753–67, pp. 43–46.
33. William G. Stanard, ed., "Jones Papers," *Virginia Magazine of History and Biography* 26, no. 2 (April 1918): 176. Another example for a very large house is found in the description of Westover written in 1783. The author stated that the front door led into "a very wide entry" (Thomas Lee Shippen, *Westover Described in 1783,* ed. L. H. Butterfield [Richmond: William Byrd Press, 1952], unpaged). Since the inventories record the dates of the owners' deaths rather than those of the construction of the houses, the disappearance of porches and entries from the inventories at midcentury may reasonably be supposed to reflect an architectural change that had occurred earlier, probably during the second quarter of the century. The earliest passage recorded in the probate inventories that is clearly a central passage is that in the house of Matthew Ballard, who died in 1719 (York County Records, no. 15, pp. 479–80). Again the actual change can be back dated.
34. Glassie, *Folk Housing,* pp. 21–26.
35. Landon C. Bell, *Cumberland Parish, Lunenburg County, Virginia, 1746–1816. Vestry Book, 1746–1816* (Richmond: William Byrd Press, 1930), pp. 380, 384.
36. Lancaster County Deeds, etc., no. 13, 1736–43, pp. 297–301; Surry County Deeds, Wills, etc., 1738–54, pp. 43–44; King George County Inventories, 1721–44, pp. 283–91.
37. Stanard, "Jones Papers," p. 176.
38. York County Wills and Inventories, no. 23, 1783–1811, pp. 492–93.
39. York County Records, no. 18, pp. 416–19, 679–80.
40. Jeffrey M. O'Dell, *Chesterfield County: Early Architecture and Historic Sites* (Chesterfield, Va.: Chesterfield County, 1983), pp. 185–86.
41. Ibid., pp. 105–6.
42. Similar plans were used at the Peyton-Randolph House, Williamsburg, and at the house site excavated at Burkes Corner, York County, in 1974 (Marcus Whiffen, *The Eighteenth-Century Houses of Williamsburg: A Study of Architecture and Building in the Colonial Capital of Virginia* [Williamsburg: Colonial Williamsburg Foundation, 1960], pp. 96–100; and Alain Outlaw, "Excavations at Burkes Corner and Survey of the Skimino Meetinghouse Lot, York County, Virginia," archaeological report, Virginia Historic Landmarks Commission, Richmond, 1974, pp. 6–21).
43. One geometrical system of visual order is described in Whiffen, *Eighteenth-Century Houses,* pp. 56–59.
44. James Gibbs, *A Book of Architecture* (1728; reprint, New York: Benjamin Blom, 1968), plate 58; Abraham Swan, *A Collection of Designs in Architecture,* vol. 1 (1757; reprint, Westmead: Gregg International Publishers, 1972), plate 11; Abraham Swan, *The British Architect* (1758; reprint, New York: Da Capo Press, 1967), plate 41.
45. Edmund S. Morgan, *American Slavery, American Freedom: The Ordeal of Colonial Virginia* (New York: W. W. Norton, 1975), pp. 215–70, 295–315; Bernard Bailyn, *The Origins of American Politics* (New York: Vintage Books, 1967), p. 74.

"Set Thine House in Order": The Domestication of the Yeomanry in Seventeenth-Century New England

ROBERT BLAIR ST. GEORGE

English society underwent a significant transition in the seventeenth century and its New England outpost was not immune to these changes. The key shift was manifested by a decided tilt toward pragmatic action, social acts in which personal initiative was highlighted. The older focus on the emotional power of religion and morality became less intense as throughout the seventeenth century New England became less God-centered and more man-centered. Such an important change was not abrupt but gradual, and more important, it could not be acknowledged by upstanding Puritans without fear of admitting that their world was approaching chaos if not total collapse. The general response to the attendant tension of these conflicting cultural alternatives was to impose a strict divisive order on daily life and Robert Blair St. George finds this order registered in architectural acts.

Animals, he notes, were kept a great distance from people as agricultural roles were confined to the barn and domestic roles to the house. Men's work took place outside the house while women's work occurred within. The ideal of the appropriate place or space for the appropriate activity was rigorously pursued. Rooms in houses, for example, came to have specific functions and names. During the early seventeenth century most rooms were fairly empty of furniture, allowing, even encouraging, some flexibility of behavior. Near the end of the century, however, all rooms by comparison were filled with specialized artifacts designed for particular social and technical functions. The more one divided up his house and filled it with special furnishings, the more one might direct and channel the behavior of visitors to one's home. They would be received in one place, talked to in another, fed in yet another room, and maybe bedded down in still another chamber. The main task of the Puritan yeoman was then to restrict the uses of the spaces around him in order to assert his will, his control. Citizens of the Bible commonwealth had taken on God's role on earth.

Perhaps the historian's persistent lack of attention to space is rooted in an unhealthy positivism. Space, after all, implies to the modern mind a kind of phenomenological absence. Facts, as "hard data," seem more dependable, or so it seems.[1] But in reality much the opposite holds true. Space is indeed substantive, and for the yeoman in seventeenth-century New England, the physical layout of the farmyard—the arrangement of barn, outbuildings, and house—was crucial both to his economic livelihood and to his psychological stability. For the yeoman, existing in a pre-Newtonian universe, the location of man-made structures helped bring coherence to an otherwise apparently chaotic world. The New England yeoman's emphasis on artifice and order demanded that his world be rigorously outlined by regular fences, well-maintained buildings, and fields plowed and cross-plowed in geometric patterns. The Englishman John Worlidge painted a complete picture of the ideal farmyard when he described how the yeoman's house should have a "garden on every side inclosed with a noble fence, and [be] Cultivated with most curious Art, and singular Industry." Overwhelmed by the power of regularity, Worlidge so worshipped "the compleat order of everything, and the height of the Trees, planted in such direct lines, and every way lineal or prospective, the Earth adorned with Plants, the fairness of the Fruits, the beauty and the order of the pleasant and fragrant Flowers . . . that he did exceedingly admire not so much at the study and diligence, as the Industry and Ingenuity of the Workman, by whom the same was so *Artificially* ordered and contrived."[2]

The seventeenth-century rhetoric in this description of the ideal farmstead goes counter to our modern belief in freedom and unrestrained action: *inclosed, Cultivated, Art, compleat order, direct, lineal, beauty and order, contrived.* Visiting Plymouth when the new town was in its eighth year, Isaack De Rasieres commented on the appearance of the streets, where each family's plot had "gardens *enclosed* behind and at the sides with clapboards, so that houses and courtyards are arranged in very good *order.*"[3] Part of the yeoman's cultural baggage was this predisposition to order; the hardy settlers of Medfield sought "to subdue the earth for the sonnes of Adam" when they founded their town in 1649, while twenty-seven years earlier Richard Cushman had lambasted the raw New England landscape as being "marred for want of manuring, gathering, ordering, &c."[4] The domestic farmstead, as the unifying force beneath a matrix of everyday functions, enabled the massive task of ordering the landscape to proceed. By examining in close detail its constituent elements—the barn, its associated outbuildings, and the house—we can approach in more specific terms the New England yeoman's success or failure in living up to Worlidge's ideal.

Upon arrival in New England, yeomen continued to build for animals and crops as they had in their native English counties. Judging from surviving examples and documentary sources, two types of farmstead seem to have made the Atlantic crossing. Most prevalent in the greater part of England at the time of settlement was the use of two principal agricultural structures: a barn for the processing and storage of grain crops and a cowhouse or beast house for housing of cattle during the winter months and for daily milking. Farmers from the Midlands and the southeastern counties of England were among those principally responsible for transferring this division of functions to the New World, where reference to it appeared occasionally in inventories throughout the century. John Fairfield of Wenham, Massachusetts, died in 1646, the owner of a separate "Cowhouse," while a 1653 writ in Essex County refers to a "barn and hay in it, with the cow house."[5] Both inventories clearly refer to two separate structures. Ten years later, the 1663 inventory of John Fish of Sandwich mentions a "beast house," and the inventory of his near neighbor Thomas Dexter includes among "the outhousing a Barne & Cowhouse" in 1686.[6] Without question the need for some yeomen to house animals away from grain, blood away from bread, was strong enough to persist into the second generation.

The second English type of farmstead that appeared in New England included the long house, or "byre-and-dwelling," most often found in the northern and western counties of England. The form itself appears to have seen only limited and short-lived use in New England, perhaps because there were fewer West- and North-countrymen

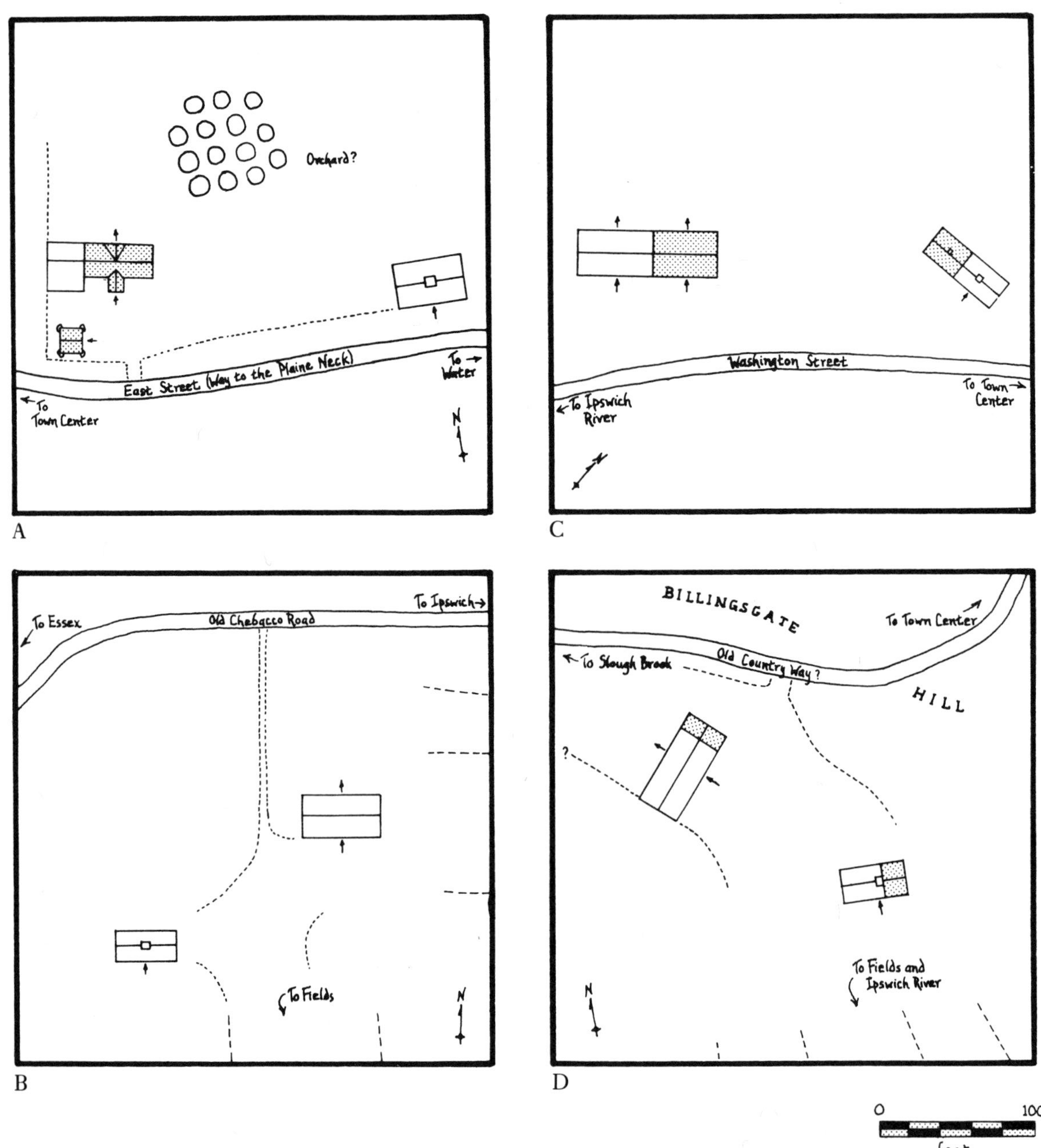

Figure 1. Four early New England farmsteads: a, Cushing Farmstead, Hingham, Massachusetts, ca. 1700; b, Giddings-Low Farmstead, Essex (formerly Chebacco Parish of Ipswich), Massachusetts, before 1702; c, Gould Farmstead, Topsfield, Massachusetts, ca. 1710; d, Stanley-Lake Farmstead, Topsfield, Massachusetts, before 1718. (From fieldwork by the author and R. F. Trent, 1979–81.)

among the immigrants and because it presented an increased fire hazard in a cold climate. The selectmen of Reading, for example, advised in 1649 that owing to "there being manni ascidentes in the Countree by fire, to the great damning of many, by joining of barne or haystacks to dwelling houses, therfor no barne or haystacks shall be set within six polles of anni dwelling house opon panilltie of twentie shillings."[7] The long house no doubt was also seen by Puritan yeomen as a less improved and less artificial structure, since the realm of beasts was viewed as unclean and debasing to the reason of man.[8]

Despite the persistence of these two farmstead plans, New England yeomen most commonly employed a third alternative: the incorporation of both animal housing and the processing and storage of grain into a single structure known generically as the "barn." From the very beginning of settlement this was the most typical meaning of the word *barn;* on the four pre-1720 New England farmsteads where both house and barn survive in situ (fig. 1) and on a fifth known only through graphic evidence, the barn definitely served this dual purpose. Exactly when use of the barn began is unclear, although its reported absence throughout much of England suggests that it was in some instances an early New England innovation.[9] Making the transformation in one leap of mind, a yeoman must have built this new kind of structure from the outset. Others made the change gradually, as did Ralph Partridge of Duxbury, who had stored "over the Cow House 1 bushell & an halfe of Corn" by 1658.[10]

The four surviving sites demonstrate three major points. First, they show that yeomen in early New England were careful to place raw food supplies and the arena of men's work at quite a distance from the house, an average of over 140 feet. In terms of sheer linear space, farmstead layout manifests a perceived disjunction between the realm of man the improver and the realm of his unimproved animals. Second, they show that in no instance was the yeoman's house placed in front of his barn. Eager to show his stock and store of supplies and thereby convince neighbors of his productivity, he pushed the barn out toward the street until it was either even with the front of the house or well beyond it. Finally, the farmstead was set strategically in regard to climatic exposure. Typically the house faced south and the barn was backed up to the northwest wind, protecting both house and animals (whose stalls were usually along the barn's south and east walls) from winter's blast. In two instances, the priority of exposure demanded that the house face directly away from the street (fig. 1b, d).

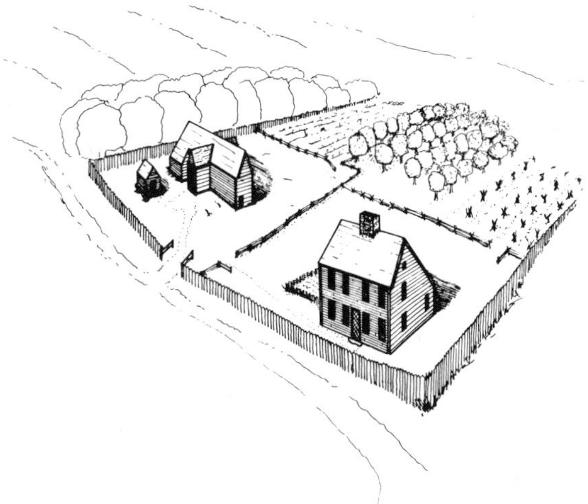

Figure 2. Perspective view of the Cushing Farmstead, Hingham, Massachusetts, ca. 1700. (From fieldwork by the author and R. F. Trent, 1979–81.)

The Cushing Farmstead in Hingham, Massachusetts (fig. 2), can serve as a paradigm for seventeenth-century New England barn planning and construction, and more generally of farmstead organization. The first reference to any barn on the property occurs in the 1693 will of Daniel Cushing, in which he gave "unto my Son Peter Cushing all my lands . . . containing twenty and four acres and halfe an acre of Land, be they more or less, with the Dwelling house and Barne and all other Buildings standing thereupon."[11] As the reference to "Barne" is clearly in the singular, it undoubtedly alludes only to the western section of the present structure, a small four-bay barn built with an integral lean-to on its south elevation (fig. 1a). With an original sill-to-plate distance of only 5½ feet, this first section was likely constructed soon after Cush-

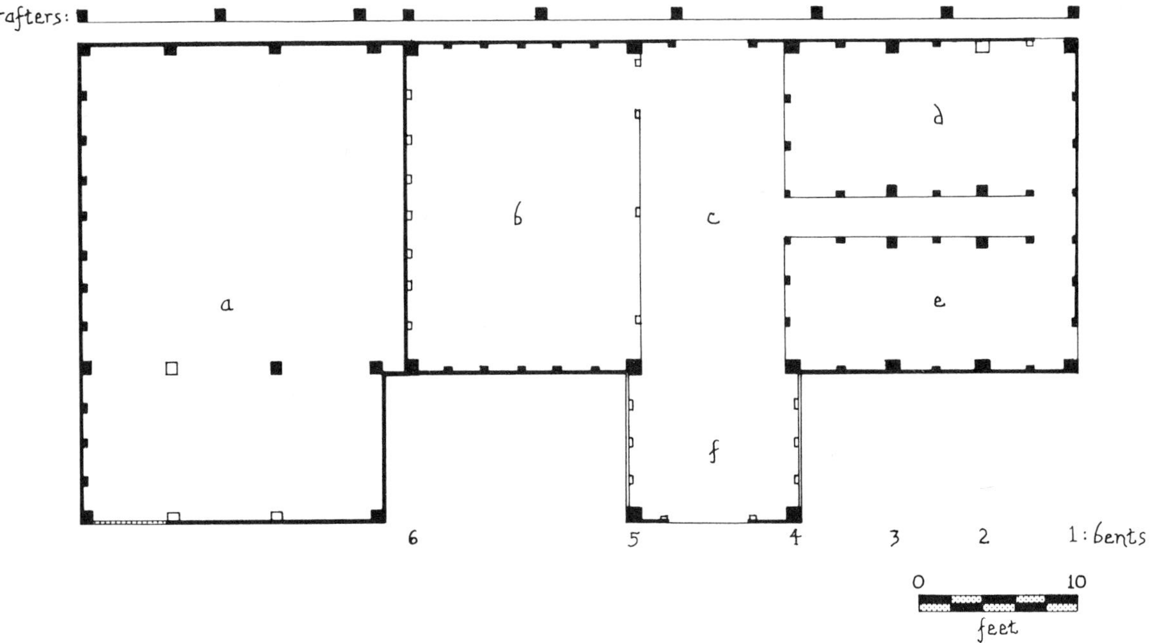

Figure 3. Plan of the Cushing barn, Hingham, Massachusetts, ca. 1693–1700. Areas within the structure include: a, probably first barn or cow-house, about 1679–93; b, storage area or section reserved for housing of untethered immature animals; c, threshing floor or runway; d, milking and feeding passage (with original planked floor); e, manuring passage (with original dirt floor); f, porch entry for loaded carts. Bents designated 1 through 6 define the boundaries of the second (ca. 1693–1700) barn structure. (From fieldwork by the author and R. F. Trent, 1979–80.)

ing built his house in 1679. At some point in the mid-1690s, the eastern portion of the barn was either damaged or dismantled, and a five-bay barn with fully articulated rear roof gable and projecting front porch was added onto its truncated remnant. As they stood during the closing years of the seventeenth century, these two structures were united under a single roof into one large barn (fig. 3).

The plan of the earlier section of the Cushing barn is unclear (fig. 3). Because of its low stud height and its low lean-to, it may even have been a cowhouse against which a dual-function barn was built. But the plan of the added barn, a complete symmetrical structure in and of itself, survives intact. Running through its center was a floored area for threshing and for unloading farm carts. In this respect, the Cushing barn was similar to one built for Philip Nelson of Rowley in 1667, which was "well nailed with a good floor, with a pair of great doors well hung for a loaded cart to go in and a pair of little doors for an unloaded cart to go out."[12] The threshing floor in the Cushing barn survives and consists of milled two-inch oak boards pegged in place with large trunnels and well-scarred by the fierce staccato of grain flails hitting its rough surface. The eastern half of the Cushing barn still contains its original open stalls used for the housing of dairy cows. Those on the north side originally had a plank floor and provided a clean passage for daily milking and feeding, while those on the south had dirt floors and were probably used as a bedding area and manuring passage. Modern farmers use grids and slatted floors as a means of combining manuring and feeding passages into a single run, but the seventeenth-century yeoman would never risk milking his cows directly over an earthen floor, recognizing that milk at all contaminated by dirt was instantly "made fit for hoggs."[13] A narrow foot passage between these areas provided the farmer with easy access to his animals. On the other side of the threshing floor, the Cushing barn provided space for the storage of processed grains and perhaps the open penning of young animals still too immature to be turned out or used for milk production. Both here and in the milking stalls, cattle would have been tethered front and rear to structural timbers; they were not enclosed in individual stalls or secured by passing their heads through hinged stanchions, as they are today.

The Cushing barn is large by any standard and owes its survival in part to its size, which could easily accommodate the changing needs of its owners during the ensuing two centuries. Other surviving agricultural structures are of similar size; both the Giddings-Low and the Gould barns are five-bay barns whose original dimensions provided an average total floor area of 1,400 square feet. Like the Cushing barn, these structures distributed livestock and storage around a central runway used for threshing. Lean-tos on barns were optional and sometimes were defined as such in contemporary contracts. As in house construction, lean-tos on barns do not indicate an inability to predict needed space but instead demonstrate a notable disregard for formal symmetry. In 1647 John Glover and Henry Dunster stipulated that Edmund Rice, in return for the privilege of working their land in Sudbury, should "build one barne, 50 foote long, 11 high on the stud, one foote above ground the sill, 20 foote if no leantos, or 18 foote wide with Leantoes on the one side."[14] A smaller barn with an integral lean-to like that on the western section of the Cushing barn once stood on the land of William Goodhue of Ipswich. After agreeing to rent his land to tenants Robert Wallis and William Smyth, Goodhue promised "to build them . . . a barn forty feet long with a leanto at one end twenty feet wide."[15] Without doubt this was a four-bay barn like the surviving Stanley-Lake barn in Topsfield. Yet these barns were all probably larger than most men in seventeenth-century New England could build or maintain without the help of servants or hired laborers. Probably more typical were the "Smale Barne biltt . . . of 20 ffoot loung and 18 ffoot wide" erected in Yarmouth in 1692 and that mentioned in the 1693 inventory of John Whitstone of Scituate, who owned "7 acres of Land and a Little house & a little Barne" worth twenty pounds.[16]

In its construction the Cushing barn is both typical and atypical. Like other surviving barns, it employs both girts and braces, which help to support the heavy loads of hay placed in loft areas (fig. 4). Although girt construction was recognized as an added expense during the period, farmers did not scrimp on the building that housed their means of economic livelihood. The Cushing barn is also fully studded, thus strengthening the walls and increasing their cost even more. Early in the seventeenth century, New England barns were all covered with riven oak clapboarding and later were sheathed with milled cedar weatherboarding, and, like the small barn illustrated by Worlidge, probably had no windows. Barn roofs were made of a variety of materials. Thatch found use far longer on barns than it did on houses; as late as 1671 two barn-building Ipswich carpenters agreed "to get laths and lath the roof for thatching."[17] Some roofs probably were shingled, but the most common technique, especially after mill-sawn lumber was widely available, was a boarded roof. Because most roof frames seem to have consisted of principal rafters supporting a series of common purlins let through trenches in their outer surfaces, roof boards probably went from ridge to eave. Certainly the roof of Nelson's barn in Rowley, which was "to be covered with pine boards well and close laid and well nailed, then to be covered with either slabs or battens on the joints and sides" suggests such an orientation.[18] Yet in other barns that, like Cushing's, employed a roof structure consisting of principal and secondary rafters with only one principal purlin per bay, roof boards must have been laid horizontally, perhaps with lapped joints to prevent leakage.

The roof of the Cushing barn is atypical in that

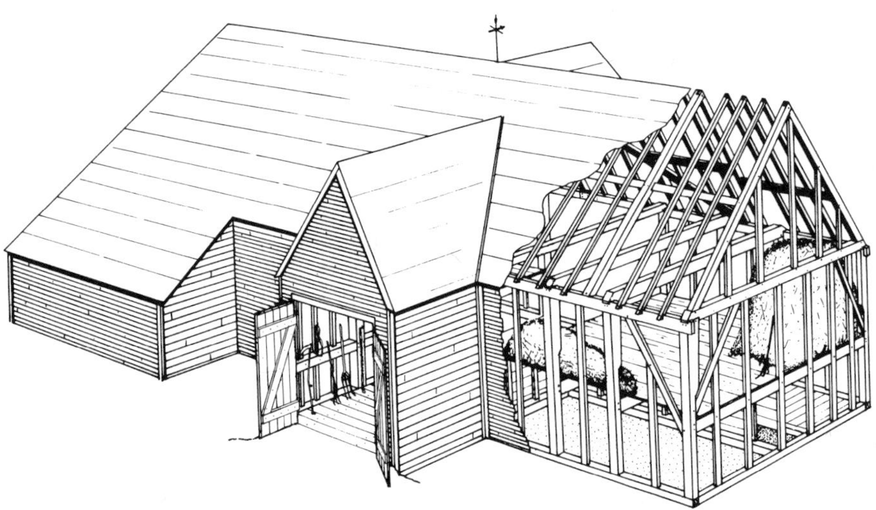

Figure 4. Perspective view of the Cushing barn, Hingham, Massachusetts, ca. 1693–1700. (From fieldwork by the author and R. F. Trent, 1979–80.)

its principal rafter feet do not meet the plates at points directly over the principal posts of the lower frame. Extant also in the Andrews House in Hingham, this roof-framing technique seems to be a direct transfer of a Norfolk carpentry technique, which persisted in Hingham owing to the town's unusually high percentage of woodworking artisans from that county.[19] As a result of this technique, the Cushing barn has evenly spaced roof bays that do not relate to the functional variations in the bay widths of the lower section. Besides this unusual merging of two systems, the Cushing barn shares with all other surviving barns the use of bents (structural framing sections) that vary with the use of particular areas in the plan (fig. 5). The Cushing barn uses different bents for the stall areas, the threshing area, and the storage area. The Stanley-Lake barn in Topsfield best demonstrates the complexity of bent design; while some of the variations result from the process of raising the frame itself, the principal areas used for animals, threshing, and, in this case, the housing of immature animals, all called for different bent designs.[20] By the late eighteenth century, functional variation in bent design had given way to standardized sections, which forced the farmer to mold his labor around an immutable form.

Since no inventory was made of Daniel Cushing's estate, exactly how many animals and how much grain he kept in his barn will never be known. But we can turn to other evidence to chart the contours of the average yeoman's farm in seventeenth-century New England. In 1652 a detailed town rate described the shape of agricultural life in Medfield, Massachusetts, a town settled by farmers from Dedham in 1649. Although the town was still relatively new, many of its residents had lived within its bounds long before its incorporation and were well established. The average house in Medfield that year had between five and six people under its roof and was worth a little less than thirty pounds, about one-sixth the value of its owner's estate.[21] In his barn and fields, the Medfield yeoman kept cattle and pigs, and he usually owned from one to three of both kinds of animals.[22] Farmers in Medfield were almost all from East Anglia and like their Dedham neighbors continued to practice mixed husbandry, with emphasis on dairying and the cultivation of cereals; the total absence of sheep is therefore not surprising. And horses, while used by an occasional New England yeoman for personal transport, were too expensive to feed over the long winter and less reliable than oxen before the plow.

During the seventeenth century agriculture var-

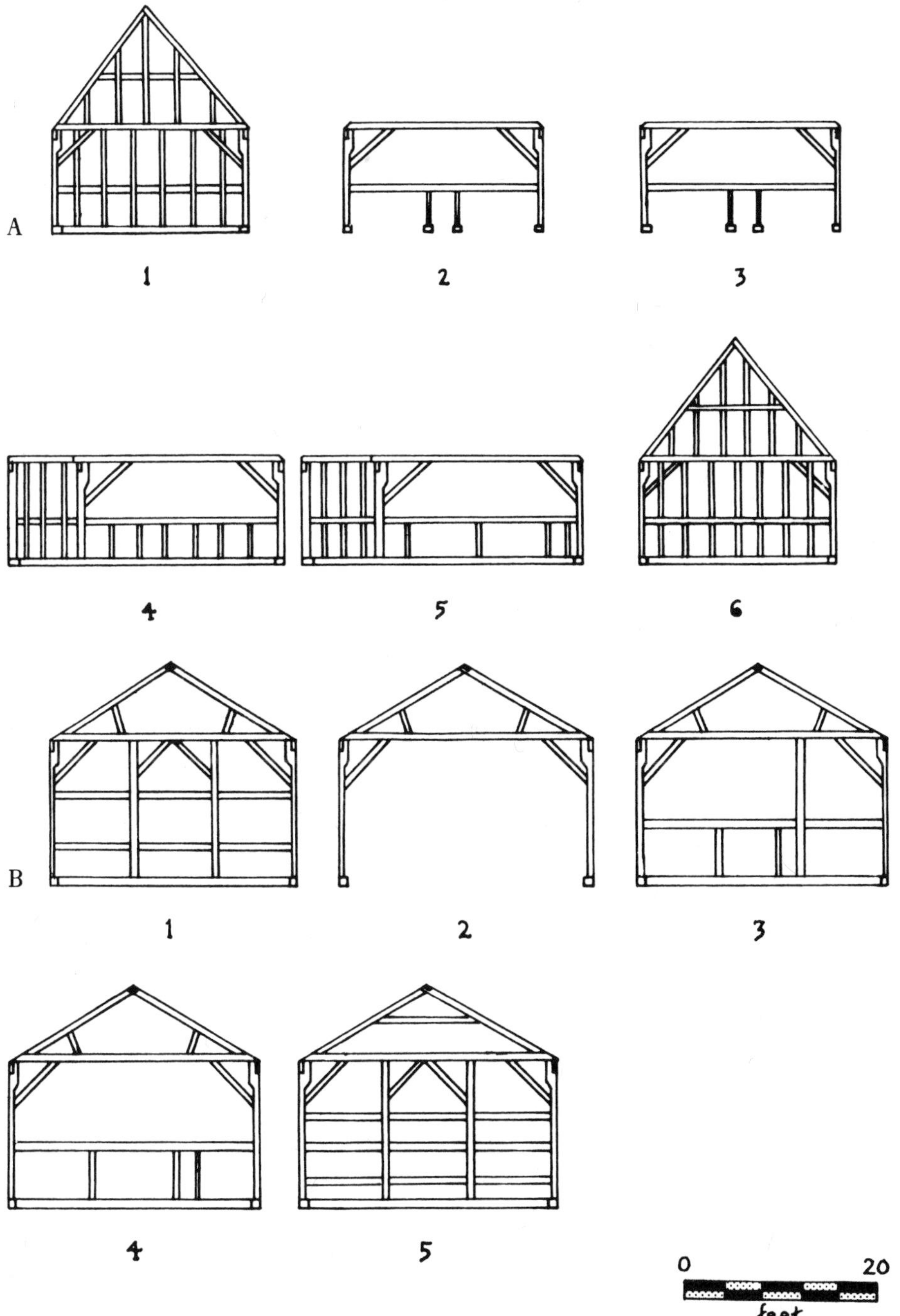

Figure 5. Bent designs of early New England barns: a, second Cushing barn, Hingham, Massachusetts, ca. 1693–1700 (see corresponding numbers on plan in figure 3); b, Stanley-Lake barn, Topsfield, Massachusetts, before 1718 (bents 1–5 proceed from southwest to north-east on plan of barn shown in figure 3). (From fieldwork by the author and R. F. Trent, 1979 and 1981.)

Table 1
Landholdings, Medfield, 1652

	Types of Land					
	Unbroken (N = 15)	Broken (N = 17)	Improved (N = 2)	Other (N = 5)		
				Fenced (N = 2)	Unfenced (N = 1)	Unspecified (N = 2)
Mean acreage owned	3.0	6.0	2.5	5.0	–	10.0
Median acreage owned	3.0	6.0	2.5	5.0	–	10.0
Value per acre	£1 12s. 0d.	£3 10s. 0d.	£6 10s. 0d.	£2 0s. 0d.	£1 0s. 0d.	£2 10s. 0d.

ied from town to town depending on the English regional preferences of first-generation yeomen. Some towns like Dedham and Medfield witnessed a continuity with the dairying and cereal crops of East Anglia, while others like Newbury had settlers from diverse backgrounds who argued over correct land use and proper husbandry techniques.[23] The size of landholdings varied with the type of animals and crops raised, as well as with the wealth and status of the owner in local affairs. In Medfield, dairying and cereal-production were processes that kept farms fairly compact; the average yeoman owned a little less than ten acres.

By contrast, the sheep-raising areas of the Narragansett Basin by the early eighteenth century saw yeomen with literally hundreds of acres available for grazing. On Aquidneck Island, Portsmouth men owned an average of 142 sheep, while their neighbors on nearby Jamestown Island owned an average of 289. And again, land was methodically categorized according to where it stood along the nature-culture continuum. The Medfield rate of 1652 is instructive, as it demonstrates how directly the monetary value of land depended on its reduction and containment (table 1). Unbroken lands were worth half as much as broken lands, which in turn were worth one-half the value of improved acreage. Similarly, fenced lands were worth twice the value of unfenced lands. Fences were vital to the stability of early New England communities, as court records repeatedly attest. Fences represented a great existential challenge. As fields gave way to plows, stones from the earth became stone fences; as trees were cut to clear needed acreage, trees on the earth became wooden fences. Fences also needed constant repair. Like the pattern cut by the yeoman's plow the containment of his land was an added step toward the ever receding edge of improvement. And containment applied not only to visible animals restrained by rail fences but also to invisible spirits, which, if not warded off by special markers, would ruin crops and cast spells on unsuspecting cattle.

Besides housing animals and grain, barns sheltered the tools needed for a wide variety of tasks. Agriculture in seventeenth-century New England was still "an art and mystery" whose practitioners were the masters of many implements. Worlidge lists a total of seventy-nine: thirteen "Belonging to the Arrable and Fieldlands," twenty-two for use in barn and stable, six peculiar only to the meadows and pasture, and twenty-three additional "necessary Instruments."[24] Of this compendium the New England yeoman used the basics: plows, harrows, shovels and spades, hoes, sickles, scythes or reap-hooks, pitchforks, rakes, flails, winnowing fans, grain measures, steelyards, sieves, hedging hooks and bills, sheep shears, trowels, plow sulls, yokes, and a variety of grain chests, bins, and pails used in feeding animals. In addition, he kept in the barn animal "furniture," such as harnesses, horse stirrups, spurs, bits and bridles, horseshoes, ox shoes, and cowbells.

Finally, barns in seventeenth-century New England seem to have found frequent use as arenas for antisocial behavior and for aggression that, for a wide variety of reasons,[25] could not find expression in the yeoman's house. Court records are full of cases of neighborly strife involving fights in barns, slander in barns, "unclean carriages" in barns, and other acts of physical violence. As the result of an argument in 1649, for example, Thomas Farrar of Lynn was "fined for throwing down Benjamin Smith and dragging him by the heels out of the barn."[26] Or when Thomas Coleman of Newbury faced charges two years later "for striking William Richardson of Newbury with the swingle of a flail . . . William Michell testified that Thomas Collman came to Goodman Sandar's barn and with a great swingell struck William Richeson across the back and ran away."[27] As one pole of the seventeenth-century New England farm plan, the barn represented the antithesis of man's artificial reason. Whether literally the realm of animals and raw cereals or whether the site of man's animal behavior, the barn was one side of a spatial dialectic balanced at its other extreme by the yeoman's house.

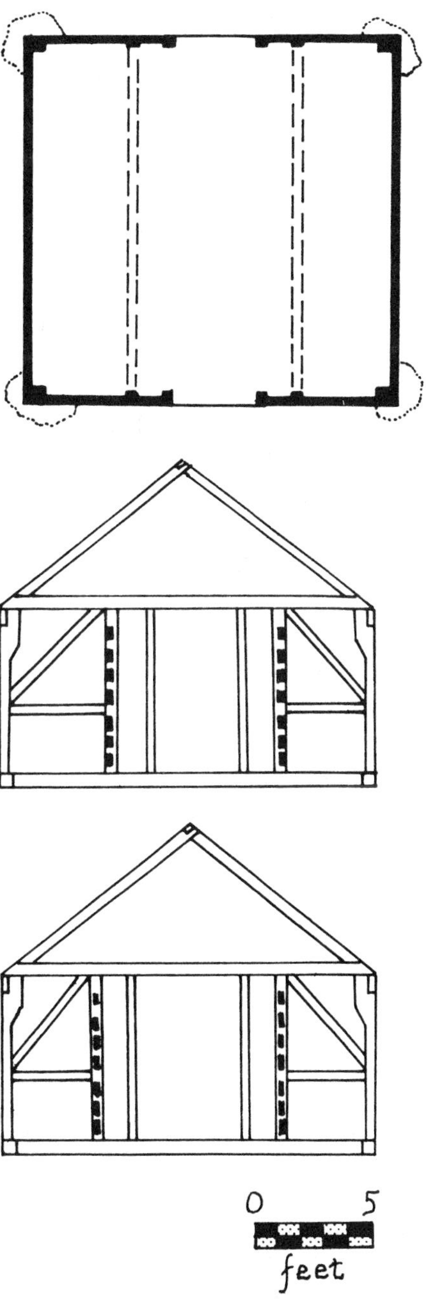

Figure 6. Plan and bent designs of the Cushing granary or "Corne barn," Hingham, Massachusetts, before 1740. (From fieldwork by the author and R. F. Trent, 1979–80.)

Situated between these two conceptual extremes were a variety of mechanical linkages, a series of smaller service structures. Some of these smaller buildings housed animals that did not belong in the barn; sheep had shippens, horses had stables, pigs had sties. Additional structures provided extra storage for grains, among them the mysterious "Small Moveable house" containing processed barley, three riddles (sieves with coarse mesh), and three flails on the property of Francis Brayton of Portsmouth, Rhode Island in 1717/18.[28] Within the pale of the Cushing barnyard still stands a corn barn or granary built before the early 1740s, in which seventeenth-century construction techniques were employed throughout its small frame. Used for the storage of husked corn and sacks of milled flour, it consists of a central walkway flanked on either side by two rows of horizontal rails, which are swung-fit into open mortises in the principal median posts to form two separate cribs (fig. 6). Under its pitched roof a loft of loose oak planks could be moved or removed, depending on the amount of storage needed. The building stands on its original stone pilings, or “staddles,” designed to keep the precious store of new corn off the damp ground and away from barnyard rodents. But by far the most numerous of outbuildings were those directly related to domestic industries, such as malt houses, brew houses, bolting houses, dairy houses, milk houses, bake houses, assorted shops for artisans, and unspecified “sheds.”

Exactly how all these structures might have been arranged remains for the most part unclear. The Cushing corn barn is placed so that a small yard is formed between it, the barn, and the house. If we look at this plan more closely, we learn that both the corn house and the added eastern barn were sited *toward* the house from the outer perimeter of the yard struck by the first barn. Instead of extending his original yard area with the placement of additional service structures, Daniel Cushing effectively opted to fill in existing space. The other extant sites reveal a similar pattern; whenever yeomen added to their barn or house, they expanded inward, keeping initial fencelines intact. The kitchen garden, another “improved” artificial space, also would have extended from the house straight into the farmyard. With new functions constantly imploding, this pattern reveals the prevailing aesthetic of seventeenth-century New England yeomen as one of pronounced formal construction; their concern for inviolate boundaries was manifest in everything from town planning and land use to portraiture and furniture construction.[29]

If the barn framed the symbolic realm of irrationality, the house signified the triumph of art and reason over disorder. New Englanders built permanent English houses within a very short time of settlement. In fact, within a decade of the end of the Great Migration, Edward Johnson attributed the material success of the Puritans to providential cause and gloated on how “the Lord hath been pleased to turn all the wigwams, huts and hovels the English dwelt in at their first coming into orderly, fair, and well-built houses, well furnished many of them, together with orchards filled with goodly fruit trees and gardens with variety of flowers.”[30] These “well-built houses” were almost without exception constructed of wood, using techniques transferred to the New World by trained carpenters and joiners. Although a few brick and stone houses punctuated the landscape, it was not until the discovery of natural limestone deposits in Rhode Island in the 1660s and near Newbury in the late 1690s that masonry buildings became feasible. The victim of a structural failure caused by a lack of necessary materials, John Winthrop lamented in 1631 how after “having erected a building of stone at Mistick, there came so violent a storm of rain, for twenty-four hours, from the N.E. and S.E. as (it not being finished, and laid with clay for want of lime) two sides of it were washed down to the ground.”[31] Over the course of the first century of settlement, a general pattern prevailed, which led from the relative heterogeneity of English regional house types to an eventual uniformity of plan and, to a lesser degree, of framing technology.

The distribution of plan types in British folk housing during the seventeenth century in some ways paralleled the pattern of local agriculture, with lowland housing and farming being noticeably different from their upland counterparts.[32] By the beginning of immigration to New England, a “revolution in housing” had swept through the British countryside, and while its results were dramatic, they were also varied.[33] In the lowlands, especially East Anglia and the southeastern counties, the interior environment became cleaner and brighter. Yet contributing a concern for presenting a clean social front was an overall tendency to push the service functions of the house toward the rear. Hiding the clutter of domestic process, the owner could now present a symmetrical product to his neighbors: the facade of his central-chimney house. Finally, as chimneys filled old smoke-holes, the open hall of the sixteenth-century house could be ceiled over to provide a second floor of chambers previously unavailable.

The eastern counties of England, then, had by 1620 made a concerted effort to disjunct the clean social front of the house from its dirty back and countered the rearward movement of services with the upward expansion of chamber space. In seventeenth-century New England this formal arrangement was dominant, owing in large part to the regional origins of the English settlers. It is well demonstrated in the earliest seventeenth-century framed house to survive, the Jonathan Fairbanks House in Dedham, Massachusetts (fig. 7). Like its regional precedents in the nucleated villages of Suffolk and Norfolk, the Fairbanks House was set in a line of similar houses and greeted its visitors with a small porch entry, a cold impersonal space that acted as a social buffer between the interior space and the external universe.

In England's upland districts the process of rebuilding was slowed both by topographical and economic circumstances and by an alternative social structure that shaped many of its remote communities. People in the uplands often lived farther from their neighbors than did their lowland brethren, partly owing to the demands of a predominantly grazing economy. They probably saw their neighbors less often and had to go farther for a visit. At some distance from one another, their houses needed no hallway or entry to ensure privacy; as a result, West- and North-country houses typically had front doors that opened directly into the hall, the principal social space of the house. Upland houses also differed from their lowland counterparts in profile. Built on windy hillsides and open to the blast of rain and wind, they hugged the ground and frequently were built into the sides of hills.[35] And, far from the critical eye of neighbors and hence not socially closed, their service rooms were not hidden from view. Because of these social and climatic conditions, upland houses followed a low, linear plan that contrasted with lowland English notions of design and social order. When West-countrymen came to New England, they continued to build their long and low houses with doors that opened into their hearts. In early Rhode Island, a colony with a high percentage of West-countrymen, houses with such open plans survive, and the Roger Mowry House in Providence is a representative single-cell example (fig. 8). In other areas these houses were built randomly. The Standish site in Duxbury, excavated in the early 1860s, reveals a plan (fig. 9) undoubtedly brought by an immigrant from a rural area of western or northern England, and two other similar house types in the Plymouth area have been unearthed more recently.[35]

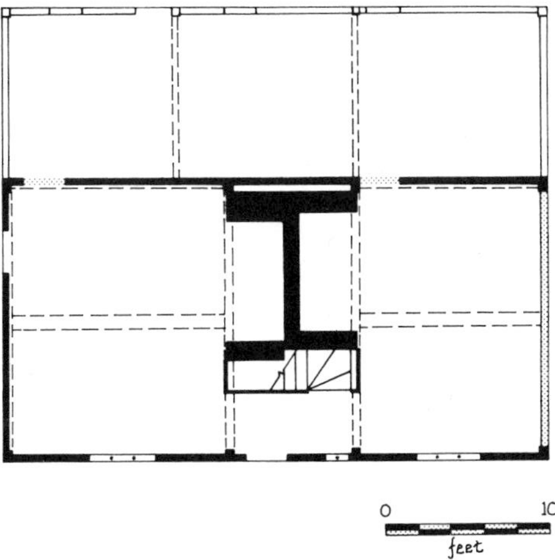

Figure 7. Plan of the Jonathan Fairbanks House, Dedham, Massachusetts, ca. 1637–46 and later. (From fieldwork by the author in 1981.)

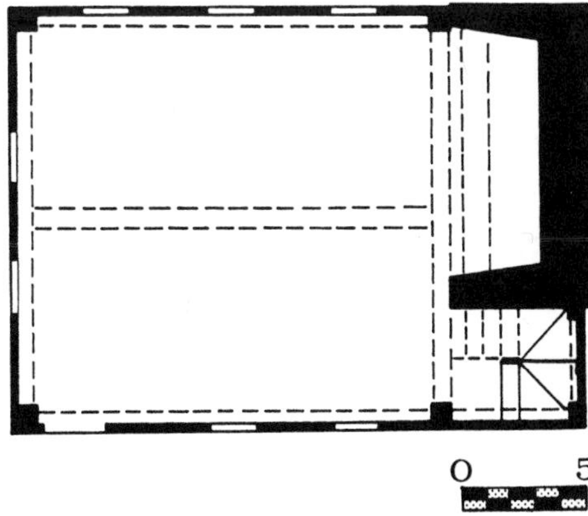

Figure 8. Plan of the Roger Mowry House, Providence, Rhode Island, ca. 1653 (now destroyed). (After Norman M. Isham, Early Rhode Island Houses, *[Providence, 1898].)*

Yet in towns like Plymouth, which saw only spotty West-country immigration, the lowland plan found

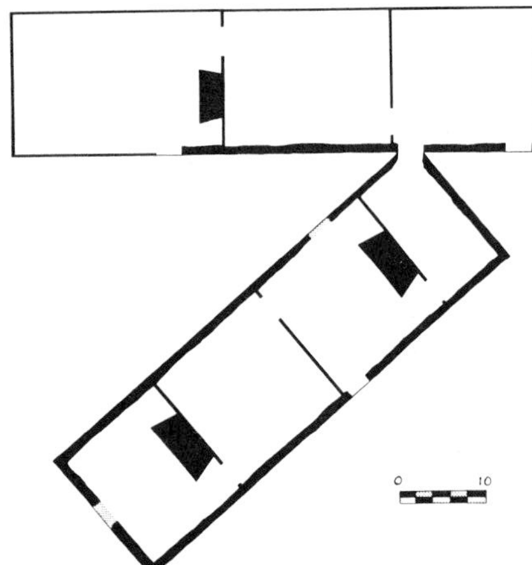

Figure 9. Plan of the Miles Standish House, Duxbury, Massachusetts, ca. 1630–50. (After original drawing made by James Hall, ca. 1861–64, now owned by the Pilgrim Society, Plymouth, Massachusetts.)

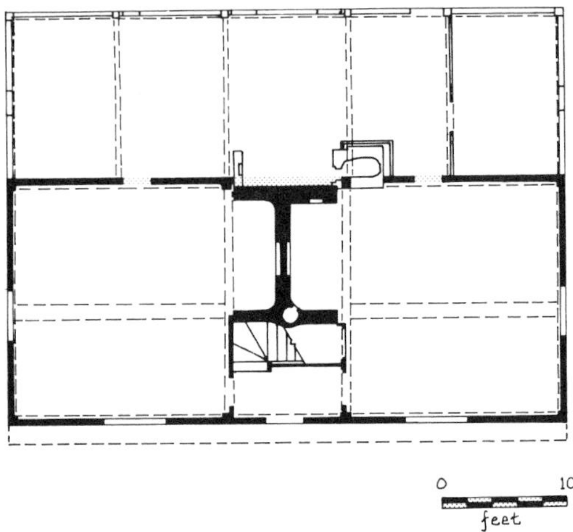

Figure 10. Plan of the William Boardman House, Saugus, Massachusetts, ca. 1687. (After Abbott Lowell Cummings, The Framed Houses of Massachusetts Bay, 1625–1725 *[Cambridge, Mass.: Belknap Press, 1979].)*

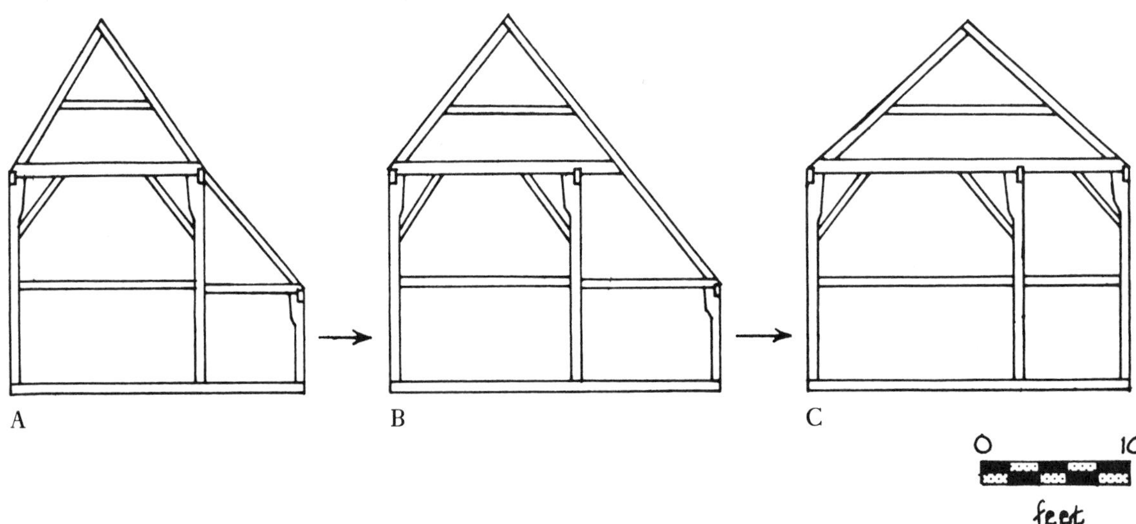

Figure 11. Development of bent designs toward external symmetry, 1640–1700: a, Fairbanks House, Dedham, showing lean-to added to original structure between about 1637–46 and 1668; b, Bradford House, Kingston, Massachusetts, showing offset integral lean-to framed at construction of house, 1674; c, Winslow House, Marshfield, Massachusetts, showing fully integrated rear service rooms framed at construction of house in 1698–99. (From fieldwork by the author in 1981.)

almost unanimous approval. Over the course of the seventeenth century, in part because of the layout of New England's nucleated villages, which concentrated housing in the middle of town in close proximity, and in part because of the sheer demographic dominance of East Anglian patrons and artisans, the "up-and-back" plan triumphed.[36] Houses with two front rooms and a working kitchen in the rear lean-to, such as the William Boardman House in Saugus, Massachusetts (fig. 10) became the rule. And by the close of the seventeenth century, the irregular profile of the long lean-to roof itself fell into disfavor, as local champions of symmetry turned their sights to the sides of houses as well as the fronts. Within a decade the ridge of the yeoman's house had shifted back to integrate the service rooms into a balanced elevation (fig. 11).

Lacking a survival rate of upland house types sufficient to permit an estimate of their average size, we can use room-by-room inventories as a means to check whether first-generation settlers reproduced cultural norms of domestic space and family density in the New World. That they did so is demonstrated by a survey of documented first-generation structures in southeastern New England known either through inventories or survival. Despite an overall similarity in family size, West- and North-countrymen built houses with less room than did immigrants from England's southeastern regions (table 2), suggesting that uplanders had different living patterns. Whether because of a stronger sense of authoritarianism in family government or rules for social interaction that admitted a higher degree of everyday contention as a norm, immigrants from northern and western England preferred to live in closer quarters. As we explore the mechanics of local ethnicity, we see that seventeenth-century New England yeomen, depending on their English regional origin, were all on separate cultural schedules and following distinct trajectories through time and society toward privacy and cleanliness. Indeed, people in different parts of early seventeenth-century England built houses that varied in size and number of rooms.[37]

Table 2
House Sizes of First-Generation Immigrants to Southeastern New England Whose English Regional Origins Are Known

	Number of Rooms	
Regional Origin	Mean	Median
East Anglia	6.4	7.0
London and Southeast	5.3	5.0
Midlands	5.2	6.0
West and North Country	4.6	4.0

Note: This table is based on N = 36 houses whose total number of rooms are known and whose owners can be traced to their native countries.

Recent research on early timber houses in New England demonstrates that a steady movement toward uniformity was also at work in framing techniques.[38] The Fairbanks House, with its primary- and secondary-rafter and principal-purlin roof scheme stabilized by falling wind braces and relatively light timbers, clearly descended from East Anglian precedents and perhaps from the specific subregion along the Suffolk-Norfolk border from which most of Dedham's first-generation woodworkers emigrated (fig. 12).[39] By contrast, structures like the Tristram Coffin House in Newbury and the Blake House in Dorchester have roofs more like those found in the cruck-built houses of western England, with rafters supporting evenly spaced common purlins. These West-country structures are frequently made of timbers heavier than those commonly used by East Anglian carpenters, suggesting that the chronic shortage of building materials in the Home Counties had so conditioned some artisans that they continued to treat trees with reverence despite their abundance in New England.

As apprenticeships and migration gradually blurred the crisp edges of English regional practices in the colonies, house plans and structure underwent subtle changes. On one hand, the melding of diverse practices could result in strange new plans. Rhode Island provides many instances of second- and third-generation structures whose odd plans resulted logically from the coalescence of West-

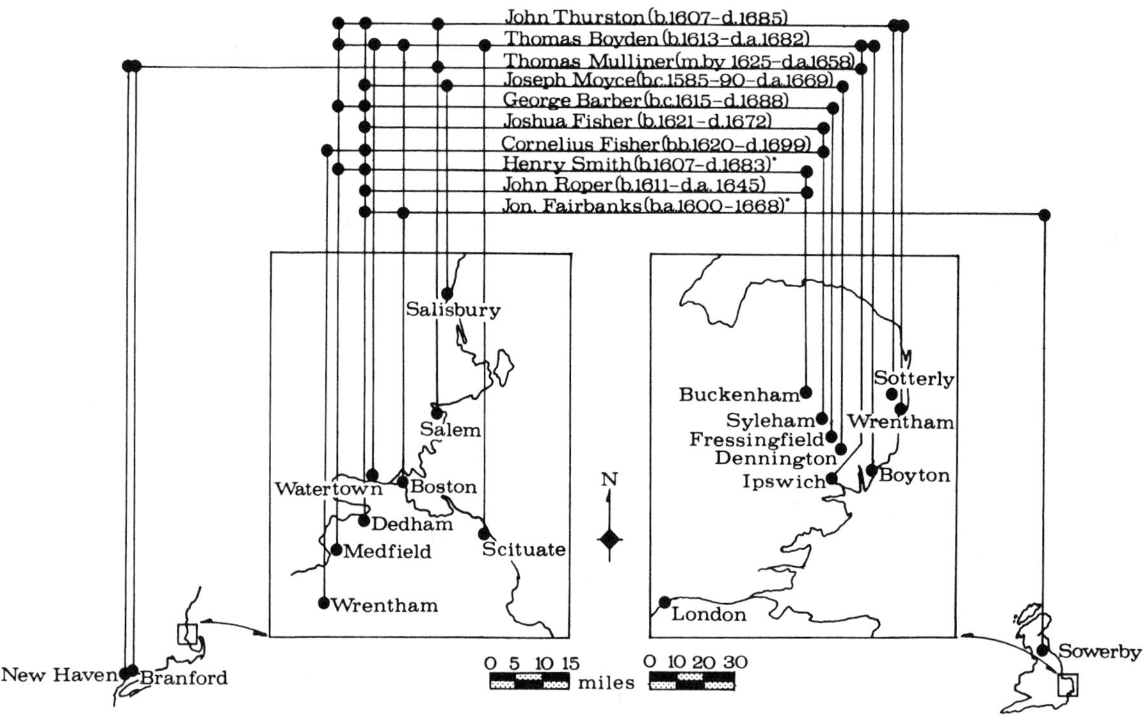

Figure 12. The English regional origins of first-generation woodworking artisans in Dedham and Medfield, Massachusetts.

country and East Anglian concepts. In the Eleazer Arnold House the door placement is common to that in West-country house plans (fig. 13), yet the roof framing (fig. 14) is as East Anglian as that on the Fairbanks House (fig. 7). Western, too, is the use of end chimneys for a multiroom dwelling, yet the plan extends not longitudinally, but backwards. On the other hand, the great majority of houses erected in New England in the fourth quarter of the seventeenth century (the Sparrow-Leach House in Plymouth is representative; figs. 15, 16) had door placements inherited from East Anglian plans combined with a roof structure derived principally from West-country prototypes.

The names used to describe the rooms of the New England house confirm the pattern toward commonality. Initially, rooms went by a great number of names. *Hall* could also be the *fier room,* the *Great Room,* or even the *kitchen.* The parlors also went as the *outer room* or the *chamber.* Rooms added to the rear of the structure were variously called *lean-to, bedroom, kitchen, dairy, new house,* or *back house.* In most cases these names came from different English regional dialects; *new house,* for example, appears to be a Yorkshire term, while *fier room* has its clear precedents in sections of Kent and Sussex.[40] Yet, beginning in the third quarter of the seventeenth century, there was a shift in room nomenclature away from idiosyncratic names based on function to a universal system based on the location of the room according to points of the compass.[41] The "prizers" (appraisers) of Thomas Hatch's estate in Scituate were in the midst of making this transition when they described his "East Chamber, Middle Chamber, West Chamber, Leantoo, West Room, Closset, [and] East Room" in 1684.[42] When Oliver Norris's house in Plymouth was appraised in 1715, his rooms included the "Northerly End of the House in the Lower Room, Southerly Lower Room, Chamber Over the Northerly Room," and an additional chamber over the "southerly Lower Room."[43]

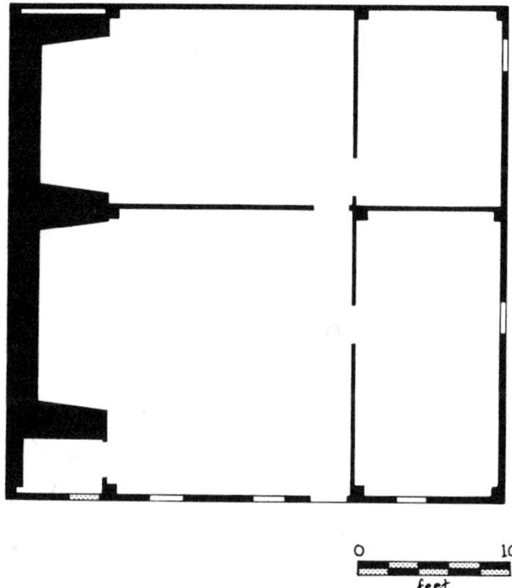

Figure 13. Plan of the Eleazer Arnold House, Lincoln, Rhode Island, ca. 1684. (From fieldwork by the author in 1981.)

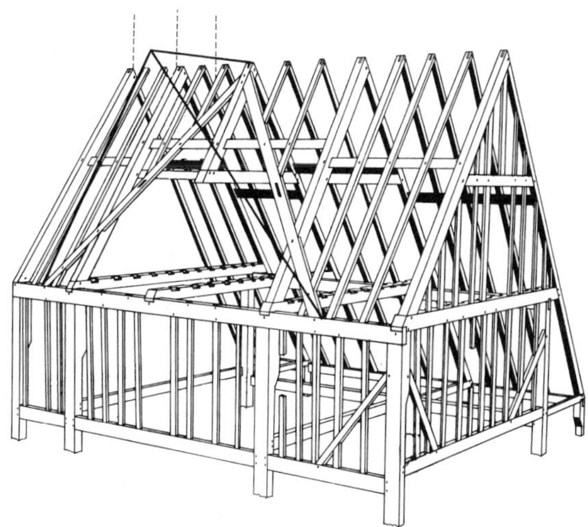

Figure 14. Roof framing of Eleazer Arnold House, Lincoln, Rhode Island, ca. 1684. (From fieldwork by the author in 1981.)

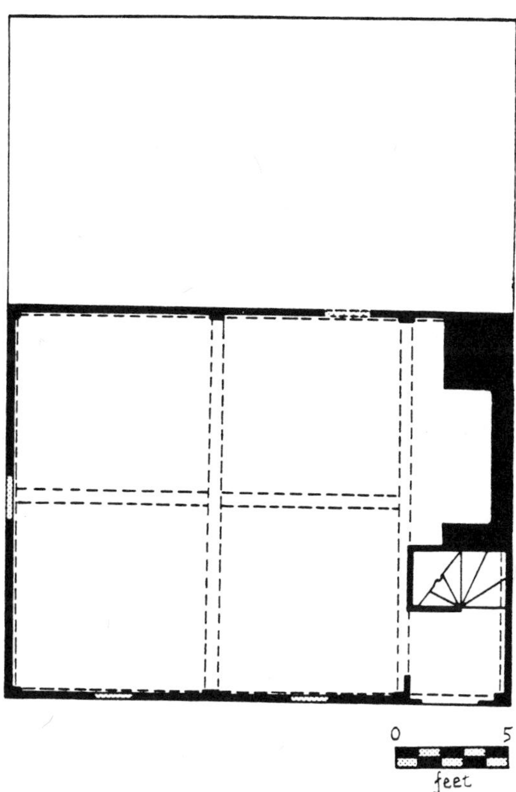

Figure 15. Plan of Sparrow-Leach House, Plymouth, Massachusetts, ca. 1679 and later.

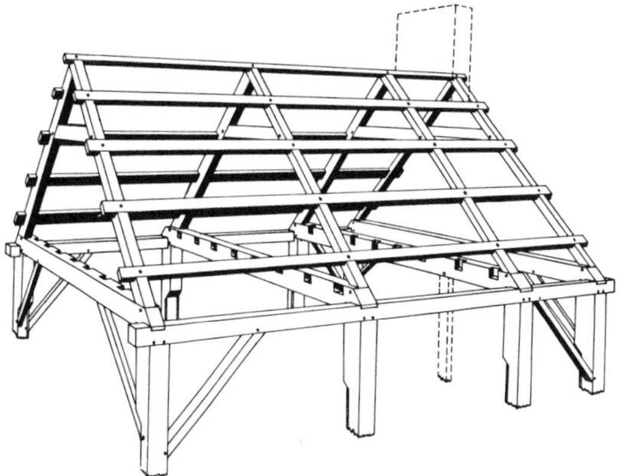

Figure 16. Roof framing of Sparrow-Leach House, Plymouth, Massachusetts, first building phase ca. 1679. (From fieldwork by the author in 1981.)

Materials used in house construction also traced a line toward convention. The diverse regions of England had provided all sorts of building materials, among which were wood (albeit increasingly rare and expensive throughout the seventeenth century), stone, cob, brick, and pisé for walls, and shingles, slate, tiles, and thatch for roofs.[44] While some of the practices, such as use of stone and thatch and even ceramic roof tiles, undoubtedly lingered in New England into the waning decades of the seventeenth century, by the turn of the eighteenth century the yeoman's buildings were almost universally constructed of wood, with either studded or planked frames sheathed in horizontal clapboards and shingled roofs.

Beyond its shape, size, and substance, the yeoman's house was a symbolic form proclaiming his victory over the wilderness. The charged language of contemporary court narratives often provides clues to its meaning. In 1679 William Morse of Newbury noticed strange events afflicting his household, and as he described the "witchcraft," he revealed much about the yeoman's attitude toward human space. To Morse, the human environment was above all a frail and vulnerable vessel, an attitude that echoed a common belief that material things were constantly changing, transient, and "mutable." During the time he perceived his household to be bewitched, Morse testified that flying sticks and stones constantly barraged the roof of his house; the door of his house was alternately secure and worthless, as hogs seemed to come and go at will; even his chimney malfunctioned, with objects coming down and in as often as they went up and out. "I had an Aule in the window," Morse reported, "which was taken away I know not how and Com Dune the chimney. I take the same aule and put it into a Cubard and fasened the Dore. The same aule Com Down 3 or 4 times."[45] Without exception he described cosmic upheaval by making symbolic reference to the fabric of his house; roof, door, window, and chimney, all thresholds between the safe interior and dangerous exterior, where violated and penetrated by spirits. With such a thin membrane of artifice mediating between chaos and control, between supernatural disorder and human order, the yeoman consciously strove to chart the edges of his universe by marking the limits of his house with decorative elements and by providing locks for doors already well wrought and securely fastened by iron hinges.

Even more helpful in understanding the significance of the house in seventeenth-century society is a close look at how the yeoman distributed functions and artifacts in its various rooms. The New England yeoman usually had between four and eight rooms, a number that indicated the middling status of most of the immigrants. In southeastern New England almost one in every two first-generation houses for which evidence survives had six or more rooms (table 3). As in England,[46] the fully developed house plan included a *hall*, or room used for a variety of purposes varying from cooking and eating to working and sleeping; a *parlor*, which seems to have been used as parents' sleeping quarters and for special ritual functions (for example, courtship, funerals, and so forth); two upstairs chambers; and sometimes a rear lean-to, which housed a working hearth and spaces for domestic industry. Finally, a long undivided garret ran under the ridge of the pitched roof.

The hall was the symbolic center of the yeoman's house, for in it burned the only continuous fire. If the kitchen area had not yet been removed to a rear lean-to, the hall was the room of the hearth, and in farming communities throughout the Anglo-Celtic world, the hearth was the center of personal social interaction.[47] In most New England houses the hall enjoyed a southern or southeastern exposure, which enabled the sun to augment the light and heat cast into the room by the fire. Yet during the seventeenth century the symbolic valence of the hall was in constant flux as working hearths gradually moved to the rear lean-to. In some ways, this separation of cooking and the constellation of women's tasks that surrounded it from the social front of the house was an evolutionary change over time. The plan of the Fairbanks House in 1668 shows the working hearth

Table 3
Sizes of Yeomen's Houses in Southeastern New England, 1630–1730

	Number of Rooms											
	Two		Three		Four		Five		Six		Total	
	N	%	N	%	N	%	N	%	N	%	N	%
1630–1670	5	11.6	8	18.6	4	9.3	7	16.3	19	44.2	43	100.0
1671–1700	14	13.7	19	18.6	12	11.8	17	16.7	40	39.2	102	100.0
1701–1730	24	19.7	22	18.0	16	13.1	14	11.4	46	37.7	122	100.0
Totals and Averages	43	16.1	49	18.4	32	12.0	38	14.2	105	39.3	267	100.0

Note: This table is based on 267 (88.1%) of 303 structures recorded. All garret and cellar spaces mentioned in inventories of the period or available for measurement in surviving examples are included.

in the hall despite the presence of a rear lean-to; the 1696 plan of the Boardman House shows the kitchen in the lean-to. Yet the disjunction of women's work from the everyday life of the family as a whole and the parallel concern for making the front rooms culturally "clean" were also related to social class. The ability to separate worlds of work and leisure, process and product, and to form abstract concepts of cleanliness depended on an economic ability to supply extra space.

In general the furniture kept in the hall was designed for bulk storage or constant use. Usually a chest or large box contained miscellaneous tools or clothing; the chest doubled as a seat if stools and chairs were too few. Sometimes the hall contained a small cupboard that held the family's everyday eating utensils as well as dry or imperishable foods. The focal point of the hall was a large table at which the family took its meals. Seating at the table was highly symbolic of social status and seniority. Especially during the lifetime of the first generation, the head of the household sat in a great armchair, a virtual throne from which he overlooked wife and children as they sat on long benches called *forms,* joint stools, or smaller chairs without arms. At times older children stood during meals. Infants were set apart by special chairs. Near the hearth were one or two additional stools and a settle, types of seating specifically designed for moving about the fire to garner heat to the best advantage.

The basic hearth equipment included trammels used for hanging cooking vessels at desired heights above a fire, andirons for the support of wood while burning, and miscellaneous iron cooking utensils. Some households also owned an elaborate clockwork jack, which kept a piece of meat rotating at a consistent speed while cooking and thus freed the woman's hands to perform other tasks. The seventeenth-century *goodwife,* whose primary work domain was the hearth, did not use her fireplace for a single large fire but instead made several smaller ones of different sizes and perhaps of different woods in order to regulate the heat produced. Heat could also be regulated by changing the height of the trammel or by changing the shape of the fire with poker and tongs. The utensils in the hearth area included those for cooking the major components of the seventeenth-century diet: liquids and cereals, bread and cakes, and meat, poultry, and fish.

The yeoman's family regularly congregated at the hall table to take meals; once for breakfast and once for dinner at midday were usual, and sometimes parents ate a late-night supper in the parlor. For everyday meals the family used bowls, plates, dishes, cups, tankards, platters, and porringers, and knives, forks, and spoons of wood, earthenware, and pewter, usually made in the same form as their counterparts in silver, glass, stoneware, and even porcelain. The arrangement of people at the table was carefully prescribed, with the head of the household seated at one end of the table (usually the end away from the fire) and other people placed on either side in order of social status, the lowest in rank being farthest from the host. The position of the standing salt was crucial, as everyone who sat "above the salt" was socially superior to those who sat below it.[48] The sheer number of utensils used by the seventeenth-century yeoman in preparing and consuming food suggests that food, and its associated activities, was probably one of the most important elements of New England culture. The hall also sometimes housed textile equipment such as scissors, cards, and wheels, which, like peels and toasters, were tools for women's work.

Because the hall was the center of family work and interaction, it was also the best-lit room. Augmenting the daylight from its south-facing windows was light from a variety of lamps, which sputtered with the heavy scent and irregular light of animal fat, as well as from candles, which gave off a gentler and more constant flame. The hall was clearly associated with two qualities in the yeoman's mind: the hearth (heat, light, warmth) and the woman of the house.

The yeoman's parlor differed dramatically from his hall. The parlor served principally as a display case for artificial products—totems of material success and, perhaps, God's favor—rather than as a frame of cultural transformation. Almost without exception the parlor was the room containing the greatest concentration of what wealth the family had accrued. The most overt display of material consciousness centered on the great bed. High-posted bedsteads decked in textile hangings filled a substantial portion of the room. When trundlebeds were pulled out at night, very little open floorspace was left. Often carved like their English counterparts, these bedsteads were enveloped with coverlets, bed rugs, pillows, curtains and valances, which themselves were often worked in needlepoint and finished with fringes and tassels. In some very wealthy households, expensive imported textiles were even used. The parlor was, after all, where parents found their only privacy and enjoyed sexual intimacy. Wrapped in fabric, the great bed was a room within a room, a cocoon of parental power metaphorically akin to the *inner room* found in smaller houses of the period.[49] The parlor was also the locus of social reflexivity, and, if their owners could afford such luxuries, looking glasses and portraits were always hung here.

In addition to the great bed, the parlor sometimes contained a large cupboard that displayed the family's *plate*—its silver, pewter, and glassware—set off by textiles called *cupboard cloths* or *cupboard cushions.* Laden with tankards, flagons, plates and large platters, the cupboard in New England as well as old England was a tour de force of overt display. If a family had sufficient glassware, it was put on view in a glass case with a decorative front grill. Other furnishings in the parlor included chairs covered in leather or a textile. Usually purchased in sets of six or twelve, they were lined up along the perimeter of the room to be pulled into use only when needed. Chairs were needed for private conferences at the parlor table, or for a late-night supper.

Parlors also contained artifacts with overt patriarchal connotations. Often yeoman kept family deeds, assorted small valuables, and cash in coffers and small cabinets. The Fairbanks parlor contained a display of weaponry: "one sword," "one Cutles," "2 gunns," "one musqut & vest," "one halfe pike," and "a pr of bandeleers."[50] Books were found most frequently in parlors, and if a member of the family could read, it was most likely the father. The parlor hearth, smaller than that of the hall, contained brass rather than iron andirons, brass or brass-tipped shovel, tongs, and poker, a bellows, and a fireback, as well as a warming pan to heat the bed before retiring. Finally, the rare clock or mechanical timepiece almost always resided in the parlor, a symbol of authority in an artificial world.[51] The parlor, charged with patriarchal prerogatives, was the most artificial space in the yeoman's house and, if whitewash were not enough to defeat the specter of the outside world, its walls were sometimes covered with textile hangings and its ceiling and floor painted with spongework and feathered patterns.[52]

Above the hall and parlor—the respective domains of women and men, process and products—were the hall chamber and parlor chamber. The use of these rooms varied from household to household depending on the size of the family, the ages of its members, and the particular kind of domestic industry they practiced. The 1696 inventory of the Boardman House lists furniture and other everyday artifacts in both, while the Fairbanks family in 1668 used only the parlor chamber on a daily basis and reserved the hall chamber for the storage of grain and tools. But one chamber in each house contained a bedstead, undoubtedly a low-posted bedstead with appointments far less grand than those of the great bed in the parlor below. Serving most frequently as sleeping quarters, these second-floor spaces seem to have been used also for the storage of finished textiles. Textiles were extremely valuable in seventeenth-century New England, and people protected them from fading and damage by placing them in chests or trunks with strong locks. Chests made along the south shore of Massachusetts Bay even have drawers of white cedar, a wood widely recognized in the period for its fragrance and ability to keep textiles free from moths.

Lean-to additions made at the rear and sides of the house contained equipment for the processing of textiles, dairy products, and food supplies. Bread was made in the deep ovens often built into the chimney when it was enlarged at the rear to provide a new working hearth. At one end of the lean-to was the dairy, filled with earthenware vessels and wooden tubs needed for the storage of milk, cream, and butter, and a cheese press and vats. Also in the lean-to was a buttery (named for the *butts* or barrels stored there, not for *butter*). The buttery housed the troughs used in the salting of meat and fish, dough troughs used in making bread, and a wide assortment of tools, including flax breaks, sieves, harnesses, and saws. The garret and cellar(s) completed the yeoman's house, both being used predominantly for the storage of food supplies.

If we link these basic room functions, they reveal the seventeenth-century house as a social machine, at once economic and symbolic. The rooms at the extreme top and bottom stored natural materials, still in the raw state in which they left the field. The rooms at the back of the house framed the transformation of raw materials (foodstuffs, unbroken animal and vegetable fibers) into workable materials, such as dressed beef, cheese, milk, cleaned linen and woolen fibers. The room containing the working hearth—usually the hall, sometimes the rear kitchen—witnessed the further transformation of these partially processed foods and fibers into artificial commodities (cooked food, spun threads). The second-story rooms were used for storage of completed artificial products (textiles); and the parlor completed the system with its bold display of improved products (plates, textiles, clocks, armor, and books). The yeoman's house was his cognition in motion, progressing from the socially open "back" regions of the house, where the unbroken was broken, through the middle regions where the broken was improved, and emerging in front amid the total control of improvement displayed:

Nature: Back	Garret, Lean-to Garret	: unbroken food/fiber stored
	Cellar Lean-to	: unbroken food/fiber → broken food/fiber
	Hearth (Hall/ Kitchen)	: broken food/fiber → improved food/fiber
	Chambers	: improved fiber stored
Culture: Front	Parlor	: improved fiber displayed[53]

In turn, this sequence of relations connected with areas of work and public display outside the house. The yeoman's world existed as a series of concentric circles around the hearth, with its crucial stage of transformation controlled by women and framed by men in the field and parlor. In effect, the dialectic of the yeoman's domain, moving his consciousness from the coarse unbroken ground to the extreme artifice of the parlor, was mediated by his wife. Despite the acknowledged role, in seventeenth-century social theory, of the Puritan father as lord of his "Little Commonwealth," his psychologi-

Table 4
Room Dimensions in the Fairbanks House, 1668

Room	H (ft)	W (ft)	D (ft)	Area (ft^2)	Volume (ft^3)
Parlor	6.2	10.2	15.5	158.1	980.2
Hall	6.2	13.1	15.5	203.1	1258.9
Parlor Chamber	6.1	10.2	15.5	158.1	964.4
New House	6.2	32.0	10.0	320.0	1984.0
New House Chamber	6.1*	32.0	10.0	320.0	976.0
Hall Chamber	6.1	12.7	15.5	196.8	1200.8
Garret Chamber	10.3	32.0	15.5	496.0	2554.4
[Porch entry]†	6.2	7.3	2.9	21.2	131.3

Note: This table does not include dimensions of the "working Cellar" or "Another Cellar" specified in the inventory because their respective sizes are impossible to determine on the basis of surviving evidence.
*Due to the rear slope of the roof, the New House Chamber is triangular in section. Hence, it is 6.1 feet high at the inside wall, while its rear wall has no height at all. The area and volume of this space are equal to and one-half of, respectively, that of the New House beneath.
†The porch entry was not specified in the inventory, although it was certainly there at the time. No artifacts, therefore, are recorded as having been in it.

cal stability on a day-to-day basis rested squarely on his wife. Indeed, it is no wonder that men remarried more quickly than women when widowed and still less wonder that three times as many seventeenth-century women as men suffered from mental and emotional disorders.[54] For in the agricultural towns and villages of early New England, women were the ones whose knowledge guided the key transformation of nature into culture. While men were the breakers and displayers of nature, women were the improvers, a role fostered by contemporary treatises on *Huswifery* and later reinforced throughout the eighteenth and nineteenth centuries.

Complementing this arrangement of functions was the organization of domestic space, which determined how much space in each room was filled by major artifacts and how much was left unfilled. How crowded was the yeoman's house? What did it "feel" like? The structure of space in the domestic environment was closely related to the shape of social interaction. As anthropologists and psychologists interested in small group ecology and proxemics have shown, individuals not only react unconsciously to distances but can also produce spaces of different qualities as a means of controlling or influencing social action.[55] One way of exploring the mechanics of space is to examine the arrangement of furniture, as a relatively stationary group of forms ranging from built-in dressers to ordinary chairs and tables, in the rooms of the house. Folklorists and geographers working in Ireland have been attending to this issue in their ethnographic work on peasant houses, and their efforts can inform our own historical task.[56] In examining two surviving seventeenth-century houses for which a room-by-room inventory of the period is also extant, we can make fairly precise estimates as to the relative "crowdedness" of their rooms.[57]

The plan of the Jonathan Fairbanks House in Dedham and the 1668 inventory of the estate of its first owner are the first documents to consider. Although originally built on a simple hall-parlor plan with a central chimney, the house had acquired by 1668 a long undivided lean-to across its rear elevation; the working hearth remained in the old hall. After measuring its rooms (table 4) and listing the location and mean sizes of all furniture in 1668 (tables 5, 6), we can arrive at gross quantitative estimates of the average space occupied by these movables (table 7). And although no method can tell us the exact arrangement of objects in relation to one another, we can at least discover the extent to which

Table 5
Location of Furniture in the Fairbanks House, 1668

Parlor	Hall	Parlor Chamber
1 bedstead	2 old tables	1 bedstead
1 trundle bedstead	1 form	1 chest
1 livery cupboard	1 chair	1 box
1 sea chest	1 box	
2 chairs		
1 little box		

Table 7
Mean Occupied Space of the Fairbanks House, 1668

	Mean Area		Mean Volume	
Room	ft^2	%	ft^3	%
Parlor	53.6	33.9	225.5	23.0
Parlor Chamber	32.4	20.5	110.6	11.5
Hall	19.1	9.4	37.9	3.0

rooms were filled, or spatially "closed," or left unfilled and "open."

The structure of space in the Fairbanks rooms is clear. Without doubt the parlor was the most densely packed, with over a third of its total area and one-quarter of its total volume occupied by furniture. By contrast the hall was only about one-tenth filled in area and about one-fiftieth filled in volume. The long lean-to at the rear contained no furniture. In the second story, only the parlor chamber contained furniture, although there it accounted for almost one-fifth of the total area and over one-tenth of its volume. The garret and lean-to garret were empty. Overall, the spaces at the front of the house were the most crowded, emphasizing the public display of artificial products, while the rear rooms were empty. And the rooms used for everyday family activity—the hall and lean-to—were sparsely furnished. The parlor chamber, used for sleeping, was a bit more "closed"; the seventeenth-century yeoman regarded sleep as a period of extreme vulnerability. The parlor, the room that the Fairbanks reserved for the rituals of courtship, death, formal entertainment, and sexual intimacy, was the most filled. Indeed, there was a hierarchic arrangement of space directly related to the kinds of activities specific to each room. In everyday life, open space manifested less control of movement; closed space exerted more authority in rooms framing socially precarious and uncertain behavior.

If we compare the distribution of space in the Fairbanks House with that of the Boardman House, built in 1687 and inventoried in 1696, we see that important changes resulted from the removal of the working kitchen to the lean-to (see fig. 13). This allowed the old hall of the house (the Boardman House, like the Fairbanks House, was first built on a two-room, central-chimney plan)[58] to become the *best room,* a secondary parlor for the entertainment of visitors, and separated the cooking from the eating of food (table 8). In addition, because both lower front rooms were clean and free of noise, the

Table 6
Mean Dimensions of Furniture in the Fairbanks House, 1668

Artifact	H (in)	W (in)	D (in)	Area (ft^2)	Volume (ft^3)
Bedstead (high post)	75.0	48.0	72.0	24.0	150.0
Bedstead (low post)	46.5	49.8	72.6	25.1	97.3
Trundle bedstead	19.5	47.5	62.0	20.4	33.2
Cupboard	49.1	45.5	21.8	6.9	28.2
Chest	26.5	42.7	18.3	5.4	12.0
Sea chest	16.5	45.7	17.5	5.5	7.6
Chair	46.8	23.0	17.7	2.8	11.0
Little box	9.7	25.2	15.9	2.8	2.7
Box	8.3	30.7	17.9	3.8	2.6
Table	25.4	47.8	19.2	6.4	13.5
Form	16.7	67.9	12.7	6.0	8.3

Table 8
Room Dimensions in the Boardman House, 1696

Room	H (ft)	W (ft)	D (ft)	Area (ft^2)	Volume (ft^3)
Best Room	7.0	17.0	18.0	306.0	2142.0
Parlor	7.0	17.0	18.0	306.0	2142.0
Hall Ch.	7.0	17.0	19.5*	331.5*	2320.5*
Parlor Ch.	7.0	17.0	19.5*	331.5*	2320.5*
Kitchen Ch.†	7.0	34.0	11.5	391.5	1368.5
Kitchen	7.0	22.0	12.5	275.0	1925.0
Milkhouse	7.0	8.0	12.5	100.0	700.0
Cellar‡	—	16.0	17.0	272.0	—

*Extra space in these front second-story rooms is due to jetty on front of house.
†Sloping lean-to roof cuts total volume of this room by half.
‡Vertical dimensions are impossible to determine on basis of surviving evidence.

Table 11
Artifact Value Distribution and Material Quality Space of the Fairbanks House, 1668

Room	Total Value of Artifacts Contained (£	s.	d.)	Material Quality Space (d/ft^2)*
Garret Chamber	0	4	0	1
New House Chamber	3	4	0	2
New House	4	15	6	4
Hall Chamber	4	15	0	6
Hall	7	0	0	8
Parlor Chamber	9	16	0	15
Parlor	21	11	10	33

*Calculated to nearest 1d.

hall chamber now became an acceptable sleeping room (table 9). The total range of spatial structure was as widespread in the Boardman House as it was in the Fairbanks House. In the latter, the most closed room was over one-third filled; in the Boardman House it was barely one-fifth full (table 10). Comparison of the two houses suggests that a leveling process was in effect in which the spatial organization of rooms was becoming more and more similar instead of being rigidly differentiated. And the "material quality" of each room (the average monetary value of each expressed in pence per square foot) confirms the same pattern (tables 11, 12). The quality of the Fairbanks rooms declines dramatically from thirty-three pence per square foot in the parlor to slightly less than one penny per square foot in the garret. The quality of the Boardman rooms, on the other hand, ranges from only twenty-one pence per square foot in the parlor to less than one penny per square foot in the cellar, even though Boardman invested over twenty percent of his estate in material chattels as compared with slightly more than fifteen percent invested by Fairbanks. With this spatial data in hand, we can restate the house as a dialectic between the different domains of men and women:

Table 9
Location of Furniture in the Boardman House, 1696

Best Room	Parlor	Hall Chamber	Parlor Chamber
1 cupboard	2 bedsteads*	1 bedstead†	1 table
2 tables	1 table	1 table	6 chairs
6 chairs	1 chest	1 chest	
		6 chairs	

*Values and description indicate that these were both high-posted bedsteads with textile furnishings.
†Value indicates that this was a low-posted bedstead.

Table 10
Mean Occupied Space of the Boardman House, 1696

Room	Mean Area ft^2	%	Mean Volume ft^3	%
Parlor	59.8	19.5	325.5	15.2
Hall Chamber	45.3	13.7	155.8	6.7
Best Room	28.1	9.2	88.2	4.1
Parlor Chamber	14.8	4.5	46.5	2.0

Gender	*Woman*	*Man*
Room	Hall	Parlor
Exposure/"Feeling"	S:Warm/Light	N:Cold/Dark
Space/Quality	Open/Low	Closed/High
Function	Process:Transformation	Product:Display

At the same time as spatial differences between rooms were becoming less pronounced and investment in household goods was increasing, houses acquired additional separate rooms as the need for individual privacy grew.

There was, of course, deviation from this general pattern in both directions. The vast estates and lengthy inventories of Boston merchants and to a lesser degree those of ministers demonstrate that wealth was not distributed evenly throughout the colonial population. Because their houses were larger, the more prosperous New Englanders had more rooms in which to distribute their possessions. The Boston merchant Henry Webb, for example, owned a house whose eleven rooms contained artifacts worth in excess of £7,000 at his death in 1660. The wealthy owned the rare and the exquisite, including maps of faraway or "outlandish" places. The houses of ministers in both town and countryside usually contained a small room called a *study,* their counterpart of the merchant's *counting room.* The study was usually located on the second floor, set apart for quiet contemplation.

The different ways in which merchants, ministers, and yeomen directed their yearly incomes toward investment capital and merchandise, books and travel, and farm equipment, respectively, demonstrate clearly the extent to which social status was determined by the kinds and quantity of artifacts accumulated. These differences illustrate too the contrast between the town of Boston and the surrounding villages. During the seventeenth century, Boston grew into a worldly commercial center, whose reputation both excited and dismayed its Puritan leaders. The Boston ministry was famed for its academic brilliance, and Cambridge, the center of learning and printing, was only a few miles distant. Yet, on the other hand, Boston was corrupted by material wealth and cursed by its apparent mercantile success. Founded with optimism and a sense of ecclesiastical mission, it soon fell into depravity and iniquity.[59] Besides its merchants, ministers, and artisans, Boston supported an endless array of transients—seamen, traders, and vagrants—whose values were in direct opposition to those cherished by the conservative rural yeomen.

New England's poorer farmers in the seventeenth century were at the opposite end of the social spectrum from the merchants. If house size alone can serve as a guide, the farmers seem to have grown in number between 1630 and 1730 (see table 3), and at the same time the gulf between them and the very wealthy became wider. While merchants in Boston counted their money and invested more and more in local industries such as ironworks and shipbuilding, at least a few of their fellow Puritans were literally starving. Traveling through the Narragansett County in 1704, Sarah Knight, a wealthy woman from Boston, reacted with disdain and amazement when she came upon a poor farmer's house: "This little Hutt was one of the wretchedest I ever saw a habitation for human creatures. It was

Table 12
Artifact Value Distribution and Material Quality Space of the Boardman House, 1696

Room	Total Value of Artifacts Contained (£	s.	d.)	Material Quality Space (d/ft^2)*
Cellar	1	0	0	1
Milkhouse	1	0	0	2
Kitchen Chamber	2	10	0	2
Kitchen	2	16	0	2
Parlor Chamber	5	0	0	4
Hall Chamber	10	0	0	7
Best Room	10	0	0	8
Parlor	27	7	0	21

*Calculated to nearest 1d.

suported with shores enclosed with Clapboards, laid on lengthways, and so much asunder, that the Light come throu' everywhere; the doore tyed on with a cord in ye place of hinges; the floor the bear earth; no windows but such as the thin covering afforded, nor any furniture but a Bedd with a glass Bottle hanging at ye head on't; an earthen cupp, a small pewter Bason, A Bord with sticks to stand on, instead of a table, and a block or two in ye corner instead of chairs."[60]

This confrontation between rich and poor in the opening years of the eighteenth century dramatizes a simple historical fact: the less space and space-structuring artifacts a person could afford—including items like elaborate bed furniture, displays of plate, and standing salts—the more his use of space as a means of expression and as a tool in social interaction was limited. Certainly, no social scientist or historian would doubt that all men, regardless of their accumulated wealth, arrange interiors according to deeply embedded cognitive patterns; the poor man's house is no less value-laden because of its sparse furnishings than that of the wealthy townsman. Yet, in ushering visitors into a parlor filled with artifacts and spatially "closed," the prosperous yeoman, and to a greater degree the Boston merchant, could exercise control over his guest's thoughts and actions. Depending on one's ability to produce it, space is a means of oppression and control as well as a cognitive design. By structuring the many rooms of his house along the continuum from open to closed space, the wealthy yeoman could better suit a specific interaction or performance to an appropriate material setting. But the man who greeted Madam Knight at the door of his "hut" had no such advantage. With less rooms and less possessions, he was further along the road leading to spatial disenfranchisement.

The amount of furniture in the New England yeoman's house increased with each passing decade, as it had in England.[61] A myriad of other artifacts increased too; yet they seem to have done so in inverse proportion to the decreasing availability of land. On the whole, then, the seventeenth century may have been less a period of unqualified accumulation than one characterized by shifting modes of accumulation. Issues of economy merge with those of ecology when we see that the rise of a "consumer culture" in New England was directly linked to both a perceived scarcity of land and the demographic and geographic stability of the nuclear family. Yet, as these markers of status shifted in Puritan culture over time, the social historian's concern with counting the artifacts of a consumer culture intersects with the anthropologist's interest in the distribution of spatial rights in society.[62] For as the locus of status-defining property increasingly became the household interior and not the land per se, the yeoman's spatial behavior also changed. Like the design of his farmyards, the movement of social space over time, from the land to deep within the house, was frighteningly implosive.

The use of space in the yeoman's house relates directly to the cultural effects of rising population density. Many old towns in New England, such as Ipswich,[63] saw their populations double at least once during the seventeenth century. Boston began with a population density higher than that of its rural neighbors, and it continued to grow. Many of the people who contributed to the fourfold rise in population during the period were residents of Boston. In most rural towns houses were lined up in even rows on either side of principal streets, with at least 150 feet separating most dwellings. But in Boston the houses shared party walls and were packed "close together on each side the streets, as in London."[64] Larger rural towns like Dedham and Hingham may have had one hundred houses by 1700, whereas Boston already had one thousand by 1698. Since all cultures have crucial points at which diminished availability of personal space contributes to social deviance,[65] it comes as no surprise that crime rates were generally higher in the colonial capital in part because of the spatial conditions in which its residents lived. Similarly, countryfolk became increasingly likely to act aggressively toward their neighbors as rural density rose. In Essex

County, court litigation rose dramatically in the closing decades of the seventeenth century owing not only to the diminishing regulatory power of the church but also to the effects of decreasing personal space on emotional stability.[66]

These ongoing changes in how the seventeenth-century yeoman conveyed his attitudes toward space had correlates in his conceptualizations of time and the human body, and, together, in many ways seem to foreshadow the eventual rise of an "enlightened" man. Houses that had been open social containers became private enclaves, individual shrines to perceived wealth, in which rooms grew increasingly function-specific. By the first decade of the eighteenth century, even separate *dining rooms* and *children's rooms* were appearing more and more frequently.

Yet despite our modern penchant to see change and consensus in a single glimpse of the past, the world of the seventeenth-century yeoman did not move at one great historical moment into the eighteenth century. The shift from quality to quantity, from "traditional" to capitalist modes of economic and cultural production, and from regional diversity to a guise of unity had already begun when the Puritans left England. Throughout the seventeenth century in both England and New England these related shifts occurred in small increments, which were probably imperceptible to the individual immersed in daily work and discourse. Indeed, these metaphoric shifts never appeared as polarities to the yeoman but presented themselves as daily alternatives for contemplation or action.

Instead of positing a linear pattern of cultural change to account for the appearance of new forms and beliefs, we must conceive of the yeoman's world as a layering of cultural options and communicative needs, which were revealed at different levels to certain sectors of colonial society in specific contexts. While hindsight grants us the ability to describe seventeenth-century culture as cognitively different from that of later periods, what really was changing was the distribution of new communicative methods and opportunities that enabled new orders of knowledge and expressive power to spread to groups in society previously weakened by cultural silence. This is what changing patterns of artifact consumption and enfranchisement ultimately embody.

Realizing the central significance of material contexts to the aesthetics of everyday life in the past, we can no longer cling to the belief that "no consistent pattern of styles related to social class can be ascertained" in seventeenth-century New England.[67] Indeed, what we must look for are emergent correlations of style and social class, not in the discrete art object but rather in the intertextuality of setting and performance.

Notes

This article is an abridged version of a chapter that was originally published in *New England Begins: The Seventeenth Century,* edited by Jonathan L. Fairbanks and Robert F. Trent (1982). All the illustrations in this article are by the author.

1. John Amsden, "Historians and the Spatial Imagination," *Radical History Review,* no. 21 (Fall 1979): 12–13; J. Sonnenfeld, "Variable Values in Space and Landscape: An Inquiry into the Nature of Environmental Necessity," *Journal of Social Issues* 22, no. 4 (October 1966): 73–74.
2. John Worlidge, *Systema Agriculturae, Being the Mystery of Husbandry Discovered and Layd Open* (London: T. Johnson, 1669), p. C 1.
3. Isaack De Rasieres, "Isaack De Rasieres to Samuel Blommaert, 1628," in Sydney V. James, Jr., ed., *Three Visitors to Early Plymouth* (Plymouth, Mass.: Plimoth Plantation, 1963), p. 76 (italics added).
4. "Records of the Town of Medfield, Massachusetts," Office of the Town Clerk, Medfield, Massachusetts, meeting of November 14, 1649; Richard Cushman, "Reasons and Considerations Touching the Lawfulness of Removing Out of England into the Parts of America," in Alexander Young, ed., *Chronicles of the Pilgrim Fathers of the Colony of Plymouth from 1602–1625* (1844; reprint, Baltimore: Genealogical Publishing, 1974), p. 243.
5. George Francis Dow, ed., *Records and Files of the Quarterly Courts of Essex County, Massachusetts,* 8 vols. (Salem, Mass.: Essex Institute, 1911–1921), 1:117–18, 293.

6. "Plymouth Colony Wills and Inventories," Office of the Town Clerk, Plymouth County Courthouse, Plymouth, Massachusetts, vol. 2, pt. 2, p. 17; "Barnstable County Wills and Inventories," Office of the Town Clerk, Barnstable County Courthouse, West Barnstable, Massachusetts, 1:7.
7. Quoted in Robert R. Walcott, "Husbandry in Colonial New England," *New England Quarterly* 9, no. 2 (June 1936): 233.
8. In some areas of New England, notably the Narragansett Basin, the long house plan may have persisted at least into the early eighteenth century. There is a single suggestive reference to a "long house" owned by Abraham Anthony of Portsmouth in 1727, which may represent an entire genre of buildings that have not survived; see "The Council Book & ye Register of Wills belonging to Portsmouth in the Colony of Rhode Island (Council Book no. 2)," 3:83–84. The long house was also common to sections of Wales and Ireland, which, though not major contributors to seventeenth-century migrations to New England, did send a few scattered settlers. The presence in New England of such carpenters as Joseph McCarthy, who came from Kinsdale in County Cork, Ireland, and died in 1680 in East Greenwich, Rhode Island, could explain the use of that plan in the region. See also Caoimhin Ó Danachair, "The Combined Byre-and-Dwelling in Ireland," *Folk Life* 2 (1964): 65; P. Smith, "The Long-House and the Laithe-House: A Study of the House-and-Byre Homestead in Wales and the West Riding," in I. Ll. Foster and L. Alcock, eds., *Culture and Environment: Essays in Honor of Sir Cyril Fox* (London: Routledge and Kegan Paul, 1963), pp. 416–24.
9. Ronald W. Brunskill, *Vernacular Architecture of the Lake Counties* (London: Faber and Faber, 1974), pp. 75–76.
10. "Plymouth Colony Wills and Inventories," vol. 2, pt. 1, pp. 69–73.
11. "Suffolk County Probate Records," Suffolk County Probate Court, Boston, Massachusetts, 14:294–300.
12. Dow, ed., *Records and Files of the Quarterly Courts of Essex County*, 6:129–30.
13. Peter Buckler, "Slatted Floors and Other Ways of Reducing the Use of Litter for Livestock," *Journal of the Royal Agricultural Society* 123 (1962): 78–80; Increase Mather, *An Essay for the Recording of Illustrious Providences* (1684; reprint, Delmar, N.Y.: Scholar's Facsimiles and Reprints, 1977), p. 147.
14. Robert W. Lovett, ed., *Documents from the Harvard University Archives, 1638–1750* (Boston: Colonial Society of Massachusetts, 1975), p. 22.
15. Dow, ed., *Records and Files of the Quarterly Courts of Essex County*, 1:368.
16. "Yarmouth Town Records," Office of the Town Clerk, South Yarmouth, Massachusetts, meeting of July 22, 1692; "Plymouth County Wills and Inventories," Plymouth County Probate Court, Plymouth, Massachusetts, 1:165.
17. Dow, ed., *Records and Files of the Quarterly Courts of Essex County*, 6:420–21.
18. Ibid., pp. 129–50.
19. Abbott Lowell Cummings, *The Framed Houses of Massachusetts Bay, 1625–1725* (Cambridge, Mass.: Belknap Press, 1979), pp. 102–5; Robert Blair St. George, *The Wrought Covenant: Source Materials for the Study of Craftsmen and Community in Southeastern New England (1620–1700)* (Brockton, Mass.: Brockton Art Center, 1979), pp. 72–102.
20. For analyses of the relationship of bent design to spatial function in barns, see John Fitchen, *The New World Dutch Barn: A Study of Its Characteristics, Its Structural System, and Its Probable Erectional Procedures* (Syracuse: Syracuse University Press, 1968), and Henry Glassie, "The Variation of Concepts within Tradition: Barn Building in Otsego County, New York," in H. J. Walker and W. G. Haag, eds., *Man and Cultural Heritage: Papers in Honor of Fred B. Kniffen*, Geoscience and Man, vol. 5 (Baton Rouge: Louisiana State University, 1974), pp. 205–7.
21. The 1652 Medfield town rate is reprinted in William S. Tilden, ed., *History of the Town of Medfield, Massachusetts, 1650–1886* (Boston: G. H. Ellis, 1887), p. 562 n. 2; John Demos, "Demography and Psychology in the Historical Study of the Family," in Peter Laslett, ed., *Household and Family in Past Time* (Cambridge: Cambridge University Press, 1972), pp. 51–56, confirms that the size of Medfield families (mean 5.6; median 6.0) is consistent with those of other New England towns of the period. Detailed information I have extracted from the 1652 Medfield town rate concerning exact house value and total estate value is available upon request in the Department of American Decorative Arts and Sculpture, Museum of Fine Arts, Boston.
22. The breeds of cattle most commonly owned and used in seventeenth-century New England depended on their purpose. Yorkshire, Derbyshire, Lancashire, and Staffordshire cattle were used as breeders, Lincolnshire for draft purposes, and Somerset and Gloucestershire as milk producers. All of these breeds gradually interbred and by the 1660s became

generically known as "New England cattle" or "Neat cattle"; see Darrett B. Rutman, *Husbandmen of Plymouth: Farms and Villages in the Old Colony* (Boston: Beacon Press, 1967), p. 47.

23. David Grayson Allen, *In English Ways: The Movement of Societies and the Transferal of English Local Law and Custom to Massachusetts Bay in the Seventeenth Century* (Chapel Hill: University of North Carolina Press, 1981), p. 100.
24. Worlidge, *Systema Agriculturae,* pp. 210–11.
25. Demos, *A Little Commonwealth: Family Life in Plymouth Colony* (New York: Oxford University Press, 1970), pp. 50–51.
26. Dow, ed., *Records and Files of the Quarterly Courts of Essex County,* 1:183.
27. Ibid., p. 225.
28. "The Council Book & ye Register of Wills belonging to Portsmouth in the Colony of Rhode Island (Council Book no. 2)," 2:188–89.
29. The Puritan aesthetic is, in other words, profoundly "intensive"; see Robert Plant Armstrong, *The Affecting Presence: An Essay in Humanistic Anthropology* (Urbana: University of Illinois Press, 1971), pp. 69–79; Henry Glassie, *Folk Housing in Middle Virginia: A Structural Analysis of Historic Artifacts* (Knoxville: University of Tennessee Press, 1975), pp. 138–57.
30. John Franklin Jameson, *Johnson's Wonderworking Providence, 1628–1651* (New York: C. Scribner's Sons, 1910), p. 11.
31. John Winthrop, *The History of New England from 1630 to 1644,* 2 vols. (Boston: Phelps and Farnham, 1825), 1:63.
32. Joan Thirsk, "The Farming Regions of England," in *The Agrarian History of England and Wales, IV: 1500–1640,* 8 vols., gen. ed. H. P. R. Finberg, vols. 4 and 8, ed. Joan Thirsk (London: Cambridge University Press, 1967), pp. 2–15; F. R. Banks, *English Villages* (London: B. T. Batsford, 1963), pp. 58–210; Ronald W. Brunskill, "Distribution of Building Materials and Some Plan Types in Domestic Vernacular Architecture of England and Wales," *Transactions of the Ancient Monuments Society,* n.s., 23 (1978): 48–51.
33. W. G. Hoskins, *Provincial England: Essays in Social and Economic History* (London: Macmillan, 1963), pp. 131–48.
34. James Walton, "Upland Houses: The Influence of Mountain Terrain on British Folk Building," *Antiquity* 30, no. 119 (September 1956): 142–44.
35. James Deetz, "Plymouth Colony Architecture: Archaeological Evidence from the Seventeenth Century," in *Architecture in Colonial Massachusetts,* Publications of the Colonial Society of Massachusetts, vol. 51 (Charlottesville: University Press of Virginia, 1979), pp. 55–59.
36. I am indebted to Dell Upton for the phrase "up-and-back" to describe the typically southern and eastern English plan for the extension of domestic architectural form. The short overview of English regional plans offered here should be augmented by the detailed account given in Dell Upton, "Early Vernacular Architecture in Southeastern Virginia," Ph.D. diss., Brown University, 1980, pp. 43–64.
37. Comparative data for four locations in rural England during the period are offered in Hoskins, *Provincial England,* p. 292; Alan Everitt, "Farm Labourers," in Thirsk, ed., *The Agrarian History of England and Wales,* pp. 443–44; M. W. Barley, "Farmhouses and Cottages, 1550–1725," *Economic History Review* 7, no. 3 (April 1955): 294; and Derek Portman, "Vernacular Building in the Oxford Region in the Sixteenth and Seventeenth Centuries," in C. W. Chalkin and M. A. Havinden, eds., *Rural Change and Urban Growth, 1500–1800: Essays in English Regional History in Honor of W. G. Hoskins* (London: Longman's, 1974), pp. 149–53.
38. See Cummings, *The Framed Houses of Massachusetts Bay.* I am grateful to Abbott Lowell Cummings for sharing his research interests with me; my use here of the Fairbanks, Coffin, Blake, and Boardman houses as descriptive examples is drawn from his own detailed analysis of these structures. Cummings's work on seventeenth-century New England houses represents the most detailed and exhaustive interpretation of the material culture of the period.
39. Ibid., p. 95; Robert Blair St. George, "Style and Structure in the Joinery of Dedham and Medfield, Massachusetts, 1635–1685," *Winterthur Portfolio 13,* ed. Ian M. G. Quimby (Chicago: University of Chicago Press, 1979), pp. 37–46.
40. Peter C. D. Brears, ed., *Yorkshire Probate Inventories, 1542–1689* (Kendal, England: Yorkshire Philosophical Society, 1972), pp. 67–68; Barley, "A Glossary of Rooms," Foster and Alcock, *Culture and Environment,* pp. 489–90.
41. I am indebted to Dell Upton for pointing out this overall pattern.
42. *Plymouth Colony Wills and Inventories,* vol. 4, pt. 2, p. 152.
43. *Plymouth County Wills and Inventories,* 3:387.
44. Alec Clifton-Taylor, *The Pattern of English Building* (London: Faber and Faber, 1972), passim; Burnskill, "Distribution of Building Materials," pp. 41–45.
45. Quoted in Joshua Coffin, *A Sketch of the History of Newbury, Newburyport, and West Newbury from 1635 to 1845* (Boston: S. G. Drake, 1845), p. 124.

46. Mildred Campbell, *The English Yeoman under Elizabeth and the Early Stuarts* (New Haven: Yale University Press, 1942), pp. 221–61; G. E. Fussell, *The English Rural Labourer: His House, Furniture, Clothing and Food from Tudor to Victorian Times* (London: Batchworth Press, 1949), pp. 1–24; W. G. Hoskins, *The Midland Peasant: The Economic and Social History of a Leicestershire Village* (London: Macmillan, 1957), pp. 293–94.
47. Caoimhin Ó Danachair, "Hearth and Chimney in the Irish House," *Béaloideas* 16, no. 1–11 (1946): 91.
48. Jay Allen Anderson, "A Solid Sufficiency: An Ethnography of Yeoman Foodways in Stuart England," Ph.D. dissertation, University of Pennsylvania, 1971, pp. 237–40. The distribution of such salts—hence the symbolic seating at table based on their position—while not universal in seventeenth-century society, at least appears to have been fairly widespread, as they were made of wood, pewter, or silver for owners of varying economic status.
49. For the function of the "inner room" in seventeenth-century houses in the Plymouth Colony, see Demos, *A Little Commonwealth,* pp. 31–34.
50. "Suffolk County Probate Record," 5:112–14.
51. Otto Mayr, "A Mechanical Symbol for an Authoritarian World," in Klaus Maurice and Otto Mayr, eds., *The Clockwise Universe: German Clocks and Automata, 1550–1650* (New York: N. Walton Academic Publications, 1980), pp. 1–8.
52. Cummings, *The Framed Houses of Massachusetts Bay,* pp. 195–97.
53. My treatment of the seventeenth-century yeoman's house owes much to Pierre Bourdieu, "The Berber House or the World Reversed," in Jean Pouillon and Pierre Maranda, eds., *Echanges et communications: Mélanges offerts a Claude Lévi-Straus à l'occasion 60eme anniversaire,* 2 vols. (The Hague: Mouton, 1971), pp. 151–69.
54. John G. Howells and N. Livia Osborn, "The Incidence of Emotional Disorder in a Seventeenth-Century Medical Practice," *Medical History* 14, no. 2 (April 1970): 197.
55. Edward T. Hall, "Proxemics," *Current Anthropology* 9, no. 2 (April–June 1968): 83–90, and *The Hidden Dimension* (Garden City, N.Y.: Doubleday, 1969), pp. 103–10; Robert Sommer, *Personal Space: The Behavioral Basis of Design* (Englewood Cliffs, N.J.: Prentice-Hall, 1969), p. 3–76; Judith Friedman Hansen, "Proxemics and the Interpretative Process in Human Communication," *Semiotica* 17, no. 2 (1976): 61–67.
56. Alan Gailey, "Kitchen Furniture," *Ulster Folklife* 12 (1966): 18–34; Glassie, *Folk Housing,* pp. 76–93; F. H. A. Aalen, "Furnishings of Traditional Houses in the Wicklow Hills," *Ulster Folklife* 13 (1967): 61–67.
57. The following analysis, in trying to define an underlying and constant spatial structure of the yeoman's house, does not include artifacts that varied in size and type (such as large sacks of grain or tools, etc.) according to the season. My description is based solely on the (relatively) stationary forms of furniture that can be measured and discussed in quantitative terms.
58. Abbott Lowell Cummings, "The 'Scotch'- Boardman House," *Old-Time New England* 43, no. 1 (January–March 1953): 53–73 and 43, no. 2 (April–June 1953): 91–102, and *The Framed Houses of Massachusetts Bay,* pp. 184–86.
59. Rutman, *Winthrop's Boston,* pp. 135–201.
60. Sarah Knight, *The Journal of Madam Knight* (Boston: D. Godine, 1972), p. 13.
61. See, for example, Gabriel Olive, "Furniture in a West Country Parish, 1576–1769," *Furniture History* 12 (1976): 21.
62. Kevin Lynch, *A Theory of Good City Form* (Cambridge, Mass.: MIT Press, 1981), pp. 205–7, provides a good summary of what constitutes five basic spatial rights: presence, use-action, appropriation, modification, and disposition. His discussion relates directly to historical issues and should be consulted by historians and geographers interested in the politics of space.
63. Susan L. Norton, "Population Growth in Colonial America: A Study of Ipswich, Massachusetts," *Population Studies* 25, no. 3 (November 1971): 435.
64. John Josselyn, "An Account of Two Voyages to New England," *Massachusetts Historical Society Collections,* ser. 3, vol. 3 (1833), p. 319.
65. Paul-Henry Chombart-de Lauwe, *La Vie quotidienne des familles ouvrières* (Paris: Centre National de la Récherche Scientifique, 1977), pp. 61–86; John McCarthy, Orner R. Galle, and William Zimmern, "Population Density, Social Structure and Interpersonal Violence," *American Behavioral Scientist* 18, no. 6 (July–August 1975): 787–88; G. Simmel, "The Metropolis and Mental Life," in Richard Sennett, ed., *Classic Essays on the Culture of Cities* (New York: Appleton-Century Crofts, 1969), passim.
66. David Thomas Konig, *Law and Society in Puritan Massachusetts: Essex County, 1629–1692* (Chapel Hill: University of North Carolina Press, 1979), pp. 89–116.
67. Alan Gowans, *The Unchanging Arts: New Forms for the Traditional Functions of Art in Society* (Philadelphia: Lippincott, 1971), p. 53.

Part Five Design and Intention

The Mansions of Alloways Creek

ALAN GOWANS

Alan Gowans's essay inaugurates this series of essays on vernacular architecture as the product of thought by placing the issue within its historiographical context. Gowans commences his discussion of a distinctive group of houses in southern New Jersey by asking whether any of the traditional ways that these well-known buildings have been interpreted is appropriate. First, he investigates ethnic connections. Can we attribute either the striking patterned-brick decoration for which the houses are famous, or their central-passage, story-and-a-half, gambrel-roofed forms to either the Swedish or the British settlers who first came to the area in the seventeenth century? Then he considers the possibility that a single builder or "school" of builders could be identified through traditional art historical techniques for aesthetic analysis, the investigation of formal influences, and the attribution of individual works. Economic factors receive brief consideration as well. Gowans concludes that, while each of these approaches might yield some insights into the brick houses of Alloways Creek, none is capable of addressing the fundamental questions of the builders' intentions, and of the reasons for the appearance and abandonment of these architectural forms. The answers to those questions lie not in ethnicity, aesthetics, or economics, but in the social dynamics of an agrarian society. In such a society, power and merit must be asserted by each new generation. A "Homeric" aristocracy—one in which social standing was based on superior individual accomplishments in a local context—arose. Its great men and women asserted their personal standing in part by building houses that shared their neighbors' architectural vocabulary, but surpassed them in magnificence.

Gowans not only challenges many of the questions traditionally asked of vernacular buildings, but he offers a model of the kinds of uses to which antiquarian local histories and other nonacademic sources can be put by the vernacular architectural historian. From those sources he extracts a portrait of a short-lived, intensely local architectural tradition of the sort that flourished in many parts of the United States until they were overwhelmed by the national vernacular forms that Kniffen described in the first essay in this collection.

The hundred or more patterned-brick houses of Salem County in southern New Jersey, roughly centering around Alloways township, are not unknown to people interested in American arts and civilization; but they are not exactly famous monuments, either.[1] Although you can find them if you take the trouble to ask, few of them are voluntarily pointed out as landmarks. Yet if you happen to be in that vicinity, they are worth looking for, and at. There is nothing quite like them in North America, at least in such a concentration. What you find are houses with blank side walls, one and one-half to two and one-half stories high, built of bricks set with vitrified headers to form elaborate patterns of zigzags, diamonds, coronets, figures, and letters (fig. 1). Almost always the vitrified bricks are burnt blue, the regular courses red. When the sun catches them, especially mornings or evenings, it flashes off the glassy surface so that the pattern seems to glow crimson and gold. They are worth seeing as aesthetic experience, worth observing as folk culture, and worth studying as historical documents of a particular area and era in American life.

The first Europeans who came to the area now centered around Salem were put there by the New Sweden Company in the 1630s and 1640s. They were not all Swedes by any means, but came from all over Northern Europe. They seem to have brought with them a North European folk building tradition of long low cottages consisting of two or three contiguous rooms roofed by what some authorities like to call "Swedish gambrels." Then in the mid-1670s a sizable English settlement of Quakers arrived, led by John Fenwick. These outnumbered and assimilated the first settlers, and in due course became first families of the region. At first they seem to have adopted the original settlers' house type—or more precisely, perhaps, the original settlers helped them get established by building houses for them.[2] John Fenwick's 1678 house in Salem sounds, from descriptions, as if it were just this Northern European gambrel-roofed three-contiguous-room sort of homestead (fig. 2). But there were all sorts of interconnections, personal and business, between the Salem colony and the much larger Philadelphia settlement established across the Delaware River in the 1680s, and soon enough the distinctive Philadelphia town-house type began appearing on farms in Salem County (fig. 3). Devised apparently by Nicholas Barbon (who may have been the first speculative contractor-builder in the modern sense) to meet a need for quickly built and easily repeatable city houses following the Great Fire of London in 1666, this was composed vertically rather than horizontally, on a few standardized plans, of units standardized in size, with standardized details like pent eaves and blank firebreak walls.[3]

That Philadelphia builders should be invited to erect houses in Salem was natural; that they would build the same types there as in Philadelphia was natural too—by the practices of traditional vernacular building, if not ours. Whence the curious sight of Salem County houses standing in the countryside with blank side walls, obviously designed as firebreaks to separate city row houses. (Of course Salem County is far from the only place you see this kind of house; it can be found all around Philadelphia, notably in Chester and Bucks County, and for the same reasons.[4]) In due course, this Philadelphia house type was coalesced by local builders with the gambrel-roofed rural type. The result: a distinctive South Jersey variant of Mid-Atlantic colonial folk building. One-and-a-half or occasionally two stories high, it typically had a "Swedish gambrel" roof, and frequently a so-called "Swedish" three-room plan as well; but its proportions, materials, use of variable standard units, and blank side walls obviously derived from city house types associated with Restoration London and Quaker Philadelphia (figs. 4 and 5).

It was on these blank side walls that the elaborate blue glazed-brick patterns appear, which give Salem County whatever architectural renown it may enjoy.

The precise origins of this tradition of patterned-brick has been a subject of considerable speculation, not to say controversy, among its small but devoted band of admirers. There is a vague tradition that the patterned brickwork was done by per-

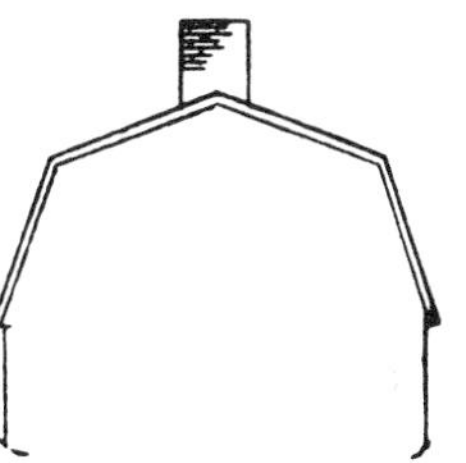

Figure 1. a (top left), West wall, John and Martha Dickinson House, Alloways Creek, New Jersey, as restored in the 1960s; b (top right), original gambrel-shaped roof line; c (right), west wall, Zaccheus and Deborah Dunn House, Woodstown (about 2½ miles from the Dickinson House), as restored in the 1970s.

Figure 2. Conjectural reconstruction of John Fenwick's 1678 homestead at Ivy Point on Fenwick Creek at the foot of Fifth Street, Salem. Demolished ca. 1820. Original North European house type in this area. (From Joseph Sickler, Old Houses of Salem County, New Jersey *[Salem: Sunbeam Publishing, 1949].)*

Figure 3. William Hancock House, 1734, Hancock's Bridge. The Philadelphia town-house type in rural Salem County as it was before the restoration of ca. 1980.

Figure 4, top and bottom left. General view and west wall of the William and Mary Oakford House (as restored ca. 1980 by Mary Acton Hamilton, lineal descendant of the Oakfords), 1736, one mile south of Alloway, New Jersey. A distinctive folk house type in brick, this one-and-a-half-story, gambrel-roofed, three-room-ground-floor house is the record of the fusion of descendants of the New Sweden settlement with those of Fenwick's English Quaker colony. This brickwork—checkerboard on the facade, ornate initials and date on the blank side wall picked out by vitrified blue headers set against finely burnt red stretchers—is the special distinguishing feature. The house was built for (and possibly the carpentry was executed by) a grandson of the Wade Oakford who by 1700 had acquired five thousand acres of land in this country.

Figure 5, top and bottom right. West wall and original "Swedish gambrel" roofline of the John and Mary Dickinson House, 1754, a few miles west of Alloway near the Wistar Glass works as restored ca. 1980 by Jerry Watland for Jeff and Louise Huber. The Dickinson House was the climax of this type. It was a full two-and-a-half stories high, as is evident from a view of ca. 1930, which also shows the original "Swedish gambrel" roofline. Enlargement to the fashionably flat Italianate bracketed roof apparently took place ca. 1850, and during its restoration in the 1930s the house was mistakenly restored to a straight gable on the analogy of other country houses belonging to the common I-type. Its west wall has been called "the most ornate glazed brickwork in all America," and it displays almost the full vocabulary of this art: date, initials of builders, and a wealth of geometric designs, diamonds, zigzags, and quasi-floral patterns. The first John Dickinson (sometimes spelled Dickeson) appears in the Salem County records as acquiring one hundred acres of land from founder John Fenwick's granddaughter in 1702. The builder of this house died in 1768.

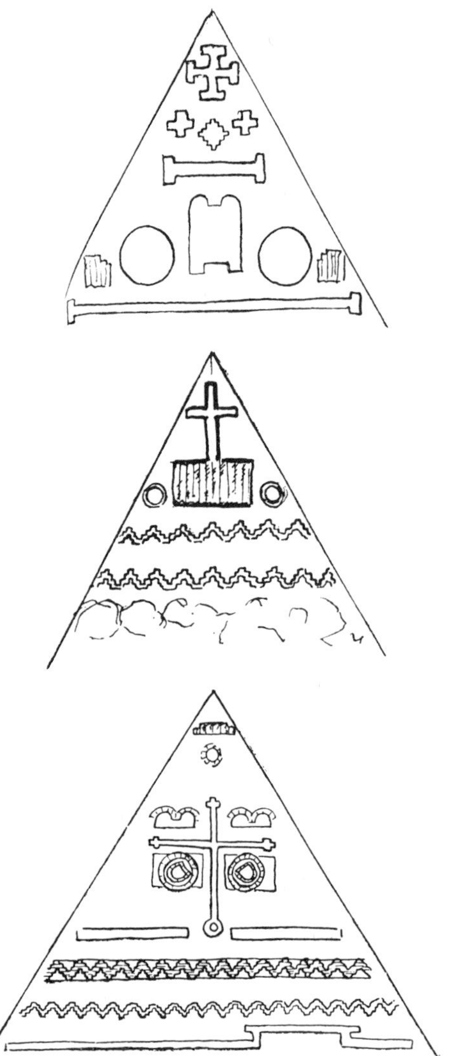

Figure 6. Gable decorations in patterned-brick from typical small Swedish churches. (From Gerda Boëthius, De tegelornerade gråstenskyrkorna *[Brick-ornamented fieldstone churches], [Stockholm: Svenska Kurkans diakenistyrelses bokförlag, 1921].) Wall hanging, patterned weaving, from the province of Blekinge, Sweden, ca. 1750. (Courtesy of the Nordiska Museet, Stockholm.)*

sons of Swedish extraction. Reviewing the 1966 tercentennial picture book *Fenwick's Colony,* Carl Williams wrote that "the identity of the man who fashioned the most elaborate of these [patterned-brick] walls has been recovered. It is surprising to learn that he was a native of Salem County, a third generation Swede in America with no known contact at all with English or European techniques and traditions in brick laying. The great west wall of the [Dickinson] house was certainly his personal creation. This craftsman was not old enough to have laid the walls of the earliest decorative examples . . . but the Samuel Bassett gable [1757] is his work."[5] Only the bricklayer's Swedish descent was remembered, apparently, not his name; and for many, that was not enough.

The notion of a Swedish influence is attractive to people who like the melting-pot theory of American culture. It also affords a satisfying demonstration of the principle that the first settlers in any region give a distinctive accent or flavor to its later culture, no matter how totally assimilated they may be. Transmission of a patterned-brick tradition from, say, Uppsala (where there are a great many elaborate examples of patterned walls on churches), presumably via patterned hangings common in Swedish folk tradition, quilts, folk-carved cradles and bedsteads, and the like, is romantic to contemplate (fig. 6).[6] Further, it can be neatly compared with parallel developments in linguistic studies of dialect. Consult the volume of *New Jersey Archives* from 1664 to 1703 and you will find land deeds and legal transactions abounding with Swedish names, not yet Anglicized.[7] As late as 1753, the celebrated visitor Peter Kalm found Swedish being spoken in this region.[8] Thus the hypothesis of a Swedish tradition behind the patterned-brick houses would parallel the principle of linguistics that the earliest speech in any region continues to provide a substratum of accent—unrecognized preferences for what "sounds right," similar to preferences for what "looks right," subtly modify later visual culture for generations thereafter.[9] Further, it opens the way for exploration of parallels in this region to community patterns of political, sociological, and ethnographic development—the sort of thing studied in C. C. Zimmerman and R. E. Du Wors's *Graphic Regional Sociology* or C. M. Arensberg's "American Communities."[10]

After all this, it is rather dull to consider the possibility that the bulk of these patterned-brick houses may represent no more than provincial survivals of English taste for such patterning going back to the Elizabethan and Jacobean periods, still being perpetuated in remote areas of rural England in the mid eighteenth century (fig. 7).[11] And so a controversy rages—modest enough by *Kunstgeschichte* standards, but raging nonetheless. Behind, and unconsciously fueling much of it, is an assumption that we may have here in visual arts something corresponding to the "mute inglorious Milton" of Gray's Elegy—some forgotten genius expressing a view of life and an awareness of materials in the simple medium of brickwork in his native country, whose origins can be looked for in much the same spirit as Iberian and African influences are traced in Picasso. For this kind of art, no such assumption is valid. Its primary value is not as art in any modern sense, but as historical documentation—a record of certain older attitudes toward life that remain significant to us living today, because we cannot escape being to some extent their products.

First, these houses are records of the art of architecture. That is, they demonstrate unequivocally, in a way our Art of architecture cannot, how architecture in most parts of the world and in most ages of the world was constructed. They remind us that our modern concept of the genius creating a great aesthetic experience for artists to enjoy is *not* the way historic architecture came into being.

Second, they are records of basic institutions in Western civilization—specifically, visual metaphors of the founding of landed families and property transmission through marriage.

These are matters worth investigating.

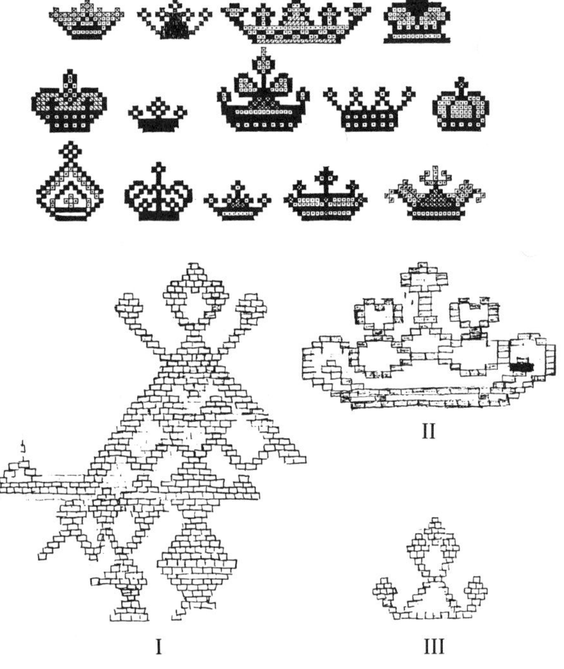

Figure 7. Illustrations of the case for English origins for the patterned brickwork of Salem County: a (top left), isometric drawing of Little Moreton Hall, Cheshire, ca. 1540, detail showing chimney with brickwork diamonds (from Thomas Garner and Arthur Stratton, Domestic Architecture of England during the Tudor Period, *2 vols., 2d ed. [London: B. T. Batsford, 1929], vol. 2); b (bottom left), black diaper pattern, spontaneously appearing on a chimney at Eastbury House, Essex, ca. 1520 (from Garner and Stratton,* Domestic Architecture of England during the Tudor Period*); c (top right), patterned-brick gable, 1748, on a rural building in southeast England (photograph by Henry Glassie); d (bottom right), comparison of typical eighteenth- and nineteenth-century traditional textile designs for weaving and embroidery with I, central design, Dickinson House; II, coronet design, Bassett House; and III, gable design, Swing House (top three rows, from Leigh Ashton,* Samplers *[London: Medici Society, 1926]).*

A Lesson in the Vernacular

No documentation reveals exactly who built south Jersey's patterned-brick houses. But we can get a good idea of the kind of people they must have been, and how they went about it, on analogy with development from early settlement to permanent house-building elsewhere. For what the documentation on early life in southern New Jersey does reveal is its great similarity to frontier life at all times and places. Homesteading in Wisconsin in the 1870s and South Dakota in the 1880s as described by Laura Wilder hardly differs in any detail from homesteading in New Jersey in the 1670s and 1680s; nor were either different from the life of settlers in Vermont or upper New York in the 1780s. Whence it follows that all these cases can profitably be collated in order to discover how a distinctive regional architecture came into existence. A paradigm emerges, roughly as follows: The first settlers who arrive are in their late twenties or thirties, with young families. They begin by erecting modest shelters of whatever materials are handy—logs in forested area, sod on the prairies; if they have pit-saws, they will shape planks. Thereafter their only building consists of additions and enlargements to their first shelters.

Whatever time is left over from the incessant round of chores frontier families have to do—neatly turned into an asset in the famous promotional blurb for Fenwick's Colony on 8 January 1675: "Here you need not trouble the Shambles for Meat, nor Bakers and Brewers for Beer and Bread, not run to a Linnen-Draper for a supply, everyone making their own Linnen, and a great part of their Woolen Cloth for their ordinary wearing"—is taken up simply clearing the land, draining it, and otherwise transforming it from forest or marsh into farm.[12] By the second or third generation, depending on time and place, this basic work is done. Chores remain, but the land is not so demanding; furthermore, it now begins to produce a surplus. So improvements like wharves (if there is a creek or river) and roads can be thought of, to get the crops to market. All going well, cash prosperity ensues. And with this development comes a "proper" house. These permanent houses, coming fifty-odd years after the original settlement, will not be built like the first dwellings, by the farmers or planters themselves. They are now able to hire someone to do it. Whom? Apparently in all cases, a transient team of some kind—the same practice followed in this style of life in every area calling for a distinct degree of specialization beyond the frontiersman's normal jack-of-all-trades abilities.

Laura Ingalls Wilder's *Farmer Boy,* for instance, describes the cobbler's visit to Almanzo Wilder's boyhood farm home near Malone, New York.[13] He stayed two or three days, long enough to make shoes for everyone in the family, then moved on to the next place. Similarly with the tinsmith and his pots and pans. Similarly with Sam Slick the clockmaker in Nova Scotia, or the Yankee Trader of frontier folk legend, with his wagonload of manufactured articles. Houses were specialized artifacts to be acquired in just this way. At a certain stage in any given settlement, houses would be going up all over. A team of carpenter and stonemason (if good stone was abundant) or bricklayer (if clay was available and a brick house preferred) could make their living for a great many years simply going about from one property to another, living on each as many months as construction of a new house required. It was the style of such teams that gave regional character to architecture in most if not all times and places, a character that traditional High Art could build on. It was on just this kind of foundation that Frank Lloyd Wright's architecture was formed. Maginel Wright Barney in *The Valley of the God-Almighty Joneses* gives the following account:

> There was, living in Uncle John's house, a Welsh stonemason named Timothy. . . .
>
> He was the stone builder for all the clan. He made the walls and foundations of their houses, their fireplaces and chimneys. He carved their mantels with mistletoe and holly and the family emblem: the old Druid symbol "Truth Against the World." . . .
>
> He was a loyal advocate of my brother. If there was a controversy concerning Frank's building, later on when he was becoming an architect, Timothy would nod his

> old head gently and say: "Trust the boy, he knows." It was he who supported Aunt Nell in the belief that Frank's idea for the windmill "Romeo and Juliet," a wooden tower of unique construction and design, would be feasible. . . .
>
> "It will stand," Timothy insisted more than once, and he made the foundations even deeper and more solid than the specifications demanded. He lived to see his faith vindicated, too . . . Romeo and Juliet still stands, almost seventy years later. It was Timothy also who built the foundations for the beautiful new school building my brother later designed for the Aunts.[14]

Things were surely no different in early eighteenth-century New Jersey. Folktales (that is the proper word) have even preserved names and ethnic backgrounds of some of these builders. Joseph Sickler, writing *Old Houses of Salem County* in the early 1930s, recorded reminiscences like Dr. Warren L. Ewen's of his ancestors in the Oakford family:

> I was told years ago by my granddad, Jonathan House (formerly Houseman [descended from one of the Germans brought over to run the Wistar Glass Works, a later racial strain in the country]) that the Oakfords, Wade and Charles, built several brick houses of the same design (hip [i.e., gambrel] roofed) on or near the Alloway Creek, and I believe they built the brick Gosling house [originally Richard Smith house, 1729, q.v.]—all of them were similar. One, just south of Alloways Creek—now standing one mile from Hancock's Bridge, another at Fogg's Landing on the Creek and on the first old road from Thompson's Bridge (now Alloway), via Sandy Ridge, to Salem, known as the old "Kentuck" road.
>
> There were also three of the same pattern in Alloway village itself—one located on our (Ewen's) Lake, which was Alloway Creek before the dam; one on Daniel P. Dorrell's farm at the upper end of Alloway; and one in the yard of my previous home on Main Street in Alloway. All three are vouched for also by William B. Willis, Esquire, et als. There is also another, now standing one mile southeast of Thompson's Bridge and owned by Mrs. Frances House Acton, of Salem [see fig. 4].

Sickler went on to add that this team also built the Friends' Meeting House of 1772 in Salem, and that they built ships as well as houses—a combination as old as Western civilization itself, by the way—out of Salem County white oak, floating them down Alloways Creek to the Delaware River.[15]

One need not delve deep into county archives to find hopeless confusion in these reminiscences. There were a Wade and Charles Oakford in the records from the late 1690s, acquiring land, along with a "Wadesamuel" Oakford who may or may not be one of the same persons. That these were the same brothers referred to as builders is possible; if they were of legal age in the 1690s they would have been in their fifties when they built the Gosling (Smith) House, about sixty when they built the Oakford/Acton House in 1736 (figs. 4, 8a,c). But to have built the Friends' Meeting House they would have been exactly one hundred . . . Does it matter? For archival accuracy, yes. To understand how meaningful folk architecture was created, no. For that, we need only realize it was the work of local carpenters, serving needs of their society. And further that they worked in collaboration—Sickler's reminiscence is surely sound that "while the Oakford brothers were undoubtedly carpenters and carpenter-contractors, whether they did their own brick work or had a sub-contractor, the records fail to reveal."[16] They gave the emergent folk house type its plan and structure, guided in this taste by the taste of the English-descended community centering in Philadelphia. The brickwork, completing the house type's distinctive character, was done by others, and deserves separate study. The point here is how the vernacular building process represented by these houses preserves a regional sense for proportions and spaces consistently through the most extraordinary changes. Henry Glassie has written acutely on this subject:

> The skins of houses are shallow things that people are willing to change, but people are most conservative about the spaces they must utilize and in which they must exist. Build the walls of anything, deck them out with anything, but do not change the arrangement of the rooms or their proportions. In these volumes—bounded by surfaces from which a person senses rebound to him—his psyche develops; disrupt them and you disrupt him.[17]

This kind of inherent taste is a visual metaphor—albeit unconscious, but perhaps all the stronger for that, of a concept of "rightness," which lies at the bottom of any objective value system. Hence the appearance of the concept of "rightness" at the very beginning of civilization is no accident; on such a concept depends natural law and practical reason, and on these all civilized institutions ultimately rest. Egyptian civilization starts with *ma'at*—created and inherited rightness, the first premise of all reason and all justice. Mesopotamian civilization with *šimtu,* the same.[18] In every Indo-European language, whereas words for "left" or "wrong" differ wildly, the word and the concept of "rightness" remains constant through all millennia: *rta* in Hindu, *ortho* in Greek, *pravda* in Russian, *dharma* in Sanskrit, *rectus* in Latin, *droit* in French, *recht* in German. So understood, folk and vernacular building is a metaphor of the foundations of civilized life itself. But South Jersey folk and vernacular building offers something more—one of our best metaphors of the institution of marriage in western society.

Founding Fathers *and* Founding Mothers

The bulk of the elaborately blue-and-red patterned-brick houses that give South Jersey most of whatever distinction in early American architecture it possesses, falls in date between 1720 and 1760. Paul Love's "Patterned Brickwork in Southern New Jersey" listed over a hundred examples from four counties.[19] The most remarkable—forty or so of them—clustered in Salem County. Presumably there were others that have been destroyed. Some are still being found, when sheds or additions built up against them are torn off or fall down for some reason (fig. 8). One of the best examples in Salem County, the Joseph Darkin House, was discovered in this manner. Even supposing that twice as many houses as are now known originally existed, however, that would still mean that one could have been erected in Salem County every eight months over a forty-year period—by no means beyond the capacity of a team of carpenter and bricklayer with some assistance. In fact, such a schedule is just about what might be expected of a building team working during the spring, summer, and fall, but not during the winter.

In other words, all the patterned-brick houses in Salem County and vicinity could have been built by one person or a small team. It follows that a sequence of dates on known houses might give a chronological list of this team's clientele and general movements over a forty-year period. In theory, they could have begun working on Joseph Darkin's house in Elsinboro township, completed in 1720. Next, Abel Nicholson's nearby, completed in 1722. Thence to other famous examples: the John Maddox Denn House of 1725, near Hancock's Bridge; the Chambless House in Lower Alloway's Creek township and the Padgett House near Harmersville between 1730 and 1733; the William Hancock House at Hancock's Bridge in 1734; working up to masterpieces—the Samuel Nicholson House of about 1752 in Elsinboro township, the famous John Dickinson House outside of Woodstown in Alloway township of 1754, the Samuel Bassett House in Pilesgrove township outside Woodstown of 1757; finally trailing off in the mid-1760s.

Here is fuel to fire the coldest art-historical soul! A neat geographical sequence, inviting a neat artistic biography of stylistic evolution. Missing links; doubtful attributions; daring inclusions or exclusions of attributions from far adjacent counties—all the necessary material to emulate Berenson in a small South Jersey way. Postulations of some Maestro di Allovacci, complete with *oeuvre,* disciples, *amici,* schools. And *Einflüsse*—Swedish influences, to top it off. Who could ask for more? Alas, the material stubbornly resists. There is no discernible evolution in this style, unless one counts the "climactic moment" from the Dickinson House of 1754 to the Samuel Bassett of 1757, and that is better explained by rivalry of patrons than by artists' self-expression. No formal development of technique can be seen. Nor would it reveal anything if it could. The reason is that traditional architecture was never created as personal or cultural self-expression. It was always done in a context of

Figure 8. Illustrations of how vernacular houses change with the generations: a (above), front view of Richard Keen House, Quinton. Seemingly a normal sort of South Jersey Georgian mansion, built in the 1820s; b (right), view of the west wall, taken in 1981 when renovations were underway; the 1820s plaster had fallen to reveal a patterned-brick wall of the familiar Salem County sort, with the prominent numerals "1759." Obviously by the 1820s the meanings and motivation for the big date numerals had been lost and were covered over as an embarrassment when the house was added to and made into a fashionable Georgian mansion. Actually the window punched into this wall dates only from 1974; c (facing page), Richard Smith (Gosling) House of 1729 in the vicinity of Salem, as it was in the 1930s. (From Old Roof Trees and Candle Ends, *rev. ed. [Salem: Salem County Historical Society, 1971].) Here too the house has been added to, and heightened so as to produce a straight gable rather than the by then old-fashioned "Swedish gambrel" (though the old outline is plainly visible); but the family initials and dates were carefully preserved.*

S
RS
1729

social function. It was always the creation of some kind of Establishment, creating visual metaphors of some established social convictions. And the particular interest of these houses is precisely that in them it is not difficult to ascertain what this Establishment was and its values were.

Where you can see that best, oddly enough—though actually it is not so odd once you realize that the old concepts of what architecture is and does in society have been preserved on the popular level—is in guides and local histories. Consider for example the handout given to tourists visiting grand Tidewater Virginia mansions like Berkeley on the James River:

> The land on which it stands was part of a grant made in 1619 by King James I to the Berkeley Company. . . . On December 4, 1619, the settlers stepped ashore there and celebrated the first Thanksgiving Day more than a year before the Pilgrims landed in New England . . . it was as the home of the Harrison family that Berkeley achieved its greatness. The early Georgian mansion which is said to be the oldest three-storey brick house in Virginia, was built in 1726 by Benjamin Harrison, a leader in colonial affairs. His son, Col. Benjamin Harrison, inherited it. Member of the Continental Congress, Signer of the Declaration of Independence, active in the Revolution and thrice Governor of Virginia, this Harrison was himself enough to bring glory to his house. . . . Further prestige came to Berkeley in the next generation through Col. Harrison's younger son, William Henry. . . . He made his reputation in the Northwest Territory of which he was the first secretary and as a great Indian fighter, he came to be called "old Tippecanoe." When he was elected President of the United States [in 1840] he returned to write his inaugural address in the room in which he had been born (despite his supporters having featured in their campaign models of the "simple log cabin, his birth place"). The Harrison family was to produce yet another President [1889–1893] in Benjamin, the grandson of William Henry. As the ancestral home of two Presidents, Berkeley has the distinction almost unique, shared only with the Adams house in Massachusetts (fig. 9).

Popular descriptions of architecture like this—like so much else in the popular arts—preserve a principle all too often obscured or neglected by formal arts and architectural study: the history of architecture does not primarily consist of analyzing aesthetics and streams of influences. It begins with, and is inseparable from, the history of the people who had architecture built for themselves. So Joseph Sickler, the local historian of Salem County, was quite correct in claiming that he "tried to preserve Salem's past in book form" by relating the history of *The Old Houses of Salem County* and their builders together; correct, too, when he observed that he had had two predecessors in that task: Thomas Shourds (1805–1891) who, "spending years in the accumulation of data [about family histories] . . . finally published, at the age of 71 . . . in 1876 his celebrated *History of Fenwick's Colony*"; and Robert Gibbon Johnson, "the first historian, but Johnson ended his text with the Revolution and made no attempt to trace the great land-owning families and their scions who made Salem."[20] Precisely. On such people and their estates Western civilization was founded, and they remained one of its fundamental institutions from the later Middle Ages into the twentieth century. Hear a French scholar, Régine Pernoud, lamenting the dissolution of this foundation of Western society in France, and blaming on it the loss of French influence throughout the modern world. According to her, family solidarity was "the essential motif" of medieval society—a family all so "united by flesh and blood that their interests are identical":

> This conception of the family rested on a material basis: The family property, generally landed property . . . the family, stretching across generations, remained in every case the true owner of the patrimonial estate. The father of the family, who received the property from his ancestors, was responsible for it to his descendents . . . he had the duty of defending, protecting, and improving the lot of all the persons and things of whom he had been appointed the natural guardian. . . . Anglo-Saxon . . . family institutions were identical with those of the French throughout the middle ages . . . unlike the French . . . [they] have continued to preserve them. Here doubtless, lies the explanation of the prodigious Anglo-Saxon expansion throughout the world, for it is in fact in this way that an Empire is founded, as a result of waves of explorers, pioneers, merchants, and adventurers . . . leaving their

Figure 9. Berkeley, Charles City County, Virginia. A visual metaphor of family success in Virginia. General view, including one of the two flanking dependencies; and detail of the datestone with initials of Benjamin and Ann Harrison. (From a tourist handout.)

> homes . . . without forgetting their native land and the tradition of their forefathers.[21]

These "family institutions" are what all colonial American houses of any pretensions are "about." Precisely how families were established and perpetuated varied, of course, from region to region within colonies, from colony to colony within British America; and nowhere in the colonies was the process exactly like England. But throughout the colonies, the idea of founding a family with an estate was a common ambition. And a "great house"—great by comparison with its neighbors—was its commonest monument.

Most famous American examples of such houses, perhaps, are the eighteenth-century mansions of Tidewater Virginia. Through them, and their counterparts in South Carolina and Maryland, can be traced a developing "Georgian" taste for restrained, balanced, classical forms—from Rosewell through Stratford, Westover, Berkeley, Carter's Grove, Gunston Hall to the banqueting room at Mount Vernon: Mulberry to Middleton to Drayton Hall: Readbourne to Whitehall. This architecture is conscious High Art, and its formal development has so preoccupied recent scholarly and appreciative writings that these mansions are now commonly thought to be related by lines of descent, as if begotten one by another in a biological sense. Such research has its uses. But it tends to obscure another and historically much more significant set of relationships of these Virginia mansions—to house-types elsewhere which are similar not in outward forms, but in social function. That is, to houses that had the same kind of "meaning." It is in this sense that famed Berkeley is related to the obscure patterned-brick houses in south Jersey.

On the side walls of all of them appear initials of the owners, husband and wife, and the date. In this apparently trivial coincidence is summed up both the differences between these two buildings and their similarities. In the one case, aspirations to English aristocracy implied in the elegant refinement of a classically lettered Georgian plaque, tastefully inconspicuous above a pedimented side door (fig. 9; one can find the same in other Tidewater mansions). In the other, simple folk pride displayed in great blue-glazed brick digits sprawling blatantly over a whole end wall. But in both, evidence of how the buildings functioned in their own time and place—and evidence that, in both cases, their social function was the same. They were visual metaphors of family success.

A second metaphor might be mentioned here—the *front parlor* or, in mansions, the *Great Hall.* At Stratford, seat of the Lee family on the Potomac, you can see a fine example of the Great Hall as metaphor of successful landed-family founding: in a room that is the focal point of the whole structure, connecting two wings, matched portraits of Thomas Lee and his wife face each other in specially inset paneling, the place of their meeting being the pivotal point of the whole mansion. Counterpart in the patterned-brick houses of Salem County are the front parlors, also with paneling, over fireplaces, with if not portraits, family souvenirs and memorabilia prominently displayed (fig. 10). Such front parlors, statements of family establishment, remained features of farm houses right into the twentieth century. A house with no other evidences of culture would have its horsehair sofa, its fireplace with ledge and paneling on which were displayed tintypes of ancestors, mementos of honeymoons to Niagara Falls or a grand trip to San Francisco. Only gradually, in the 1920s, did this feature begin to fade out of American houses, its disappearance corresponding to and manifesting erosion of the concept of the landed family or indeed of family solidarity at all.

And, of particular interest nowadays, perhaps, *family* success—*not* career success of the head of the house. These houses were not built by and for Mr. Harrison, or Mr. Smith, with "Mrs." tagging along somewhere obscurely. They were built for Benjamin and Ann, for Richard and Sarah. They are metaphors of the traditional Western concept of marriage, as the founding of a landed family in a *joint* enterprise. To speak of Founding Fathers only is not to speak like the founders themselves. They thought of both Founding Fathers and Founding Mothers, together.

Homeric Aristocracies in North America

Everywhere in North America from the seventeenth well into the twentieth century, erection of a substantial house in some architectural style distinct from a utilitarian log cabin or barn was a recognized mark of successful family founding. It follows, that differences in house type or style from region to region, or colony to colony, were heavily influenced, if not dictated, by differences in the way landed families were established and their status understood.

In "Politics and Social Structure in Virginia," Bernard Bailyn pointed out how, although Virginia's settlement went back to 1607, its "first families" came considerably later than that:

> Most of Virginia's great eighteenth-century names, such as Bland, Burwell, Byrd, Carter, Digges, Ludwell, and Mason, appear in the colony for the first time within ten years either side of 1655. Favored . . . by circumstance, a small group within the second generation migration moved toward setting itself off in a permanent way as a ruling landed gentry. . . . The establishment of this group was rapid. Within a decade of their arrival they could claim, together with a fortunate few of the first generation, a marked social eminence and full political authority at the county level. . . . By the end of the century the most difficult period of adjustment had passed and there was an acceptance of the fact that certain families were distinguished from others in riches, in dignity, and in access to political authority. The establishment of these families marks the emergence of Virginia's colonial aristocracy.[22]

This social evolution was a result of the introduction of slavery on a great scale, and the consequent practicality of amassing huge blocks of land. Virginia's first settlers, though they had cleared the land, lacked the capital and connections necessary to develop it on a big scale. Possessing both, immigrants of the 1640–1670 wave gained control and took leadership. Thus the famous "mansions of Virginia" that began to appear in the 1720s symbolized the success of families whose progenitors had arrived sixty-odd years before.

It was the same in Salem County, New Jersey.

There too the "mansions of Alloways Creek" represented the success of families who arrived in the 1670s. The 1664–1703 volume of *New Jersey Archives* reveals precisely how it happened.[23] First, lordship over the land was directly delegated from the British Crown to substantial gentlemen of the realm, and they in turn secured their grants from the actual occupants, the Amerinds:

> 16th Charles 2d. March 12. Patent. King Charles II. to the Duke of York, for the land from the St. Croix River on the East, to the River Canada on the North and the Delaware R. on the West and South.
>
> 1664 June 24. Do. James, Duke of York, to John, Lord Berkeley and Sir George Carterett, Knight, for the land West of Long Island and Manhatas Island, bounded East by the main sea and Hudson's River, West by Delaware Bay or River, extending South to Cape May and North as far as the Northernmost branch of said river, called New Jersey.
>
> 1673–4 March 18. Deed. John, Lord Berkeley. Baron of Stratton, to John ffenwick of Binfield, Co. of Berks, Esqre, for one half of New Jersey.
>
> 1676–7 March 14. Indian Deed. Mohutt and other Indians to John Fenwick, for the land along Delaware River from Game of fforcus or ffenwick's Creek to Cannahockinch Creek and up the last named creek, then from its head to the head of Allowayes Creek, thence to the head of the first named and down the same to Delaware R.

Then come a long series of deeds recording transfer of land blocks—anywhere from five hundred to ten thousand acres—to substantial bourgeois and gentlemen:

> 1675 April 8. Patent. John Fenwick to Edward Wade, citizen and cloth-worker of London, and wife Prudence, for 1000 acres to be surveyed in N.J.
>
> 1675 May 6. Do. Same to Thomas Anderson of the Parish of St. James Clerkenwell, Co. of Middlesex, bricklayer, and wife Ann, for 1000 acres in Fenwick's Colony.
>
> 1675 May 6. Do. Same to Edward Bradway of St. Paul Shadwell, Co. of Middlesex, lighterman, and wife Mary, for 1000 acres in Fenwick's Colony.
>
> 1675 May 10. Do. Same to Richard Hancock of Bromley near Bow, Co. of Middlesex, upholsterer, and wife Margaret, for 500 acres in Fenwick's Colony.

And so on and on. Also there follow a few patents to occupants of Salem County land from the New Sweden settlement, such as:

> 1679 Oct. 12. Patent. John Fenwick to Matthyas Johnson of West Fenwick Township, N.J., planter, Andrea Anderson, Lawrence alias Lance Cornelious and Annica Henricks, for 600 acres between the mouth of Bastowe Creek on the South, Purling Creek on the North and Fenwick's River on the East.

Succeeding deeds evidence how the settlers considered themselves to be founding new landed family estates. Over and over there are references to the names of estates, pathetically grandiloquent when one considers that in the late 1670s and 1680s they must have consisted mostly of bush and swamp, with a log house set in the middle of a few acres of cleared land. Typically, Hipolit (Hypolitus) Lefevor calls his land Hollybourne, and the nine hundred acres his son Hypolitus junior acquires from him in 1687 is called Lefevors Chase. Samuel Hedge calls his land Hedgefeild. Widow Ann Craven "late of Lymehouse . . . Middlesex . . . now of New Salem" proposed to call the three hundred acres she acquired in 1679 along Alloways Creek Craven's Choice, thus perpetuating a family name for her sons even after she married Charles Bagaley and gave the land to him.

Of course substantial images of these aspirations could be built only after the land was cleared, and the inevitable shakedown established which of the early settlers could make a go of the venture and which could not. That means the 1720s—contemporaneously with the Virginia mansions, but earlier than Virginia relative to the founding of the colony because, although New Jersey did have some slavery and (as Jackson Turner Main pointed out) there was a tendency toward larger estates in south than in north Jersey, these never became factors requiring outside resources on such a scale as to upset the evolution of local society, as happened in Virginia.[24]

So in roughly the same decade, mansions serving similar social functions began to rise along Alloways Creek as along the James River. Their difference in outward form was a measure of differing wealth and power resulting from concentration of land and slavery (and other factors of course, such as Quaker principles).

Thus, the image of family success in Virginia was cast in Georgian, a high style whose forms had conscious aristocratic connotations. In the minds of designers and owners of eighteenth-century mansions, whether in Britain or Virginia (or Bombay or Barbados, for that matter), Georgian forms were associated with the aristocracy of Rome; that was the source of their appeal—with especially powerful logic in Virginia, where powerful slaveowning Roman patricians could be pointed to as exemplars of the benefits accruing from aristocratic rule. Had not the great Roman families taken their nation to world leadership, wealth and power? Would not oligarchic rule do the same for England and Virginia?

The image of family success in Salem and surrounding New Jersey counties was cast in outwardly very different forms. Yet these folk house types likewise proclaim the convictions of an aristocracy—and quite as validly as the mansions of Virginia. Only the type of aristocracy was different. In essential ethos, it was closer to what is described in the *Odyssey*, for instance:

> Kings and nobles have a right, of course, to sit sometimes and feast, listen to minstrels singing, watch the young lads toss their balls and dance, or take a hand themselves in a contest of boxing, racing, or pitching weights, but only as a rest between labors. Like any great ranch owners, the more they and their wives possess in the way of practical skills, the more their affairs are likely to prosper. The lady Penelope is renowned not only for her beauty but for her weaving and competence as a housewife. Odysseus has the reputation of having in the past done every job on the place better than anyone else could do it . . . drive the straightest furrow . . . mow the biggest stretch of meadow in a day, breed the best strains of oxen and swine. He was adept at carpentry, too. There stand his room and the unique bed he built . . . he was the surest marksman with his great bow.[25]

In social base and outlook, it was like the aristocracy Laura Ingalls Wilder described in her books on pioneer life in the American Middle West during the 1870s and 1880s—where, again, leaders founded families and created estates through demonstrable personal superiority, "the reputation of having in the past done every job on the place better than anyone else could." So Almanzo Wilder's mother made the best butter in the State of New York, and his father raised the finest horses; Laura's father could build everything from a house to a sleigh, and build it to perfection; and her mother, like Lady Penelope, was "renowned not only for her beauty but for her weaving and her competence as a housewife." In all these households, in Ithaca on the Adriatic or Malone in upper New York, the preeminent values were aristocratic local pride and fierce independence:

> Father told her that Mr. Paddock wanted to take Almanzo as a [wheelwright] apprentice. . . . "Well!" Mother snapped. She was all ruffled, like an angry hen. "A pretty pass the world's coming to, if any man thinks it's a step up in the world to leave a good farm and go to town! How does Mr. Paddock make his money, if it isn't catering to us? I guess if he didn't make wagons to suit farmers, he couldn't last long!"
>
> "That's true enough," said Father. "But——"
>
> "There's no 'but' about it!" Mother said. "Oh, it's bad enough to see Royal [their older son] come down to being nothing but a storekeeper! Maybe he'll make money, but he'll never be the man you are. Truckling to other people for his living, all his days—He'll never be able to call his soul his own."[26]

This was a Lincolnesque kind of aristocracy, if you like—"primitive" in the original and good sense of that word; "pristine," best.

These parallels with archaic Greek aristocracy are, historically speaking, entirely fortuitous; but they are nonetheless real and significant. Wherever found, leaders of "pristine aristocracy" not only work their own lands and run their own households, they help design, build, and decorate their own houses. What they call their houses varies, of course, from "palace" in archaic Greece where every leader called himself king and his wife queen, to the American "home place," "main house," or "farm." No matter; everywhere, in social function and basic character these buildings were similar.

Pristine aristocracies everywhere necessarily hold

the conviction that inequality is now and ever has been inherent in society, hence that some families will always be superior to others—but at the same time, that this superiority is not fixed in any order of the universe, hence that family superiority in intelligence, ability, and energy must be reproven in each successive generation. Consequently, the architectural image of pristine aristocracies everywhere is never too far from folk building. Families who have the same recent origins as their neighbors but believe themselves superior, require the visual metaphor of a building similar in type to their neighbors', in the traditional style of their common race and region, but proclaiming superiority by being larger, solider, and above all, showier.

Showiness is characteristic of architecture functioning to proclaim the convictions of pristine aristocracy. Menelaus's palace in Sparta is "blazing with copper and gold, silver and ivory, like the mansions of Olympian Zeus." In eighteenth-century America, brickwork was commonly used to infuse buildings with the required magnificence. The elegant brickwork of Christ Church, Lancaster County—actually, as I have shown in *King Carter's Church,* a mausoleum-chapel functioning as a visual metaphor of the rise of the Carter family—is an outstanding example; the ruined walls of Rosewell nearby suggest that this may have been the principal means of providing the required meaning to Carter's own mansion, Corotoman.[27] Surely the original owners of south Jersey's patterned-brick houses felt comparable satisfactions when a rising or setting sun flashed ruddy off vitrified walls, over broad family acres stretching away on every side.

Once you interpret architecture in terms of social function, you solve all sorts of problems inexplicable by conventional formalistic analysis. For example:

(1) What are the origins of the patterned brickwork? If you opt for a theory of Swedish origins or tradition, your great problem is that the comparable brickwork occurs on church, not house gables, and the comparable motifs on nonarchitectural forms like textiles, folk carvings, and wall hangings. If you opt for English origins or tradition, you have to explain why the best comparable examples come two centuries earlier, circa 1530–1560, and why the only comparable eighteenth-century examples are crude, provincial, and obscure.[28] No logical chain of descent or influences can be established, hence no convincing theory of origins is possible. But the moment you think of how brickwork functioned to dramatize these houses as monuments to successful landed-family founding, these difficulties melt away. It will be obvious why the most comparable buildings occur in England circa 1530–1560—that was when new landed families were being founded all over the country following Tudor triumph in the civil wars, redistribution of wealth after dissolution of the monasteries, and so on. Obvious, too, why any transmission of Swedish motifs would be through media like textiles and folk carvings translated into brick in the New World—brick in Sweden was a rare enough material that patternings to set off revered monuments to community values and purposes were usually restricted to churches, whereas in south Jersey, where brick-making clay was better and more plentiful than anywhere else in the world, its use for comparable purposes on houses was natural.[29] Thus the brick patternings on south Jersey houses are products of a double stream of tradition, just as the house types they adorn are fusions of North European rural and Philadelphia city house types.

(2) Why did the custom of patterning brick walls die out? It became superfluous, along with the distinctive regional folk house type it adorned, because the social function of that house type was subsumed by what cultural geographers call the I-type vernacular (fig. 10).[30]

Peter Kalm, Swedish traveler of the 1740s, records that while Swedish language and traditions were still being maintained in the Swedesboro-Racoon parish of New Jersey, in the other two nuclei of old New Sweden (Christiana, now Wilmington, Delaware, and Wicoa, now Philadelphia) it was already well on the way to assimilation by the English majority, and he predicted that Swedish traditions would soon die out in New Jersey too.[31] This pro-

Figure 10. Focus of interiors of Salem County patterned-brick houses was the hearth-fireplace. If it did not provide space for portraits of the family founders—home builders, it offered a shelf for family memorabilia. Examples: a (top), front parlor of the Dickinson House, Alloway, before restoration (photograph by Jeff and Louise Huber); b (middle), same parlor after restoration by Jerry Watland; c (bottom), front parlor of the Zaccheus and Deborah Dunn House, Woodstown, as restored by Jerry Watland for Gordon and Eleanor Engel.

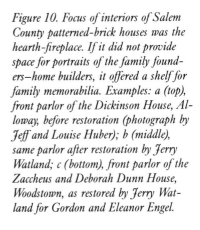

cess is in fact recorded in south Jersey's patterned-brick houses. One after another their gambrel-roofed walls were expanded into regular gable ends, conforming thereby to the I-type form (figs. 11, 12). By around 1770 the practice of patterned-brick end walls was dying out also. Thenceforth only a faint speech accent recalled the early Swedish substratum in that region, just as only imperceptible touches distinguished I-types built there from I-types elsewhere.

By the late nineteenth century, the patterned-brick houses of south Jersey had long been forgotten, but the I-type was still flourishing in Colorado and Louisiana, British Columbia and the prairies—all over rural North America. Its appeal, according to Kniffen, was its consistent set of proportions and living space, which made it a symbol: "These constant qualities, a continuous distribution, still-extant logical evolutionary stages, and an almost exclusive association with economic success in an agricultural society, indicate a common fundamental concept and thus describe a type. . . . Early in its movement southward the I-house became symbolic of economic attainment by agriculturists and remained so."[32]

That is to say, the I-type vernacular house came into being and was perpetuated as a visual metaphor of pristine aristocracy (or, less pretentiously, of "economic attainment by agriculturists"). The principal means of infusing it with the meaning that enabled it so to function was consistent proportion—the primordial image of "rightness." This broader and more universal kind of symbolism carried the I-type across the country, subsuming local folk styles like the south Jersey types, or merging with high style vernaculars like Georgian or Greek Revival as circumstances inspired. As long as the need for visual metaphors of rural success continued—that is, as long as farmers continued pushing into new lands, setting up new landed families—I-types continued to be built. When that need ceased, a distinctive era in American culture and architecture came to an end. But the kind of

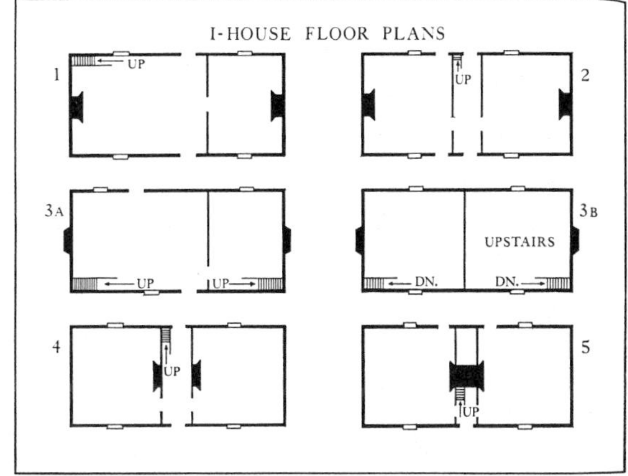

Figure 11. Plans and a typical example of the "I-type vernacular" rural homestead. "The I-type," wrote Fred Kniffen, "is one of several compounded from the old English unit consisting of one room and end chimney. It is recorded full-blown for the Delaware-Chesapeake section by at least the late seventeenth century." (From Fred Kniffen, "Folk Housing: Key to Diffusion," Annals of the Association of American Geographers *55, no. 4 [December 1965], reprinted in this volume.)*

impulse that produced south Jersey's patterned-brick houses has not entirely ceased yet.

(3) Descendants of patterned-brick houses are in the popular and commercial arts. It is the popular and commercial arts, not avant-garde Establishment art, that carries on the social functions of traditional arts in modern life. In comic strips like *Thimble Theatre* (Popeye the Sailor) classic High Art themes of utopian visions and social commentary are car-

Figure 12. With Kniffen's identification of the I-type vernacular in mind, it is easy to recognize how the local south Jersey colonial variant conformed to it. The Dickinson House is only the most famous example of the one-and-a-half-story, gambrel-roofed type being transformed into an I-type by an enlargement that must have been done more to conform to the fashionable I-type status symbol than for additional space, since what it adds is hardly commensurate with the expense and inconvenience involved. Others are the Richard Smith (Gosling) House (fig. 8c) and the Padgett-Evans House, 1733, near Hammersville, New Jersey, seen here enlarged to its present I-type form some time after 1790.

ried on; television today tells stories by means of sequential pictures as traditional illustrative arts did; and so on.[33] And here again the principle holds. If you want to find descendants of the patterned-brick houses of south Jersey, look in popular and commercial architecture.

Drive across the American Midwest, for example, through rural Minnesota, Nebraska, Iowa; or over the Canadian prairies, for that matter. You will see all sorts of houses roofed with commercial asbestos shingles in all sorts of fancy patterns, sometimes with owner's names and dates picked out in them. Even more strikingly, you find great silos through all the corn country, built of commercial cement block in elaborate checkered patterns with initials, dates and the like. For what purpose? Such roofs do not keep the rain out any better, or make tastier silage. Their purpose is the same as the old patterned-brick walls of Salem County—to proclaim the prosperity and success of the landed proprietors who built them. They are popular and commercial metaphors of latter-day Homeric aristocracy.[34]

Notes

This article was originally published in *RACAR: Revue de l'Art Canadien/Canadian Art Review* (1976).

1. The basic works on the patterned-brick houses of southern New Jersey are Joseph Sickler, *Old Houses of Salem County,* rev. ed. (1934; reprint, Salem, N.J.: Sunbeam Publishing, 1949), and Paul Love, "Patterned Brickwork in Southern New Jersey," *Proceedings of the New Jersey Historical Society* 73, no. 3 (July 1955): 182–208. The earliest reference to them is in 1758, when Israel Acrelius, reporting on the state of Swedish churches in America, remarked that "the houses along the Delaware [i.e., in former New Sweden] are built of bricks, after the English fashion, without coating, every other brick glazed" (quoted in George Fletcher Bennett, *Early Architecture of Delaware* [1932; reprint, New York: Bonanza Books, n.d.], p. 16). An 1876 Centenary reminiscence of Thomas Shourds (1805–91), a member of a founding family of Salem County, refers to them only to mention that the first patterned-brick buildings were the work of Richard Woodnutt, a Quaker bricklayer who arrived from England via Philadelphia about 1695 and was instrumental in building Salem County's first brick meeting-house on Abel Nicholson's property (Thomas Shourds, *History of Fenwick's Colony* [Bridgeton, N.J.: G. F. Nixon, 1876], p. 368).
2. On Swedish, Dutch, and Finnish settlement patterns in New Jersey, see Peter O. Wacker, *Cultural Geography of New Jersey* (Trenton: New Jersey Historical Commission, 1975), esp. pp. 169–72. In the case of Philadelphia, Swedish participation in early building is documented. Land for the new city was bought from Swedes and they helped with building the first houses. See Amandus Johnson, *Swedish Settlements on the Delaware* (1911; reprint, New York: B. Franklin, 1970), 2:113. Hugh Morrison quotes William Penn's 1684 instructions to his immigrants to "build, then, a House of thirty foot long and eighteen broad, with a partition near the middle, and an other to divide one end of the House into two small Rooms" as, in fact, advice to adopt a Swedish-style plan (*Early American Architecture* [New York: Oxford University Press, 1952], p. 505).
3. On folk architecture generally, a very good study—perhaps the best so far—is Henry Glassie, *Pattern in the Material Folk Culture of the Eastern United States* (Philadelphia: University of Pennsylvania Press, 1969). Glassie discusses Philadelphia–Restoration London house types on pp. 58–59.
4. See the discussion, and illustrations, of the variations on Philadelphia house types, and the effect of the "Wertenbaker line" dividing brick- from stone-building country in the Delaware Valley, in Alan Gowans, *Images of American Living: Four Centuries of Architecture and Furniture as Cultural Expression* (Philadelphia: Lippincott, 1964), pp. 80–86.
5. Carl Williams, review of *Fenwick's Colony, New Jersey Genesis* 13, no. 3 (1966): 588.
6. On patterened-brick in Swedish churches, see *Sveriges Kyrkor: Konsthistoriskt Inventarium,* founded in 1912 by S. Curman and J. Roosval and still continuing under the direction of Armin Tuulse of the Art History Institute, University of Stockholm. Specifically: the standard work on Swedish medieval churches is Gerda Boëthius, *De Tegelornerade grästenskyrkorna* (Stockholm: Svenska Kyrkans drakonistyrelses bökförlag, 1921); comparable churches in Finland are studied in Carolus Lindberg, *Om teglets användning i finska medeltida grästenskyrkor* (Stockholm: H. Schildsts tryckeri, 1919); there are also a number of older books of a general nature, such as O. Stiehl, *Der Backsteinbau romanischer Zeit, besonders in Oberitalien und Norddeutschland* (Leipzig,

East Germany: Baumgartner, 1891); F. Adler, *Mittelalterlich Backsteinbauwerke der Preussischen Staates* (Berlin: Ernst and Korn, 1859–69, 1896–98, etc.). I am grateful for advice on the survival of brickwork in the seventeenth and eighteenth centuries from Sten Karling, professor emeritus of the University of Stockholm Institute of the History of Art. All around the provinces of Stockholm, Uppsala, or Dalarna—the very provinces, by the way, whence the majority of settlers in New Sweden came, according to Amandus Johnson (*Swedish Settlements*, vol. 1, distribution map 28)—can be found Swedish brickwork obviously composed in the deliberate manner of the south Jersey examples, rather than like the natural and spontaneous decoration of Tudor England. All the characteristic designs of south Jersey for which Paul Love reported "no duplicate, no echo found in either America or England" are found there. Most, to be sure, belong to the fourteenth through the sixteenth centuries, but there are examples from all centuries up through the nineteenth. Being on such prominent and visible buildings as the churches of villages and hamlets, this Swedish brickwork has been continuously before the eyes of succeeding generations. Also, it apparently was more than ornamental; it had some symbolic significance that kept the idea of a figured or patterned wall from being dulled through familiarity. A good discussion of this can be found in Dietrich Ellger, "Der Dom zu Ratzeburg und die Frage nach der Farbigkeit romanischer Backsteinkirchen zwischen Niedersachsen und Seeland," *Nordelbingen* 38 (1969). Though almost entirely concerned with German brickwork, this study has obvious implications for Sweden, which then, as long subsequently was in the German cultural orbit. Ellger argues that the appearance in the twelfth and thirteenth centuries of "niche patterning" (*fügennetz*) in brickwork which obviously has no structural origins or connotations, indicates that "symbolic significances" are to be sought. Tentatively he suggests that this symbolism would be in the area of architectonic simulations of ideal proportional systems. I would be inclined to think: (1) that symbolic value, perhaps of a prophylactic sort, would be inherent in the shapes themselves—just as this is not modern ornament "in the nature of materials," so the meaning of these shapes was explicit; (2) that the original meaning of these shapes was set in pre-Christian Nordic times; (3) that such an interpretation is strengthened by the existence of Swedish examples of actual figures set into the brickwork, as for example at Stora Tuna in Dalarna where figures of St. Olaf and St. Erik appear, 3 meters high, made of brick and plaster; (4) that there may be some relationship in origin therefore between this Swedish patterned brickwork and external painting of houses (e.g., in Switzerland) and barns (e.g., the Pennsylvania German "hex" signs). But all such matters are beside the point here, as would be any getting into the vexed question of Pennsylvania German "hex" signs, whether they have any antiquity at all, and if so, what they mean, or meant. What matters in our connection is that symbolic value would inhibit anyone from covering the brickwork over. Evidence for the visible survival of this brickwork into and beyond the eighteenth century comes from *Sveriges Kyrkor;* also the fact that some of these medieval churches were later refurbished in Renaissance and Baroque times. The west gable of Oster Lövsta is an example (Boëthius, *De Tegelornerade grästenskyrkorna*. See also Friedrich Fischer, *Norddeutscher Ziegelbau* [Munich: G. D. W. Callway, 1944]).

For examples of folk patterns in textiles and other arts, see Eleanor Whitmore, "Origins of Pennsylvania Folk Art," *Antiques* 38, no. 3 (September 1940): 106–10; Albert Eskeröd, *Swedish Folk Art* (Stockholm: Nordiska Museet, 1964–65), pp. 22–29 and passim; Verla Birrell, *The Textile Arts* (New York: Harper, 1959). Specifically: in her unpublished Winterthur thesis Ruth Cox illustrates a linen bed hanging from Hancock's Bridge, descended in the Ware family, and comments that it is more elaborate than ordinary textiles of the Philadelphia region ("Textiles Used in Philadelphia, 1760–1775," Master's thesis, University of Delaware, 1960, p. 15).

7. *New Jersey Archives* (Newark, N.J.: Daily Advertiser Printing, 1897), 1st ser., p. 21.
8. Peter Kalm, *The America of 1750: Peter Kalm's Travels in North America,* ed. Adolph B. Benson (New York: Erickson, 1937), pp. 683, 687–89.
9. On linguistic patterns in early settlement, see M. Pei, *Language for Everybody* (New York: Pocket Books, 1958), p. 53; the University of Michigan linguistic atlas of the United States has not yet reached this part of New Jersey. John Geipel, *The Viking Legacy: Scandinavian Influence on the English and Gaelic Language* (Newton Abbot, Eng.: David and Charles, 1971), is a good example of an interrelated study of folk art and language forms, although it deals with the reverse situation—the imposition of alien forms on an existing culture. But it does show how, in linguistics and place names, the influence of Scandinavians as a substratum or overlay, depending

on whether they settled empty land or imposed themselves on earlier inhabitants, is decisively demonstrable. That there was a comparable influence on taste for design, proportions, and so forth, is obvious, but less easily demonstrable because the surviving evidence for it is chiefly in the form of manuscripts, which are movable, and sculptured ornament, whose markers by their profession move about.

10. C. C. Zimmerman and R. E. Du Wors, *Graphic Regional Sociology* (Cambridge, Mass.: Phillips Book Store, 1952), "Basic Regions Map 1"; C. M. Arensberg, "American Communities," *American Anthropologist* 57, no. 6 (December 1955): 1143–62.
11. This was Paul Love's conclusion: "There was a comparatively large colony of Swedes already located in the neighborhood of Salem before 1675," he wrote in "Patterned Brickwork" (p. 185). "Here we have no evidence whatsoever of brick architecture which might have influenced the English colonists. It is nevertheless of interest to discover that patterned brickwork was also known and used in Sweden during this same period. [But he never seems to have looked at any, to ascertain resemblances.] It is apparent that . . . in most examples, we can safely assume an influence directly from England." Glassie follows him in this position (*Pattern in the Material Folk Culture,* pp. 150–54).
12. Charles E. Peterson, ed., "Houses for New Albion, 1650," *Journal of the Society of Architectural Historians* 15, no. 3 (October 1956): 2. John Fenwick's exuberant prospectus "The Description of a happy country, Delaware Bay . . ." is preserved in the archives of the Pennsylvania Historical Society and has been reprinted with other works in a booklet published by the Salem County Historical Society, titled "An Early Advertisement by John Fenwick" (*Colonial Roof Trees and Candle Ends* [1934; rev. ed., 1971], pp. 2–3). He ends by citing "a late Writer" who said, "If there be any terrestrial happiness to be had by any People, especially of any inferior rank, it must certainly be here." Corn and cattle, streams and grapevines, hunting and fishing in a countryside teeming with game of all sorts, "But that which adds happiness to all the rest, is the healthfulness of the Place, where many people in twenty years time never know what Sickness is; where they look upon it as a very great Mortality, if two or three die out of a Town in a years time. . . . if there be any terrestrial 'Canaan' 'tis surely here, where the Land floweth with Milk and Honey." This is New Jersey? Someday we may see a treatise on the art of selling the joys of pioneer life, an art that helped populate North America, whose high points must surely include this treatise, a direct ancestor of prospectuses on farming and prairies in the 1870–1900 period.
13. Laura Ingalls Wilder, *Farmer Boy* (1933; new ed., New York: Harper and Row, 1971).
14. Maginel Wright Barney, *The Valley of the God-Almighty Joneses* (New York: Appleton-Century, 1965), pp. 85–86.
15. Sickler, *Old Houses of Salem County,* pp. 98–100.
16. Ibid., p. 100.
17. Henry Glassie, "Eighteenth-Century Cultural Process in Delaware Valley Folk Building," *Winterthur Portfolio 7,* ed. Ian M. G. Quimby (Charlottesville: University Press of Virginia, 1972), pp. 29–59 (reprinted in this volume).
18. See, for example, the discussions of *ma'at* in John Wilson, *The Burden of Egypt* (Chicago: University of Chicago Press, 1951), pp. 48–49, 119–23, and passim; of *šimtu* in A. Leo Oppenheim, *Ancient Mesopotamia: Portrait of a Dead Civilization* (Chicago: University of Chicago Press, 1964), pp. 201–2, 204–5.
19. *Proceedings of the New Jersey Historical Society* 73, no. 3 (July 1955): 182–208.
20. Sickler, *Old Houses of Salem County,* p. 68; Shourds, *History of Fenwick's Colony,* p. 68.
21. Régine Pernoud, *La Lumière du moyen-age* (Paris: B. Grasset, 1944), p. 1.
22. Bernard Bailyn, "Politics and Social Structure in Virginia," in *Seventeenth-Century America: Essays in Colonial History,* ed. James Morton Smith (Chapel Hill: University of North Carolina Press, 1959), pp. 98, 100, 106.
23. Excerpts from *New Jersey Archives,* 1st ser., 21:559–60: Salem no. 1 (numbers refer to page entries in that register).
24. Jackson Turner Main, *The Social Structure of Revolutionary America* (Princeton: Princeton University Press, 1965), pp. 25, 33. From early times the southern part of New Jersey had a character quite different from the north—a distinctiveness based on a pattern of land use in "West Jersey" much closer to the southern plantation model than to the small holdings typical of "East Jersey" and the central or northern colonies generally. "New Jersey's tax records for the years 1774–1788 demonstrate clearly the contrast between East and West Jersey. . . . The distribution of land . . . reveals that the counties near New York (such as Bergen, Morris, Essex, and Monmouth) were occupied almost entirely by small farmers, whereas the southwestern section (notably Burlington and Gloucester) contained many large estates. . . .

"The tax lists of Burlington County, New Jersey, reveal a prosperous farm society in the Delaware Valley. A very high proportion—considerably over half—of the men had no land, a fact which indicates the presence of many farm laborers. New Jersey farms were seldom large, but these southwestern communities had many more 500-acre estates than did the townships near New York. Especially striking is the concentration of real estate. Nearly half of the Burlington land was owned by 10% of the taxpayers. The same concentration existed in nearby Salem and Gloucester counties" (Main, *Social Structure,* p. 33). In the nineteenth century, this social pattern produced the disruptive strife and strong pro-Confederate sentiment of the Civil War period in south Jersey. In the twentieth century, it made possible the consolidation of great tracts into the vegetable farms that gave New Jersey its name of the "Garden State." In the eighteenth century, it was manifested in south Jersey's distinctive patterned-brick houses.

25. Louise Ropes Loomis, Introduction to Homer's *Odyssey,* trans. Samuel Butler (Roslyn, N.Y.: Walter J. Black, 1944), pp. xxvi–xxvii.
26. Wilder, *Farmer Boy,* pp. 366–67.
27. Alan Gowans, *King Carter's Church: Being a Study in Depth of Christ Church, Lancaster County, Virginia* (Victoria, B.C.: University of Victoria Maltwood Museum, 1969), pp. 10–41.
28. The building commonly cited for comparisons with Salem County brickwork is Little Leigh's Priory in Essex, built ca. 1536; thus typically Sickler (*Old Houses of Salem County,* p. 6) states that "the zigzag designs of the Hancock and Chambless houses came directly from there [Leigh's Priory] as did the Darkin and Nicholson diaper designs," without attempting to explain the two-hundred-year hiatus.
29. On brickmaking in the Delaware Valley, from Edwin Atlee Barber, *The Pottery and Porcelain of the United States* (New York: G. P. Putnam and Sons, 1901), p. 47, comes the famous quote of a Philadelphian writing to a friend in England in 1753: "The greatest vein of Clay for Bricks and Pottery, begins near Trenton Falls [Trenton, N.J.], and extends a mile or two in Breadth on the Pennsylvania side of the River to Christine [Wilmington, Del.]; then it crosses the River and goes by Salem [N.J.]. The whole world cannot afford better bricks than our town is built of." This claim has been substantiated in modern times by figures from Test Hole 2, Tidewater Oil Company, Delaware. (Heinrich Ries, et al., *High Grade Clays of the Eastern United States* [Washington, D.C.: Government Printing Office, 1922], pp. 202–3; Heinrich Ries, "Report of the Clays of Maryland," *Maryland Geological Survey* 4 (1902): 203–505). Modern analyses show that in this belt the highest percentage (75 percent) of kaolinite, principal mineral of kaolins and other high-quality potting and firing clays, was on the Wilmington-Salem axis; it tapered off to around 60 percent by the Baltimore area. Illite and illitic mixtures (clay minerals of good quality though not as refractory as kaolinite) were consistent throughout the belt at about 24 percent. How early this clay was used is attested by a 1683 law in Fenwick's Colony that required bricks to be well-burnt and a uniform 9½ × 4½ × 2¾ inches—dimensions slightly larger than English statutory size either before 1625 (9 × 4½ × 2¼ inches) or after 1625 (9 × 4⅜ × 2¼ inches) and longer also than the average 8½-inch bricks used in eighteenth-century Virginia and on the Pennsylvania Delaware side of the Delaware River. For references to nineteenth-century brickwork in southern New Jersey, see Harry B. Weiss and Grace M. Weiss, *Early Brickmaking in New Jersey* (Trenton: New Jersey Agricultural Society, 1966), pp. 52–56. Almost all of this book deals with brickmaking after 1750, and much of it with the nineteenth century. The Weisses have discovered a few early records, for example, those that identify Thomas Kendall as builder of the first St. Mary's Episcopal Church of 1702–3 at Burlington.
30. A vernacular style in building or speech (whence the word was originally borrowed by architectural writers, Sir George Gilbert Scott being the first to use it, apparently, in 1857) is flexible in meaning according to situation. Essentially it means an unaffected, unselfconscious way of building (speaking). Like folk building, it has intrinsic meaning so that it functions as visual metaphor of conviction. But a vernacular style shows some degree of influence from high arts (e.g., formal high art styles in architecture, foreign or educated ways of speaking, etc.); and it is propagated to some extent by mass media—published builders' guides, lithographs, etc. In type, therefore, vernacular arts could be categorized as midway between folk art and modern mass or popular arts. As cultural expression, therefore, vernacular styles indicate a melting pot of different racial and folk traditions. Thus vernacular styles in North America are peculiarly nineteenth- and twentieth-century products, though their folk origins go back to the eighteenth and nineteenth centuries.

31. Kalm, *America of 1750,* pp. 683, 687–89.
32. Fred B. Kniffen, "Folk Housing: Key to Diffusion," *Annals of the Association of American Geographers* 55, no. 4 (December 1965): 549–77 (reprinted in this volume).
33. Alan Gowans, "Remarks on Arts and Utopias in the 1930s, apropos of some excerpts from 'Popeye's Art,'" *RACAR* 1 (1974): 5–22. This material, slightly reworked, is included in Alan Gowans, *Prophetic Allegory: Popeye and the American Dream: Two Classics by E. C. Segar* (Watkins Glen, N.Y.: American Life Foundation, 1983).
34. For a full statement of this theory, see Alan Gowans, *Learning to See: Historical Perspectives of Modern Popular/Commercial Arts* (Bowling Green, Ohio: Popular Press, 1981).

Eighteenth-Century Cultural Process in Delaware Valley Folk Building

HENRY GLASSIE

Central to this essay by Henry Glassie is the assumption that the things people make reveal something about their cultural concepts. Focusing on the Delaware Valley, he reviews the evolution of English and German house types and farm layouts. What is most significant about Glassie's examination is that he reads buildings as more than technical accomplishments; he sees them as indications of thought. For him house types are not merely plans for buildings but "plans for production," and as such, when enough of them are considered collectively, they can reveal the wishes of a community as well as its actual achievements. Once we see buildings as Glassie does—as the products of desire and emotion—we are then ready to understand houses from the inside out rather than from the outside in. We can then pursue the design process from the moment that a house is an idea in the mind to the moment when it is a building on the ground. But first one must understand that material expression is but a mask for mind.

By methodically surveying mainly nineteenth-century buildings, Glassie sets out to determine the outcome of a period of extensive change in domestic architecture that began in the middle of the eighteenth century. He finds that eighteenth- and nineteenth-century builders used fashionable forms regardless of the building's context; that they designed more from abstract concepts than pragmatic conditions. With the example of central-passage house plans he next gives a description of the dynamic of thought in folk society showing that a design solution is not reached by direct imitation of a fashionable source but by cautious testing, negotiation, and consideration. When change occurs then in folk building, it is slow change, modest change. The same point is also made with the evidence of Mid-Atlantic farm plans.

The people of the past wrote little. A progressive agriculturist may have left a diary in a trunk for modern discovery; an egotistic public servant may have endured his sunset years longhanding reminiscence, but most of those who are now dead wrote formally about themselves no more than people do today. Like us, they allowed posterity to depend on the external observer for a record of their thought. Reliance on the journalist or the literate elite for our glimpses of deceased cultures skews our view of the past in a definite direction—the direction formalized in those history texts to which the intellectual reformer and the black spokesman for today's minorities object. Reading the words of the past, we can accumulate the fragments for a fair mosaic of the life of the wealthy, which they and their literate retainers bequeathed to us, and we can uncover occasional references, usually maddeningly superficial, to workaday life in the chancy journals of travelers. The comments of an Andrew Burnaby or a Pehr Kalm are invaluable, but we have been left no understanding of the culture of the majority: those who farmed or tinkered with sufficient success—the kind of people who now live in modest, solid brick houses, drive a late model sedan, and spend the day tightening bolts at the Caterpillar factory or keeping the house clean to the rhythm of "The Secret Storm"; just folks who are more excited by the World Series than they are by the latest show at the Museum of Modern Art.

Today, the average person is a consumer; in the eighteenth century he was a maker. If he left no books, he did leave artifacts by the thousands. The wagon or the rifle or the shape of a field outlined by walls of rock is as direct an expression of culture as the book—all are artifacts. These artifacts, many now inflated in value as antiques, have attracted different sorts of scholars. Some, trained as historians, have selected a few things associated with specific events—a blood-stained chair from Ford's Theater, say—to use as visual props for historical notions set in print. Others have treated objects as if they were art, selecting the few which measure up to modern taste and arranging these about the walls of museums in chronological schemata to illustrate the sequence of detail called "style." Selection on the basis of contemporary need has demonstrable social worth, whether it is mythological (in the case of the historian striving to justify the current situation) or aesthetic (in the case of the antiquarian working to preserve some old-fashioned charm in a drab and jerry-built present); but as scholarship it is incomplete, and incompleteness is wrong—except by accident.

A methodological limitation to print binds the scholar to studying only the handful of people who were literate. The artifact is potentially democratic; artifacts from the past are so abundant that they can be utilized to replace romantic preconceptions with scientifically derived knowledge.[1] This is not, however, inevitable. Often the historian treats only the genealogically relevant things, artifacts which fit the scheme of progress. To parody Herbert Read's statement on art history,[2] the history of artifacts is often presented as a line from progressive thing to progressive thing. The usual historical treatment of agricultural implements, for example, is not a description of the tools in use at given times and places; rather, it is a chronological list of rare tools that suggests the "evolution" of modern machinery. This constrictively linear approach to the past, as Claude Lévi-Strauss has shown in his magnificent book *The Savage Mind*,[3] leaves most people and most artifacts out of consideration.

A similarly ethnocentric approach treats past artifacts only if they are judged appealing by contemporary standards. The prevailing opulent taste of most critics causes them to single out some things as better than others on the basis of their richness of decoration. The application of modernist aesthetic criteria to past artifacts causes a violent change; it eliminates from greatness the things that are untrue to their media.[4] Chippendale highboys and Gothic cathedrals are banished (both have characteristics appropriate to sculpture rather than to furniture and architecture), and their places in art appreciation classes are taken by milking stools and the stone cabins of the Hebrides. Taste is an important subject for study, but the modern critics' evaluations teach not of past but of present culture. Connoisseurship and the optimistic notion of progress have prevented the study of artifacts from becoming a means for making history the rigorous study of past cultures.

Some scholars—they may be historians, archaeologists, cultural geographers, anthropologists, or folklorists—have begun to appreciate the artifact as a powerful source of information. They view objects as books that, no matter how pretty the bindings, are worthless until read. A hammer and a quilt may look nice behind the museum's glass, but they are merely chance associations of hard or soft substances unless enough is known about their source and function to make accurate interpretation possible.[5] A building may enhance the landscape, but it remains a heap of old wood and stone until it is analyzed. The analysis leads away from a concern with the fabric itself toward the ideas that were the cause of the fabric's existence. Strictly speaking, the ideas in the mind of a maker can never be enumerated, but the scholar can venture near a comprehension of the mind's activities and the maker's intent through deep play with components, sources, and models of process, as John Livingston Lowes did in his study of Samuel Taylor Coleridge's two greatest poems.[6] From sticks of wood joined into a chair, from the burned clay mortared into a dwelling, we can get an idea of ideas, a feeling for the concepts that are culture, an understanding, perhaps, of the anguish and pleasure, the joy of innovation and the pain of compromise of men long dead.

The spoor of culture on the land is amazing and easily followed. The dangers in interpreting from artifact back through behavior to culture are obvious, but it is the best means we have; we will never understand the eighteenth century if we read only books. By reading artifacts, if we will read enough of them and not be trapped by a shapely cabriole leg or a scrap of molding, we can learn of past culture, the repertoire of learned concepts carried by those people who framed not only our basic law, but our environment and social psychology as well.

In using things to teach of the past, some classes of artifacts are more useful than others. This usefulness is a function of the ease with which objects can be related to their time and place, of a complexity sufficient to eliminate the probability of polygenesis, and of the existence of enough material to prevent theory from being built on chance survival. Architecture—complex objects that can be sensed inside and out and are such direct and conscious expressions of culture that for both scholar and builder they become symbol—is one of the most useful kinds of objects.

This paper deals with two matters of Delaware Valley architecture—houses and farm plans. It is based on fieldwork conducted in the eastern United States between 1961 and 1970. It is intended not as a study but as a metaphor for a study. The paper itself is an abstraction, an impression of study based on social-scientific rather than art historical philosophy. It does not include the kind of information normally presented in art historical publications but is made of the stuff familiar to readers of cultural geographic or folkloristic publications. It is offered in this context to increase understanding and communication and to illustrate an alternative to art historical considerations of vernacular architecture and is intended not to replace but to complement. The full study of a subject as large as building in the Delaware Valley should involve the art historian's emphasis on diachronic methodology, concentrating on the few fine houses and public buildings remaining and on the decorative elements of a dwelling's facade. It should also involve the social scientist's emphasis on synchronic methodology, focusing on the quantitatively dominant humble buildings, and on the economic functions of a building's internal volumes.

The attempt to account for all building is fundamental to the social scientist's approach to architecture. When the totality of building is taken into account, the mansions and gems considered worthy of preservation form such a tiny portion of the whole that they deserve little attention. Similarly, by considering all of each building, crockets, brackets, and twitches of stylish trim become unimportant when compared with matters of basic form. The architect Clovis Heimsath expressed the notion succinctly in his intriguing book on Texas architecture: "It's the form that really counts in architecture. Decoration buzzes around the form to dress it up."[7]

It is easy and voguish but incorrect to think of these basic forms as following function (folk buildings frequently have a Bauhaus clarity, which calls to mind the functional style of recent architecture). The basic forms were useful; people lived and worked in them, and they did function—to return to the anthropological sense of the word—both economically and aesthetically. But they were not designed to suit idiosyncratic need; they were traditional components, traditionally structured into traditional organizations of space required for psychological comfort. The forms lay in the minds of their makers until some problem caused them to be drawn out. When drawn out, the forms were defined by some material, stone, log, or brick, frame filled or sided. Then, the form might have been decoratively encrusted, and it might have had other, distinct forms added onto it. Forms are types—plans for production—and buildings are examples of types or composite types. It is definitively characteristic of folk buildings, and most buildings are folk buildings, to be examples of types that persist with little change through time. The invariant aspects of a form are the aspects of deepest necessity to the people who must use the form.[8]

This paper, accordingly, will concentrate on basic folk types and will be concerned more with architecture as internally usable space than as externally viewed art. A democratic examination of Delaware Valley building leads to a series of conclusions about the cultures of the area during the eighteenth century. These will be exemplified through an examination of certain forms, but the major regional patterns are sketched here as forewarning.

Since Fred Kniffen's classic paper "Louisiana House Types,"[9] scholars have used folk architecture to suggest spatial patterning in the United States. Fieldwork reveals that the Delaware River runs through two major American cultural regions. The Delaware Valley is divided horizontally at about the southern limits of the Pocono and Kittatinny mountains; the portion above this line belongs with New England and New York in the broad culture region of the North, the portion below fits into the Mid-Atlantic, the architectural region including southern Pennsylvania and parts of adjacent Maryland, Delaware, and New Jersey. There is an approximate consensus on the regional boundaries among scholars from different disciplines working with different manifestations of culture. The Mid-Atlantic architectural region outlined on the accompanying map (fig. 1) is quite similar to Midland speech areas seven and eight in Hans Kurath's *A Word Geography of the Eastern United States.*[10] The northern border is in close agreement with that on the map, "Folk Housing Areas: 1850," recently offered by Kniffen.[11] On the southern and western boundaries there is less general agreement, though the line through southern Maryland is compatible with the one drawn by Wilbur Zelinsky after studying several different cultural traits.[12] Though some of the disagreement in the various maps of cultural phenomena is the result of a difference of interpretation,[13] most of the apparent disagreement results from the distributional differences exhibited by varying aspects of culture. Alan Lomax's map of the English language folk song styles of North America[14] locates the southern boundary of the cultural region of the North far south of the line in figure 1 or the divisions made by Kurath or Kniffen. This reflects the actual state of difference in the spatial patterns of dialect and folk architecture as opposed to song and fiddle style. The differences in the cultural maps of the East offered to date are small when contrasted with the truly striking similarities. Cultural regions are scientifically valid; they can be clearly delineated even in these days of supposed national homogeneity.

The lower Delaware Valley, an area, dominated by Philadelphia, that fits into the Mid-Atlantic region, will be the focus of this paper. The lower valley's areas of close cultural connection are found throughout the remainder of the Mid-Atlantic region. The Mid-Atlantic region has been defined by compromising the distribution of major architectural forms and techniques of construction: for example, north of the region, log construction is rare;[15] the Dutch barn found nearby in New Jersey and New York is generally absent from the region;[16]

Figure 1. The Mid-Atlantic folk architectural region and major Mid-Atlantic subregions with directions of extraregional connection.

and the external west British[17] chimney, which is characteristic of areas south of the region, is restricted to a handful of examples in Chester County, Pennsylvania,[18] and in the Alleghenies. The boundaries of the regions are not arbitrary lines scratched through the border country between influential centers. Locations within a region, even when greatly separated, are culturally more alike than juxtaposed locations in different regions. Still, the culture of the Mid-Atlantic exhibits certain extraregional connections (fig. 1), especially between central New Jersey and Long Island, between southern New Jersey and the Chesapeake Bay area, and among southeastern Pennsylvania, central Maryland, and the Valley of Virginia.[19]

Also, the region is not perfectly homogeneous; it can be divided and subdivided into subregions by plotting the distribution of traits restricted to but not found throughout the region, by establishing the local proportions of traits found everywhere in the region, and by examining the difference in association and significance of regional traits. For example, the drive-in corncrib, called "old fashioned" in *Radford's Practical Barn Plans,*[20] is found for the length and breadth of the Mid-Atlantic region, but it is more common in some areas than in others and is treated differently in the subregions. In New Jersey the drive-in corncrib is a major farm building located in a position of importance within the farmyard; it is fitted with doors and sheds and serves multiple purposes, such as implement storage (fig. 2). In Pennsylvania it is a dependency of the barn, generally located to one side of the barn's ramp; it often lacks sheds, occasionally, the doors, and frequently serves only as a corncrib (fig. 3). In the Midwest the drive-in corncrib is a large building with a cupola,[21] and in the southern Appalachian region it is a small structure frequently built of logs.[22]

Figure 2. Drive-in corncrib west of Roadstown in Cumberland County, New Jersey.

Paradoxically, although the Delaware River is the threshold of the Mid-Atlantic, it also amounts, roughly, to a boundary between the major Mid-Atlantic subregions, separating the almost wholly English New Jersey sphere from the syncretistic British and Germanic Pennsylvania sphere (fig. 1). But there are major intrusions across the river, so that in western New Jersey around Phillipsburg, Pennsylvania characteristics are in evidence, and parts of Chester, Delaware, and New Castle counties are as English as the country to the east. The observable pattern is readily explainable by settlement history, but settlement history might not suggest that this river is as neat a regional border as contemporary fieldwork reveals it to be.

In viewing the Delaware Valley from the other organizational coordinate, time, it is possible to distinguish distinct building phases. By focusing on decorative detail, the architectural historian can chop the past into a lengthy and complicated series

Figure 3. Drive-in corncrib at Clear Spring, south of Dillsburg, York County, Pennsylvania; see also figure 25.

of style periods.[23] Most buildings were completely unaffected or only superficially affected by the sequence of "style," so only three major phases emerge from a consideration of the totality of building. The first, lasting in the Mid-Atlantic area from the period of first settlement to about 1760, was a time of ethnic solidarity in architecture, of the retention of diverse Old World forms and techniques with a resultant heterogeneity on the land. The second major time segment included an initial acceptance of new ideas and a blending of the old and new to create a New World repertoire with resultant regional homogeneity on the land. The point at which the regional culture lost its dominance in building practice (though it is nowhere entirely dead and its manifestations still rule the environment) varies from region to region. R. W. Brunskill writes that the end of English regional building can be marked by the coming of the railway in 1840.[24] About the same date seems to hold for the northeastern United States. In the Mid-Atlantic area, regional building practices were retained more tenaciously, and it was not until the era of the First World War that the regional culture was dissolved into the national. In the South the date was still later.[25] Temporally this paper will focus on the early part of the second building phase—the time of extensive and intensive innovation—the third quarter of the eighteenth century; for better than a century later, its legacy was the stable pattern of Delaware Valley building, and the patterns that continue to characterize the landscape today are the products of cultural clash and mesh in the mid eighteenth century.

It should be noted that most of the illustrations for this paper picture nineteenth-century expressions of eighteenth-century ideas. Late buildings, rather than structures that actually date to the eighteenth century, were chosen to illustrate the points in this paper for two reasons, both of them crucial to the paper's intent. In the first place, basic house forms, because of the conservatism of builders and inhabitants, persisted unchanged despite the fluctuations of taste represented by architectural detail. Secondly, the major Mid-Atlantic house types of the eighteenth century continued to be erected for better than a century after their introduction or development, so that forms of eighteenth-century origin are not now rarities on the landscape. Buildings worth study are not difficult to locate, and contemporary fieldwork can teach much about eighteenth-century cultural patterns.

The earliest forms of human shelter in the valley changed with the insertion of the Georgian house type (figs. 4, 5a) into the awareness of builders in the middle of the eighteenth century. As a form it was a century old in England and on the Continent; as a geometric structure of geometric components, it was a Renaissance-inspired notion of classical planning. The form, primly symmetrical, was employed in America as early as 1700 and was accepted for the home of affluent gentlemen the length of the Atlantic seaboard for the last three quarters of the eighteenth century, although its impact was not great until after the publication of handbooks advocating the Georgian style in the 1740s and 1750s.[26] Like the drama of an earlier period, the Georgian form is an English interpretation of an Italian interpretation of Roman practice (with an optional half-step through Dutch interpreters). The Georgian form is usually considered an English contribution to American domestic architecture, but while that notion connotes accurately the acculturative situation, English Georgian was part of an international Renaissance style. Distinctively Scottish and Germanic expressions of the style were built in Pennsylvania, and the fact that the basic Georgian form was known in seventeenth-century central Europe facilitated its acceptance by Continental settlers in the Mid-Atlantic region.[27] The definitive elements of the type rarely varied; externally, a low pitched roof (hipped on finer houses but usually gabled) and two openings per floor on the ends, five on the facade; internally, a double pile plan with two rooms on each side of a central hall containing the stair.

The new idea was not radically different from older European folk practice. Medieval building was not wholly lacking in symmetry; bilateral symmetry

Figure 4. The Georgian house type. With its double pile plan and rhythm of five openings per floor on the front and two per floor on the end, this house is a perfect example of the eighteenth-century Georgian form expressed in a nineteenth-century structure. Note the Gothicized Palladian window. The plan of this house type can be found in figure 5a; other examples of the type can be found in figures 10 and 21. Middleburg, Snyder County, Pennsylvania.

was, in fact, an essential feature of western European folk design. The roof of the new type was shallow, but it was still a triangle that could be framed and covered in the old manner. A central passage, though hardly a formal hall was, as M. W. Barley points out in his excellent *The English Farmhouse and Cottage,* "a characteristic feature of the medieval house."[28] The idea of a symmetrical cover for a two-room depth was alien to most old British building, but it was familiar enough to those who came in great numbers from central Europe. The Georgian form was new, but not too new, and backed by the taste makers of the period, it became firmly lodged in the Mid-Atlantic architectural repertoire. From the middle of the eighteenth century to the close of the nineteenth, the type was constructed as a stalwart farm house in stone, brick, log, or frame throughout the Mid-Atlantic region, achieving dominance at the region's western end in the area of Somerset County, Pennsylvania, and standing as a very familiar form along the Delaware River and throughout New Jersey.

Being an idea, existing fully in the mind before its achievement as an object, the Georgian type was not only built of a variety of materials (form and techniques being separate architectural subsystems),[29] it was subject to formal modification. The most common transformation within the Georgian type consisted of a subtractive step yielding two-thirds of the complete idea, a house with two rooms on one side of the hall (figs. 5b, 6). Houses of this kind are seen occasionally as farm houses through southern Pennsylvania and adjacent Delaware and Maryland. It is also the predominant, traditional town house type even beyond the region, being found commonly in cities such as Washington, D.C., and Richmond, Virginia,[30] where Georgian house subtypes are unusual in the surrounding countryside. In New Jersey the two-thirds Georgian type is extremely common on the farm and in the village. Generally, it has a kitchen wing, lower and narrower than the bulk of the basic house, built off the gable along which the hall runs. An additional rural New Jersey Georgian modification amounts to a two-thirds form in a single story expression (fig. 22). The occurrence of this house in central New Jersey is an example of the connections between New Jersey and Long Island, where the

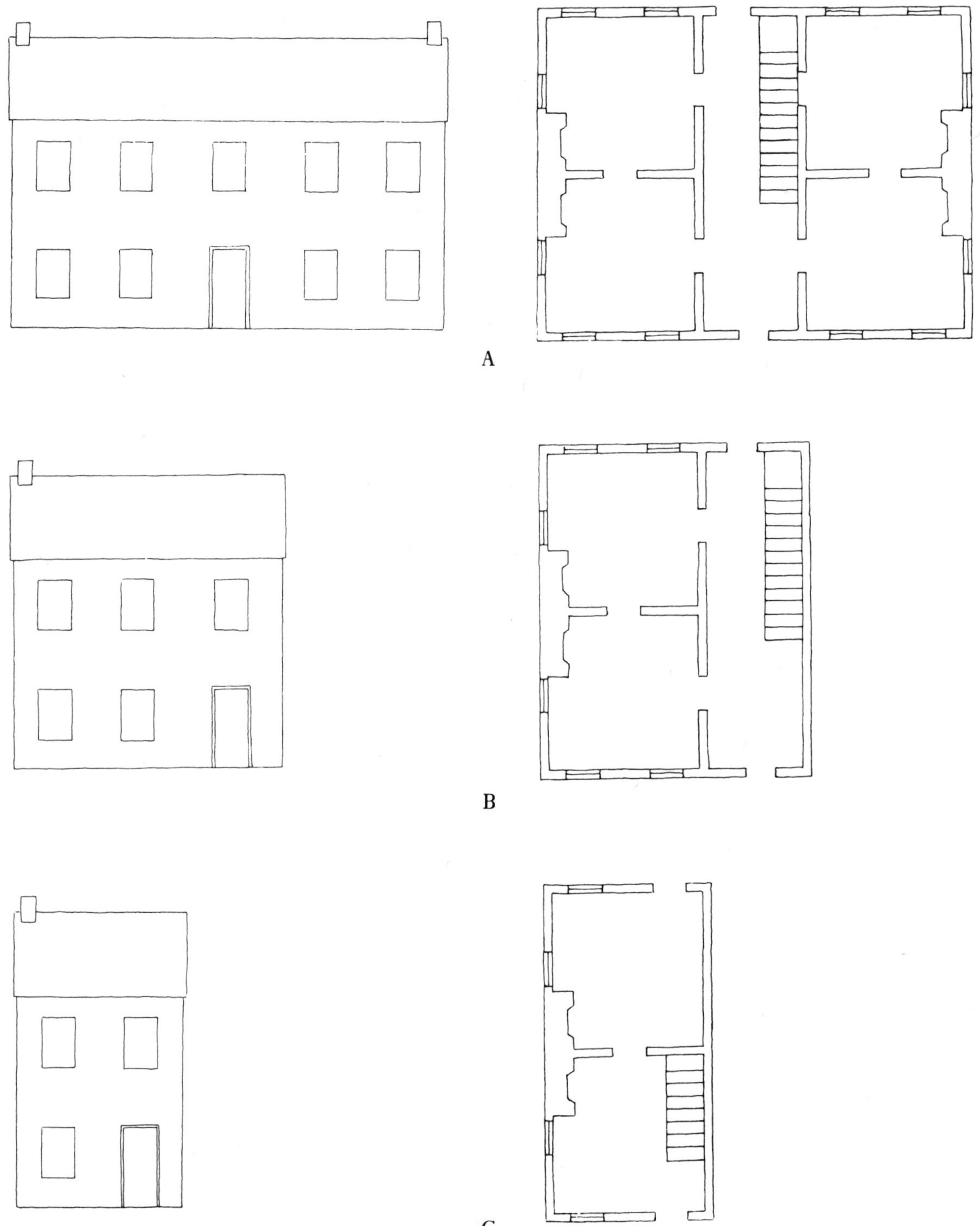

Figure 5. Major transformations of the Georgian house type: a, full (see also figures 4, 10, 21); b, two-thirds (see also figures 6, 9, 22); c, one-third (see also figures 7, 8).

Figure 6. Two-thirds Georgian house type. The plan of this house is basically that of figure 5b. The wing off the hall gable is characteristic of country New Jersey. Northeast of Mt. Airy, Hunterdon County, New Jersey.

type is also found with frequency. On Long Island and in northeastern New Jersey, the chimney was often placed internally, New England fashion; in the part of New Jersey located within the Mid-Atlantic region, chimneys were built inside the gable end as they were nearly always in Pennsylvania and Maryland.

If the Georgian form could be reduced by one-third, it could be reduced by two-thirds, and the new form, one-room wide and two deep, was a common town house in the Delaware Valley, as it was in London (fig. 5c). Like larger town houses, it was often built as half a pair in the vicinity of the Delaware (fig. 7). In southeastern Pennsylvania, nearby Delaware, and particularly in the area of New Jersey just east of Philadelphia, it can be found, built of frame or log, brick or stone, as a farm house, generally with a wing off the non-chimney gable (fig. 8). The gable of this house, one-third of the Georgian type, is the same as that of houses that are two-thirds or all of the fundamental form, but the openings per floor on the facade are reduced from five to three to two (fig. 5).

The transformations of the Georgian type tell a simple story. Ernest Allen Connally teaches the same lesson in his study of Cape Cod houses.[31] People, being innovative, can modify ideas and fragment forms to suit economic and environmental needs. Houses that are portions of the entire idea were doubtless built by the same masters who built the full houses, though for people who had smaller families, less cash, or a smaller piece of land. The narrow, deep proportions of the one-third and two-thirds Georgian subtypes made them suited to small lots and crowded situations. The fact that when the architectural repertoire was rummaged for town houses partial Georgian subtypes were chosen as the forms to fit the context[32] reveals a traditional, rural element in Mid-Atlantic town planning. If the builder were designing from a problem rather than out of a limited collection of folk components, he would likely have constructed a thin house, its gable

Figure 7. An urban row composed of houses of the one-third Georgian house type. These houses—some masonry, some wooden; some of the eighteenth century, some of the nineteenth—illustrate the variety of one-third Georgian facades. This sketch represents the 200 block of North Darlington Street in West Chester, Chester County, Pennsylvania.

Figure 8. One-third Georgian house type. The basic house is of the type pictured in figure 5c. It is located between New Hope and Wrightstown, Bucks County, Pennsylvania.

to the street, like the ones found in pictures of old European towns or in the late nineteenth-century mill and mine company towns of Pennsylvania. But the planner's repertoire was rural, and even though it meant that the rafters had to span a long distance, he wanted his house in the town to be structured and positioned as it was in the country. Behind the house he had a plot for a garden and a tiny barn, so that the town consisted of rows of miniature farms, the houses, country fashion, with their long sides, or what purported to be their long sides, to the road (fig. 9). Our innovator was a conservative man: he comforted his innovation by placing it in a traditional structure (the relationship between entrance, ridge line, and road), and he limited his innovations to simple matters of addition and subtraction—addition because the partial form could be enlarged subsequent to its building to produce the full form, and the full form could be enlarged by an additional one-third or two-thirds (fig. 10).

The little family of house types on the Georgian plan is a major characteristic of the Mid-Atlantic region. In neither of the adjacent coastal regions, North or South, did the Georgian set of ideas become as deeply embedded in the thinking of traditional builders. The existence of the Georgian type did more than inspire novel forms that collectively signal a new, impurely folk phase in architectural chronology. The basic form was dissected, and some of its components were fused with elements from pre-Georgian building to produce, in a flurry of eighteenth-century innovation, two new house types, both of which showed much more creative thought than occasional refinements within the Georgian form and style such as Cliveden in Germantown or Mount Pleasant in Philadelphia's Fairmount Park.[33]

Figure 9. Mid-Atlantic townscape. This photograph shows the characteristic orientation of traditional urban housing in the Mid-Atlantic region. To the left is a house of the two-thirds Georgian type. The next house is an example of the Pennsylvania farm house type, as in figure 13. The main street through Dover, York County, Pennsylvania.

Figure 10. Full Georgian house with additions. The stone house is of the full Georgian form. It has had an additional one-third in frame added with lateral symmetry to one gable; beyond that is another frame addition. The house is situated south of Norton, Hunterdon County, New Jersey.

Figure 11. Continental central chimney house type. Weatherboarded log house. The plan of this house is as in figure 12a. The small upstairs windows and bunched window spacing are typical of early houses of this kind. The one story rear ell is a washhouse—common in southern Pennsylvania as an appendage or detached dependency; see too figures 13, 27. Between Bermudian and York Springs, Adams County, Pennsylvania.

In the German areas of the region, including spots in West Jersey[34] as well as the more predictable broadening arc in Pennsylvania from Northampton to York counties, an off-center chimney characterizes a common house type, built regularly up to about 1770. Rendered, generally, in stone or log, it exists in one and two story examples. Typically, it has a three room plan; an offset door opens into a long, narrow kitchen incorporating the house's deep fireplace. Behind the chimney, a broader front room serves as a parlor, a smaller back room as the chamber (figs. 11, 12a).[35] The size of the house cues internal modifications, such as partitioning the kitchen of a larger house or eliminating the wall between bedroom and parlor in a small house.[36] The plan is like that of peasant dwellings in Switzerland and the Rhine Valley.[37] Its depth and proportions, products of the late medieval Continent, are not completely incompatible with the Georgian intent; its plan is not wholly unlike the two-thirds Georgian house subtype. This similarity surely supported acceptance of the new Georgian form, and it facilitated the merger of the old and new forms into the type most common in the heartland of the Mid-Atlantic area from Bethlehem, Pennsylvania, to Frederick, Maryland (figs. 12b, 13). The flattish roof and external quasi symmetry of the common house type fool scholars into assigning its origin to England and neoclassicism. But that shell masks an aged Continental interior. The type's gable end is strictly Georgian (fig. 14), but its front is pierced by four rather than five openings in order to accommodate the three room plan inside. One door still brings the visitor into a long, narrow room, but there is usually, though not

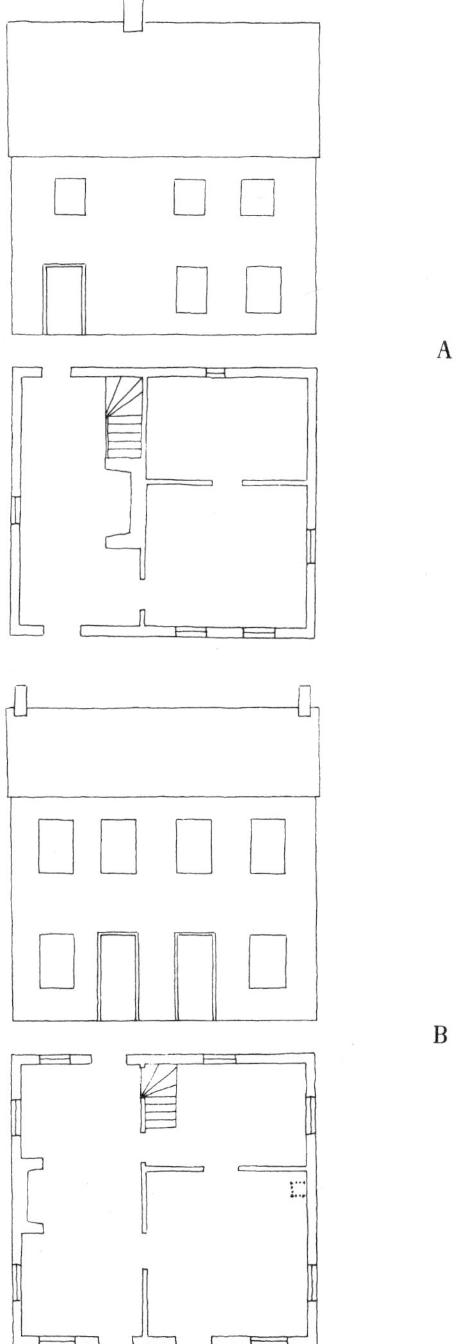

Figure 12. Schematic representation of the development of the Pennsylvania farm house type: a, continental central-chimney house type; b, Pennsylvania farm house type—the continental central-chimney house altered to suit the Georgian aesthetic. The chimney at the right serves a stove to heat the parlor.

always, another front door leading into the parlor. Rarely used, often lacking a screen door, and explained in a variety of amusing ways, this second door seems to be a stab at symmetrical arrangement, but as the old kitchen was thinner than the parlor, a close look at window spacing shows the symmetry on the facade is frequently a sham. The large central chimney has been replaced by chimneys in the gables (fig. 23). If the viewer rumbling by on the road does not look too critically, he thinks he is seeing the latest word, a Georgian house with a formal hall; that is the impression the builder wished to convey while his wife went about her work inside in the old way, speaking German to her offspring. The Pennsylvania farm house, an eighteenth-century compromise, was constructed into the twentieth century of log, stone, brick, or frame, sided with weatherboards under which there was often a nogging of brick. Like other kinds of houses around the Delaware River, it was frequently stuccoed.

This synthetic type is the result of the same kind of mental activity that generated the common New England house type, which packaged the old English saltbox house in a symmetrical container.[38] In both houses, Old World interiors were externally disguised to be acceptable. Both house forms teach us that the skins of houses are shallow things that people are willing to change, but people are most conservative about the spaces they must utilize and in which they must exist. Build the walls of anything, deck them out with anything, but do not change the arrangement of the rooms or their proportions. In those volumes—bounded by surfaces from which a person's senses rebound to him—his psyche develops; disrupt them and you can disrupt him.[39]

The kind of house that preceded the Georgian type as predominant in the intensely English sections around Philadelphia and across the river in New Jersey was as venerable a folk form as the Germanic three room house. It has been named, by Kniffen, the I-house (its tall, thin gable might be envisioned as an upper case *I*). Its definitive charac-

Figure 13. The Pennsylvania farm house type. This is an orderly and elegant nineteenth-century example of the synthetic Georgian-Germanic house; other examples can be seen in figures 9, 12, 14, 23, and 27. It is located south of Wellsville, York County, Pennsylvania.

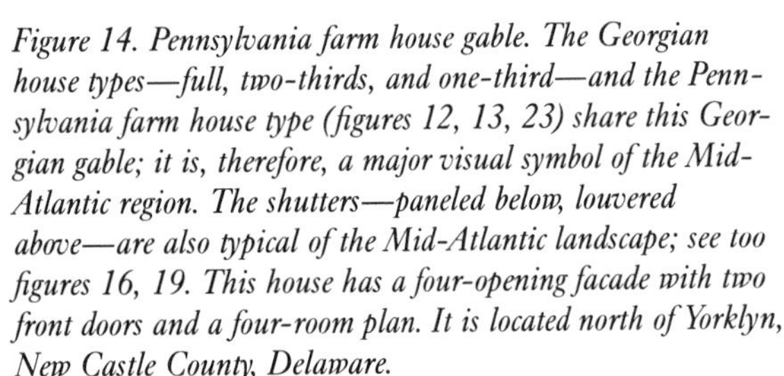

Figure 14. Pennsylvania farm house gable. The Georgian house types—full, two-thirds, and one-third—and the Pennsylvania farm house type (figures 12, 13, 23) share this Georgian gable; it is, therefore, a major visual symbol of the Mid-Atlantic region. The shutters—paneled below, louvered above—are also typical of the Mid-Atlantic landscape; see too figures 16, 19. This house has a four-opening facade with two front doors and a four-room plan. It is located north of Yorklyn, New Castle County, Delaware.

teristics are two story height, one room depth, and length of two or more rooms. Known across England at the time of initial settlement in the New World,[40] it was commonly built in all the English colonies north of the middle of the North Carolina coast during the seventeenth and early eighteenth centuries. The early form, in most instances, consisted of two rooms on the ground floor, one of which was square, called a hall, and used for most living; it was often a bit longer than the other room, the parlor.[41] In New England, logically enough, the East Anglian[42] central chimney form was most usual; in the Chesapeake Bay area, west British external chimneys were most characteristic. In the Mid-Atlantic area, the chimneys were built flush within each gable wall.[43]

The introduction of the Georgian form into I-house country engendered the same results in the Chesapeake and Mid-Atlantic areas. The I-house retained its one room depth (without which an example would be classified as a different type), but its new plan approximated the front half of the Georgian house with rooms of about equal size separated by a hall (figs. 15, 16, 17). The five-opening facade became standard, so that from the front a Georgian house and a Georgian-influenced I-house are indistinguishable. The gable view, however, is quite different. The gables of early I-houses were normally blank (fig. 16), though an off-center window per floor became common on later Pennsylvania houses. Particularly throughout southern New Jersey and the Maryland Eastern Shore, there are often two windows on each floor, disguising the old I-house even more completely as a Georgian house (fig. 17).

Most extant Mid-Atlantic I-houses are frame, though some in the Alleghenies, on the region's western frontier, are log. In Bucks and Chester counties particularly they are of stone. They were frequently built of brick, most notably in southern New Jersey, and in Salem and Cumberland counties where glazed headers were worked into elaborate diamond and zigzag patterns and into dates and initials (fig. 18)[44]—a mode of decoration that was quite common in Tudor England and occasional along the southern Atlantic coast.[45]

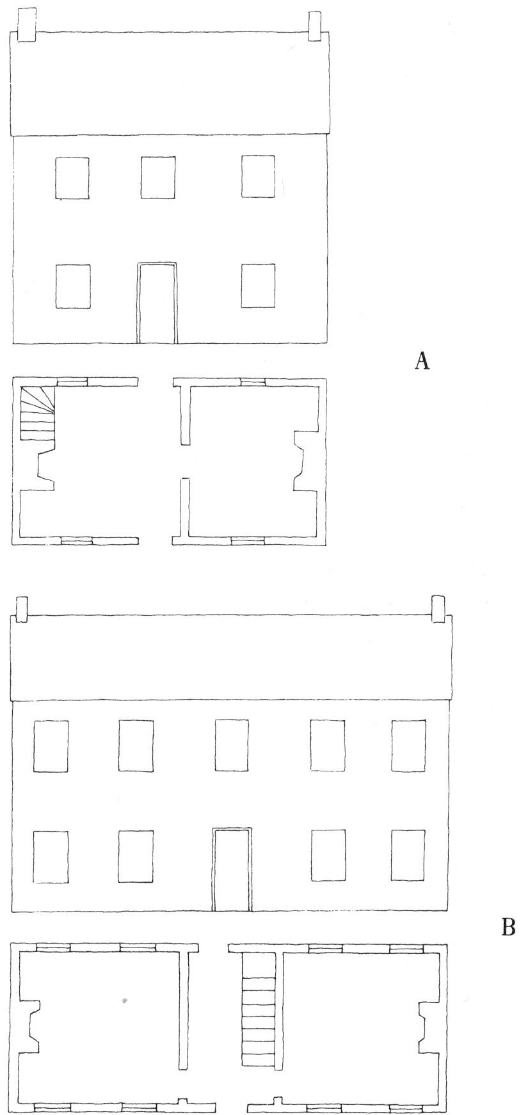

Figure 15. Schematic representation of the development of the Georgian I-house type: a, an early two room— "hall and parlor"—plan; b, Georgian I-house plan (see also figures 16, 17, 24).

Figure 16. Georgian I-house type. Stone house with a brick facade. Northwest of Middletown, Dauphin County, Pennsylvania.

Figure 17. Georgian I-house type. Greek revival era I-house. The gable fenestration is typically Georgian (see figures 4, 14), though the tall, narrow proportions of the old British yeoman's house remain intact. The exposed chimney back of the internal end chimney, which is characteristic of New Jersey and southeastern New York, is found occasionally throughout the southern United States; the automatic ascription of this feature to some continental—Dutch or Flemish—source is simplistic at best. South of Norton, Hunterdon County, New Jersey.

Figure 18. I-house. The original section of this building was an early two-room I-house. The gable was subsequently altered—the roof flattened and a double chimney added—in accordance with Georgian taste, and a room (laid in common bond where the original house was laid up in Flemish bond) was added bringing the house into the double parlor form. The overall zigzag pattern on the gable is less common in the fancy brickwork of southern New Jersey than dates and initials. The house stands south of Hancocks' Bridge, Salem County, New Jersey.

The I-house concept, expressed like all basic concepts in diverse materials, underwent expansion through various kinds of shed and ell additions to the rear (figs. 17, 19, 20)—if not actual additions, these are still conceptual additions like suffixes on words. Also, a two-story room—square in good English fashion, like the house's main rooms—was occasionally added onto one gable, producing a double-parlor house (fig. 18), a form that, owing to its popularity in England, one would expect to have been more usual in America. Like the Georgian house, the I-house could be split, and houses that are two-thirds of the full form, one room and a hall, are found in Pennsylvania villages and in the countryside of southwestern New Jersey and eastern Delaware (fig. 19).

Once introduced, the Georgian form was worked upon in many ways: it was built unaltered of a variety of materials; it was reduced and enlarged systematically to fit spatial or economic requirements; and it was broken down so that some of its components could be combined with components from pre-Georgian architectural repertoires, both British and Germanic, to produce new house types.

Culture is an inventory of learned concepts. The cultural process consists of selecting from among the concepts, some of them new, some of them old, when a problem such as walking, courting, or building a barn has to be solved. Some concepts are fully

Figure 19. Two-thirds Georgian I-house type. The perfect Gothic trim and frontal gable and the rear appendages do not entirely obscure the basic house, which conforms to the two-thirds Georgian I-house type, a hall along one gable with a room with a fireplace next to it; compare this house with figures 15b, 16, 17. This late nineteenth-century expression of an old concept is located east of Woodstown, Salem County, New Jersey.

accepted, some are modified, some are torn apart and combined with others, and some are rejected. The acceptance of the Georgian form meant not only the appearance of new things but also the disappearance of old things. Some old ideas were specifically incompatible: if the Georgian ideal of chimneys poking up at either gable were embraced, the central fireplace of the three room Continental house could not remain, despite the elaborate flues constructed to that end in at least one house. Some ideas were lost as a part of the general but rapid move during the third quarter of the eighteenth century toward a prosperous homogeneity—a move facilitated by a new and prestigious architectural concept, offered at once to all people, and to all somewhat foreign, somewhat familiar. A few manifestations of the ethnically distinct architectural ideas of the early period in Mid-Atlantic building can still be found to give the fieldworker an impression of the early heterogeneity—of the ideas that were rejected. Among the lost forms was the Swiss bank house,[46] although its multilevel concept may have survived in the semisubterranean cooking cellars of many Mid-Atlantic farm houses. The low, stone Scotch-Irish cabin[47] was also lost as New World Ulstermen moved into larger, more fashionable dwellings. Although translated into log or frame, the little northern Irish cabin did persist with tenacity on the Appalachian frontier.[48] Apparently never of much importance, Scandinavian log construction, too, was lost during this period when an acceptable but limited folk architectural repertoire was built up in the New World out of Old World stuff.[49] By mid-century Scandinavian log construction had been completely overwhelmed by the totally different kind of log construction usual in America, which was introduced from central Europe.[50]

The houses and other folk buildings that typify the Mid-Atlantic landscape—the barns and mills, meeting houses and corncribs—can be explained as artifacts largely by reference within the architectural system. Unlike a utopian designer, the folk planner employs an old and established form, despite changes of use and environment. In arranging a complete form in a spatial relationship to other forms, the folk planner finds himself with an abundance of problems. The lay of the land, the ranges of wind, rain, and temperature, the changes in the social and economic systems—all make adherence to a type, a traditional template for correctness, more difficult in the construction of composite, noncontinuous forms, such as towns or farms, than it is in the construction of unitary, continuous forms, such as houses or bridges. Exactly the same house type might work nicely in a metropolis or a wilderness, but different settings obviously require quite different relationships between the house and other structures.

Two distinct, fundamental farm plans exist in the Delaware Valley; in their ideal forms they stay pretty obediently on opposite sides of the river, though both tend to lose the rigor of their pattern at the Delaware and especially on the Jersey bank above Philadelphia. In southern New Jersey, the ideal from which reality varies is a hollow square (figs. 20, 21).[51] It consists of a house, an I-house or some Georgian subtype, generally, facing the road with the barn, almost always a three-bay, side-opening barn of one level, such as was most common in England,[52] directly behind it or set a bit to one side. In some cases the ridge lines of house and barn are set at right angles (fig. 20) though a parallel arrangement is more common and seems to have been the ideal (fig. 21). On one side a line of buildings, consisting mainly of a long shed open on the inside, connects the spheres of house and barn. A few other dependencies are placed opposite this line forming a courtyard, a hollow rectangle—house at

Figure 20. New Jersey farm. Built on the courtyard plan with the house and barn at right angles. The house is a late nineteenth-century I-house; the barn is an example of the three-bay English barn type. East of Canton, Salem County, New Jersey.

Figure 21. New Jersey farm. This farm is built on the most common courtyard pattern with the house and barn related within a parallel structure. The house is of the full Georgian type; the barns and the open shed are of English derivation and are typical of New Jersey. South of Elmer, Salem County, New Jersey.

Figure 22. New Jersey farm. This farm is not built on the courtyard plan. There is some suggestion of the parallel relation of house and barn, except, unlike the true courtyard plan (figure 21), in this case the house faces the barn, and the layout is composed of separate house and barn areas. The house is a two-thirds Georgian house of one story; as with two-story houses of the kind, the kitchen wing is lower than the basic dwelling (compare figure 6); the barn is the usual English three-bay type. Between Unionville and Wertsville, Hunterdon County, New Jersey.

the front, barn at the rear, with one boundary typically a little ragged. As one moves northward through New Jersey, this tight plan loosens up. Some farms exhibit the major structural elements, the parallel relation of house and barn, but they lack the sheds enclosing the square. In others the barn and sheds form a courtyard of sorts—what would be called a *foldyard* in England[53]—but the house is not a part of the rectangular layout. This situation is common in the North and suggests that such farms may be products more of Northern than of Mid-Atlantic thinking.

When the house is rarely an I-house and the barn is usually a Yankee-style basement barn,[54] the fieldworker is likely to be near the Kittatinny Mountains, and his suspicion that he is leaving the Mid-Atlantic region is confirmed. In this hilly section of western New Jersey, farms on which there is no clear statement of the square are common; there is instead the simple clustering of some outbuildings around the barn and others around the house with a psychological separation between the two areas (fig. 22). The groups of buildings may be considered, respectively, as extensions of house or barn and the two areas as spheres of sexual control, the barn being the man's domain, the house, the woman's. While it takes different forms in different subregions, this loose dual arrangement appears to be an Americanism with multiple origins, lacking sufficient precision to enable the scholar to make confident assertions about Old World provenance or New World antiquity. The hollow square, which predominates in flat southern New Jersey but breaks up in the stony hills of the upper Delaware Valley, is an English form. Probably related to similar plans in northern Europe,[55] the hollow square, including or omitting the house, dates to Saxon times in England, where it is still regularly found, and in Ireland it is restricted to the English-planted areas.[56] In America, derivative plans are found not only in New Jersey but also on Long Island and in upstate New York.[57] The farms of New England[58] occasionally consist of a house and barn in a parallel arrangement, though the two are joined by a service wing; the similarities are suggestive of a possible genetic relationship in old England between these two tight farm plans, which are outstanding in a country characterized by loose farm planning.

The ideal in southern Pennsylvania and its areas of cultural continuity, west central New Jersey, central Maryland, and the northern Valley of Virginia, consists of lining up the house and barn gable to gable and positioning this linear structure so that the fronts of both the house and the barn face south, east, or somewhere in between (figs. 23, 24, 26a). The front of the house is obvious, but the barn's front, in traditional terms, is the side with the doors into the stables—the side on which the manure, a sign of agricultural success, is displayed in early spring—and not necessarily the side into which one would drive a wagon or truck. Many different kinds of houses and barns were plugged into the slots in this linear structure. Around the southern and western borders of the Mid-Atlantic region, in Maryland and Virginia particularly, the house slot was usually filled with an I-house (fig. 24). Through the center of the region the house was generally a Georgian or Germanic farm house (fig. 23), and one often sees modern bungalows neatly inserted in the dwelling's traditional position on the farm. In hilly areas of rocks and subsistence farming, eastern Northampton, northern Chester and York, and Bedford counties, Pennsylvania, especially, the barn is often one level. Through most of the western subregion of the Mid-Atlantic area, the barn slot in the farm structure is filled with some variety of bank barn. Prefab and cement block barns, even those lacking any formal connection with the old tradition, still tend to be related traditionally to the rest of the farm's buildings.

As long as the barn was one level, the problems involved in the achievement of the ideal layout were not hard to conquer. With the development of the bank barn, the planning problem became complicated. The bank barn developed at about the same time as the pair of syncretistic Mid-Atlantic house types, and it was, like them, a product both of the fragmentation of preexisting forms and of the reordering and meshing of their elements. It seems to

Figure 23. The linear Mid-Atlantic farm plan. This farm consists of (from left to right) hog house, bank barn (of the Charles H. Dornbusch and John K. Heyl, Pennsylvania German Barns *[Allentown: Pennsylvania German Folklore Society, 1958], type f–g), chicken coop, washhouse, and Pennsylvania farm house type. Southwest of Dillsburg, York County, Pennsylvania.*

Figure 24. The linear Mid-Atlantic farm plan. This farm consists basically of a Georgian I-house and a bank barn (of Dornbusch and Heyl type h). Later nineteenth-century Georgian I-houses in the Mid-Atlantic region, such as this one, tend to have three rather than five openings per floor on the front; compare this house with figures 16, 17. North of Frederick, Frederick County, Maryland.

be an application of the multilevel, banked concept, common on barns in northwestern England and on barn and house combinations in north central Switzerland and the Black Forest, to the single level double-crib barn of Swiss ancestry.[59] The bank barn of the Mid-Atlantic is typified by a cantilevered forebay over the stabling doors at the front and a ramp leading to its upper level at the rear (figs. 23, 24, 25, 27).[60] The problems involved in planning a farm that included a bank barn were not solely the linear arrangement and southerly exposure but also the location of a grade into which the barn could be built. Despite the complexity of the requirements, the ideal generally materialized on the land although topography occasionally caused compromise. In some areas houses were not traditionally backed into a bank, so that the barn was constructed slightly uphill of the house, crooking the plan. Generally, the house and the barn were positioned squarely to the rise of the land, like English bank barns,[61] which seem to have provided part of the suggestion for the Pennsylvania barn, so that a curved piece of terrain caused the buildings to be related along the contour, bending the plan (fig. 25). In these ways topography served to distort the ideal.

When it became fashionable to have the house front on the road, an additional factor of confusion was introduced. If the road ran east-west and the farm were on the north side of the road, no trouble arose (fig. 26a). If the farm were on the road's south side, a choice had to be made. Some farm planners ignored the road, situating the house with its back turned to it, leaving the house and barn in alignment facing the early sun. Others compromised by placing the front of the house and the back of the barn to the road (fig. 26b); in this way, the aesthetic arrangement of ridge lines was retained, though the practical tradition of the dwelling's orientation was lost. A road running in an inconvenient direction, northwesterly say, presented even greater problems. Many ignored the road, letting it run through or by the farm without influencing the organization of the buildings (fig. 26c), so that an appropriate slope for

Figure 25. The linear Mid-Atlantic plan, bent to correspond to the topography. The house and barn of this farm were constructed directly parallel to slopes that intersect at an angle, causing the linear plan to bow. The bank barn is of the Dornbusch and Heyl type f–g; in front of it, built into the stone wall around the barnyard, is a hog house; behind it is a drive-in corncrib. The house is an altered example of a two-thirds Georgian type. The farm is situated near Clear Spring, south of Dillsburg, York County, Pennsylvania.

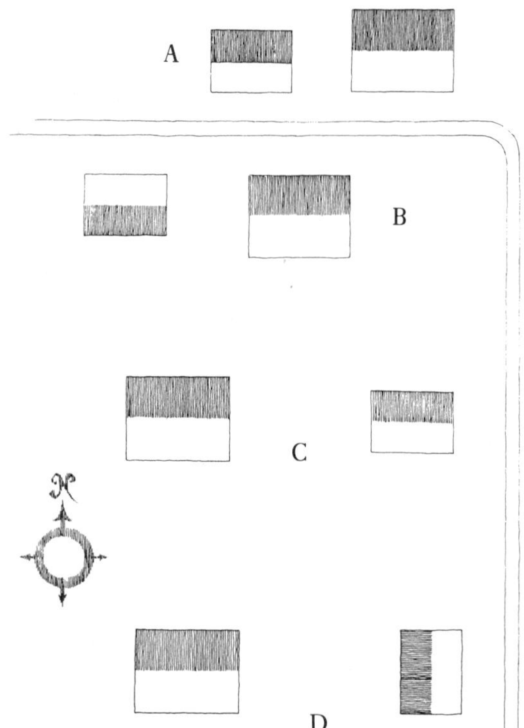

Figure 26. Variety in the relationship between the linear plan and the road; a, house and barn face the road and the south (see also figures 23, 24); b, house faces the road, barn faces the south; c, house and barn face the south, ignoring the road; d, house faces the road, barn faces the south (see also figure 27).

the barn and the cardinal points were the only factors considered in the accomplishment of the ideal. Others built the house on the road, even if it meant that the house faced into the coldest winds. The barn could have been placed in alignment, preserving the aesthetic tradition while violating the practical tradition; however, the barn was left so that the morning sun bathed the barnyard, and the farm's plan became L-shaped—a compromise that is frequently seen (figs. 26d, 27). When neither hillside nor road allowed the expression of the ideal, disruption of both the practical and aesthetic—economic and artistic—traditions resulted. But the first step in planning was site selection, and such sites were usually avoided; farms lacking any suggestion of linear organization and southern orientation are rare.

The forces that affect change in the cultural process are easily ordered in an examination of the problems solved in structuring a farm's components. Given an ideal, there are aesthetic forces for its continuation (the familiarity of the linear or the rectangular plans) and aesthetic forces for its disruption (the desire to orient the house to the road). There are practical forces for its continuation (the warmth of the southerly aspect, the utility of the courtyard arrangement) and practical forces for its disruption (the need for a slope in Pennsylvania, the need for flat land in New Jersey).

The two ideal farm layouts of the Delaware Valley act as modulations between European and American farm patterns. In both, unlike the plans found throughout most of the United States, the house and barn were considered as parts of a single, formal unit rather than as separate foci for units related only by extra-architectural systems. The separation one senses between the house and barn in the Midwest, or indeed in southwestern Pennsylvania or northwestern New Jersey, is not present in the older Delaware Valley farms. Still, in general, the Delaware Valley farm plans, as sets of spaces set aside for particular uses, were not as tight or integrated as farm plans in the Old World.

The origin of the linear plan may lie in buildings or ranges of buildings that housed the farmer at one end and his stock at the other. These are found in many of the parts of the Old World from which the Mid-Atlantic settlers came: in England, Wales, Ireland, Scotland, Switzerland, and the Rhine Valley.[62] Germans in nineteenth-century Wisconsin erected buildings housing both people and stock, and there are reports by a traveler and two tax assessors of similar buildings in Pennsylvania.[63] The first house built by the Moravians at Bethlehem, Pennsylvania, was a 20′ × 40′ log building that housed people at one end and animals at the other.[64] But clearly the pattern was never usual. Arriving in the New World with the tradition of a combined house and barn, the farm planner seems

Figure 27. The L-shaped variant of the linear Mid-Atlantic plan. The house of this farm faces the road, while the barn faces southward. The house is of the Pennsylvania farm house type (as in figure 13); the barn is Dornbusch and Heyl type f–g. The locations of the hog and chicken houses at the front of the barn and the washhouse at the rear of the dwelling are characteristic of southern Pennsylvania and adjacent Maryland. This farm is north of Bermudian in York County, Pennsylvania.

to have exploded the old building. The building's components were individually unaltered, and they were ordered linearly, but he let daylight in between them.

The activities on the farm were spread out and separately housed; the holdings that were loosely bound into the agricultural community were similarly scattered. In Britain before and during the Roman presence, farms were independently possessed and isolated.[65] This ancient European pattern survived through the Middle Ages only in those mountainous areas of the Continent and the British Isles that were relatively undisturbed by the waves of violence called history.[66] In the most densely settled sections, where the land had many stomachs to support and was worth fighting over, the agricultural village with its clustered habitations, outfield system, and cooperative style became the norm. But the old, individualistic sense of status dependent upon the accumulation of territory and chattels was not wholly lost in the medieval, communal setting;[67] and although tight agricultural villages were planned in Spanish, French, and English America, the settlers of those villages scattered rapidly and greedily into the countryside, claiming and working isolated holdings,[68] with exceptions only in extremely authoritarian situations such as those that existed in early New England and Mormon Utah.[69] With antecedents in the land-use patterns of the Scotch-Irish and with support from the land allotment schemes of William Penn,[70] the separate, single-family farm became the usual pattern for the Mid-Atlantic and for the United States.[71]

The availability of land is the most obvious among the factors that made up the New World environment and that functioned causally to encourage an abrupt change in planning. The Delaware Valley settler's holding was much larger than his European father's; he could spread his buildings and farms around; more significantly, he probably felt that he had to. After the fact, we can wax ecstatic about the vastness of the new country, though at the time only a few philosophers gloried in the creeks and trees. We might wish that those folk who found themselves on the banks of the Delaware two hundred and fifty years ago had related to the environment like Thoreau or a crusading member of the Sierra Club, but they were peasants. The forests were enemies, strange and evil, existing only to be cleared. The forests caused the immediate invention of nothing—men do not work that way—but they did cause the selection and elaboration of old traditions through which the trees could be utilized—or rather, exploited, for wood was wasted and what was used was ripped out of natural shape and hidden. Then as now, the ash-tough American on the move felt that the physical environment was something to devastate. America to the newcomer, as Leo Marx has pointed out, was "*both* Eden and a howling desert," a wilderness and a garden,[72] the idea of wilderness produced fear, but the idea of the garden gave him strength, and the American "environment-buster"[73] tore fearfully and optimistically through the land. The limitless spaces he faced had to be controlled to eliminate the fear and to realize the optimism. Great expanses of land had to be turned from wilderness into material culture; they had to be subdued by the surveyor's chain and mile upon mile of fencing; they had to be claimed by buildings, tall, inharmonious signs of conquest dropped across the landscape—man-made forms spread out as far and lonesome as they could be, without leaving too much space between for the wilderness to slip in.

Transition can be read in the characteristic spatial arrangements of the Delaware Valley; there is a lingering sense of the tightness of the English or German peasant with his clustered, cooperative modes, but there is also the beginning and fulfillment of the dominant style of America, loose, worried, acquisitive individualism. Dispersion—separate buildings, separate holdings—is the major material manifestation of cultural response to the New World environment, and it has been from the beginning of European settlement. Jamestown was only fifteen years old when an English visitor complained that the buildings seemed scattered about.[74] Three hundred and thirteen years later, Le Corbusier noted that the American desire for "a little garden, a little house, the assurance of freedom"[75] —the capitalistic possession of a bit of land—had resulted in the failure of the American city and the American way of life. From the Delaware Valley westward go separate holdings where the nuclear family works for itself, where ownership is an end in itself, where noncooperative capitalism flourishes. The single farmstead, symbol of individualistic endeavor, is compatibly systematic with other segments of the culture: the constricted, unaccompanied solo singing,[76] the literature demanding authority, the art and architecture stressing symmetry, the strict sex roles, the restrictive morality with its attendant modesty, guilt, and patrifocality,[77] the politics of individual power, and the hope for upward mobility within what Henry Nash Smith calls "the fee-simple empire."

Individualism suggests conformity and breeds repetition. The irony of cultural freedom in America has not been better expressed than by D. H. Lawrence:[78] masterless, the American is mastered; free, the American has conservatively chosen to restrict freedom. The land of the free is paradoxically not a land of endless variety. The critic might react differently to an eighteenth-century farm house and a modern rambler (and the old house is objectively assisted in its appeal by the soft edges that come with age and the subtlety that, as James Agee wrote,[79] results from the attempt to achieve stark symmetry with less than perfect hand methods), but there are no more basic eighteenth-century farm house types in the Delaware Valley than there are different house models in many subdivisions. The colonial American would have had no more trouble finding the whitewashed kitchen in the home of an unknown contemporary than today's suburbanite would have finding the knotty pine rec room in the split-level of a new neighbor.

Books may not tell us, but buildings do. The eighteenth-century average guy in the Delaware Valley was an individualist but a conformist—a wary adventurer. He felt anxious in his adjustment to the changing times and chose to appear modern while acting conservatively. He cared more for economics than for aesthetics. He does not sound unfamiliar.

Notes

This article was originally published in the *Winterthur Portfolio* (1972). All illustrations in this article are by the author.

1. Ivor Noël Hume, *Historical Archaeology* (New York: Alfred A. Knopf, 1969), p. 20.
2. "The history of art is a graph traced between points which represent the appearance in history of a great artist." Herbert Read, *Art and Alienation: The Role of the Artist in Society* (New York: Viking Press, 1969), p. 22.
3. Claude Lévi-Strauss, *The Savage Mind* (Chicago: University of Chicago Press, 1969), chaps. 8, 9, esp. p. 257.
4. For an interesting statement of modernist criticism, see Clement Greenberg, "Modernist Painting," in Gregory Battcock, ed., *The New Art: A Critical Anthology* (New York: E. P. Dutton, 1966), pp. 100–110.
5. See J. Geraint Jenkins, "Folk Museums: Some Aims and Purposes," *Museums Journal* 69, no. 1 (June 1969): 17–20; William C. Sturtevant, "Does Anthropology Need Museums?" *Proceedings of the Biological Society of Washington* 82 (1969): 619–50.
6. John Livingston Lowes, *The Road to Xanadu* (1927; reprint, New York: Vintage Books, 1959).
7. Clovis Heimsath, *Pioneer Texas Buildings: A Geometry Lesson* (Austin and London: University of Texas Press, 1968), p. 100.
8. The adjective *folk* when applied to an object indicates that the object was produced out of ideas that were old to the producer and out of style with regard to the overtly supported mass culture. For more on the subject, see Henry Glassie, "Artifacts: Folk, Popular, Imaginary and Real," in Marshall Fishwick and Ray B. Browne, eds., *Icons of Popular Culture* (Bowling Green: Bowling Green University Popular Press, 1970), pp. 103–22, and "Folk Art," in Richard M. Dorson, ed., *Folklore and Folklife: An Introduction* (Chicago: University of Chicago Press, 1972), pp. 253–80.
9. Fred Kniffen, "Louisiana House Types," most recently published in Philip L. Wagner and Marvin W. Mikesell, eds., *Readings in Cultural Geography* (Chicago: University of Chicago Press, 1962), pp. 157–69.
10. Hans Kurath, *A Word Geography of the Eastern United States* (1949; reprint, Ann Arbor: University of Michigan Press, 1967), fig. 3.
11. Fred Kniffen, "Folk Housing: Key to Diffusion," *Annals of the Association of American Geographers* 55, no. 4 (December 1965): 571 (reprinted in this volume).
12. Wilbur Zelinsky, "Where the South Begins: The Northern Limit of the Cis-Appalachian South in Terms of Settlement Landscape," *Social Forces* 30, no. 2 (December 1951): 172–78.
13. The greatest conflicts lie in the South, which has been less efficiently studied than the Mid-Atlantic and the North. The problem relevant to the Mid-Atlantic is whether or not the Upland South is an extension of the Mid-Atlantic or a separate region. Crucial to the solution of this problem is the source of the major Upland house types, most significantly the I-house. Kniffen in "Folk Housing," p. 561, feels that the I-house of the Upland South and the Midwest is a Mid-Atlantic contribution. He is followed by Peirce F. Lewis, "The Geography of Old Houses," *Earth and Mineral Sciences* 39, no. 5 (February 1970): 34. On the other hand, I feel that the I-house of the middle of the United States comes out of the Chesapeake Bay area and that both Kniffen and Lewis have vastly underestimated the influence and cultural significance of the coastal South. See Henry Glassie, *Pattern in the Material Folk Culture of the Eastern United States* (Philadelphia: University of Pennsylvania Press, 1969), pp. 37–39, 64–67, 75.
14. Alan Lomax, *The Folk Songs of North America in the English Language* (Garden City, New York: Doubleday, 1960), front endpapers.

15. Fred Kniffen and Henry Glassie, "Building in Wood in the Eastern United States: A Time-Place Perspective," *The Geographical Review* 56, no. 1 (Jan. 1966): 40–66, esp. 60, 64, 66 (reprinted in this volume).
16. For some reason John Fitchen, *The New World Dutch Barn* (Syracuse: Syracuse University Press, 1968), considers only the Dutch barns of upstate New York. A couple remain on Long Island and there are many just outside the Mid-Atlantic region in New Jersey; see Peter O. Wacker, *The Musconetcong Valley of New Jersey: A Historical Geography* (New Brunswick: Rutgers University Press, 1968), pp. 94–97.
17. M. W. Barley, *The English Farmhouse and Cottage* (London: Routledge and Kegan Paul, 1961), pp. 98, 112, 145, 156, 221; Sir Cyril Fox, "Some South Pembrokeshire Cottages," *Antiquity* 16, no. 64 (Dec. 1942): 312.
18. Eleanor Raymond, *Early Domestic Architecture of Pennsylvania* (New York: William Helburn, 1931), pp. 72–77.
19. The Valley of Virginia is the area between the Blue Ridge and the Allegheny mountains in western Virginia.
20. William A. Radford, *Radford's Practical Barn Plans* (New York: Radford Architectural Co., 1909), p. 274. The drive-in corncrib can also be found in Byron David Halsted, *Barn Plans and Outbuildings* (New York: Orange Judd, 1881), pp. 219–30.
21. Kniffen, "Folk Housing," pp. 576–77.
22. Henry Glassie, "The Old Barns of Appalachia," *Mountain Life and Work* 40, no. 2 (Summer 1965): 22–25.
23. A fine recent work is Marcus Whiffen, *American Architecture since 1780: A Guide to the Styles* (Cambridge: MIT Press, 1969).
24. R. W. Brunskill, "The Study of Vernacular Architecture," *Architecture North West* (April 1966).
25. Henry Glassie, "The Impact of the Georgian Form on American Folk Housing" (abstract), in Austin and Alta Fife and Henry Glassie, eds., *Forms upon the Frontier* (Logan: Utah State University Press, 1969), pp. 23–25.
26. Hugh Morrison, *Early American Architecture from the First Colonial Settlements to the National Period* (New York: Oxford University Press, 1952), pp. 288–91, 317.
27. Charles Morse Stotz, *The Early Architecture of Western Pennsylvania* (New York and Pittsburgh: William Helburn, 1936), pp. 89–91; William J. Murtagh, *Moravian Architecture and Town Planning* (Chapel Hill: University of North Carolina Press, 1967), pp. 79–82, 101–4, 124–25; C. Gillardon, "Das Safierhaus," *Schweizerisches Archiv für Volkskunde* 48, no. 4 (1952): 201–32; see also G. Edwin Brumbaugh, *Colonial Architecture of the Pennsylvania Germans* (Lancaster: Pennsylvania German Society, 1933), pp. 7–8.
28. Barley, *The English Farmhouse and Cottage,* p. 24.
29. On this and many other points essential to the understanding of building, Christian Norberg-Schulz, *Intention in Architecture* (Cambridge: MIT Press, 1968) is extremely useful; for this matter see p. 102.
30. Paul S. Dulaney, *The Architecture of Historic Richmond* (Charlottesville: University Press of Virginia, 1968), pictures many examples.
31. Ernest Allen Connally, "The Cape Cod House: An Introductory Study," *Journal of the Society of Architectural Historians* 19, no. 2 (May 1960): 47–56.
32. Christopher Alexander, *Notes on the Synthesis of Form* (Cambridge: Harvard University Press, 1967), pp. 18–24.
33. Irwin Richman, *Pennsylvania's Architecture* (University Park: Pennsylvania Historical Association, 1969), pp. 17–19.
34. For an example: Peter O. Wacker and Roger T. Trindell, "The Log House in New Jersey: Origins and Diffusion," *Keystone Folklore Quarterly* 13, no. 4 (Winter 1968): 253.
35. Donald Millar, "An Eighteenth Century German House in Pennsylvania," *The Architectural Record* 63, no. 2 (Feb. 1928): 161–68; Henry Kinzer Landis, *Early Kitchens of the Pennsylvania Germans* (Norristown: Pennsylvania German Society, 1939), pp. 15–16; Robert C. Bucher, "The Continental Log House," *Pennsylvania Folklife* 12, no. 4 (Summer 1962): 14–19; Henry Glassie, "A Continental Log House," *Pennsylvania Folklife* 18, no. 2 (Winter 1968–69): 32–39.
36. For examples, see Glassie, *Pattern in the Material Folk Culture,* pp. 50–51.
37. Max Gschwend, *Schwyzer Bauernhauser* (Bern: Paul Haupt, 1957), pp. 20–21; Franz von Pelser-Berensberg, *Mitteilungen über Trachten, Hausrat Wohn- und Lebenweise im Rheinland* (Dusseldorf: L. Schwann, 1909), pp. 49–53; Karl Rumpf, *Deutsche Volkskunst: Hessen* (Marburg: Simons, 1951), p. 23.
38. Ralph Nevill, *Old Cottage and Domestic Architecture in South-West Surrey, and Notes on the Early History of the Division* (Guildford: Billing, 1889), pp. 13, 58. It is almost fashionable to criticize the Darwinian aspect of J. Frederick Kelly, *Early Domestic Architecture of Connecticut* (1924; reprint, New York: Dover, 1963). If it took place at all, the evolution of most of his New England types occurred in old England, but one

step, from asymmetrical to symmetrical cover for the central chimney plan (his fifth period, pp. 12–13), was probably taken in the New World.

39. Domestic architecture can be viewed as the product of spatial perception, as man's personal bubble frozen, as a material manifestation of proxemic patterning; a couple of engaging and readable books relevant to these considerations are: Robert Sommer, *Personal Space: The Behavioral Basis of Design* (Englewood Cliffs: Prentice-Hall, 1969); Edward T. Hall, *The Hidden Dimension* (Garden City: Doubleday, 1969).
40. Barley, *The English Farmhouse and Cottage,* p. 178.
41. A good English plan of the type can be found in W. Galsworthy Davie and W. Curtis Green, *Old Cottages and Farmhouses in Surrey* (London: Batsford, 1908), p. 16.
42. For English plans: Harry Forrester, *The Timber-Framed Houses of Essex* (Chelmsford: Tindal Press, 1965), p. 15; Elizabeth Melling, *Kentish Sources: V: Some Kentish Houses* (Maidstone: Kent County Council, 1965), p. 44.
43. For a good example, see Ned Goode, "An Album of Chester County Farmhouses," *Pennsylvania Folklife* 13, no. 1 (Fall 1962): 20.
44. Joseph S. Sickler, *The Old Houses of Salem County* (Salem, N.J.: Sunbeam, 1949); Paul Love, "Patterned Brickwork in Southern New Jersey," *Proceedings of the New Jersey Historical Society* 73, no. 3 (July 1955): 182–208; Roger T. Trindell, "Building in Brick in Early America," *Geographical Review* 58, no. 3 (1968): 484–87.
45. Harry Batsford and Charles Fry, *The English Cottage* (London: Batsford, 1950), p. 109; "Brickwork Details," in Thomas Garner and Arthur Stratton, eds., *The Domestic Architecture of England during the Tudor Period* (1911; reprint, Boston: Architectural Center, 1923); Lewis Coffin, Jr., and Arthur C. Holden, *Brick Architecture of the Colonial Period in Maryland and Virginia* (New York: Architectural Book Publishing, 1919), p. 8; Henry Chandlee Forman, *The Architecture of the Old South: The Medieval Style, 1585–1850* (Cambridge: Harvard University Press, 1948), p. 150.
46. Robert C. Bucher, "The Swiss Bank House in Pennsylvania," *Pennsylvania Folklife* 18, no. 2 (Winter 1968–69): 2–11. The Schaeffer, Spangler, and Ley houses pictured are good examples of the type; the Matz House is a good example of a German–Georgian Pennsylvania farm house with a banked cellar.
47. Ake Campbell, "Irish Fields and Houses: A Study in Rural Culture," *Béaloideas* 5, no. 1 (1935): 57–74; E. Estyn Evans, "The Ulster Farmhouse," *Ulster Folklife* 1 (1955): 27–31.
48. Henry Glassie, "The Types of the Southern Mountain Cabin," in Jan H. Brunvand, *The Study of American Folklore: An Introduction* (New York: W. W. Norton, 1968), pp. 338–70.
49. Harold R. Shurtleff, *The Log Cabin Myth* (1939; reprint, Gloucester: Peter Smith, 1967), pp. 166–71.
50. Kniffen and Glassie, "Building in Wood in the Eastern United States" (reprinted in this volume). It has been more difficult to kill the erroneous notion of the Swedish-Finnish origin of American log construction, traceable to Henry C. Mercer's pioneer article, than it was for Harold R. Shurtleff to do away with the idea that log construction was the earliest building mode in the English colonies. Some scholars, probably as a result of American affection for the underdog and the melting pot, seem bent on giving the little settlement of New Sweden—whose population never reached a thousand souls and which was destined for early acculturation—credit for the introduction of a host of major American cultural traits. Martin Wright, for example, traced the essentially English dogtrot house of the Deep South to Scandinavia, and Thomas Tileston Waterman somehow located Swedish origins for the Germanic three-room house and for the most usual kind of English town house. The best scholars continue to write about the Scandinavian provenance of American log construction, yet the hewn, chinked, box-cornered log construction that predominates in the United States is definitely different from that of Sweden and Finland. Sigurd Erixon, the foremost authority on Scandinavian building, came to America believing that American log construction was Swedish in origin; after examining a few houses, he decided that it definitely could not be. Henry C. Mercer, "The Origin of Log Houses in the United States," *Old-Time New England* 18, no. 1 (July 1927); 18, no. 2 (October 1927), and in *Collection of Papers Read before the Bucks County Historical Society,* 5:568–83; Stevenson Whitcomb Fletcher, *Pennsylvania Architecture and County Life: 1640–1840* (Harrisburg: Pennsylvania Historical Museum Commission, 1950), pp. 42–44; Martin Wright, "Antecedents of the Double-Pen House Type," *Annals of the Association of American Geographers* 48, no. 2 (June 1958): 109–17; Thomas Tileston Waterman, *The Dwellings of Colonial America* (Chapel Hill: University of North Carolina Press, 1950), pp. 43, 125, 128–34; information on Erixon comes from an interview with Professor Stith Thompson, internationally known folktale scholar, Cooperstown, New York, May 1, 1965. Erixon is the author of, among other things, "The North-Euro-

pean Technique of Corner Timbering," *Folkliv* 1 (1937): 13–60, a description of Scandinavian log construction that implicitly reveals the vast difference between north European and North American construction.

51. Fred Kniffen mentions the New Jersey courtyard plan in his "Neglected Chapters of Pioneer Life," *Pioneer America Society Newsletter* 2, no. 4 (July 1969 [supplement]): 1–4.
52. George Ewart Evans, *The Farm and the Village* (London: Faber and Faber, 1969), pp. 82–83.
53. Joscelyne Finberg, *Exploring Villages* (London: Routledge and Kegan Paul, 1958), pp. 70–71.
54. Glassie, *Pattern in the Material Folk Culture of the Eastern United States,* pp. 135–41.
55. Hollow square plans are found in many parts of Northern Europe. Their appearance in northern Schleswig and Denmark is most relevant to the historic situation of England: R. Mejborg, *Nordiske Bøndergaarde* (Copenhagen: Lehman and Stages, 1892), 1:169–220; six of the farmsteads at the Danish Open-Air Museum (from Eastern Jutland, Sweden, Zealand, and Funen) are of the type, as Kai Uldall's valuable guide shows, *Frilandmuseet* (Lyngby: Danish National Museum, 1966), nos. 42, 54, 55, 63, 68, 71.
56. M. E. Seebohm, *The Evolution of the English Farm* (Cambridge, Harvard University Press, 1927), p. 100; Finberg, *Exploring Villages,* pp. 70–71; C. Henry Warren, *English Cottages and Farm-Houses* (London: Collins, 1947), p. 26; Sydney R. Jones, *English Village Homes and Country Buildings* (London: Batsford, 1947), pp. 72–75, 115; E. Estyn Evans, *Irish Folk Ways* (New York: Devin-Adair, 1957), p. 112.
57. Henry Glassie, "The Wedderspoon Farm," *New York Folklore Quarterly* 23, no. 3 (Sept. 1966): 163–87.
58. See Wilbur Zelinsky, "The New England Connecting Barn," *The Geographical Review* 48, no. 4 (Oct. 1958): 540–53.
59. See Henry Glassie, "The Double-Crib Barn in South Central Pennsylvania," 4 parts, *Pioneer America* 1, no. 1 (Jan. 1969): 9–16; 1, no 2 (July 1969): 40–45; 2, no. 1 (Jan. 1970): 47–52; 2, no. 2 (July 1970): 23–34, esp. part 4.
60. For the Pennsylvania bank barn see: Charles H. Dornbusch and John K. Heyl, *Pennsylvania German Barns* (Allentown: Pennsylvania German Folklore Society, 1958); Alfred L. Shoemaker, ed., *The Pennsylvania Barn* (Kutztown: Pennsylvania Folklife Society, 1959); Henry Glassie, "The Pennsylvania Barn in the South, Part Two," *Pennsylvania Folklife* 15, no. 6 (Summer 1966): 12–25.
61. James Walton, "Upland Houses: The Influence of Mountain Terrain on British Folk Building," *Antiquity* 30, no. 119 (Sept. 1956): 144.
62. Sidney Oldall Addy, *The Evolution of the English House* (London: Swan Sonnenschien, 1898), pp. 69–74; Seebohm, *The Evolution of the English Farm,* pp. 282–328; P. Smith, "The Long-House and the Laithe-House: A Study of the House-and-Byre Homestead in Wales and the West Riding," in Idris Ll. Foster and L. Alcock, eds., *Culture and Environment* (London: Routledge and Kegan Paul, 1963), pp. 415–37; Christopher Stell, "Pennine Houses: An Introduction," *Folk Life* 3 (1965): 16, 20–21; Barley, *The English Farmhouse and Cottage,* pp. 110–12; Iowerth C. Peate, *The Welsh House, a Study in Folk Culture* (Liverpool: Hugh Evans, 1946), pp. 51–84; Alwyn D. Rees, *Life in a Welsh Countryside* (Cardiff: University of Wales Press, 1950), pp. 47–51; Caoimhin Ó Danachair, "The Combined Byre-and-Dwelling in Ireland," *Folk Life* 2 (1964): 58–74; I. F. Grant, *Highland Folk Ways* (London: Routledge and Kegan Paul, 1961), pp. 75, 145, 150; Hans Schwab, "Das Bauernhaus in der Schweiz," *Schweizerisches Archiv für Volkskunde* 31, no. 3–4 (1931): 177–78. A very important study with relevance to this topic is Richard Weiss, *Häuser und Landschaften der Schweiz* (Erlenbach, Zurich, and Stuttgart: Eugen Rentsch, 1959), especially the fourth and fifth sections; see also Adolph Spamer, *Hessische Volkskunst* (Jena: Eugen Diedrichs, 1939), pp. 20, 24–25; Heinrich Götzger and Helmut Prechter, *Das Bauernhaus in Bayern* (Munich: Callwey, 1960), pp. 81–180.
63. Richard W. E. Perrin, "German Timber Farmhouses in Wisconsin," *Wisconsin Magazine of History* 44, no. 3 (Spring 1961): 199–202; and the same scholar's " 'Fachwerkbau' Houses in Wisconsin," *Journal of the Society of Architectural Historians* 18, no. 1 (Mar. 1959): 29–33; Don Yoder, ed., "The Pennsylvania Sketchbooks of Charles Leseur," *Pennsylvania Folklife* 16, no. 2 (Winter 1966–67): 34; Shoemaker, *The Pennsylvania Barn,* p. 9.
64. Murtagh, *Moravian Architecture and Town Planning,* p. 23.
65. A. L. F. Rivet, *Town and Country in Roman Britain* (London: Hutchinson, 1966), pp. 39–40, 43, 108–21.
66. Hermann Kallbrunner, "Farms and Villages: The European Pattern," *Landscape* 6, no. 3 (Spring 1957): 13–17.

67. H. S. Bennett, *Life on the English Manor: A Study of Peasant Conditions, 1150–1400* (Cambridge: Cambridge University Press, 1962), chap. 2.
68. John W. Reps, *Town Planning in Frontier America* (Princeton: Princeton University Press, 1969), pp. 3, 66, 68, 89, 92, 147–53, 183, 259, 386.
69. See Sumner Chilton Powell, *Puritan Village: The Formation of a New England Town* (Garden City: Doubleday, 1965); Lowry Nelson, *The Mormon Village: A Pattern and Technique of Land Settlement* (Salt Lake City: University of Utah Press, 1952).
70. E. Estyn Evans, "The Scotch-Irish: Their Cultural Adaptation and Heritage in the American Old West," in E. R. R. Green, ed., *Essays in Scotch-Irish History* (London: Routledge and Kegan Paul, 1969), pp. 73–74, 84–85; Anthony N. B. Garvan, "Proprietary Philadelphia as Artifact," in Oscar Handlin and John Burchard, eds., *The Historian and the City* (Cambridge: MIT Press, 1966), p. 187.
71. Lowry Nelson, *American Farm Life* (Cambridge: Harvard University Press, 1954), chap. 5.
72. Leo Marx, *The Machine in the Garden: Technology and the Pastoral Ideal in America* (New York: Oxford University Press, 1967), p. 43.
73. The phrase is from Wallace Stegner, "The Meaning of Wilderness in American Civilization," in Roderick Nash, ed., *The American Environment* (Reading, Mass.: Addison-Wesley, 1968), p. 194.
74. Nathaniel Butler, quoted in Wayne Andrews, *Architecture, Ambition and Americans: A Social History of American Architecture* (New York: Free Press, 1967), pp. 1–2.
75. Francis E. Hyslop, Jr., trans., *When the Cathedrals Were White* (1947; reprint, New York, Toronto, London: McGraw-Hill, 1964), p. 174.
76. Alan Lomax, *Folk Song Style and Culture* (Washington: American Association for the Advancement of Science, 1968), pp. 99–100.
77. Conrad M. Arensberg and Solon T. Kimball, *Culture and Community* (New York: Harcourt, Brace, and World, 1965), chaps. 11–13.
78. D. H. Lawrence, *Studies in Classic American Literature* (1923; reprint, Garden City, New York: Doubleday, 1953), chap. 1.
79. James Agee, *Let Us Now Praise Famous Men*, ed. Walker Evans (1941; reprint, New York: Ballantine, 1966), pp. 131–33.

Just Folks Designing: Vernacular Designers and the Generation of Form

THOMAS HUBKA

It was once common to sentimentalize vernacular architecture as the product of simple, intuitive people who built as if by instinct, or at least by rote. We can no longer accept the notion that vernacular building is "unselfconscious." It is the product of thought, constructed by intelligent, conscious human beings who generally know what they want and who have methods for achieving it. Consequently we must ask about idea and intention as carefully as in any other aspect of architectural history.

Thomas Hubka's brief article is an admirable summary of this point of view. Hubka carefully distinguishes the vernacular builder's process of design, in which existing models are conceptually taken apart and then reassembled in new buildings, from the professional designer's manner of working, in which elements from disparate sources are combined to solve design problems anew. He characterizes the vernacular architect's process as "preconstrained"; by choosing *to limit architectural ideas to what is available in the local context, the vernacular architect reduces the design task to manageable proportions. Although this mode of composition seems superficially to generate monotonously similar structures, it allows in fact for considerable individuality within its boundaries, permitting the designer to focus on the skillful solution of particular problems rather than on reinventing whole forms. Hubka also observes that the apparent dichotomy between vernacular and professionally trained "modern" designers is mitigated by a reliance by professionals on their own traditions of composition, which are nearly as strong, if less frankly acknowledged, as those of the vernacular builder.*

Folk builders are not often given the status of architectural designers. This is unfortunate because folk builders have rigorous, highly structured design methods for generating and refining spatial form. Although folk design methods differ from those employed by modern architectural designers, their object is the same—the conversion of ideas into spatial form.

The fundamental principles of folk or vernacular design methods are embodied in tradition. In order to understand the folk design method one must understand how architectural forms are generated within a system of thought dominated by tradition. By working within tradition the folk designer explores a much narrower design field than a modern designer, but he is no less creative than his modern counterpart. His creative method, however, is different.

The intent of this paper is to outline the general strategy by which folk builders design structures. It is my hope that an understanding of the design methods of these architects will provide a valuable means of enriching our own methods of form generation in architecture. The hypotheses of this paper are an extension of my research of folk builders in northern New England.[1]

Misconceptions about Folk Design Method

Folk builders are also folk designers. Since most vernacular architectural scholarship tends to focus attention on buildings (often because the designers are either anonymous or deceased) it is not surprising that the design skills of these architects should remain largely unrecorded. When a design method is allowed to folk builders, it is often couched in explanations amounting to naturalistic determinism—as if these people, like birds, naturally make shelter.[2] Although no serious study of folk architecture could negate the design role of folk builders, the myth of the spontaneous vernacular builder seems to be an idea with wide acceptance in our culture, especially among architectural designers.

It seems important to begin this study by outlining a group of pervasive misconceptions about folk architecture before analyzing the design method of its builder.

MYSTICAL CAUSATION

The myth of naturalistic determinism is sometimes perpetrated by the strongest advocates for vernacular studies. Bernard Rudofsky's charming and energetic books are typical of many surface investigations of vernacular architecture[3]—strong on exotic images and weak on critical analysis of building and design method. While studies like these are well-intentioned, they actually serve to diminish the real accomplishments of vernacular builders by ascribing to their designs and buildings misconceptions about their purpose and method, such as the exaggerated notion of intuitive (divine?) genius and methodologies amounting to mystical causation. Consequently the reader is left with pretty pictures but no explanation for how vernacular buildings were designed.

HISTORICAL ELITISM

Vernacular architecture examples have always suffered the neglect of the architectural history establishment, and it is no surprise that the design method of vernacular builders would also go unnoticed and unrecorded. Even when scholarship is directed at vernacular examples, it usually assumes the elitist metaphor: high style leaders and folk followers.[4] This platonic model hypothesizes that folk designers merely copy, often crudely, the forms of high style or elite architecture. Although there are good folk architectural investigations to suggest otherwise,[5] the general acceptance of this model has often prevented a serious appraisal of folk design method. (Folk and elite architecture overlap on many levels and influences occur both ways, but certainly not only one way.)

Folk designers have seldom been granted design method because most researchers have failed (or never attempted) to place a human designing mind behind these structures and failed to see folk architecture as the product of real people making real design decisions. Frequently this neglect can be traced to a contemporary desire to perceive folk architecture through a narrow aesthetic or moralistic filter, to confirm hypotheses about simple life styles, pure unadorned forms, or holistic-naturalistic environments.

PRIMITIVE SOCIETIES

In most architectural definitions, primitive architectural examples would be placed at one end of a vast folk-vernacular architecture scale. Although today primitive buildings make up only a very small and exotic portion of vernacular architecture examples, they are usually given a disproportionate emphasis in the total spectrum of vernacular buildings worldwide.

Vernacular architecture is found in all the world's cultures; ancient and modern, and, most important, it continues throughout the world today in various relationships to modern world culture—certainly not only the most primitive relationship. Many vernacular cultures exist in some relationship to a larger, or dominant culture—as do all American folk cultures today.

The application of the word *primitive* to vernacular architectural studies is unfortunate because it tends to imply that vernacular cultures are stagnant and unchanging. This is particularly unfortunate because it tends to mask and fossilize the generative design method of its builders.

UNSELFCONSCIOUS DESIGNERS

Most contemporary architectural writers have used or implied the term *unselfconscious* to describe vernacular design and building practices. (Christopher Alexander's book *Notes on the Synthesis of Form* has been one of the most influential in this respect.) While the term is a productive means to exaggerate the weaknesses in contemporary design process (the gap between design method and building practice today) it has come to imply a naive spontaneity about the working methods of vernacular designers and tends to conceal the thinking and designing mind behind the architecture called vernacular.

Vernacular building method is unselfconscious only to the degree that the design system is not articulated in drawings or written words, and is not continuously analyzed by its practitioners. It is, however, a systematic method of design facilitated by a highly structured, traditional mental language (or architectural grammar). The tacitly accepted notion of the unselfconscious designer is a major stumbling block in the path toward understanding vernacular builders as designers with real methods of going about designing and building.

THE OWNER AND THE DESIGNER

One of the most pervasive misconceptions about folk architecture is the myth of the spontaneous owner-builder. In the majority of Indo-European vernacular societies, where information is available, the frequently complex building traditions are maintained by highly trained individuals in their societies (called architects by our own standards). It is easy to misinterpret the role of folk builders because in many societies the owner or occupant is also an active participant in the building process. Unfortunately this collective building practice tends to conceal the fundamentally important role of the vernacular builder as designer. The widespread acceptance of this notion has the obvious side effect of belittling the creative design abilities of folk builders by making their contribution seem insignificant or available to just about anyone in the society.

Purpose and Method in Folk Design

Folk design method is circumscribed by habit and tradition. In order to understand this method, folk design process must be analyzed according to the way "thinking traditionally" structures the designer's approach to problem solving. From a modern perspective, a design strategy relying on tradition and habit might seem like a poor method for creative problem solving and form generation, but this is probably only because contemporary designers have often selected change or the search for new form as a starting point for design study. Folk designers start with the unchanging and accommodate change. They are not less creative than contemporary designers; they just create differently.

TRADITION

Folk design method is carried exclusively in the human mind and maintained within its culture by tradition—the handing down of information by word of mouth, observation, replication, and apprenticeship. It is distinguished from modern design process because it is a nonliterary method of design that stores its complex traditions, not in treatises and drawings, but in the minds of its builders. To understand this method one must be prepared to hypothesize about the way the human mind works to transform tradition into complex architectural designs.

The folklorist Henry Glassie has developed several models for interpreting the design methods of folk builders. By borrowing theory from linguistic philosophy, semiology, anthropology, and folklore, he has constructed models for understanding the generative aspects of the human mind within traditional thinking.[6] In his interpretations an abstracted mental language of basic rules and relationships is manipulated by the folk designer according to cultural principles encoded in the traditional building method. This system is transformed and manipulated by the folk builder according to generative rules similar to those of language acquisition and creation (where finite means produce infinite variety). The mental language that defines the folk designer's rules of competence—the folk building tradition—is seen as a kind of highly abstracted architectural grammar, or schemata, which codifies habitualized responses or typical reaction to a situation. The mental language or schema structure used by folk builders should not be seen as mental pictures or symbols of houses or doorways, but ideas abstracted far beyond representation and symbolizing fundamental ideas in culture. It is important to emphasize that this explanation is no more, but no less, than a model for understanding how habit and tradition are reinforced and manipulated in the human mind. Without a model such as this one for understanding traditional thought it would be difficult to interpret folk design method, because folk builders design in their minds.

FORM GENERATION

Folk builders share a common strategy for generating design ideas that can be described as a continuous process of composition and decomposition within a vocabulary of existing building forms (fig. 1). Folk designers operate in a narrow, culturally defined field of possibility that is structured by tradition. This field consists largely of the existing building examples available to each builder and the design repertoire contained within each builder's particular tradition. (Of course, modern designers

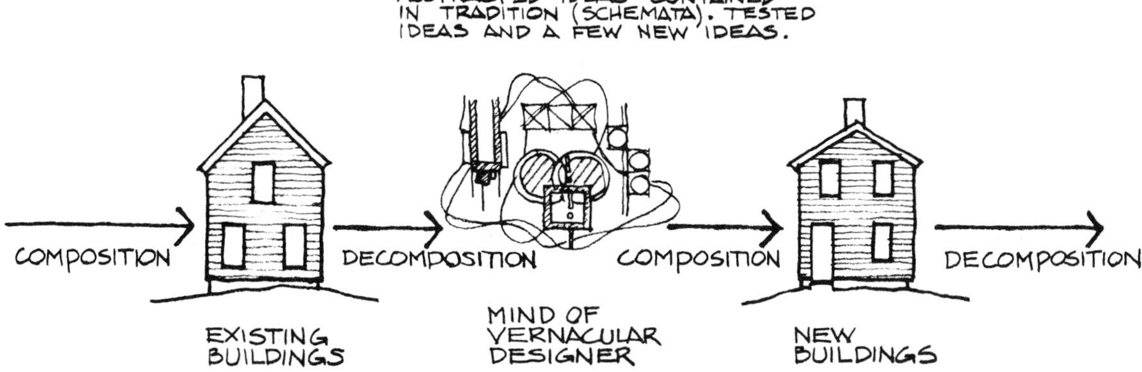

Figure 1. The generative process in the vernacular design method.

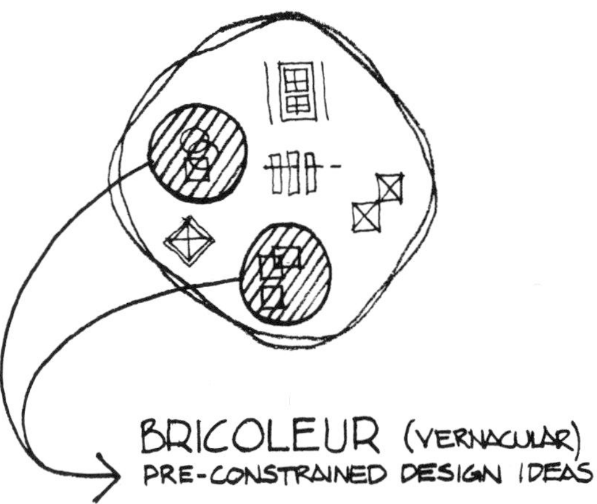

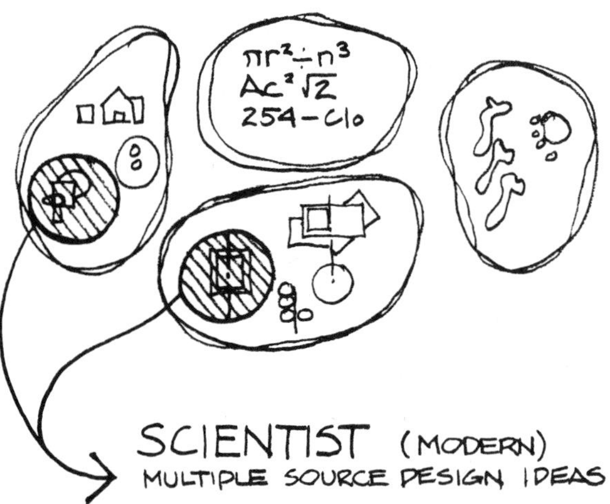

Figure 2. A comparison of the design ideas available to the vernacular and the modern designer.

also work within a limited personal and culturally defined field, but the quantitative difference is significant.)

Folk designers solve design problems by relying on past precedent, but it is inaccurate to say that they merely copy old forms. It is more accurate to say that they generate design ideas by disassembling or decomposing existing forms and composing new forms out of the abstracted ideas of bits and pieces of existing forms. The folk designer accomplishes change by reordering the hierarchy of ideas (schemata) contained within the known grammar or tradition of existing structures. In the folk system, new forms are conservatively generated out of old forms and old ideas, while in modern design practice new forms may be generated from both old and new forms and ideas. To use Lévi-Strauss's terms the *bricoleur* (handyman) or folk designer works within a severely limited field of preconstrained ideas derived from existing buildings while the *scientist* or modern designer is free to go beyond the constraints of the context or building tradition and manipulate theoretically unlimited design explorations (fig. 2).[7] The folk builders' dependence on the existing context and tradition for design ideas is what fundamentally distinguishes this mode of design from more modern or scientific approaches.

The distinction between the folk design mind and the modern design mind extends to the very nature of the ideas they consider. To use Lévi-Strauss's distinction again, the folk designer operates with a finite world of ideas and signs structured by the physical world and preconstrained by the local building tradition. The modern designer, however, operates in an infinite world of ideas and abstract concepts that have an unlimited capacity to hold new forms and ideas. While both design minds rely on abstract thought to manipulate ideas, the modern designer's use of abstracted concepts to stand for unlimited associations is a qualitative difference of great importance.

Advantages to the Folk Design Method

At first glance the benefits of the modern design method seem overwhelming, but the plodding folk turtle has some persistent advantages over the quick modern rabbit. One commonly recognized advantage of the folk method of design is the benefits of a narrower field of design exploration (it may even be argued that what designers primarily do is to impose limits on the design field to make problems manageable). By choosing to operate within tradition, the folk designer's real problems are small and manageable, but not insignificant. Since the traditional buildings are summaries of problems already solved, the folk designer is free to focus design attention on areas that need repair or change. This is the type of misfit problem solving strategy that theorists like Christopher Alexander have in mind when they speak of the repair of the existing environment.[8]

The structure of folk design method allows for a significant degree of individual interpretation and variety. Common to most folk method is a strategy of focusing attention on critical areas of design while allowing a variety of individual interpretations in subordinate areas. This design method is characterized by a primary (dependent) and a secondary (independent) design component in which the primary or gross architectural arrangement is rigorously structured while allowing the designer a range of individual design interpretations in the secondary systems. For example, the basic room proportional system and plan arrangement of English and Germanic housing in the New World (the key to the design replication strategy) was steadfastly maintained for hundreds of years in America while the same settlers were relatively free to experiment in various building materials (log, brick, heavy timber, and even sod). The stylistic transformation of the Cape Cod house in northern New England is another example of an unchanging structural organizational system freely interpreted in a wide variety of architectural styles according to the latest fashions and stylistic trends. The strategy of ordered frameworks or grids for accommodating individual variety is often taken up by systems advocates but seldom with as solid a basis for success as long established folk design methods.

Folk designers are often perceived as unimaginative copiers because much of their architecture appears to be simple repetition. It is often assumed that the constraints of traditional design emasculate the individuality or creativity of the folk designer. This is simply not borne out in documentation which suggests that proud, individualistic, creative designers are folk societies' rule—although the folk designer manifests individuality in different ways than contemporary designers. The folk designer simply signs his signature much smaller but by no means less forcefully. This signature is in the details, in the care, and in the craft of building (and while the modern observer might not see this signature you can be sure his contemporaries saw it).

Folk architecture that appears unified, homogeneous, even identical becomes, on closer inspection, rich, diversified, and individualistic. New England barns that seem grossly uniform from the car become, on closer inspection, so diverse that it is risky to generalize about their structural system over even a small country area. Without denying the strong collective uniformity of folk architecture, it is possible to construct a strong case for individuality in the smaller scale based on care, refinement, and craft. The folk designer offers a much-needed interpretation of creativity within an ordering framework or established tradition.

Similarities between Folk and Modern Design Methods

Although the differences might seem extreme, there are basic similarities between the folk design mind and the modern design mind. The most important similarity between these methods is that both have their basis in tradition, although the modern debt to its traditional sources has been seriously undervalued, especially in design education.

Until quite recently contemporary research into creativity and design was dominated by models emphasizing new or unique creation (often these models are used as handmaidens to the contemporary search for new form or uniqueness). This research has not demonstrated the degree to which architects actually rely on this type of creative reasoning in design, nor has it fundamentally addressed the role of replication and tradition in contemporary design practice. The study of folk architecture design with its necessary emphasis on the working of the human mind should lead to a more reasoned assessment of the modern design mind, especially its debt to tradition.

What I find most exciting about the study of folk design method is the relative closeness of this "primitive" method to the way architects actually think and work—the way a modern designer must internalize vast amounts of complex information into symbolic mental grammar; and the vastly underemphasized role of tradition, replication and examples in the architect's creative process. Although the development of this assertion is beyond the scope of this paper, it is the model from vernacular architecture that is most intriguing to me at the present time.

Lessons from Folk Design Method

The folk design method is not a working model of form generation for modern times, nor is it an instant panacea for the problems of contemporary design. It does however offer a tough, thoroughly tested, approach to design that has significant differences to contemporary methods.

The folk design method carries out design according to a nonliterary method based on tradition. It is worth considering simply because it is a design model based on different assumptions about the meaning and purpose of architecture. Since the role of tradition is especially emphasized in folk method and seemingly de-emphasized by modern designers, it is worthy of serious study in order to reevaluate the value of traditional thinking for design. It is, therefore, encouraging to report that vernacular architecture method has no problem integrating tradition with design process. Basic to all vernacular design method is the dominant role of tradition—an entire epistemological structure geared to replication and maintenance of tradition.

The tough message from folk architecture is that its design method is no fluke; it is not a flash-in-the-pan strategy. A case can, and should, be made for folk design method as one of the most pervasive and well-conceived design methods in the history of civilization. The fact that it is not studied by architects as a serious method is indicative of essential differences in purpose and method in folk and modern strategies; and of a lack of understanding of folk design as method. Folk design seems worthy of careful study.

Notes

This article was originally published in the *Journal of Architectural Education* (1979). The illustrations for this article are by the author.

1. Thomas C. Hubka, "The Connected Farm Buildings of Southwestern Maine," *Pioneer America* 9, no. 2 (December 1977): 143–79.
2. Although many books make this basic assumption it is particularly evident in Bernard Rudofsky's *Architecture without Architects: A Short Introduction to Non-Pedigreed Architecture* (New York: Doubleday, 1964).
3. Bernard Rudofsky, *The Prodigious Builders* (New York: Harcourt Brace Jovanovich, 1977), p. 12.
4. See, for example, Wilbur Zelinsky, "The New England Connecting Barn," *Geographical Review* 48, no. 4 (October 1958): 540–53.
5. See, for example, Henry Glassie, "The Variation of Concepts within Tradition: Barn Building in Otsego County, New York," in *Man and Cultural Heritage: Papers in Honor of Fred B. Kniffen*, ed. H. J. Walker and W. G. Haag, Geoscience and Man (Baton Rouge: Louisiana State University School of Geoscience, 1974), 5:177–235.
6. Henry Glassie, *Folk Housing in Middle Virginia: A Structural Analysis of Historic Artifacts* (Knoxville: University of Tennessee Press, 1975).
7. Claude Lévi-Strauss, *The Savage Mind* (Chicago: University of Chicago Press, 1966), p. 16.
8. Christopher Alexander, *Notes on the Synthesis of Form* (Cambridge: Harvard University Press, 1968), p. 50.

Vernacular Building and Victorian Architecture: Midwestern American Farm Homes

FRED W. PETERSON

Like Alan Gowans and Thomas Hubka, Fred W. Peterson is concerned in the following essay with the local character of vernacular building; however, Peterson looks beyond the local context as well to ask what influence architectural ideas from outside had on vernacular traditions. He is particularly interested in the architectural style books that appeared in growing numbers from the 1830s. These were intended to "reform" the tastes of ordinary Americans by showing them the errors of traditional ways. Peterson assesses the success of these arguments by comparing the midcentury treatises with a group of standing buildings in Minnesota. He concludes that a "practical wisdom" embodied in local building traditions developed from the farmer's experience produced a method of architectural composition that, in contrast to the integrated design methods advocated in the books, proceeded additively, with little concern for an end result that resembled any single current architectural style. But the alternative to fashionable emulation was not a shapeless nonentity. Despite the fundamental difference of approach from that of the urban professional, it is clear that Midwestern vernacular builders did work with an eye for appearance that often gave their products a pleasing aspect. As final evidence of the operation of a vernacular aesthetic, Peterson notes that his examples represent the most popular forms among twelve basic formal types of farm house designs that can be found in Minnesota. If they were not impressed by the arguments of professional arbiters of architectural taste, Minnesota's late nineteenth-century builders did have a visual ideal of their own.

Art historians tend to treat only the large and ostentatious examples of Victorian architectural styles and relegate to limbo the more commonplace and simple structures of the vernacular tradition of American building. Cultural geographers have investigated aspects of the vernacular farm home, but they have concentrated upon external features of these structures in order to document the dissemination of various kinds of farm houses or analyze the evolution of a particular type of farm house in a given region. No study has been made that attempts a thorough treatment of the farm home as a distinctive and significant generic art form. Some urgency prompts the beginnings of such a study because of the disappearance of primary source materials. Because of urban growth, freeway construction, and large acreage agribusiness that absorbs the small family farm, many nineteenth-century farm houses are gone from the rural landscape. The preservation of local and family history becomes more difficult with the passing of each generation and the dispersion of photographic and written documents that comprise family memorabilia. The nineteenth-century American farm home is a vanishing phenomenon that merits recognition and evaluation as a significant part of American architecture and culture.[1]

The second half of the nineteenth century in America saw one of the greatest building booms this nation has experienced. From elaborate mansions on the east coast to claim shanties on the western frontier, from multistoried steel frame commercial buildings in Chicago to the false front clapboard general stores of rural towns, the variety and richness of the era is documented in a full range of architectural styles, building types, methods, and materials. During this period when the frontier was rhetorically celebrated as the Garden of Eden and when the frontier was actually settled, the midwestern American farm home came into being as the result of a complex interplay of cultural, environmental, economic, and ethnic factors. On the one hand, the dominant Anglo-Saxon aesthetic and ethic established ideals of soundness, stability, picturesque beauty, and sentiment as necessary qualities of the American home. On the other hand, the yeoman confronted realities of the new land and created a homestead according to standards of economy and expediency. Utilizing the efficient and economical balloon frame structural system, the rural homes that these new Americans built constituted a separate and distinct aesthetic which is quite different from that fostered by the professional architect of the period. It seems a significant task to discern the essential traits of this vernacular style of building. The qualities of that style may lie half concealed beneath a superficial frosting of decoration or may be clearly revealed in the simple unadorned units of the nineteenth-century farm home.

The prevailing architectural taste of the period was formed by architects of English origin or allegiance. The revival styles that they promulgated in America were those that were initially accepted and practiced among the educated and wealthy in England. From midcentury to the 1890s, first and subsequent editions of plan books supplied the American family or builder with numerous styles of pictorial designs and practical specifications to aid in the realization of a substantial home. When the economy of the nation was expansive, large quantities of such building guides reached the market to meet the demands of the building boom. Only during the Civil War, the depression of the 1870s, and the disappearance of the frontier in the 1890s did the publication of these architectural plan books decrease.[2]

First among those authors to preach the need of an appropriate style for domestic life was Andrew Jackson Downing. As one of the most influential theorists and planners, Downing did not ignore the significance of the farm home as central to the physical and moral well-being of the yeoman and his family. In *The Architecture of Country Houses* he devoted the sixth section of the work to six plans for farm homes. The plans and elevations for these houses are relatively simple when compared to the other projects for thirteen cottages and twenty-three country villas that were also included in the volume. Of the proposed farm homes, some are German, English, Swiss, or Gothic in origin. The single design labeled "American" is a simplification of an English plan from John Claudius Loudon. Downing seemed to believe that there was no American style for the farm home and offered a single model for this building type to suit his romantic conception of the virtuous yeoman and to establish an ideal of domestic architecture for the farm that would exceed merely simple and expedient measures of building.[3]

Figure 1. American bracketed farm house, 1848. (From A. J. Downing, The Architecture of Country Houses *[New York: Dover Publications, 1967], figure 70.)*

Downing's image of the American farmer was that of "the man of nature—more sincere, more earnest than men of any other class." "His dwelling ought to suggest simplicity, honesty of purpose, frankness, a hearty genuine spirit of goodwill . . . the true farmer despises affectation; he loves a blunt and honest expression of the truth." The farmer's home, therefore, "should be frank, genuine, and open-hearted like its owner" and wear no borrowed ornaments from any class of different habits and tastes.[4]

Because the farmer's house would be built in the expanse of the countryside, its proportions should be broad and ample. A large porch of a simple design should reflect the manly work of the farmer as well as sincere hospitality. The roof of the home should be high and wide because it sheltered a large family and covered large stores of nature's gifts of harvest. Many chimneys should break the profile of the roofline to indicate the warm-hearted reception one would receive inside the home at the hearth and the table. This rustic and plain style of building was intended to reflect a class of Americans who were preoccupied with the practical rather than the fine arts.

Many of Downing's designs were realized by Alexander J. Davis, a professionally trained architect. These designs were picturesque rather than plain and frequently were derived from elements of Swiss and English rural homes and the Gothic style (fig. 1). Although it may seem strange that Downing (and Davis) sought to house such a genuine American pioneer in a structure of medieval or European style, the desire to create a dwelling that would reflect its environment explains the choice of styles. The countryside was considered picturesque. The simple forms of the neoclassical style or the fundamental simplicity of a vernacular structure would clash with such an environment, but the irregular and varied filigree elaborations of the Gothic style or the rusticated qualities of rural Swiss and English homes would provide patterns that would repeat and reflect the picturesque elements perceived in nature.

In his love of picturesque beauty, Downing rejected the classical style of the Federal period. He was also deeply concerned about the apparent lack of architectural taste among the rural population. He lamented the kind of farm homes that were plain rectangles with purely functional roofs, doors, and windows. These homes, he claimed, were devoid of taste and expressed nothing more than a need for shelter. Further, he considered it false to label such simple farm homes as true architecture because they lacked the element of true sentiment that gave romantic meaning to man's endeavors. Downing intended to find that which was architecturally appropriate for each situation in life and for each class of persons in society whether they lived in sophisticated urban centers of the nation or on the developing frontier.

A desire to classify and codify what was considered proper and improper was a trait common to Victorian architects. Appropriate building on the frontier was considered extremely important because sound, stable, and tastefully executed homes were believed to reflect secure family values and reveal the level of civilized life established on the edge of the wilderness. Those who desired to see the vast spaces and resources of the nation settled and developed viewed the wilderness as a negative reality that should be transformed from a savage to a civilized state. The creation of a pastoral environment (consistent with picturesque modes of perception) was believed to be the suitable stage for the nurture of sound civilized values, for the pastoral afforded an escape from the over-sophisticated forms of the city and protected one from the savage qualities of the wilderness. Central to the realization of this Eden-like vision was the creation of the appropriate landscape and architectural environment that would reveal the social and moral values that transcend the basic physical needs of man.

The "Bracketed American Farm House" was Downing's (and Davis's) offering for such an ideal environment (fig. 1). The design of the home was an attempt to present a "more blunt and honest expression of the truth." Although the dwelling exhibits the rural traits that Downing prized, such as broad proportions, large and simple porch, high roof line broken by chimneys, and absence of borrowed ornament, the house is essentially a simplification and slight modification of a farm home he proposed in "the English Rural Style." Like other Americans, Downing was dependent upon English or European prototypes of architectural building styles when attempts were made to create an American mode in the arts. The floor plan proposes spaces for the practical aspects of farm life and supplies as many as five bedrooms for a large rural family. The overall dimensions of the home are 40′ × 55′—a space to be enclosed by a mortise-and-tenon frame of heavy timbers and covered with vertical boards on the exterior. Estimated cost of the project without furnishing was given from $1,676 to $2,000.[5]

Downing's concern for the absence of the established taste evident in the plain masses of many farm homes of 1850 was repeated and amplified by professional architects in following decades. These planners labeled such farm homes as plain, simple, cheap, nondescript, or ugly. In many plan books of the period, projects were offered for the remodeling of such architectural blunders. Henry Hudson Holly in *Country Seats* lamented that such remodeling projects were the most difficult that confronted the architect, because he must develop "harmony out of discord, beauty out of ugliness, elegance out of the commonplace." Like Downing, Holly attempted to attain that quality called *sentiment* that refined and elevated the home and those who inhabited it. In Holly's judgment, the simple vernacular or "carpenter's" architecture could not attain that quality. To Holly and his contemporaries educated in Victorian taste, the unadorned functional object, tool, or home was perceived as lacking beauty.[6]

The picturesque styles that were fostered by the professional architects embodied a way of seeing that made itself manifest in a way more pervasive than the pictorial effects of the home. The proliferation of images of the proper and stylish home during the second half of the nineteenth century established the picturesque dwelling as an essential element of an expanding but cultured and civilized nation that was based upon sound family life and established taste. In addition to the architectural plan books, journals on etiquette frequently included sections that visually instructed the reader in the virtues of the picturesque. Through repeated rhetoric and contrasting images, the lesson was clear that the picturesque as the proper style offered visual variety and interest as well as vitality and promise.

From the vantage point of the dominant Anglo-Saxon ethic, those who did not achieve what was portrayed as the proper lifestyle were believed to be not only unfortunate but somehow physically, mentally, and morally incapable of an acceptable place in society. This insidiously discriminatory ethic, set in the categories of social Darwinism, provided a competitively based morality to justify an ostentatious life style. Those who could not or would not assimilate the Anglo-Saxon ethic were condemned and relegated to an appropriately wretched state within the categories of this social morality. Victorian guides to etiquette either implied or clearly stated the qualities of different life styles resulting from inherited traits and acquired virtues that determined success or failure in life. Morality was considered to be not an individual affair; virtue was also a social and national concern especially when related to domestic architecture.[7]

Examples of such public concern for the proper domestic environment for the farmer can also be discovered in the agriculture journals of the period. In 1879 *The Independent Farmer and Fireside Companion* published images and commentary to encourage the virtuous yeoman to achieve an acceptable domestic environment. Through a striking contrast, the remarkable transformation from an original homestead to a miniature Versailles visualizes an admirable, if not miraculous, establishment of culture, morality, and material well-being on the American frontier. This achievement was described as a result of hard work, discipline, and refinement of taste. The regularity of each structure, garden, orchard, fountain, and field reflects a resolute desire to establish order and civilized values on the edge of the wilderness.[8]

These crusades to convert an existing building type and architectural style to the fold of acceptable taste and redeeming life style give ample evidence of the existence of the apparently lost souls of domestic environments—that is, the vernacular. Despite earnest rhetoric and vivid illustrative materials used by the aesthetically educated, vernacular building in the nineteenth century persisted. Based upon experience rather than theory, established upon frugality rather than riches, the simple, plain structures of the nineteenth-century farm home document a set of values and practices that resulted in a distinct and relatively different architectural style from the complexities and varieties of the revival fashions.

In the agricultural journals of the period one can discover scattered statements made by farmers who articulated some principles upon which the building of a home and farm were based. As early as 1839 *The Cultivator* of Albany, New York, published a floor plan for a farm home submitted by a farmer who offered primarily practical advice on building. The effort was praised by Solon Robinson, who recognized on the basis of his own experience on the frontier that practical and economic factors had to be considered before aesthetic factors when building on the edge of the wilderness.

Robinson was a pioneer in Indiana in 1830. During the 1840s he wrote articles on various topics for *The Cultivator, The Plough,* and *The American Agriculturist* and from 1853 to 1880 was the agricultural editor for the *New York Tribune.* He articulated an orientation toward the farm home that stood in opposition to the professional architect and planner. His response to the published plan in *The Cultivator* in 1839 was to submit the plan of his own large log cabin in northeastern Indiana with the suggestion

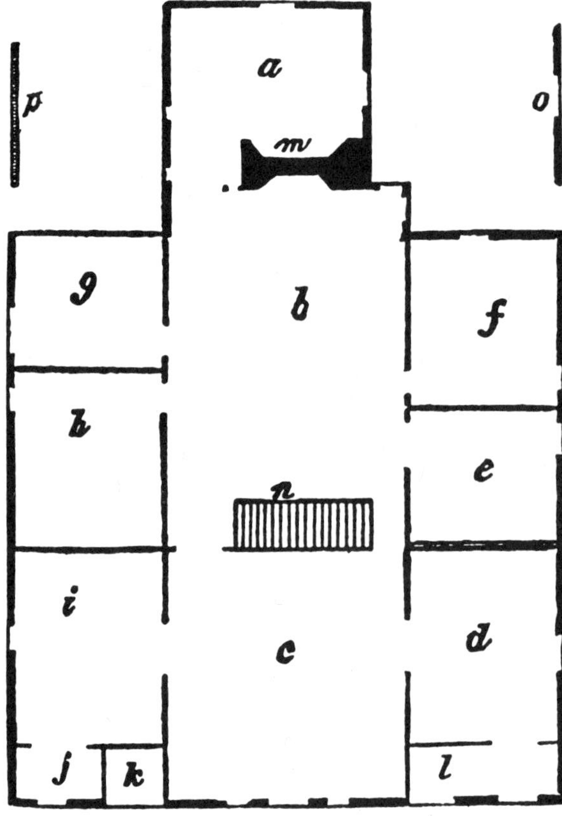

Figure 2. A cheap farm house. (From Solon Robinson, American Agriculturist *5 [February 1846]: figures 11, 12.)*

that "comfort and convenience should never be dispensed with by the farmer for show." His plan for "A Cheap Farm House" was published in February 1846 (fig. 2). The comments that accompanied the plan recognized the "high character and adaptability of Mr. Downing's works," but they suited only the "upper ten thousand" of the rural population and did not serve the wants of the lower "ten hundred thousand." Robinson's farm home was to be constructed in the economic and efficient balloon frame method rather than the heavy mortice-and-tenon system used by Downing and other architects. Robinson's plan was to be realized in stages when the farm family could afford additions to the house. A modest room measuring 13′ × 13′ provided the initial shelter until the entire home could be completed to the ample dimensions of 36′ × 53′. Although Robinson did not provide the total cost of the home, it can be estimated that it would not have cost more than $1,000.[9]

Other farmers submitted plans of and opinions on farm homes to these agricultural journals. These rural offerings consistently expressed a practical and economic point of view. A New York state farmer was critical of plans printed in *The Cultivator* that necessitated a $2,000 to $3,000 expenditure. He requested projects within the range of $1,000 and suggested eliminating paint from the building budget because he had lived in a farm home for fifty-nine years that had not been painted. "Let paint, therefore, be set down to taste, not to profit."[10]

The categories of economy, utility or convenience, and comfort provided the basis for the practical home builder on the farm. These were the criteria most often used by farmers who submitted plans and comments to agricultural periodicals during the second half of the nineteenth century. Concern for creating an image of cultivated taste in the categories of the picturesque irregularities of plan and elevation of the home were absent. These periodicals did, however, print many articles and plans for farm homes that were contributed by professional architects. Accepting the farmers' practical orientation, the editors of these journals also felt the

Figure 3. The J. C. Hutchins Farm House, Pope County, Minnesota. (Courtesy of the Pope County Historical Museum, Glenwood, Minnesota.)

need to educate the taste of their rural subscribers and to encourage the acquisition of some culture beyond the purely expedient measures according to which the majority of farmers built and furnished their homes.[11]

A practical wisdom about building developed from the experience of the farmer in meeting daily needs in a direct and practical manner. The values that grew out of such experience were manifest in the farm home whether that home was the result of a single building project or the product of generations. The J. C. Hutchins House (fig. 3) is a typical example in which the final structure of the home was the result of successive stages of building. Hutchins homesteaded in Minnesota in 1861 and built a log cabin to meet minimal shelter needs for his family of seven. That cabin was destroyed in 1862 during the Sioux Indian uprising. After returning from the sanctuary of a nearby town, Hutchins built the cabin seen on the far left of the photograph. Through the next three decades he enlarged the house until it took the form of a telescoped T-plan. Two log units climaxed in the balloon frame unit on the far right. The home grew according to a simple additive process with minimal, if any, projected concern to achieve the appearance of an established architectural style of the period. Dormers and the chimneys break the roof line, two larger units of the home create cross gables, and a bay window adorns the southern facade of the balloon frame unit. These are elements of professional Victorian buildings, but here these structural qualities and elements are also the result of economy and expediency in construction. The dormers enlarge space and provide illumination beneath low ceilings on the second floor, the chimneys serve the heating sources and cooking stoves, and the cross gable structure was the most effective way to join the smaller to the larger unit in order to align interior spaces. The bay window is a peculiar four-sided affair made of standard sash units set into a frame that is tacked on rather than integrated into the facade. The window hardly affords vignette views into a picturesque garden. Other window sizes follow no regular proportions. The second story window on the center of the wall to the far right is the largest and illuminates a stairwell. Other windows appear when structure and interior space allow and necessitate such openings.

Expediency and economy not only determined the size, materials, and spatial division of the home, but also its placement on the building site. A grove of trees protected the home from northwesterly winds during bitterly cold winters. The southern facade of the home remained exposed to the sun for warmth in winter and cooling winds in the hot summers. The wood supply near the house allowed easy access to fuel from the protected side of the house during winter storms. The makeshift appearance of the home and surroundings is misleading. Efficiency and survival determined the lives of these people, not surface appearance in a display of fashion. The home developed from experience and necessity, not from externally acquired axioms and laws of architectural design. Few pioneers surpassed this level of lifestyle and environment except to utilize in their own way the industrially produced lumber to construct homes according to the balloon frame method.

In response to the critical labels given to vernacular buildings, people did not erect any kind of structure that was "plain" or "nondescript" in the absolute sense. If one were to imagine such a building, it would lack all elements of design and exist as a geometric cube, totally unadorned and unarticulated. Illustrations of such nonpicturesque designs in architectural plan books did approach such ultimate simplicity but these were fictitious exaggerations used to make the professionally remodeled home appear more elaborate and stylish.

The photograph of the Syver Ellingson farm home documents the structure when it was in mint condition about 1890 (figs. 4, 5). Although the house reveals a unity of design and appearance, it was constructed in two phases. The unit to the far right and the central portion of the structure initially provided the family with a kitchen, pantry, dining room, and bedrooms. The wing on the left added a parlor, porch, and another bedroom.[12]

The Ellingson House may lack picturesque variety in appearance, but it does not lack unity of design. The proportioned whole derived from the size of the balloon frame members lends itself to a clear articulation of units through the horizontal and vertical divisions of the simple planar walls. The window and door frames as well as the end boards and eave boards are painted a dark earth color to create a clear and sharp delineation of the several functional and decorative units of the exterior. The eye can easily perceive and appreciate the height and width of the entire structure as well as the measured placement of windows and doors. Decoration is not added to the design (except in the minor filigree units on the porch) but is an element that arises from the nature of the structure itself and the straightforward manner in which it was put together. The end boards and the eave boards were used because they were efficient and effective ways to finish and seal extremities of walls and turn corners with the clapboard siding. The function of these structural units does not in any way distract from the subtle and sufficient way that they decorate and clarify the structure of the house.

One can imagine the builders of the home calculating the dimensions of the entire structure and carefully measuring each piece of lumber so that economy and ease of construction would be achieved. There is inherent in such a process not only a thorough rational analysis of means to an end but also a wisdom derived from much experience of construction with wood. Through a fruitful combination of reason and experience, the elements of the home design fall naturally into place; the window levels and the height of the porch reveal the taller height of the ground floor rooms in relation to those of the upper story. The horizontality of the clapboard siding and simple lines of the roof sug-

Figure 4. The Syver Ellingson Farm Home, Grant County, Minnesota. Built ca. 1890. (Courtesy of the Grant County Historical Museum, Elbow Lake, Minnesota.)

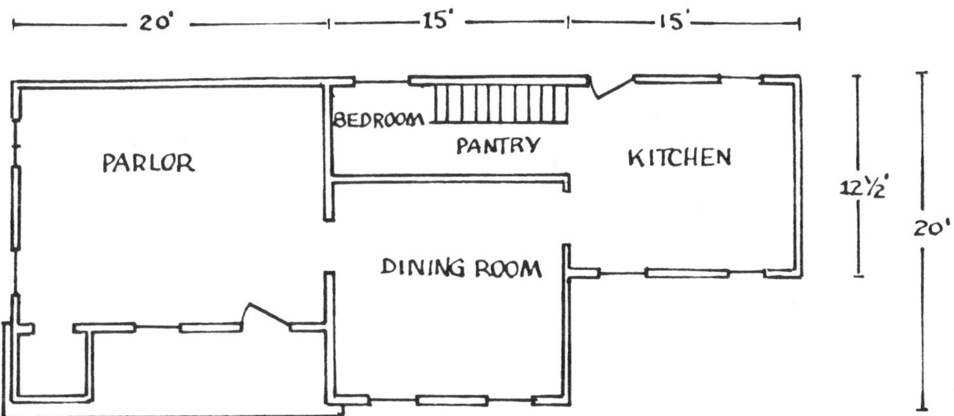

Figure 5. Plan of the Syver Ellingson Farm Home. (Drawing by the author.)

Figure 6. The Sanford Olson Farm Home, Pope County, Minnesota. Built 1881–1895. (Photograph by the author.)

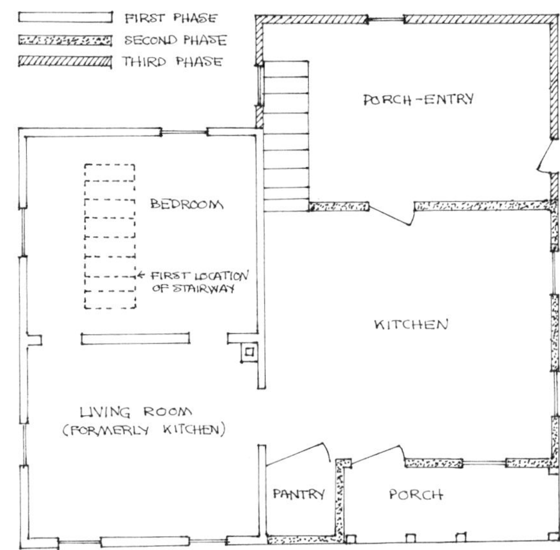

Figure 7. Plan of the Sanford Olson Farm Home. (Drawing by the author.)

gest the ample but not ostentatious extension of the structure into its site. The full clear sunlight that sharply etches in shadow the basic volumes of the house also creates a regular and simple pattern over the clapboard. The Ellingson home may not be a Parthenon of the plains, but it does possess in its plan and elevation the qualities of a straightforward and intelligent creation.

Another typical example of vernacular building is the Sanford Olson farm home (figs. 6, 7). The front view of the structure bears a likeness to Downing's "Bracketed American Farm House" (fig. 1). Each has two basic units set at right angles to one another, forming a T- or L-shaped plan. The placement of porch and broken line of the roof and eave are also similar. The Olson home, however, is half the size of Downing's project, was built in three stages, not one, and at a cost of approximately $900, not $1,676 to $2,000. The initial portion of the home, constructed in 1881, measured 22′ × 14′ and cost approximately $400. This balloon frame unit was crowned by a centrally peaked roof and divided into two equal parts containing a kitchen, living room, and two upstairs bedrooms. The bedrooms were reached by a steep staircase placed centrally in the living room. The wing on the right was added approximately a decade later when Olson was married. This unit provided a new kitchen of 14′ × 15′ and freed the former kitchen to become a living or dining room. Two more bedrooms were also added to accommodate the couple and future family. Finally, a rear entrance space was added to enclose a pump and sink and allow separate access to the upstairs bedrooms. A root cellar under the initial unit was the only excavated space beneath the structure.

It would be inaccurate to claim in this and other farm homes discussed here that the farmer or rural carpenter consciously and knowingly aspired toward a norm in which form followed function. It seems true that the farmer did seek convenience and efficiency in a domestic dwelling, but one cannot infer from such goals that building projects were designed according to the sophisticated norm of form following function. No elaborate blueprints or plans predetermined the precise form of the structure. The first unit of the Olson home, for instance, was built without any consciousness of an aesthetic ideal. After the length of the joists for the Olson home were known, the thick foundation of granite could be set in the excavation. Because the home was built on light sandy gravel, the foundation was exaggerated in dimensions to measure 5′ thick at its base and 3′ wide at its top. Upon this foundation the framework of the house rose to form a simple rectangle that was divided in half, fenestrated at equal intervals, and crowned with an economical pointed roof.

Such a simple structure was what Olson could afford and was based, no doubt, upon general conceptions of homes that the farmer had already observed. In the same conservative manner in which the heavy foundation for the house was set, farmers seldom sought innovations in building. They adopted standard construction systems and adapted them to their specific needs. In the Olson home interior spaces could fulfill various functions at different times—a kitchen could become a dining room and a living room could serve as a bedroom. The form of any architectural space did not seem to predestine its function.

The most consistent need exhibited by Olson was for economy expressed in the conservation of money, materials, and labor in building projects. When Olson added the kitchen wing to his home, he situated it so that it related most efficiently to the spaces of the first unit. He also apparently learned that a heavy foundation was not necessary for the light weight of a balloon frame structure and used a base of stone and mortar only 12″ thick as a support for the kitchen wing. There is an essential difference between an approach to building that inductively realizes a building in stages and a method that initially creates a design through blueprint specifications and deduces the form and function of architectural spaces from such an *a priori* standard. The rural builder most often followed the former path to realize his home.

The relationship of the Olson home to its site was primarily practical. Trees mitigated the winter's winds that blew from hills north of the farm site. The drainage of heavy rain and melting snow was achieved by the natural slope of the land toward a small prairie river that flows approximately 1,200 feet west of the house. A supply of fresh, cold water was provided from natural springs that flowed from the base of the hills in several locations. Provisions for the pantry came from a garden that always had water; wild game from the river and hunting places on the farm supplied the family larder. Well-being consisted in adaptation to local conditions rather than the imposition of a predetermined aesthetic or design upon the land.

A sense of place was an important factor in the experience of farm families. The houses themselves fulfilled the basic need of shelter and the simple function of food preparation and storage, eating, and sleeping. One large room (a parlor) when present was used for family and community functions. Here wakes, funerals, weddings, parties, and dances were held. Descriptions by farm families usually recall the quality of life and events that took place in or near their farm homes. Little, if any, attention was given to descriptions of the physical or architectural appearance of the structures themselves. What was vividly remembered were the personal experiences of place that encompassed both the extraordinary and the commonplace.[13]

The Ellingson and Olson homes are not unique. Other farm homes repeat almost identical plans and elevations so as to constitute distinct and separate types of vernacular dwellings. On the basis of geographical surveys, it is possible to identify approximately twelve types of farm homes ranging from one-and-a-half-roomed small rectangular structures to large two-story dwellings. Each house exhibits its own unique variation of roofline, porch, fenestration, or proportion within a type, but each is easily recognized as an example within a type. The Ellingson and Olson homes were chosen for consideration because they are examples of the most prevalent types of farm homes; they also both illustrate and embody an aesthetic quality that is inherent in almost all vernacular structures.[14]

The Ellingson and Olson homes in particular and the others in general were the results of practical wisdom that was an essential ingredient of such a generic tradition of building. If the homes are not picturesque in appearance or in relation to the site, it is because American farmers were not trained in or did not care for the aesthetics of vision. They were schooled in the practical, day-to-day, season-to-season schedule of labors that were best accomplished in the most simple and efficient way. If the farmer's eye was trained at all, it was to sight a straight furrow in a field that was bordered by straight fence lines within the square or rectangle of the homestead farm. He would also visually test the trueness of line in the walls and placement of the outbuildings on his and others' farms.

It was this experience of simple repetition of tasks and appreciation for the correctness and straightness of things that provided a basis for the aesthetics of vernacular building. The formal qualities that exist in vernacular architecture also are evident in the design of tools, utensils, furniture, and machinery that were created and used in the same context of American life. Simplicity, absence of ornament, economy of production and cost, and flexibility in use and adaptation were essentials to this kind of design in the practical arts. The geometric volumes of farm homes created by joining the mass-produced parts of balloon frame construction were not only the results of such a process of easy assembly, but were also expressions of an economy of form consistent with the farmers' experience. The severe and plain appearance of farm homes that grew on the frontier may seem out of place when viewed as the means of realizing the dream of a lush and verdant garden that would rival the richness of Eden. These homes did, however, express an economy of thought and practice necessary to reach goals with a minimum of means and materials. As such the most menial of frontier farm homes reveals more of the American frontier experience than any stylish mansion. The people who settled and developed this land either migrated from the eastern states or immigrated from European nations. The majority of them were farmers or peasants who knew and cared little for a sophisticated taste in architecture.

This article has focused primarily upon social, economic, aesthetic, and environmental factors that have contributed to the formation of a vernacular style in American architecture. Further study is needed to explore various ways that ethnic and traditional values and preferential matters of taste influenced vernacular building. Such factors certainly shaped the types of vernacular building in America from the seventeenth through the nineteenth century, but questions remain unanswered about the ways in which these values and techniques were translated into the new balloon frame construction method after the 1830s. Division and function of interior space, methods of cutting and joining frame members, or type and location of interior and exterior decorative elements may be some areas in which European cultural traits were assimilated into the new building technique. These considerations indicate the exploratory nature of research in a complex historical phenomenon spread over a vast geographical area of the nation. To document and interpret those historical moments when farm houses came into being and functioned as homes for farm families is to recognize a valid and meaningful style that was generated by the untutored and anonymous artists of vernacular building.

Notes

This article was originally published in the *Journal of Interdisciplinary History* (Winter 1982).

1. The primary material upon which this essay focuses is the work of art. In this case it is the farm homes created by the professional architect or the vernacular builder. The literature of historical studies is considered essential to establish the frame of reference in which the farm homes are perceived. The author recognizes that a term as broad and controversial as Victorian culture is used in this essay without extended definition. Sources that have contributed to a historical comprehension of the period are: John Higham, "From Boundlessness to Consolidation: The Transformation of American Culture, 1848–1860" (Ann Arbor: University of Michigan, 1969); Daniel Walker Howe, "American Victorianism as Culture," *American Quarterly* 27, no. 4 (December 1975): 507–32; Howard Mumford Jones, *The Age of Energy: Varieties of American Experience, 1865–1915* (New York: Viking, 1970). For a fuller description of methodology in art history see: Meyer Shapiro, "Style," in *Anthropology Today,* ed. A. L. Kroeber (Chicago: University of Chicago Press, 1953), pp. 287–312.
2. See Henry-Russell Hitchcock, *American Architectural Books: A List of Books, Portfolios, and Pamphlets on Architecture and Related Subjects Published in America before 1895,* new expanded ed. (New York: Da Capo, 1976).
3. John Claudius Loudon, *Encyclopaedia of Cottage, Farm, and Villa Architecture and Furniture* (London: Longman, Rees, Orme, Brown, Green and Longman, 1833). Andrew Jackson Downing was not only familiar with specific plans presented in this larger work, but he also used it as a model for his smaller, simpler *The Architecture of Country Houses* (1850; reprint, New York: Dover, 1969).
4. Andrew Jackson Downing, *Rural Essays,* ed. George William Curtis (1853; reprint, New York: Da Capo, 1974), p. 138; Downing, *Architecture of Country Houses,* p. 139.
5. Compare design 17 and design 18 from Downing, *Architecture of Country Houses.*
6. Henry Hudson Holly, *Holly's Country Seats* (New York: D. Appleton, 1863), pp. 37–38.
7. See Thomas E. Hill, *Never Give a Lady a Restive House* (Berkeley: Diablo Press, 1967), p. 128. Through word and image Hill contrasts the homes of the vicious and the honest, stating that success in life is the result of "inheritance of good brain and physical constitution." Similar visual and verbal contrast appeared in the farm journals of the period to instruct the reader in the relationship between morality and domestic environment.
8. Thomas McLean Newson, ed., *The Independent Farmer and Fireside Companion* (St. Paul, Minn.: St. Paul Independent Farmer and Fireside Companion, 1879), pp. 164, 170.
9. Herbert A. Kellar, ed., *Solon Robinson, Pioneer and Agriculturist* (Indianapolis: Indiana Historical Bureau, 1936), p. 36; Solon Robinson, "Plan of a Western

Prairie Cottage," *The Cultivator* 6 (November 1839): 109; Solon Robinson, "A Cheap Farm House," *American Agriculturist* 5 (February 1846): 57.

10. N. Reed, Letter to the Editor, *The Cultivator* 7 (March 1840): 93.
11. The following periodicals were used as source material: *The American Agriculturist,* 1855–1885; *The Plough,* 1850–1858. For the amount of advice offered concerning farm facilities, including farm houses, contained in such journals see Richard T. Farrell, "Advice to Farmers: The Content of Agricultural Newspapers, 1860–1910," *American Agriculturist* 51, no. 1 (January 1977): 209–17.
12. A module of five or fifteen feet seems to have determined the proportions of the house in terms of lengths and widths of units as well as heights of walls. The length of the floor and ceiling joists obtained from a lumberyard or directly from a railroad shipment of lumber to the region no doubt established these measurements.
13. For a description of a sense of place by those who lived in midwestern farm houses, see Ruben L. Parson, *Ever the Land: A Homestead Chronicle* (Staples, Minn.: Adventure Press, 1978); *The North Dakota Oral History Project: 792 Interviews with Early Settlers and Long Term Residents of the State* (Bismarck: North Dakota Historical Society, 1978); Erna Oleson Xan, *Wisconsin, My Home* (Madison, Wis.: University of Wisconsin Press, 1950). A pamphlet published in Alexandria, Minnesota, in 1876 entitled *Cheap and Pleasant Homes in Douglas County* describes only the positive values of community such as business, farming, education, religion, and family life. No description whatsoever is given to the architectural appearance of such a community.
14. See Fred B. Kniffen, "Folk Housing: Key to Diffusion," *Annals of the Association of American Geographers* 55, no. 4 (December 1965): 549–77 (reprinted in this volume); Robert Finley and E. M. Scott, "A Great Lakes to Gulf Profile of Dispersed Building Types," *Geographical Review* 30, no. 3 (July 1940): 412–19, for discussions of general types of vernacular houses.

Jacob W. Holt: An American Builder

CATHERINE W. BISHIR

It is sometimes convenient to lump distinct cultural experiences together under broad collective labels such as the "folk," the "elite," the "middle class." Studies like this one by Catherine W. Bishir remind us, however, that life and history are never so simple as to allow generalized descriptions to be accepted without question. When we allow the makers of history to be individuals rather than anonymous participants in a vaguely defined community, we soon discover how complicated their experiences were and how ingenious their solutions to their everyday problems may have been. Or we may find out how catastrophically stupid they were. In any case, when we confront the actual builders of vernacular structures we should learn more precisely how they solved their design problems.

Jacob Holt, the builder described in the following article, thought more grandly than his community. We see in his own house built between 1855 and 1856 an aspiration to participate in the latest Italianate fashion. At the same time most of his clients would not have any but the plainest boxy house graced by only a few brackets. The forward-thinking artist in Holt was held in check by his conservative southern milieu and although we can only speculate about how he must have felt, it is not too presumptuous to imagine him as somewhat rankled by requests to build I-houses. Yet he did build them, but always with distinctive touches of style and fashion that show that his aesthetic instincts were not altogether forsaken. No doubt the planters for whom he worked were nudged by Holt's expertise into accepting new ideas and images of house and home. As Bishir observes, the tug and pull of tradition and fashion were at work in the Virginia–North Carolina border lands and in such circumstances Holt had to creatively balance those opposing forces. He was simultaneously an agent of architectural change and a source for the continuity of older house plans.

Jacob W. Holt, a builder who worked in North Carolina and Virginia in the mid nineteenth century, is representative of an important group in the development of American architecture. He was one of the many practical builders—carpenters, housewrights, masons, and mechanics—who not only constructed but also shaped the design of much of the nation's architecture.

The study of American architecture has considered mostly the top and bottom layers with far less attention to the vast body of architecture in between or to the men responsible for it. Most architectural histories focus on the procession of elite, high-style buildings and their popular influence and, hence, upon the constellation of major architects and authors of architectural books that disseminated styles. Folk studies, on the other hand, examine the building patterns of the bedrock of traditional culture and thus the habits of craftsmen expressing ancient folkways. The buildings that lie between these two extremes are often dismissed as naive versions of academic models or as dilutions of traditional patterns. In either case, their importance on their own terms is not assessed.

But in fact the vast fabric of American architecture, stretching from elite to folk, contains a broad middle section where stylish and vernacular threads weave a lively pattern of national unity and regional diversity. The meaning of this midlevel architecture, which includes most American buildings, lies in the diverse resolutions of popular and traditional forces and in the accommodation of aesthetic and practical demands. Its energy springs from the tension between continuity and change at work at different rates across the country.[1]

Such architecture was the work principally of practical builders. Trained in the apprentice system as carpenters or masons, these men worked closely with their clients in the unified process of design and construction. They used the models in popular architectural guides but translated them into locally appropriate forms that satisfied people of different regions, social situations, economic levels, and ethnic origins.

The creativity of these builders lay not so much in exploring new concepts as in finding workable syntheses of popular and traditional elements that expressed their communities' accommodation to these forces. In the proficient hands of these artisans, ideas promulgated by popular publications became livable, three-dimensional realities. The builders' design decisions as well as their skill with plane or trowel lay behind the regional variations on national themes that form the great body of midlevel American architecture.

Jacob W. Holt (1811–80) was such a builder. His career spanned the decades from the 1840s to the 1870s and illustrates how a builder worked to accommodate the changing demands of regional custom and current style. Because of his highly identifiable personal idiom, the survival of a high proportion of his work, and the continued presence of strong local and family traditions about him in a region little altered by economic growth, his career can be traced in considerable detail. The quantity of his work—as many as twenty buildings documented and about seventy more attributed to him—permits assessment not only of individual structures but also of broader patterns of his development. In his responses to the needs and tastes of his patrons, the possibilities as well as the limitations of local technology, the models of popular pattern books, and the dramatic changes of his period, Holt like thousands of his counterparts created his own synthesis of continuity and change.

Holt's Career

Jacob Holt was born and grew up in Prince Edward County, Virginia, a moderately prosperous agricultural, tobacco-producing region in the rolling southern piedmont section of the state (fig. 1). Remote from port cities, the county's economic and political life focused on small trading towns and remained agrarian and conservative.[2]

Holt was the older son of David Holt, a carpenter, and Elizabeth McGehee Holt, daughter of a prominent planter family. At their mother's death in 1821, Jacob, his younger brother Thomas, and his two older sisters were entrusted by their father to the care of their maternal uncle John McGehee. Within three years David Holt died, leaving a poignantly meager estate of carpenter's tools "left at different places" about the community. Jacob and

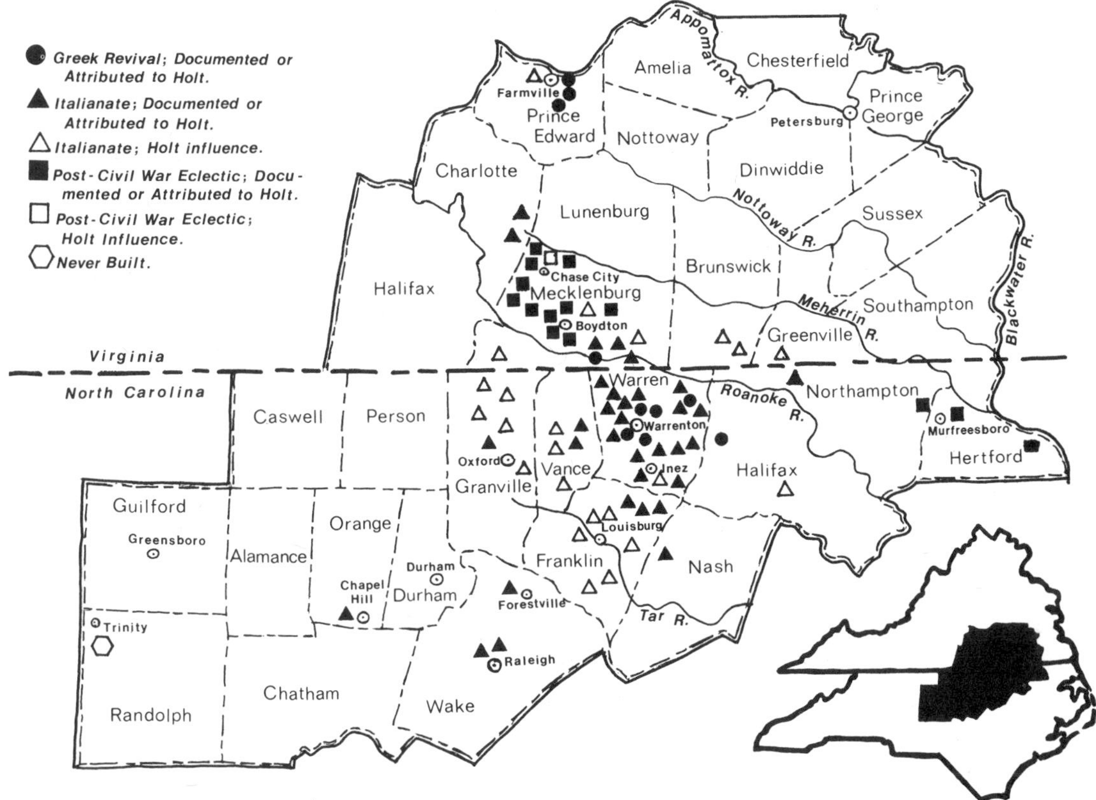

Distribution of the Work of Builder Jacob W. Holt in North Carolina and Virginia, ca. 1840 - 1880

Figure 1. Distribution of buildings built by and attributed to Jacob W. Holt, as well as those reflecting influence of his work. (Map by Michael T. Southern, 1980.)

Thomas probably entered into apprenticeships, for this was the customary means of supporting and training orphans. The most likely master for Jacob and possibly Thomas is William A. Howard, a successful carpenter working in Prince Edward and nearby counties, who was the builder of Jeffersonian courthouses, colleges, and other buildings in the 1820s and 1830s.[3]

By his late twenties Jacob Holt had gained a solid place in the community. In 1837 he joined the Baptist church and the next year married sixteen-year-old Aurelia Phillips, also a new Baptist.[4] He began to acquire real estate and slaves and by 1840 commanded the second largest nonagricultural work force in the county—nineteen young freemen and twenty-nine young male slaves. By age thirty Holt had established a way of life that persisted throughout his career: strong family and church ties and his own unusually large and presumably self-sufficient work force.[5] Despite his large shop, little is known of Holt's work in Prince Edward County. There is no tradition of his role in the county's architecture, and comparison with his later work suggests only three houses as his, one of which, Rotherwood, circa 1840, is supported by documentary evidence.[6]

In the early 1840s Holt, his growing family, and his household of black and white workmen joined a throng of Prince Edward County craftsmen who abandoned their native Virginia to move south to Warrenton, North Carolina. Whatever the reason for their apparently abrupt mass departure, these skilled artisans soon gained wide success in their new community and reshaped the architectural character of the town and outlying county.

Warrenton offered much promise to ambitious young builders and cabinetmakers. Although isolated and rural like most of antebellum North Carolina, it had long been a fashionable little town, the trading and political center of Warren County, the wealthiest county in the South's poorest state.[7] The county's close-knit network of affluent planter families dominated a population of slightly more than 4,000 whites and 8,000 black slaves. The plantation system depended heavily upon slave labor and production of tobacco sold in Virginia markets. Mineral-spring spas and a famous racetrack lent panache to the social life of planters and town residents alike, and frequent trips to Petersburg, Richmond, Baltimore, Philadelphia, and New York whetted the gentry's appetite for stylish goods. Warrenton, with about 1,000 people, prided itself on its fine schools, fashionable shops, political leadership, and lively social season. Ambitious lawyers, doctors, and merchants lived alongside planters in the town and supported a surprisingly cosmopolitan collection of teachers, musicians, hotelkeepers, carriage makers, tailors, and artists from northern states and distant lands.[8]

With the coming of the railroad in the late 1830s, a general upswing after recovery from the panic of 1837, and increasing agricultural improvements, Warren County and Warrenton stood in the 1840s at the edge of a period of unprecedented prosperity. For a builder, a glance at the modest and, by 1840, old-fashioned dwellings that lined its streets confirmed a ready market for new and stylish construction. Memoirist Lizzie Wilson Montgomery later recalled:

> In the early forties the town of Warrenton began to improve in business and in numbers; new citizens moved in, and a colony of skilled mechanics and their families from Prince Edward County, Virginia, and adjoining counties, all Baptists, came there to reside. No community ever received a more valuable acquisition than did Warrenton in the settlement of that colony as her citizens. It embraced the callings of architecture, carpentry, brick-laying, lathing and plastering. They were all experienced and capable managers or workers. The individuals, without exception, were religious, sober, honest, truthful, orderly, and industrious. They were all intelligent, well informed, and possessed of sufficient education to meet the demands of their several callings.[9]

By 1845, Holt was at work in Warrenton along with Edward T. Rice and Francis Woodson, brickmasons and plasterers from Prince Edward. In 1849 Jacob's younger brother, Thomas, who had been in Lunenburg County, Virginia, joined him. The two brothers lived in neighboring households, and Thomas took responsibility for supervising some of Jacob's construction projects.[10] Rice and Woodson owned a small number of slaves, but Jacob Holt listed forty-two slaves and seventeen free whites in his household by 1850. His workshop was by far the largest in the building trade in the county and the state. His free employees included twelve young men from Virginia, who had presumably come with him to Warrenton, and five others from North Carolina.[11] Holt's carpentry shop, sometimes working in association with Woodson and Rice or subcontracting with another mason, undertook the entire process of design and construction, as Holt's several extant contracts show. He assumed responsibility for every detail from cutting and curing the timber and sketching a ground plan to such finishing touches as window hardware or decorative painting and graining. Projects ranged from building a smokehouse for the Episcopal rectory to the construction of an entire plantation complex to the execution of the contract for carpentry for a large public building.[12]

The shop gained a broad practice and growing reputation in Warrenton and beyond. Working for the community's wealthiest families, Holt and his associates produced a series of substantial new buildings, first in a Greek revival mode and, by the 1850s, in a more eclectic Italianate style. In Warrenton, Holt developed a distinctive architectural idiom that marked his work throughout his career. As many as twenty-seven Warrenton buildings from this period are attributed to Holt's shop through documents, family tradition, or stylistic evidence.[13] In less than a decade the town's small-scale streetscape gave way to the rapid construction of big new buildings, fronted by columned porches that lent sudden elegance and a more generous scale to the dusty old streets.

In the 1850s Holt reached into the county beyond Warrenton and then to more and more distant communities in North Carolina and Virginia (see fig. 1). His bold, personalized style appealed to the region's thriving planters and merchants, and his large work force enabled him to compete successfully for low bid on a series of major institutional buildings stimulated by the state's increasing prosperity. As many as twenty buildings in Warren County and about thirty more in eleven counties beyond demonstrate the dramatic expansion of his work in the antebellum period. Perhaps a dozen others exhibit similarities that suggest his influence or possibly the activity of former employees.

By the eve of the Civil War, Holt like many North Carolinians enjoyed unprecedented success. He had established a broad regional business and gained a degree of prosperity. At age forty-nine, he lived with his wife and six children in a towered villa he had built near the center of Warrenton. His oldest son and namesake worked with him, and his reputation as a builder attracted young artisans from distant communities to his shop. The 1860 census listed nineteen young men in his household, all different from those with him a decade earlier, natives of nine North Carolina and Virginia counties.[14]

Holt's brother, Thomas, after a decade in Warrenton, had moved south to Raleigh where he began to style himself "architect." He won first prize for architectural drawing at the 1860 state fair and became chief architect for the Raleigh and Gaston Railroad. His commissions included a massive railroad repair shop and the Peace Institute near the northern end of the city.[15]

Jacob Holt, in contrast to his brother, made no claim to the title "architect." He had called himself "carpenter" in 1850, and to the 1860 census taker he identified himself proudly as "master mechanic." In this role, he bid successfully on several big building projects in the region, enlarging his sphere of activity to Saint John's College in Oxford, Peace Institute in Raleigh, and Trinity College near Asheboro. Following a common builders' custom on major contracts, Holt served as contractor working from an architect's designs. At Saint John's, he took only the carpentry contract, with Hillsborough brickmason John Berry executing the masonry, but at Trinity and Peace he gained the contracts for both carpentry and masonry. In the meantime, he continued to undertake both design and construction on smaller jobs.[16]

Holt's increasing activity across the state won attention in the newspapers. One reporter observed in 1860, "Mr. Holt, the contractor [for Trinity] is one of the first architects in the state. He is a Virginian by birth, but has resided in Warrenton for several years. He has put up many fine residences and public buildings in the eastern part of the state."[17]

For Holt, as for so many others, the Civil War halted business. The Peace project stopped and work on Trinity never began.[18] Several plantation houses stood unfinished. After the war, Warrenton struggled to recover amid a county and region whose plantation economy was irretrievably wrecked. The builder found occasional repairs and modest construction jobs, as an 1868 issue of the Warrenton newspaper reported: "Our friend Jacob Holt, Esq., so well known in North Carolina and Virginia, is busily employed in repairing [Warrenton's Central Hotel]."[19] But the once-wealthy planters straining to retain their property could offer scant patronage to an ambitious builder.

So once again Holt, nearing sixty and with a grown family, moved to a more promising community. In and around the village of Christiansville in neighboring Mecklenburg County, Virginia, activity was stirring amid the ruins of the plantation economy. Two Pennsylvanians, John E. Boyd and George Endly, arrived in 1868, bought land cheaply, and advertised widely for immigrants and investors. People came from the North and established their farms on the plantation land bought at low prices from cash-poor owners. The village grew as new businesses were established. Christiansville, renamed Chase City in 1873, became one of the South's most successful postwar development efforts. Holt quickly recognized that Boyd, Endly, and the stream of energetic and ambitious immigrants would require—and could afford—new buildings. He moved there in 1869 and gained key patronage by erecting big new houses for the two entrepreneurs. More work followed rapidly as he established himself as leading builder for the growing community.[20] His slave work force gone, Holt hired hands as needed, and he adapted his work to reflect the growing ornateness demanded by current taste.

Soon Holt expanded his activity to remodeling and new construction in Boydton, the old Mecklenburg county seat. He erected a handsome new brick church and several dwellings. The local newspaper reported in 1870 that Holt, "master carpenter and genius," was "turning things upside down in Boydton," and continued, "We are satisfied that he can and does do more work than one can hire the labor by the day, and have it executed. . . . Yes, give us plenty of mechanics, and we will make Boydton and Mecklenburg County look like a new country. See what Mr. Holt and his brawny armed assistants have done for Christiansville." In March 1871, the paper observed, "We learn from Mr. J. W. Holt that he is being offered large quantities of work in the county. We have no idea that Mr. Holt will be able to do half of the carpenter's work that will be needed in the county this year. There is a fine field in the county for other house carpenters. Lands we think must now advance in some sections of the county."[21]

A firm base established, Holt again reached beyond the county for work. In the mid-1870s he undertook a number of houses in and around Murfreesboro, North Carolina, about ninety miles downriver from Chase City. There he erected his last and most floridly finished dwellings, including the David A. Barnes House. Holt's Murfreesboro reputation, however, extended beyond the houses he built. In 1877 one "J. P. Phillips, Builder," announced: "Having served my apprenticeship under the well-known Contractor and Builder, J. W. Holt, Esq., I hereby notify the [public] that I am prepared to execute all kinds of BUILDING, REPAIRING, &c., in the best and most modern styles."[22]

Holt died September 21, 1880, at age sixty-nine. His eldest son, Jacob Whitington Holt, continued in the trade in Petersburg. Another son, William Howard Kenneth Holt, practiced building in North Carolina and Virginia. At least three grandchildren also followed careers in building, making four generations of builders in the family.[23]

Continuity Amid Change

Holt's career spanned a period of tremendous social, technological, and economic change. He was part of a generation that grew up in an agrarian, still largely traditional, and, in the South, slave-dependent culture, but that survived—even thrived—in the late nineteenth century's increasingly urban and industrialized culture and a new economic and labor system.

For builders the period brought dramatic developments in the practice of building and in the character of popular styles. Rapid developments in building technology—the invention of the circular saw, the proliferation of sash and blind factories producing vast quantities of ready-made decoration, and the spread of the balloon frame—introduced new flexibility of form and decoration as well as new roles for the builder. Architectural publications shifted not only from classicism to eclecticism but also from builders' guides to the house pattern books with models for complete buildings and their settings. Growing separation of the processes of design and construction came with the emerging distinction between the professional architect and the contractor.

Holt's generation of builders had to adapt to all these changes and found different ways of surviving. Some clung to old ways and avoided the mainstream. Others, such as Holt's younger brother, Thomas, dismissed their traditional identity as carpenters or builders to lay claim to the title "architect," and, jettisoning all vestiges of earlier customs, plunged into the mainstream of new styles and practices.

Jacob Holt charted his own course through this turbulent transitional era, combining old and new elements to create for himself a workable synthesis. His long career exemplifies the persistence of traditional practices into the middle and late years of the nineteenth century, of antebellum culture into the postwar era, and of individualization into a period of growing standardization. He was no hidebound reactionary but a man of practical good sense who knew his market and his own capabilities. He combined reliance upon accustomed techniques with flexibility and accommodation to new ways. He began in a slave-dependent economy and relied upon slave labor for much of his career but quickly adapted to the labor situation of the postwar economy. He established himself as principal builder for one community yet left it in pursuit of new patronage when times changed. He undertook the entire process of design and construction in traditional fashion, but he bid successfully as contractor for other architects on major projects as well.

Just as his career reflected his resilience in the face of changing situations, so Holt's personal architectural idiom sprang from his resolutions of the disparate demands of his time and place. For builders the tension between traditional and popular forces found expression in the tenacity of traditional regional habits and the attraction of changing architectural fashions. Holt, like so many others, responded to both. He knew the architectural publications of his day, but he also knew his community. He used popular models to create buildings peculiarly suited to—and hence expressive of—his regional clientele. Although his work was more novel and fashionable than anything else in his vicinity, in a broader context it was nevertheless conservative. He executed popular motifs with boldness and vigor but nearly always within the framework of the vernacular artisan.

Holt's design process involved several components: use of popular publications, vernacular reliance on a conservative form and plan, the nature of his shop operation, and the character of his clientele.

The impact of popular architectural publications is obvious throughout Holt's forty years of building. Like builders nearly everywhere, he relied on these volumes to keep his work current and appealing to the tastes of his wealthy patrons. He employed a sequence of widely circulated books that are credited with shaping the nation's architectural development.

Holt's earliest work reflected the influence of Owen Biddle's *Young Carpenter's Assistant* (1805).[24] He copied Biddle's restrained Federal style molding, foliated stair brackets, and design for stairs (figs. 2, 3). In Prince Edward and in the imposing house of William Eaton in Warrenton (figs. 4, 5) he combined Biddle's Federal motifs with Asher Benjamin's Grecian designs which appeared in the widely circulated *Practical House Carpenter,* first published in 1830.[25]

In the 1840s Holt moved to a robust simplification of Benjamin's Grecian taste, executing Benjamin's motifs in a highly plastic, three-dimensional form. Holt built big, boxy houses fronted with broad porches whose columns and plain entabulatures suggest Benjamin's 1835 economical hybrid Tuscan-Doric order of *The Practice of Architecture* (figs. 6, 7).[26] He emphasized the cubic forms of his buildings with broad, exaggerated linear strokes—wide water tables, heavy corner pilasters, and a plain frieze beneath the roofline. His *in antis* entrances reflected Minard Lafever's *The Young Builder's General Instructor* (figs. 8, 9).[27] The generous interiors boasted heavy woodwork typical of Greek revival designs. Burly, Doric columned mantels (fig. 10) reinterpreted Benjamin's models (fig. 11). Also following Benjamin's example, Holt used Grecian key moldings at unexpected spots inside

Figure 2. Design for stair and detail for bracket from Owen Biddle's The Young Carpenter's Assistant *(Philadelphia: Benjamin Johnson, 1805), plate 31. Holt used the curving form of Biddle's stair in various ways, as seen in subsequent illustrations, and used a simpler ramped two-flight stair (Biddle, plate 30). He did not use Biddle's bud-and-spiral bracket seen in the enlarged detail of plate 31, however, but rather in his earliest houses used the simpler bracket visible in the general view of Biddle's stair. In later work Holt used only a plain molding at the end of each tread. (Courtesy of the Henry Francis du Pont Winterthur Museum.)*

Figure 3. Stair of Rotherwood (Edwin Edmunds House), attributed to Jacob W. Holt. Prince Edward County, Virginia, ca. 1840. The plan of this house features a front cross hall and rear parlors with the stair rising along the rear hall wall. This occurs again in at least three Holt houses of the 1850s. (Photograph by the author, 1978.)

Figure 4. William Eaton House, attributed by local tradition to Jacob W. Holt. Warrenton, North Carolina, 1843. (Photograph by JoAnn Sieburg-Baker, 1976, North Carolina Division of Archives and History.)

Figure 5. Stair hall, William Eaton House, attributed by local tradition to Jacob W. Holt. Warrenton, North Carolina, 1843. (Photograph by JoAnn Sieburg-Baker, 1975, North Carolina Division of Archives and History.)

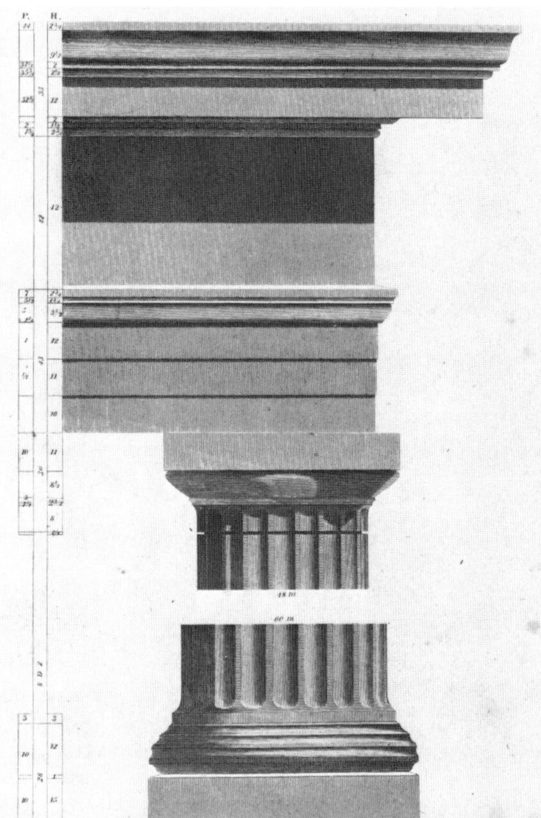

Figure 6. Design for column and entablature from Asher Benjamin's The Practice of Architecture *(Boston: By the author and Carter, Hendee, 1833), plate 7. (Courtesy of the Henry Francis du Pont Winterthur Museum.)*

Figure 8. Design for a front door from Minard Lafever's The Young Builder's General Instructor *(Newark, N.J.: W. Tuttle, 1829), plate 15.*

Figure 7. Porch and entrance, Somerville House, attributed by family tradition to Jacob W. Holt. Warrenton, North Carolina, ca. 1850. Although the dentil and fret motifs are unusual, the column and entablature are otherwise characteristic of Warrenton's Greek revival work. (Photograph by JoAnn Sieburg-Baker, 1976, North Carolina Division of Archives and History.)

Figure 9. Entrance to the T. E. Wilson House, attributed to Jacob W. Holt. Warrenton, North Carolina, ca. 1850. (Photograph by JoAnn Sieburg-Baker, 1975, North Carolina Division of Archives and History.)

Figure 10. Mantel at Reedy Rill, attributed by family tradition to Jacob W. Holt. Warren County, North Carolina. The oak-grained mantel is in a section of the house built about 1850 and is essentially identical to others throughout Warrenton. (Photograph by JoAnn Sieburg-Baker, 1978, North Carolina Division of Archives and History.)

Figure 11. Design for a chimney piece from Asher Benjamin's The Architect; or, The Practical House Carpenter *(Boston: Benjamin B. Mussey, 1850), plate 51. (Courtesy of the Henry Francis du Pont Winterthur Museum.)*

Figure 12. Somerville House, attributed by family tradition to Jacob W. Holt. Warrenton, North Carolina, ca. 1850. The window sash is altered. A typical but unusually grand example of Holt's Greek revival work; the scale and form are typical as well, but the detail is unusually elaborate. (Photograph by JoAnn Sieburg-Baker, 1975, North Carolina Division of Archives and History.)

and out but not the floral decorativeness found in Lafever's or Benjamin's later anthemions and acanthus.[28] The large, boldly Grecian houses (for example, fig. 12) rose rapidly throughout Warrenton and in the nearby countryside. Unified in their repetitive form and detail, no two were alike, as the builder played a series of recombinations on a theme.

In the early 1850s Holt introduced a new note, replacing the simple classicism of Benjamin's models with the more ornate and eclectic vocabulary taken from William Ranlett's *The Architect* (fig. 13), Samuel Sloan's *The Model Architect*, and possibly A. J. Downing's *Cottage Residences*.[29] He extracted from Ranlett's handsome plates of villas and cottages a series of brackets to punctuate the broad eaves of his houses, to clump in miniature at the caps of corner pilasters and porch posts, or to march up the raking cornices of temple-form public buildings. He filled his large rectangular windows with round, ogee, or lancet paired arches and enriched entrances with pinwheel and scallop motifs (fig. 14). Instead of the Doric simplicity of his columned porches, he created luxuriant trellises of swags, pendants, arches, and brackets. He replaced his Doric mantels with an eclectic Ranlett model (fig. 15), and he lavished a series of Gothic trefoil and quatrefoil motifs on mantels, panels, and stair newels. He reshaped door and window moldings and gave arched heads to the panels of his doors (fig. 16). Sometimes handled with restraint as at Engleside in Warrenton (fig. 17) or at the more full-

Figure 13. Exterior details accompanying design 20 from William Ranlett's The Architect, *2 vols. (New York: Dewitt and Davenport, 1849), 1: plate 57. (Courtesy of the Henry Francis du Pont Winterthur Museum.)*

Figure 14. Details accompanying design 18 from William Ranlett's The Architect, *2 vols. (New York: DeWitt and Davenport, 1849), 1: plate 52. (Courtesy of the Henry Francis du Pont Winterthur Museum.)*

Figure 15. Mantel at Engleside, John White's house, attributed to Jacob W. Holt. Warrenton, North Carolina, ca. 1850. Compare with the Ranlett mantel design but note the frieze roll carried over from the Greek revival mantel. This feature is common in Holt's Italianate houses of the 1850s. (Photograph by JoAnn Sieburg-Baker, 1975, North Carolina Division of Archives and History.)

Figure 16. Entrance to Vine Hill, built by Jacob W. Holt. Franklin County, North Carolina, 1856. This is a typical Holt entrance. Vine Hill is documented by a Holt contract of September 5, 1856, listing all components for construction. Although the surviving fabric of the house provides a key point of comparison to substantiate traditional Holt attributions of the 1850s, it has lost its porch and fallen into decay, so that it does not serve well for photographic illustrations. Surviving features of plan and detail are essentially identical to those of contemporary houses illustrated here. (Photograph by JoAnn Sieburg-Baker, 1976, North Carolina Division of Archives and History.)

Figure 17. Engleside, the John White House, attributed to Jacob W. Holt. Warrenton, North Carolina, ca. 1850. Simple box modillions from Ranlett's details for design 20 (see figure 13) are rare in Holt's work. The porch gallery balustrade is unusual, and, although apparently commonly used in Holt's work originally, few have survived. Descendants living in other houses recall early use of a gallery, as illustrated here. (Photograph ca. 1876, North Carolina Division of Archives and History.)

Figure 18. Cherry Hill, attributed to Jacob W. Holt and, by family tradition, to his associate, John A. Waddell. Warren County, North Carolina, ca. 1859. (Photograph by Greer Suttlemyre, 1974, North Carolina Division of Archives and History.)

blown Cherry Hill (fig. 18), sometimes piled on extravagantly at every possible spot as at Reedy Rill (fig. 19), Holt's new collection of details when applied to his boldly outlined cube of a house created an eclectic and obviously modish idiom unique in the region.

Although at first straitened by economy, during the postwar period Holt continued the use of many of the 1850s elements. His penchant for incorporating new motifs kept his work current, and his buildings grew increasingly ornate in the 1870s. The source of his new postwar motifs is unknown. He treated the roofline of his houses with a raised central gable, following the ubiquitous late nineteenth-century roofline feature seen in Ranlett's villas and in Downing's cottages. He adorned the gable with a cluster of sawn decorations (figs. 20, 21). Here and along the raking cornices of churches and at the brackets of porches, Holt introduced a curious, tightly coiled spiral motif that must spring from some pattern book of the time (fig. 22). He took from Ranlett's details an elongated quatrefoil to adorn porch brackets or compose a gallery balustrade. By his last work in the 1870s (figs. 23, 24) he had accumulated a wealth of wooden decoration to apply to his accustomed, firmly outlined cubic building form. The energetic design and copiousness of the brackets, coils, quatrefoils, faceted bosses, polygons, lattices, arches, and pendants expressed vividly the ornateness of the era.

Holt's sequence of pattern-book motifs from the late federal to the mid Victorian era is precisely what the peruser of nineteenth-century architectural books might expect from a builder of his period. Yet comparison of the published plates with Holt's actual buildings shows immediately that these models were only one of many factors Holt considered in creating his architectural idiom.

As significant as what books he used is how he used them. He handled the entire sequence of publications in the conservative fashion established by the early builders' guides, thus working within the framework of the vernacular builder.

Holt began work with traditional builders' guides. Like their predecessors, Biddle, Lafever, and Benjamin aimed their books at the provincial builder who would take from their pages correct techniques for framing structures or for designing classical orders, as well as ideas for mantels, stairs, moldings, and the like. Seldom did these books present elevations or ground plans; they focused primarily on the

Figure 19. Reedy Rill, second phase of construction attributed by family tradition to Jacob W. Holt. Warren County, North Carolina, late 1850s. (Photograph ca. 1890, courtesy of the family of Panthea Twitty, North Carolina Division of Archives and History.)

Figure 20. Shadow Lawn, attributed by family tradition to Jacob W. Holt. Chase City, Virginia, ca. 1869. (Photograph by the author, 1977, North Carolina Division of Archives and History.)

Figure 21. House attributed to Jacob W. Holt. Boydton, Virginia, 1870s. This modest dwelling illustrates Holt's repetition of motifs from expensive to simple buildings in each period. (Photograph by the author, 1977.)

Figure 22. Burwell House, attributed to Jacob W. Holt. Near Chase City, Virginia, 1870s. Although altered somewhat by the application of aluminum siding, this farm house exhibits bracket caps, bracket cornices, porch spirals, and a curious row of curls along the front gable. (Photograph by the author, 1977, North Carolina Division of Archives and History.)

Figure 23. David A. Barnes House, built by Jacob W. Holt. Murfreesboro, North Carolina, 1875. The surviving contrasting paint scheme probably suggests the original character of many Holt houses now painted white. (Photograph ca. 1880, courtesy of Frank and Margaret Stephenson, North Carolina Division of Archives and History.)

presentation of details for application to various compositions. In the 1840s and 1850s, however, architectural propagandists like A. J. Downing, Calvert Vaux, Samuel Sloan, and William Ranlett redirected architectural publications. Their house pattern books, unlike the earlier builders' guides, promoted entire compositions of picturesque buildings with appropriate landscaping schemes, painting examples, and even furnishings for their users to emulate in toto with the object of improving the entire life-style of the prospective resident. Details like mantels, windows, brackets, and panels appeared to insure their proper execution as part of the exemplary picturesque whole.[30]

Holt, however, used the new pattern books not as their authors intended, nor perhaps as architectural historians depending on these volumes might assume, but selectively, as he had used the builders' guides. Rather than reproducing for his clients the glamorous villas of the plates, he chose a collection of appealing details, such as mantels, pinwheels, brackets, arches, trefoils, and the like, that he applied enthusiastically and repeatedly to his ac-

Figure 24. Vinson House, attributed to Jacob W. Holt and his apprentice, J. P. Phillips. Murfreesboro, North Carolina, 1870s. (Photograph ca. 1890, courtesy of Frank Stephenson, North Carolina Division of Archives and History.)

customed house form without substantially disturbing the basics.

Despite the changing character of detail, Holt's buildings remained essentially the same from the 1840s through the 1870s. The most extravagant application of decorative veneer never obscures the inherent conservatism of his work. The boxy three-dimensional double-pile plan of the ornate 1875 Barnes House (fig. 25) is essentially identical to the Greek revival Somerville House of 1850 (fig. 26) and the Italianate Vine Hill of 1856 (fig. 27).

Thus we can look through the fashionable veil to see Holt operating as a vernacular builder. Holt's approach embodied many characteristics considered to define the "folk" or vernacular artisan, whether furniture maker or builder. Folklorist Henry Glassie points out that the folk artisan, consciously or unconsciously, extracts from his tradition a few basic forms that are old at the time of his use and different from those promoted by popular culture. Working in his tradition he defines for himself a minimal concept of the essentials of the object and arrives at "a small set of rules that define the limits within

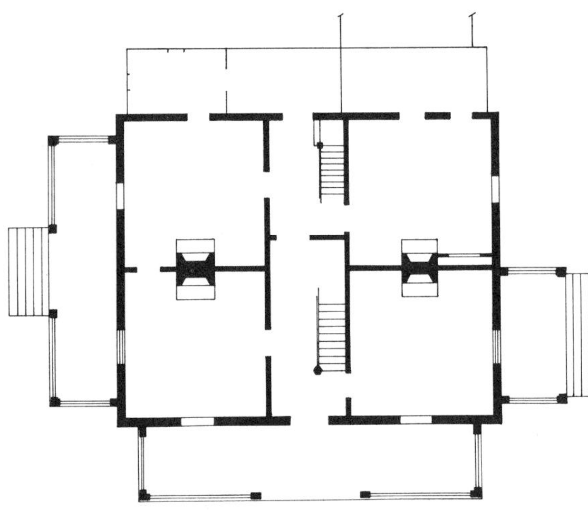

Figure 25. Ground plan of the David A. Barnes House, built by Jacob W. Holt, Murfreesboro, North Carolina, 1875. (Drawing by Margaret L. Stephenson, 1979.)

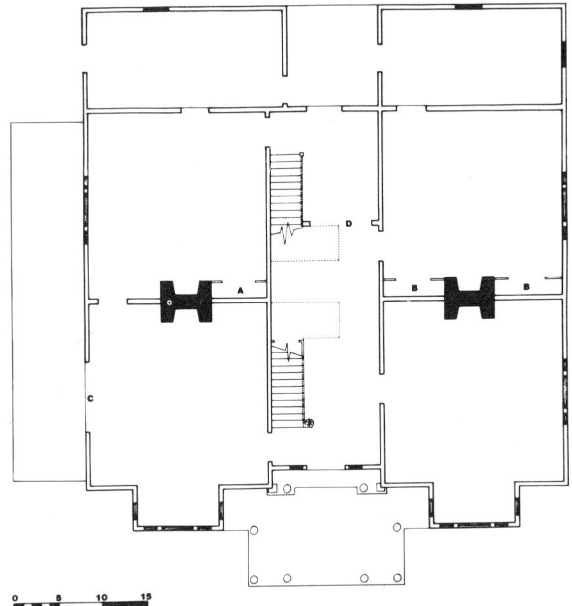

Figure 26. Ground plan of the Somerville House, attributed by family tradition to Jacob W. Holt. Warrenton, North Carolina, ca. 1850. (Drawing by Carl Lounsbury, 1979.)

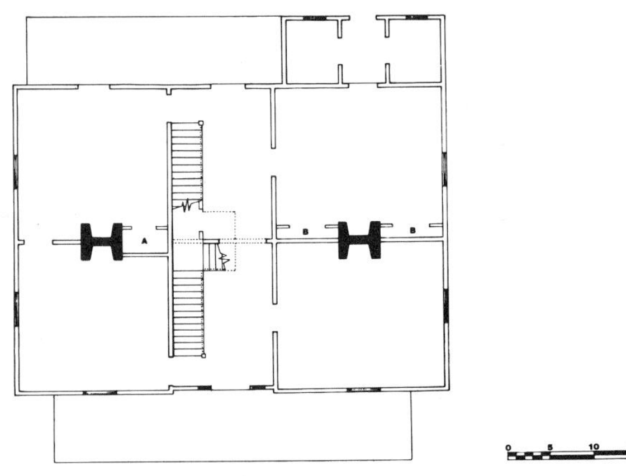

Figure 27. Ground plan of Vine Hill, built by Jacob W. Holt. Franklin County, North Carolina, 1856. (Drawing by Carl Lounsbury, 1979.)

which he can modify the concept according to his taste and talent and the taste and pocketbook of his clientele."[31] Within the concept thus defined the artisan can work freely, varying nonessential details as he chooses.

Typically the folk artisan responds to novelty or changing ideas by breaking down the new concept and translating it into terms compatible with the old. Usually this means that the artisan keeps the accustomed basic form and updates only the most obvious elements and those that are most easily changed.[32] The result is a composite of new and old, "a novel and synthetic idea . . . a compromise of fashionable and unfashionable ideas." The fundamental rules of folk art—"the dominance of form and the desire for repetition"—rather than academic models govern the folk artisan.[33] However convoluted it may become, the ornament is characterized by symmetry and repetition; it never obscures and, in fact, emphasizes the basic form (see figs. 12, 18).

Holt gleaned from his tradition a "small set of rules" that defined his work. He relied on basic forms and plans that were old when he adopted them, and continued them throughout his work without changing or obscuring them behind the increasingly abundant ornament. He took as his basic model the shallow-roofed, cubic house form, usu-

Figure 28. Pool Rock Plantation House, attributed to Jacob W. Holt. Vance County, North Carolina, 1850s. This is one of several examples of Holt's additions to existing dwellings. (Photograph by Michael T. Southern, 1978, North Carolina Division of Archives and History.)

ally three bays wide and two deep, a Georgian (double-pile) plan—a central hall with two rooms on either side. By the mid nineteenth century this plan, originally introduced in the eighteenth century in fashionable English houses, had supplanted the standard two-room vernacular house for middle- and upper-middle-class people in northeastern North Carolina and southern Virginia.[34] Well over half of Holt's houses follow this plan.

Holt used as well a few variations that also had been introduced to the region in fashionable eighteenth-century buildings but were antiquated by the mid nineteenth century. He sometimes reduced the double pile to a single-room depth (the common I-house form), especially in less costly houses or in additions to existing dwellings (fig. 28). Occasionally he used a side-hall plan or a two-story central cross-hall block flanked by one-story wings—forms seen in modish Virginia and North Carolina houses of the eighteenth and early nineteenth centuries.[35] In all public buildings (one courthouse and five churches), Holt followed the simple rectangular temple form that had dominated Virginia and North Carolina public architecture since Jefferson introduced it in 1785 (figs. 29, 30, 31).

When Holt began building in the 1840s, these plans, although conservative, were still within the current Greek revival vocabulary. However, his retention of the eighteenth-century plans through the 1850s, 1860s, and 1870s became increasingly conservative as the popular pattern books of the midcentury promulgated increasingly complex forms. Holt had extracted the set of rules that defined for him and his clients what the plan and form of a house or public building should be, and he held to these rules with conservative tenacity. Within this framework, Holt was indeed free to work eclectically to suit the taste, comfort, and pocketbook of his client in addition to his own desires.

Respecting the budget of his client, Holt unabashedly adapted scale and ornamentation to economic requirements. On occasion he built plain, even old-fashioned houses—one for his own household, another for a farming family, and another for an associate, Warrenton cabinetmaker

Figure 29. Warren County Courthouse, built by Jacob W. Holt with brickmasons Francis Woodson and Edward Rice. Warrenton, North Carolina, 1853–57. (From Lizzie Wilson Montgomery, Sketches of Old Warrenton *(Raleigh: Edwards and Broughton, 1924), facing p. 212; photograph ca. 1890–1900, North Carolina Division of Archives and History.)*

Figure 30. Warrenton Presbyterian Church, attributed to Jacob W. Holt. Warrenton, North Carolina, 1855. (Photograph by JoAnn Sieburg-Baker, 1975, North Carolina Division of Archives and History.)

Figure 31. Boydton Methodist Episcopal Church, built by Jacob W. Holt. Boydton, Virginia, 1871. (Photograph by the author, 1977, North Carolina Division of Archives and History.)

Samuel N. Mills, who had come with Holt and the other artisans from Prince Edward County.[36] These inexpensive structures resembled their vernacular contemporaries more than they did Holt's distinctive and stylish work for the local elite. At the same time Holt applied to more pretentious buildings whatever degree of luxury properly announced the affluence of the client without straining his purse. He frankly concentrated costly decoration on the main facade (fig. 32) and front rooms where it would be most visible, restricting the finish of rear facade (fig. 33) and secondary rooms to cheaper components. Even in principal rooms, he used skillful woodgraining and marbleizing to enrich native pine doors, mantels, stairs, and sometimes plastered walls at far less cost than fine woods or marble (fig. 34; see also fig. 10).[37]

To accommodate the comfort and convenience of his patron, Holt improved the standard plan without making fundamental changes. Enhancing the air circulation already permitted by the central-hall plan, he partitioned the hall midway by adding a doorway filled with folding doors with movable louvers.[38] These could be adjusted to allow any degree of air flow and privacy. The two halls thus created each contained a stair, separating activity in the front and rear portions of the house so that guests, residents, children, and servants could move freely within the house (fig. 35; see also fig. 34). He also inserted a series of closets, presses, and cupboards flanking the fireplaces, providing unusually capacious storage space for the period. Often small service and storage rooms flanked an open rear porch, which is similar to regional vernacular use of shed rooms flanking rear central porches (see ground plans, figs. 25, 26, 27).[39]

All of Holt's variations of adjustable ornamentation, decorative painting, and functional improvements remained within the limits of the basic plan, from which in his work for his clients Holt never strayed, despite his familiarity with novel and often admirably functional pattern-book models. As with any vernacular artisan, the question arises: who defined the limitations, the artisan or the patron?[40] For Holt, it appears that both the practical requirements of his shop and the character of his clientele were involved.

Figure 32. Archibald Taylor House, attributed to Jacob W. Holt. Franklin County, North Carolina, ca. 1857. (Photograph by Michael T. Southern, 1975, North Carolina Division of Archives and History.)

Building technology obviously had an impact on Holt's design. Repetition of form and detail were singularly compatible with the operation of his prolific shop. Whether Holt expanded his operation so rapidly and undertook projects miles and miles apart because he had developed a standardized style or whether his method of production necessitated adopting a repetitive idiom is unclear. Certainly the two coincided conveniently.

Holt incorporated both traditional and innovative methods. Like his contemporaries, he relied on his own and on his clients' slave labor until the end of the Civil War.[41] He utilized traditional labor-intensive construction techniques, including heavy timber framing. (This old technique persisted in substantial construction until the late nineteenth century in many areas, notwithstanding the invention of the faster balloon frame in 1833, probably because of its obvious sturdiness, workers' familiarity with it, and the easier access to labor than to machinery.) The framing method, of course, restricted the complexity of Holt's building forms to those that could be framed with heavy timbers and thus dictated the composition of a cubical format.

Figure 33. Rear and side view of the Archibald Taylor House, attributed to Jacob W. Holt. Franklin County, North Carolina, ca. 1857. (Photograph by JoAnn Sieburg-Baker, 1976, North Carolina Division of Archives and History.)

Figure 34. Front stair hall of the Archibald Taylor House, attributed to Jacob W. Holt. Franklin County, North Carolina, ca. 1857. The plastered walls are painted to resemble blocks of ochre, slate blue, and ivory marble. Pieces of a painted trompe l'oeil frame once encircling a portrait survive on the soffit of the stair. Note the rear stair. (Photograph by JoAnn Sieburg-Baker, 1976, North Carolina Division of Archives and History.)

Figure 35. Stair hall of the Somerville House, attributed by family tradition to Jacob W. Holt. Warrenton, North Carolina, ca. 1850. (Photograph by JoAnn Sieburg-Baker, 1975, North Carolina Division of Archives and History.)

In contrast with this conservative technology was Holt's somewhat unusual introduction of standardized, perhaps machine-made or mass-produced, decorative motifs long before his community boasted a sash and blind factory.[42] Little is known for certain about the technology of his production, but Mrs. Montgomery recalled that on the lot behind his Warrenton house "was located an old lumbering shop, in which the materials for the handsome homes and stores of the town and county were kept. The shaving pile outside of the building was the favorite place for the school boys of the town to play 'circus' and other games. On the lot was also the kiln, used by Mr. Holt for drying the lumber needed in his business. Large quantities of brick were burnt there."[43] Her description, plus the recurrence of the same details in building after building, and the standard itemization and pricing of components of woodwork in his contracts—bracket cornice by the foot, front doors at a set rate, various grades of mantels, cupboards, pilasters, windows, and so on—suggest that Holt employed an early system of mass producing the millwork required to complete the many buildings under way at any one time. That he did so with elements of his own idiosyncratic design represents an intermediate stage in building technology.

To produce items expediently, Holt typically adapted pattern-book motifs to forms that could be easily reproduced by his shop. For example, the paired arched windows and doorways of Ranlett's designs (see figs. 14, 16, 18, 19, 20) required arched openings far more difficult and unfamiliar than the customary rectangular openings. Holt simply placed Ranlett's forms within a rectangular frame and created a composite that was adequately stylish and far easier to execute. His style of building therefore accommodated, and indeed exploited, this standardization in its design. Thus, the vernacular penchant for repetition of ornament paralleled the demands of technological advance.

Not only the production of quantities of woodwork but also his reliance on a few basic plans enabled Holt to erect many buildings concurrently at widely separated sites. With many projects under way at a time in the late 1850s, Holt deployed workmen to several sites and entrusted their direction to his most experienced associates, including his brother, Thomas, and two employees from Prince Edward County, John A. Waddell and John C. McCraw. With buildings following familiar formulae in plan and detail and using standard components presumably sent from the Warrenton shop, workmen could construct buildings more quickly and reliably, and with less supervision, than if new decisions had to be made every day.

Beyond the practical requirements of shop technology, however, there lies the role of the taste of the client in the builder's designs. Was it merely the convenience of standardization in construction or perhaps Holt's lack of sophistication that restricted

Figure 36. Jacob W. Holt House, built by Jacob W. Holt. Warrenton, North Carolina, ca. 1855–56. (Photograph ca. 1900, North Carolina Division of Archives and History.)

his response to new ideas to a traditional framework? Or did the conservatism lie within his clientele? As one specialist puts the question: "Did the . . . [craftsman] produce only what pleased himself or did he work to please his neighbors and customers?"[44]

Although the question of the artisan's tastes versus those of his patrons must nearly always remain a mystery, Holt provided a vital clue in the design of his own house in Warrenton, erected in the mid-1850s (fig. 36).[45] Here in a vigorously executed little wooden villa, he demonstrated unmistakably his full comprehension of the meaning of Downing's and Ranlett's volumes. Although for his clients' dwellings he took only a collection of details from these books, for his own house Holt replicated not merely the decoration or even the facade but the boldly three-dimensional massing of Downing's "Cottage in the Italian, or Tuscan Style" (fig. 37). Holt's forceful statement of his sophistication as a builder, and presumably of his willingness to venture into the complexities of current pattern books, was far different from his work for his patrons or, for that matter, anything else in the region.[46]

Yet despite its obvious claim to the latest fashion, the little villa remained an anomaly. There is no evidence that Holt's vivid billboard of his abilities whetted the appetites of the community for novel villas or cottages from Downing or any other volume. Nowhere in the region did the builder find a patron venturesome enough to follow his lead, to break free from the box, and to explore the novel offerings of the pattern books' forms and plans.

Community reaction to Holt's villa is suggested by Mrs. Montgomery's recollection: "On the south on the corner Jacob Holt built . . . [an] unusually shaped house for that time, as people knew little else than a square house. This was built for his own use, and he resided there as long as he remained in Warrenton."[47] Her description, together with the dramatic contrast between Holt's own house and his work for his patrons, suggest that perhaps he was more attuned to popular innovations than were those for whom he built. It was, then, not Holt's lack of understanding or appreciation of new ideas that kept his work within a vernacular framework but rather his keen understanding of his clients.

The piedmont plantation gentry were, for all their travels to northern cities and appetites for the latest in fashionable luxuries, at core inherently conservative. Wedded to an entrenched, slave-based agrarian economic system that was threatened by political or ideological change, accustomed to political hegemony, and established among the intricate family connections and elite social position of a provincial aristocracy, the gentry as a class naturally avoided any challenge that might fundamentally change their way of life.

Figure 37. "A Cottage in the Italian, or Tuscan Style," from Andrew Jackson Downing's Cottage Residences; or, A Series of Designs for Rural Cottages and Cottage-Villas, and Their Gardens and Grounds, Adapted to North America *(New York and London: Wiley and Putnam, 1842), figure 72. (Courtesy of the Henry Francis du Pont Winterthur Museum.)*

The personal style Holt developed for these patrons in the antebellum period struck a deep and responsive chord, as expressed in their rapid acceptance of his work. Families who needed a new house contracted with him as did many who wanted to update an older house in his distinctive mode. In Warrenton, construction of the courthouse (see fig. 29), drastic remodelings of the modest Episcopal church (figs. 38 and 39), and construction of a new Presbyterian church (see fig. 30) placed his stamp on public as well as private structures. Holt's exaggerated trim set off his buildings as unmistakably new, far more "modern" than the conservative, plain architecture that dominated the region; yet the familiar form and plan implied no substantial departure from ingrained custom.

Local understanding of "old" and "new" in the mid nineteenth century is suggested by contemporary or later descriptions, including Mrs. Montgomery's early twentieth-century recollections of Warrenton, along with those of her friend Mrs. Pendleton. Consistently they labeled the modest dormered dwellings of the eighteenth and early nineteenth centuries "old fashioned" and in fact remarked that Holt's plainer buildings for modest residents looked "old fashioned" considering their 1840s construction dates. The Greek revival buildings, on the other hand, they deemed "fine" and "handsome." John White's bold Italianate house of 1850–52 was described by Mrs. Montgomery as late as 1910 as a "large, modern house." In 1870 the *Mecklenburg Herald* praised Holt's outstanding "architectural taste" as well as his "faithfulness to comply with his contracts." And in 1877, Holt's former apprentice declared that his training with Holt had enabled him to build in the "best and most modern styles." Clearly for Holt's patrons his work was "modern" indeed.[48]

Both the design and the repetitiveness of Holt's

Figure 38. Emmanuel Episcopal Church, Warrenton, North Carolina, 1827, 1845–58. Remodeling by Jacob W. Holt included tower and front facade and probably the side brackets. Holt modeled the design after a plate for a "Village Church" in Sloan's Model Architect. *(Photograph pre-1906, North Carolina Division of Archives and History.)*

work enhanced rather than detracted from his appeal. The builder's authorship far more than the personal taste of the owner was apparent in his buildings. Clusters of Holt-built houses indicate that one member of a family or neighborhood after another sought his services. Several contracts even refer to the finish or components of a nearby Holt house to be emulated in the new construction—a stair, for example, to be "like Mr. Williams' rear one" or the finish to be "like Col. W. R. Baskervilles or not inferior."[49] The homogeneity of scale, form, and even detail affirmed the basic unity and shared viewpoint of Holt's clients, with only minor differences suggesting individuality.

For Holt, as for most of his counterparts, conclusions about his design decisions, pattern-book sources, and relations with his patrons come mostly from circumstantial and stylistic evidence. Seldom do documents explicitly state the builder's processes; the buildings remain the principal record. The fullest firsthand confirmation of many aspects of Holt's approach is found in the Baskerville family papers.[50]

The earliest work Holt did for the Mecklenburg County, Virginia, family was the 1855–56 remodeling of a house (now destroyed) for planter William Rust Baskerville. For the alteration of a gabled dwelling of about 1825 into a decorated three-part villa, the builder provided a ground plan to show what was to be done—the sketch is the only carefully detailed ground plan of Holt's known to survive. He accompanied it with a contract listing work to be done and materials needed, and together the client and the builder worked out payment in the exchange of provisions and labor for the work.[51]

Baskerville's satisfaction with his newly fashionable house evidently stimulated his son, Dr. Robert D. Baskerville, to engage Holt in 1857 to erect a grand new mansion. Eureka was probably Holt's most elaborate structure, and the documents surviving from its construction provide the most complete accounting of his work. Here he and his wealthy client conferred to produce a highly original composition.

The initial contract for Eureka set forth clearly the multiplicity of influences that shaped its design and suggested the creative interaction between artisan and patron:

> A Bill for Dweling House to be built [for] Dr. R. D. Baskerville of Mecklenburg County Va. agreeable to the following specifications and to be built by Design 31st plate 19th Volume 2nd Ranlets Architect (Except) in length of Veranda which is to be 40 ft long and not to extend on the ends & to have in the rear of the Building a piazza 8 by 32 feet in place of kitchen Bedrooms &c as described on Ground plan drawn by J. W. Holt. . . . The style and finish of the work is to be like Col. W. R. Baskervilles or not inferior. . . .
>
> J. W. Holt on his part agrees to execute in a good and workmanlike manner the aforesaid Building and defray every expense necessary to completion of the work and to have the building finished by about the 15th of August 1858. Dr. R. D. Baskerville on his part agrees to pay the above mentioned sum of $4885.[52]

The contract cited the pattern-book model but acknowledged functional adjustments to suit the client. The role of the builder in creating the final design and undertaking the entire construction process was clear.

Figure 39. "A Village Church" in Samuel Sloan's Model Architect *(1852) was used literally by Holt in his remodeling of Emmanuel Church. (Courtesy of the Henry Francis du Pont Winterthur Museum.)*

Curiously, the complex floor plan of Ranlett's "Italian villa" (fig. 40) rather than the elevations (fig. 41) and the details, served as model for Eureka. The cross form with grand rear saloon and swirling stair offered a dramatic expansion on the standard central-hall plan. Holt, as the contract specified and his ground plan illustrates, modified the cross plan to a T (fig. 42) and altered the rear room arrangement. He placed the kitchen in a separate structure (following standard southern usage)

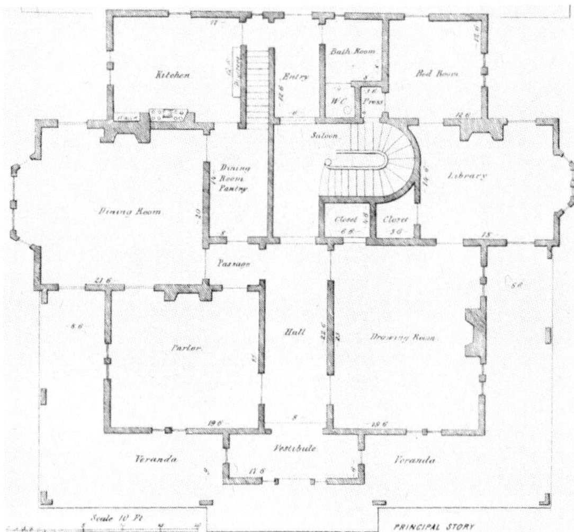

Figure 40. Ground plan for a villa, design 31, from William Ranlett's The Architect, *2 vols. (New York: Dewitt and Davenport, 1849), 2: plate 20. (Courtesy of the Henry Francis du Pont Winterthur Museum.)*

Figure 41. Design for a villa, design 31, from William Ranlett's The Architect, *2 vols. (New York: Dewitt and Davenport, 1849), 2: plate 19. (Courtesy of the Henry Francis du Pont Winterthur Museum.)*

but retained the crucial aspects of Ranlett's plan.

With the "style and finish of the work" like Baskerville's father's house "or not inferior," Eureka's lavishly applied detail epitomizes Holt's repetitive, eclectic vocabulary combined from several of Ranlett's plates (fig. 43).[53] The mantels, brackets, windows, stairs (fig. 44), and other elements are identical to those in most of Holt's other buildings of this period rather than replications of the relatively simple treatment advocated by Ranlett for the villa.

Baskerville and Holt aggrandized the composition by adding a dominant central tower, perhaps inspired by Holt's own house or, more likely, a plate for an "Italian Villa" (design VI) in Sloan's *Model Architect.* The result was a spacious villa of original design, far removed from Ranlett's plate cited in the contract.

The initial contract was but the first step in the design of Eureka. Whether at the suggestion of builder or patron, the form of the building continued to evolve. Construction progressed slowly partly because of problems Holt experienced in obtaining manufactured goods. Changes in the design also required additional work. "Extra work on dwelling house" included "Building 2 side piazzas" for $96 each, "Changing roof and building Tower difference" for $45, "Lengthening back piazza from 32 to 49 ft." for $26, and so on, to a total of nearly $1,000.[54] In such ways the design of the house continued to depart from the published model to accommodate the tastes and life-style of the client. The resulting building was perhaps Holt's grandest private project, bearing the stamp of his standardized detail but in its dramatic towered form and atypical plan reflecting the productive cooperation of builder and adventuresome client.

A far less ambitious Holt project for the Baskervilles is even more revealing of the builder's approach. After he completed Eureka, Holt corresponded with the elder Baskerville about remodeling a church:

> Dear sir—Inclosed I send you an estimate for the addition & Alteration to the Church and may seem to you to be too much, but by reference to the Items in the

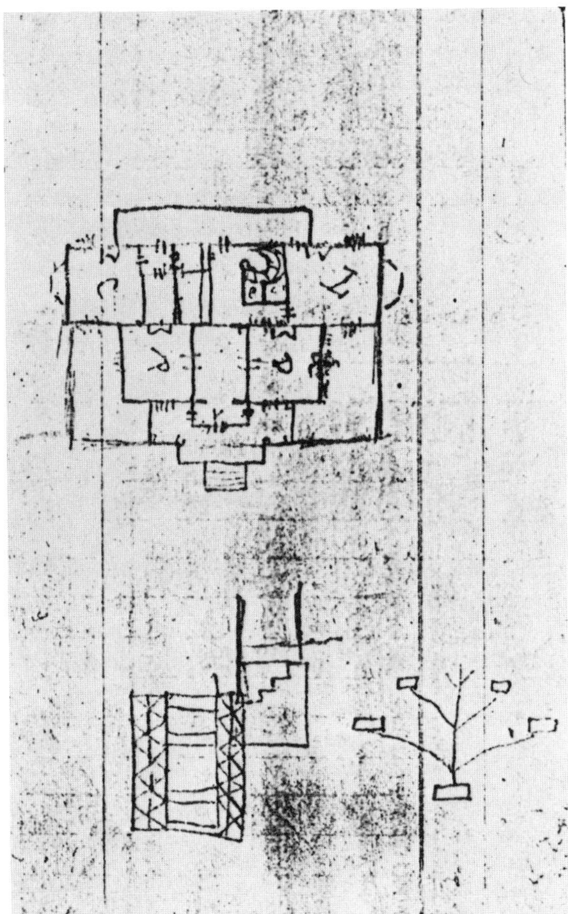

Figure 42. Sketch of the ground plan for Eureka, drawn by either Jacob W. Holt for Robert D. Baskerville or by Baskerville himself, 1857. The letters refer to rooms as shown in figure 40: parlor, dining or drawing room, library, chamber. The small treelike sketch at lower right is a scheme for the arrangement of the house and its outbuildings. (From a small personal notebook used by Robert D. Baskerville, Baskerville Papers, private collection.)

Figure 43. Eureka, built by Jacob W. Holt. Mecklenburg County, Virginia, 1857–59 or 1860. (Photograph by the author, 1977, North Carolina Division of Archives and History.)

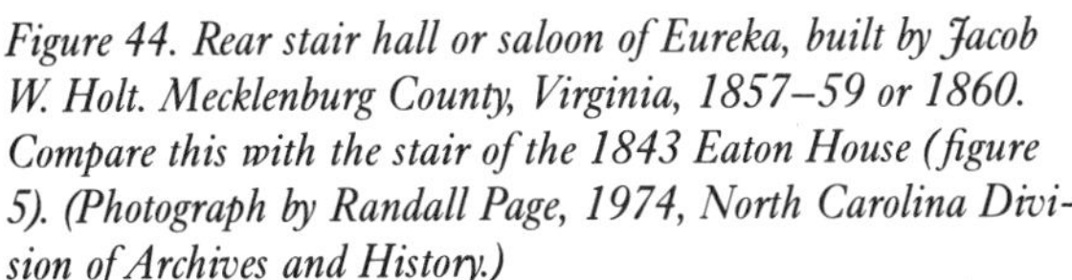

Figure 44. Rear stair hall or saloon of Eureka, built by Jacob W. Holt. Mecklenburg County, Virginia, 1857–59 or 1860. Compare this with the stair of the 1843 Eaton House (figure 5). (Photograph by Randall Page, 1974, North Carolina Division of Archives and History.)

bill you will see that it is not[.] I have put several Items lower than I have been charging for several years, the framing, weatherboarding, sheeting & shingling. Cornice & seats all are lower. The bill is made to have the work done in a manner & style that will suit you, but can be done for less money if done in a plainer manner. I have concluded to put the bill at $1150, you will please let me know whether [you] wish the bill changed to less work & plane. If such a building be entirely new it would be worth about $1900 dollars.[55]

Holt's letter reveals explicitly and unpretentiously the cool confidence, stout practicality, and unerring awareness of his client's taste and purse that undergirded his success. He knew precisely what "manner & style . . . will suit" yet expressed frankly his willingness to accommodate elegance to budget, for he would adjust his work to require "less money if done in a plainer manner."

Holt's contracts, correspondence, and sketches for the Baskerville family confirm the attitudes that permeate all his work. He was a practical builder who established priorities to focus on the needs of his patrons. He erected structures within stipulated budgets using the technology at his command. Like the folk artisans Henry Glassie has described who serve far less self-conscious cultures than Holt's mid nineteenth-century piedmont planters, Holt and his clients collaborated, "mutually influencing each other's decisions, sharing an unspoken aesthetic, discussing artifacts from the angle of practicality."[56]

Although others of his generation accepted the growing separation of design and construction, Holt continued the integration of the processes well into the 1870s, devising a highly individualized personal style and a system of production that combined standardization and an idiosyncratic version of pattern-book detail.

Because of Holt's identifiable style and the survival of many buildings and documents, his career reveals the outlines of a pattern that informs the work of many other builders across the country. This kind of builder formed a vital bridge between waning traditional culture and the rising challenges of popular culture. Holt was neither the major architect serving the elite nor the unselfconscious artisan of folk dwellings nor even the literal copyist of popular pattern books. Integrating national styles into the framework of the vernacular artisan, he was able to design and build in ways that satisfied his clients' needs for regional and traditional continuity and that also acknowledged the attraction of changing fashions. From such builders' varied and often creative resolutions of these forces springs much of the lively, expressive character of America's architecture.

Notes

This article was originally published in the *Winterthur Portfolio* (Spring 1981).

1. See Doug Swaim, "North Carolina Folk Housing," and Michael T. Southern, "The I-House as a Carrier of Style in Three Counties of the Northeastern Piedmont," *Carolina Dwelling, Towards Preservation of Place: In Celebration of the North Carolina Vernacular Landscape,* ed. Doug Swaim (Raleigh: North Carolina State University, 1978), pp. 28–45, 70–83.
2. Herbert W. Bradshaw, *History of Prince Edward County* (Richmond: Dietz Press, 1955).
3. Prince Edward County deeds, wills, estates papers, guardian bonds, Prince Edward County Courthouse, Farmville, Virginia. Howard built courthouses in Lunenburg (1824–27) and Mecklenburg (1838–42), campus buildings at Randolph-Macon College, Boydton, and perhaps others at Hampden-Sydney College. He was often associated with Dabney Cosby, prolific brick contractor in the region who had worked on the University of Virginia under Thomas Jefferson. Holt's possible association with Howard is suggested by the similarity between Holt's early work and the details of the two college campus buildings of the 1830s, the prominence of Howard and his large shop in the 1820s and 1830s, and the fact that Holt named his second son William Howard Kenneth Holt; see Prince Edward, Lunenburg, and Mecklenburg county court records; and Richard Irby, *History of Randolph-Macon College, Virginia* (Richmond: Whittet and Shepperson, 1898), p. 24.
4. Minutes of Sharon Baptist Church, Prince Edward County, Virginia State Library, Richmond; Prince Edward County marriage bonds, Prince Edward County Courthouse; Aurelia Holt tombstone, Woodland Cemetery.

5. Prince Edward County deeds; Manuscript population schedule, Prince Edward County, Virginia, 6th U.S. Census (1840), microfilm copy, North Carolina Archives. Holt was later a founding member of the Baptist church in Warrenton, North Carolina, and a member of Concord Baptist Church, Mecklenburg County, Virginia; Jacob W. Holt obituary, *Religious Herald* (Richmond, Virginia) (October 28, 1880).
6. Built in the Sandy River section of Prince Edward County, Linden, Walnut Hill, and Rotherwood, all ca. 1840, are similar to each other and to later Holt work. Edwin Edmunds, for whom Rotherwood was built, made several entries in his farm accounts that link Holt to the building of Rotherwood; Edwin Edmunds account books, Southern Historical Collection, University of North Carolina, Chapel Hill.
7. Warren County's aggregate personal and real property value per free person in 1860 was by far the highest in the state at $3,092; next highest was Edgecombe County with $2,499; other counties ranged between $200 and $1,800; see Dwight B. Billings, Jr., *Planters and the Making of a "New South"* (Chapel Hill: University of North Carolina Press, 1979), p. 48. Warren County's planters with 2,000 to 10,000 or more acres and thirty to eighty slaves—and a few with far more—ranked in the upper one-half of one percent of population in the state, where average farm size was between 300 and 400 acres, and slightly more than 30,000 out of nearly a million people owned any slaves; see Hugh T. Lefler and Albert Ray Newsome, *The History of a Southern State: North Carolina* (Chapel Hill: University of North Carolina Press, 1973), pp. 391, 420.
8. Lizzie Wilson Montgomery's excellent memoir, *Sketches of Old Warrenton* (Raleigh: Edwards and Broughton, 1924), describes the town's social history and people; it is supplemented by Victoria L. Pendleton's "Reminiscences" (two undated [ca. 1910] ms. notebooks, Warren County Historical Association File, Warren County Memorial Library, Warrenton). See also Manley Wade Wellman, *History of Warren County* (Chapel Hill: University of North Carolina Press, 1959); manuscript population schedules, Warren County, North Carolina, 6th–9th U.S. Census (1840, 1850, 1860, 1870), Miscellaneous Records, Archives Section, Division of Archives and History, North Carolina Department of Cultural Resources, Raleigh (hereafter North Carolina Archives). See also Catherine W. Bishir, "The Montmorenci–Prospect Hill School," in Swaim, *Carolina Dwelling,* pp. 84–103.
9. Montgomery, *Sketches,* pp. 196–97. The impact of these builders coming to Warrenton and Warren County and some inkling of why they came are suggested by data recorded in the 1840 census. In 1840, a few years before these craftsmen came to Warren County, the census taker recorded that only thirteen wooden houses and no brick or stone ones were built in the entire town and county. Thirty men worked on the construction of these houses, and the value of the structures was estimated at $5,030. Holt's shop alone exceeded thirty men, and two of his houses would have far exceeded $5,000. By comparison, in Prince Edward County, Virginia, where Holt and his shop were working when the 1840 census was taken, thirty stone or brick houses and fifty-eight wooden ones were built in that year, to a total value of $58,100; the work employed a total of 183 men. *Compendium of the Enumeration of the Inhabitants and Statistics of the United States* (Washington, D.C.: Department of State, 1841), pp. 184–85, 160–61.
10. Bill, M. T. Hawkins to J. W. Holt, 1850. Thomas Pittman Collection, Private Collections, North Carolina Archives.
11. Manuscript population schedule, Warren County, North Carolina, 7th U.S. Census (1850), North Carolina Archives. Carl Lounsbury's survey of builders listed in the 1850 and 1860 censuses revealed that Holt's household shop was the state's largest.
12. Emmanuel Episcopal Church Records, microfilm copy, North Carolina Archives; county accounts and claims, Courthouse Building Accounts, Warren County Records, North Carolina Archives; addition to contract for building Sylva Sonora, Warren County, North Carolina (1857–58), private collection, photocopy in possession of author.
13. Montgomery, *Sketches,* p. 197. List of Holt's buildings in possession of author, with author's notes.
14. Manuscript population schedule, Warren County, North Carolina, 8th U.S. Census (1860), North Carolina Archives.
15. After the Civil War, T. J. Holt practiced architecture in Raleigh and in Charlotte, North Carolina. Manuscript population schedule, Wake County, North Carolina, 8th U.S. Census (1860), North Carolina Archives; cornerstone of Raleigh and Gaston Company Shops building (surviving corner of ruin), Raleigh, North Carolina; *Raleigh Register* (October 24, 1860); *Weekly Raleigh Register* (May 2, 1860); *Daily Observer* (Charlotte, North Carolina) (October 10, 1869).
16. *North Carolina Standard Weekly* (Raleigh) (October 31, 1860); *Proceedings of the Grand Lodge of Ancient York Masons of North Carolina* (Raleigh: Printed by

Will C. Daub, 1855), p. 28; Nora Chaffin, *Trinity College, 1839–1892: The Beginnings of Duke University* (Durham: Duke University Press, 1950), pp. 189–92. On John Berry, see Eva Ingersoll Gatling, "John Berry of Hillsboro, North Carolina." *Journal of the Society of Architectural Historians* 10, no. 1 (March 1951): 18–22.

17. *North Carolina Standard Weekly* (Raleigh) (October 31, 1860).
18. Elizabeth C. Waugh, *North Carolina's Capital, Raleigh* (Raleigh: Junior League of Raleigh and North Carolina State University Print Shop, 1967), p. 107; Chaffin, *Trinity College,* pp. 189–92, 217–20.
19. The county's land, valued at over $3.3 million in 1860, fell to about $1.6 million by 1870, and Warrenton's population dwindled from 1,520 in 1860 to 941 in 1870 (Wellman, *History,* p. 163); *Warren Indicator* (February 14, 1868).
20. Aurelia Holt obituary (*Religious Herald* [October 3, 1895]) states that she moved to Chase City in 1869. See also Douglas Summers Brown, *Chase City and Its Environs, 1765–1975* (Richmond: Whittet and Shepperson, 1975), pp. 103–16. Interview with Gladys McKinney and Mary McKinney, March 1978.
21. *Mecklenburg Herald* (Boydton) (December 14, 1870, March 8, 1871). See also Susan L. Bracey, *Life by the Roaring Roanoke: A History of Mecklenburg County, Virginia* (Richmond: Whittet and Shepperson, 1978).
22. *Norfolk Virginian* (April 21, 1875); *Murfreesboro Enquirer* (January 11, 1877).
23. *Chataigne's Petersburg Directory* (1879–80, 1882–83, 1886–87); *J. L. Hill Printing Company's Directory of Petersburg, Virginia* (1905–6, 1907–8, 1909–10, 1911–12, 1913–14, 1915–16, 1917), Petersburg Public Library; *Manufacturer's Record* (Baltimore) (July 27, 1884).
24. The volume was published in Philadelphia in 1805 with editions through 1858 and was widely used in North Carolina and Virginia; see Henry-Russell Hitchcock, *American Architectural Books* (Minneapolis: University of Minnesota Press, 1962).
25. Montgomery (*Sketches,* p. 285) credits Eaton's house to Holt; Jack Quinan, "Asher Benjamin and American Architecture," *Journal of the Society of Architectural Historians* 38, no. 3 (October 1979): 244–56; Hitchcock, *Architectural Books,* pp. 11–12.
26. *The Practice of Architecture* was published in Boston in 1833 and six more editions through 1851. Included was a column and entablature that Benjamin explained in his preface was "selected from the Grecian antiquities and standing, with regard to expense, between the Tuscan and Doric orders."
27. Lafever's first book was published in 1829 and had but one edition. Holt's use of it is not as certain as the other volumes, but certainly Holt's columned door treatment resembles Lafever's plate more than those of Benjamin.
28. See Clay Lancaster, "Adaptations from Greek Revival Builders' Guides in Kentucky," *Art Bulletin* 32, no. 1 (March 1950): 62–70.
29. Ranlett provided designs for the popular periodical *Godey's Lady's Book,* and two North Carolina houses—Wessington in Edenton and Cooleemee in Davie County—replicated his plates in the 1850s. For Cooleemee, see Thomas T. Waterman and Frances Benjamin Johnston, *The Early Architecture of North Carolina* (Chapel Hill: University of North Carolina Press, 1947), pp. 180, 240–41.
30. See Hitchcock, *Architectural Books,* p. iii.
31. Henry Glassie, "Folk Art," in *Folklore and Folklife: An Introduction,* ed. Richard M. Dorson (Chicago and London: University of Chicago Press, 1972), pp. 253–80.
32. John T. Kirk, *Early American Furniture,* 4th ed. (New York: Alfred A. Knopf, 1977), pp. 81–82.
33. Glassie, "Folk Art," pp. 260–271.
34. Concerning the long use of the Georgian plan in American vernacular architecture, see also Swaim, "North Carolina Folk Housing"; Henry Glassie, "The Impact of the Georgian Form on American Folk Housing (Abstract)," in *Forms upon the Frontier: Folklife and Folk Arts in the United States,* ed. Henry Glassie, Austin Fife, and Alta Fife, Utah State University Monograph Series 16, no. 2 (April 1969): 23–25; and Howard W. Marshall, "Houses," unpublished manuscript.
35. Waterman and Johnston, *Early Architecture of North Carolina,* pp. 37–40.
36. Pendleton, "Reminiscences," notebook 1, p. 152. The house was built for Holt and his family about 1849–50 and sold to the Johnson family shortly after. Warren County deed books, vol. 30, p. 98, and vol. 31, p. 71, Warren County Courthouse, Warrenton, North Carolina.
37. Holt billed John E. Boyd in 1857–58 for "Extra graining in back rooms of house, $25.00" (private collection; photocopy in possession of author). The 1856 contract for Vine Hill, Franklin County, North Carolina, called for some "best style" mantels and some "plain" ones, evidently for principal and secondary rooms, respectively (private collection; photocopy in possession of author).

38. The Vine Hill contract called for "Blind door across passage (four fold) pivot, or stationary slats, $15." Other contracts include similar items. The most extravagant proliferation of doors, porches, stairs, and halls occurred at Sunnyside, a house described as built by Holt in 1850 for T. W. and Martha Harriss. It stood near Littleton, North Carolina, and burned in 1873. The house had a great front piazza with tall fluted columns. Inside were front, middle, and rear halls, each partitioned by folding (louvered?) doors. More folding doors led from the middle hall to porches on either side and from the rear hall to a porch. Stairs rose from the front and rear halls to the second floor and descended from the middle and rear hall to the basement. (Notes of Annie B. Thorne, Littleton, probably 1930s or 1940s; photocopy in possession of Edgar Thorne, Warren County.)
39. The Vine Hill contract mentions "1 Piazza in the rear 8 ft by 48 Including 2 pantries or closets," and an undated estimate that may be for Cherry Hill refers to "Back porch and closets, $80.00" (unsigned estimate for house for P. G. Alston, Henry G. Williams Collection, Southern Historical Collection, Chapel Hill, North Carolina).
40. For a discussion of this issue, see John D. Morse, ed., *Country Cabinetwork and Simple City Furniture* (Charlottesville: University Press of Virginia, 1969).
41. Holt augmented his work force through the common practice of hiring slaves by the year. He deployed both slave and free workers on his building sites, where often the client paid their board or Holt paid the client for supplying the board.
42. A steam-powered sawmill operated in Warren County by 1860, following earlier water-powered ones, but no sash and blind factory. These mass-production operations were rare in antebellum North Carolina outside a few cities but became prevalent during the industrialization and urbanization of the late nineteenth century; manuscript schedule of industry, Warren County, North Carolina, 8th U.S. Census (1860), North Carolina Archives. The development of building technology in North Carolina is discussed in Carl Lounsbury's Ph.D. dissertation for The George Washington University.
43. Montgomery, *Sketches,* p. 332.
44. See the comments of Edward F. LaFond, Jr., in "Conclusions," in Morse, *Country Cabinetwork,* pp. 282–83.
45. Montgomery, *Sketches,* p. 332; Holt leased the property for residence and workshop, Warren County deeds.
46. A. J. Davis designed Blandwood in Greensboro for John Motley Morehead in the 1840s. It was among the few towered villas in North Carolina at this time. Architect William Percival built some florid villas in Raleigh and Tarboro in the late 1850s, but this work postdates Holt's Warrenton villa. See William B. Bushong, "William Percival, an English Architect in the Old North State, 1857–1860," *North Carolina Historical Review* 57, no. 3 (July 1980): 310–39. The only other known extant North Carolina reference to this particular Downing plate, which Downing acknowledged as coming from a design by John Notman, is a brick house with Grecian detail, which served for some years as Ravenscroft School in Asheville, North Carolina. See Constance M. Greiff, *John Notman, Architect 1810–1865* (Philadelphia: Athenaeum of Philadelphia, 1979), pp. 79–80.
47. Montgomery, *Sketches,* p. 332.
48. Pendleton, "Reminiscences," notebook 1, pp. 106, 152; Montgomery, *Sketches,* p. 350; *Mecklenburg Herald* (Boydton) (April 20, 1871).
49. Unsigned, undated P. G. Alston contract possibly for Cherry Hill, Warren County, and Baskerville family papers, private collection, photocopies in possession of author. References to another building as an example in Holt's contracts continues an ancient practice among English as well as American builders; H. M. Colvin, *A Biographical Dictionary of English Architects, 1660–1840* (Cambridge: Harvard University Press, 1954), p. 6.
50. William R. Baskervill(e) papers. Baskervill(e) papers, Virginia Historical Society, Richmond (hereafter Baskerville Papers, VHS): Baskervill(e) Family Papers, private collection, photocopies in possession of author (hereafter Baskerville Papers, PC); and William R. Baskervill(e) Papers, Manuscript Collection, Perkins Library, Duke University, Durham (hereafter Baskerville Papers, DU).
51. Baskerville Papers, VHS.
52. Baskerville Papers, PC.
53. Baskerville Papers, PC.
54. Baskerville Papers, PC.
55. Holt to Col. W. R. Baskerville, June 29, 1860, Baskerville Papers, DU.
56. Glassie, "Folk Art," p. 278.

Aesthetic Ideology and Urban Design

BARBARA RUBIN

Vernacular builders confront new ideas not just as raw materials to be accepted or rejected in their own designs, but as ideological statements—interpretations of the world and the way it ought to be. In this sense, the existing landscape can be read as the product of conflicts among competing concepts of land use and the social order.

Barbara Rubin's essay is a sensitive reading of the "debate" embodied in the commercial strip. She questions the widely held assumption that the urban commercial landscape is ugly and "probably immoral." Instead, she suggests, pleas for aesthetic unity in cities are one aspect of a bid for elite control of valuable urban space. This bid is not merely ignored, but is directly opposed, by the commercial builders whose works are the subject of the following article.

Rubin locates the first direct expression of the conflict for control of the city in the World's Columbian Exposition held at Chicago in 1893. There the values of America's elite were enshrined in the carefully planned "White City" portion of the fair. Its architects ensured visual unity by adhering to common design standards. Small entrepreneurs were relegated to the narrow, crowded strip called the Midway Plaisance, where they utilized strident, individualistic structures to call attention to themselves. At the Panama-Pacific International Exposition, held in San Francisco in 1915, these techniques of self-advertisement were further refined through the use of buildings that were giant nonarchitectural sculptures. They were the ancestors of the fondly remembered giant ducks, giant milk bottles, giant coffee pots, and other curiosities that once lined America's highways. Ironically, the elements of this antiestablishment aesthetic have recently been coopted by arbiters of elite taste in an effort to draft them into the service of the official culture that once scorned them.

In the early 1970s, the Atlantic Richfield Oil Company (ARCO) sponsored a series of advertisements that appeared in popular magazines in the United States. Entitled "The Real . . . The Ideal," the series featured full-color, full-page institutional ads intended to draw attention not to ARCO and its products, but to the American social malaise and

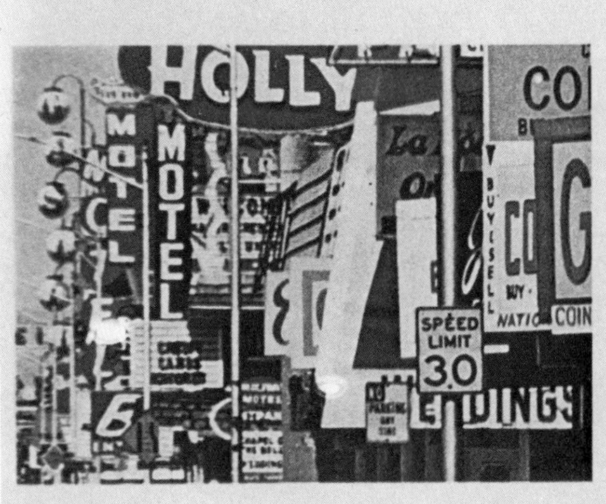

Figure 1. "The Real" as seen by the Atlantic Richfield Oil Company in its advertising campaign of the early 1970s. (From Time, *September 3, 1973, p. 26.)*

especially to its urban manifestations. In one typical ad, "The Real" was depicted as an urban commercial street described generically as "Main Street garish . . . neon nightmares . . . graceless buildings . . . billboards [that] block out the sun" (fig. 1). By contrast, ARCO's "The Ideal" was represented not by a commercial environment, but by Frank Lloyd Wright's famous Fallingwater, a residence built for a wealthy client in rural Bear Run, Pennsylvania. ARCO's description of "The Ideal" called for "structures designed for beauty and long life as well as for practicality. Man's greatest architectural achievements are those that blend in perfectly with the natural environment, or somehow create an environment of their own. They become as permanent as their natural surroundings."

Implicit in ARCO's juxtaposition of these images of a national "real" and a national "ideal" is the assertion that urban commercial environments are inevitably ugly and probably immoral, and, by contrast, that rural or suburban environments are wholesome and beautiful. Implied also through the medium of advertisement is the notion that we all share a uniform and homogeneous perception of environmental wholesomeness and beauty, and that we are in agreement that Fallingwater might be an attainable reality for everyone if only we clean up the garish neon nightmares that have become our cities.

An even less sympathetic view of the urban environment was promulgated in advertisements published by Volvo, the Swedish auto maker. In promoting the reliability of its product, Volvo presented its auto as a mobile fortress—"A Civilized Car Built for an Uncivilized World." The "uncivilized world," to Volvo, is the contemporary city symbolically represented in its ad as a wall dense with graffiti (fig. 2). Graffiti, as we well know, have come to be associated with juvenile gangs, urban poverty, alienation, lawlessness, and racial minorities—the stereotypic components of the "uncivilized world" as viewed by the predominantly white, upper middle class American to whom Volvo markets its cars.

The diversity of an urban population, or the cos-

A CIVILIZED CAR BUILT FOR AN UNCIVILIZED WORLD.
VOLVO

Figure 2. The Uncivilized World according to Volvo: the company's 1973 multimedia promotional theme for radio, television, and the press. (From Time, *November 12, 1973, p. 42.)*

mopolitan range of goods and services exchanged, is rarely taken as an index of urban success by students of urban culture. Instead, urban success is found in a catalog of a city's noncommercial, nonindustrial institutions: a philharmonic orchestra, art museums, parks, religious and historical shrines, theaters, fine-arts architecture, and unified, monumentalizing plans.

This dichotomy between urban function and urban "culture" reflects a deeper polarization in Western civilization wherein sensitivity to art, music, poetry, and other "exalted manifestations of the human spirit" are appreciated essentially and ostensibly for their own intrinsic formal qualities. By placing a primary value upon aesthetic behaviors associated with transcendental aspirations, students of culture have been unable to come to terms with the city—the modern city—as a symbolic manifestation of values mediated by forms. As a result, we have not yet been provided with demystified and pragmatic characterizations of urban form and urban function and the ideological relationships between the two. Instead, the modern city is persuasively characterized as an environment of "endless string commercial strips," "thickets of billboards," "unsightly mixed usages," "cheap, tawdry honky-tonk store fronts," "a gross commercial carnival," "a Barnum and Bailey world." These are aesthetic responses to urban function which reflect unspoken but deep antipathies toward a society "committed to the maintenance of efficiency and preservation of individual liberties through free enterprise."[1]

Who Designs the Cities?

In the history of urbanization in the United States, the few master plans that transcended functional prerequisites can be exemplified by George Washington's late eighteenth-century commission to Pierre L'Enfant to design the nation's new capital city. In contrast to the planned design of Washington, D.C., most cities in the United States evolved as pragmatic mosaics of individual functions within a geomorphological framework. By 1890, almost thirty percent of the entire U.S. population was living in cities as a result of unprecedented urban growth during the nineteenth century.[2]

In the shift from a rural culture to an increasingly urban one, the centers of social and economic power in the United States also shifted. In the nineteenth century, the inventor-entrepreneur was chiefly responsible not only for the growth of cities already in existence, but also for the new towns and cities that developed around his workshop or factory.[3] As an "old money" agrarian aristocracy shifted its base of operation from the rural estate to the city, it confronted a "new money" entrepreneur indigenous to the metropolitan environment. This confrontation engendered conflict. In coming to the city, the agrarian aristocracy "wished more than indulgence in a lavish style of life . . . it also wished general acquiescence in its position . . . The aristocracy—genuine and putative—wished to bring with them the commodious features of their landed estates. They expected the city to provide them with the elegant squares to set off their homes, with picturesque monuments, and with parks and boulevards . . . for the gentleman on horseback and for the lady in her carriage."[4]

City-building entrepreneurs were neither to the manor born nor yet socialized by the responsibilities and protocols of economic power. The urbanizing agrarian aristocracy, unable to compete in numbers or in economic strength with the urban entrepreneur, nonetheless asserted its birthright claim to preeminence. Seizing upon the transcendental symbols of high culture, the agrarian elite "transformed the theater, the opera and the museums into institutions, to display its dominance. . . . [It] turned music into classics, art into old masters, literature into rare books, possessions symbolic of its status."[5]

Following suit, the inventor-entrepreneur similarly staged himself according to his own standards and priorities for measuring success and accomplishment. He built his corporate and commercial buildings as monuments to, and advertisements of, himself. While the culture elite were competing for Old Master paintings, the emergent titans of industry were competing for preeminence on the urban horizon (fig. 3). A city's capacity to support museums, operas, theaters, and art galleries was limited by civil interest and collective financing; a city's capacity for monuments to commerce and industry was constrained only by the limitations of space.

Predictably, the culture elite could find little comfort in their control of "enculturating" institutions. By the latter part of the nineteenth century, they had moved their theater of operation to aesthetic criticism of the urban environment. Because they controlled the institutions of "official culture," their aesthetic campaigns carried weight and credibility. They found urban commercial streets to be "bizarre, blatant, and distracting." Although they understood well the competitive nature of "free enterprise" with its base in individual liberty, they objected to the use of the city as a backdrop for "hideous advertisements . . . [buildings with] striking colors . . . great height [and] sudden littleness in a wilderness of skyscrapers."[6]

The inventor-entrepreneur, on the other hand, despite his anarchic and individualistic approach to economic competition as manifested in his use of urban space in the late nineteenth century, entertained "cultural" aspirations commensurate with his wealth.[7] These aspirations became a source of vulnerability. Employing the tyranny of high culture aesthetics—*terra incognita* to the entrepreneur—the culture elite soon joined forces with architects, designers, planners, and social reformers, a highly cosmopolitan corps of professional tastemakers. By this alliance, they attempted to codify and dissemi-

Figure 3. An example of commercial competition for skyline dominance: the Bromo-Seltzer Tower Building in Baltimore, Maryland. (From a postcard in possession of the author.)

Figure 4. An "Architectural Aberration": The Record Building in Philadelphia. (From Architectural Record *1, no. 3 [January–March 1892]: 262.)*

nate standards of "good taste" in the latter half of the nineteenth century.[8] The "good taste" industry was relatively new, however, and no hierarchical ranking of "schools of good taste" or "morally correct" style was available. Merchant kings and entrepreneurs, industrialists and inventors, employed architects or designers whom they believed respectable, only to find photographs of their new corporate headquarters illustrating "Architectural Aberrations," a regular feature in the professional journal *The Architectural Record* (fig. 4). Under these circumstances, confusion prevailed.

Confusion Resolved

The promulgation of legislated aesthetics would not occur until the middle of the twentieth century.[9] In the late nineteenth century persuasion by example alone was to suffice, and a very effective program it became. The medium which was to carry the message was already in place.

A series of international expositions and world's fairs had been held in England, Germany, France, Austria, and in the United States (New York and Philadelphia) during the second half of the nineteenth century. These events were arenas in which nations vied with each other to display cultural and economic superiority; they were showcases in which technological innovation could be disseminated worldwide.[10] An implicit dimension of all these fairs became, eventually, quite explicit: the forms of architectural packaging came to be as important as the didactic displays they contained. The occasion of the 400th anniversary celebration of Columbus's discovery of the New World provided the opportunity for the culture elite, in alliance with professional taste-makers, to create the first world's fair explicitly intended to set a standard for architectural and urban design. The fair was held in Chicago in 1893. According to Daniel Burnham, its supervising architect, the overall plan of the exposition and its individual buildings had definite intentions:

> to inspire a reversion to the pure ideal of the ancients. . . . The intellectual reflex of the Exposition will be shown in the demand for better architecture, and designers will be obliged to abandon their incoherent originalities and study the ancient masters of building. There is shown so much of fine architecture here that people have seen and appreciated this. It will be unavailing hereafter to say that great classic forms are undesireable. The people have a vision before them here, and words will not efface it.[11]

In other words, the prevailing aesthetic confusion of the late nineteenth century called for the imprinting, by example, of appropriate architectural design. A precedent, of a sort, existed. In France, l'Ecole des Beaux Arts increasingly had sought to train architects whose designs would blend artfully with the earlier buildings that crowded most of the major cities of Europe.[12] The Beaux Arts style received its first major American showing at the Chicago Fair of 1893. For the United States, the imported historicism of Beaux Arts design had not to reconcile new urban construction with sanctified architectural relics; American cities were too new to be so demanding of architects' sensitivity and erudition. Instead, the importation of this eclectic Classic-Renaissance-Baroque idiom was intended to codify, by virtue of its "high culture" associations with Europe and Antiquity, the hierarchical framework by means of which "good taste" in America could be distinguished from "bad taste."

The Economics of the Ideal

The Columbian Exposition at Chicago, or "White City" as it was popularly called, had a phenomenal impact. Its courts, palaces, arches, colonnades, domes, towers, curving walkways, wooded island, ponds, and botanical displays elicited ecstatic responses from visitors to whom the "White City" was little short of a fairyland. Its monumental sculptures and gondola-studded water courses and lagoons (created expressly for the Exposition) were tangible references to the "jewel of Italy"—Venice (fig. 5). And its ground plan, complex and curvilinear, was the antithesis of the nineteenth-century urban grid pattern characteristic of most American cities.

The fair as a three-dimensional architectural pattern book opened—and closed—to mixed reviews. Some found in its historic references to European architecture evidence of America's economic and cultural maturity; to others it was a blatant and calculated exploitation of architectural style as social and cultural propaganda, masking "the monstrous evils and injustices of *fin-de-siècle* America."[13] Arguments over the implications of the fair's imported Beaux Arts style masked a more portentous feature, to wit: that its grand-planning design and monumental architecture derived from a single, unified, imposed aesthetic program, and was possible only under circumstances of centralized, authoritarian control. In addition, the realization of so grand a scheme was possible only through decentralized funding, and most of the funding was derived from the public. Public guarantee of debenture bonds purchased by banks and railroads and other corpo-

Figure 5. At the World's Columbian Exposition of 1893, Daniel Chester French's Statue of the Republic rises from the waters of the Grand Basin in front of the arched peristyle crowned with quadriga. (From Shepp's World's Fair Photographed *[Chicago: Globe Bible Publishing, 1893], p. 25.)*

rations, public subscription through stock purchases (unbacked and unguaranteed, and subsequently unredeemed), and public admission fees to the fair itself, made construction of the Exposition possible.[14] The Exposition represented no financial burden to the elite taste-makers, their lobbyists, theoreticians, and technicians, or to the city builders and commercial-industrial magnates for whom it was intended as an object lesson in design. Such were the economics of "The Ideal."

The Economics of the Real

It was intended that the Chicago Exposition of 1893 create an image of an urban ideal that would be "widely understood and approved."[15] To accomplish that end, individual liberties and competitive enterprise were suspended for the higher good of unified planning and aesthetic qualities. These ideals, as exemplified by the "White City," seemed to require no visible means of economic support. Nonetheless, the success of the Exposition was definitely measured in economic terms—increased railroad revenues and an estimated $105,000,000 left in Chicago by the 3,000,000 visitors to the fair.[16]

By the late nineteenth century, the demographics peculiar to international expositions had given rise to a class of petty entrepreneurs who specialized in exploiting the commercial opportunities the fairs made possible. At the Philadelphia Centennial Exposition of 1876, for example, "shrewd outsiders" developed a "play area" beyond the sacrosanct precincts of the city-owned Exposition grounds, in a section that became known as Shantyville.[17] By 1893, the offerings of these businessmen were for the first time acknowledged as a formal component of an Exposition.[18] But because the emerging ideology of urban aesthetics could not admit commerce, and since by definition commerce could not be aesthetic, a separate quarter within the walled precincts of the Chicago Exposition was set aside for these commercial activities—a quarter that became known as the Midway Plaisance or amusement zone.

The Midway Plaisance was a separate strip, arranged in a rigid grid pattern, set perpendicular to the grounds of the Exposition proper. In stark contrast to the sinuous arrangement of parks, ponds, and palaces in the "White City," the Midway was a street one mile long by one city block wide, with a central axis upon which commercial attractions lined up neatly along each side. In its straightforward presentation of commercial functions and in its morphology, the Midway Plaisance anticipated the twentieth-century string commercial strip or linear shopping center.

Originally, the Midway had been conceived as "Department Q of the Ethnological Division," established for the purpose of gathering "the peculiar and unknown peoples of the world" for display.[19] Because a living museum of mankind did not conform to the aesthetic program of the fair, Department Q was assigned quarters adjacent to, rather than integrated with, the Exposition city, and was left to its own devices for funding. By virtue of the necessity of turning a profit simply to exist, the "living museum" and its attendant support activities (curio stands, food stands, amusement rides and entertainments) quickly became a "hilarious amusement zone . . . synonymous for masked folly."[20]

Environments, more or less authentic, were constructed to display their exotic inhabitants: Dahomean, Dutch, Turkish, and American Indian villages, a Moorish Palace, a Chinese Pagoda, and a street in Cairo (fig. 6). Cultural merchandising proved effective. The raucous, colorful, competitive commerce of the Midway developed as the antithesis of the noneconomic aesthetic ideal of the Beaux Arts "White City." Although the Midway may have sacrificed some veracity in environmental design in favor of sensational impact, visitors judged its impact to be "far better than any dead collection of antiquities. To see the people themselves, alive, moving, acting in their costumes, manners, build-

Figure 6. "The Streets of Cairo," a popular exotic environment of the Midway Plaisance, World's Columbian Exposition, 1893. (From Shepp's World's Fair Photographed, *p. 507.)*

Figure 7. An urban "Ideal" confronts an urban "Real": Dewey Arch versus Heinz Pickles in Madison Square, New York. (From Municipal Affairs *4 [1900]: 275.)*

ings, businesses, is far more instructive than to look at their remains in art, or their empty armor, or their skeletons."[21]

The Midway Plaisance and the "White City" alike were architectural illusions. Each was an ephemeral environment in which structures were built merely of stucco applied over lath (attached to framing). The stucco had been ingeniously worked to create the impression of permanent materials: brick, marble, travertine, granite, and other materials and techniques of construction that suggested a material and structural integrity. Almost all the buildings on both the Midway Plaisance and in the "White City" were dismantled and discarded at the conclusion of the Exposition. It was only the "White City," however, which was intended "to leave a residue in the minds of men and in printer's ink."[22]

The Exposition's spiritual residue was made manifest in tangible programs and artifacts that appeared outside the walled city. The Chicago fair was credited with stimulating the "City Beautiful" movement that spread nationwide through the organization of local municipal arts societies.[23] It was a movement concerned solely and exclusively with urban aesthetics and not with the economic realities of urban function or the social realities of poverty and class stratification that made the city "ugly."

Civic beautification programs developed the Exposition's Baroque and Neoclassical architectural vocabulary and planning syntax in new banks, city halls, schools, skyscrapers, fire stations, and urban squares throughout the United States (fig. 7). Urban furniture, such as Dewey Arch in New York City, "stirred local pride and national interest, and for a mile up Fifth Avenue to the top of Murray Hill its features are most prominent in the view of that thronged thoroughfare. For the whole distance, in a blaze of color by day and a glare of electric flashlights by night, the sculpture and the lines of the Arch . . . stand out."[24] Dewey Arch was not alone in commanding this spectacular vista; set against it "in the daytime, [is] a thirty foot cucumber, in bright green on an orange background above a field of scarlet, lettered in white. . . . In the evening the dancing flash-light of the '57 varieties' of beans, pickles, etc. [is] thrown in the faces of all who throng Madison Square."[25] The sacred "ideal" of the "White City" as well as the profane "real" of the Midway had escaped the controlled precincts of the Exposition, but in the urban milieu the boundaries separating the "real" from the "ideal" blurred. No form was sacrosanct, and no medium was immune to exploitation (fig. 5). Even the sculptural centerpiece of the Chicago Exposition—Daniel Chester French's monumental Statue of Columbia—ultimately found its way into billboard advertising, and is, in reproduction, an awesome presence in Hollywood's commercial necropolis, Forest Lawn (fig. 8.)[26]

Overwhelming the aesthetic program so clearly delineated by the Chicago Exposition, the "advertising curse" proliferated across urban landscapes of America. Its progress was viewed by taste-makers as "a measure at once of progress of civilization and lack of culture."[27] Fundamentally different from the outset, "The Real," unlike "The Ideal," had to pay its own way.

Figure 8. One-third the size of the original Statue of the Republic, Forest Lawn's "Republic" stands opposite a monumental statue of George Washington in the cemetery's Court of Freedom. Also an original, this Republic was one of two produced by Daniel Chester French after the World's Columbian Exposition. Height: 18 feet 2 inches; head and arms of Carrara marble, remainder cast in bronze with draperies overlaid with gold. (Photograph by the author.)

Migrations of the Propaganda Machine

Despite the massive initial impact of the "White City," the Exposition's aesthetic propaganda almost immediately began to dissipate over space and time. To capitalize on the energy and momentum begun by the Chicago Exposition, a series of similar fairs throughout the United States quickly followed: in 1897, Nashville; in 1898, Omaha; in 1901, Buffalo; in 1904, St. Louis; in 1905, Portland. At each, the separation of commerce and culture was maintained essentially as had been the case at Chicago. Beaux Arts "White Cities," with minor variations and in a different scale, were reproduced at each new site to reinforce the ideals of architectural and urban design (fig. 9). Whereas the aesthetic ideal for urban design remained more or less static, the competitive ethic of commerce fueled the continued evolution of Midway merchandising.

Midway concessionaires migrated with the expositions. In continuously adjusting and adapting their entertainments and attractions, they sought the optimum synthesis of art and commerce. It was a dual concern that made the Midway zone a dynamic environment for architectural merchandising (fig. 10). No environment was too exotic and no experience too alien to escape commercial exploitation on the Midway. At the Buffalo Pan-American Exposition of 1901, where Midway visitors were offered a trip to the moon, an enervated critic lamented:

> The prodigal modern Midway is fairly using up the earth. A few more Expositions and we shall have nothing left that is wonderfully wonderful, nothing superlatively strange; and the delicious word "foreign" will have dropped out of the language. Where shall we go to get us a new sensation? Not to the heart of the Dark Continent; Darkest Africa is at the Pan American. Not to the frozen North; we have met the merry little fur-swathed, slant-eyed Eskimos behind their papier-mache glacier at Buffalo. Not to the far islands of the Pacific; Hawaiians, and little brown Filipinos are old friends on the new Midway. Not to Japan; tea-garden geisha girls, and trotting, jin-riksha men have rubbed the bloom off that experience. Not Mexico, not Hindoostan, not Ceylon, not the Arabian Desert, can afford us a thrill of thorough-going surprise. . . . The airship Luna leaves in three minutes for a Trip to the Moon . . . not satisfied with exhausting the earth, they have already begun upon the universe. Behold, the world is a sucked orange.[28]

Figure 9. In the Beaux-Arts tradition, a "White City" constructed for the Louisiana Purchase Exposition, St. Louis, 1904: Festival Hall and the Grand Basin. (From The Universal Exposition *[St. Louis: Official Publication, 1904].)*

The exposition impulse had migrated to California by 1915. On the occasion of the opening of the Panama Canal, California was host to not one, but two, international expositions. Grand design for expositions had not been substantially altered in the westward migration of world's fairs. At the San Francisco Exposition of 1915, the Beaux Arts architectural environment was a polychrome version of Chicago's "White City." At the San Diego Exposition, held simultaneously with San Francisco's, the same building technology (stucco applied to lath attached to framing) was used to create an Hispanic-colonial "mission style" architecture that would ultimately make its own distinctive contribution to the architectural history of California.[29]

As an object lesson for urban designers, the San Francisco Beaux Arts landscape was anachronistic even before it opened; it represented the last grand florescence of what had begun with the Chicago

Figure 10. An extraordinary facade on the Zone: the entrance to Dreamland, "A Midway Mystery at the Pan-American Exposition," Buffalo, 1901. The "mystery" was how to exit after entering. "Dreamland" was a maze. (From The World's Work Magazine, *August 1901.)*

Exposition of 1893. The entertainment zone at San Francisco, however, was to be of some consequence in its impact upon urban design.

The Midway at the San Francisco Exposition was host, for the most part, to attractions and concessions of proven commercial viability. For the first time at an Exposition, the fair's administrators and designers turned their attention to Midway design. Not only were the professional services of Exposition designers offered to Midway concessionaires, but the Exposition management announced the requirement that all concessions were to be self-identifying without the aid of billboards or signs.[30]

As a result of the sanction against signing, the Midway at the San Francisco Exposition became a zone of out of scale "signature architecture." Each attraction became an advertisement of itself either in its three-dimensional form or by means of visual cues—"facade architecture"—attached to the front of the structure. A gigantic Golden Buddha announced the presence of a Japanese concession (fig. 11). "Tin soldiers," approximately ninety-feet tall, housed merchandise booths in their feet (fig. 12). The Atchison, Topeka, and Santa Fe Railway constructed a scale model of the Grand Canyon of Arizona; the Union Pacific Railway reproduced Yellowstone Park (with Old Faithful and the Inn); a large and realistic pueblo was occupied by real Indians, and a scale model of the Panama Canal had an actual working canal with an ocean at each end. Other exhibits included the Blarney Castle, a Samoan Village, and a troupe of Maori tribesmen who also camped on the zone.[31] Amusements and displays, as advertisements of themselves, depended on their architectural merchandising for continued commercial success.

On the opening day of the Exposition, all but twenty-six feet of the entire Midway footage of six-

Figure 11. The golden Buddha claiming attention for the "Japan Beautiful" exhibit on "The Zone" at the Panama Pacific International Exposition in San Francisco, 1915. (Courtesy of the Special Collections, University Research Library, University of California, Los Angeles.)

Figure 12. Ninety feet tall, these monumental toy Tin Soldiers housed stores in their feet on "The Zone" at the Panama-Pacific International Exposition in San Francisco, 1915. (Courtesy of the Special Collections, University Research Library, University of California, Los Angeles.)

thousand feet had been sold to concessionaires. Along these empty twenty-six feet, the concessions manager ordered that false fronts be erected and painted to make the vacant footage appear to belong to adjacent occupied booths and theaters.[32] In an aesthetic peculiar to commerce, any sign of activity—however illusory—was preferable to a void. Emptiness disrupted economic symmetry and signaled dysfunction and blight.

Leaving the Walled City

Midway design was acknowledged to be of "a necessary garishness," whereas the Exposition proper had been designed for another sort of impact: "to refine and uplift and dignify the emotions."[33] Both were architecturally didactic. It is hardly surprising, however, that American entrepreneurs chose to exploit the idiom of the amusement zone for the architecture of commerce: the Midway mode was the end result of two decades of intensive experimentation and refinement of commercial forms, in the hothouse environment of Midway competition.

In California, and especially in southern California, the transition from Midway to urban commercial street was relatively simple. The stucco construction methods employed to produce ephemeral structures for the expositions were particularly suited to southern California's mild climate. The addition of cement to the stucco mixture—a technological breakthrough that occurred in time for the San Diego and San Francisco

Expositions and that enabled the stucco to carry pigment—was the essential ingredient for stabilizing this previously unreliable building material.[34]

This new genre of commercial architecture was most apparent in Los Angeles, where the streets seemed choked with windmill bakery shops, giant tamales, Sphinx heads, outdoor pianos, owls, and landlocked ships (fig. 13).[35] The ultimate origin of these structures was confirmed by a visitor to Los Angeles in the 1920s who noted that here was a city where "one must even buy one's daily bread under the illusion of visiting the Midway Plaisance."[36] The unreality of this dispersed Midway landscape was heightened by the presence of the film industry in Hollywood. A Swiss visitor to Los Angeles in 1929 wondered "Why do they build special Hollywood towns? One hardly knows where the real city stops and the fantasy city begins. Did I not see a church yesterday and believe it belonged to a studio—only to find out it was a real church? What is real here and what is unreal? Do people live in Los Angeles or are they only playing at life?"[37]

The convergence of urban commercial realities and Hollywood commercial fantasies, in addition to the profusion of Midway-style structures in southern California, began to earn for the region its reputation as the home of the hard sell—a region in which "culture" did not vitiate commercial densities, but where commerce became instead the predominant form of culture. Nonetheless, Midway-style architecture was not unique to southern California. A poultry store on Long Island established itself in the Big Duck; a dairy stand in Boston could be found in a gigantic milk bottle; a Cincinnati snack shop was built into a giant sandwich flanked by monumental salt and pepper shakers; a Texas gas station was built in the shape of an oil derrick, and one in North Carolina was built as a seashell; in Iowa, a giant coffee pot housed a diner, and in New Orleans a nightclub named Crash Landing was partially constructed from the front end of a Lockheed Constellation (complete with wings).[38] These, and countless examples that have escaped documentation, bore witness to the nationwide exploitation of Midway "signature architecture" in which form often quite literally followed function.

Architectural idiosyncracy in the Midway genre quickly established itself as a successful medium for merchandising. By the late 1920s, suburban business districts (which followed suburban residential subdivision and development) had their share of "signature" structures and facade architecture. The encroachment of commerce upon the suburban residential fringes became synonymous, to critics, with social pathology. Displeasing architectural design seemed to represent an environmental threat equivalent to garbage dumps.

> In American cities of any considerable size our new outlying business centers frequently are becoming the ugliest, most unsightly and disorderly parts of the entire city. . . . Buildings of every color, size, shape and design are being huddled and mixed together in a most unpresentable manner. A mixture of glowing billboards, unsightly rubbish dumps, hideous rears, unkempt alleys, dirty loading docks, unrelated, uncongenial mixtures of shops of every type and use, with no relation to one another; shacks and shanties mixed up with good buildings; perfectly square, unadorned buildings of poor design, are bringing about disorder, unsightliness and unattractiveness that threaten to mar the beauty and good appearance of the residential regions of American cities.[39]

But the spatial organization of a society ideologically committed to the maintenance of efficiency and preservation of individual liberties through free enterprise permitted and even required the areal repetition of commercial centers and the competitive and economical design of the structures which comprised them.

Franchise Architecture

By the middle of the twentieth century, the rhetoric of economic competition, fundamental to Midway philosophy and morphology, had become formula. Signature architecture ultimately served as the cornerstone upon which a massive franchise industry

Figure 13. Clockwise, from top left: A windmill bakery in Los Angeles in the 1920s (courtesy of the Los Angeles Public Library); a tamale food stand in Los Angeles in the 1930s (courtesy of the Los Angeles Public Library); an evangelical ship of good hope: The Haven of Rest Radio Studio, constructed in the mid-1930s and still in use in North Hollywood (photograph by the author); The Hoot Owl Ice Cream Shop in Los Angeles in the 1920s (courtesy of the Special Collections, University Research Library, University of California, Los Angeles); The Big Red Piano Store, built in Los Angeles in the 1930s and a survivor until the mid-1970s when preservationists attempted to transplant it (courtesy of Seymour Rosen, SPACES, *Inc.); and a real estate office in the head of a Sphinx, Los Angeles (undated) (photograph by John Pastier).*

MALTED
MILK
AS YOU LIKEM
THE TAMALE
HAMBURGERS · HOT TAMALE PIE · CHILI · SPANISH DELIGHT · TAMALES
6421

HOOT HOOT
I SCREAM

HAVEN OF REST

developed in the United States after World War II.

Franchising in the United States has been a method of marketing and distribution of goods and services based upon a clear delineation of territory. The geographic foundations for American franchising can be traced to the system of merchandising devised by the Singer Sewing Machine Company at the end of the Civil War. Later, the auto industry developed a similar system of franchised dealers for achieving a national distribution of cars, and with the proliferation of auto franchises, a national network of franchised service stations was also established. Similarly, at the turn of the century, Coca-Cola and Pepsi Cola launched their soft drink empires based solidly upon the use of franchised distributors. By the 1920s, the well-known names of Howard Johnson and A&W Root Beer had entered the American franchise scene. This franchise method of distribution, however, did not inspire widespread emulation until the 1950s.[40]

Often mistaken for a giant corporate monolith intent upon smothering the nation with its corporate presence, each unit within a franchise is actually a locally owned business operated by independent entrepreneurs. Owners typically buy the right or privilege to do business in a franchisor's prescribed manner, in a specific geographic region, and for a specific period of time. The purchase of a franchise generally involves the use of the parent company's methods, symbols, trademarks, architectural style, and network of wholesale suppliers.[41] The effort to produce a "packaged appearance" and to maintain a "chain identity" despite independent ownership has made modern franchising successful within the context of multiple competitors for the same market.[42]

The franchise system was almost a century old when it suddenly became a widespread phenomenon in the United States. At the end of World War II, a growing pool of economically alienated Americans, especially returning veterans and displaced farmers, dreamed the dream of financial and personal independence conferred through private ownership of a business.[43] So successful were some franchise operations that the United States seemed, in the 1950s and 1960s, to be overrun by franchised hamburgers, ice cream, donuts, fried chicken, motels, and rental cars, all engaged in mortal combat for national, regional, and local markets. In almost every case, a franchise was closely identified with its signature architecture. One of the most successful franchises—McDonald's hamburgers—underwent in twenty years an architectural evolution indicative of the manner in which values are mediated by forms.

McDonald's became a franchise operation in 1955. The original McDonald's stand was built in San Bernardino, California, by the brothers McDonald who owned and operated a drive-in, fast-food stand under their name. The transformation of this single stand into an international franchise network was made by Ray Kroc, a traveling salesman impressed by the volume of business generated by this single store.[44] Integral to the transformation was the McDonald's name and the signature structure that was to become synonymous with the product in its initial phase of expansion: a building with red and white stripes, touches of yellow, oversized windows, and a distinctive set of arches that went up through the roof. These "golden arches," when viewed from the proper angle, described the letter *M* (fig. 14). A generation of Americans has proved that such highly abstract signature architecture can effectively come to signify standardized hamburgers, milk shakes, and french-fried potatoes.

As the franchise system began to expand, however, the original McDonald's signature structure was found to be inappropriate in temperate climates. The building had been designed for San Bernardino's semidesert location; it had a wide roof overhang, huge windows, no basement, and required only an evaporative cooler on its roof, with no space provided for a heating plant.[45] Acknowledging the importance of signature architecture to franchise success, the corporation designed a series of adaptations for different climatic conditions that would result in no discernible displacement of signature elements. By the mid-1960s, McDonald's "golden

Figure 14. Original McDonald's architecture of the 1950s. Advertising postcard offering one free hamburger for redemption of card. (Photograph by the author.)

arches" blanketed the nation, each stand keeping score of the number of hamburgers (by then in the billions), that had been sold by McDonald's. At the same time, evidence began to accumulate from California—the hearth region which had generated the original form—that golden-arched hamburger sales were in decline.[46] Because Los Angeles had been the cradle of drive-in restaurants, the parent company sent an investigator to the city. He conducted his field research in front of "an invitingly clean" McDonald's that was doing no business, and observed "the flow of people in bizarre looking cars and the pedestrians walking brightly ribboned dogs, typical Angelinos in their habitat. [He concluded]: 'The reason we can't pull people in here is because these golden arches blend right into the landscape. People don't even see them. We have to do something different to get their attention.' "[47] The Los Angeles experience highlighted a major limitation of the extreme forms of signature architecture: in a hypercompetitive commercial environment, by some Alice-in-Wonderland inversion, the extraordinary becomes normal and thus invisible; the restrained and understated stand out.

In the mid-1960s, McDonald's initiated a new architectural style for its franchised structures. Agreeing now with critics who had long decried the original flat-roofed, candy-striped, golden-arched design as a major contributor to visual blight in America, McDonald's "new" architectural recipe drew upon "elite," conventional forms, materials, and behavioral modes: brick-surfaced buildings with mansard roofs, pseudo-antique furnishings and fixtures, and interior eating areas.[48] Because the franchise logo was heavily invested in the "golden arch" motif, that element, in an abbreviated, scaled-down, detached, two-dimensional version, was preserved as the signature feature, completely indepen-

Figure 15. The McDonald's "new look" of the late 1960s: brick walls, mansard roof, and interior dining spaces. Constructed in Santa Monica in the 1960s. (Photograph by the author.)

Figure 16. Jack-in-the-Box in Los Angeles: a rectangular building with a changeable facade and freestanding sign. (Photograph by the author.)

Figure 17. *Colonel Sanders' Kentucky Fried Chicken in Santa Monica, with brick detailing, mansard roof, and freestanding sign. (Photograph by the author.)*

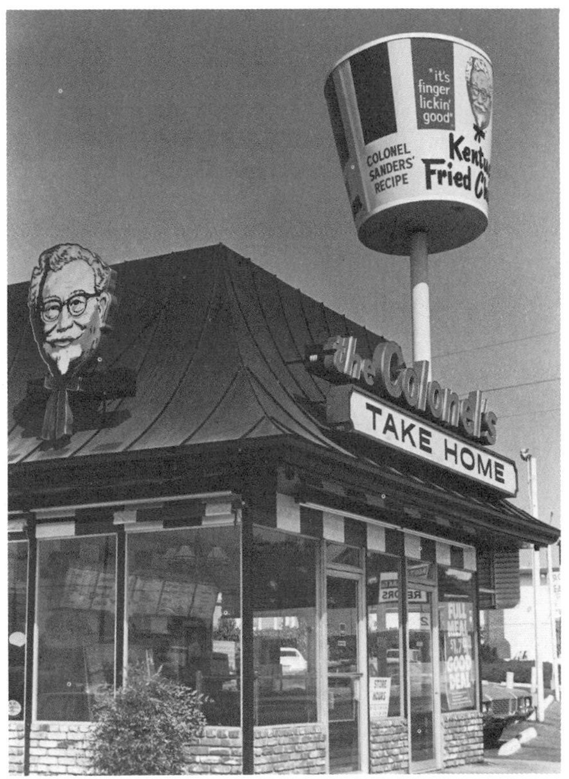

dent of the structure itself (fig. 15). The separation of the signature element from the structure made good economic sense because it eased the transition in recycling a building to other commercial uses.

Following the McDonald's example, many franchises in the 1960s eschewed signature architecture in favor of portable statements of franchise identities placed adjacent to the relatively conventional buildings they occupied (figs. 16, 17). Others, however, elected to accept the risk of investing identity and success in a continuation of Midway merchandising (fig. 18). Moreover, the earlier stages of franchise architecture seem to have stimulated a renaissance in architectural design based more

Figure 18. The first successful Taco Bell made its appearance in Los Angeles in 1963 and became a franchise in 1965. By the mid-1970s, 325 franchises had been sold, with the largest concentration of Taco Bells in the Middle West, California, and Texas. This one, photographed in Santa Monica, was constructed in 1966. (From Barbara Rubin, "A Promising Manana," Forbes *120, no. 3 [August 1, 1977]: 62.)*

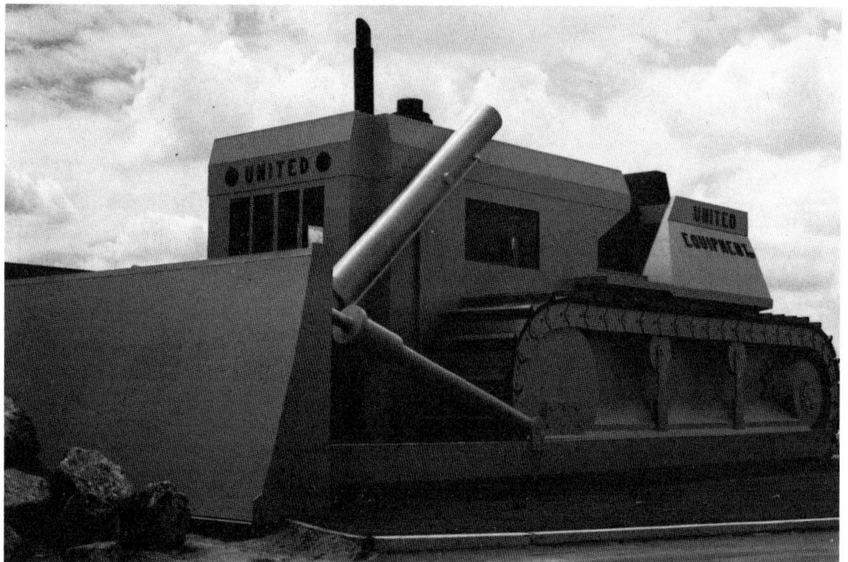

Figure 19. Office building in a two-story tractor, built by the United Equipment Company near Fresno, California; the architect-designed structure was completed in 1977. (Photograph by the author.)

Figure 20. Old Town Mall, an enclosed shopping center constructed in the early 1970s in Torrance, California, was designed with Disneyland's Main Street as its architectural model. (Photograph by the author.)

closely on Midway principles. Entrepreneurs operating businesses unassociated with franchise networks began, in the late 1960s, once again to exploit unusual forms and architectural assemblages intended to arrest, amaze, and delight. Gigantism as exploited in the 1915 San Francisco Exposition, and subsequently in the 1920s and 1930s in regions sustaining urbanization and suburbanization, began to reappear (fig. 19). Unlike the early stucco structures, these latter twentieth-century architectural whimsies represent substantial economic investments: a bulldozer office building for a heavy equipment company; Victoria Station (from whose initial success was cloned a chain and numerous independent imitators) as a restaurant in an assemblage of freight cars and cabooses; and Best Products Company has claimed national attention with its "indeterminate facade" buildings—among others, a showroom in Sacramento that appears to have had a bite taken out of one corner (actually its entryway).[49]

Under these circumstances of heightened architectural merchandising, it was inevitable that the architecture of modern urban commerce would be drawn ever more closely to its source. "Theme" shopping centers and malls of the 1970s now provide the illusion of other times and other places. Like the Midway Plaisance they emulate, they represent walled enclaves wherein are merchandised an international panoply of products, services, and exotic experiences (fig. 20). The ultimate architectural statement in this regard is, of course, Disneyland, itself a synthesis of the great American world's fairs of the nineteenth and twentieth centures.[50] There is, in fact, less and less to distinguish between the conventional forms of retail merchandising and the Disney version of wonderland: an architectural review of the opening of a new regional shopping center in Los Angeles was entitled "A New Kind of Amusement Park."[51]

The Compelling Aesthetic

As the styles and forms of the architecture of urban commerce evolved in the United States, so too did the actors competing for dominance of the social and economic life of the city. The main features of urban morphologies had been, for the most part, delineated and established by industrialists and entrepreneurs during the late nineteenth and early twentieth centuries. The latter part of the twentieth century might be characterized as a period of the filling-in of the urban interstices. Key economic functions—industrial, commercial, and governmental—continue to occupy central places and satellite nodes, and within them, express increasing densities through vertical expansion. Less costly horizontal expanses of the city are still claimed by the petty entrepreneur, however.

The problems of gaining control of urban space—and ultimately of urban life—that engaged the rural agrarian elite in contending for the nineteenth-century city are the same problems that confront the corporate elite today. Not surprisingly, members of the contemporary elite exploit the same institutions through which their predecessors had sought to accomplish the same objective. Centers of culture and their taste-making, trend-setting, culture-validating functions have come to be controlled on a national scale by political, corporate, and elite family dynasties. Business and genealogy play the same role on regional and local scales. Higher education, in particular, has been acknowledged as probably "the single most powerful factor" in the standardization of taste, and indeed, in the standardization of culture.[52] Thus it is also not surprising to find in the latter half of the twentieth century that the corps of professional taste-makers has expanded to include educators whose role it is to disseminate "official culture" as defined by those who increasingly control their institutions. Just as the nineteenth-century agrarian elite sought to neutralize and divert the growing economic power of the corporate entrepreneur, the corporate elite, now dominant, seeks to control and manipulate mass culture and the petty entrepreneur.

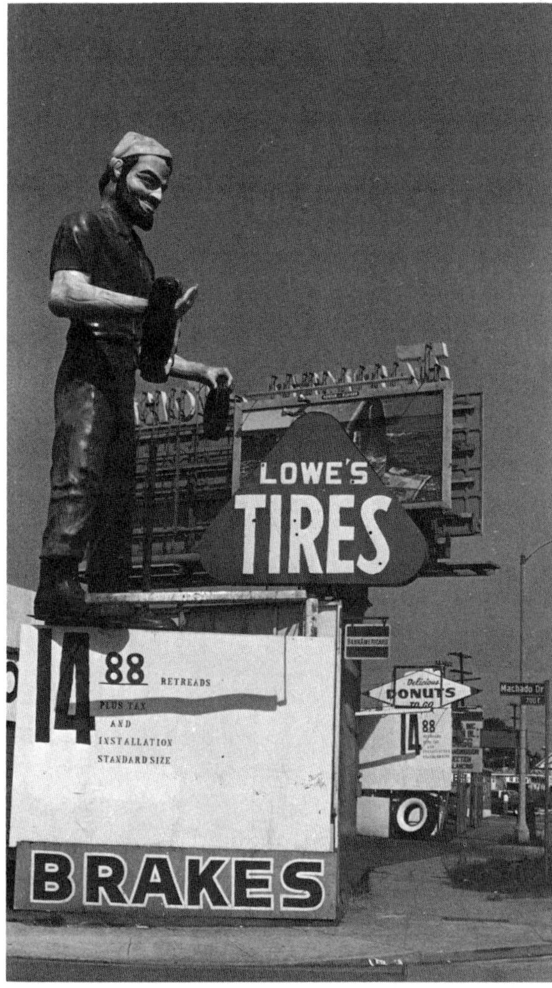

Figure 21. Lowe's Tire Man, an attention getter on Lincoln Boulevard, a commercial route in Los Angeles. (Photograph by the author.)

The exploitation of the American ideology of urban aesthetics is difficult to refute. Its objectives are appealing, and it seems not to conflict with that other American ideology which postulates a society committed to the preservation of individual liberties through free enterprise. In the nineteenth century, the culture elite and professional taste-makers excoriated the corporate monoliths that had begun to dominate the urban skyline. Their twentieth century counterparts devote their critical faculties to condemnation of the myriad small businesses that have filled in the urban interstices and occupy now-valuable urban space. The contemporary urban boulevard is characterized as "a gross carnival of signs and billboards . . . with no style or unity, little architecture and few aesthetics."[53] Urban commerce is described as a "relentless, oppressive attack on the senses . . . the beat of the sell is nearly constant, like living under a tin roof in a monsoon."[54] The small businessman is accused of "crude architectural huckstering which never helped the economy of a town. It helped kill it. It destroyed not only the integrity of old buildings but also the town's integrity—the image of innocence, wholesomeness and honesty."[55]

The canons of these critics would thus exclude from the marketplace of the city those who are usually the most lively and the most vulnerable—the small businessmen and entrepreneurs whose capital is so limited and whose footholds so tenuous that their survival depends upon maximally effective, portable icons: neon signs, billboards, and fiberglass totems (fig. 21). Not surprisingly, aesthetic campaigns gain momentum when urban commercial space appreciates in value.

Where "crude architectural huckstering" metamorphoses into massive corporate success, however, the contempt of taste-makers is supplanted by respect. When it became evident that the McDonald's formula was working, its architectural aspect soon became "the object of much serious discussion in architectural classes. James Volney Righter, who teaches architecture at Yale, says he believes the [new] style 'holds great potential in that it links the energy of the lively American *pop* forms with functional utility and quality construction.' "[56] Ada Louise Huxtable, architecture critic for the *New York Times* began to find "aesthetic merit and cultural meaning" in these urban vernacular commercial forms.[57] And with transparent cynicism, Charles Jencks, writer and teacher of architectural history has suggested that "Since you can't escape Bad Taste any more, the only thing you can do is apply standards to it and discover when it is really subversive and enjoyable. Today, most man-made things are horribly mediocre, but happily, a few of them are really awful. We have to cultivate principles of banality not just to survive but to keep the lovably ridiculous from slipping into the merely no-account."[58]

Professional taste-makers are doing precisely that. In 1976, the Society for Commercial Archaeology was founded "to promote the understanding, documentation and preservation of significant structures and symbols of the commercial built environment."[59] Earlier, Yale architect Robert Venturi paid tribute to a spectacular efflorescence of gambling architecture in his book *Learning from Las Vegas*.[60] In the process of manufacturing academic and professional capital, taste-makers have begun to invest the remnants of an earlier age of architectural refugees from world's fair Midways with the aura of transcendental meaning. Los Angeles's few surviving hotdogs, donuts, and derbies are now being apotheosized as significant Urban Art.

> Of all the landmarks threatened with eventual extinction by bulldozer and high rise, none will be mourned with such mixed feelings as the[se] grandly eccentric monuments. . . . Holdovers from a more rococo era, they gave Southern California a colorful and often unwelcome stamp in the 20s and 30s as the home of architectural anarchy. . . . In retrospect, the worst of the kookie structures seems less abortive than ill-timed. With the advent of pop art and "camp" movements, they might have found homes in art galleries rather than on street corners.[61]

In the ideology of American aesthetics, it is understood that those who make taste make money, and those who make money make taste. In the twentieth century, this logic manifests itself primarily in an urban context: it is pivotal in the battle for urban territory and urban markets. No one worries the farmer for his unaesthetic barns. All ideologies have their time and their space.

This Is Not a Conclusion

A fundamental contradiction is evident in examinations of the forms and structures of contemporary American commerce in its urban context. Investigations of function and morphology have revealed the operation of coherent, efficient systems. The inherent instability of the urban economic environment is accepted as a corollary of the "free enterprise" system. Nevertheless, urban economic networks have been abstracted and analyzed quantitatively and cartographically, revealing evidence of logic and order accepted by most scholars and policymakers. In contrast, the material culture of urban commerce, the framework within which networks of distribution and consumption are operationalized, has been portrayed in diametrically opposite terms. Few students of culture would claim that the architectural forms and the syntax of commercial competition conform to discernible patterns deriving from a coherent system of belief and behavior, parallel to the "free enterprise" logic that provides a rational basis for the analysis of economic behavior. The three-dimensional space occupied by urban commerce—the heritage of World's Fair amusement zones—is invariably characterized as dysfunctional, even pathological. How is this conceptual disjunction, originating in different aspects of one and the same urban space, and within a single framework of objectives, to be explained?

One explanation resides in the fact that the "aesthetic impulse" which filters perception of three-dimensional space has little to do with the formal appreciation of shapes, colors, or combinations thereof. As chronicled in this paper, the merchandising of "good taste" in urbanizing America long ago coalesced as an aesthetic ideology that has permeated public policy and public programs. Urban "ugliness" and urban "blight," variously defined, have been employed as rhetorical gambits in propaganda campaigns to control the use of appreciating urban space. Typically, the costs of aesthetic programs, beginning with the "White City" of 1893, have been borne most heavily by those who benefit from them the least. Yet aesthetic ideology continues to mold attitudes toward environmental design and urban development because it is reinforced by academics and policymakers who operate as powerful allies of "official culture." Aesthetic ideology remains a potent vehicle for the perpetuation of urban, economic, and social inequalities, and serves as reinforcement for another oppressive ideology: that our economy is based upon the maintenance of efficiencies through free enterprise.

It is only a matter of time before academics and policymakers will be forced to confront the inconsistencies and disjunctions arising from the evidence of their own research. Ultimately they will have to go beyond the quantifiers' and cartographers' two-dimensional discussions of the mechanics of urban economics and the impressionistic value judgments of critics and historians of architecture. To begin, they will have to examine the manipulations and special pleadings which have operated to distort and impede their understanding of the symbolic, syncretic, and integrated nature of that dauntingly complex nexus which is the modern American city. In that vast no-man's-land separating "The Real" from "The Ideal" lie many opportunities for enlightenment.

Notes

This article was originally published in the *Annals of the Association of American Geographers* (September 1979).

1. Brian J. L. Berry, *Commercial Structure and Commercial Blight,* Research Paper no. 85, Department of Geography, University of Chicago, 1963, p. 2.
2. Oscar and Mary F. Handlin, *The Wealth of the American People* (New York: McGraw-Hill, 1975), p. 143.
3. Richard L. Meier, "The Organization of Technological Innovation in Urban Environments," in *The Historian and the City,* ed. Oscar Handlin (Cambridge: MIT Press, 1963), p. 76.
4. Handlin and Handlin, *Wealth of the American People,* pp. 21–22.
5. Ibid.
6. Charles Mulford Robinson, *Modern Civic Art* (New York: G. Putnam's Sons, 1901), p. 132.
7. Russell Lynes, *The Taste-Makers* (New York: Harper and Brothers, 1955), p. 167.
8. Periodicals such as *Cassel's, Harper's New Monthly, Lippincott's, Atlantic Monthly, Scribner's,* and others regularly featured treatises on appropriate and inappropriate development or embellishment of urban space, and appropriate life styles for urban culture.
9. In 1949, Congress passed the Federal Housing Act, making available a number of Federal aids to local redevelopment agencies for the rehabilitation of substandard housing. The Housing Act required that displaced families be found housing, but it was not necessary to return them to the original site. As a result, virtually any urban site could be declared blighted by a local authority, and then reclaimed for shopping centers, luxury housing, or other high-yielding projects developed by private companies benefiting from public subsidies. By 1954, urban redevelopment was no longer viewed with alarm as a form of social engineering; rather, its programs were increasingly interpreted as the Federal sanctioning of the use of police power to achieve aesthetic ends by seizing urban properties through condemnation of areas judged (by developers, planners and politicians) to be "blighted," and to rebuild these areas in conformity with imposed "master plans." (Mel Scott, *American City Planning since 1890* [Berkeley: University of California Press, 1969], p. 491.)
10. C. E. Pickett, "The French Exposition of 1878," *San Francisco Examiner,* Oct. 26, 1877.
11. "Last Words about the World's Fair," *Architectural Record* 3, no. 3 (January–March 1894): 292.
12. Talbot Hamlin, *Architecture through the Ages* (New York: G. P. Putnam's Sons, 1953), pp. 605–9. Many aspiring American architects received their training at l'Ecole des Beaux-Arts in the nineteenth century and returned to the United States to promote a revival of its particular form of architectural historicism. The principal designer of the World's Columbian Exposition of 1893, Daniel Burnham, had not been trained at l'Ecole, but clearly subscribed to its principles.
13. James Marston Fitch, *American Building: The Historical Forces That Shaped It* (Boston: Houghton Mifflin, 1948), p. 127. For a summary of reactions to the Chicago exposition, see William A. Coles and Henry Hope Reed, Jr., *Architecture in America: A Battle of Styles* (New York: Appleton-Century Crofts, 1961), pp. 137–211.
14. "The World's Fair Balance Sheet," *Review of Reviews* 8, no. 5 (November 1893): 522–23.
15. John C. Cawelti, "America on Display: The World's Fairs of 1876, 1893, 1933," in *The Age of Industrialism in America,* ed. Frederick Cople Jahar (New York: Free Press, 1968), p. 319.
16. "World's Fair Balance Sheet," pp. 522–23.
17. Edo McCullough, *World's Fair Midways* (New York: Exposition Press, 1966), pp. 31–34.
18. Ibid.

19. Richard H. Barry, *Snap Shots on the Midway of the Pan-American Exposition* (Buffalo: R. A. Reid, 1901), p. 8.
20. Ibid.
21. Denton J. Snider, *World's Fair Studies* (Chicago: Sigma Publishing, 1895), pp. 360–61.
22. Hubert Howe Bancroft, *The Book of the Fair* (Chicago: Bancroft, 1893), p. 4.
23. Robinson, *Modern Civic Art,* p. 275; Charles Mulford Robinson, "Improvement in City Life," *Atlantic Monthly* 83, no. 6 (June 1899): 780. See also George Kriehn, "The City Beautiful," *Municipal Affairs* 3, no. 4 (December 1899): 597; Edwin Howard Blashfield, "A Word for Municipal Art," *Municipal Affairs* 3, no. 4 (December 1899): 582–93.
24. John DeWitt Warner, "Advertising Run Mad," *Municipal Affairs* 4, no. 2 (June 1900): 276.
25. Ibid.
26. An illustration of a cutout Statue of Columbia gracing a billboard in Newark Meadows can be found in Warner, "Advertising Run Mad," p. 274. For an analysis of the development of Forest Lawn Cemetery, see Barbara Rubin, "The Forest Lawn Aesthetic: A Reappraisal," Los Angeles Institute of Contemporary Art, *Journal,* no. 9 (1976): 10–15.
27. Warner, "Advertising Run Mad," p. 269.
28. Mary Bronson Hartt, "The Play Side of the Fair," *The World's Work,* Pan-American Exposition 2, no. 4 (August 1901): 1096.
29. The Hispanic-colonial tradition in California architecture is discussed in Barbara Rubin, "A Chronology of Architecture in Los Angeles," *Annals of the Association of American Geographers* 67, no. 4 (December 1977): 521–37.
30. Frank Morton Todd, *The Story of the Exposition* (New York: G. P. Putnam's Sons, 1921), p. 155.
31. Ibid., pp. 147–58.
32. Ibid., p. 158.
33. Ibid., pp. 155, 173.
34. The World's Columbian Exposition of 1893 had been called "The White City" because technicians were unable to introduce pigments successfully into the stucco. The fair's promoters thus made a virtue out of a limitation in bestowing on the colorless landscape the title "White City." ("The Great International Pan-Pacific Exposition," *Scientific American* 112, no. 9 [February 27, 1915]: 194–95; "The Color Scheme at the Panama-Pacific International Exposition—A New Departure," *Scribner's Magazine* 56, no. 3 [September 1914]: 277; Paul E. Denieville, "Texture and Color at the Panama-Pacific Exposition," *Architectural Record* 38, no. 5 [November 1915]: 563–70.)
35. The structures illustrated, and others, are discussed and illustrated in Morrow Mayo, *Los Angeles* (New York: Alfred Knopf, 1933); "Low Camp—A Kook's Tour of Southern California's Fast-Disappearing Unreal Estate," *Los Angeles Magazine* 10, no. 11 (November 1965): 35–36; Charles Jencks, "Ersatz in L.A.," *Architectural Design* 43, no. 9 (September 1973): 596–601; David M. Fine, "L.A. Architecture as a Blueprint for Fiction," *Los Angeles Times Calendar,* December 11, 1977, pp. 20–21.
36. Sara Comstock, "The Great American Mirror: Reflections from Los Angeles," *Harper's Monthly* 156, no. 6 (May 1928): 715–23.
37. Felix Moeschlin, *Amerika vom Auto aus* (Zurich: Erlenbach, 1931), p. 98.
38. Long Island's Big Duck is illustrated in Peter Blake, *God's Own Junkyard* (New York: Holt, Rinehart and Winston, 1964), p. 101, and discussed in Robert Venturi and Denise Scott Brown, "Ugly and Ordinary Architecture of the Decorated Shed," *Architectural Forum* 135, no. 4 (November 1971): 64–67, and James Wines, "Case for the Big Duck," *Architectural Forum* 136, no. 3 (April 1972): 60–61. The Sankey Milk Bottle and seashell service station are illustrated in Chester H. Liebs, "Remember Our Not-So-Distant Past?" *Historic Preservation* 30, no. 1 (January–March 1978): 30–35.
39. Charles N. Glaab and A. T. Brown, *The Emergence of Metropolis: A History of Urban America* (London: MacMillan, 1967), pp. 294–95, quoting real estate developer Jesse C. Nichol's 1926 observation.
40. *Franchised Distribution* (New York: Conference Board, 1972), pp. 1–2.
41. Charles L. Vaughn, *Franchising, Its Nature, Scope, Advantages, and Development* (Lexington, Mass.: Lexington Books, 1974), p. 2.
42. Robert Rosenberg with Madelon Bedell, *Profits from Franchising* (New York: McGraw-Hill, 1969), p. 44.
43. Vaughn, *Franchising,* p. 2.
44. Two books chronicle Ray Kroc's machinations in transforming a San Bernardino drive-in hamburger stand into an international franchise: Ray Kroc with Robert Anderson, *Grinding It Out: The Making of McDonald's* (Chicago: Henry Regnery, 1977); and Max Boas and Steven Chain, *Big Mac: The Unauthorized Story of McDonald's* (New York: New American Library, 1977).
45. Kroc with Anderson, *Grinding It Out,* p. 70.
46. Ibid.
47. Ibid., p. 127.

48. Ibid., p. 161. More recent McDonald's construction has superseded the mansard style, with emphasis on conforming to regional architectural flavor. A McDonald's constructed in 1977 in Santa Monica features a red-tiled roof and stucco walls in keeping with southern California's largely fabricated Spanish colonial tradition. In San Francisco, near City Hall, a McDonald's completed in August, 1978, exhibits a formal modernism consistent with the most up-to-date construction in civic buildings and avant garde residential construction: greenhouse windows, large expanses of concrete wall meeting at unusual angles, and ornamental graphics.
49. David M. Kinchen, "Indeterminate Facade Building Opens," *Los Angeles Times,* April 17, 1977, part 8, p. 5.
50. Evidence for the origins of Disneyland is discussed in Barbara Rubin, "Monuments, Magnets and Pilgrimage Sites: A Genetic Study in Southern California," Ph.D. diss., University of California, Los Angeles, 1975, pp. 445–62.
51. Art Seidenbaum, "A New Kind of Amusement Park," *Los Angeles Times,* May 9, 1976, part 7, p. 1.
52. Gilbert Burck, "How American Taste is Changing," *Fortune* 60, no. 1 (July 1959): 196. The role of education and its impact on the "American Way of Life" is cogently discussed in James O'Toole, *Work, Learning and the American Future* (San Francisco: Jossey-Bass, 1977). Objections to the use of public cultural institutions and public monies for the dissemination and validation of "official culture" were outlined in *an anti-catalog* (New York: Catalog Committee of Artists Meeting for Cultural Change, 1977).
53. Gerald Faris, "Santa Monica Boulevard: The Grotesque and the Sublime," *Los Angeles Times,* February 17, 1974, part 11, p. 1.
54. John Chapman, "Los Angeles Is Just Too Much," *Los Angeles Times,* June 28, 1977, part 2, p. 7.
55. Wolf Von Eckhardt, "The Huckster Peril on Main Street, U.S.A.," *Los Angeles Times,* December 5, 1977, part 2, p. 11.
56. Kroc with Anderson, *Grinding It Out,* p. 161.
57. Ada Louise Huxtable, "Architecture for a Fast Food Culture," *New York Times Magazine,* February 12, 1978, p. 23.
58. Jencks, "Ersatz in L.A.," pp. 596–601.
59. Leibs, "Remember Our Not-So-Distant Past?" p. 35.
60. Robert Venturi, Denise Scott Brown, and Stephen Izenour, *Learning from Las Vegas: The Forgotten Symbolism of Architectural Form* (Cambridge: MIT Press, 1972).
61. "Low Camp," pp. 35–36.

Further Reading

The twenty-three essays reprinted in *Common Places* have given you a mere glimpse of vernacular architecture and landscapes studies. As the field has expanded in the last decade, so has its scope. We have been as selective in the following bibliography as we were in choosing the articles themselves. Our list does not pretend to be comprehensive or even to include every good work. Rather it offers further readings along the lines that the authors in our collection have pursued and fills in some of the glaring gaps that a mere twenty-three articles necessarily leave. (Publications that have been issued in paperback are marked with an asterisk.)

Introduction

We have organized this bibliography along the same lines as the rest of the book. The entries are placed according to which of our five parts they seem to fit most closely. For more orthodox approaches, the publications in this section of the bibliography may serve as guides.

BIBLIOGRAPHIES

There is as yet no comprehensive bibliography of all of American vernacular architecture and landscapes, but the following are useful starting places for your own work.

Dunbar, Gary S. "Illustrations of the Earth: An Essay in Cultural Geography," *American Studies: An International Newsletter* 12, no. 1 (Autumn 1973): 3–15. A bibliography of works on American cultural geography.

Hitchcock, Henry-Russell. *American Architectural Books: A List of Books, Portfolios, and Pamphlets on Architecture and Related Subjects Published in America before 1895.* New expanded ed. New York: Da Capo, 1976. A comprehensive bibliography of pattern books and builders' guides that is the place to start for most research on nineteenth-century vernacular architecture.

Jakle, John A. *Past Landscapes: A Bibliography for Historic Preservationists Selected from the Literature of Historical Geography.* Exchange Bibliography 651. Monticello, Ill.: Council of Planning Librarians, 1974.

*Marshall, Howard Wight. *American Folk Architecture: A Selected Bibliography.* Publications of the American Folklife Center, no. 8. Washington, D.C.: American Folklife Center, Library of Congress, 1981. The most comprehensive bibliography available.

Roos, Frank J., Jr. *Bibliography of Early American Architecture: Writings on Architecture Constructed before 1860 in the Eastern and Central United States.* Rev. ed. Urbana: University of Illinois Press, 1968.

Schlereth, Thomas J. "Material Culture Studies and Social History Research," *Journal of Social History* 16, no. 4 (Summer 1983): 111–43.

———, ed. "American Studies and Students of American Things," *American Quarterly* 35, no. 3 (Bibliography 1983): 236–338. This special issue contains essays on the cultural landscape by Pierce Lewis, on vernacular architecture by Dell Upton, on decorative arts and household furnishings by Kenneth L. Ames, on technology and material culture by Carroll W. Pursell, Jr., and on material culture in American folklore by Simon J. Bronner.

Upton, Dell. "Ordinary Buildings: A Bibliography on American Vernacular Architecture," *American Studies International* 19, no. 2 (Winter 1981): 57–75.

SURVEYS

There is no survey of American vernacular architecture or landscapes as defined in *Common Places.* The closest we have are Henry Glassie, **Pattern in the Material Folk Culture of the Eastern United States* (Philadelphia: University of Pennsylvania Press, 1969), and John R. Stilgoe, **Common Landscape of America, 1580 to 1845* (New Haven: Yale University Press, 1982).

All surveys of American architectural history give some attention to vernacular architecture, though it is usually confined to the chapters on colonial architecture. Few do well with the subject. Of such surveys, the most satisfactory treatments of vernacular architecture can be found in the following works.

*Fitch, James Marston. *American Building: The Historical Forces That Shaped It.* 2d ed. New York: Schocken, 1973.

*Gowans, Alan. *Images of American Living: Four Centuries of Architecture and Furniture as Cultural Expression.* Philadelphia: J. B. Lippincott, 1964.

*Kimball, Fiske. *Domestic Architecture of the American Colonies and of the Early Republic.* 1922. Reprint. New York: Dover Publications, 1966.

*Pierson, William H., Jr. *American Buildings and Their Architects: The Colonial and Neo-Classical Styles.* Garden City, N.Y.: Anchor Books, 1976.

*———. *American Buildings and Their Architects: Technology and the Picturesque; The Corporate and the Early Gothic Styles.* Garden City, N.Y.: Anchor Books, 1978.

Waterman, Thomas Tileston. *The Dwellings of Colonial America.* Chapel Hill: University of North Carolina Press, 1950.

*Wright, Gwendolyn. *Building the Dream: A Social History of Housing in America.* New York: Pantheon, 1981.

PERIODICALS

A major resource for vernacular architecture and landscape studies is the Vernacular Architecture Forum's quarterly *Vernacular Architecture Newsletter,* which publishes news, notes, queries, and reviews, as well as a current bibliography. The latter is particularly helpful since, as a result of the disparate and interdisciplinary nature of the field, relevant articles might appear in any one of dozens of historical, archaeological, and design journals. The following, however, are the principal American vehicles for scholarship of the vernacular.

APT Bulletin (Association for Preservation Technology)
Annals of the Association of American Geographers
Geographical Review
Historical Archaeology
Journal of Cultural Geography
Journal of Historical Geography
Journal of the Society of Architectural Historians
Landscape
Landscape Journal
Material Culture (formerly *Pioneer America*)
Pennsylvania Folklife
Winterthur Portfolio

Definitions and Demonstrations

OVERVIEWS

*Hart, John Fraser. *The Look of the Land.* Englewood Cliffs, N.J.: Prentice-Hall, 1975.

Kniffen, Fred. "The Geographer's Craft: Why Folk Housing?" *Annals of the Association of American Geographers* 69, no. 1 (March 1979): 59–62.

Lewis, Pierce. "Common Houses, Cultural Spoor," *Landscape* 19, no. 2 (January 1975): 1–22.

*Meinig, D. W., ed. *The Interpretation of Ordinary Landscapes: Geographical Essays.* New York: Oxford University Press, 1979. An excellent collection.

*Rapoport, Amos. *House Form and Culture.* Englewood Cliffs, N.J.: Prentice-Hall, 1969. Good discussion of common presuppositions about vernacular architecture.

*Zelinsky, Wilbur. *The Cultural Geography of the United States.* Englewood Cliffs, N.J.: Prentice-Hall, 1973.

OVERSEAS ANTECEDENTS

Many American vernacular forms have European, African, or Asian antecedents and parallels. The following are a sample of works treating them. Our list is weighted toward Britain because most surviving American vernacular building was British-rooted and because the literature available in the United States is weighted in that direction. We have been very selective here and have favored book-length treatments of major regional traditions that were sources of American vernacular environments.

Ayres, James. *The Shell Book of the Home in Britain: Decoration, Design and Construction of Vernacular Interiors.* Boston: Faber and Faber, 1981.

Barley, M. W. *The English Farmhouse and Cottage.* London: Routledge and Kegan Paul, 1961. A classic study, based mostly on probate inventories, that should now be supplemented by Eric Mercer's book (see below).

Bedal, Konrad. *Historische Hausforschung: Eine Einführung in Arbeitsweise, Begriffe und Literatur.* Münster, West Germany: F. Coppenrath Verlag, 1978.

*Brunskill, R. W. *Illustrated Handbook of Vernacular Architecture.* 2d ed. London: Faber and Faber, 1978. A manual intended for fieldworkers.

Chapman, Stanley D., ed. *The History of Working-Class Housing: A Symposium.* Totowa, N.J.: Rowman and Littlefield, 1971.

*Danaher, Kevin. *Ireland's Vernacular Architecture.* Cork: Mercier Press for the Cultural Relations Committee of Ireland, 1975.

Demangeon, Albert. "L'habitation rurale en France—essai de classification," *Annales de géographie* 29, no. 161 (1920): 352–73. A standard survey.

*Denyer, Susan. *African Traditional Architecture: An Historical and Geographical Perspective.* New York: Holmes and Meier, 1978.

Dunzhen, Liu. *La maison chinoise.* Traduction et adaptation française augmentée d'une présentation et d'un lexique par George et Marie-Hélène Métailie, Sophie Clément-Charpentier, et Pierre Clément. Paris: Editions Berger-Levrault, 1980.

Erixon, Sigurd. "The North-European Technique of Corner Timbering," *Folkliv* 1 (1937): 13–60.

———. *Svensk Byggnadskultur: Studier och skildringar belysande den svenska byggnadskulturens historia.* 1947. Reprint. Stockholm: Walter Ekstrand Bokförlag, 1982.

Feduchi, Luis. *Spanish Folk Architecture.* New York: Editorial Blume, 1977.

Fenton, Alexander, and Bruce Walker. *The Rural Architecture of Scotland.* Edinburgh: John Donald, 1981.

Glanville, Ranulph. "Finnish Vernacular Farmhouses," *Architectural Association Quarterly* 9, no. 1 (1977): 36–52.

Glassie, Henry. *Passing the Time in Ballymenone: Culture and History of an Ulster Community.* Philadelphia: University of Pennsylvania Press, 1982. A model of the integration of material and non-material culture.

*Hoskins, W. G. *The Making of the English Landscape.* 1955. Reprint. Harmondsworth: Pelican Books, 1970.

Ito, Nobuo. *Traditional Japanese Houses.* Trans. Charles Terry. Tokyo and New York: Kodansha, 1982.

Letenoux, Guy. *Architecture et vie traditionnelle en Normandie.* Paris: Editions Berger-Levrault, 1980.

Meirion-Jones, Gwyn I. *The Vernacular Architecture of Brittany: An Essay in Historical Geography.* Edinburgh: John Donald, 1982.

*Mercer, Eric. *English Vernacular Houses: A Study of Traditional Farmhouses and Cottages.* London: Her Majesty's Stationery Office, 1975.

*Muthesius, Stefan. *The English Terraced House.* New Haven: Yale University Press, 1982.

*Oliver, Paul, ed. *Shelter in Africa.* New York: Barrie and Jenkins, 1971.

Smith, Peter. *Houses of the Welsh Countryside: A Study in Historical Geography.* London: Her Majesty's Stationery Office, 1975.

Stany-Gauthier, Joseph. *Les maisons paysannes de vieilles provinces de France.* Paris: Charles Massin, 1951.

Vlach, John Michael. "Affecting Architecture of the Yoruba," *African Arts* 10, no. 1 (October 1976): 48–53.

Voskuil, J. J. *Van Vlechtwerk tot Baksteen: Gescheidenis van de Wanden van het Boerenhuis in Nederland.* Arnhem, The Netherlands: Stichting Historisch Boerderij-onderzoek, 1979. English summary.

Weiss, Richard. *Häuser und Landschaften der Schweiz.* 2d ed. Erlenbach-Zurich: Eugen Rentsch Verlag, 1973. The standard work on the Rhenish tradition.

*Zippelius, Adelhart. *Das Bauernhaus am unteren deutschen Niederrhein.* Wuppertal, West Germany: Verlag A. Martini und Grüttefein Gmbh., 1957. Revelant both to Germany and the Netherlands.

INDIVIDUAL STUDIES

*Ahlborn, Richard. *The Penitente Moradas of Abiquiu.* Contributions from the Museum of History and Technology, paper 63. Washington, D.C.: Smithsonian Institution, 1968.

Alanen, Arnold, and William H. Tishler. "Finnish Farmstead Organization in Old and New World Settings," *Journal of Cultural Geography* 1, no. 1 (Fall–Winter 1980): 66–81.

Andrew, Laurel B. *The Early Temples of the Mormons: The Architecture of the Milennial Kingdom in the American West.* Albany: State University of New York Press, 1978.

*Arthur, Eric, and Dudley Witney. *The Barn: A Vanishing Landmark in North America.* Greenwich, Conn.: New York Graphic Society, 1972.

Baer, Kurt. *Architecture of the California Missions.* Berkeley and Los Angeles: University of California Press, 1958.

Blackmar, Elizabeth. "The Urban Landscape," *Journal of Architectural Education* 30, no. 1 (January 1976): 12–14.

Bucher, Robert C. "The Contintental Log House," *Pennsylvania Folklife* 12, no. 4 (Summer 1962): 14–19.

———. "The Swiss Bank House in Pennsylvania," *Pennsylvania Folklife* 18, no. 2 (Winter 1968): 1–11.

*Bunting, Bainbridge. *Early Architecture in New Mexico.* Albuquerque: University of New Mexico Press, 1976.

Candee, Richard M. "A Documentary History of Plymouth Colony Architecture, 1620–1700," *Old-Time New England* 59, no. 3 (Winter 1969): 59–69; 59, no. 4 (Spring 1969): 105–11; 60, no. 2 (Fall 1970): 37–53. A good short account of the colony's architectural history.

Connally, Ernest Allen, "The Cape Cod House: An Introductory Study," *Journal of the Society of Architectural Historians* 19, no. 2 (May 1960): 47–56.

Daniels, Ted. "A Philadelphia Squatter's Shack: Urban Pioneering," *Pioneer America* 13, no. 2 (July 1981): 43–46. A study of the least glamorous of housing forms.

Dornbusch, Charles H., and John K. Heyl. *Pennsylvania German Barns.* Pennsylvania German Folklore Society, no. 21. Allentown, Pa.: Schlechter's, 1956. A pioneering attempt at a comprehensive study of a single building type, with emphasis on classification.

Downing, Antoinette Forrester. *Early Homes of Rhode Island.* Richmond, Va.: Garrett and Massie, 1937.

*Fairbanks, Jonathan L., and Robert F. Trent, eds. *New England Begins: The Seventeenth Century.* 3 vols. Boston: Museum of Fine Arts, 1982. An exhibit catalog with major essays on architecture, landscapes, and decorative arts.

Fife, Austin E., and James M. Fife. "Hay Derricks of the Great Basin and Upper Snake River Valley," *Western Folklore* 7, no. 3 (July 1948): 225–39.

*Fishwick, Marshall, and J. Meredith Neil, eds. *Popular Architecture.* Bowling Green, Ohio: Bowling Green Popular Press, 1975.

Francaviglia, Richard V. *The Mormon Landscape: Existence, Creation and Perception of a Unique Image in the American West.* New York: AMS Press, 1979.

———. "Western American Barns: Architectural Form and Climatic Consideration," *Yearbook of the Association of Pacific Coast Geographers* 34 (1972): 153–60.

Garvan, Anthony N. B. *Architecture and Town Planning in Colonial Connecticut.* New Haven: Yale University Press, 1951.

Glassie, Henry. "A Central Chimney Continental Log House from Cumberland County," *Pennsylvania Folklife* 18, no. 2 (Winter 1968–69): 32–36.

———. "The Double-Crib Barn in South Central Pennsylvania," *Pioneer America* 1, no. 1 (January 1969): 9–16; 1, no. 2 (July 1969): 40–45; 2, no. 1 (January 1970): 47–52; 2, no. 2 (July 1970): 23–34.

———. "The Pennsylvania Barn in the South," *Pennsylvania Folklife* 15, no. 2 (Winter 1966–67): 8–19; 15, no. 4 (Summer 1967): 12–15.

———. "The Types of the Southern Mountain Cabin." In Jan H. Brunvand, *The Study of American Folklore: An Introduction.* 2d ed. New York: Norton, 1978, pp. 391–420.

Gowans, Alan. *Architecture in New Jersey: A Record of American Civilization.* Princeton: A. D. Van Nostrand, 1964.

Griffith, James S. "The Folk-Catholic Chapels of the Papagueria," *Pioneer America* 7, no. 2 (July 1975): 21–36.

Gutman, Richard J. S., and Elliot Kaufman. *The American Diner.* New York: Harper and Row, 1979.

Hart, John Fraser. "The Bypass Strip as an Ideal Landscape," *Geographical Review* 72, no. 2 (April 1982): 218–23.

Hart, John Fraser, and Eugene Cotton Mather. "The Character of Tobacco Barns and Their Role in the Tobacco Economy of the United States," *Annals of the Association of American Geographers* 51, no. 3 (September 1961): 274–93.

Harvey, Thomas. "Mail-Order Architecture in the Twenties," *Landscape* 25, no. 3 (1981): 1–9.

Hattersley-Drayton, Karana. "Folk Housing in Pioneer California: A Preliminary Typology," *Southwest Folklore* 4, no. 2 (Spring 1980): 42–61.

Hayward, Mary Ellen. "Urban Vernacular Architecture in Nineteenth-Century Baltimore," *Winterthur Portfolio* 16, no. 1 (Spring 1981): 33–63. With William J. Murtagh's article on Philadelphia, a rare study of urban vernacular architecture.

Hirshorn, Paul, and Steven Izenour. "Learning from Hamburgers: Architecture of 'White Tower' Lunch Counters," *Architecture Plus* 1, no. 5 (June 1973): 46–55.

———. *White Towers.* Cambridge: MIT Press, 1979. More complete but less interesting than the article.

Hubka, Thomas. "The Connected Farm Buildings of Northern New England," *Historical New Hampshire* 32, no. 3 (Fall 1977): 87–115.

*Jackson, J. B. *Landscapes: Selected Writings of J. B. Jackson.* Ed. Ervin H. Zube. Amherst: University of Massachusetts Press, 1970. A collection of Jackson's most provocative articles, but with the illustrations unaccountably omitted.

Jakle, John A. "The American Gas Station, 1920–1970," *Journal of American Culture* 1, no. 3 (Fall 1978): 520–42.

Johnson, Hildegard Binder. *Order upon the Land: The U.S. Rectangular Land Survey and the Upper Mississippi Country.* New York: Oxford University Press, 1976.

*Kelly, J. Frederick. *Early Domestic Architecture of Connecticut.* 1924. Reprint. New York: Dover Publications, 1963.

King, Anthony D. *The Bungalow: The Production of a Global Culture.* Boston: Routledge and Kegan Paul, 1984.

Kniffen, Fred B. "Louisiana House Types," *Annals of the Association of American Geographers* 26, no. 4 (December 1936): 179–93. The pioneering study of American folk housing from a geographical perspective.

Kubler, George. *The Religious Architecture of New Mexico in the Colonial Period and Since the American Occupation.* Albuquerque: University of New Mexico Press, 1972.

Lohof, Bruce A. "The Service Station in America: The Evolution of a Vernacular Form," *Industrial Archaeology* 11, no. 1 (Spring 1974): 1–13.

McHenry, Stewart G. "Vermont Barns: A Cultural Landscape Analysis," *Vermont History* 46, no. 3 (Summer 1978): 151–56.

Marshall, Howard Wight. *Folk Architecture in Little Dixie: A Regional Culture in Missouri.* Columbia: University of Missouri Press, 1981.

———. "The 'Thousand Acres' Log House, Monroe County, Indiana," *Pioneer America* 3, no. 1 (January 1971): 48–56.

Mather, Eugene Cotton, and John Fraser Hart. "Fences and Farms," *Geographical Review* 44, no. 2 (April 1954): 201–23.

Meinig, D. W. "The Mormon Culture Region: Strategies and Patterns in the Geography of the American West, 1847–1964," *Annals of the Association of American Geographers* 55, no. 2 (June 1965): 191–220.

Murtagh, William J. *Moravian Architecture and Town Planning.* Chapel Hill: University of North Carolina Press, 1967.

———. "The Philadelphia Row House," *Journal of the Society of Architectural Historians* 16, no. 4 (December 1957): 8–13.

Nelson, Lowry. *The Mormon Village: A Pattern and Technique of Land Settlement.* Salt Lake City: University of Utah Press, 1952. A classic.

Raup, H. F. "The Fence in the Cultural Landscape," *Western Folklore* 6, no. 1 (January 1947): 1–12.

Reps, John W. *The Making of Urban America.* Princeton: Princeton University Press, 1965. The first of a series of more specialized works, of which the following is an example.

*———. *Town Planning in Frontier America.* Princeton: Princeton University Press, 1969.

Robinson, Willard B. "Colonial Ranch Architecture in the Spanish-Mexican Tradition," *Southwestern Historical Quarterly* 83, no. 2 (October 1979): 123–50.

*Rubin, Barbara, Robert Carlton, and Arnold Rubin. *L. A. in Installments: Forest Lawn.* Santa Monica, Calif.: Westside Publications, 1979.

*Rugo, Bob. *Boston's Triple-Deckers.* Boston: Office of Program Development, Boston Redevelopment Authority, 1978.

*Sande, Theodore A. *Industrial Archaeology: A New Look at the American Heritage.* Brattleboro, Vt.: Stephen Greene Press, 1976.

———. "The Textile Factory in Pre–Civil War Rhode Island," *Old-Time New England* 66, nos. 1–2 (Summer–Fall 1975): 13–31.

Simmons, Marc. "Settlement Patterns and Village Plans in Colonial New Mexico," *Journal of the West* 8, no. 1 (January 1969): 7–21.

Spencer, Joseph E. "House Types of Southern Utah," *Geographical Review* 35, no. 3 (July 1945): 444–57.

*Stern, Robert A. M., ed. *The Anglo-American Suburb.* London: Architectural Design, 1981.

Stewart, Janet Ann. *Arizona Ranch Houses: Southern Territorial Styles, 1867–1900.* Tucson: Arizona Historical Society, 1974.

*Swaim, Doug, ed. *Carolina Dwelling: Toward Preservation of Place; In Celebration of the Vernacular Landscape.* Student Publication of the School of Design, vol. 26. Raleigh: North Carolina State University, 1978. Excellent collection of essays on many aspects of the North Carolina vernacular landscape.

*Venturi, Robert, Denise Scott Brown, and Steven Izenour. *Learning from Las Vegas: The Forgotten Symbolism of Architectural Form.* Rev. ed. Cambridge: MIT Press, 1977. Arrogant and often superficial, but essential.

*Vieyra, Daniel I. *Fill 'er Up: An Architectural History of America's Gas Stations.* New York: Macmillan, 1979.

Vlach, John Michael. "The 'Canada Homestead': A Saddlebag Log House in Monroe County, Indiana," *Pioneer America* 4, no. 2 (July 1972): 8–17.

Wallis, Allan. "Drawn Quarters," *Natural History* 13, no. 3 (March 1984): 42–52. An analysis of the forms of the house trailer.

*Wells, Camille, ed. *Perspectives in Vernacular Architecture.* Annapolis: Vernacular Architecture Forum, 1982. Papers from the first two annual meetings of the VAF.

*Wroth, William. *The Chapel of Our Lady of Talpa.* Colorado Springs: Taylor Museum of the Colorado Springs Fine Arts Center, 1979. Good study of a New Mexico church.

Zelinsky, Wilbur. "The Pennsylvania Town: An Overdue Geographical Account," *Geographical Review* 67, no. 2 (April 1977): 127–47.

______. "Walls and Fences," *Landscape* 8, no. 3 (Spring 1959): 14–20.

Construction

Log and timber framing are the most conspicuous and best-studied of vernacular building systems, but brick, stone, adobe, and other forms of earth construction and metal buildings are all common and have been investigated to varying degrees. Little attention has been given to the technologies of plumbing, heating, and lighting that make a building usable. If technologies and materials have been treated spottily, the *process* of building—the structure of the building trades, the organization of work, the physical process of building, and the financing of building projects—has been almost ignored.

**Adobe, Past and Present.* Santa Fe: Museum of New Mexico, 1972.

Ball, Norman. "Circular Saws and the History of Technology," *APT Bulletin* 8, no. 3 (1975): 79–89.

Carson, Cary, Norman F. Barka, William M. Kelso, Garry Wheeler Stone, and Dell Upton. "Impermanent Architecture in the Southern American Colonies," *Winterthur Portfolio* 16, nos. 2–3 (Summer–Autumn 1981): 135–96.

*Condit, Carl. *American Building: Materials and Techniques from the First Colonial Settlements to the Present.* Chicago: University of Chicago Press, 1967. The only single-volume survey of American building technology, but unfortunately out of date and unreliable on vernacular building.

*Cummings, Abbott Lowell. *The Framed Houses of Massachusetts Bay, 1625–1725.* Cambridge: Harvard University Press, 1979. The best book on New England architecture; a comprehensive treatment that also discusses plans, decoration, and use.

Curtis, John O. "The Introduction of the Circular Saw in the Early Nineteenth Century," *APT Bulletin* 5, no. 2 (1973): 162–89.

Darnall, Margaretta Jean. "Innovations in American Prefabricated Housing: 1860–1890," *Journal of the Society of Architectural Historians* 31, no. 1 (March 1972): 51–55.

Field, Walker. "A Reexamination into the Invention of the Balloon Frame," *Journal of the Society of Architectural Historians* 2, no. 4 (October 1942): 3–29. The starting point for studies of balloon framing.

*Fields, Curtis P. *The Forgotten Art of Building a Stone Wall.* Dublin, N.H.: Yankee Press, 1971.

*Fitch, James Marston. *American Building: The Environmental Forces That Shape It.* Boston: Houghton Mifflin, 1966.

*Fitchen, John. *The New World Dutch Barn: A Study of Its Characteristics, Its Structural System, and Its Probable Erectional Procedures.* Syracuse: Syracuse University Press, 1968.

Hopson, Rex C. *Adobe: A Comprehensive Bibliography.* Santa Fe: Lightning Tree, 1979.

*Isham, Norman Morrison, and Albert F. Brown. *Early Connecticut Houses: An Historical and Architectural Study.* 1900. Reprint. New York: Dover Publications, 1965. A more extensive and more detailed study on the same model as *Early Rhode Island Houses.*

*Jordan, Terry G. *Texas Log Buildings: A Folk Architecture.* Austin: University of Texas Press, 1978.

Lounsbury, Carl. "The Building Process in Antebellum North Carolina," *North Carolina Historical Review* 60, no. 4 (October 1983): 431–56.

*McKee, Harley J. *An Introduction to Early American Masonry: Stone, Brick, Mortar and Plaster.* Washington, D.C.: National Trust for Historic Preservation, 1973. Essential.

Marzio, Peter C. "Carpentry in the Southern Colonies during the Eighteenth Century with Emphasis on Maryland and Virginia." In *Winterthur Portfolio 7,* ed. Ian M. G. Quimby. Charlottesville: University of Virginia Press, 1972, pp. 229–50.

Mercer, Henry Chapman. *Ancient Carpenters' Tools.* Doylestown, Pa.: Bucks County Historical Society, 1929.

*Merrilees, Doug, and Evelyn Loveday. *Pole Building Construction.* Charlotte, Vt.: Garden Way Publishing, 1973.

Nelson, Walter R. "Some Examples of Plank House Construction and Their Origins," *Pioneer America* 1, no. 2 (July 1969): 18–29.

*Peterson, Charles E., ed. *Building Early America: Contributions toward the History of a Great Industry.* Radnor, Pa.: Chilton, 1976.

Stone, May N. "The Plumbing Paradox: American Attitudes toward Late Nineteenth-Century Domestic Sanitary Arrangements," *Winterthur Portfolio* 14, no. 3 (Autumn 1979): 283–309.

Tishler, William H. "Stovewood Architecture," *Landscape* 23, no. 3 (1979): 28–31.

Upton, Dell. "Traditional Timber Framing." In *Material Culture of the Wooden Age,* ed. Brooke Hindle. Tarrytown, N.Y.: Sleepy Hollow Press, 1981, pp. 35–93. Treats traditional eastern Anglo-American, Dutch, and German framing, as well as plank and balloon framing.

Vlach, John Michael. "'Us Quarters Fixed Fine': Finding Black Builders in Southern History." In *Perspectives on the American South,* ed. Charles Wilson and James Cobb, vol. 3. 1984.

Welsch, Roger L. *Sod Walls: The Story of the Nebraska Sod House.* Broken Bow: Purcells, 1968.

*Welsh, Peter C. *Woodworking Tools, 1600–1900.* Contributions from the Museum History and Technology, paper 51. Washington, D.C.: U.S. Government Printing Office, 1966.

Wood, Peter H. "Whetting, Setting, and Laying Timbers: Black Builders in the Early South," *Southern Exposure* 8, no. 1 (Spring 1980): 3–8.

Function

The works in this section treat the uses of space in two senses: the furnishing and decoration of spaces, particularly domestic ones, for use; and the social dimensions of spaces as manifestations and reinforcements of social relations.

Belasco, Warren James. *Americans on the Road: From Autocamp to Motel, 1910–1945.* Cambridge: MIT Press, 1979.

Blackmar, Betsy. "Re-Walking the 'Walking City': Housing and Property Relations in New York City, 1780–1840," *Radical History Review* no. 21 (Fall 1979): 131–50.

*Borchert, James. *Alley Life in Washington: Family, Community, Religion and Folklife in the City, 1850–1970.* Urbana: University of Illinois Press, 1980.

Bronner, Simon J. "Manner Books and Suburban Houses: The Structure of Tradition and Aesthetics," *Winterthur Portfolio* 18, no. 1 (Spring 1983): 61–68.

*Bunting, Bainbridge, Thomas R. Lyons, and Margil Lyons. "Penitente Brotherhood Moradas and Their Architecture." In *Hispanic Arts and Ethnohistory in the Southwest: New Essays Inspired by the Work of E. Boyd,* ed. Marta Weigle. Santa Fe: Ancient Arts Press, 1983, pp. 31–80.

*Carson, Cary. "Doing History with Material Culture." In *Material Culture and the Study of American Life,* ed. Ian M. G. Quimby. New York: Norton, 1978, pp. 41–64. A valuable consideration of the utility of vernacular architecture and landscapes to historians.

*Cohen, Lizabeth A. "Respectability at $50.00 Down, 25 Months to Pay!: Furnishing a Working-Class Victorian Home." In *Victorian Furniture,* ed. Kenneth L. Ames. Philadelphia: Victorian Society in America, 1982, pp. 231–42.

Cummings, Abbott Lowell, ed. *Rural Household Inventories: Establishing the Names, Uses and Furnishings of Rooms in the Colonial New England Home, 1675–1775.* Boston: Society for the Preservation of New England Antiquities, 1964.

*Deetz, James. *In Small Things Forgotten: The Archaeology of Early American Life.* Garden City, N.Y.: Anchor Books, 1977.

Duis, Perry. "Whose City? Public and Private Places in Nineteenth-Century Chicago," *Chicago History* 12, no. 1 (Spring 1983): 2–27; 12, no. 2 (Summer 1983): 2–23.

Duncan, Carol, and Alan Wallach. "The Museum of Modern Art as Late Capitalist Ritual: An Iconographic Analysis," *Marxist Perspectives* 1, no. 4 (Winter 1978): 28–51. A perceptive analysis of the ways that circulation patterns in a museum are used to reinforce an interpretation of modern art history.

*Groth, Paul. *AC 15: Oakland as a Cross Section of America's Urban Cultural Landscape.* Oakland, Calif.: Paul Groth, 1980. A short course in the close analysis of the ordinary urban landscape, disguised as a tour guide.

———. "Streetgrids as Frameworks for Urban Variety," *Harvard Architectural Review* 2 (Spring 1981): 68–75.

*Kasson, John F. *Amusing the Millions: Coney Island at the Turn of the Century.* New York: Hill and Wang, 1978.

Lane, Jonathan. "The Period House in the Nineteen-Twenties," *Journal of the Society of Architectural Historians* 20, no. 4 (December 1961): 169–78. Discusses the effect of sociological changes on the middle-class American house.

Laumann, E. O., and J. S. House. "Living Room Styles and Social Attributes: The Patterning of Material Artifacts in a Modern Urban Community," *Sociology and Social Research* 54, no. 3 (April 1970): 321–42.

*Leone, Mark P. "Archaeology as the Science of Technology: Mormon Town Plans and Fences." In *Historical Archaeology: A Guide to Substantive and Theoretical Contributions*, ed. Robert L. Schuyler. Farmingdale, N.Y.: Baywood Publishing, 1978, pp. 191–200.

*Little, Nina Fletcher. *American Decorative Wall Painting, 1700–1850.* Enlarged ed. New York: E. P. Dutton, 1972.

*Lyon, Irving W. *The Colonial Furniture of New England: A Study of the Domestic Furniture in Use in the Seventeenth and Eighteenth Centuries.* 1890. Reprint. New York: E. P. Dutton, 1977. With Isham and Brown's *Early Rhode Island Houses*, the pioneering study of early American material culture, and still useful.

*McDaniel, George. *Hearth and Home: Preserving a People's Culture.* Philadelphia: Temple University Press, 1981. Black material culture in southern Maryland since the Civil War.

Michel, Jack. "'In a Manner and Fashion Suitable to Their Degree': A Preliminary Investigation of the Material Culture of Early Rural Pennsylvania," *Working Papers from the Regional Economic History Research Center* 5, no. 1 (1981): 1–83.

*Schlereth, Thomas J. *Historic Houses as Learning Laboratories: Seven Teaching Strategies.* History News Technical Leaflet no. 105. Nashville: American Association for State and Local History, 1978.

Shammas, Carole. "The Domestic Environment in Early Modern England and America," *Journal of Social History* 14, no. 1 (Fall 1980): 3–24.

Twombley, Robert C. "Saving the Family: Middle Class Attraction to Wright's Prairie House, 1901–1909," *American Quarterly* 27, no. 1 (March 1975): 57–72. The social process of vernacular architecture affects high-style buildings as well.

*Warner, Sam Bass, Jr. *Streetcar Suburbs: The Process of Growth in Urban Boston, 1870–1900.* New York: Atheneum, 1971.

Wood, Joseph S. "Village and Community in Early Colonial New England," *Journal of Historical Geography* 8, no. 4 (October 1982): 333–46.

History

Some vernacular buildings and landscapes change slowly, others very rapidly, but none is unaffected by time. Change is an element that must be confronted in all vernacular studies, but those in the following list address the issue directly.

*Banham, Reyner. *Los Angeles: The Architecture of Four Ecologies.* New York: Penguin, 1971.

*Bloomberg, Britta, et al. *Minnesota Farmscape: Looking at Change.* St. Paul: Minnesota Historical Society, 1980.

*Bunting, Bainbridge, Jean Lee Booth, and William R. Sims, Jr. *Taos Adobes: Spanish Colonial and Territorial Architecture of the Taos Valley.* Fort Burgwin Research Center, publication no. 2. Santa Fe: Museum of New Mexico Press, 1964.

Carson, Cary. "The 'Virginia House' in Maryland," *Maryland Historical Society Magazine* 69, no. 2 (Summer 1974): 185–96.

*Emmet, Alan. *Cambridge, Massachusetts: The Changing of a Landscape.* Cambridge: Harvard University Press, 1978.

*Handlin, David P. *The American Home: Architecture and Society, 1815–1915.* Boston: Little, Brown, 1979.

*Jackson, J. B. *American Space: The Centennial Years, 1865–1876.* New York: Norton, 1972.

Jakle, John A., and Richard L. Mattson. "The Evolution of a Commercial Strip," *Journal of Cultural Geography* 1, no. 2 (Spring–Summer 1981): 12–25.

Kulik, Gary. "A Factory System of Wood: Cultural and Technological Change in the Building of the First Cotton Mills." In *Material Culture of the Wooden Age*, ed. Brooke Hindle. Tarrytown, N.Y.: Sleepy Hollow Press, 1981, pp. 300–335. The best treatment of early textile mills to date.

Lewis, Pierce. "The Geography of Old Houses," *Earth and Mineral Sciences* 39, no. 5 (February 1970): 33–37.

Marshall, Howard Wight, and John Michael Vlach. "Toward a Folklife Approach to American Dialects," *American Speech* 48, nos. 3–4 (Fall–Winter 1973): 163–91. Compares patterns in folk architecture with patterns in folk speech.

Peterson, Fred W. "Norwegian Farm Homes in Steele and Traill Counties, North Dakota: The American Dream and the Retention of Roots, 1890–1914," *North Dakota History* 51, no. 1 (Winter 1984): 4–13.

Rubin, Barbara. "A Chronology of Architecture in Los Angeles," *Annals of the Association of American Geographers* 67, no. 4 (December 1977): 521–37.

Shank, Wesley L. "Eighteenth-Century Architecture of the Upper Delaware River Valley of New Jersey and Delaware," *Journal of the Society of Architectural Historians* 31, no. 2 (May 1972): 137–44.

Stilgoe, John R. *Metropolitan Corridor: Railroads and the American Scene.* New Haven: Yale University Press, 1983.

Streatfield, David C. "The Evolution of the California Landscape," *Landscape Architecture* 66, no. 1 (January 1976): 39–46; 66, no. 2 (March 1976): 117–26; 67, no. 3 (May 1977): 229–39; 67, no. 5 (September 1977): 417–24.

*Upton, Dell. "The Origins of Chesapeake Architecture." In *Three Centuries of Maryland Architecture: A Selection of Presentations Made at the Eleventh Annual Conference of the Maryland Historic Trust.* Annapolis: Maryland Historic Trust, 1982, pp. 44–57.

Wright, Gwendolyn. *Moralism and the Model Home: Domestic Architecture and Cultural Conflict in Chicago, 1873–1913.* Chicago: University of Chicago Press, 1980.

Design and Intention

Vernacular building is thought as well as made and used. The works below address the design process and the elusive issue of the "meaning" of vernacular forms understood from the point of view both of the maker's intent and the user's affective response.

Ames, Kenneth L. "Material Culture as Non-Verbal Communication: A Historical Case Study," *Journal of American Culture* 3, no. 4 (Winter 1980): 619–41.

Appleyard, Donald. "Home," *Architectural Association Quarterly* 11, no. 3 (1979): 4–20.

*Carter, Tom. "Folk Design in Utah Architecture, 1849–1890." In *Utah Folk Art: A Catalog of Material Culture,* ed. Hal Cannon. Provo: Brigham Young University Press, 1980, pp. 34–59.

Clark, Clifford E., Jr. "Domestic Architecture as an Index to Social History: The Romantic Revival and the Cult of Domesticity in America, 1840–1870," *Journal of Interdisciplinary History* 7, no. 1 (Summer 1976): 33–56.

Cromley, Elizabeth Collins. "Modernizing: Or, 'You Never See a Screen Door on Affluent Homes,'" *Journal of American Culture* 5, no. 2 (Summer 1982): 71–79.

*Deetz, James. *Invitation to Archaeology.* Garden City, N.Y.: Natural History Press, 1967.

Dole, Philip. "The Calef Farm: Region and Style in Oregon," *Journal of the Society of Architectural Historians* 23, no. 4 (December 1964): 200–209.

Edwards, Jay D. "Cultural Syncretism in the Southern Louisiana Creole Cottage," *Louisiana Folklore Miscellany* 4 (1976–80): 9–40.

*Glassie, Henry. "Folk Art." In *Folklore and Folklife: An Introduction,* ed. Richard M. Dorson. Chicago: University of Chicago Press, 1972, pp. 253–80.

———. *Folk Housing in Middle Virginia: A Structural Analysis of Historic Artifacts.* Knoxville: University of Tennessee Press, 1975. Absolutely essential. A difficult but rewarding study with a thorough bibliography that serves as an excellent guide to the ideas Glassie uses.

———. "Structure and Function, Folklore and the Artifact," *Semiotica* 7, no. 4 (1973): 313–51. A good warm-up for *Folk Housing in Middle Virginia* that summarizes the geometrical relationships of the latter without the linguistic analysis.

———. "The Variation of Concepts within Tradition: Barn Building in Otsego County, New York." In *Man and Cultural Heritage: Essays in Honor of Fred B. Kniffen,* ed. H. J. Walker and W. G. Haag. Geoscience and Man, no. 5. Baton Rouge: Louisiana State University School of Geoscience, 1974, pp. 177–235.

*Gould, Peter, and Rodney White. *Mental Maps.* Baltimore: Penguin Books, 1974.

*Hayden, Dolores. *Seven American Utopias: The Architecture of Communitarian Socialism, 1790–1975.* Cambridge: MIT Press, 1976.

Hayward, D. Geoffrey. "Home as an Environmental and Psychological Concept," *Landscape* 20, no. 1 (October 1975): 2–9.

Horwitz, Richard. "Architecture and Culture: The Meaning of the Lowell Boarding House," *American Quarterly* 25, no. 1 (March 1973): 64–82.

*Isaac, Rhys. *The Transformation of Virginia, 1740–1790.* Chapel Hill: University of North Carolina Press, 1982. A brilliant use of architecture and landscape in a social historical study.

Jackson, J. B. "The Abstract World of the Hot-Rodder," *Landscape* 7, no. 2 (Winter 1957–58): 22–27.

*Jones, Michael Owen. "L.A. Add-Ons and Re-Dos: Renovation in Folk Art and Architectural Design." In *Perspectives on American Folk Art,* ed. Ian M. G. Quimby and Scott T. Swank. New York: Norton, 1980, pp. 325–63.

*Leone, Mark P. "The New Mormon Temple in Washington, D.C." In *Historical Archaeology and the Importance of Material Things,* ed. Leland Ferguson. Special Publication Series, no. 2. N.p.: Society for Historical Archaeology, 1977.

Lockwood, Yvonne. "The Sauna: An Expression of Finnish-American Identity," *Western Folklore* 36, no. 1 (January 1977): 71–84.

Lowenthal, David. "Past Time, Present Place: Landscape and Memory," *Geographical Review* 65, no. 1 (January 1975): 1–36.

———. "Geography, Experience, and Imagination: Towards a Geographical Epistemology," *Annals of the Association of American Geographers* 51, no. 3 (September 1961): 241–60.

McGuire, Randall H., and Michael B. Schiffer. "A Theory of Architectural Design," *Journal of Anthropological Archaeology* 2, no. 3 (September 1983): 277–303. Based on Anasazi architecture.

Rapoport, Amos. *The Meaning of the Built Environment: A Non-Verbal Communications Approach.* Beverley Hills, Calif.: Sage Publications, 1982.

*Sommer, Robert. *Personal Space: The Behavioral Basis of Design.* Englewood Cliffs, N.J.: Prentice-Hall, 1969.

Staub, Shalom. "The Near East Restaurant: A Study of the Spatial Manifestation of the Folklore of Ethnicity," *New York Folklore* 7, nos. 1–2 (Summer 1981): 113–27.

*Tuan, Yi-Fu. *Topophilia: A Study of Environmental Perception, Attitudes, and Values.* Englewood Cliffs, N.J.: Prentice-Hall, 1974.

*Trent, Robert F. *Hearts and Crowns: Folk Chairs of the Connecticut Coast, 1740–1820.* New Haven: New Haven Colony Historical Society, 1977.

Upton, Dell. "Toward a Performance Theory of Vernacular Architecture in Tidewater Virginia," *Folklore Forum* 12, nos. 2–3 (1979): 173–96.

______. "Pattern Books and Professionalism: Aspects of the Transformation of American Domestic Architecture, 1800–1860," *Winterthur Portfolio* 19, nos. 2–3 (Summer–Autumn 1984): 107–50.

*Vlach, John Michael. *The Afro-American Tradition in Decorative Arts.* Cleveland: Cleveland Museum of Art, 1978.

Do It Yourself: Research

The primary data of vernacular architecture and landscapes are the physical objects themselves, and there is no substitute for first-hand fieldwork. Since few vernacular environments have been extensively documented, research in the field requires some familiarity with recording and analytical techniques. There is no comprehensive primer, but the following works will be helpful.

Borchert, James. "Analysis of Historical Photographs: A Method and a Case Study," *Studies in Visual Communication* 7 (Fall 1981): 30–63.

Brunskill, R. W. "Recording the Buildings of the Farmstead," *Transactions of the Ancient Monuments Society,* n.s., 21 (1975–76): 115–50.

______. "A Systematic Procedure for Recording English Vernacular Architecture," *Transactions of the Ancient Monuments Society,* n.s., 13 (1965–66): 43–126. The Brunskill essays were prepared for English audiences, but the methods proposed have been used in several American and Canadian surveys as well.

Clay, Grady. *Close-Up: How to Read the American City.* New York: Praeger, 1973.

*Collier, John. *Visual Anthropology: Photography as a Research Method.* New York: Holt, Rinehart and Winston, 1967.

*Derry, Anne, H. Ward Jandl, Carol D. Shull, and Jan Thorman. *Guidelines for Local Surveys: A Basis for Preservation Planning.* Washington, D.C.: National Register of Historic Places, 1977.

*Leach, MacEdward, and Henry Glassie. *A Guide for Collectors of Oral Traditions and Folk Cultural Material in Pennsylvania.* Harrisburg: Pennsylvania Historical and Museum Commission, 1968. Includes a section on recording buildings and other material culture.

McKee, Harley J. *Recording Historic Buildings.* Washington, D.C.: National Park Service, 1970. General description of the methods used by the Historic American Buildings Survey.

Renk, Thomas B. "A Guide to Recording Structural Details of Historic Buildings," *Historical Archaeology* 3 (1969): 34–48.

*Roberts, Warren E. "Fieldwork: Recording Material Culture." In *Folklore and Folklife: An Introduction,* ed. Richard M. Dorson. Chicago: University of Chicago Press, 1972, pp. 431–44.

Watts, Mae Thielgaard. *Reading the Landscape of America.* New York: Macmillan, 1975.

Notes on Contributors

KENNETH L. AMES, who holds a degree in art history from the University of Pennsylvania, is the chairman of the Office of Advanced Studies, Henry Francis du Pont Winterthur Museum, and adjunct associate professor of art history at the University of Delaware. A specialist in nineteenth-century American material culture, Ames is the editor of *Victorian Furniture* and the author of *Beyond Necessity: Art in the Folk Tradition,* along with many articles on American furniture, folk art, and gravestones.

CATHERINE W. BISHIR is the head of the Survey and Planning Branch of the Division of Archives and History in the North Carolina Department of Cultural Resources. She serves on the board of directors for both the Vernacular Architecture Forum and the Society of Architectural Historians and has published articles on a wide range of topics including the preservation of courthouses and the history of beach cottages.

JAMES BORCHERT, who holds a doctorate in American studies from the University of Maryland, is an associate professor of history at Cleveland State University. He is the author of *Alley Life in Washington* as well as several articles on the use of photographs in historical research.

EDWARD A. CHAPPELL is the director of architectural research at Colonial Williamsburg. Having earned a master's degree in architectural history at the University of Virginia, he also served as architectural surveyor for the state of Kentucky. His publications include articles on both historical architecture and archaeology.

LIZABETH A. COHEN is a graduate student in history at the University of California, Berkeley, where she is writing a dissertation entitled "From Welfare Capitalism to the Welfare State: Mass Production Workers in Chicago Between the Wars, 1919 to 1939." She has worked in museums and with public history projects in California and Massachusetts. Among her publications is "Respectability at $50.00 Down, 25 Months to Pay!: Furnishing the Working-Class Victorian Home," in *Victorian Furniture,* edited by Kenneth L. Ames.

ABBOTT LOWELL CUMMINGS is Charles F. Montgomery Professor of American Decorative Arts at Yale University. A renowned scholar of New England architecture and material culture, he was for many years executive director of the Society for the Preservation of New England Antiquities and served as first president of the Vernacular Architecture Forum. He edited *Bed Hangings, A Treatise on Fabrics and Styles in the Curtaining of Beds, 1650–1850* and *Architecture in Colonial Massachusetts* and is the author of *Architecture in Early New England* and *The Framed Houses of Massachusetts Bay, 1625–1725.*

HENRY GLASSIE is a professor of folklore and folklife at the University of Pennsylvania. He is the author of numerous publications on traditional culture both in the United States and Ireland. His two books on American vernacular architecture, *Pattern in the Material Folk Culture of the Eastern United States* and *Folk Housing in Middle Virginia,* are both landmark studies.

ALAN GOWANS founded the Department of History in Art at the University of Victoria and for ten years taught in the Winterthur Program. He currently teaches during fall and winter in Victoria and spends spring and summer working at the National Images of North American Living Research and Archival Center in Washington, D.C. He is the author of a widely used survey, *Images of American Living: Four Centuries of Architecture and Furniture as Cultural Expression,* as well as many other books on architecture, art, and popular culture in the United States and Canada, including *Church Architecture in New France, Architecture in New Jersey, Building Canada, King Carter's Church, The Unchanging Arts,* and *Learning to See.*

THOMAS HUBKA is an architect teaching at the University of Oregon and practicing in the state of Maine. His extensive fieldwork in the vernacular architecture of Maine has resulted in several articles and a recently published book, *Big House, Little House, Back House, Barn: The Connected Farm Buildings of New England.*

NORMAN MORRISON ISHAM (1864–1943) was a Providence, Rhode Island, architect and an instructor at Brown University and the Rhode Island School of Design. In his long career he produced *Early Rhode Island Houses* (1895) and *Early Connecticut Houses* (1900) with Albert F. Brown, then went on to publish a brief survey, *Early American Houses* (1928); *A Glossary of Early American Architectural Terms* (1939) that is still widely consulted; and many articles. Isham was an original member of the Walpole Society, a group of wealthy antiquarian collectors. As an architect he was responsible for restoring many of the famous colonial buildings of Rhode Island and eastern Connecticut, including the Colony House and Trinity Church in Newport and the First Baptist Church in Providence. ALBERT F. BROWN was an architect who did no other known work on vernacular architecture after his two books with Isham.

FRED B. KNIFFEN is Boyd Professor Emeritus in the Department of Geography and Anthropology at Louisiana State University. His books include *The Natural Landscape of the Colorado Delta, Culture Worlds,* and *Louisiana: Its Land and People.* A pioneering scholar in the field of folk housing, his articles are some of the key building blocks for vernacular architecture research.

CLAY LANCASTER has taught art history at Columbia University, New York University, and Vassar College. He is the author of many books on the architecture of the eastern United States, including *Old Brooklyn Heights, Ante Bellum Houses of the Blue Grass,* and *The Architecture of Historic Nantucket.* His study of *The Japanese Influence in America* was recently reissued in a new edition by Abbeville Press, which will also publish his book *The American Bungalow: 1880s–1920s* in the spring of 1985.

STEWART G. MCHENRY, a cultural geographer trained at Syracuse University, has taught at the University of Vermont. His publications have focused on the cultural landscape of New England and include two studies on Vermont barns.

FRASER D. NEIMAN, a graduate student in anthropology at Yale University, was director of the Stratford Archaeological Project when the article reprinted here was written. He has worked as an archaeologist for the Virginia Research Center for Archaeology and the St. Mary's City Commission as well. Neiman is currently completing a dissertation based on his excavations at the Clifts Plantation.

FRED W. PETERSON is a professor of art history at the University of Minnesota, Morris. His interest in vernacular architecture, which grew out of his work as a watercolorist, has resulted in the publication of several studies on the vernacular architecture of the Upper Midwest, including "Norwegian Farm Homes in Steele and Traill Counties, North Dakota: The American Dream and the Retention of Roots, 1890–1914," in *North Dakota History* (1984).

EDWARD T. PRICE is a professor emeritus of geography at the University of Oregon. His research interests cover Europe, the Caribbean, and the southern United States and his publications are equally diverse. They include the following articles: "The Melungeons: A Mixed-Blood Strain of the Southern Appalachians," "The Redlegs of Barbados," and "The Matter of Housing."

THEODORE H. M. PRUDON is a senior associate with the Ehrenkrantz Group, where he is principal restoration architect for the restoration, rehabilitation, and historic preservation projects of the firm. His specialties have included theaters and the preservation of architectural terra-cotta. He has taught in the historic preservation program at Columbia University since 1970, and has published over forty articles on restoration, rehabilitation, and architectural history in American, Canadian, and European periodicals.

Warren E. Roberts, a professor of folklore at Indiana University, has written extensively on verbal art and material culture. In addition to many articles on folk architecture and traditional craftsmen, he is the author of the forthcoming book *The Log Buildings of Southern Indiana* (Bloomington, Ind.: Trickster Press).

Barbara Rubin, a geographer with a doctorate from the University of California, Los Angeles, teaches geography at Northwestern University. Her publications on vernacular architecture and landscapes include *L. A. in Installments #1: Forest Lawn.*

Robert Blair St. George is an assistant professor of American and New England studies at Boston University. Trained as a folklorist, his published studies deal principally with seventeenth- and eighteenth-century Anglo-American architecture and furniture. These include *The Wrought Convenant,* "The Stanley-Lake Barn in Topsfield, Massachusetts," and "Style and Structure in the Joinery of Dedham and Medfield, Massachusetts."

Dell Upton, who holds a doctorate in American studies, teaches architectural history in the Department of Architecture at the University of California, Berkeley. He edits the *Vernacular Architecture Newsletter* and is the author of *Holy Things and Profane: Anglican Parish Churches in Colonial Virginia* (Architectural History Foundation/MIT Press, forthcoming).

John Michael Vlach is an associate professor of American civilization and anthropology and director of the Folklife Program at The George Washington University. He is the author of *The Afro-American Tradition in Decorative Arts* and *Charleston Blacksmith.*

Index